MCSA Guide to
Administering Microsoft® Windows Server® 2012/R2, Exam 70-411

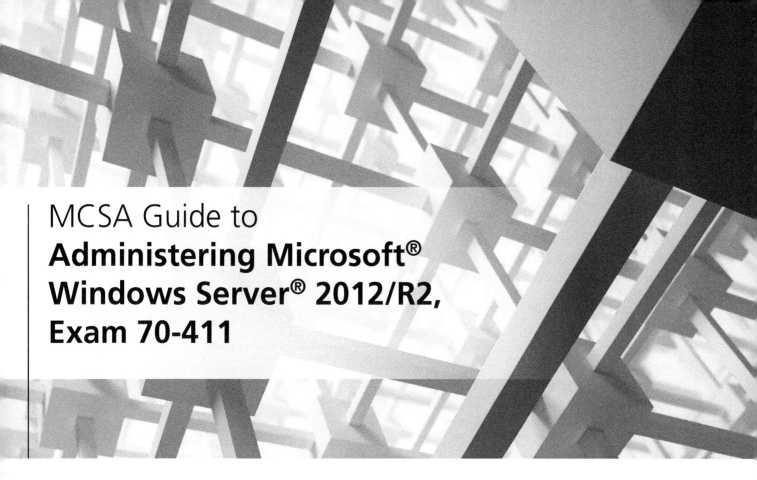

MCSA Guide to
Administering Microsoft®
Windows Server® 2012/R2,
Exam 70-411

Greg Tomsho

CENGAGE
Learning·

Australia • Brazil • Japan • Korea • Mexico • Singapore • Spain • United Kingdom • United States

CENGAGE
Learning·

**MCSA Guide to Administering
Microsoft® Windows Server® 2012/R2,
Exam 70-411**
Greg Tomsho
Contributors: Matt Tomsho and Jack Hogue

Vice President, General Manager: Dawn Gerrain

Product Director: Kathleen McMahon

Product Team Manager: Nick Lombardi

Director, Development: Marah Bellegarde

Product Development Manager: Leigh Hefferon

Senior Content Developer:
   Michelle Ruelos Cannistraci

Development Editor: Lisa M. Lord

Product Assistant: Scott Finger

Marketing Manager: Eric La Scola

Senior Production Director: Wendy Troeger

Production Manager: Patty Stephan

Senior Content Project Manager:
   Brooke Greenhouse

Art Director: GEX Publishing Services

Cover image: ©iStockphoto.com/agsandrew

For product information and technology assistance, contact us at
Cengage Learning Customer & Sales Support, 1-800-354-9706

For permission to use material from this text or product,
submit all requests online at **www.cengage.com/permissions**
Further permissions questions can be e-mailed to
permissionrequest@cengage.com

Library of Congress Control Number: 2014943050

ISBN-13: 978-1-285-86834-9

ISBN-10: 1-285-86834-X

Course Technology
20 Channel Center Street
Boston, MA 02210
USA

Cengage Learning is a leading provider of customized learning solutions with office locations around the globe, including Singapore, the United Kingdom, Australia, Mexico, Brazil, and Japan. Locate your local office at **www.cengage.com/global**

Cengage Learning products are represented in Canada by Nelson Education, Ltd.

To learn more about Cengage Learning, visit **www.cengage.com**

Purchase any of our products at your local college store or at our preferred online store **www.cengagebrain.com**

Printed in the United States of America
3 4 5 6 7 8 9 21 20 19 18 17

Brief Contents

Contents

Introduction

MCSA Guide to Administering Microsoft® Windows Server® 2012/R2, Exam 70-411, gives you in-depth coverage of the 70-411 certification exam objectives and focuses on the skills you need to administer Windows Server 2012/R2. With almost 100 hands-on activities and dozens of skill-reinforcing case projects, you'll be well prepared for the certification exam and learn valuable skills to perform on the job.

After you finish this book, you'll have an in-depth knowledge of Windows Server 2012/R2, including Windows deployment, maintenance and monitoring, advanced file services, remote access, network policy, Active Directory, Group Policy, and DNS. Both the original release of Windows Server 2012 and the R2 release are covered.

Intended Audience

MCSA Guide to Administering Microsoft® Windows Server® 2012/R2, Exam 70-411, is intended for people who want to learn how to administer a Windows Server 2012/R2 network and earn the Microsoft Certified Solutions Associate (MCSA) certification. This book covers in full the objectives of the second exam (70-411) needed to be MCSA: Windows Server 2012 certified. This book serves as an excellent tool for classroom teaching, but self-paced learners will also find that the clear explanations and challenging activities and case projects serve them equally well. This book builds on the topics you learned in *MCSA Guide to Installing and Configuring Microsoft® Windows Server® 2012/R2, Exam 70-410*, and adds some new topics. It's critical that you learned the 70-410 exam's objectives before continuing your learning with this book.

What This Book Includes

- A lab setup guide is included in the "Before You Begin" section of this introduction to help you configure a physical or virtual (recommended) lab environment for doing the hands-on activities.

- Step-by-step hands-on activities walk you through tasks ranging from a basic Windows Server 2012 R2 installation to complex multiserver network configurations involving Active

Directory, Group Policy, DNS, and many other services. All activities have been tested by a technical editor, reviewers, and validation experts.

- Extensive review and end-of-chapter materials reinforce your learning.

- Challenging case projects require you to apply the concepts and technologies learned throughout the book.

- Abundant screen captures and diagrams visually reinforce the text and hands-on activities.

- A list of 70-411 exam objectives is cross-referenced with chapters and sections that cover each objective.

About Microsoft Certification: MCSA/MCSE

This book prepares you to take the second exam in the Microsoft Certified Solutions Associate (MCSA) Windows Server 2012 certification. The MCSA Windows Server 2012 certification is made up of three exams, which should be taken in order as follows:

- Exam 70-410: Installing and Configuring Windows Server 2012

- Exam 70-411: Administering Windows Server 2012

- Exam 70-412: Configuring Advanced Windows Server 2012 Services

Taking the exams in order is important because the objectives build on one another, with some topics introduced in an earlier exam and reinforced in subsequent exams.

Microsoft Certified Solutions Expert (MCSE): The Next Step

After achieving the MCSA Windows Server 2012 certification, you can move on to the MCSE certification. Microsoft offers three main options, and all require the three MCSA exams as a prerequisite:

- MCSE: Server Infrastructure

  - Exam 70-413: Designing and Implementing a Server Infrastructure

  - Exam 70-414: Implementing an Advanced Server Infrastructure

- MCSE: Desktop Infrastructure

  - Exam 70-415: Implementing a Desktop Infrastructure

  - Exam 70-416: Implementing Desktop Application Environments

- MCSE: Private Cloud

  Exam 70-246: Monitoring and Operating a Private Cloud with System Center 2012

  Exam 70-247: Configuring and Deploying a Private Cloud with System Center 2012

Chapter Descriptions

Each chapter in this book covers one or more important Microsoft Windows Server 2012 technologies. The 70-411 exam objectives are covered throughout the book, and you can find a mapping of objectives and the chapters in which they're covered on the inside front cover, with a more detailed mapping in Appendix A. The following list describes this book's chapters:

- **Chapter 1,** "Deploying Windows Server," covers Windows Deployment Services (WDS), including situations in which WDS is used and installation and configuration of WDS. You also learn to work with WDS images and configure DHCP for WDS.

- **Chapter 2,** "Windows Server Update Services," describes the Windows Server Update Services (WSUS) role and shows you how to install and configure WSUS. You learn a basic WSUS configuration as well as how to configure WSUS synchronization and approval rules.

- **Chapter 3**, "Advanced File Services Configuration," explains how to work with Distributed File System (DFS) to create a reliable and highly available file-sharing system. You also learn how to work with File Server Resource Manager (FSRM) to configure quotas, file screens, storage reports, and file management tasks. Last, you learn about securing files with file and disk encryption.

- **Chapter 4**, "Server Monitoring and Auditing," discusses how to monitor a Windows server with tools such as Event Viewer, Task Manager, and Performance Monitor. You also learn how to monitor a network by using a protocol analyzer. The chapter ends with an explanation of file and folder auditing.

- **Chapter 5**, "Remote Access Configuration," discusses remote access technologies, such as dial-up, virtual private networks (VPNs), routing, NAT, and DirectAccess. You begin by installing the Remote Access server role and configuring and testing a VPN. You learn how to configure routing and NAT and finish by configuring a DirectAccess connection.

- **Chapter 6**, "Network Policy Configuration," describes the components and flow of Network Policy Server and RADIUS. You learn how to configure centralized authentication and authentication policies by using Network Policy Server and RADIUS. You also learn how to configure Network Access Protection to protect the health of the network from computers that don't meet policies for security configuration and malware protection.

- **Chapter 7**, "Domain Controller and Active Directory Management," describes the key concepts and components of Active Directory. You learn about cloning virtual domain controllers and read only domain controllers. Next, you learn about sites and working with operations master roles. Finally, you learn how to maintain Active Directory with backups and diagnostics.

- **Chapter 8**, "User and Service Account Configuration," reviews user accounts and group policies so that you have a fresh context for learning how to configure account policies in a domain environment and on a local computer. You learn how to make exceptions in account policies with PSOs so that you can designate more stringent or more lenient policies for groups of users when needed. You also learn to configure service authentication with a variety of methods.

- **Chapter 9**, "Group Policy Settings and Preferences," starts with a quick review of Group Policy and how to create, configure, and link Group Policy objects. You then delve into different areas of group policies, including software installation policies, script deployment, folder redirection, administrative templates, security templates, and group policy preferences.

- **Chapter 10**, "Managing Group Policies," teaches you how to configure group policy scope, precedence, and inheritance. You learn more about group policy client processing and how to use the Group Policy Results and Group Policy Modeling tools. Finally, you learn to back up, restore, copy, and migrate Group Policy objects.

- **Chapter 11**, "Managing and Configuring DNS," teaches you how to configure zones, the main structural component of DNS, and resource records, the data component of DNS. You learn how to create and configure host resource records as well as mail server, name server, service locator, and start of authority records. You also learn the advantages of using an Active Directory–integrated zone and how to tune replication between DNS servers. Finally, you learn about round-robin DNS, which allows you to load-balance a variety of network services.

- **Appendix A**, "MCSA 70-411 Exam Objectives," maps each 70-411 exam objective to the chapter and section where you can find information on that objective.

Features

This book includes the following learning features to help you master the topics in this book and the 70-411 exam objectives:

- *Chapter objectives*—Each chapter begins with a detailed list of the concepts to be mastered. This list is a quick reference to the chapter's contents and a useful study aid.
- *Hands-on activities*—Almost 100 hands-on activities are incorporated into this book, giving you practice in setting up, configuring, and managing a Windows Server 2012/R2 server. The activities give you a strong foundation for carrying out server installation and configuration tasks in production environments. Much of the learning about Windows Server 2012/R2 comes from doing the hands-on activities, and a lot of effort has been devoted to making the activities relevant and challenging.
- *A requirements table for hands-on activities*—A table at the beginning of each chapter lists the hands-on activities and what you need for each activity.
- *Screen captures, illustrations, and tables*—Numerous screen captures and illustrations of concepts help you visualize theories and concepts and see how to use tools and desktop features. In addition, tables are used often to give you details and comparisons of practical and theoretical information and can be used for a quick review.
- *Chapter summary*—Each chapter ends with a summary of the concepts introduced in the chapter. These summaries are a helpful way to recap and revisit the material covered in the chapter.
- *Key terms*—All terms in the chapter introduced with bold text are gathered together in the Key Terms list at the end of the chapter. This list gives you a way to check your understanding of all important terms.
- *Review questions*—The end-of-chapter assessment begins with review questions that reinforce the concepts and techniques covered in each chapter. Answering these questions helps ensure that you have mastered important topics.
- *Case projects*—Each chapter closes with one or more case projects. Many of the case projects build on one another, as you take a small startup company to a flourishing enterprise.
- *Trial Version Software*—To download the trial version software, go to https://www.microsoft.com/en-US/evalcenter/evaluate-windows-server-2012.

Text and Graphics Conventions

Additional information and exercises have been added to this book to help you better understand what's being discussed in the chapter. Icons throughout the book alert you to these additional materials:

 Tips offer extra information on resources, how to solve problems, and time-saving shortcuts.

 Notes present additional helpful material related to the subject being discussed.

 The Caution icon identifies important information about potential mistakes or hazards.

 Each hands-on activity in this book is preceded by the Activity icon.

 Case Project icons mark the end-of-chapter case projects, which are scenario-based assignments that ask you to apply what you have learned in the chapter.

CertBlaster Test Preparation Questions

MCSA Guide to Administering Microsoft® Windows Server® 2012/R2, Exam 70-411, includes CertBlaster test preparation questions for the 70-411 MCSA exam. CertBlaster is a powerful online certification preparation tool from dti Publishing that mirrors the look and feel of the certification exam.

To log in and access the CertBlaster test preparation questions for *MCSA Guide to Administering Microsoft® Windows Server® 2012/R2, Exam 70-411*, go to *www.certblaster. com/login/*. The CertBlaster user's online manual describes features and gives navigation instructions. Activate your CertBlaster license by entering your name, e-mail address, and access code (found on the card bound in this book) in their fields, and then click Submit. CertBlaster offers three practice modes and all the types of questions required to simulate the exams:

- *Assessment mode*—Used to determine the student's baseline level. In this mode, the timer is on, answers aren't available, and the student gets a list of questions answered incorrectly, along with a Personal Training Plan.

- *Study mode*—Helps the student understand questions and the logic behind answers by giving immediate feedback both during and after the test. Answers and explanations are available. The timer is optional, and the student gets a list of questions answered incorrectly, along with a Personal Training Plan.

- *Certification mode*—A simulation of the actual exam environment. The timer as well as the number and format of questions from the exam objectives are set according to the exam's format.

For more information about dti test prep products, visit the Web site at *www.dtipublishing.com*.

Instructor Companion Site

Everything you need for your course in one place! This collection of book-specific lecture and class tools is available online via *www.cengage.com/login*. Access and download PowerPoint presentations, images, the Instructor's Manual, and more.

- *Electronic Instructor's Manual*—The Instructor's Manual that accompanies this book includes additional instructional material to assist in class preparation, including suggestions for classroom activities, discussion topics, and additional quiz questions.

- *Solutions Manual*—The instructor's resources include solutions to all end-of-chapter material, including review questions and case projects.

- *Cengage Learning Testing Powered by Cognero*—This flexible, online system allows you to do the following:
  - Author, edit, and manage test bank content from multiple Cengage Learning solutions.
  - Create multiple test versions in an instant.
  - Deliver tests from your LMS, your classroom, or wherever you want.

- *PowerPoint presentations*—This book comes with Microsoft PowerPoint slides for each chapter. They're included as a teaching aid for classroom presentation, to make available to students on the network for chapter review, or to be printed for classroom distribution. Instructors, please feel free to add your own slides for additional topics you introduce to the class.

- *Figure files*—All the figures and tables in the book are reproduced in bitmap format. Similar to the PowerPoint presentations, they're included as a teaching aid for classroom presentation, to make available to students for review, or to be printed for classroom distribution.

Acknowledgments

I would like to thank Cengage Learning Product Manager Nick Lombardi for his confidence in asking me to undertake this challenging book project. In addition, thanks go out to Michelle Ruelos Cannistraci, the Senior Content Developer, who assembled an outstanding team to support this project. A special word of gratitude goes to Lisa Lord, the Development Editor, who has a knack for taking an unrefined product and turning it into a polished manuscript. Lisa's good humor and understanding as well as her commendable skills as an editor made my life considerably easier during the many months it took to complete this book. Serge Palladino, from the Manuscript Quality Assurance staff at Cengage Learning, tested chapter activities diligently to ensure that labs work as they were intended, and for that, I am grateful. I also want to include a shout-out to a student, Stephanie Garcia, who provided an extra layer of QA for hands-on activities.

Of course, this book wasn't written in a vacuum, and the peer reviewers offered thoughtful advice, constructive criticism, and much needed encouragement: Kara Brown, Sinclair College; Matt Halvorson, Yavapai College; Heith Hennel, Valencia College; and Michael Linkey, University of Illinois.

Finally, my family: My beautiful and supportive wife, Julie; daughters Camille and Sophia; and son, Michael, deserve special thanks and praise for their patience and understanding while I left them mostly husbandless and fatherless for so many months. Without their happy greetings when I did make an appearance, I could not have accomplished this.

Additional Contributors

Matt Tomsho and Jack Hogue tackled three difficult chapters in this book: 3, 4, and 6. Without their help, this book could not have been published on time. I want to give particular thanks to them for taking on this project and fitting it into their otherwise very busy lives.

Matt Tomsho has 35 years of computer programming and network experience. Currently an independent database consultant in Pittsburgh specializing in Web-based applications, Matt has been an IT director at several Internet companies, managing Web and database servers running Windows and Linux. Matt was a co-author of *MCTS Guide to Microsoft® Windows Server® 2008 Application Infrastructure Configuration*.

Jack Hogue has 25 years of computing and network experience. He currently specializes in Microsoft Windows environments and supports integration of Mac and Linux OSs into Windows networks. Jack is the co-owner of Chordata Technologies in Pittsburgh, which supports more than 150 clients across the United States and Canada. Jack was a co-author of *MCTS Guide to Microsoft® Windows Server® 2008 Application Infrastructure Configuration*.

About the Author

Greg Tomsho has more than 30 years of computer and networking experience and has earned the CCNA, MCTS, MCSA, A+, Security+, and Linux+ certifications. Greg is the director of the Computer Networking Technology Department and Cisco Academy at Yavapai College in Prescott, Arizona. His other books include *MCSA Guide to Installing and Configuring Microsoft® Windows Server® 2012/R2, Exam 70-410*; *MCTS Guide to Microsoft® Windows Server® 2008 Active Directory Configuration*; *MCTS Guide to Microsoft® Windows Server® 2008 Application Infrastructure Configuration*; *Guide to Networking Essentials*; *Guide to Network Support and Troubleshooting*; and *A+ CoursePrep ExamGuide*.

Contact the Author

I would like to hear from you. Please e-mail me at *w2k12@tomsho.com* with any problems, questions, suggestions, or corrections. Your comments and suggestions are invaluable for shaping the content of future books. You can also submit errata, lab suggestions, and comments via e-mail. I have set up a Web site to support my books at *http://books.tomsho.com*, where you'll find lab notes, errata, Web links, and helpful hints for using my books. If you're an instructor, you can register on the site to contribute articles and comment on articles.

Before You Begin

Windows Server has become more complex as Microsoft strives to satisfy the needs of enterprise networks. In years past, you could learn what you needed to manage a Windows Server–based network and pass the Microsoft certification exams with a single server, some good lab instructions, and a network connection. Today, as you work with advanced technologies—such as Hyper-V, Storage Spaces, and DirectAccess, to name just a few—your lab environment must be more complex, requiring two or even three servers and at least one client computer. Setting up this lab environment can be challenging, and this section was written to help you meet this challenge. Using virtual machines in VMware Workstation or VMware Player is highly recommended; other virtual environments work as well.

If you can't set up a lab environment exactly as described in this section, you still have some options to help you gain the skills learned through hands-on activities:

- *Configure a partial lab*—If you have just one Windows Server 2012 R2 server available, you can still do many of the hands-on activities. Having one server and one client is even better, and having two servers and one client enables you to do the majority of the book's activities. If you can't do an activity, it's important to read the activity steps to learn important information about Windows Server 2012/R2.

- *Purchase the Web-Based Labs*—Cengage Learning offers Web-Based Labs for this book. This product gives you access to a real lab environment over the Internet by using a Web browser. Step-by-step lab instructions are taken directly from the hands-on activities in the book. See your sales representative or the Cengage Learning Web site for more information.

Lab Setup Guide

The lab equipment for hands-on activities consists of three computers. All three computers should be configured before beginning the first chapter. The first chapter requires a client computer for testing Windows Deployment Services (WDS). You can deploy another client machine (no OS required) or use the Windows 8.1 client for this purpose. Figure 1 shows a diagram of the network.

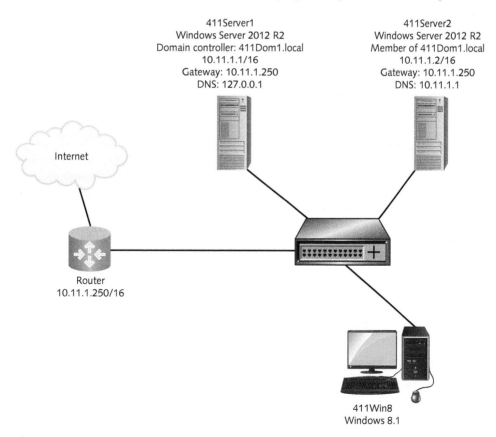

Figure 1   A diagram of the lab configuration

A few words about this diagram:

- The router address is suggested, but you can use a different address. You can do most activities without a router to the Internet, except those requiring Internet access.
- DNS is handled by 411Server1 which already has Active Directory installed and configured with domain 411Dom1.local.
- Specific installation requirements for each server are explained in the following sections.

411Server1

This server should be configured as follows before beginning the activities in Chapter 1:

- Windows Server 2012 R2 Standard or Datacenter
- Server name: 411Server1
- Administrator password: Password01
- Active Directory and DNS installed
- Domain: 411Dom1.local
- DHCP installed
- Scope: 10.11.1.50—10.11.1.60
- DNS server option: 10.11.1.1—10.11.1.1
- Memory: 1 GB or more
- Hard disk 1: 60 GB or more
- Hard disk 2: 60 GB or more
- Network interface card
- IPv4 address: 10.11.1.1/16
- DNS: 127.0.0.1
- Default gateway: 10.11.1.250 (or an address supplied by the instructor)
- Windows Update: Not configured
- Requires Internet access for Chapter 2, "Windows Server Update Services"
- If you're using an evaluation version of Windows Server 2012 R2, you can rearm the evaluation up to five times. To do so, follow these steps:

1. Open a command prompt window as Administrator.

2. Type `slmgr -xpr` and press **Enter** to see the current status of your license. It shows how many days are left in the evaluation. If it says you're in notification mode, you need to rearm the evaluation immediately.

3. To rearm the evaluation, type `slmgr -rearm` and press **Enter**. You see a message telling you to restart the system for the changes to take effect. Click **OK** and restart the system.

411Server2

This server should be configured as follows before beginning the activities in Chapter 2:

- Windows Server 2012 R2 Standard or Datacenter
- Server name: 411Server2
- Administrator password: Password01
- Domain: Member of 411Dom1.local
- Memory: 1 GB or more (4 GB or more for the Hyper-V activities in Chapter 12)
- Hard disk 1: 60 GB or more

- Hard disk 2: 60 GB or more
- Network interface card 1
  - IPv4 address: 10.11.1.2/16
  - DNS: 10.11.1.1
  - Default gateway: 10.11.1.250 (or an address supplied by the instructor)
- Network interface card 2 (used starting in Chapter 5)
  - IPv4 address: 192.168.1.1/24
  - DNS: Not configured
  - Default gateway: Not configured
- Windows Update: Not configured

411Win8

This computer should be configured as follows before beginning Chapter 2:

- Windows 8.1 Enterprise Edition
- Machine name: 411Win8
- Sign in with a local account, not a Microsoft account
- Settings: Express settings
- Local administrator account with the username Win8User and the password Password01
- Domain: Member of 411Dom1.local
- Memory: 1 GB or more
- Hard disk: 60 GB or more
- Network interface card: DHCP enabled
- Windows Update: Not configured

WDS Client

This computer is used only for activities in Chapter 1 to test Windows Deployment Services (WDS) configuration. You can use the computer you plan to use for 411Win8, if you want. If you're using virtualization, you can create a virtual machine with no OS. You must be sure the NIC is PXE compatible. Use the following settings:

- No OS is installed.
- Reference name: WDSClient (It's used only to refer to the machine; there's no computer name because no OS is installed.)
- Memory: 1 GB
- Hard disk: 20 GB
- Network interface card: PXE compatible

In addition, a router to the Internet is recommended. The recommended address is 10.11.1.250/16, but any address in this subnet will work.

Deployment Recommendations

Using virtualization to configure your lab environment is recommended. If you're using physical computers, the requirements are much the same, but you need many more physical computers. If you're using physical computers, you can set up the network as shown previously in Figure 1 and configure the computers as described earlier.

Avoiding IP Address Conflicts

Whether you're using physical computers or virtual computers, you must have a method for avoiding IP address conflicts. There are two setups for working in a classroom environment:

- *All students computers are on the same physical subnet*—In this setup, IP addresses and computer names must be changed to avoid conflict. One strategy for avoiding IP address conflicts is using the third octet of the address. Each student is assigned a number, such as one from 1 to 50. When assigning IP addresses, simply change the third octet to the student-assigned number. For example, for student 15, address 10.11.1.1 becomes 10.11.15.1. Use the same number as a suffix for the computer and domain names. For example, 411Server1 becomes 411Server1-15, 411Server1-16, and so forth. The domain name also changes accordingly, such as 411Dom1-15.local, 411Dom1-16.local, and so on.

- *Each student works in a "sandbox" environment*—This setup is preferred, if it's possible. A router using NAT separates each student's sandboxed network environment, so there are no conflicts. This setup is easier to configure with virtualization. One possibility, as described later in the "Sample Configuration for Virtualization" section, is to configure an extra Windows Server 2012 VM as a NAT router with RRAS and as a DNS server. This machine can then route from the private network to the public Internet when needed. It also serves as the initial DNS server required for some activities, but its main purpose is to hide students' VMs from each other so that there are no address or name conflicts.

Using Virtualization

Using virtualization is highly recommended, and you have the following options for virtualization software:

- *VMware Workstation*—This sophisticated virtualization environment is a free download if your school or organization is a member of the VMware Academic Program (*http://vmapss.onthehub.com*). The advantage of VMware Workstation is that you can take periodic snapshots of VMs and revert to one if something goes wrong with a virtual machine.

- *VMware Player*—This product is a free download from the VMware Web site. You can't take snapshots, but otherwise, it's an excellent virtual environment.

- *Hyper-V*—If you install Windows Server 2012 R2 or Windows 8.1 on your host computers, you can run Hyper-V as your virtual environment. The advantage of using Hyper-V is that you need not install any third-party software on student computers. The disadvantage of using Hyper-V is that you need Administrator access to your host computers to use Hyper-V Manager.

- *VirtualBox*—This excellent open-source virtualization product from Oracle has many advanced features, as VMware Workstation does, but it's free.

Host Computer Requirements When Using Virtualization

The following are recommendations for the host computer when you're using virtualization:

- Dual-core or quad-core CPU with Intel-VT-x or AMD-V support. You can see a list of supported Intel processors at *http://ark.intel.com/products/virtualizationtechnology*.

- 8 GB RAM.

Most activities can be done with 4 GB RAM installed on the host. Only those requiring three VMs running at the same time need more than 4 GB.

- 150 GB free disk space.

- Windows 7 or Windows 8/8.1 if you're using VMware Workstation, VMware Player, or VirtualBox.

- Windows Server 2012 R2 or Windows 8.1 Pro or Enterprise 64-bit if you're using Hyper-V.

Sample Configuration for Virtualization

Figure 2 shows a diagram of a setup that includes a virtual machine acting as a router and DNS server. The virtual networks are labeled for both Hyper-V and VMware setups. The virtual machine set up as a router has two virtual NICs, one connected to the private network with lab computers and one connected to an external (Hyper-V) or bridged (VMware) network that connects to the physical network. The router VM is running RRAS and NAT for routing.

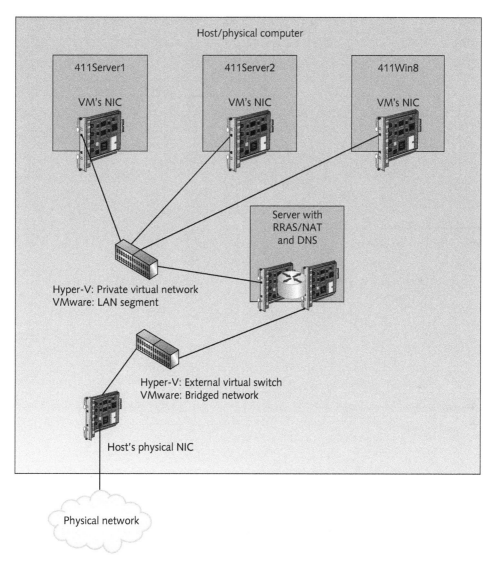

Figure 2   A sample virtual lab configuration

© 2015 Cengage Learning®

Where to Go for Help

Configuring a lab and keeping everything running correctly can be challenging. Even small configuration changes can prevent activities from running correctly. If you're using virtualization, use snapshots if possible so that you can revert virtual machines to an earlier working state in case something goes wrong. The author maintains a Web site that includes lab notes, suggestions, errata, and help articles that might be useful if you're having trouble, and you can contact the author at these addresses:

- Web site: *http://books.tomsho.com*
- E-mail: *w2k12@tomsho.com*

chapter 1

Deploying Windows Server

After reading this chapter and completing the exercises, you will be able to:

- Describe the Windows Deployment Services process
- Describe situations in which Windows Deployment Services is used
- Install and configure the Windows Deployment Services role
- Work with Windows Deployment Services images
- Configure DHCP for Windows Deployment Services

Installing Windows Server 2012/R2 on a single server isn't difficult, as you learned in *MCSA Guide to Installing and Configuring Windows Server 2012/R2, Exam 70-410* (Cengage Learning, 2015). However, on a network of dozens or hundreds of servers, you're best served by using a deployment system that enables you to configure roles and services and manage patches and updates remotely. Windows Server 2012/R2 has a server role designed for just this purpose: Windows Deployment Services. This role is targeted at networks with more than a couple of servers, but you'll see that its utility is indispensable as more servers are added to a network.

This book covers Windows Server 2012 and the newer Windows Server 2012 R2. When a topic or feature is relevant to both the original release of Windows Server 2012 and R2, the name Windows Server 2012/R2 is used. If a feature is particular to the R2 version, Windows Server 2012 R2 is used (without the "/" character). Microsoft has added a number of enhancements in Windows Server 2012 R2, and the new and modified features will have found their way into the Windows Server 2012 certification exams by the time this book is published.

An Overview of Windows Deployment Services

Before you begin this chapter, make sure you have completed *MCSA Guide to Installing and Configuring Windows Server 2012/R2, Exam 70-410* or have equivalent knowledge. The topics covered in this book assume prerequisite knowledge of the topics the 70-410 certification exam covers. In addition, to do the hands-on activities, you must configure your lab environment according to the lab setup instructions in the "Before You Begin" section of this book's introduction. Table 1-1 lists the resources needed for the hands-on activities.

Table 1-1   Activity requirements

Activity	Requirements	Notes
Activity 1-1: Installing Windows Deployment Services	411Server1	411Server1 must be configured according to instructions in the "Before You Begin" section.
Activity 1-2: Configuring Windows Deployment Services	411Server1	
Activity 1-3: Viewing WDS Server Properties	411Server1	
Activity 1-4: Adding a Boot Image to WDS	411Server1	A Windows Server 2012 R2 installation DVD or an .iso file that can be mounted as a DVD
Activity 1-5: Testing a Boot Image	411Server1, WDSclient	
Activity 1-6: Creating a Capture Image	411Server1	
Activity 1-7: Adding an Install Image	411Server1	A Windows Server 2012 R2 installation DVD or an .iso file that can be mounted as a DVD
Activity 1-8: Adding an Active Directory Prestaged Device	411Server1	

© *2015 Cengage Learning®*

Windows Deployment Services (WDS) is a server role that facilitates installing Windows OSs across a network. With WDS, you don't need to have installation media ready and sit at the server console as Windows performs the usually uneventful task of OS installation. In addition, you can configure many OS properties (such as computer name and IP address) before deployment, instead of having to perform these tasks at the server console after installation. WDS in Windows Server 2012/R2 can deploy the following OSs: Windows XP, Windows Server 2003, Windows Vista SP1, Windows Server 2008/R2, Windows 7, Windows Server 2012/R2, and Windows 8/8.1.

To use WDS, you need a working knowledge of Active Directory, DHCP, and DNS, all covered in *MCSA Guide to Installing and Configuring Windows Server 2012/R2, Exam 70-410* (Cengage Learning, 2015).

Starting with Windows Server 2008, WDS replaced the older technology Remote Installation Services (RIS).

Before you get into the details of installing and configuring WDS, review the following terms used with this server role:

- *Preboot eXecution Environment*—**Preboot eXecution Environment (PXE)**, pronounced "pixie," is a network environment built into many NICs that allows a computer to boot from an image stored on a network server (referred to as a "network boot") rather than from local storage. During a network boot, PXE sends packets to the network looking for a WDS server to send it an installation image. PXE uses Dynamic Host Configuration Protocol (DHCP) to acquire an IP address and Trivial File Transfer Protocol (TFTP) to transfer data.

- *Image file*—An **image file** contains other files, much like a zip file contains multiple files. In WDS, an image file is a boot image or an install image. A **boot image** contains the Windows PE (defined next) that allows a client computer to access a WDS server so that it can access an install image. An **install image** contains the actual operating system (OS) being deployed to the client computer. A **discover image** can be used to boot a client computer that can't use PXE; usually from a CD/DVD or flash device. A **capture image** is a special boot image that creates an install image from a reference computer (described later in "Working with Boot Images"). WDS supports three image file formats: `.wim`, `.vhd`, and `.vhdx`. Files with the `.wim` extension are **Windows Imaging Format (WIM)** files, the most common image file type used by WDS and the method for storing installation files on a Windows installation DVD. VHD and VHDX files are virtual disk formats also supported by WDS, but their use in WDS is not covered in this book.

- *Windows Preinstallation Environment*—**Windows Preinstallation Environment (PE)** is a minimal OS that has only the services needed to access the network, work with files, copy disk images, and jump-start a Windows installation. Windows PE also has a command-line interface that can be used for troubleshooting startup problems or recovering from a damaged OS installation. When you boot Windows Server 2012/R2 or Windows 8.1 into Recovery Mode, you're booting into Windows PE. Windows PE is used in the boot image for remote installation with WDS.

- *Multicasting*—**Multicasting** is a network communication method for delivering data to multiple computers on a network simultaneously. It's used in WDS when the same installation image should be sent to multiple computers on the network at the same time. Multicasting reduces bandwidth use more than unicasting does because with unicasting, you have to send data across the network separately for each computer that should receive it. With multicasting, data is sent once and received by all computers configured to receive it.

- *Network boot*—As discussed, a computer with a PXE-compatible NIC has the capability to boot from the network rather than local storage, called a **network boot**. A computer with a PXE-compatible NIC performs a network boot in the following situations:

  o The computer does not have an OS installed on the local hard drive and there is no bootable media inserted into any of the removable drives.

  o The BIOS is configured to attempt a network boot before attempting to boot from local media.

  o The F12 key is pressed during computer startup (but before a locally installed OS boots), which initiates a network boot.

- wdsnbp.com—The bootstrap program **wdsnbp.com** is a WDS component that a WDS client downloads when performing a network boot. It contains basic instructions on how to perform a network boot operation, such as whether F12 must be pressed to continue the network boot and which file to request from the WDS server.

The WDS Process

So how do all the technologies described so far work together in WDS? An illustration of the process can help answer this question. Suppose you're deploying Windows Server 2012/R2 to 20 computers with WDS. Your servers must have a NIC that's PXE compatible and must be configured to use PXE when they're powered on. The following steps (shown in Figure 1-1) apply to each computer that's powered on. The computer where Windows Server 2012/R2 is being installed by using WDS is called the "client computer." The DHCP server and WDS server can be the same machine.

1. The client computer is powered on, and its NIC starts the PXE process by querying a DHCP server for an IP address.

2. The DHCP server on the network responds, and an IP address is assigned to the client.

3. The client requests the bootstrap file from the WDS server via TFTP.

4. The WDS server uses TFTP to send the client the wdsnbp.com bootstrap program.

5. The client runs wdsnbp.com and requests a boot image containing Windows PE and Windows Setup from the WDS server.

6. The WDS server sends the boot image to the client computer.

7. Windows PE and Windows Setup are started.

8. The client requests an install image.

9. The WDS server sends the install image to the client computer.

10. The install image runs on the client computer, and Windows Server 2012/R2 is installed.

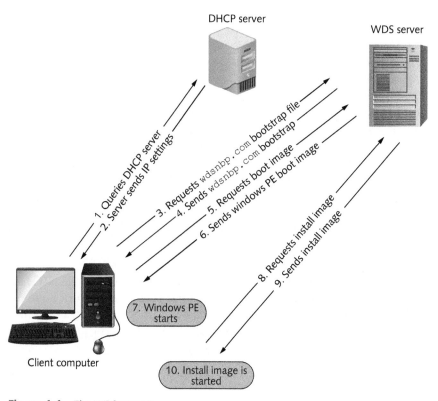

Figure 1-1   The WDS process

© 2015 Cengage Learning®

These steps are an overview of the process in one possible WDS situation. Some details were omitted to simplify the process, but these steps show the basic procedure for OS deployment with WDS. There are a host of methods and options for OS deployment with WDS; several are explained later in "Windows Deployment Services Situations."

WDS Requirements

The WDS server role doesn't stand on its own; it requires several support technologies on the network:

- *Windows Server 2012/R2*—WDS is also available in Windows Server 2008 and as a downloadable installation with Windows Server 2003 R2, but these requirements apply to installing the role on a Windows Server 2012/R2 server.
- *Active Directory*—In Windows Server 2012, Microsoft introduced a stand-alone option for WDS that doesn't require Active Directory, but installing it on a domain controller or member server is recommended and provides the most features.
- *DHCP Server*—A DHCP server must be available, ideally on a Windows server. Having WDS and DHCP on the same server requires fewer configuration steps because some required DHCP options are configured automatically when WDS is installed.
- *DNS Server*—Part of the WDS process in an Active Directory environment requires user authentication from the client computer; a DNS server is needed for the client to locate a domain controller. Even in a stand-alone WDS implementation, DNS is required for name resolution.
- *PXE-compatible NICs*—A PXE-compatible NIC on WDS client computers isn't a strict requirement because client computers can be booted to a discover image; but using PXE is preferable.
- *Suitable storage*—An NTFS volume with enough free space for storing the boot and installation images is required.

Windows Deployment Services Situations

WDS has a number of implementation options to fit most OS deployment situations. For example, you can configure OS deployments that require user interaction and those that are unattended installations. You can install just the base OS as it is on the installation medium, or you can install an OS that has applications installed already. The following sections examine several situations in more detail.

Attended Deployment of a Noncustomized Install Image

The simplest WDS implementation requires a user to attend the client computer and step through the OS deployment by using the install image on the OS installation medium. This type of deployment is suitable for installing an OS on 10 to 25 computers. If you're installing on fewer computers, it might not be worth the extra time to install and configure WDS. If you're installing on more computers, configuring an unattended installation might be worth the extra time.

As an example of the procedure for a basic attended OS deployment, Mike works for IT Consulting Services and receives a call from a small business customer, CSM Tech Publishing, asking him to install Windows 8.1 on its 15 desktop computers. The customer tells Mike to install Windows 8.1 Enterprise, for which the customer has an installation DVD and licenses. No other applications are to be installed at this time. Mike is familiar with CSM Tech Publishing's network environment because he installed a new Windows Server 2012 R2 computer last month. He has confirmed that CSM has the following roles installed on its server: Active Directory Domain Service, DNS, and DHCP.

When Mike gets on site, he verifies that the client computers are PXE compatible. He installs the WDS server role on the server and configures a boot image and an install image for Windows 8.1 Enterprise. Both images are available on the Windows 8.1 installation medium in the \sources directory. Because Mike will be doing a basic installation of Windows 8.1 with no additional applications, he can use the following images straight from the Windows 8.1 DVD:

- \sources\boot.wim—This image contains the Windows PE and Windows setup program. Client computers request this image when booting to the PXE environment.

- \sources\install.wim—This image contains the Windows 8.1 Enterprise installation files. It's the same image a computer uses if Windows installation is started by booting directly from the installation DVD.

With WDS installed, Mike powers on the first computer. All computers are configured for a network boot with PXE. The network boot starts, and the client is assigned an IP address from the DHCP server and the wdsnbp.com file is downloaded. Mike is prompted to press F12 to start the network service boot. When he presses F12, the client contacts the WDS server to download the boot image. If more than one boot image is configured, a menu to select the correct image is displayed. In this case, only the boot.wim boot image is available, which Mike configured earlier. The boot image, containing Windows PE and Windows Setup, is downloaded to the client and started, and then the Windows Setup process starts. Mike chooses the location information and clicks Next, which takes him to the window where he must enter his network credentials (see Figure 1-2). Credentials must be entered in the UPN format or as *domain\user*. The next window shows the familiar prompt to select the OS to install. At this point, the installation continues like a typical install; Mike can move on to the next computer while installation files are copied to the first client.

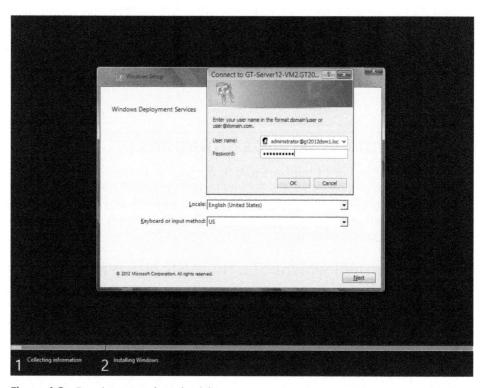

Figure 1-2   Entering network credentials

This situation requires someone to attend the installation, responding to prompts as in a typical installation. The main advantage of using WDS in this situation is that you don't need installation media ready for each client. However, suppose you have to install several applications after the OS installation is finished. In this case, you can create a custom install image that can be deployed to client computers with the applications already installed, which is discussed next.

Attended Deployment of a Customized Install Image

The power of WDS is evident when you create and deploy a custom installation image. By creating a custom image, you can install applications and perform other configuration tasks on the OS before you deploy it.

Returning to the example from the previous section, CSM Tech Publishing wants two of its applications installed on each client. Mike has two options: He can use the same procedure described previously and return to each client and install the applications, or he can install Windows 8.1 and the applications on one computer and then use it as the reference computer to create a custom install image. A **reference computer** is one that has been configured with the OS and applications you want to deploy and is used to create an install image that can be deployed to other computers by using WDS.

Mike decides a reference computer is the most efficient approach. To create it, he can use a traditional installation DVD or use WDS and the standard `install.wim` image. After Windows 8.1 is installed, Mike installs the two applications and is then ready to create the custom image by following these steps:

1. Use WDS to create a capture image.
2. Run `sysprep` on the reference computer.
3. Boot the reference computer to the capture image by using a network boot.
4. The install image is created and uploaded to the WDS server.

Now Mike can perform a network boot on the other computers. This time, he has the option to choose the custom image (see Figure 1-3). When the installation is finished, Windows 8.1 and the applications are installed on each client.

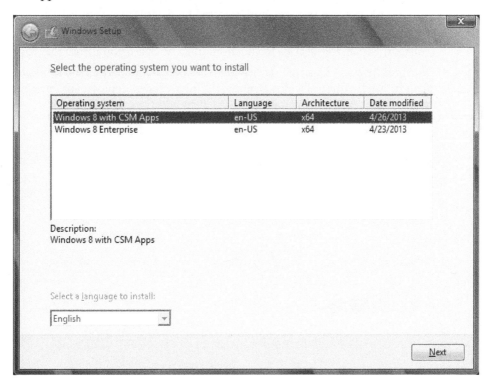

Figure 1-3   Choosing a custom install image

Unattended Deployment of a Customized Install Image

Performing attended installations with WDS for 10 or 15 computers is reasonable because of the time it takes to configure an unattended installation. If you're installing Windows on several dozen or several hundred computers, however, the extra steps for unattended installations make sense.

To do unattended installations, you need an **answer file**, which contains responses to the prompts and questions (such as clicking Next or selecting the installation partition) Windows asks during an OS installation. This file can be created with a text or an XML editor, but the preferred method is the System Image Manager (SIM), a tool that's part of the Windows Assessment and Deployment Kit (ADK). The ADK has several tools designed to make deploying Windows easier. It doesn't come with Windows Server 2012/R2, but it's available as a free download from the Microsoft Download Center.

 You can find the ADK for Windows 8.1 at *www.microsoft.com/en-us/download/details.aspx?id=39982*, or just do a search for Windows 8.1 ADK at the Microsoft Download Center.

Now that you have an idea of some situations in which you can use WDS and the basic steps, continue to the next section on installing and configuring a WDS environment.

Installing and Configuring the WDS Role

You can install WDS, like most Windows server roles, by using Server Manager or PowerShell. The real work begins after the role is installed. WDS is a complex server role and has numerous configuration options and associated tasks. This section covers some of the most common configurations you'll encounter.

In Server Manager, you install the WDS role as you do any other role. In the Role Services window, you're prompted to install the Windows Deployment Services tools, and you have the option to install two role services, both selected by default (see Figure 1-4):

- *Deployment Server*—This role service provides full WDS features and depends on the Transport Server role service to function. In most cases, you install this role service.

- *Transport Server*—This role service provides necessary services for Deployment Server, but it can be used without Deployment Server in advanced deployment environments, such as those without Active Directory and DHCP. In addition, Transport Server supports image multicasting (discussed later in "WDS Server Properties").

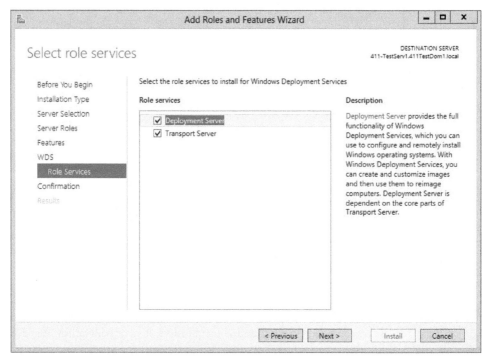

Figure 1-4   Selecting role services for WDS

You can also install the WDS role with PowerShell. To do so, open a PowerShell command prompt, and enter the following command:

```
Install-WindowsFeature WDS
```

By default, this command installs the necessary features and both role services.

WDS Initial Configuration

After WDS is installed, the management console is added to the Tools menu in Server Manager. Before you can use WDS, you must perform initial configuration. When you first open the Windows Deployment Services MMC, you see a message informing you that WDS isn't configured. To configure WDS, right-click the server name in the left pane and click Configure Server to start the WDS Configuration Wizard. The Before You Begin window explains the requirements for configuring WDS (see Figure 1-5).

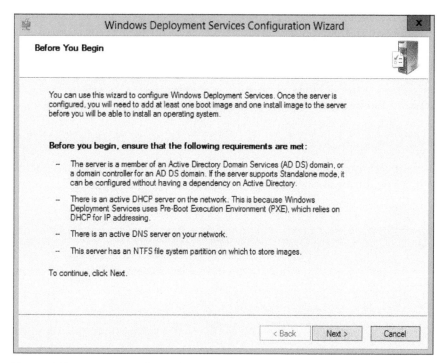

Figure 1-5   Prerequisites for configuring WDS

The next window gives you the choice of installing WDS integrated with Active Directory or as a stand-alone server (see Figure 1-6). The default option, an Active Directory–integrated installation, is recommended if your network includes Active Directory. With this option, you can prestage client computers by creating computer accounts for them in Active Directory. **Prestaging** enables you to do a basic unattended installation by specifying the computer name, selecting the boot and install images a client should receive, and joining the client to the domain. You can also specify which WDS server a client should use when more than one server is on the network. In addition, you can specify that only prestaged clients can access the WDS server, thereby enhancing security.

In the next window, you decide where to store boot and install images, PXE boot files, and WDS management tools. Install images can be quite large, so you need to choose a folder on an NTFS-formatted volume with plenty of free disk space. By default, this folder is C:\RemoteInstall.

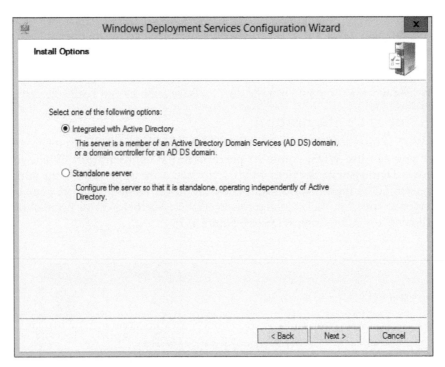

Figure 1-6   Selecting install options

For the best performance, you shouldn't choose the System volume (where the \Windows folder is located). If you do, a warning message is displayed, shown in Figure 1-7.

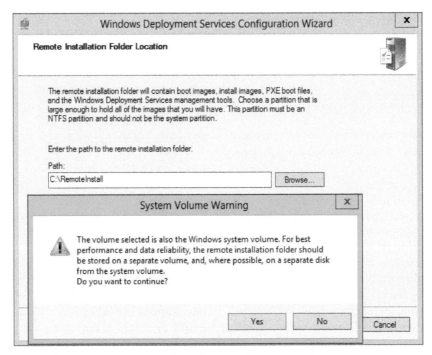

Figure 1-7   Warning message about choosing the System volume

If DHCP is installed on the server, you see the window shown in Figure 1-8, where you configure how DHCP works with WDS. There are two options in this window:

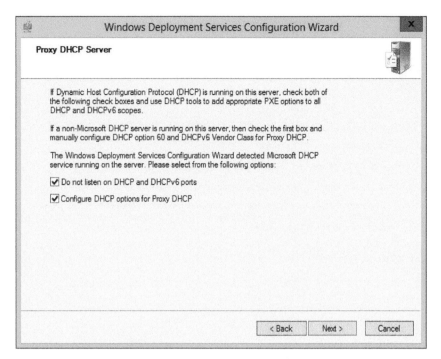

Figure 1-8   DHCP settings

- *Do not listen on DHCP and DHCPv6 ports*—Select this check box when the WDS server is also configured as a DHCP server. This option tells the WDS server not to listen on UDP port 67 to avoid a conflict with DHCP, which uses this port to listen for client IP configuration requests.
- *Configure DHCP options for Proxy DHCP*—If the DHCP server installed on the WDS server is the Microsoft DHCP server, this check box should be selected so that the WDS configuration wizard automatically configures DHCP to forward PXE requests to the WDS server. If a non-Microsoft DHCP server is in use or if DHCP is configured on another server, Proxy DHCP must be configured manually.

If Microsoft DHCP is running on the same server as WDS, both options should be selected. You use the next window to define which PXE clients the WDS server should respond to. There are three options (see Figure 1-9):

- *Do not respond to any client computers*—This option essentially disables WDS, an option you might want to choose until you have finalized WDS configuration.
- *Respond only to known client computers*—With this option set, WDS responds to only prestaged clients. This option is more secure because it prevents a rogue computer from attempting to acquire an install image, but it requires more upfront configuration.
- *Respond to all client computers (known and unknown)*—WDS responds to all clients that attempt a PXE boot, whether they're prestaged or not. If this option is set, you can choose whether administrator approval is required before WDS responds to unknown computers. Unknown clients requiring administrator approval are placed in the Pending Devices node in the WDS management console.

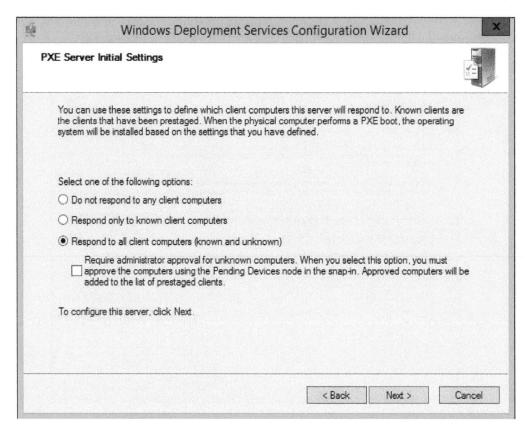

Figure 1-9   PXE server settings

All the options configured with the WDS configuration wizard can be changed later in the Properties window of the WDS server.

The WDS service attempts to start after the last window of the WDS configuration wizard. If the WDS server is also a DHCP server, a DHCP scope must be configured so that WDS can configure proxy DHCP; otherwise, WDS won't start.

If the WDS service doesn't start after finishing the wizard, right-click the server in the WDS console, point to All Tasks, and click Start.

Activity 1-1: Installing Windows Deployment Services

Time Required: 25 minutes
Objective: Install Windows Deployment Services.

Required Tools and Equipment: 411Server1 with Windows Server 2012R2 Standard or Datacenter Edition installed according to instructions in "Before You Begin." Active Directory, DNS, and DHCP must be installed on 411Server1 for WDS to work according to this activity.
Description: You want to streamline the Windows 8.1 installation process on your computers and decide to install WDS to help with remote Windows 8.1 installations. In subsequent

activities, you configure WDS and experiment with a basic WDS implementation, using the standard boot and install images.

1. Start 411Server1 and log on as **Administrator** with the password **Password01.** Server Manager opens automatically.

2. Click **Manage, Add Roles and Features** from the menu to start the Add Roles and Features Wizard. In the Before You Begin window, click **Next.**

3. In the Installation Type window, click **Next.** In the Server Selection window, click **Next** again.

4. In the Server Roles window, scroll down and click the **Windows Deployment Services** check box. Click **Add Features,** and then click **Next.**

5. In the Features window, click **Next.** The WDS window describes WDS and lists the prerequisites for installing it. Read this information, and then click **Next.**

6. The Role Services window shows the two role services you can install: Deployment Server and Transport Server. Leave the check boxes next to both role services selected, and then click **Next.**

7. In the Confirmation window listing your installation selections for review, click **Install.**

8. The Results window shows a progress bar for the installation. Wait for the installation to finish, and then click **Close.**

9. Open the Windows Deployment Services console by clicking **Tools, Windows Deployment Services** from the Server Manager menu.

10. Click to expand **Servers** in the left pane. A yellow caution triangle is shown on the server icon, indicating that you have to configure WDS before you can use it. You use the configuration wizard in the next activity.

11. If you're continuing to the next activity, stay logged on; otherwise, log off or shut down 411Server1.

Activity 1-2: Configuring Windows Deployment Services

Time Required: 15 minutes
Objective: Use the WDS configuration wizard.

Required Tools and Equipment: 411Server1
Description: You have installed WDS so that you can streamline the Windows 8.1 installation process, and now you're ready to configure WDS. In subsequent activities, you experiment with a basic WDS implementation, using the standard boot and install images.

1. Start 411Server1 and log on as **Administrator,** if necessary. Open the Windows Deployment Services console, if necessary.

2. In the WDS console, click to expand **Servers,** if necessary. Right-click **411Server1.411Dom1. local** and click **Configure Server.**

3. In the Before You Begin window, read the requirements for WDS, and then click **Next.**

4. In the Install Options window, be sure **Integrated with Active Directory** is selected, and then click **Next.**

5. In the Remote Installation Folder Location window, accept the default **C:\RemoteInstall,** and then click **Next.** In the System Volume Warning message box, click **Yes.**

6. In the Proxy DHCP Server window, accept the default selections by clicking **Next.**

7. In the PXE Server Initial Settings window, click the **Respond to all client computers (known and unknown)** option button. You can change this option later to improve security. Click **Next.**

8. WDS configuration begins, and you're shown a Task Progress window. After configuration is completed, click **Finish**.

9. In the WDS console, look at 411Server1.411Dom1.local. If a green triangle icon is displayed next to it, the WDS service started successfully, and you can go to the next step. If it shows a black square icon, the service didn't start. In this case, right-click the server, point to **All Tasks**, and click **Start**. You should see the message "Successfully started Windows Deployment Services." Click **OK**.

10. Your WDS server is ready to go. If you're continuing to the next activity, stay logged on; otherwise, log off or shut down your computer.

WDS Server Properties

After the initial configuration of WDS, you could start adding boot and install images, but having a more detailed understanding of WDS server properties first is best. In addition, if you need to change any settings you made with the WDS Configuration Wizard, you do so in the server's Properties window. The following activity walks you through viewing the WDS server properties, and the subsequent sections describe each tab in the Properties window.

Activity 1-3: Viewing WDS Server Properties

Time Required: 10 minutes
Objective: View the WDS server's properties.

Required Tools and Equipment: 411Server1
Description: You'll be working with WDS to perform several OS installations and want to be familiar with the default property settings and where to change them on your WDS server.

1. Start 411Server1 and log on as **Administrator** with the password **Password01**, if necessary. Server Manager starts automatically.

2. If necessary, click **Tools, Windows Deployment Services** from the menu to open the WDS console.

3. Click to expand the **Servers** node, if necessary. Right-click **411Server1.411Dom1.local** and click **Properties**. You see the General tab (shown in the following section).

4. Click each tab, and read the information in it. The following sections describe each tab briefly. Take your time reviewing this information so that you have a good idea of where to configure different aspects of WDS. When you're finished reviewing these tabs, click **Cancel**.

5. If you're continuing to the next activity, stay logged on; otherwise, log off or shut down your computer.

WDS Properties: General   The General tab (see Figure 1-10) has no information you can edit. It simply displays the computer name, the location of the remote installation folder where images and other WDS-related files are stored, and the mode in which WDS is running. (Only native mode is supported in Windows Server 2012/R2; mixed mode is a deprecated mode that's backward-compatible with Remote Installation Services.)

WDS Properties: PXE Response   The PXE Response tab, shown in Figure 1-11, defines which client computers the WDS server responds to and contains the same options as the last window of the WDS Configuration Wizard, explained previously. In this window, you can also adjust how quickly the WDS server responds to PXE clients. This value should be set to the default value, 0, unless other servers on the network responding to PXE requests should have a higher priority than this WDS server.

Figure 1-10   The General tab

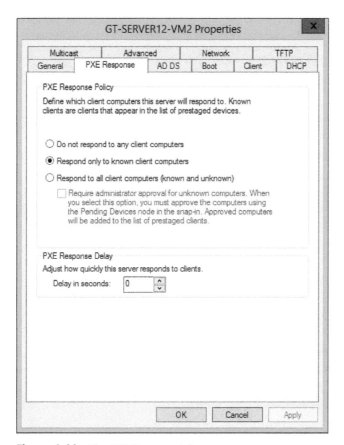

Figure 1-11   The PXE Response tab

WDS Properties: AD DS   The AD DS tab (see Figure 1-12) defines the naming policy for unknown client computers (ones that aren't prestaged). The default string creates a computer account named the same as the user who first logs on to the computer, followed by a number. You can also specify where the computer account is created in Active Directory.

You can find a list of variables to use for the computer-naming policy at *http://technet.microsoft.com/en-us/library/cc771624.aspx.*

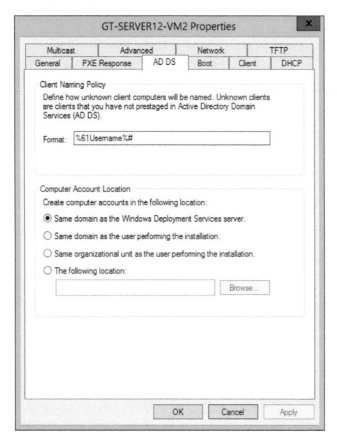

Figure 1-12   The AD DS tab

WDS Properties: Boot   The Boot tab (see Figure 1-13) specifies the PXE boot policy for both known and unknown clients. It defines what happens after a network boot is started with the following options:

- *Require the user to press the F12 key to continue the PXE boot*—If this option is set, someone must be attending the computer when it boots, and the F12 key must be pressed to continue a PXE boot; otherwise, the network boot is aborted, and a local boot is attempted.

- *Always continue the PXE boot*—If this option is set, the network boot proceeds without user intervention, and the boot image is downloaded and started.

- *Continue the PXE boot unless the user presses the ESC key*—This option is similar to the previous option, except a user can cancel the network boot by pressing Esc.

- *Never continue the PXE boot*—This option effectively cancels the network boot process, and the client always attempts a local boot.

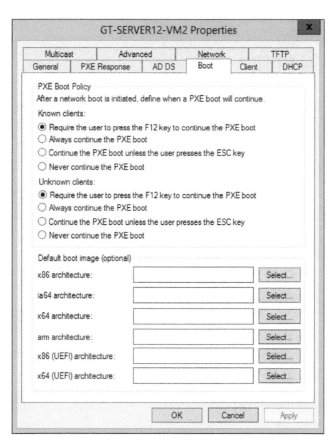

Figure 1-13   The Boot tab

You can also use the Boot tab to specify a default boot image, depending on the client's CPU architecture. If no default boot image is specified in this section, the client uses the boot images in the Boot Images folder of the WDS management console.

WDS Properties: Client   You use the Client tab (see Figure 1-14) to enable unattended installations for client computers, depending on the CPU architecture. You can also specify that the computer shouldn't join the domain after the installation is finished. By default, client computers installed with WDS join the domain automatically. At the bottom of this tab, you can enable client logging (disabled by default) and specify the level of messages that should be logged. These messages might be important when troubleshooting WDS. You can view the log in Event Viewer under the Applications and Services Logs node in the Microsoft\Windows\Deployment-Services-Diagnostics folder.

WDS Properties: DHCP   The DHCP tab (see Figure 1-15) enables you to change how WDS and DHCP work together. You see the same options shown previously in Figure 1-8, but strangely, they're named differently than in the WDS Configuration Wizard.

WDS Properties: TFTP   You use the TFTP tab (see Figure 1-16) to fine-tune TFTP, which is used to transfer image and other files between the client and WDS server. The default value of 0 means no maximum block size is specified, so the default block size of 1456 bytes is used. Variable Window Extension is a new feature that allows Windows to adjust the transfer window size dynamically according to current network conditions. This option is enabled by default.

WDS Properties: Network   The Network tab (see Figure 1-17) enables you to change the UDP port policy, which allows you to change the range of UDP ports used by WDS. By default, Winsock assigns UDP ports dynamically, and you usually don't have to change this option. You can use the network profile to set the network connection speed, but it's usually grayed out if WDS can detect it automatically.

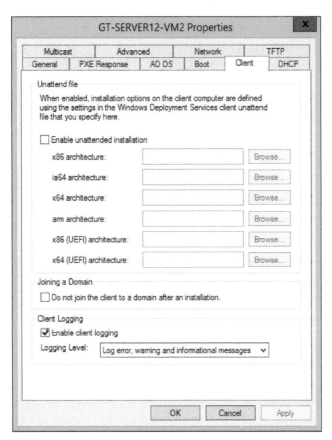

Figure 1-14   The Client tab

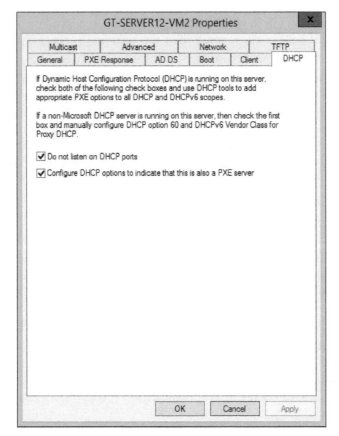

Figure 1-15   The DHCP tab

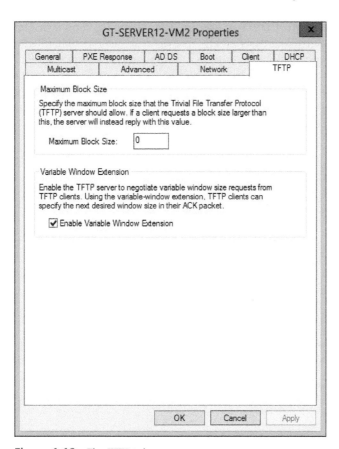

Figure 1-16   The TFTP tab

Figure 1-17   The Network tab

WDS Properties: Advanced You use the Advanced tab, shown in Figure 1-18, to have WDS discover domain controllers dynamically (the default and recommended option) or to set a specific domain controller and global catalog server manually. Usually, the default option is best; you should change it only if you have a good reason (performance, for example) to direct WDS to a specific domain controller. You use the DHCP Authorization section to authorize the WDS server in DHCP; although this option isn't necessary, it can be used to prevent incorrectly configured or rogue servers on the network.

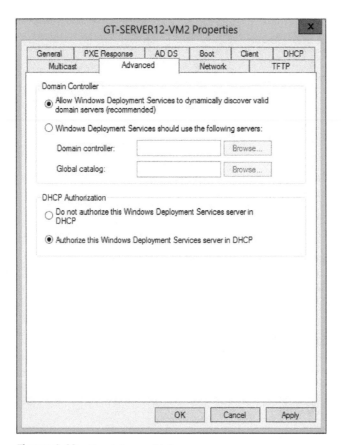

Figure 1-18 The Advanced tab

WDS Properties: Multicast The Multicast tab (see Figure 1-19) is used to specify whether multicast addresses should be assigned via DHCP or with a specific range of addresses (the default). You can also specify whether all clients should be delivered images at the same speed or in groups at different speeds. With the latter option, you can disconnect clients that are transferring data below a specified threshold.

Working with WDS Images

Now that you're familiar with installing the WDS server role and how to configure its properties, it's time to turn your attention to working with WDS images so that you can begin performing remote installations. Images are the heart of the WDS server role. Boot and install images, along with a client that has a PXE-compatible NIC allow an administrator to install an OS remotely on a computer that has neither an OS installed on its hard disk nor locally bootable media. You can use WDS images customized for your environment, the stock OS installation, or a combination of both, depending on the needs of those using the target client computer. The following

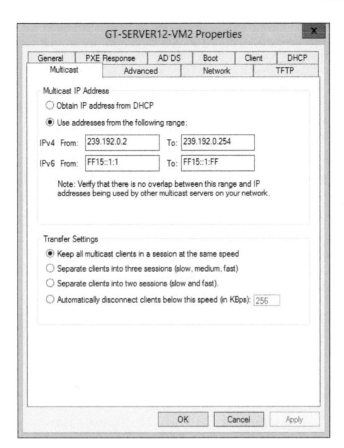

Figure 1-19 The Multicast tab

sections go into more detail on boot and install images and explain discover images and how to update an existing image.

Working with Boot Images

As discussed, a boot image contains Windows PE and Windows Setup, which a client computer uses to select and download an installation image and begin the OS installation. The boot image used in WDS contains the same code on a Windows installation DVD that a client computer boots from when performing a local installation. The main difference is that with WDS, the installation image is loaded across the network, allowing many installations to occur at the same time without requiring multiple copies of the installation medium.

Adding a boot image is really the first step in working with images because without one, you can't boot clients from the network. After a boot image is configured, you can do testing of your WDS setup. In most cases, you should use the boot.wim file on the Windows Server 2012/R2 (or Windows 8.1) installation DVD. The following activity walks you through configuring a boot image in WDS.

Activity 1-4: Adding a Boot Image to WDS

Time Required: 15 minutes
Objective: Configure a boot image in WDS.

Required Tools and Equipment: 411Server1, a Windows Server 2012 R2 installation DVD or an .iso file that can be mounted as a DVD

Description: WDS is installed and the initial configuration is finished; now it's time to configure a boot image. This activity uses the standard `boot.wim` boot image on the Windows Server 2012/R2 installation DVD.

1. Start and log on to 411Server1 as **Administrator,** if necessary.

2. Insert the Windows Server 2012/R2 installation DVD in 411Server1's DVD drive. If you have an ISO image of the DVD, right-click the `.iso` file in File Explorer and click **Mount** (a new feature in Windows Server 2012/R2).

3. Open the WDS console, if necessary.

4. Click to expand the **Servers** node, if necessary, and then click to expand **411Server1.411Dom1. local.**

5. Right-click **Boot Images** and click **Add Boot Image** to start the Add Image Wizard. In the Image File window, click **Browse.**

6. In the Select Windows Image File window, browse to the drive where you inserted the Windows Server 2012/R2 installation DVD. Open the **sources** folder and click **boot.wim** (see Figure 1-20). Click **Open.**

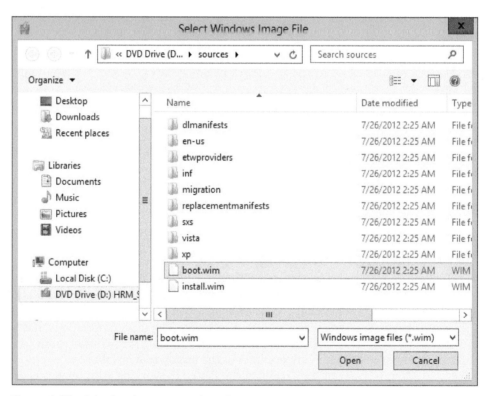

Figure 1-20   Selecting the `boot.wim` boot image

7. Click **Next.** In the Image Metadata window, you can type a descriptive name for the image and a description, or you can accept the default values (see Figure 1-21). Accept the default values, and then click **Next.**

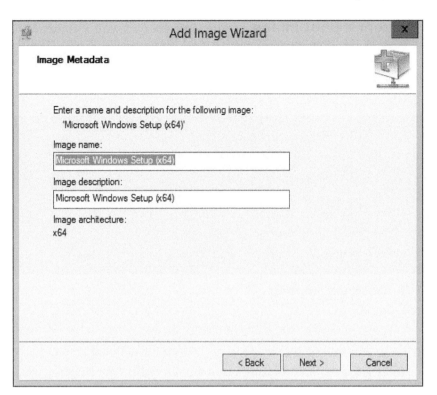

Figure 1-21 Entering an image name and description

8. In the Summary window, click **Next**. The image is added to the Boot Images folder. Windows must copy `boot.wim` from the DVD to the \RemoteInstall folder. Click **Finish** to return to the WDS console. The boot image is shown in the right pane (see Figure 1-22).

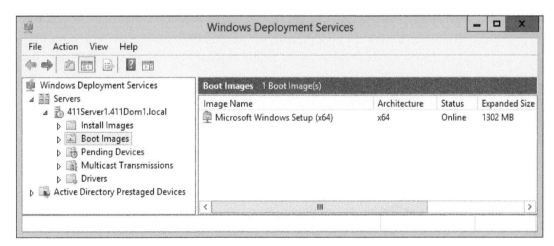

Figure 1-22 WDS with a boot image added

9. That's it! You've created a boot image, and your clients are ready to boot from it. To see the possible actions you can take on the boot image, right-click it. The menu shows options for actions such as viewing the images properties, disabling the image, exporting the image, and creating capture and discover images. Press **Esc** to close this menu.

10. If you're continuing to the next activity, stay logged on; otherwise, log off or shut down 411Server1.

Booting from a Boot Image   Quite a bit goes on with a computer when it's getting ready to boot an OS, even more so when it performs a network boot. Figure 1-23 shows the typical screen you see when you do a network boot and DHCP and WDS respond to the client computer's requests. Take a look at the contents of this screen:

```
Network boot from Intel E1000e
Copyright (C) 2003-2008  VMware, Inc.
Copyright (C) 1997-2000  Intel Corporation

CLIENT MAC ADDR: 00 50 56 20 4E 05   GUID: 564D5BA7-AC2D-3EE9-75E8-2CEF54EFF656
CLIENT IP: 172.31.210.200  MASK: 255.255.0.0  DHCP IP: 172.31.210.102

Downloaded WDSNBP from 172.31.210.102 GT-Server12-VM2.GT2012Dom1.local

Press F12 for network service boot
_
```

Figure 1-23   The network boot screen

- The first three lines show the type of network card performing the PXE boot.
- The fourth line displays the client's MAC address and globally unique identifier (GUID).
- The fifth line shows the IP address information the client got from the DHCP server. If you see this line, your DHCP server is working correctly, and your client was able to contact it.
- The sixth line shows that the WDSNBP file (wdsnbp.com) was downloaded from the WDS server.
- The last line prompts you to press F12 to continue the PXE boot. If you don't press F12 quickly, the PXE boot times out, and the computer attempts to boot from a local OS, if available.

As you've learned, WDSNBP is a basic bootstrap program that allows the PXE client to request the actual boot image (boot.wim). It has some configurable options in the Boot tab of the WDS server's Properties window. For example, you can specify that pressing F12 isn't necessary to continue the network boot process; you might select this option for unattended installations. After you press F12, the boot.wim file is downloaded and started, and you begin Windows setup.

Activity 1-5: Testing a Boot Image

If you're using VMware Workstation or Player, you need to turn off the VMware DHCP service for this activity to work correctly.

Time Required: 15 minutes
Objective: Test a boot image.

Required Tools and Equipment: 411Server1 and WDSclient (configured according to instructions in "Before You Begin")
Description: Now that you have a boot image added to WDS, you can test the WDS configuration by trying to boot a client. This activity uses the standard boot.wim boot image on the Windows Server 2012/R2 installation DVD.

1. Start 411Server1, if necessary.

2. Start WDSclient. If WDSclient already has an OS installed and the BIOS isn't configured with a network boot first in the boot order, press F12 to activate the boot menu. When a network boot has been initiated, you should see the screen shown previously in Figure 1-23.

3. If you missed the prompt, restart the server and be ready to press F12 when you see the prompt. You see a message similar to Figure 1-24 showing the progress of downloading `boot.wim`.

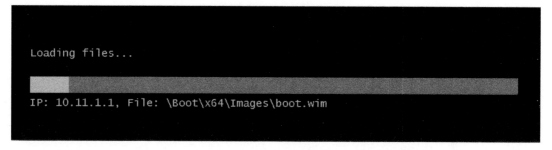

Loading files...

IP: 10.11.1.1, File: \Boot\x64\Images\boot.wim

Figure 1-24   Loading `boot.wim`

4. After `boot.wim` is loaded, Windows Setup begins. You see a window asking for locale and keyboard settings (see Figure 1-25). You can accept the default settings or change them as needed for your location. Click **Next**.

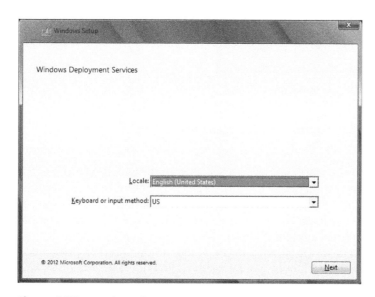

Figure 1-25   Locale settings

5. Next, you're prompted for domain credentials. In the User name text box, type **administrator@411dom1.local,** and in the Password text box, type **Password01.** Click **OK.**

6. The last window of Windows Setup is where you normally select an OS to install. Because you haven't added an installation image, you see a window indicating that no OS image is available.

7. At this point, you know that your basic WDS configuration works; in the next activity, you add an install image. For now, power off your client computer.

8. If you're continuing to the next activity, leave 411Server1 running; otherwise, log off or shut down 411Server1.

Creating and Using a Capture Image   A capture image is a specialized boot image used to capture the state of an OS already installed and configured on a reference computer. A reference computer, as you've learned, is like a prototype where you have installed an OS, made configuration changes, and installed some applications. It serves as the model for other computers. You then boot the reference computer to the capture image and capture the OS and applications to an install image that's applied to other computers. You create a capture image in the WDS management console, using an existing boot image as a template.

Before you boot the reference computer with the capture image, it must be prepared with `sysprep`, which resets system identifiers and other information unique to the computer (such as computer name). In most cases, when you run `sysprep` (in the \Windows\system32\sysprep folder), you should choose the following options (see Figure 1-26):

- Enter System Out-of-Box Experience (OOBE)
- Generalize
- Shutdown

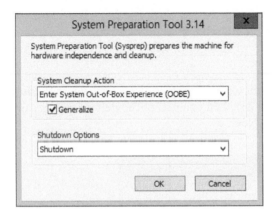

Figure 1-26   Selecting `sysprep` options

You can also run `sysprep` from the command line:

```
C:\windows\system32\sysprep\sysprep /oobe/generalize /shutdown
```

The `/oobe` option causes the computer to start in the usual startup mode, allowing users to perform initial configuration tasks. The `/generalize` option removes the unique identifiers on the system; they're created the next time the system boots. This option also clears system restore points and deletes event logs. The `/shutdown` option causes the target computer to shut down after `sysprep` is finished running. You can also choose `/reboot`, but the `/shutdown` option makes sure your WDS server is ready and you can be prepared to press F12 to do a network boot. If you miss the network boot, your target system boots into Windows and you need to run `sysprep` again.

One caution when using a capture image on the target computer: There must be enough space on the target to store the resulting install image. A network drive can be used, but it isn't recommended because a failed network link can cause image corruption. The next activity walks you through creating a capture image.

Activity 1-6: Creating a Capture Image

Time Required: 20 minutes or longer
Objective: Create a capture image from the boot image already installed and add it to WDS.

Required Tools and Equipment: 411Server1
Description: Now that you have a boot image added to WDS, you can create a capture image for later use when you want to create a custom install image.

1. Start 411Server1 and log on as **Administrator,** if necessary.
2. Open the WDS console. If necessary, click to expand the **Servers** node and click to expand **411Server1.411Dom1.local.**

3. Click the **Boot Images** folder, if necessary. In the right pane, right-click the **Microsoft Windows Setup** boot image you added in Activity 1-4 and click **Create Capture Image**. The Create Capture Image Wizard starts.

4. In the Metadata and Location window (see Figure 1-27), type **Capture Image** in the Image name text box. In the Image description text box, type **Capture and create a custom install image**. In the Location and file name text box, type **C:\RemoteInstall\Capture.wim**, and then click **Next**.

The path to the `capture.wim` file places the capture file in the \RemoteInstall folder. The next step moves it to the WDS image store. You can save a step by specifying the path to the image store (\RemoteInstall\boot\x64\images\capture.wim).

Figure 1-27   The Metadata and Location window

5. The Task Progress window shows the progress of creating the capture image, which can take several minutes. When the process is finished, click the **Add image to the Windows Deployment Server now** check box (see Figure 1-28) to move the image to the WDS image store. Click **Finish**.

6. The Add Image Wizard starts. In the Image File window, accept the path to the image and click **Next**. Click **Next** in the Image Metadata window.

7. Click **Next** in the Summary window. In the Task Progress window, click **Finish** when the task is completed. The WDS management console window updates and displays the new image in the Boot Images folder. The next time you PXE boot a client, a menu shows both boot images, and you can select Capture Image when you want to capture an OS installation or the Microsoft Windows Setup image when you want to install from an installation image.

8. If you're continuing to the next activity, leave 411Server1 running; otherwise, log off or shut down 411Server1.

Figure 1-28   Adding an image to WDS

Working with Install Images

Install images, unsurprisingly, contain the data and instructions for installing an OS. You can use the stock install image (\sources\install.wim) on the Windows installation DVD, or you can create an install image with a reference computer and a capture image. The `install.wim` file on a Windows installation DVD might contain multiple installation images. For example, a Windows Server `install.wim` file might contain four images: Standard and Datacenter editions in both the Server Core and GUI versions. While adding the image to WDS, you can select which edition and version you want to include.

Using a Stock Windows Install Image   This section and the following activity describe adding an install image from a Windows installation DVD. When you use the standard `install.wim` image on the installation DVD, the installation experience is the same as though you booted the client to the installation DVD. The only difference might be the choices of which OS to install. When you boot to the installation DVD, you see all the installation choices on the DVD (for example, Datacenter Edition Server Core or with a GUI). However, when you configure the install image with WDS, you can limit which choices the person attending the installation sees.

When you configure an install image in WDS, the image must be added to an image group. An **image group** is just a container where you can organize images with common properties. For example, you can create an image group for Windows Server 2012 install images and one for Windows 8.1 install images. You can also group images according to which users should have access to them. You can create an image group before adding an install image or by using the Add Image Wizard. The following activity guides you through adding the `install.wim` file from the Windows Server 2012 R2 installation DVD.

Activity 1-7: Adding an Install Image

Time Required: 20 minutes or longer
Objective: Add an install image to WDS.

Required Tools and Equipment: 411Server1 and the Windows Server 2012/R2 installation DVD or ISO file

Description: You're ready to add an install image to WDS. For now, you use the stock install image from the Windows Server 2012 R2 installation DVD. This activity uses the Windows Server 2012 R2 evaluation DVD downloaded from the Microsoft Web site.

1. Start 411Server1 and log on as **Administrator,** if necessary. Insert the Windows Server 2012 R2 installation DVD, if necessary.

2. If necessary, open the WDS console. Click to expand the **Servers** node and click to expand **411Server1.411Dom1.local.**

3. Right-click **Install Images** and click **Add Install Image.** (You can also create an image group in this menu, but you do it with the Add Image Wizard instead.)

4. In the Image Group window (see Figure 1-29), make sure the **Create an image group named** option button is selected, type **Windows Server 2012 R2 Images** for the image group name, and then click **Next.**

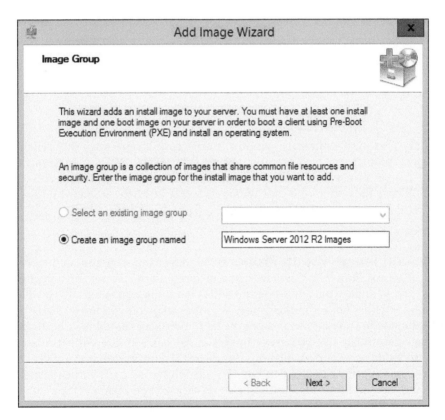

Figure 1-29   Creating an image group

5. In the Image File window, browse to the DVD drive where the installation disc is inserted, and open the **\sources** folder. Click the **install.wim** file and click **Open.** Click **Next.**

6. The Available Images window lists the installation images in the install.wim file (see Figure 1-30). By default, all images are available, or you can clear the check box next to any images you don't want to add. To reduce the time it takes to add images, clear all check boxes but **Windows Server 2012 R2 SERVERSTANDARD,** and then click **Next.**

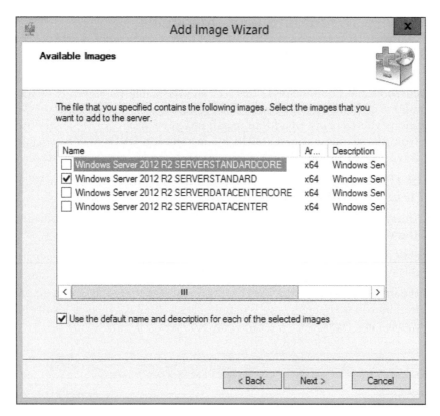

Figure 1-30   Selecting images to be available in WDS

7. Click **Next** in the Summary window. In the Task Progress window, click **Finish** when the task is completed, which can take several minutes. The WDS management console updates and displays the image in the Install Images folder. The next time you PXE boot a client, you'll have the option to install Windows Server 2012 R2 Standard Edition.

8. If you're continuing to the next activity, leave 411Server1 running; otherwise, log off or shut down 411Server1.

Image and Image Group Properties   After an image is added to WDS, it's ready for clients to access. However, there are some properties you can set for image groups and install images. For example, you can set permissions on an image group to allow only particular users or groups to access images in the group. So, for example, if you have created a Windows Server 2012/R2 image group that members of the IT Department should have access to and a Windows 8.1 image group that all employees can access, you can set different permissions on each image group. To set image group permissions, right-click the image group in WDS and click Security to open a standard permissions dialog box. The default setting gives authenticated users read access to all the images in the group. You can also set different permissions for an image inside a group by right-clicking the image and clicking Properties, and then clicking the User Permissions tab. Permissions for image groups and images work just like NTFS permissions on folders and files; image groups are similar to folders, and images are like files inside the folder. One caveat: Users who authenticate to the WDS server to access an image must have at least read permissions to the image group.

Another option for restricting access to an install image is to disable it. You might have an image in WDS that you don't want available to any clients at the moment. To disable this image in WDS, right-click it and click Disable. Disabling an image makes it unavailable to clients without having to change permissions or remove it from WDS. Clients currently using the image can continue the installation, but new clients won't be able to access the image.

Other image tasks include exporting and replacing an image. To use these functions, right-click the image in WDS. If you need to make changes to an image, you can export it, make changes to it with the Windows ADK, and then replace the existing image.

Creating Multicast Transmissions If you need to send a single image to multiple clients, you can conserve network bandwidth by using multicast transmissions. In a multicast transmission, packets sent across the network that contain the image's contents are transferred only once and received by all clients listening for the multicast.

You can set up a multicast transmission in the WDS console by right-clicking the install image and clicking Create Multicast Transmission or by right-clicking the Multicast Transmissions node and clicking Create Multicast Transmission. In either case, a wizard walks you through the process. There are two types of multicast transmissions you can create (see Figure 1-31):

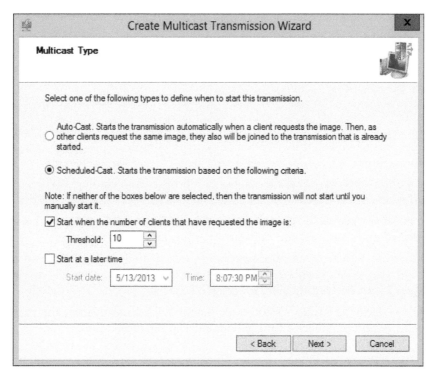

Figure 1-31   Multicast transmission types

- *Auto-Cast*—The image transmission starts as soon as a client requests the image; if other clients request the same image, they're joined to the ongoing transmission. When a client joins an ongoing transmission, it starts receiving packets from the point at which it joined. When the transmission has ended, WDS starts sending packets from the beginning of the file for the clients joining the transmission late.

- *Scheduled-Cast*—The transmission begins when the minimum number of clients have joined the transmission or at a particular date and time, or you can choose both options.

Multicast transmissions are also configured in the Multicast tab of the WDS server's Properties window (shown previously in Figure 1-19), where you can control the IP address and transfer settings. Review these settings to make sure they're correct before you create a multicast transmission. After you have created a multicast transmission, clients can connect to it, and you can monitor the progress in the WDS console (see Figure 1-32).

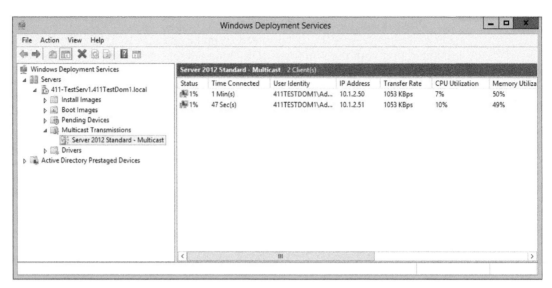

Figure 1-32   Monitoring a multicast transmission

You can perform a few tasks on a multicast transmission after it's created. In the Multi-cast Transmissions node of the WDS management console, right-click a transmission to get the following options:

- *Properties*—You can view a transmission's properties, including its status, multicast type, and number of connected clients. However, you can't edit these properties.

- *Start*—If you created a Scheduled-Cast transmission and don't want to wait until the specified criteria is met, you can start the transmission manually.

- *Deactivate*—An active transmission can be deactivated; connected clients continue the install, but no new clients can connect to the transmission. After all current clients are finished with the transmission, it's deleted.

- *Delete*—Deleting a transmission stops the multicast transmission; any currently connected clients begin using unicast for the remainder of the installation.

Adding Drivers to WDS   Before Windows Server 2008 R2, an install image that required special drivers for a client computer had to be updated with the command-line tool dism.exe (discussed later in "Updating Images"). Driver management is now built into the WDS console in the Drivers node. To add drivers to WDS, right-click the Drivers node in the WDS console and click Add Driver Package. You can install a specific driver by specifying an .inf file, or you can specify a folder containing multiple drivers. After drivers are specified, they're imported to WDS and made available to client computers during OS installation.

After drivers are imported to WDS, you can create a driver group by right-clicking the Drivers node and clicking Add Driver Group. A **driver group** is a collection of one or more driver packages you can restrict to specific client computers based on client hardware and software specifications, such as BIOS, manufacturer, model, OS edition, install image, and so forth. By default, all driver packages are available to all clients, but if you find a conflict with a particular type of client, you can use driver groups to prevent the conflict.

Creating Unattended Installations

WDS is useful in attended mode, when somebody has to answer prompts at the client computer, but its real power comes when used in unattended mode. An unattended installation frees you from having to answer prompts at the client computer while stepping through the installation. Not surprisingly, then, an unattended installation requires an answer file, described earlier. An answer file is often called an "unattend answer file" or just "unattend file." Because WDS uses the term "unattend file," it's been used in this chapter.

Aside from using a text editor or an XML editor, there are two main ways to create an unattend file. You can use the System Image Manager tool that comes with the ADK, which is recommended for more advanced installations, or you can use the Active Directory Prestaged Devices option in WDS.

Active Directory Prestaged Devices When you create an Active Directory prestaged device with WDS, a computer object is created in Active Directory. When the WDS client installs the image, the client is joined to the Windows domain, using the name of the computer object. The Add Prestaged Device Wizard also gives you the option of creating an unattend file for the client, in which you specify basic installation options. The following activity walks you through creating an Active Directory prestaged device.

Activity 1-8: Adding an Active Directory Prestaged Device

Time Required: 20 minutes
Objective: Add an Active Directory prestaged device.

Required Tools and Equipment: 411Server1
Description: You want to begin deploying computers and want the computers to be members of your domain. Instead of doing the server installation and then adding computers to the domain as a separate step, you decide to prestage them and create a basic unattend file so that you don't have to answer installation prompts.

1. Start 411Server1 and log on as **Administrator**, if necessary.

2. If necessary, open the WDS console, and click to expand the **Servers** node.

3. Right-click **Active Directory Prestaged Devices** and click **Add Device** to start the Add Prestaged Device Wizard.

4. In the Identity window (see Figure 1-33), type **WDS-Client1** in the Name text box. In the Device ID text box, you can use the MAC address of the client computer or the device GUID. Both are displayed in the PXE boot window, and there are other ways to get this information. Figure 1-33 uses the device GUID. Because you won't actually be testing it, you can use any value, as long as it's in the correct MAC address or GUID format.

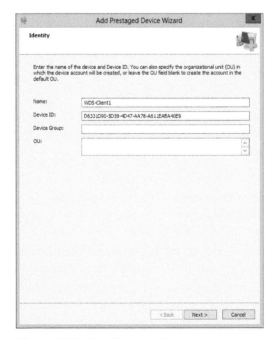

Figure 1-33 Specifying an identity

5. The Device Group setting is optional and is only an identifier used in the WDS management console. The organizational unit (OU) is also optional; the computer account is created in the Computers folder in Active Directory by default unless you specify another OU here. Click **Next**.

6. In the Boot window (see Figure 1-34), you can select the referral server if the client should download the boot image from a server other than the current server. The PXE prompt policy determines whether the user is prompted to press F12 to continue to PXE boot. Because you want an unattended installation, click **Always continue the PXE boot**.

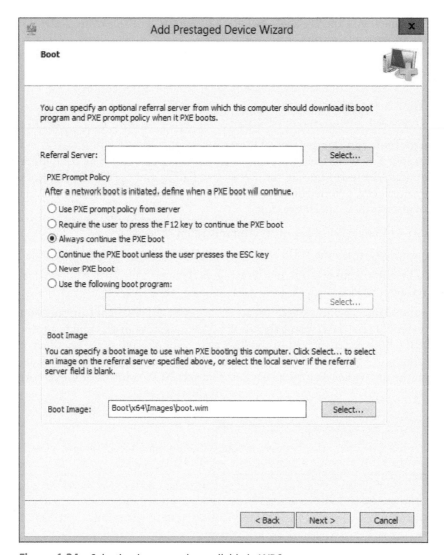

Figure 1-34   Selecting images to be available in WDS

7. In the Boot Image section, specify a boot image if more than one image is available on your WDS server. Because you have both the default boot image and the capture image, click **Select**. Click **Microsoft Windows Setup**, and then click **OK**. Click **Next**.

8. In the Client Unattend window, leave the Referral Server text box blank because you're not using another server. You can create a new unattend file or use an existing one. Click **Create New**.

9. Examine the Create Client Unattend dialog box (see Figure 1-35). The first two text boxes are filled in for you; note that WDS creates an unattend file with the same name as the computer account. This file is stored in the WdsClientUnattend folder in the default image directory (C:\RemoteInstall\WdsClientUnattend). Select the language to be used for Windows Setup.

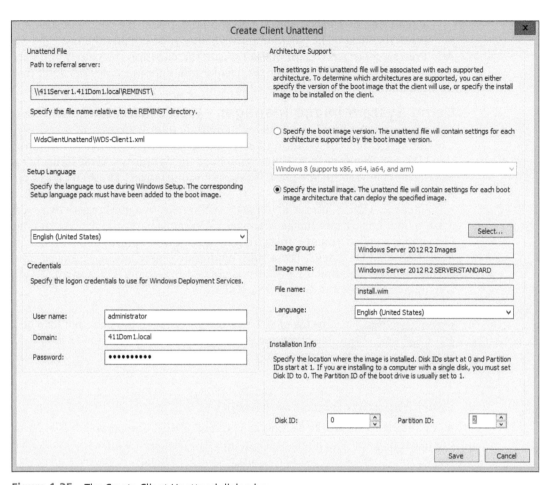

Figure 1-35   The Create Client Unattend dialog box

10. Credentials are required to access the WDS server. Normally, you don't use the Administrator account because this information is stored in the unattend file. You should create a user with limited permissions to use for this purpose. For this activity, however, use the Administrator account. Fill in the rest of the information as shown in Figure 1-35, and then click **Save**. Click **Next** in the Client Unattend window.

11. In the Join Rights window, you can specify a user who has permissions to join the computer to the domain. If you don't, any user can join the computer to the domain. Click **Finish**. In the message box stating that the device was added successfully, click **OK**.

12. Now when you PXE boot a client computer with the specified ID, it installs the specified install image named WDS-Client1 (or whatever you configure) and is joined to the Windows domain. To see the resulting unattend file, open File Explorer and browse to **C:\RemoteInstall\WdsClientUnattend**. Right-click the **WDS-Client1.xml** file and click **Edit** to open it in Notepad. You can review this file to get an idea of the unattend file's format and see why you probably don't want to create it manually. Close Notepad.

13. If you're continuing to the next activity, leave 411Server1 running; otherwise, log off or shut down 411Server1.

Using the MAC address for the device ID in the prestaged device doesn't seem to work fully in unattend mode. The WDS client PXE boots unattended and chooses the selected boot and install image, but it doesn't name the computer or join it to the domain. Therefore, use the GUID as the device ID.

When using prestaged devices, you should consider the choice of disk and partition where you install the image. The partition must already exist because the unattend file created with the Add Prestaged Device Wizard doesn't create the partition for you. If you need this function or other options, such as entering the product key, that prestaged devices don't offer, you need to use the System Image Manager, discussed next.

Using System Image Manager As mentioned, the System Image Manager is a component of the Windows ADK, which you can download and install from the Microsoft Download Center. For Windows Server 2012 R2 and Windows 8.1 deployments, download the ADK for Windows 8.1. When you start the Windows ADK setup program, the default installation choices are adequate for most circumstances. The ADK takes up more than 3 GB disk space.

After the ADK is installed, you start the System Image Manager by searching for this program name. The **System Image Manager** (**SIM**) automates the process of creating an unattend file, similar to what you saw in Activity 1-8, but more options are available for automatic configuration of WDS clients. For a fully unattended installation, you need two unattend files: a client unattend file, similar to what was created in Activity 1-8, and an OS unattend file, which responds to the prompts during OS installation.

The use of SIM is beyond the scope of this book, but for a good tutorial, see *http://technet.microsoft.com/en-us/library/cc722301(v=ws.10).aspx.*

Working with Discover Images

As discussed, WDS works as long as you have PXE-boot-capable NICs. Most NICs now have this capability, but you might still run into a situation in which you can't PXE boot from a client station. That's when a discover image comes in handy. A discover image is a boot image you burn to a CD/DVD. You insert the disc with the discover image in the client computer, and the client boots to the disc and starts Windows PE. From there, a WDS server is contacted and the process proceeds as usual. As with a capture image, you create a discover image from an existing boot image in WDS. Here are the steps:

1. Open the WDS console.

2. Open the Boot Images folder. Right-click the standard Microsoft Windows Setup boot image and click Create Discover Image.

3. The Create Discover Image Wizard starts. In the Metadata and Location window (see Figure 1-36), you can usually leave the default name and description; just specify where you want the image saved. The WDS server's name can be left blank if the current server should respond to clients.

4. Click Next and then click Finish when the Task Progress window indicates that the image is completed.

5. The next step is creating an ISO image that can be written to a DVD or other bootable media. This step requires using the `oscdimg` command (found in the Windows ADK), which converts the WIM format to a bootable ISO image format.

6. The last step is burning the image to a DVD and booting to it. The boot process is almost identical to the PXE boot you have already seen. For more details, see *http://technet. microsoft.com/en-us/library/dd759146.aspx.* The steps are for Windows Server 2008 R2, but the main difference is that in Windows Server 2012/R2, you need the Windows ADK (called Windows AIK in Windows Server 2008 R2).

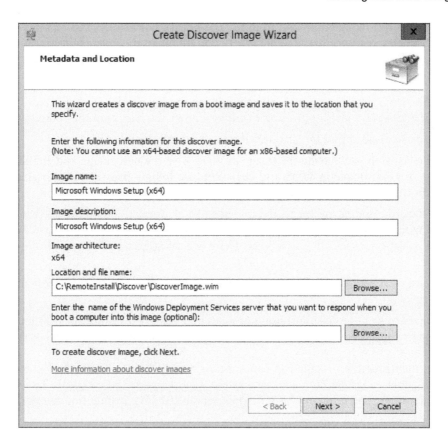

Figure 1-36　Creating a discover image

Updating Images

You can make changes to images after they're created. For example, you've created an install image with several customizations and installed applications, and you don't want to go through the same process each time a patch or service pack is released. With the **Deployment Image Servicing and Management** (`dism.exe`) command-line tool, you can update an image with patches, drivers, hot fixes, and service packs without having to re-create the entire image. The `dism.exe` command can be used on an offline image that you've mounted by using `dism /mount-wim` or on an online image if you include the `/online` switch. It can also be used to display information about an image.

As a typical example of using `dism.exe` on an existing image, say you've created a Windows Server 2012 R2 custom install image from a reference computer. After creating the image, you learn that Microsoft has published a hot fix containing a security patch for the DNS Server role service. You plan to deploy DNS on several servers that will use the install image, so including the hot fix in the install image is critical. The following steps describe the procedure; each step can take a lot of time because of the size of image files:

1. First, take the image you need to apply the hot fix to offline by right-clicking it in WDS and clicking Disable. Then right-click the image again and click Export Image. Make note of where you placed the exported image and the name you gave it. (*Note*: If the image was never added to WDS, you don't need to perform this step.)

2. Create a folder where you'll mount the image. Mounting an image is like mounting a drive, making its contents available as though they were just files and folders on a disk. This example uses C:\mount as the location. Use the following command to mount the `install.wim` image in the C:\RemoteInstall\Export folder. The `/index` parameter specifies which installation image to use if the `.wim` file contains more than one.

```
dism /mount-wim /wimfile:c:\remoteinstall\export\install.wim
  /index:1 /mountdir:c:\mount
```

3. Use the following command to apply the hot fix named `DNSfix.cab`. After the `/image` parameter, you specify the folder where you mounted the image but not the image's filename.

```
dism /image:c:\mount /add-package /packagepath:c:\hotfixes\dnsfix.cab
```

4. Use the following command to commit the changes to the `.wim` file and dismount the image. The `/commit` option writes the changes to the image file you exported in Step 1. You can use `/discard` instead of `/commit` if you don't want to keep the changes you made.

```
dism /unmount-wim /mountdir:c:\mount /commit
```

5. The last step is replacing the image in WDS with the new image and enabling it. Right-click the original image in WDS and click Replace Image. Browse to and select the image you exported in Step 2. Finally, enable the image so that clients can access it.

When you update an image, the updates can be applied to computers that already installed an OS with WDS. Some updates require a system restart after being applied, but you might not want this action, especially for servers. There are two `dism` options for dealing with automatic restarts:

- `/preventpending`—Prevents updates that require a restart from being installed on the target computer.

- `/norestart`—Allows installing updates that require a restart but prevents an automatic restart; the computer must be restarted manually before the update takes effect.

As mentioned, an image file can contain multiple install images. To see a list of images available in a `.wim` file, for example, use the `/Get-imageinfo` option. To see a list of images in the `install.wim` file on the Windows Server 2012/R2 installation medium in drive D:, use the following command:

```
dism /get-imageinfo /imagefile:d:\sources\install.wim
```

Any errors that occur while running `dism.exe` are reported in the Windows log at C:\Windows\Logs\DISM.

Enabling and Disabling Features in Images   Similar to applying hot fixes and patches, you can enable and disable features in an existing image by using the `dism.exe` command. To enable a feature in an image, it must be taken offline and mounted first. In the following examples, the DHCPServer feature is enabled in the first command and disabled in the second command. The third command displays a list of available features (and indicates whether they're enabled or disabled in the mounted image) and can be used to get the names of features you want to enable or disable.

```
dism /image:c:\mount /enable-feature /featurename:dhcpserver
dism /image:c:\mount /disable-feature /featurename:dhcpserver
dism /image:c:\mount /get-features
```

After you enable or disable features, be sure to commit the changes and dismount the image, and then replace the image in WDS, if necessary.

For more information on `dism.exe`, including options and parameters, see *http://technet.microsoft.com/en-us/library/dd744382(v=ws.10).aspx*.

Using PowerShell with WDS

PowerShell 4.0 in Windows Server 2012 R2 and Windows 8.1 introduced more than 30 cmdlets for managing WDS. Table 1-2 lists some PowerShell cmdlets you can use to configure WDS and work with install images. For a full list, see *http://technet.microsoft.com/en-us/library/dn283416.aspx*.

Table 1-2   PowerShell cmdlets for managing WDS

PowerShell cmdlet	WDS function
Set-WdsBootImage	Modify boot image settings
Set-WdsInstallImage	Modify install image settings
Get-WdsBootImage	View boot image properties
Get-WdsInstallImage	View install image properties
Enable-WdsBootImage	Enable a boot image
Disable-WdsBootImage	Disable a boot image
Enable-WdsInstallImage	Enable an install image
Disable-WdsInstallImage	Disable an install image
Add-WdsDriverPackage	Add a driver to a boot image
New-WdsInstallImageGroup	Create an install image group
New-WdsClient	Create a prestaged client

© 2015 Cengage Learning®

Configuring DHCP for WDS

As discussed, if a Microsoft DHCP server and WDS are on the same server and all potential WDS clients are on the same network as the WDS server, you don't have to make any other DHCP configuration changes. You just need to be sure both check boxes in the DHCP tab of the WDS server's Properties window are selected. However, if DHCP is on a different server on a different subnet, you need to make some changes. Here are the most common setups:

- *DHCP is on a different server but the same subnet*—Make sure the DHCP options are set correctly. In the DHCP tab of the WDS server's Properties window (shown previously in Figure 1-15), clear both check boxes to ensure that the WDS server is listening for PXE boot requests on port 67. No changes are needed for the DHCP server. In this setup, when the PXE client boots, the DHCP server responds with an IP address for the client, and the WDS server indicates that it can provide PXE boot services. After the client has an IP address supplied by the DHCP server, it contacts the WDS server to request the boot image.

- *DHCP is on a different server or a different subnet*—You must configure two DHCP server options. For Option 066, the boot server's hostname, you can supply the IP address or server name. Option 067 is the boot file's name and path in relation to the \RemoteInstall directory, so this value is something like boot\x64\wdsnbp.com. If you're using 32-bit computers, replace x64 with x86.

- *DHCP is installed on the same server as WDS but it's not a Microsoft DHCP server*—In this case, you need to add the 060 PXEClient option to the DHCP server manually and make sure the option for not listening on DHCP ports is selected in the WDS server's Properties window.

WDS is a complex feature in Windows Server 2012/R2, so you need to work with it to understand all its settings. After you have mastered it, you'll have a powerful tool for deploying Windows operating systems. However, you can't sit back and relax after deployment. One of a server administrator's ongoing tasks is to keep servers and workstations up to date, the topic of Chapter 2.

Chapter Summary

■ The WDS server role facilitates installing Windows OSs across a network. In Windows Server 2012/R2, WDS can deploy these OSs: Windows XP, Windows Server 2003, Windows Vista SP1, Windows Server 2008/R2, Windows 7, Windows Server 2012/R2, and Windows 8.

■ The WDS process starts with a client computer that has a PXE-compatible NIC. An IP address is assigned to the client via DHCP. A bootstrap file is transferred to the client, which uses it to boot and request a boot image file. Windows Setup is started, and an install image is sent to the client. The client runs the install image, and the OS is installed.

■ The WDS server role requires Active Directory (recommended), a DHCP server, DNS, clients with PXE-compatible NICs, and suitable storage for boot and install images.

■ WDS is used in several situations, including attended deployments of a standard image, attended deployments of a customized image, and unattended deployments. Attended deployments are generally for smaller networks or when only a few computers need to be deployed. Unattended deployments require more setup and are for larger networks.

■ The WDS server role has two role services: Deployment Server and Transport Server. In most cases, both role services are installed. WDS must be configured before it can be used. A configuration wizard walks you through basic settings, and then you can make changes in the WDS server's Properties window.

■ To use WDS, you need both boot and install images. A boot image contains Windows PE and Windows Setup, which are used to access and run install images. A capture image is a specialized boot image used to create a custom install image from a reference computer. Install images contain the OS deployed to the client computer. The Windows installation DVD contains a standard install image that can be used if no OS customizations are needed. When you add an install image, you must place it in a WDS image group, used to organize images and set permissions.

■ An unattended installation requires an answer file or unattend file. An unattend file is an XML file that can be created in the System Image Manager that's part of the ADK. You can also create a basic unattended installation by using prestaged devices.

■ If you have clients that can't PXE boot, you can create a discover image, which allows a client to boot from a CD/DVD and access a WDS server for the install image. Discover images are specialized boot images that need to be converted to an ISO file before burning to bootable media.

■ Install images can be updated with patches, hot fixes, and service packs by using the dism.exe command. Images are generally taken offline, updated with the necessary packages, and then added back to WDS. Using dism.exe, you can also enable and disable Windows features.

■ You might need to make additional configurations to DHCP, depending on your environment. If DHCP and WDS are on the same server, WDS makes the necessary changes in DHCP. If DHCP is on a different server but the same subnet, you must make sure WDS is listening on port 67, but no changes to DHCP are needed. If DHCP is on a different subnet, you must configure options 066 and 067 on the DHCP server. If DHCP is on the same server as WDS but is not a Microsoft DHCP server, you must configure option 060 on DHCP.

Key Terms

answer file   A text file containing information that answers the prompts and questions occurring during an OS installation.

boot image   An image file containing the Windows Preinstallation Environment (PE) that allows a client computer to access a WDS server so that it can access an install image. *See also* Windows Preinstallation Environment (PE).

capture image   A special boot image that creates an install image from a reference computer. *See also* install image *and* reference computer.

Deployment Image Servicing and Management (`dism.exe`)   A command-line tool for updating an image file with patches, drivers, hot fixes, and service packs without having to re-create the entire image.

discover image   An image file that can be used to boot a client computer that can't use PXE, usually from a CD/DVD or flash device.

driver group   A collection of one or more driver packages you can restrict to specific client computers based on client hardware and software specifications.

image file   A file containing other files, much like a zip file containing multiple files; WDS image files can be one of three formats: `.wim`, `.vhd`, and `.vhdx`.

image group   A container for organizing images with common properties.

install image   An image file containing the OS being deployed to client computers.

multicasting   A network communication method for delivering data to multiple computers on a network simultaneously.

network boot   The process by which a computer loads and runs an OS that it retrieves from a network server.

Preboot eXecution Environment (PXE)   A network environment built into many NICs that allows a computer to boot from an image stored on a network server.

prestaging   A feature that enables you to perform a basic unattended installation by specifying the computer name, selecting the boot and install images a client should receive, and joining the client to the domain.

reference computer   A computer that has been configured with the OS and applications you want to deploy; it's then used to create an install image that can be deployed to other computers by using WDS.

System Image Manager (SIM)   A tool in the Windows Assessment and Deployment Kit (ADK) that automates creating unattend files.

`wdsnbp.com`   A bootstrap program; a WDS component that a WDS client downloads when performing a network boot.

Windows Deployment Services (WDS)   A server role that facilitates installing Windows OSs across a network.

Windows Imaging Format (WIM)   The most common image file type used by WDS and the method used to store installation files on a Windows installation DVD.

Windows Preinstallation Environment (PE)   A minimal OS that has only the services needed to access the network, work with files, copy disk images, and jump-start a Windows installation.

Review Questions

1. Which operating system can be deployed with WDS? (Choose all that apply.)

   a. Windows Server 2003

   b. Windows 2000

   c. Windows 8

   d. Windows XP

2. Which of the following is a special boot image that creates an install image from a reference computer?

   a. Discover image

   b. Capture image

   c. Install image

   d. Update image

3. Which of the following best describes the `wdsnbp.com` file?

    a. Discover image

    b. Install image

    c. WIM file

    d. Bootstrap program

4. Of the following steps in the WDS process, which occurs last?

    a. Windows PE is started.

    b. The client requests a bootstrap.

    c. The client requests an install image.

    d. The client runs `wdsnbp.com`.

5. Which of the following do you need if your client NICs aren't PXE compatible?

    a. Capture image

    b. Discover image

    c. ReFS file system

    d. Update image

6. When performing an attended installation, what key must be pressed to cause the PXE-compatible client to begin downloading the boot image?

    a. F12

    b. F5

    c. Alt+Esc

    d. Alt+Insert

7. You want to deploy Windows 8.1 with some of your company's applications already installed so that you don't have to install them on each computer after the OS is installed. All your client computers have PXE-compatible NICs. Which of the following is a step you should take? (Choose all that apply.)

    a. Add the `install.wim` file from the Windows 8.1 DVD to WDS.

    b. Create a capture image.

    c. Run `sysprep` on a reference computer.

    d. Create a discover image by using `dism.exe`.

8. Which of the following is a WDS component that supports multicasting?

    a. Windows ADK

    b. `sysprep`

    c. Deployment Server

    d. Transport Server

9. Which WDS option should you choose if you want to be able to prestage devices?

    a. Active Directory integrated

    b. Stand-alone server

    c. No listening on DHCP ports

    d. Responding only to known clients

1

10. Which WDS properties tab should you use to define which client computers the WDS server responds to?

    a. General

    b. PXE Response

    c. Boot

    d. TFTP

11. Which WDS properties tab do you use to specify whether all clients should be delivered images at the same speed or in groups at different speeds?

    a. Boot

    b. Advanced

    c. Multicast

    d. Client

12. What protocol does WDS use to transfer files from the server to the client?

    a. TFTP

    b. TCP

    c. SMB

    d. NFS

13. If you want to deploy an image to multiple client computers at the same time but send data packets only once, what WDS feature should you use?

    a. PXE boot

    b. Prestaged devices

    c. Discover images

    d. Multicast

14. When a client performs a PXE boot, which of the following does it download from the WDS server first?

    a. `boot.wim`

    b. `wdsnbp.com`

    c. `PXE-boot.com`

    d. `install.wim`

15. You're creating a reference computer for the purpose of creating a custom install image. You have installed the OS, made your configuration changes, and installed the applications you want. What should you do next?

    a. Boot the reference computer by using `boot.wim`.

    b. Prestage the reference computer.

    c. Run `sysprep` on the reference computer.

    d. Use the `dism.exe` command on the reference computer.

16. Which of the following is true about the Windows Server 2012/R2 `install.wim` file? (Choose all that apply.)

    a. It's in the C:\Windows directory.

    b. It can contain multiple installation images.

    c. It always contains a single OS installation.

    d. It's on the DVD in the \sources folder.

17. Which of the following is true about image groups? (Choose all that apply.)

    a. They're optional.

    b. They're used to organize boot images.

    c. You can set access permissions on them.

    d. All installation images must be placed in an image group.

18. Which should you do if you want to make an image temporarily unavailable to clients but allow currently connected clients to continue an installation in progress?

    a. Disable the image.

    b. Stop the WDS service.

    c. Delete the image.

    d. Deny read access to the image.

19. You want to deploy a new Windows 8.1 image to 30 computers and make sure this deployment doesn't saturate the network. You want the image transfer to begin only after at least 25 of the computers have connected to the server. Which WDS option should you configure?

    a. Pending devices

    b. Auto Cast

    c. Prestaged devices

    d. Scheduled-Cast

20. Which of the following is true about the Add Prestaged Device Wizard? (Choose all that apply.)

    a. A computer object is created in Active Directory.

    b. You can specify instructions to create and format partitions on the client computer.

    c. An unattend file is created automatically for the client computer.

    d. You can specify instructions to set a static IP address on the client computer.

21. You're using WDS to deploy Windows to several dozen computers and have been testing your environment before you begin deployment. Most of your computers seem to have no problem connecting to the WDS server and running the boot image. However, six older computers can't connect. You find that there's no network boot option in their BIOS. What should you do so that these computers can connect to the WDS server to access the install image?

    a. When these computers boot, press F5 to display a boot menu.

    b. Create a discover image and burn it to a CD/DVD.

    c. Change the permissions on the `boot.wim` file.

    d. Configure the clients to use TFTP instead of a network boot.

22. Last week, you created a custom install image from a reference computer with plans to deploy the image tomorrow. The reference computer has already been put into service for other purposes. Today, you discover that a critical security patch for IIS has been released. IIS is a necessary part of your install image. What's the most efficient solution for ensuring that your computers will have this security patch?

    a. Disable IIS in the image, deploy the image, and then install the patch.

    b. Create a new reference computer that includes the patch.

    c. Deploy the image and then run Windows update on all your computers.

    d. Use `dism.exe` to modify the image before deploying it.

23. Which of the following is true when a Microsoft DHCP server is installed on the same computer as WDS?

    a. WDS should be configured to not listen on DHCP ports.

    b. You need to add the 060 PXEClient option to DHCP manually.

    c. DHCP option 066 must be configured so that clients can find the WDS server.

    d. WDS and DHCP can't be installed on the same server.

24. Which of the following is true when DHCP is installed on a different server than WDS is?

    a. WDS must be configured to provide IP addresses to clients.

    b. WDS should be configured to listen on DHCP ports.

    c. The DHCP server must provide the path to the wdsnbp.com program.

    d. WDS won't work; both services must be on the same server.

25. Which program should you use if you need to create an unattend file that creates and formats partitions during installation?

    a. Prestaged Device Wizard

    b. Deployment Image Servicing and Management

    c. System Image Manager

    d. wdsutil.exe

Case Projects

Case Project 1-1: Describing WDS Benefits

You have recently hired a server administrator who will help with some new server deployments you have planned. This administrator has worked in environments with only a few servers and computers and has never deployed OSs on a large scale before. He's unfamiliar with WDS and wants to know the benefits of using it. What can you tell him?

Case Project 1-2: Updating a WDS Image File

You have a Windows Server 2012 R2 custom install image named Server2012Standard that you use to deploy new servers. The current image doesn't have Remote Desktop Services enabled, and you find you have to enable it on every server you deploy. You want to enable Remote Desktop Services in the image so that it's enabled on all future servers you deploy with the image. The image is currently enabled in WDS. What steps should you take to make sure Remote Desktop Services is enabled in the image for all future deployments?

Case Project 1-3: Performing a Large Deployment

A new customer who wants to install Windows 8.1 on about 100 computers has contacted you. She tells you that the network uses Windows Server 2012 R2 in a domain configuration, and all new computers should be added as members of the domain. All Windows 8.1 computers should have three applications installed. What are some questions you need to ask this customer before beginning the deployment, and which features of WDS are you likely to use?

chapter 2

Windows Server Update Services

After reading this chapter and completing the exercises, you will be able to:

- Describe Windows Server Update Services
- Install the WSUS role
- Perform initial WSUS configuration
- Configure WSUS synchronization and approval rules
- Describe additional WSUS configuration tasks

Installing Windows on a number of desktop computers and servers can be a time-consuming task, and Windows has Windows Deployment Services (WDS) for assisting with this task. After Windows is installed, however, you can't just sit back and relax. Hackers and malware designers are constantly looking for and finding vulnerabilities in operating systems. When a vulnerability is discovered through malicious activities or by Microsoft's own software engineers, a patch is developed and made available for users to update their computers. In addition, bugs are found and OS enhancements are made, and updates to address both are made available. This chapter discusses the Windows Update program for downloading and installing available updates. In large networks, you usually want to centralize and control the update process—enter Windows Server Update Services (WSUS). This chapter discusses how to install the WSUS role and then configure the role and the client computers using WSUS.

An Overview of Windows Server Update Services

Completing the hands-on activities in this book is important because they contain information about how Windows Server 2012/R2 works and the tools to manage it that's best understood by hands-on experience. If, for some reason, you can't do some of the activities, you should at least read through each one to make sure you don't miss important information. Table 2-1 summarizes the requirements for hands-on activities in this chapter.

Table 2-1   Activity requirements

Activity	Requirements	Notes
Activity 2-1: Installing the WSUS Role	411Server2	
Activity 2-2: Performing WSUS Postinstallation Tasks	411Server2	Internet connection required
Activity 2-3: Creating a Custom Computer Group	411Server2	
Activity 2-4: Configuring Windows Update with Group Policy	411Server1, 411Win8	
Activity 2-5: Configuring WSUS Synchronization and Approval Rules	411Server2	

© 2015 Cengage Learning®

Windows Server Update Services (WSUS) is a server role that makes it possible for administrators to take control of Microsoft product updates on computers running Windows. Another term for this process is **patch management.** When patch management is done with WSUS, administrators can control which product updates are allowed as well as the source and timing of these updates. In a typical WSUS setup, the WSUS server downloads patches, security updates, bug fixes, and other updates from the Microsoft Update servers, and then distributes these updates to Windows computers after they have been approved. This means updates are downloaded from the Internet only once to the WSUS server instead of once for each computer needing the update.

You install WSUS on a Windows Server 2012/R2 computer like any other server role. After it's installed and configured, you configure Windows clients to use the WSUS server for Windows updates. Ideally, clients are configured by using Group Policy, so your clients need to be domain members. The WSUS server can be a stand-alone server or a domain member, but installing WSUS on a domain controller isn't recommended. In most cases, you configure WSUS to download updates for all the products your clients are running. You can then approve which updates you want your clients to actually install. Some advantages of using WSUS for Windows updates include the following:

- Centralized control over Microsoft product updates
- Reduced Internet bandwidth usage
- Only approved updates are installed
- Easy to determine which patches and updates have been applied

Before you delve into the details of WSUS, it's useful to review how the Windows Update process works by default, when no WSUS server is available.

Windows Update

Windows Update is a built-in function of all Windows OSs. When Windows is installed, one of the first things you're asked to configure is Windows Update. Microsoft recommends configuring Windows Update to download and install important updates automatically, but you can also check for updates manually and select the updates you want to install. In either case, you must configure Windows Update settings before updates can be downloaded and installed.

In Windows Server 2012/R2, Windows Update is disabled by default (see Figure 2-1). You can enable Windows Update and accept the default settings by clicking "Turn on automatic updates." For a server, this option isn't recommended because some updates require a system restart, and you probably don't want your server to restart without you being aware of it. A better choice is the "Let me choose my settings" option, which results in the window shown in Figure 2-2.

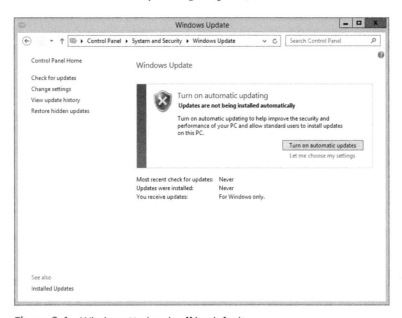

Figure 2-1   Windows Update is off by default

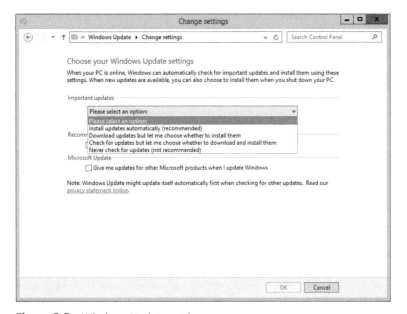

Figure 2-2   Windows Update settings

Figure 2-2 shows the options for how important updates should be handled. **Important updates** usually solve a security or reliability issue in Windows. For a Windows desktop computer, the "Install updates automatically" option is usually suitable because typically, it's okay for a desktop computer to restart automatically. For a server, you probably want to select "Download updates but let me choose whether to install them" so that you have control over whether and when an update is installed. In Figure 2-2, there are also two check boxes you can select. **Recommended updates** make minor improvements to Windows but aren't critical to security or reliability. If you want this option, select the "Give me recommended updates the same way I receive important updates" check box. If you don't select this option, you don't get recommended updates. The last type of update is called Microsoft updates. If you select the "Give me updates for other Microsoft products when I update Windows" check box, you get updates for other Microsoft products.

When Windows Update is enabled, Windows does the following, according to which option is selected:

- *Install updates automatically*—Windows checks for updates on the Microsoft update servers periodically, and when updates are found, they're downloaded in the background. Updates are installed automatically during the **maintenance window,** a time configured for performing maintenance tasks. It's set at 2:00 a.m. by default but can be set to a time of your choosing. By default, if your computer is in a power-saving state, it's awakened at the scheduled time to install updates and then resumes the power-saving state.

- *Download updates but let me choose whether to install them*—Windows checks for updates on the Microsoft update servers periodically, and when updates are found, they're downloaded in the background. Windows alerts you in the notification area that updates are ready to install. You use the Windows Update program to select and install updates manually.

- *Check for updates but let me choose whether to download and install them*—Windows checks for updates on the Microsoft update servers periodically and informs you via the notification area when updates are available, but you choose whether and when to download and install them.

It's important to realize that if you have configured dozens or hundreds of computers to download updates automatically, you're likely to notice a substantial strain on the Internet connection. To prevent this problem, it's best to set up a WSUS server and configure your computers to check for updates on the WSUS server. This way, only the WSUS server needs to contact Microsoft update servers to download updates.

 You can see when a computer checked for updates and which updates were downloaded and installed by viewing the `WindowsUpdate.log` file in C:\Windows.

Installing the WSUS Role

The WSUS role is installed by using Add Roles and Features in Server Manager. Some requirements for running the WSUS role on Windows Server 2012/R2 are as follows:

- 1.4 GHz CPU
- 10 GB available disk space (40 GB recommended)
- 2 GB RAM
- 100 Mbps network interface

The disk requirements for the WSUS server vary depending on which products you need to update, how many updates you need to store locally, and how many clients will be served. In an environment with multiple client and server OS versions, disk requirements will probably be higher. In addition, the WSUS server shouldn't be installed on a domain controller.

See *http://technet.microsoft.com/en-us/library/cc708483(v=ws.10).aspx* for a table to help you determine the hardware requirements for a WSUS server based on how many clients are being served. This table is for WSUS 3.0 running on Windows Server 2008 and earlier, but it can be used as a general guide.

WSUS Storage Requirements

WSUS has the following requirements for storage:

- *WSUS database*—This database stores the WSUS configuration data and update metadata, along with information about WSUS client interactions. All WSUS servers require a WSUS database. The default database is the built-in Windows Internal Database (WID), which is essentially a light version of a SQL database with no management interface. You can configure WSUS to use a SQL Server Express or full SQL Server installation, too. The WID database provides the same performance as a SQL database. Using the WID database is recommended unless you're already running a SQL server for other applications or plan to deploy WSUS with network load balancing (NLB). The database requires a minimum of 2 GB free space on the volume where it's stored.

- *Local file system storage*—In most situations, you want to store the actual update files on the local WSUS server and configure clients to download updates from the WSUS server. This setup constitutes the bulk of the WSUS disk space requirement. However, when client computers have a faster connection to the Internet than to the WSUS server (perhaps in some branch office arrangements), you can opt to store only update metadata in the WSUS database and have clients download approved updates directly from the Microsoft Update servers.

WSUS Deployment Options

WSUS can be installed as a single-server solution, supporting from a few dozen to several hundred clients at a single site, or a multiple-server solution, providing update services to large multiple-site enterprises. In the single-server solution, the WSUS server is deployed in the company intranet and communicates directly with Microsoft Update servers. Client computers then contact the WSUS server to download and install approved updates (see Figure 2-3).

For a multiple-server solution (see Figure 2-4), a single WSUS server is configured to contact Microsoft Update servers to get updates and then distributes updates to additional WSUS servers located on different parts of the network. Client computers can then contact the nearest WSUS server to download updates.

When using a multiple-server deployment, you have two WSUS administration options:

- *Autonomous mode*—**Autonomous mode** provides distributed administration and is the default option when you install WSUS. Using autonomous mode, an administrator for each WSUS server has the responsibility of approving updates and managing WSUS client groups (discussed later in this chapter).

- *Replica mode*—**Replica mode** provides centralized administration of update approvals and client groups. An administrator maintains client groups and approves updates on the server that connects to Microsoft Update and the information is inherited by downstream WSUS servers.

Regardless of the deployment, WSUS uses the HTTPS protocol on TCP port 443 by default to collect updates from Microsoft Update servers and between WSUS servers in a multiple-server deployment. You can change these ports, but be aware that the configured ports must be open on the network firewall.

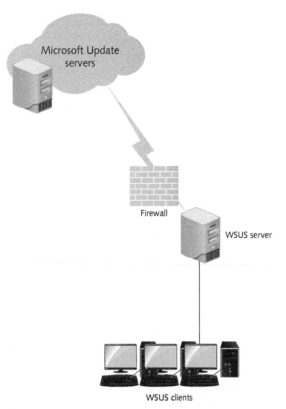

Figure 2-3   A single-server WSUS deployment

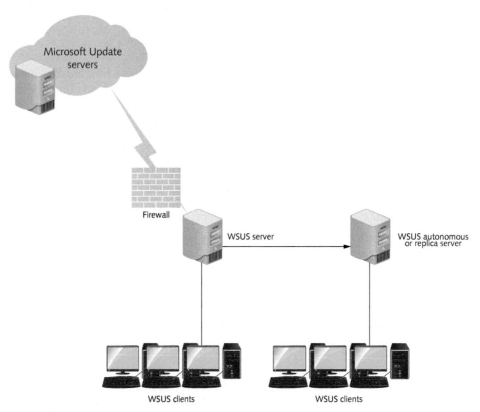

Figure 2-4   A multiple-server WSUS deployment

Installing WSUS

To install WSUS, use the Add Roles and Features Wizard in Server Manager. During installation, you're prompted to install additional features that are required for WSUS. Next, you select role services. In the Role Services window shown in Figure 2-5, you see the following options:

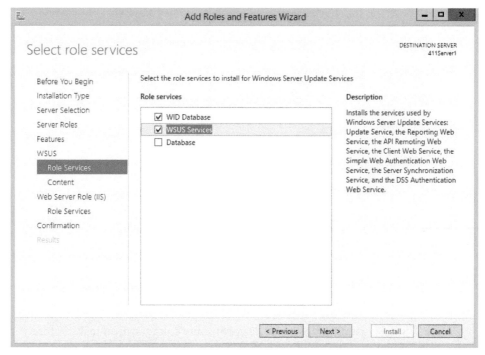

Figure 2-5   Selecting role services

- *WID Database*—When this option is selected, WSUS uses the Windows Internal Database, which is adequate for most applications. This check box should be selected unless you plan to use SQL server.

- *WSUS Services*—This check box should be selected. This option installs a number of services WSUS needs; you can see a list in Figure 2-5.

- *Database*—This check box should be selected only if you aren't going to use the WID database. The wizard doesn't let you select both this check box and the WID Database check box. If you select this check box, you need to enter the details of the database server you plan to use in a subsequent window.

After you select role services, you see a window where you can choose to store the update files on the local server along with the path (see Figure 2-6). The path can be a local drive letter and folder or a UNC path to a share on another server. If you decide not to store update files on the local server or a network share, the files are downloaded from the Microsoft Update servers as needed by clients. You can change whether updates should be stored locally and change the storage path after WSUS has been installed.

As part of the WSUS installation, the Web Server role and related role services are also installed. After you click Install in the Confirmation window, the WSUS installation begins. Installation can take quite a while because of the amount of software that must be installed.

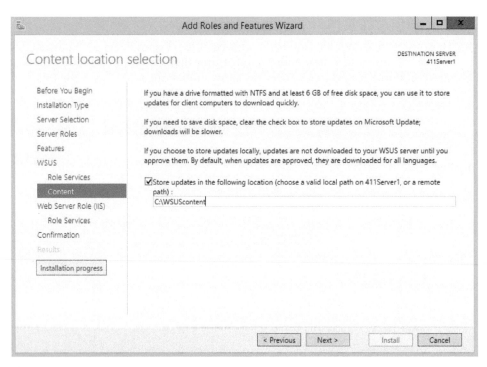

Figure 2-6   Selecting the content location

After WSUS is installed, you must perform some configuration tasks before you can begin using WSUS. When you first open the WSUS management console, a wizard guides you through these tasks:

- Choose the **upstream server.** Decide whether to get updates from the Microsoft Update servers on the Internet or another WSUS server. If this is the first WSUS server, you select Microsoft Update servers. If there's already one or more WSUS servers on your network, you can have the new server synchronize updates with an existing WSUS server.

- Configure network settings, such as whether WSUS should use a proxy server when synchronizing.

- Specify which languages the updates should include.

- Select the products the WSUS server should collect updates for.

- Specify the update classifications that should be synchronized; for example, you can choose whether the server should get critical updates, security updates, definition updates, service packs, drivers, tools, and so forth.

- Configure updates to occur automatically or manually.

All the settings configured with the WSUS Configuration Wizard can be changed in the Update Services console by clicking Options (shown in Figure 2-7). You can also run the configuration wizard again by clicking Options and then WSUS Server Configuration Wizard.

You're almost ready to start using WSUS, but before clients can begin using the WSUS server for automatic updates, several configuration tasks must be performed, which are discussed in the next section.

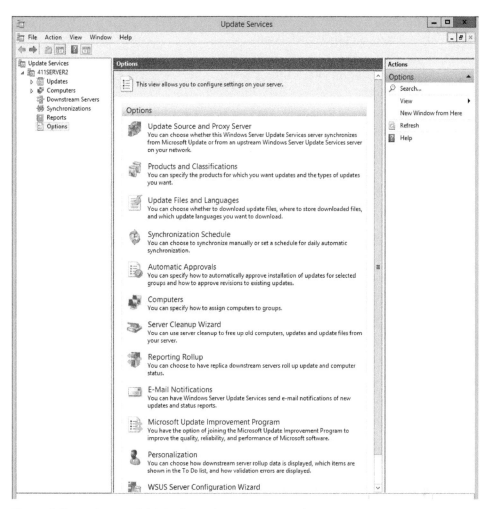

Figure 2-7 Options available in the Update Services console

Activity 2-1: Installing the WSUS Role

Time Required: 35 minutes

Objective: Install the WSUS role and required additional roles and features.

Required Tools and Equipment: 411Server2

Description: Your desktop computers are using substantial Internet bandwidth to download Windows updates, and you want more control over when desktop computers and especially servers install updates. You decide to install a WSUS server to manage updates.

1. Start 411Server2 and log on as **Administrator**, if necessary.

2. Open Server Manager, and click **Manage, Add Roles and Features** from the menu. In the Add Roles and Features Wizard, click **Next** until you get to the Server Roles window.

3. Scroll down the list of roles, and click the box next to **Windows Server Update Services**.

4. In the dialog box asking you to confirm the additional features needed for this role, click **Add Features**, and then click **Next**.

5. In the Features window, click **Next**. Read the window describing WSUS, and then click **Next**.

6. In the Role Services window, make sure the **WID Database** and **WSUS Services** check boxes are selected, and then click **Next**.

7. In the Content window shown previously in Figure 2-6, make sure the **Store updates in the following location** check box is selected, type **C:\WSUScontent** in the text box, and then click **Next**.

8. In the Web Server Role (IIS) window, read the information about IIS, and then click **Next**. In the Role Services window, click **Next**.

9. In the Confirmation window, click **Install**.

10. The next window shows the progress of the installation. (*Note*: You can close this window and view the progress later by clicking the Notifications flag on the command bar of Server Manager.) For now, wait until the installation is finished, which might take several minutes, and then click **Close**.

11. Click the Notifications flag (see Figure 2-8), and then click **Launch Post-Installation tasks**. Additional features are installed.

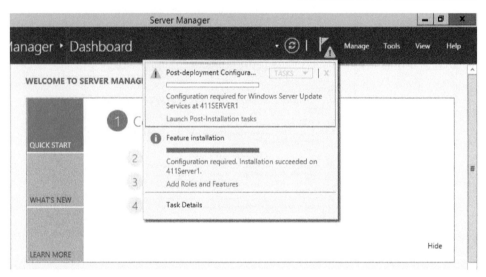

Figure 2-8   Viewing notifications

12. Stay logged on for the next activity.

Activity 2-2: Performing WSUS Postinstallation Tasks

Time Required: 35 minutes
Objective: Perform postinstallation tasks for the WSUS role.

Required Tools and Equipment: 411Server2 and an Internet connection
Description: You have just installed WSUS and related roles and features. Now you need to open the Update Services console and perform the initial configuration tasks.

1. In Server Manager, click **Tools, Windows Server Update Services** from the menu to start the Windows Server Update Services Configuration Wizard.

2. In the Before You Begin window, read the information, and then click **Next**.

If you need to run the wizard again, you can do so in the Update Services console by clicking Options in the left pane.

3. In the Microsoft Update Improvement window, click to clear the check box to decline joining the program, and then click **Next**.

4. In the Choose Upstream Server window, make sure **Synchronize from Microsoft Update** is selected, and then click **Next**. Click **Next** in the Specify Proxy Server window.

5. In the Connect to Upstream Server window, click **Start Connecting**. This step downloads information about the types of updates available, products that can be updated, and available languages. It requires the server to have a working Internet connection and might take several minutes to finish. Click **Next** when the Next button is available.

6. In the Choose Languages window, select the language or languages for your region, and then click **Next**.

7. In the Choose Products window, all Windows products are selected by default. To reduce the download time and disk space used, click to clear the **Windows** check box, click to select the **Windows 8.1** and **Windows Server 2012 R2** check boxes, and then click **Next**.

8. In the Choose Classifications window, accept the default selections (Critical Updates, Definition Updates, and Security Updates), and then click **Next**.

9. In the Configure Sync Schedule window, accept the default option, **Synchronize manually**, and click **Next**.

10. In the Finished window, you have the option to begin synchronizing with the Microsoft Update servers on the Internet. Accept the default option to not start synchronization now, and click **Next**.

11. The What's Next window shows additional tasks you might need to complete before using the WSUS server. Click **Finish**. The Update Services console opens and displays a summary of the update status of computers on the network. Close the Update Services console.

12. If you're continuing to the next activity, stay logged on; otherwise, log off or shut down 411Server2.

Configuring WSUS

Before the clients in your network can begin using WSUS for automatic updates, you need to perform a few configuration tasks on WSUS. Some of these tasks are done in the Update Services console, and others use Group Policy to configure WSUS clients remotely:

- Create computer groups.
- Assign computers to groups.
- Configure Windows Update on client computers.
- Configure WSUS synchronization and approval rules.

Creating Computer Groups

With computer groups, you can target specific computers for different types of updates. There are two default groups: All Computers and Unassigned Computers. When a client computer contacts the WSUS server, it's added to both groups by default. You can also create custom groups to meet your needs.

As the name implies, the Unassigned Computers group holds all computers you haven't assigned to a custom group. After you've created custom groups, you move computers from the Unassigned Computers group to your custom groups. The All Computers group always contains every computer that has contacted the WSUS server. Figure 2-9 shows the relationship between these groups.

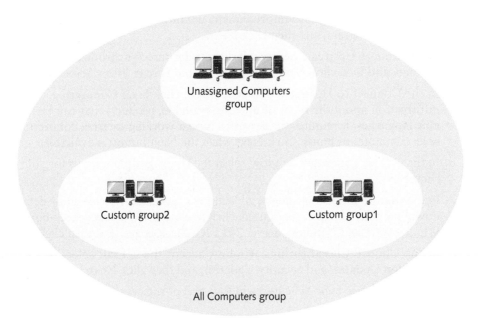

Figure 2-9   WSUS computer groups

© 2015 Cengage Learning®

Custom groups can be used to organize computers for targeting specific updates and to test updates on a limited number of computers before deploying updates to the rest of the network. Creating at least one custom group for update testing is recommended.

Assigning Computers to Groups

You select the method for assigning computers to groups in the Update Services console, where you click Options in the left pane and then Computers in the center pane. The Computers dialog box shown in Figure 2-10 opens with these options: "Use the Update Services console" (which specifies server-side targeting) and "Use Group Policy or registry settings on computers" (which specifies client-side targeting). These options are described in the following list.

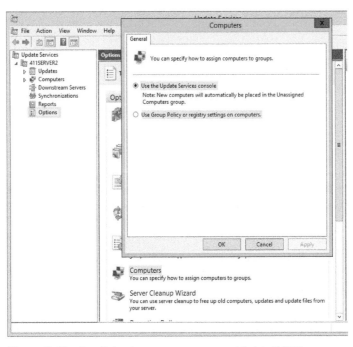

Figure 2-10   Specifying how computers are added to WSUS groups

After selecting the option you want, there are three ways to add computers to WSUS groups:

- *Update Services console*—This method is called **server-side targeting** because the action takes place at the WSUS server. Server-side targeting is enabled by default. After creating custom groups, simply move computer accounts from the Unassigned Computers group to the custom group. To use this method, select the "Use the Update Services console" option.

- *Group Policy*—This method, **client-side targeting**, is the preferred one. To use it, you must have a domain controller in your network, and clients must be domain members. The term "client-side targeting" is used because the Group Policy setting changes the relevant Registry setting on client computers that are in the scope of the group policy in Active Directory. The affected Registry setting instructs the client to add itself to the specified group. The Group Policy setting called "Enable client-side targeting" is in Computer Configuration, Policies, Administrative Templates, Windows Components, Windows Update. As shown in Figure 2-11, this policy causes affected clients to add themselves to a WSUS group named MyWindows7PCs. To use this method, select the "Use Group Policy or registry settings on computers" option.

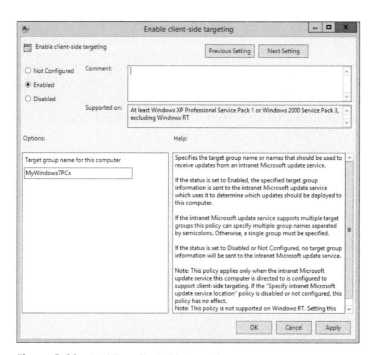

Figure 2-11   Enabling client-side targeting

- *Local Group Policy*—You can use the Local Group Policy Editor (`gpedit.msc`) to configure clients for client-side targeting. This option is satisfactory only for small networks with no domain controller because you have to change the settings on every computer. The setting is the same as what's shown in Figure 2-11. To use this method, make sure "Use Group Policy or registry settings on computers" is selected.

In Activity 2-3, you create a custom computer group and explore the options for adding computers to custom groups.

Activity 2-3: Creating a Custom Computer Group

Time Required: 25 minutes

Objective: Create a WSUS custom computer group after exploring the Update Services console.

Required Tools and Equipment: 411Server2

Description: You have done the initial configuration of the WSUS server. Now you explore the Update Services console and create a computer group.

1. Start 411Server2 and log on as **Administrator,** if necessary. In Server Manager, open the Update Services console.

2. In the left pane, click to expand **411Server2,** and then click **Updates.** This window shows an overview of the updates. Click to expand **Updates,** and then click **All Updates.** No updates are shown yet because you haven't synchronized with the Microsoft Update servers.

3. In the left pane, click to expand **Computers** and then **All Computers.** You see a group named Unassigned Computers, which contains all computers that haven't been assigned to another group. The All Computers group contains all computer groups and the computers in those groups.

4. Right-click **All Computers** and click **Add Computer Group.** Type **Desktops** for the name, and then click **Add.**

5. Repeat Step 4 to create a group named **Servers.** You now have two computer groups you can use to organize desktop computers and servers so that you can specify different update rules for them. You add computers to these groups later.

6. In the left pane, click **Downstream Servers.** If any servers were using this server as the update source, they would be listed here.

7. In the left pane, click **Synchronizations.** You see a history of synchronization attempts and the resulting status.

8. In the left pane, click **Reports.** You can generate a number of reports on updates with this option.

9. In the left pane, click **Options.** All the options you set with the Windows Server Update Services Configuration Wizard in the previous activity and more can be configured here. If you want to run the wizard again, for example, click WSUS Server Configuration Wizard at the bottom of the Options pane.

10. You're using client-side targeting, which is enabled in the Update Services console and then configured with Group Policy next in Activity 2-4. To enable client-side targeting, click **Options** in the left pane, and click **Computers** in the center pane. Click the **Use Group Policy or registry settings on computers** option button, and then click **OK.** Client-side targeting is now enabled.

11. The next step is to enable client computers to use this server for Windows Update, which you do in the next activity. Close all open windows, and log off or shut down the server.

Configuring Windows Update on Client Computers

You're almost ready to start using the WSUS server. First, your clients must be told to use the WSUS server instead of the Microsoft Update servers on the Internet to find and download updates. If your computers are domain members, you can use group policies on a domain controller to configure Windows Update; otherwise, you can configure clients separately with the Local Group Policy Editor. Activity 2-5 walks you through the process of configuring Windows Update with group policies.

When you use group policies to configure WSUS clients, it's best to create one or more Group Policy objects (GPOs) for configuring WSUS. By doing so, you can find the policy easily if you need to make adjustments later to client configurations for a group of computers.

If you have a lot of computers in your network, you can divide computer accounts into different Active Directory organizational units (OUs) and link a GPO with different WSUS parameters to each OU. This tactic allows you to, for example, stagger the update schedule so that the computers in each OU attempt to download and install updates from the WSUS server at different times of the day.

The policy settings for Windows Update can be found in Computer Configuration, Policies, Administrative Templates, Windows Components, Windows Update, where you found the setting for client-side targeting. The main settings for enabling your clients to access the WSUS server to download and install updates are Configure Automatic Updates and Specify intranet Microsoft update service location (highlighted in Figure 2-12).

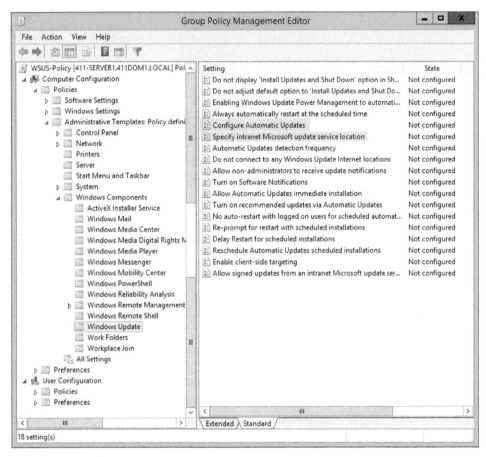

Figure 2-12   Windows Update settings in Group Policy

The Configure Automatic Updates policy (shown in Figure 2-13) has the following settings:

- *Not Configured, Enabled, Disabled*—If you enable automatic updates through Group Policy, users can see automatic update settings, but they're grayed out and can't be changed. If you disable automatic updates, updates must be downloaded and installed manually. If they aren't configured, the policy has no effect on automatic updates settings on client computers.

- *Configure automatic updating*—There are four options for this setting:

   o Notify for download and notify for install: This setting places the responsibility of downloading and installing updates on the computer's user.

   o Auto download and notify for install: This is the default setting; however, it puts the responsibility of installing updates on the computer's user.

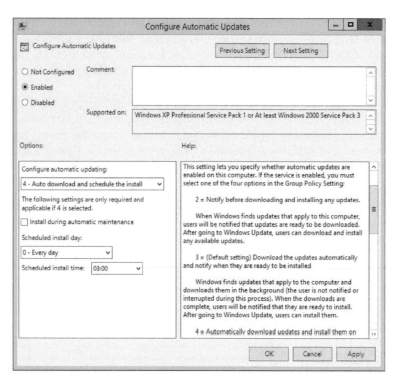

Figure 2-13   Configuring automatic updating

    o Auto download and schedule the install: This is the recommended setting because it puts the most control of when updates are installed in the administrator's hands.

    o Allow local admin to choose setting: This setting allows a user with local administrator credentials to configure Windows Update on the client computer.

- *Install during automatic maintenance*—If this option is enabled, Windows 8 and later computers install updates during automatic maintenance rather than on a specific schedule. Automatic maintenance occurs when the computer is not in use and not on battery power. Automatic maintenance can be configured with the Group Policy setting in Computer Configuration, Policies, Administrative Templates, Windows Components, Maintenance Scheduler.

- *Scheduled install day*—If "Auto download and schedule the install" is selected, you select the day of the week to install updates, or you can choose to install updates every day, which is the default setting.

- *Scheduled install time*—If "Auto download and schedule the install" is selected, you select the time of day to install updates in a 24-hour time format; the default time is 3:00 a.m.

The next policy to configure is "Specify intranet Microsoft update service location," which has the following settings (see Figure 2-14):

- *Not Configured, Enabled, Disabled*—If this policy is enabled, client computers download approved updates from the specified WSUS server. If it's disabled or not configured, client computers download updates from the Microsoft Update servers on the Internet (unless automatic updates are disabled).

- *Set the intranet update service for detecting updates*—You specify the URL to the WSUS server in the format `http://WSUSServer:8530`; `WSUSServer` is the name of the Windows Server 2012/R2 server with the WSUS role installed and configured. You should also specify the port number 8530, the default port WSUS uses. If you're using HTTPS for updates, the default port is 8531.

- *Set the intranet statistics server*—Specify the server to collect update statistics from WSUS clients. You can use the same URL as for the update server in the previous setting, or you can specify a different server name.

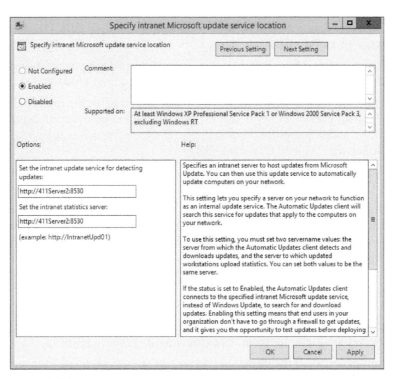

Figure 2-14   Specifying an intranet server to host updates

After you have configured automatic updates in a GPO, you can link it to the domain or an OU containing computer accounts. If you have several OUs containing computer accounts, you can create a GPO with different settings for each OU, if needed. If all computers require the same settings, the GPO can be linked to the domain. However, if it's linked at the domain level, the automatic update settings also affect servers and domain controllers (DCs). You might want different settings for servers and DCs; in particular, you probably don't want servers and DCs to install updates automatically because the updates could require an automatic restart. Automatic update settings don't affect user accounts.

 When configuring Windows Update on client computers, you can use the Local Group Policy Editor to configure clients that aren't members of a domain. The policy settings are the same as in the domain-based GPO.

Activity 2-4: Configuring Windows Update with Group Policy

Time Required: 10 minutes
Objective: Create a GPO to configure Windows Update on client computers.

Required Tools and Equipment: 411Server1 and 411Win8
Description: Now that WSUS is configured, you need to configure clients to use the WSUS server for their updates. You also enable client-side targeting by using Group Policy on a domain controller. To use the new GPO you create, you create an OU in Active Directory, move a computer account to it, and link the GPO to the OU.

1. Start 411Server1 and log on as **Administrator,** if necessary. In Server Manager, click **Tools, Group Policy Management** from the menu.

2. In the left pane of the Group Policy Management console, click to expand **Domains,** if necessary, and click to expand **411Dom1.local.** Right-click **Group Policy Objects** and click **New.**

3. In the New GPO dialog box, type **WSUS-Desktops,** and then click **OK.** Right-click the GPO you just created and click **Edit.**

4. In the Group Policy Management Editor, navigate to **Computer Configuration, Policies, Administrative Templates, Windows Components, Windows Update.**

5. In the right pane, double-click **Enable client-side targeting.** In the Enable client-side targeting window (shown previously in Figure 2-11) click the **Enabled** option button. In the "Target group name for this computer" list box, type **Desktops,** which is the name of the group you created in Activity 2-3, and then click **OK.**

6. In the right pane of the Group Policy Management Editor, double-click **Configure Automatic Updates.** Click the **Enabled** option button.

7. In the Options section, make sure the default option **3 - Auto download and notify for install** is selected. Because you aren't configuring clients to install update automatically, you don't configure a scheduled day and time. This is the option you would likely choose for servers. For desktop computers, the option "4 - Auto download and schedule the install" is a better choice. However, for the purposes of this activity, accept the default option, and click **OK.**

8. Next, you tell clients the name of the WSUS server where they should download updates. In the right pane of the Group Policy Management Editor, double-click **Specify intranet Microsoft update service location.** Click the **Enabled** option button.

9. In the Options section, type **http://411Server2:8530** in both text boxes, and then click **OK.**

10. Browse through the other policies available for Windows Update so that you know what you can configure with Group Policy. When you're finished, close the Group Policy Management Editor and the Group Policy Management console.

11. Next, you need to link the GPO to an OU containing the target computer accounts. Open Active Directory Users and Computers, and create an OU named **Desktops.** Move the **411Win8** computer account from the Computers folder to the Desktops OU you just created. When prompted to confirm that you want to move the object, click **Yes.**

12. Create a user in the Users folder named **Windows8 User** with the logon name **Win8User** and the password **Password01.** Set the password to never expire. You use this user to log on to the domain from your 411Win8 computer. Close Active Directory Users and Computers.

13. Open Group Policy Management, and then right-click the **Desktops** OU and click **Link an Existing GPO.** In the Select GPO dialog box, click **WSUS-Desktops,** and then click **OK.**

14. Start 411Win8, and log on to the 411Dom1.local domain as **Win8User.**

15. Right-click **Start,** click **System,** and click **Windows Update** at the bottom of the left pane. You should see that the settings you configured through Group Policy have been applied, and updates are managed by your system administrator (see Figure 2-15). (If the settings haven't been applied, type **gpupdate /force** at an elevated command prompt and press **Enter.** Then refresh the Windows Update window. The **gpupdate** command causes the computer to download and apply group policies immediately.)

16. Shut down 411Win8. If you're continuing to the next activity, stay logged on to 411Server1, but close all open windows; otherwise, log off or shut down 411Server1.

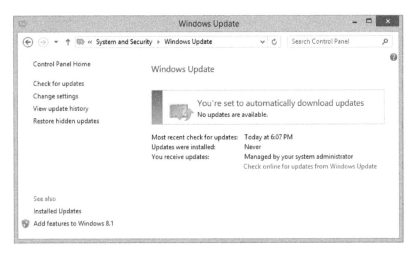

Figure 2-15   Windows Update settings configured through Group Policy

WSUS Synchronization and Approval Rules

WSUS clients can download and install only approved updates from the WSUS server. The administrator can configure automatic approval for certain types of updates and for particular groups of computers. Other updates can be approved manually. Updates that aren't approved are not downloaded and installed by WSUS clients. Before updates are approved, the WSUS server must synchronize with the Microsoft Update servers on the Internet.

Manual synchronization of updates is the default setting, but you have the option to configure automatic synchronization on a set schedule. To do this, in the Update Services console, click Options and then Synchronization Schedule. The synchronization schedule (shown in Figure 2-16) has two options:

Figure 2-16   Configuring a synchronization schedule

- *Synchronize manually*—If this option is selected, the administrator must click Synchronizations in the left pane of the Update Services console and click Synchronize Now in the Actions pane. The WSUS server then attempts to contact a Microsoft Update server on the Internet. If you choose this option, manual synchronization should be done at least once a week to make sure your computers have the latest critical security updates.

- *Synchronize automatically*—If you select this option, you can configure what time of day the first synchronization should occur and the number of synchronizations per day. If you choose more than one synchronization per day, the WSUS server attempts to synchronize every 24/*n* hours, with *n* representing the number of synchronizations per day. The maximum synchronizations per day is 24.

Using Automatic Approvals

The Automatic Approvals option in WSUS enables you to approve specific types of updates for groups of computers automatically. After updates are approved, clients can download and install updates according to the settings of the Windows Updates client. You configure automatic approvals in the Update Services console by clicking Options and then Automatic Approvals to open the dialog box shown in Figure 2-17.

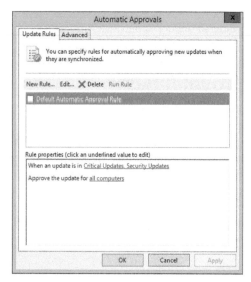

Figure 2-17   Automatic approval settings

A default automatic approval rule, if enabled, approves all critical and security updates for all computers. You have the option to edit the default rule, but creating a new rule with the parameters you want is usually better. You create a new rule by clicking New Rule in the Automatic Approvals dialog box, which opens the Add Rule dialog box (see Figure 2-18).

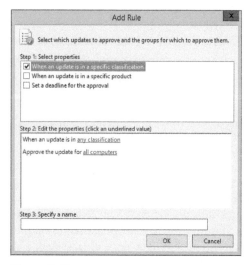

Figure 2-18   Creating a new approval rule

The rule can include one or more of the following criteria:

- *Update classification*—You choose one or more update classifications (shown in Figure 2-19).

Figure 2-19   Update classifications for a new rule

- *Specific product*—You choose which products are included in the approval rule.
- *Approval deadline*—If you set a deadline, updates are installed automatically when the deadline expires, even if a client computer is set to install updates manually instead of automatically.

By default, the All Computers group is the target of a new approval rule. You can change this setting by choosing one or more WSUS groups.

Configuring Manual Approval

You can approve updates manually in the Update Services console by clicking Updates and then clicking All Updates, Critical Updates, Security Updates, or WSUS Updates, as shown in Figure 2-20. You see a list of updates that have been synchronized with the Microsoft Update servers. Click an update to see its description in the lower pane. Right-click an update to see a shortcut menu (shown in Figure 2-20) you can use to approve or decline an update or get additional status information about it. You can also select more than one update in the list before right-clicking so that you can approve multiple updates at once.

Clicking Approve in the shortcut menu displays a list of WSUS groups. For each group, you can approve the update for installation or removal or choose not to approve a previously approved update (see Figure 2-21). If you approve the update for installation or removal, you can also set a deadline that forces the update even if the client is configured to install updates manually.

Having a test group for each OS and application configuration in your organization is recommended. This way, you can approve updates for test groups and verify that the updates don't cause any problems with the OS or installed applications before approving updates for production systems. This practice is particularly important for servers.

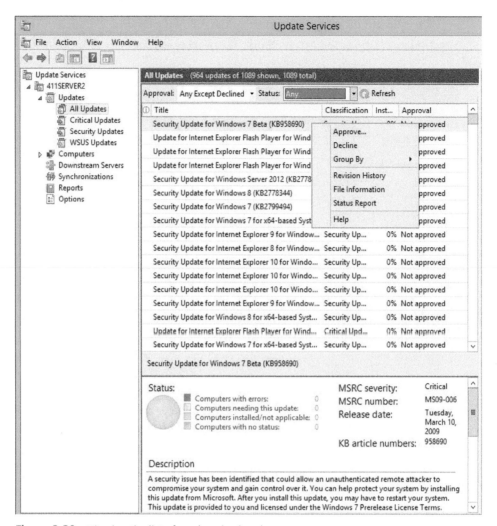

Figure 2-20   Viewing the list of synchronized updates

Figure 2-21   Approving updates

Activity 2-5: Configuring WSUS Synchronization and Approval Rules

Time Required: 15 minutes
Objective: Configure synchronization and approval rules.

Required Tools and Equipment: 411Server2
Description: You have WSUS mostly configured, but two important tasks you need to finish are configuring synchronization and approval rules.

1. Start 411Server2 and log on as **Administrator**, if necessary. In Server Manager, open the Update Services console.

2. In the left pane, click **Options**. In the center pane, click **Synchronization Schedule**.

3. In the Synchronization Schedule dialog box (shown previously in Figure 2-16), click the **Synchronize automatically** option button. You set the first synchronization for the day by typing the time or clicking the hour, minute, second, or AM/PM and using the up and down arrows. Set the time for **1:00:00 AM**.

4. Click the **Synchronizations per day** list arrow. Notice that you can synchronize up to 24 times per day or once per hour. Leave the default of **1** synchronization per day, and click **OK**. Your server then synchronizes with Microsoft Update servers once a day at 1:00 a.m. (*Note*: If you don't want the server to synchronize automatically, change the setting back to "Synchronize manually." Ask your instructor for guidance.)

5. In the center pane of the Update Services console, click **Automatic Approvals**. In the Rule properties list box, click the **all computers** link (refer to Figure 2-17).

6. In the Choose Computer Groups dialog box (see Figure 2-22), click to clear the **Unassigned Computers** and **Servers** check boxes so that only the Desktops check box is selected. The automatic approval rule then applies only to computers in this group. Updates for all other computers and servers must be approved manually. Click **OK**.

Figure 2-22   Selecting computer groups for automatic approval

7. Click the **Default Automatic Approval Rule** check box to enable the rule.

8. Click **New Rule** to see how you can create your own approval rules (see Figure 2-23). You can approve rules by update classification (for example, critical updates, security updates, service packs) and for specific products (Windows 8.1, Office, and so forth). You can also set an approval deadline. Click **Cancel**, and then click **OK** to close the Automatic Approvals dialog box.

9. Now that you've finished configuring WSUS, shut down 411Server2.

Figure 2-23   Creating approval rules

Additional WSUS Configuration Tasks

You've learned the basics of configuring WSUS. Now you look into some additional configuration options you might need, depending on your environment. In the following sections, you examine these options:

- Configuring update sources and proxy servers
- Update files and languages
- Configuring SSL
- Upgrading a WSUS server
- Creating WSUS reports

Configuring Update Sources and Proxy Servers

The update source for a WSUS server is the Microsoft Update servers or another WSUS server. If you need to change the current configuration, open the Update Services console, click Update Source and Proxy Server, and click the Update Source tab (see Figure 2-24). You have the following options in this dialog box:

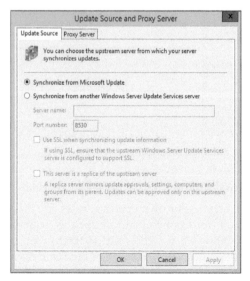

Figure 2-24   The Update Source and Proxy Server dialog box

- *Synchronize from Microsoft Update*—This is the default setting and the only option available if you have only one WSUS server in the network.

- *Synchronize from another Windows Server Update Services server*—This setting is available when you have a multiple-server WSUS deployment. If you choose this option, you specify the following:

  o Server name: Enter the upstream WSUS server name in this text box.

  o Port number: By default, port 8530 is used to communicate between WSUS servers. If you're using SSL, the port number is 8531 by default. The firewall on the WSUS servers must allow inbound traffic on these ports.

  o Use SSL when synchronizing update information: Choose this option if you want communication between WSUS servers to use SSL.

  o This server is a replica of the upstream server: Choose this option if the server should operate in replica mode. The default setting is autonomous mode.

Using a Proxy Server   If the firewall between a WSUS server and the update source (Microsoft Update servers or an upstream WSUS server) blocks the communication ports WSUS uses to synchronize updates, you can configure the WSUS server to use a proxy server in the Proxy Server tab (see Figure 2-25). A proxy server uses port 80, which should be allowed by almost all firewalls. You specify the proxy server name and optionally a port number and user credentials, if needed, to connect to the proxy server. Configuring the proxy server is beyond the scope of this book.

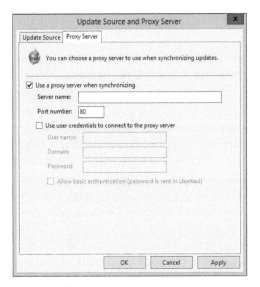

Figure 2-25   Configuring WSUS to use a proxy server

Updating Files and Languages

During the initial configuration of WSUS, you decided whether to download update files and store them on the WSUS server or store updates on Microsoft Update servers. On the first WSUS server, you have the choice of storing files locally or letting WSUS clients install approved updates from Microsoft Update servers. In the Update Services console, click Options, Update Files and Languages to change or refine these settings (see Figure 2-26).

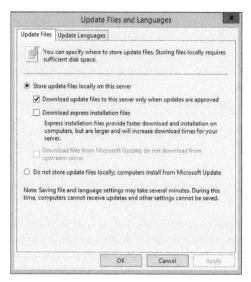

Figure 2-26   Updating files and languages

In this dialog box, you have two main options:

- *Store update files locally on this server*—If you select this option, you have three additional options:
  - o Download update files to this server only when updates are approved: This is the default option. If you disable this option, all update files are downloaded whether they're approved or not.
  - o Download express installation files: If this option is selected, the downloaded files are larger and take up more space on the server, but WSUS clients are able to download and install updates faster from the WSUS server.
  - o Download files from Microsoft Update; do not download from upstream server: This option is available only on a **downstream server** when you have a multiple-server WSUS deployment. By default, downstream servers get update files from upstream servers. If this option is selected, the server gets files directly from Microsoft update servers.

- *Do not store update files locally; computers install from Microsoft Update*—If you select this option, update must still be approved before clients can install them, but approved updates are downloaded by clients directly from Microsoft Update servers, not stored on local servers.

If your organization uses Windows in several languages, click the Update Languages tab shown in Figure 2-26, and choose the languages you want to download updates for.

Changing the Update Files Location   After you have used WSUS for a while, you might need to move the location for update files because, for example, you're running out of space on the current volume or want to offload files to a different disk to improve performance. To do this, you use the command-line tool wsusutil.exe with the movecontent option to change the path and optionally copy existing update files to the new location. You use this command to manage aspects of your WSUS server from the command line, many of which you can't do with Update Services console. This command is in the folder where WSUS is installed, which is usually C:\Program Files\Update Services\Tools. So to change the location from C:\WSUSContent to D:\WSUScontent, you do the following:

1. Create a new folder on the D volume named WSUScontent.

2. Open a command prompt window and change to the C:\Program Files\Update Services\ Tools directory.

3. Enter the command wsusutil movecontent D:\WSUScontent\movelog.log.

By default, `wsusutil.exe` copies the existing content to the new location. If you want to change the path but not copy existing content, add the `-skipcopy` option at the end of the command.

Configuring SSL

You can configure WSUS servers to use SSL for a more secure WSUS deployment. By using SSL, update metadata is encrypted and WSUS servers are authenticated. To configure SSL, follow these steps:

1. Install a certificate for the WSUS Web site. You can use the Active Directory Certificate Services role for this purpose. Active Directory Certificate Services is covered in *MCSA Guide to Configuring Advanced Windows Server 2012 Services, Exam 70-412* (Cengage Learning, 2015).

2. Change the bindings on the WSUS Web site to use HTTPS.

3. Configure the WSUS Web site's virtual roots to use SSL.

4. To tell WSUS to use SSL, issue the command `wsusutil.exe configuressl` *WSUSServerName* (replacing *WSUSServerName* with the name of the WSUS server configured on the installed certificate).

5. Finally, you configure clients to use SSL. Using Group Policy, configure the Microsoft update service location setting to use HTTPS in the URL instead of HTTP.

> The details of configuring the WSUS Web site are beyond the scope of this book, but in the 70-411 certification exam, you're expected to know the general steps for configuring WSUS to use SSL. For details, go to *http://technet.microsoft.com* and search for "Secure WSUS with the Secure Sockets Layer Protocol."

Upgrading a WSUS Server

You must take special care when upgrading a Windows server running WSUS. If you're running a version of Windows Server before Windows Server 2012 and the server is running WSUS, you must uninstall WSUS first. If you attempt to update your server to Windows Server 2012 before uninstalling WSUS, the installation is blocked. However, if you attempt to update your server to Windows Server 2012 R2, even though the installation isn't blocked, postinstallation tasks for WSUS in Windows Server 2012 R2 fail, and Windows Server 2012 R2 must be reinstalled.

Creating WSUS Reports

You might want to periodically see the results of WSUS client updates and WSUS server synchronizations. WSUS has a built-in report generator to show you the following types of information (see Figure 2-27):

- *Update reports*—These reports show summary or detailed information about each update, including which computers received each update.

- *Computer reports*—These reports show summary or detailed information about each computer getting updates, including which updates were installed by each computer.

- *Synchronization reports*—This report shows the results of the last synchronization.

The reports feature requires installing Microsoft Report Viewer 2008 Redistributable before you can view reports. If you click a report in the Update Services console without installing this component, you're prompted to install the report viewer.

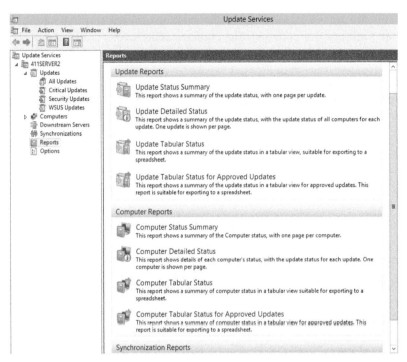

Figure 2-27   WSUS reports

Configuring WSUS with PowerShell

As with most features in Windows Server 2012/R2, WSUS has a bevy of PowerShell cmdlets for automating some configuration tasks. Table 2-2 lists PowerShell cmdlets you can use to configure most aspects of WSUS.

Table 2-2   PowerShell cmdlets for configuring WSUS

Cmdlet	Description
Add-WsusComputer	Adds a client computer to a WSUS group.
Approve-WsusUpdate	Approves an update.
Deny-WsusUpdate	Declines an update.
Get-WsusClassification	Shows a list of WSUS classifications.
Get-WsusComputer	Shows a list of WSUS client computers registered on the WSUS server.
Get-WsusProduct	Shows a list of all products by category currently available on WSUS.
Get-WsusServer	Shows the WSUS server.
Get-WsusUpdate	Shows a list of all updates currently available, including the classification and approval status of each update.
Invoke-WsusServerCleanup	Cleans up old update files on a WSUS server; including unused update files, old revisions, superseded updates, and inactive computer accounts.
Set-WsusClassification	Enables or disables an update classification for synchronization. For example, you can enable or disable drivers or service packs.
Set-WsusProduct	Enables or disables a product for synchronization.
Set-WsusServerSynchronization	Sets the source for WSUS synchronization: Microsoft Update or an upstream server. Also allows you to set the upstream server name, port number, and SSL.

To see a list of these 12 WSUS-related PowerShell cmdlets, type `Get-Command *-Wsus*` at a PowerShell prompt. For more information on a cmdlet, type `Get-Help CmdletName` (replacing `CmdletName` with the name of the cmdlet).

Some of these cmdlets are useful only when used with another command. For example, `Approve-WsusUpdate` should be used with `Get-WsusUpdate`. The following command uses `Get-WsusUpdate` to produce a list of updates that have the classification "Critical" and are currently not approved. This list is then piped to the `Approve-WsusUpdate` cmdlet, which approves each update for installation by all computers.

```
Get-WsusUpdate -Classification Critical -Approval
  Unapproved | Approve-WsusUpdate -Action Install
  -TargetGroupName "All Computers"
```

Remember, you can add the `-whatif` parameter to a command to see the results of the command without actually performing the action. Figure 2-28 shows the output of the this command with the `-whatif` parameter.

```
PS C:\Users\administrator.411DOM1> Get-WsusUpdate -Classification Critical -Approval Unappr
ction Install -TargetGroupName "All Computers" -whatif
What if: Performing the operation "Approve-WsusUpdate" on target "Office XP Alternative Use

What if: Performing the operation "Approve-WsusUpdate" on target "Office XP Input Method Ed
tilingual User Interface Pack".
What if: Performing the operation "Approve-WsusUpdate" on target "Office XP Input Method Ed
anese User Interface Pack".
What if: Performing the operation "Approve-WsusUpdate" on target "Update for Office XP (KB9
What if: Performing the operation "Approve-WsusUpdate" on target "Update for Office XP Proo
What if: Performing the operation "Approve-WsusUpdate" on target "Update for PowerPoint 200
What if: Performing the operation "Approve-WsusUpdate" on target "Update for Word 2002 (KB9
What if: Performing the operation "Approve-WsusUpdate" on target "Office XP Update: KB83725
What if: Performing the operation "Approve-WsusUpdate" on target "Office XP Update: KB83385
What if: Performing the operation "Approve-WsusUpdate" on target "Update for Access 2002 (K
What if: Performing the operation "Approve-WsusUpdate" on target "Microsoft Office File Val
PS C:\Users\administrator.411DOM1> _
```

Figure 2-28   Output of the `Get-WsusUpdate` command piped to `Approve-WsusUpdate`

Chapter Summary

- Windows Server Update Services (WSUS) is a server role that allows an administrator to take control of Microsoft product updates on computers running the Windows OS. After it's installed and configured, you configure Windows clients to use the WSUS server for Windows updates. Clients are best configured with Group Policy, so your clients need to be domain members.

- The WSUS role is installed with Add Roles and Features in Server Manager. Some requirements for running the WSUS role on Windows Server 2012/R2 are 10 GB available disk space (40 GB recommended), 2 GB RAM, and a 100 Mbps network interface.

- WSUS can be installed as a single-server solution, supporting from a few dozen to several hundred clients at a single site, or a multiple-server solution, providing update services to large multi-site enterprises.

- Before clients in a network can begin using WSUS for automatic updates, you need to perform some configuration tasks on WSUS: creating computer groups, assigning computers to groups, configuring Windows Update on client computers, and configuring WSUS synchronization and approval rules.

- Other WSUS configuration tasks you might need to undertake include updating the source and proxy server, updating files and language settings, configuring SSL, upgrading a WSUS server, and creating WSUS reports.

Key Terms

autonomous mode   A WSUS server mode that decentralizes administration of update approvals and client groups; the default option when you install WSUS.

client-side targeting   A method for adding computers to WSUS groups in which a Registry setting on the client machine instructs the client to add itself to the specified WSUS group.

downstream server   A server in a multiple-server WSUS deployment that accesses other (upstream) WSUS servers for synchronizing updates.

important updates   Updates that usually solve a security or reliability issue in Windows.

maintenance window   A set time of day at which your computer wakes up, if needed, to perform periodic maintenance tasks, including automatic updates if configured.

patch management   A procedure that enables administrators to control which product updates to allow as well as the source and timing of these updates.

recommended updates   Updates that make minor improvements to Windows but aren't critical to security or reliability.

replica mode   A WSUS server mode that centralizes administration of update approvals and client groups.

server-side targeting   A method for adding computers to WSUS groups in which the server takes action to add the computer to the WSUS group.

upstream server   A server in a multiple-server WSUS deployment that other (downstream) WSUS servers use for synchronizing updates.

Windows Server Update Services (WSUS)   A server role that makes it possible for administrators to take control of Microsoft product updates on computers running Windows.

Review Questions

1. How are client computers usually configured to access a WSUS server?

   a. Using the Windows Update Control Panel applet

   b. Using Group Policy in a domain environment

   c. Using WSUS discover mode

   d. Using `regedit` to configure Windows Update manually

2. Which of the following is true of using WSUS for Windows updates? (Choose all that apply.)

   a. It increases Internet bandwidth use.

   b. It centralizes control over product updates.

   c. Only approved updates are installed.

   d. Determining which updates have been applied is easy.

3. Which of the following is a Windows Update option after Windows Update is enabled? (Choose all that apply.)

   a. Install updates automatically.

   b. Do not download updates; install directly from Microsoft Update servers.

   c. Download updates, but let me choose whether to install them.

   d. Check for updates, but let me choose whether to download and install them.

4. Which of the following is a reason to use WSUS in your network?

   a. No server is required.

   b. Client computers always get updates faster.

   c. It requires less Internet bandwidth.

   d. All updates are installed automatically.

5. Which of the following is a requirement for running the WSUS role in Windows Server 2012/R2? (Choose all that apply.)

   a. Must be installed on a domain controller

   b. 10 GB available disk space

   c. 2 GB RAM

   d. Full SQL Server installation

6. Which WSUS server mode centralizes administration of update approvals and client groups?

   a. Replica mode

   b. Clone mode

   c. Autonomous mode

   d. Automatic mode

7. Which of the following is true about installing WSUS? (Choose all that apply.)

   a. You must install SQL Server before you install WSUS.

   b. Update files can be stored on a share on another server.

   c. The Web Server role is also installed.

   d. Clients can begin using WSUS as soon as it's installed.

8. Which of the following is an update classification that you can configure the WSUS server to synchronize with? (Choose all that apply.)

   a. Critical updates

   b. Service packs

   c. Information updates

   d. Security updates

9. What should you do if you want to target specific computers for different types of updates?

   a. Create custom groups.

   b. Configure Windows Update on the client.

   c. Install additional WSUS servers.

   d. Put computers on separate networks.

10. Which of the following is a method for adding computers to WSUS groups? (Choose all that apply.)

    a. Server-side targeting

    b. Local Group Policy

    c. Client-side targeting

    d. Windows Update configuration

11. Which of the following is a method for configuring clients to use a WSUS server?

    a. On the client, go to Control Panel, Windows Update.

    b. Enable WSUS discovery on clients.

    c. Use Group Policy for domain members.

    d. Configure the client list in WSUS options.

12. Which of the following is true about the Automatic Updates policy when it's enabled?

    a. One option is "Allow WSUS Operators group to Change Settings."

    b. Users can't change Automatic Update settings.

    c. You must choose a specific schedule for installing updates.

    d. The default scheduled install time is 9:00 a.m.

13. Automatic Updates policies affect user or computer accounts, depending on which OU they're linked to. True or False?

14. If you configure a WSUS server for automatic synchronization twice per day, which of the following is true?

    a.   Client computers are sent updates every 12 hours.

    b.   The WSUS server contacts the Microsoft Update servers every 12 hours.

    c.   Updates don't require approval before clients are updated.

    d.   The second synchronization is attempted only if the first one fails.

15. Which of the following is true about automatic approvals? (Choose all that apply.)

    a.   The default automatic approval rule is enabled by default.

    b.   The default automatic approval rule applies only to unassigned computers.

    c.   You can change the update classification of the default rule.

    d.   You can set a deadline to force an update.

16. If you want WSUS clients to download and install updates faster from the WSUS server, which WSUS server option should you configure?

    a.   Download express installation files.

    b.   Do not store update files locally.

    c.   Synchronize from another WSUS server.

    d.   Synchronize from Microsoft Update.

Case Projects

Case Project 2-1: Unable to Configure Windows Update

You have recently hired a server administrator to help maintain your servers and desktops. He was working with a desktop computer and found he couldn't configure Windows Update. Write a memo explaining why he was unable to configure Windows Update and describing four advantages of using WSUS.

Case Project 2-2: Designing a WSUS Deployment

You manage a network with 4 domain controllers running Windows Server 2012 R2, 7 member servers running Windows Server 2012 R2, 4 member servers running Windows Server 2008 R2, 100 Windows 8.1 computers, and 35 Windows 7 computers. You need to maintain updates and patches on all these computers. Explain how you would set up WSUS to do so. Which WSUS features would you use? What method would you use to be able to target specific computers with different types of updates? What method would you use to configure Windows Update on client computers?

chapter 3

Advanced File Services Configuration

After reading this chapter and completing the exercises, you will be able to:

- Configure Distributed File System servers
- Configure the File Server Resource Manager role service
- Configure file and disk encryption

All screenshots, unless otherwise noted, are used with permission from Microsoft Corporation.

As networks continue to grow and the need for easy access to documents and other types of files increases, making sure your users have the access they need becomes more challenging. In addition, you must ensure the security and availability of their files. The Distributed File System (DFS) is a tool for meeting all these challenges. In this chapter, you learn how to configure DFS namespaces and replication, two of the main components of the DFS role service.

Although storage is inexpensive, resources are not infinite, and there are costs in maintaining and backing up a large network's storage volumes. Media files can fill up disks quickly if they aren't limited, which can increase costs, and the possibility of users storing unauthorized materials adds a legal risk for organizations in the form of copyright violations. File Server Resource Manager can help reduce these risks and organize the enormous number of files stored on organizations' servers. In this chapter, you learn how this feature can help with managing and classifying file storage. Securing access to files is paramount in many networks containing sensitive data. Although file and folder permissions are the first line of defense, they can often be thwarted if an attacker has physical access to disk media. This chapter shows you how to protect files with encryption by using Encrypting File System and BitLocker.

An Overview of the Distributed File System

Table 3-1 summarizes what you need for the hands-on activities in this chapter.

Table 3-1 Activity requirements

Activity	Requirements	Notes
Activity 3-1: Uninstalling Unneeded Services	411Server1, 411Server2	
Activity 3-2: Installing the DFS Namespace and DFS Replication Role Services	411Server1, 411Server2	
Activity 3-3: Creating a Domain-Based Namespace	411Server1, 411Server2	
Activity 3-4: Creating a Replication Group	411Server1, 411Server2	
Activity 3-5: Installing the File Server Resource Manager Role Service	411Server1	
Activity 3-6: Creating and Applying a Quota Template	411Server1	
Activity 3-7: Creating a File Screen	411Server1	
Activity 3-8: Encrypting Files with EFS	411Server1	
Activity 3-9: Sharing an Encrypted File with Another User	411Server1	
Activity 3-10: Installing BitLocker Drive Encryption	411Server1	

© 2015 Cengage Learning®

A network can have any number of file servers, each with its own storage. Shares make it easy for users to access parts of this storage, but as the number of servers grows, so does the number of shares, and productivity suffers when users must try to navigate a complex maze of server names and share names. **Distributed File System (DFS)** is a role service under the File and Storage Services role that enables you to group shares from different servers into a single logical share called a **namespace**. Users see each namespace as a share with subfolders, giving them access to files that are actually stored on different servers. The DFS Namespaces role service is used to create and manage these logical shares.

DFS has four main components, shown in Figure 3-1:

- *Namespace server*—A **namespace server** is a Windows server with the DFS Namespaces role service installed.

- *Namespace root*—The **namespace root** is a folder that's the logical starting point for a namespace. It contains one or more folders or folder targets but no files. To access it, you use a UNC path, such as \\Domain1\AllShares or \\DFSServer\AllShares. In Figure 3-1, AllShares is the name of the namespace root. The domain name is used in the UNC path for a domain-based namespace; the server name is used for a stand-alone namespace. (Domain-based and stand-alone namespaces are discussed later in "Creating A Namespace.")

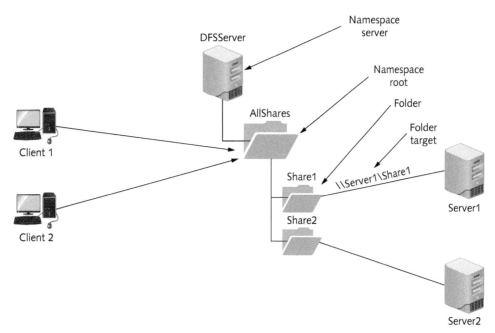

Figure 3-1   Namespace organization
© 2015 Cengage Learning®

- *Folder*—A folder can be used to organize the namespace without containing any actual files, or a folder can contain one or more folder targets. A folder without folder targets simply adds structure to the namespace hierarchy. For example, a folder named Marketing Docs might contain one or more folders with folder targets that are shared folders containing files for the Marketing Department. In Figure 3-1, Share1 and Share2 are folders, and both contain folder targets.

- *Folder target*—A **folder target** is a UNC path that points to a shared folder hosted on a server. A folder can have one or more folder targets. If there's more than one folder target, the files are usually replicated between servers to provide fault tolerance. In Figure 3-1, the folder target for Share 1 is \\Server1\Share1, and for Share2, it's \\Server2\Share2. The folder names can be the same as the share name, but they don't have to be.

In Figure 3-1, the two client computers need to know only the name of the namespace server (or the domain name) and the DFS root folder to access Share1 and Share2, even though the shares are actually hosted on Server1 and Server2.

Increasing ease of access, however, increases the consequences of file loss (because more users have access to files) and means files must be more available throughout an organization. Increased loads mean servers might go down, which makes the files stored on them inaccessible to users. One way to help ensure reliable access to files is to use **replication** to make copies of files in different locations, as shown in Figure 3-2. In this figure, the shares are replicated between the two file servers, so if either server becomes unavailable, the files in the shares are still accessible through the other server. There are several ways to use DFS replication, including replicating the entire DFS namespace. In this example, the DFS Replication role service must be installed on Server1 and Server2.

Combining these two server roles makes it possible to set up access to files in easy-to-access logical groups and maintain copies of critical files to minimize loss and downtime in case of a server failure. You can also configure them to work together to provide failover to help ensure continuous access for users.

DFS replication isn't designed to be a substitute for regular backups, but it can be used to enhance backup effectiveness and efficiency. For example, files can be replicated to a central location where a single backup can be done.

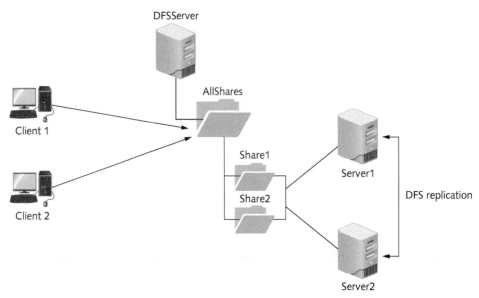

Figure 3-2   DFS replication
© 2015 Cengage Learning®

Using DFS Namespaces and DFS Replication

To use namespaces and replication, you must install the DFS Namespaces and DFS Replication role services. In the Add Roles and Features Wizard, these role services are under the File and Storage Services role and the File and iSCSI Services role service. After installing the two role services, you need to do some basic configuration that mostly involves choosing what servers and shares are to be used and organized. The default settings, however, might not meet your network's needs. To fine-tune configuration of these role services, you need to understand Active Directory and how it's deployed in your network, understand share permissions and NTFS permissions, and have general knowledge about the traffic load on your network.

Activity 3-1: Uninstalling Unneeded Services

Time Required: 10 minutes
Objective: Uninstall the WDS and WSUS server roles from 411Server1 and 411Server2.

Required Tools and Equipment: 411Server1 and 411Server2
Description: The WDS and WSUS server roles are no longer needed for this book, so to reduce the resources required on servers, you uninstall them in this activity.

1. Start 411Server1 and 411Server2, and log on to both as **Administrator,** if necessary.

2. On 411Server1, open Server Manager. Click **Manage, Remove Roles and Features.** Click **Next,** and then click **Next** again. In the Server Roles window, click to clear the **Windows Deployment Services** check box.

3. Click the **Remove Features** button, and then click **Next.** In the Features windows, click **Next.**

4. In the Confirmation window, click **Remove.** When the removal is finished, click **Close.**

5. On 411Server2, open Server Manager. Click **Manage, Remove Roles and Features.** Click **Next,** and then click **Next** again. In the Server Roles window, click to clear the **Windows Server Update Services** check box.

6. Click the **Remove Features** button, and then click **Next.** In the Features windows, click **Next.**

7. In the Confirmation window, click **Remove.** When the removal is finished, click **Close.**

8. Stay logged on to 411Server1, and leave 411Server2 running if you're continuing to the next activity.

Activity 3-2: Installing the DFS Namespace and DFS Replication Role Services

Time Required: 10 minutes
Objective: Install the DFS Namespace and DFS Replication role services.

Required Tools and Equipment: 411Server1 and 411Server2
Description: Install the DFS Namespace and DFS Replication role services on 411Server1, which will maintain the namespace, and install just the DFS Replication role service on 411Server2. Then you create shares on both servers to be used in the next activity.

1. Start 411Server1 and 411Server2, and log on to 411Server1 as **Administrator**, if necessary. Open Server Manager, and start the Add Roles and Features Wizard.

2. In the Server Roles window, click to expand **File and Storage Services** and **File and iSCSI Services**. Click to select **DFS Namespaces** and **DFS Replication**. Accept all the default installation options. When the installation is finished, close the Add Roles and Features Wizard.

3. Log on to 411Server2 as **Administrator**, if necessary. Open Server Manager, start the Add Roles and Features Wizard, and install the DFS Replication role service only. When the installation is finished, close the Add Roles and Features Wizard, and restart both servers. When they have restarted, log on to both as **Administrator**.

4. On 411Server2, create a folder on the C volume named **AcctDocs**. Share this folder by using simple file sharing. (*Note*: Right-click the folder, click **Share with**, and click **Specific people**.) Add **Everyone** with **Read** permission to the list of accounts to share the folder with.

5. On 411Server1, create a folder on the C volume named **MktDocs**. Share this folder by using simple file sharing. Add **Everyone** with **Read** permission to the list of accounts to share the folder with.

6. Stay logged on to 411Server1, and leave 411Server2 running if you're continuing to the next activity.

Creating a Namespace

A namespace doesn't actually contain the shares (and the files in them); instead, it's a list of pointers to the shares referred to in the namespace. Review Figure 3-1; the Namespace server doesn't actually host the shares but contains pointers to the shares residing on other servers.

There are two types of namespaces: domain-based and stand-alone. The type you choose depends on several factors: whether you're using Active Directory, the availability requirements of the namespace, the number of folders needed in a namespace, and the need for access-based enumeration (which allows users to see only files they actually have access to).

A namespace must be stored somewhere on the network, and the type of namespace determines the storage location. A domain-based namespace enables you to increase its availability by using multiple namespace servers in the same domain. This namespace type doesn't include the server name in the namespace, making it easier to replace a namespace server or move the namespace to a different server. A stand-alone namespace stores information only on the server where it's created and includes the server name in the namespace. If this server becomes unavailable, the namespace becomes unavailable, too. However, you can improve the availability of a stand-alone namespace by creating it on a failover cluster.

Stand-alone namespaces in Windows Server 2012 R2 can support up to 50,000 folders and access-based enumeration. The maximum number of folders and whether access-based enumeration is supported depend on whether you choose Windows Server 2008 mode or Windows 2000 Server mode. Windows Server 2008 mode is available if the domain uses the Windows Server 2008 (or higher) functional level, and all the namespace servers are running Windows Server 2008, Windows Server 2008 R2, Windows Server 2012, or Windows Server 2012 R2. If you choose Windows 2000 Server mode (or have no choice because of the domain's structure), domain-based namespaces are limited to 5000 folders and don't support access-based enumeration.

In organizations with different types of users (for example, mobile and guest users in addition to regular users) and a wide variety of documents and media with varying degrees of sensitivity, being able to control file permissions is crucial. File security in DFS namespaces is managed via the same permissions as for standard files and folders: share permissions and NTFS permissions. As a general rule, adjusting permissions on shares before configuring DFS is best. However, if multiple servers and folder targets are used with DFS replication, permissions on files and folders are replicated by DFS.

Activity 3-3: Creating a Domain-Based Namespace

Time Required: 15 minutes
Objective: Create a domain-based namespace and add shares to it.

Required Tools and Equipment: 411Server1 and 411Server2
Description: Use DFS to create a domain-based namespace, and then add several shares from 411Server1 and 411Server2 to this namespace. This new namespace allows users to access shared folders from a single location without needing to know on which server files are actually stored.

1. Start 411Server2, and log on to 411Server1 as **Administrator**, if necessary. Open Server Manager, and click **Tools, DFS Management** from the menu to open the DFS Management console.

2. In the left pane, right-click **Namespaces** and click **New Namespace** to start the New Namespace Wizard.

3. In the Namespace Server window (see Figure 3-3), type **411Server1**, the server hosting the new namespace, and then click **Next**.

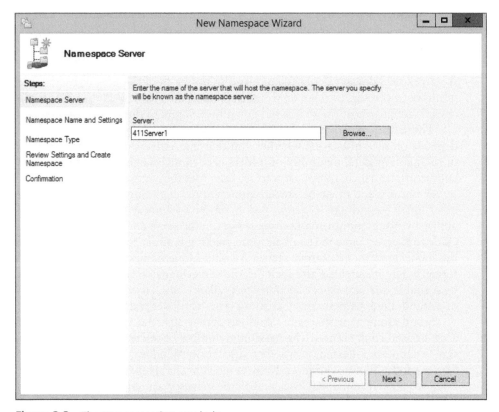

Figure 3-3   The Namespace Server window

4. In the Namespace Name and Settings window, you specify the name of the namespace you're creating. Type **AllShares** in the Name text box. Users will access the namespace by using the UNC path \\411Dom1\AllShares or \\411Server1\AllShares. Click the **Edit Settings** button to change the shared folder location and permissions (see Figure 3-4). By default, the namespace is located at C:\DFSRoots*Namespace* (with *Namespace* representing the name of the namespace). All users have read-only permission by default. You can choose any of the predefined permission settings or create custom permissions. Leave the defaults and click **OK** to close the Edit Settings dialog box. Click **Next** to continue.

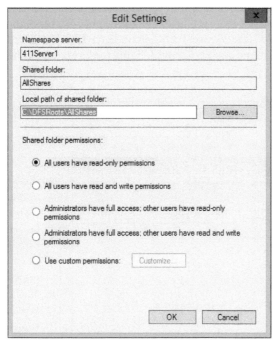

Figure 3-4   Editing namespace settings

5. In the Namespace Type window (see Figure 3-5), you choose a domain-based or stand-alone namespace. Both types show a preview of the namespace's full name. Notice that for a

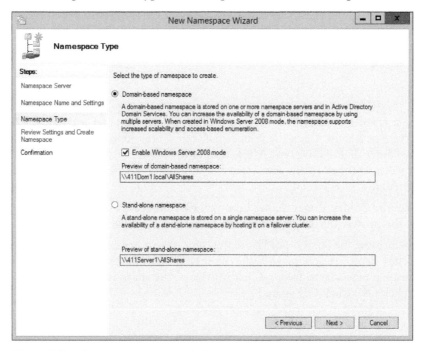

Figure 3-5   The Namespace Type window

domain-based type, the name starts with the domain name, and for a stand-alone type, it starts with the server name. Leave the default settings **Domain-based namespace** and **Enable Windows Server 2008 mode**, and then click **Next**.

6. Verify the settings in the Review Settings and Create Namespace window. (If necessary, you can click the Previous button to change a setting.) If everything is correct, click **Create**.

7. In the Confirmation window, you should see a message indicating success. Click **Close**.

8. In the DFS Management console, click to expand **Namespaces** in the left pane, and then click the **411Dom1.local\AllShares** namespace you created. In the middle pane, you see four tabs. The Namespace tab shows the shares that are members of the new namespace. Because you haven't added any shares, it's empty. Click the **Namespace Servers** tab to see the servers configured with the namespace (see Figure 3-6). As you learn later, more than one server can be configured with the same namespace to provide fault tolerance and load balancing.

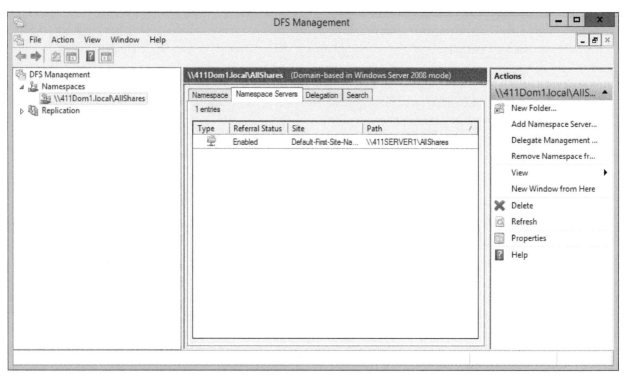

Figure 3-6　The Namespace Servers tab

9. Now it's time to add some folders to the namespace. You can add existing folders and shares or create new ones. Click the **Namespace** tab. In the Actions pane, click **New Folder**. In the New Folder dialog box, type **Marketing** in the Name text box. This name is what users see when they connect to the namespace, and it can be different from the actual share name. Click **Add**.

10. In the Add Folder Target dialog box, you can enter the folder target with its UNC name or click the Browse button and select the folder target. Click **Browse**.

11. In the Browse for Shared Folders dialog box, the shares on the current server are listed. You can click Browse to choose a different server, select an existing share on the current server, or create a new shared folder. Click **MktDocs**, the share you created in the previous activity, and click **OK**. Click **OK** again.

12. Back in the New Folder dialog box, notice that the UNC path to the MktDocs share is added to the Folder targets list. You can add folder targets to provide fault tolerance. Click **OK**. Now add the share from 411Server2. Click **New Folder** again in the Actions pane of the DFS Management console. Type **Accounting** in the Name text box, and click **Add**. Click **Browse**.

13. In the Browse for Shared Folders dialog box, click **Browse** to select a different server. In the Select Computer dialog box, type **411Server2**, click **Check Names**, and click **OK**.

14. In the Browse for Shared Folders dialog box, click **AcctDocs**, if necessary, and then click **OK**. Click **OK** twice more to return to the DFS Management console, which should now look like Figure 3-7 with both shares listed in the Namespace tab.

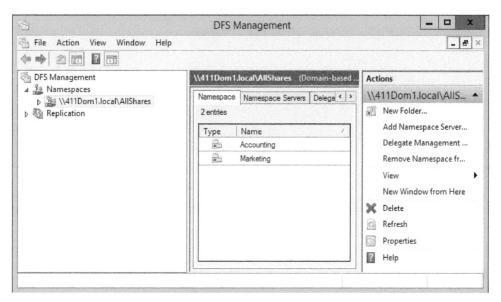

Figure 3-7   A namespace with two shares

15. To see how users would use this feature, right-click **Start**, click **Run**, type **\\411dom1\ allshares**, and press **Enter**. You see both shares, Accounting and Marketing, in File Explorer. Users could also enter the name of the server hosting the namespace, \\411Server1\allshares. A drive letter can be mapped to the namespace, too.

16. Stay logged on to 411Server1 if you're continuing to the next activity.

Installing DFS role services on 411Server2 isn't required in this activity; a share can be added to a namespace from any server in the domain. Only 411Server1 requires the DFS Namespace role service because it's hosting the namespace.

Configuring Referrals and Advanced Namespace Settings

A simple DFS namespace with a single server for hosting the namespace and a single folder target for each folder might not require more configuration. However, if you want to add fault tolerance and load sharing to a DFS namespace, you might want to configure the namespace's properties. To do so, right-click the namespace in DFS Management and click Properties. The namespace Properties dialog box has three tabs: General, Referrals, and Advanced.

The General tab just supplies information about the namespace, such as name, type (Windows Server 2008 or Windows 2000 Server), an optional description, and the number of folders in the namespace.

You use the Referrals tab (shown in Figure 3-8) to configure how DFS works when there are multiple servers for a namespace root or folder target. Recall that the namespace root can have multiple servers hosting it, and each folder can have multiple targets. When a client attempts to access a namespace root or the underlying folders, it receives a **referral**, which is a list of servers (targets) that host the namespace or folder. The client then attempts to access the first server in the referral list. If the first server is unavailable, the client attempts to access the second server in the referral list and so forth. The first option in the Referrals tab is the cache duration, which is the time (300 seconds by default) a client keeps a referral before requesting it again. By caching the referral, the client doesn't have to request the referral list each time it accesses the namespace, thereby maximizing access speed and reducing the bandwidth needed to access the namespace.

Figure 3-8   Namespace settings for referrals

The next option is the ordering method, which determines the order in which servers are listed in a referral and can be set to the following values:

- *Lowest cost*—Lists servers in the same Active Directory site as the client first. If there's more than one server in the site, servers in the same site as the client are listed in random order. Servers outside the client's site are listed from lowest cost to highest cost. Cost is based on the cost value assigned to a site in Active Directory Sites and Services.

- *Random order*—Similar to the "Lowest cost" option, servers in the same Active Directory site as the client are listed first. However, servers outside the client's site are ordered randomly, ignoring cost.

- *Exclude targets outside of the client's site*—The referral contains only servers in the same site as the client. If there are no servers in the client's site, the client can't access the requested part of the namespace. This method can be used to ensure that low-bandwidth connections, such as virtual private networks (VPNs), can't access shares containing large files.

The last option in the Referrals tab, under the Ordering method list box, is "Clients fail back to preferred targets." It's important only if referral order has been overridden in the properties of the namespace server or folder target, which essentially configures a preferred target.

If the option is selected and the preferred server fails, the client chooses another server from the referral list. If the preferred server comes back online, the client begins using it again.

The Advanced tab has options for configuring polling and access-based enumeration (see Figure 3-9). When namespaces change, changes are reflected instantly in a stand-alone namespace. If a domain-based namespace changes, however, information must be relayed to all the namespace servers. Namespace changes are first reported to the server in the domain holding the PDC emulator Flexible Single Master Operation (FSMO) role. The PDC emulator then replicates this information to all other domain controllers.

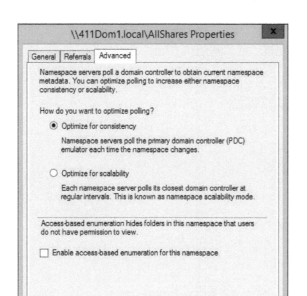

Figure 3-9   Namespace settings for polling and access-based enumeration

By default, namespace servers poll the PDC emulator to get the most current information for a namespace. In DFS configurations with many namespace servers, polling can place a considerable load on the PDC emulator. The more namespace servers in a domain, the larger the load is on the PDC emulator because of increased polling. If necessary, you can configure these polling options to reduce the load on the PDC emulator:

- *Optimize for consistency*—This setting is the default. In a domain with 16 or fewer namespace servers, this method is preferred because namespace servers poll the PDC emulator, which is the first DC updated after a namespace change.

- *Optimize for scalability*—This setting causes namespace servers to poll the nearest DC for namespace changes. This setting reduces the load on the PDC emulator but should be used only when there are more than the recommended 16 namespace servers in the domain. Because there's a delay between the PDC emulator getting a namespace update and the other DCs receiving it, users might have an inconsistent view of a namespace.

The last option in the Advanced tab is for enabling access-based enumeration for the namespace. Making sure only authorized users have access to sensitive data is a concern in most organizations. Restricting permissions on files and folders certainly helps, but to improve security, you can enable access-based enumeration to prevent users from even seeing files and folders they don't have permission to access.

Overriding Referral Order   You can use the namespace Properties dialog box to configure referral settings that affect all folder targets in the namespace. However, you might want to override these settings for a particular folder target. For example, you have a folder in the namespace with two folder targets. One target is a high-performance file server, and the other server has lower performance. In this example, you might want the high-performance server to be the preferred server clients use when accessing the folder instead of using the normal referral order.

To make changes to specific targets, you configure the properties of folder targets. In the DFS Management console, click the folder you want to change, and then right-click the folder target and click Properties. In the folder's Properties dialog box, click the Advanced tab and select the "Override referral ordering" check box (see Figure 3-10). Then select one of the following target priorities:

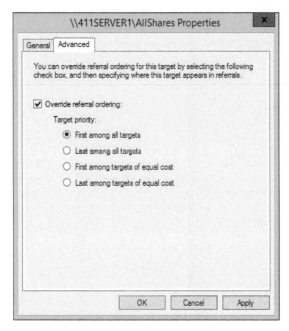

Figure 3-10   Configuring properties of a folder target

- *First among all targets*—This server is the default target if it's available. Use this option if you want clients to always use this target to access the folder.
- *Last among all targets*—You want clients to use this target only if no other targets are available.
- *First among targets of equal cost*—If more than one target exists in a site, this target is always listed first in the referral list.
- *Last among targets of equal cost*—If more than one target exists in a site, this target is always listed last in the referral list.

Creating DFS Replication Groups

A **replication group** consists of servers, known as members, that synchronize data in folders so that when a change occurs, all replication group members are updated at once. To create a replication group, you must have a minimum of two servers. One server is designated as the primary and the other as the secondary. After a replication group is defined, you add folders to it. Files in replicated folders on the secondary server, if any, are overwritten. There are several maximums to take into account when creating a replication group:

- A single file to be replicated must be less than 250 GB.
- The number of files to be replicated on a volume must be less than 70 million.
- The total size of all replicated files on a server must be less than 100 TB.

3

There are two types of replication groups: a multipurpose replication group and a replication group for data collection. A multipurpose replication group contains two or more servers and is used for content sharing and document publication when you want to provide fault tolerance and load balancing for file shares. A replication group for data collection consists of only two servers and is used mainly to transfer data from one server to another for backup purposes. For example, a server in a branch office that hosts a shared folder can use this type of replication group to transfer the share's contents to a server in the main office for centralized backups.

The folders specified in replication groups need not be shared folders or part of a DFS namespace, but they often are. You can create a replication group for folders that are already part of a DFS namespace to provide fault tolerance, or you can create a replication group on a shared or nonshared folder and add them to a DFS namespace later, if needed.

A server participating in a DFS replication group must have the DFS Replication role service installed.

Optimizing DFS Replication

In many situations, simply using the default settings when creating a replication group could cause problems by overusing network bandwidth. For example, accepting the default replication schedule between servers in a replication group that communicate over a low-bandwidth WAN link could create excessive network traffic. Several features, discussed in the following sections, can be configured to meet special bandwidth, network configuration, and server load needs:

- Replication topology
- Replication scheduling
- Remote differential compression

Replication Topology   A *replication topology* describes the connections used to replicate files between servers. Three topologies are available for replication groups: hub and spoke, full mesh, or no topology. With hub and spoke, all members of the group synchronize with the hub only. So a change on one member is updated on the hub, and then the hub replicates the change to all other members. This topology is available only if the group has three or more servers. You can specify a primary hub and a secondary hub for each spoke member. With a secondary hub in place, if one of the hubs goes down, members are configured to recognize the secondary hub, and replication occurs with it. The two hubs synchronize with each other. This topology reduces the overall network load because the spokes don't synchronize with each other, only with the hub. However, there can be a slight delay in propagating changes throughout the group because the hub must distribute all the changes.

With a full mesh topology, which is the default, synchronization is bidirectional, meaning all members synchronize with each other. It's ideal when you have just a few servers. In a larger network with 10 or more members or when you have a main office connected to several branch offices, switching to a hub and spoke topology might be best to reduce network traffic. With large replication groups, the network load of communicating between all servers could become severe, depending on the replication schedule (discussed in the next section), the total number of files, the number of changes, and the overall size of files.

The "no topology" option is exactly what it sounds like: There are no initial connections, so you must define them. When would defining your own connections be useful? Say you have a central server where changes are being made and several other servers where you want files available locally, but they should be read-only. You could configure a hub and spoke topology, with the central server as the hub where files are updated and the other servers as spokes with read-only copies of files (which is an option when configuring a replication group). The hub synchronizes changes with the spokes, but it's a one-way synchronization: The members never change the files, so they never replicate them back to the hub or to other members.

DFS Replication Scheduling   Scheduling can help manage peak bandwidth needs by forcing replication to occur in off hours. This option can be particularly good when you have large files that need to be replicated across lower bandwidth connections. However, keep in mind that changes made on one end of a connection usually aren't available to the other end until the next day. If the information is time sensitive, scheduling replication during off hours could cause problems because files might not be synchronized. The trade-off for the delay is more bandwidth available for other functions during peak hours.

By default, DFS replication tries to use the connection's full bandwidth when replicating files, which might not be what you want. Luckily, you can throttle (reduce) the bandwidth so that replication uses a specified maximum percentage of available bandwidth. To configure this scheduling, follow these steps in the DFS Management console:

1. In the left pane, select the replication group you want to adjust. In the Actions pane, click Edit Replication Group Schedule.

2. The Edit Schedule dialog box opens, showing the existing schedule and bandwidth use setting. You can select a maximum percentage in the Bandwidth usage drop-down list box. If you want to adjust the schedule, click Details. Select a day and click Edit, and you can adjust the times as needed.

Remote Differential Compression   Copying the contents of hundreds or thousands of files across a network can waste bandwidth, especially when the amount of data that actually changed is fairly small. DFS replication uses an algorithm known as **remote differential compression (RDC)**, which replicates only the changes made in files. By default, RDC is used during replication. Because only pieces of files are transmitted across the network, the use of network bandwidth is reduced. The trade-off is increased CPU and disk I/O overhead on servers because they do extra work to update files with the replicated changes. When you have a good combination of enough bandwidth and fewer files to synchronize, you might want to disable RDC. To configure RDC, follow these general steps:

1. In the DFS Management console, click the replication group in the left pane, and in the center pane, click the Connections tab.

2. Right-click a member server and click Properties. Next, clear the "Use remote differential compression (RDC)" check box, and then click Apply.

Activity 3-4: Creating a Replication Group

Time Required: 15 minutes
Objective: Configure a replication group.

Required Tools and Equipment: 411Server1 and 411Server2
Description: In this activity, you create a multipurpose replication group, which allows replicating a share on one server to another server for fault tolerance and load balancing. If one server becomes unavailable, users can access files from the other server. You use a full mesh topology so that changes made to either server are synchronized and replicated on the other.

1. Log on to 411Server1, if necessary. Create a folder on the C drive named **ReplShare**, and share it with the same settings as the shares you created in Activity 3-2. Repeat this step on 411Server2. Leave File Explorer open on both servers.

2. On 411Server1, create a text file named **testfile1.txt** in the ReplShare folder. On 411Server2, create a text file named **testfile2.txt** in the ReplShare folder. Close File Explorer on both servers.

3. On 411Server1, open the DFS Management console, if necessary. In the left pane, click to expand **Replication**. A replication group named Domain System Volume is listed, which replicates the SYSVOL share for replication of GPOs and other system files.

4. Right-click **Replication** and click **New Replication Group** to start the New Replication Group Wizard.

5. In the Replication Group Type window, accept the default type **Multipurpose replication group**, and then click **Next**.

6. In the Name and Domain window, type **Share Replication Group** in the "Name of replication group" text box. Leave the domain set at **411Dom1.local**, and then click **Next**.

7. In the Replication Group Members window, you add servers to participate in the group. Click **Add**, and in the Select Computers dialog box, type **411Server1;411Server2**, click **Check Names**, and click **OK**. You see a progress indicator while Windows verifies that the DFS Replication service is running on the specified servers. After the servers have been added (see Figure 3-11), click **Next**.

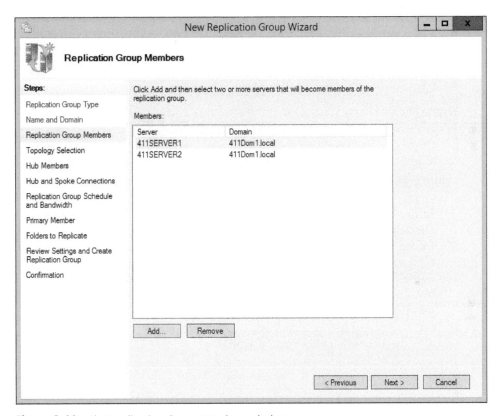

Figure 3-11   The Replication Group Members window

8. In the Topology Selection window, leave the default option **Full mesh**. Notice that the "Hub and spoke" option is grayed out because you have fewer than three servers. If you wanted to configure a custom replication topology, you would select the "No topology" option. Click **Next**.

9. In the Replication Group Schedule and Bandwidth window (see Figure 3-12), you configure scheduling and bandwidth throttling. Leave the default option **Replicate continuously using the specified bandwidth** and **Full** for the Bandwidth setting. If you select "Replicate during the specified days and times," you can configure the replication schedule by clicking the Edit Schedule button. Click **Next**.

10. In the Primary Member window, click **411Server1** in the Primary member list box to make this server's contents authoritative for the replication, which means files are copied from 411Server1 to 411Server2, and any existing files on 411Server2 are overwritten. Click **Next**.

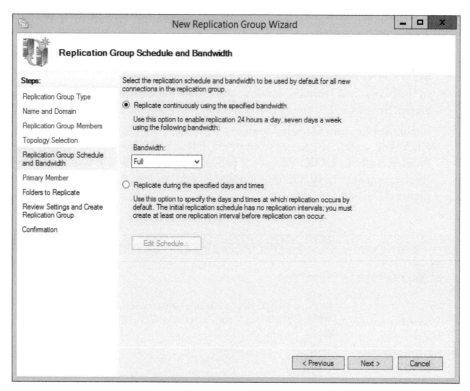

Figure 3-12 The Replication Group Schedule and Bandwidth window

11. In the Folders to Replicate window, click **Add**. In the Add Folder to Replicate dialog box, click **Browse**. In the Browse For Folder dialog box, click **ReplShare**, and then click **OK**. Any folder, whether it's shared or not, can be in the replication group, but in this activity, you replicate the ReplShare folder you just created (see Figure 3-13). You can change the folder name by clicking the "Use custom name" option button or leave the default folder name. You can also change permissions for the folder, if needed. Leave the default option **Existing permissions**, click **OK**, and then click **Next**.

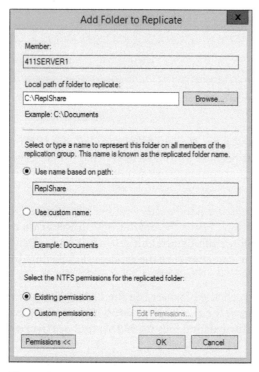

Figure 3-13 The Add Folder to Replicate dialog box

12. In the Local Path of ReplShare on Other Members window, click **411Server2**, if necessary, and click **Edit**. In the Edit dialog box, click **Enabled** to enable replication on 411Server2. Click **Browse** to select the path where data will be replicated. Click the **ReplShare** folder, and then click **OK** twice. Because 411Server1 is the primary member, files in the ReplShare folder on 411Server2 will be overwritten. Click **Next**.

13. In the Review Settings and Create Replication Group window (see Figure 3-14), verify your choices, and then click **Create**.

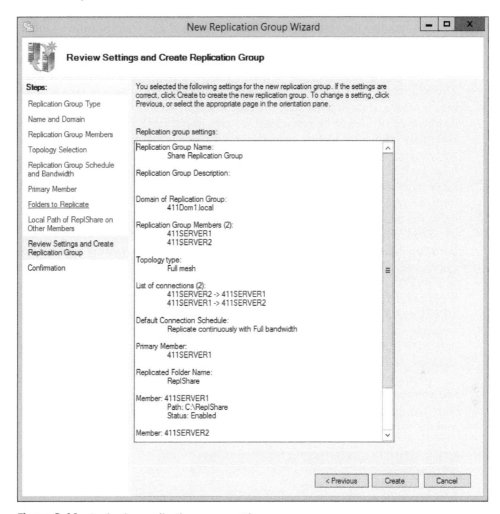

Figure 3-14   Reviewing replication group settings

14. In the Confirmation window, you see the results as well as a link to a help file on staging folder optimization, which has important information on replication staging, discussed next. Click **Close** to finish the wizard. You see a message explaining that the replication process isn't instantaneous but depends on each member server picking up the configuration from Active Directory Domain Services. Click **OK**.

15. On 411Server2, open File Explorer and navigate to **C:\ReplShare**. You should see only `testfile1.txt` because replication occurred from 411Server1 to 411Server2, erasing the `testfile2.txt` file you created on 411Server2. (If you still see `testfile2.txt`, give replication a minute to work, and then close and open the ReplShare folder again.)

16. On 411Server2, open **`testfile1.txt`** in Notepad. Type your name in the file, save it, and close it. On 411Server1, open File Explorer and navigate to **C:\ReplShare**. Open **`testfile1.txt`** to see that your change was replicated. On 411Server1, create a file named **`testfile2.txt`** in the ReplShare folder.

17. On 411Server2, refresh File Explorer, if necessary, to see that `testfile2.txt` has been replicated.

18. If needed, you could add the replicated folder to the DFS namespace you created earlier by selecting the replication group in the DFS Management console, clicking the Replicated Folders tab, and then right-clicking ReplShare and clicking Share and Publish in Namespace. For now, log off 411Server2, but stay logged on to 411Server1 if you're continuing to the next activity.

Managing the Staging Folder and the Conflict and Deleted Folder

An important consideration when configuring replication groups is making sure there's enough space on each drive that hosts a replicated folder. Each drive must have space to house not only the files, but also the Staging folder and the Conflict and Deleted folder. Only a local administrator can access these folders. The Staging folder is where changed files are cached until they're replicated; compression is performed on the sending server and decompression on the receiving server. By default, each replicated folder contains a hidden Staging folder: DFSRPrivate\Staging. The Staging folder's size acts as a quota, and its default size is 4 GB. When the Staging folder reaches 90% of its defined size, the oldest staged files are deleted until it's at 60%. Depending on the type of files to be replicated, its size might need to be adjusted, especially if you have extremely large files, such as multimedia files. For initial replication, which occurs from the primary server to other servers in the group when the group is created, the Staging folder should be at least as big as the combined size of the largest 32 files in the replicated folder on the primary member. If the folder is read-only, you can use the combined size of the largest 16 files. To improve replication performance or if you need more space for caching changed files, you can move the Staging folder to a different volume.

The Conflict and Deleted folder stores files that were deleted and files that have a conflict. If both copies of a file—the main copy and the replicated copy—were modified during a replication cycle, it results in a conflict between which copy to use and which one to cache. When a conflict occurs, DFS replication uses a "last writer wins" model to make this determination. The losing file is cached in the Conflict and Deleted folder, a hidden folder in the replicated folder named DFSRPrivate\ConflictandDeleted. Its default size is 4 GB. The log of the original names of files stored in this folder is written to the `ConflictandDeletedManifest.xml` file, which is also in the DFSRPrivate folder. Like the Staging folder, the Conflict and Deleted folder's size can be changed, and the path can be changed to move the folder to another volume.

To manage these settings in the DFS Management console, select the replication group. In the Memberships tab, open the properties for the replicated folder and replication member you want to change. The Staging folder's settings can be changed in the Staging tab (see Figure 3-15), and the Conflict and Deleted folder can be changed in the Advanced tab (see Figure 3-16).

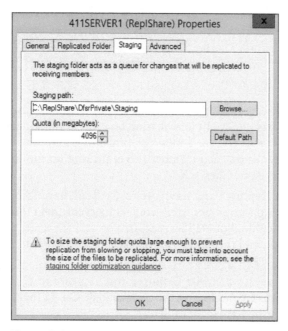

Figure 3-15   Changing the Staging folder's settings

Figure 3-16   Changing the Conflict and Deleted folder's settings

DFS Fault Tolerance and Load Balancing

DFS fault tolerance ensures continuous access to users' files; when a server goes down, DFS fault tolerance automatically "fails over" to another server with replicated copies of files. Load balancing is achieved when a user requests a file in a replicated DFS namespace and is directed, via a referral, to one of the DFS servers hosting the namespace. By using DFS namespaces and DFS replication together, you can have both fault tolerance and load balancing on all namespace servers.

To configure fault tolerance and load balancing, create identical folders on at least two servers and share them. Add the folders to an existing replication group or create a replication group for this purpose. Replicating the files ensures that you have an up-to-date copy on at least two servers for fault-tolerance and load-balancing purposes. The preferred topology for this replication group is full mesh because it makes sure all copies of files in the replication folders are consistent so that users aren't using outdated files. Using a hub and spoke topology might cause delays in the replication process that could result in inconsistent file contents when a server fails. Finally, create a DFS namespace that includes targets of all folders in the replication group. If one server in the namespace goes down, the next target server is selected. When the original server is backed up, any files that were modified are updated in the next replication cycle. Load balancing is achieved naturally because clients use the first available server returned in the referral list.

Using Replication Diagnostics

To help troubleshoot replication groups, DFS includes a useful diagnostic report utility. To use it, right-click the replication group in the left pane of the DFS Management console and click Create Diagnostic Report. A wizard guides you through selecting criteria to generate one of three types of reports:

- *Health report*—This report describes the efficiency of replication and states whether there are any problems. It shows the number of backlogged files, bandwidth savings, and whether any servers in the group have reported errors or warnings.

- *Propagation test*—This option conducts a propagation test but doesn't actually produce a report. The test creates a test file in a replicated folder and then tests the replication (propagation) of that file to other servers in the replication group.

- *Propagation report*—This report, generated from the results of the propagation test, shows how long it took to replicate the test file to each server in the replication group.

Cloning and Recovering a DFS Replication Database

One of the most resource-heavy parts of replication is the setup the system must do when adding replication targets, replacing a server, or recovering from the loss or corruption of a DFS replication database. The files and file metadata must be copied and set up. Much of this work can be eliminated by cloning the DFS replication database, a new feature in Windows Server 2012 R2. Importing a clone of the replication database can substantially reduce this synchronization time—up to 99%, depending on the number of changes to the database that occur between exporting the clone and importing it. To create a clone, use the `Export-DfsrClone` command at a PowerShell prompt:

```
Export-DfsrClone -Volume D: -Path D:\DFSRclone
```

In this command, `D:` is the drive letter of the volume containing the DFS database you want to export, and `D:\DFSRclone` is the destination folder the exported replication database files are written to. You then copy the folder with the exported files to a destination server for import. Next, you use the following command at a PowerShell prompt to import the clone:

```
Import-DfsrClone -Volume D: -Path D:\DFSRclone
```

A DFS replication database could become corrupted. Although Windows Server 2012 R2 has added features to automatically rebuild a corrupted database much faster than in previous versions, this rebuilding might not work and could still take a lot of time. Importing a clone can save more time than allowing the system to do the recovery automatically. There are a few factors to take into account when recovering a replication database with a clone:

- Make sure there's no replicated folder on the destination volume. You can't merge a clone with an existing replication database.

- Make sure there's no write access to shares on the destination replication folders.

- Remove the destination server from the affected replication group before importing the clone.

For more on DFS replication cloning, see
http://technet.microsoft.com/library/dn482443.aspx.

An Overview of File Server Resource Manager

A major challenge in network management is the use—or abuse—of storage space. Although storage has gotten less expensive, it's not free, and filling a volume can have adverse consequences on other processes and system efficiency. Users often need read and write access to file server shares but might not be careful about what, and how much, they save to these shares. Worse, users might not be aware that certain files (such as audio or video files) violate copyright law and could pose a legal risk for the organization. In addition, as the number of files on a network grows, finding files becomes a time-consuming task.

The **File Server Resource Manager (FSRM)** role service has services and management tools for monitoring storage space, managing quotas, controlling the types of files users can store on a server, creating storage reports, and classifying and managing files. When this role service is installed, you can open the File Server Resource Manager console from the Tools menu in Server Manager. This console contains five tools (see Figure 3-17):

- *Quota Management*—Monitor and create quotas for volumes and folders and apply preconfigured quota templates to volumes and folders.

- *File Screening Management*—Create file screens for volumes and folders to prevent users from storing certain types of files in the volume or folder. For example, if you set up a file screen to keep users from storing audio and video files, a user who attempts to store a blocked file sees an "Access denied" message. File screening can also be set to allow saving the screened file on the volume and sending the user an e-mail informing him or her of the violation.

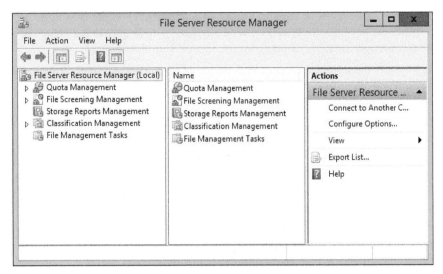

Figure 3-17   The File Server Resource Manager console

- *Storage Reports Management*—Define use thresholds on volumes and folders, and any use above these thresholds generates reports on several possible storage parameters. You can save reports in a variety of formats, including HTML and text.

- *Classification Management*—Categorize files by setting classification properties on files or folders, which are additional file attributes saved as part of a file's metadata. They can be used to search for files based on a certain value or to identify files containing certain types of information. For example, a file can be classified as "Sensitive," indicating that it contains information that must be handled discreetly.

- *File Management Tasks*—Use them to act on files based on classification properties and other attributes. For example, files classified as sensitive can be encrypted with EFS, or files can be archived or deleted based on their last accessed date. A host of tasks can be performed, including custom commands.

Using FSRM

To use quotas, file screens, storage reports, and file classification and management, you install the File Server Resource Manager role service, which is part of the File and Storage Services server role. In Activity 3-5, you install FSRM and then explore some of its features.

Activity 3-5: Installing the File Server Resource Manager Role Service

Time Required: 10 minutes
Objective: Install the File Server Resource Manager role service.

Required Tools and Equipment: 411Server1
Description: Install the File Server Resource Manager role service and explore some of its features.

1. Log on to 411Server1 as **Administrator,** if necessary.

2. Open Server Manager, and start the Add Roles and Features Wizard. In the Server Roles window, click to expand **File and Storage Services** and **File and iSCSI Services**. Click to select **File Server Resource Manager.** Install the role service with the default settings.

3. After the installation is finished, click **Tools, File Server Resource Manager** from the Server Manager menu.

4. In the left pane, click to expand **Quota Management**. You see two nodes: Quotas and Quota Templates. You use the Quotas node to create custom quotas for folder or volumes. You can also create predefined quotas from the Quota Templates node.

5. In the left pane, click to expand **File Screening Management**. You create file screens to restrict the types of files users can store on your servers. There are predefined templates for this feature, too.

6. In the left pane, click **Storage Reports Management**. You can create reports for duplicate files, large files, least recently used files, quota use, and many more criteria.

7. In the left pane, click to expand **Classification Management**. You see the Classification Properties and Classification Rules nodes. Click **Classification Properties** to see three pre-defined classification properties for folders. For files, you create your own properties by clicking Create Local Property in the Actions pane. You can also create classification rules to specify which files the classification properties should be applied to and when.

8. In the left pane, click **File Management Tasks**. You create new file management tasks based on file classification properties and other file attributes.

9. Leave the File Server Resource Manager console open if you're continuing to the next activity.

Creating Quotas and Quota Templates

Simply put, **quotas** are limits on the amount of storage users have on a volume or in a folder. They differ from NTFS quotas, which limit a user to a specified amount of storage on a volume. Quotas can be hard or soft. **Hard quotas** actually prevent users from saving files if their files in the target folder already meet or exceed the quota limit. **Soft quotas** alert users when they have exceeded the quota but don't prevent them from saving files.

You can use a predefined quota template or create your own. There are several advantages to using quota templates. For example, you can apply a quota template across different volumes and folders, and a quota template can be applied to volumes and folders to assign quotas automatically to new folders or subfolders. You also have the option of applying changes you make to a quota to all or some of the volumes or folders that used the quota template previously.

Activity 3-6: Creating and Applying a Quota Template

Time Required: 10 minutes
Objective: Configure a quota template and apply it to a folder.

Required Tools and Equipment: 411Server1
Description: In this activity, you configure a quota template and apply it to a folder. You then test the quota and quota notifications by copying files to the folder.

1. Log on to 411Server1 as **Administrator,** and open the File Server Resource Manager console, if necessary.

2. Click to expand **Quota Management**, if necessary. Click **Quota Templates** to see the list of defined templates in the middle pane. Right-click **Quota Templates** and click **Create Quota Template**.

3. In the Create Quota Template dialog box, notice that you can copy settings from an existing template by clicking the Copy button. Type **MktQuota** in the Template name text box and **Quota for Marketing Share** in the Description text box (see Figure 3-18).

4. Set the space limit to **20 MB**. This amount of storage is small by today's standards, but it's suitable for this example. Leave the default option **Hard quota**.

5. Click the **Add** button to add a notification threshold. In this dialog box, you can generate notifications when the folder or volume use reaches a certain percentage of the quota limit (see Figure 3-19). In the E-mail Message tab, you can send an e-mail to administrators, the user who exceeded the threshold, or both. You can customize the message by adding text with variables, as you can see in Figure 3-19. If you enable any of the e-mail options, the server must be configured with an SMTP e-mail server.

3

Figure 3-18   Creating a quota template

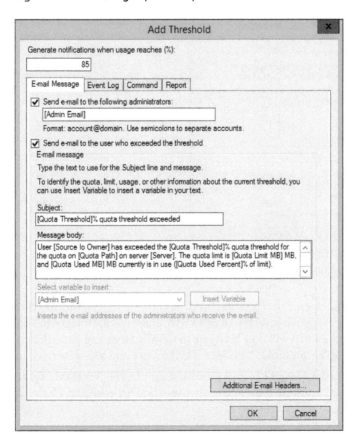

Figure 3-19   The Add Threshold dialog box

6. Click the **Event Log** tab. Here you can specify creating a warning event, which you can customize much like the notification message. The event is created in the Application log with event ID 12325 and event source SRMSVC. You view this log with Event Viewer. In the "Generate notifications when usage reaches (%)" text box, type **50**, and click **Send warning to event log** to enable event notifications.

7. Click the **Command** tab, where you can specify that a command or script should run when the threshold is exceeded. For example, you could specify a script that deletes all temporary files.

8. Click the **Report** tab. You can specify generating a storage report if the threshold is exceeded and e-mailing reports to selected administrators, users who exceeded the threshold, or both. Click **Cancel** to return to the Create Quota Template dialog box. Note that you can create multiple notification thresholds, each with its own notification messages and events. Click **OK**.

9. Now that you have a custom template, you can create a quota from it. Right-click the **MktQuota** template and click **Create Quota from Template** to open the Create Quota dialog box.

10. Click the **Browse** button to specify the path you want to apply the quota to. In the Browse For Folder dialog box, navigate to **C:\MktDocs**, click the **MktDocs** folder, and click **OK**. You can select "Create quota on path" (the default settings) to create the quota for just that folder or have the template automatically applied to the existing folder and any new subfolders. If you wanted to create a custom quota, you could select "Define custom quota properties." Leave the defaults, as shown in Figure 3-20, and click **Create**.

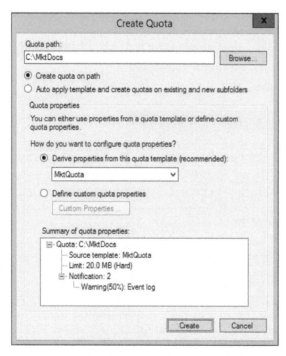

Figure 3-20 Creating a quota from a template

11. To test the quota, open File Explorer and navigate to **C:\Windows\System32**. Find the **twinui.dll** file, which is a little less than 13 MB, and copy it. (If you can't find this file, another file between 10 and 20 MB will do.) Navigate to **C:\MktDocs** and paste the file. You should have just exceeded the 50% threshold. You'll see whether an event was generated in a moment.

12. Rename the file **twinui2.dll**, and paste it again in the **MktDocs** folder. In the message stating there's not enough disk space in the MktDocs folder, click **Cancel**. Close File Explorer.

13. In Server Manager, click **Tools, Event Viewer**. Click to expand **Windows Logs** and click **Application**. You should see the event ID 12325 and event source SRMSVC. Double-click the event to read the details. Click **Close** and close Event Viewer.

14. Open the File Server Resource Manager console, and click **Quota Management** and then **Quotas**. You should see that C:\MktDocs is at around 60% of its limit. Right-click the quota for C:\MktDocs and click **Delete** to delete the quota. Click **Yes** to confirm. If you're continuing to the next activity, stay logged on to 411Server1 and leave the File Server Resource Manager console open.

Modifying Quota Templates and Monitoring Quota Use

There are two ways to modify a quota: editing the quota or editing the template the quota was generated from. In the FSRM console, you can click Quotas under Quota Management and double-click a quota in the middle pane to edit its properties. When you do so, the template the quota was created from remains unchanged, but the changes affect the quota applied to the folder or volume you're editing. If you change the quota limit or notification threshold and cause the threshold to be exceeded, no notifications are created for existing files. Only attempts to add new files that exceed the threshold generate a notification.

When you edit a quota template, the changes can be applied to all, some, or none of the quotas created from this template. When you save template changes, the dialog box shown in Figure 3-21 opens. You can configure the following settings:

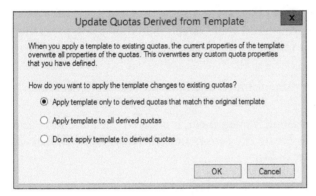

Figure 3-21   The Update Quotas Derived from Template dialog box

- *Apply template only to derived quotas that match the original template*—The changes are applied only to quotas that haven't been changed manually since the template was applied.

- *Apply template to all derived quotas*—The template is applied to all quotas generated by the template, even if the quota was changed manually.

- *Do not apply template to derived quotas*—No changes are made to existing quotas.

Often you need to make a quick check on the status of quotas you have set up or get some details on quota use. To review their current status, under Quota Management in the FSRM console, click Quotas. The center pane lists quotas along with the percent used and a summary of quota settings. Select a quota in the list to see additional details, including peak use, peak time, and available space. Figure 3-22 shows an example of this simple report.

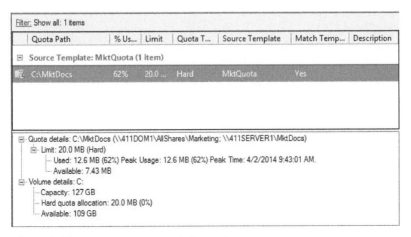

Figure 3-22   Viewing quota use information

Using File Screens

Sometimes it's better to not allow storing certain types of files on a server, even if there's enough space. For example, you might not want users storing their MP3 and video libraries on the company file servers or storing executable files on server shares. **File screens** enable you to monitor and control the type of files allowed on the server. FSRM includes file screen templates you can use as is or as a starting point for more detailed file screens.

To begin controlling the types of files stored on servers, you need to create and apply a file screen. There are two types of file screens. **Active screening** prevents users from saving unauthorized files, and **passive screening** simply monitors and notifies when unauthorized files are saved. Exceptions can be defined to allow special cases (such as a video presentation that needs to be in a central location).

Activity 3-7: Creating a File Screen

Time Required: 10 minutes
Objective: Create a file screen.

Required Tools and Equipment: 411Server1
Description: In this activity, you create a file screen that allows you to restrict the type of files users can save in a particular folder. It also alerts you if users attempt to save unauthorized files in the folder.

1. Log on to 411Server1 as **Administrator,** and open the File Server Resource Manager console, if necessary.

2. Click to expand **File Screening Management**, if necessary. Right-click **File Screens** and click **Create File Screen**. In the Create File Screen dialog box, type **C:\MktDocs** in the "File screen path" text box (see Figure 3-23).

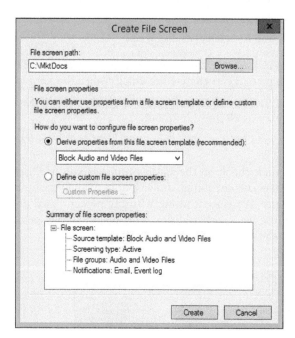

Figure 3-23   The Create File Screen dialog box

3. In the "How do you want to configure file screen properties?" section, the default option enables you to select an existing template. Click the **Define custom file screen properties** option button, and then click the **Custom Properties** button.

4. In the File Screen Properties dialog box, click the **Settings** tab, if necessary. Here you choose active screening or passive screening and select the file groups to block. Accept the default setting **Active screening**, and click the **Compressed Files** check box in the list of file groups (see Figure 3-24).

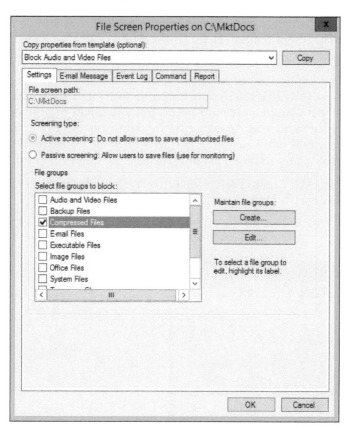

Figure 3-24 Setting custom properties for a file screen

5. Click the remaining tabs: **E-mail Message, Event Log, Command,** and **Report**. You see options similar to the ones available for creating quotas. In the Event Log tab, click to select the **Send warning to event log** option, and then click **OK**. Click **Create** to create the file screen for the MktDocs folder.

6. If you want, you can save a template based on the screen you've created. For this activity, however, click **Save the custom file screen without creating a template**, and then click **OK**.

7. To test the file screen, open File Explorer, and navigate to the **C:\MktDocs** folder. Your file screen prevents storing compressed files, which includes zipped files. Right-click the file you copied there in Activity 3-6, point to **Send to**, and click **Compressed (zipped) folder**. In the message stating "File not found or no read permission," click **OK**. It's not the most enlightening error message, but it lets you know you can't create the file, so the file screen works.

8. Open Event Viewer from Server Manager, and click **Windows Logs** and then **Application**. Verify that a warning event was generated based on the attempt to save a compressed file in the MktDocs folder.

9. Close the File Server Resource Manager console. If you're continuing to the next activity, stay logged on to 411 Server1.

Unfortunately, global restrictions often interfere with real business needs. You can use file screen exceptions, however, to restrict general file types yet allow certain files or folders.

For example, audio and video files have been blocked, but the Human Resources Department needs to show a training video to employees. To create a file screen exception, follow these steps:

1. In the left pane of the File Server Resource Manager console, right-click File Screens and click Create File Screen Exception to open the Create File Screen Exception dialog box.

2. Enter the exception path in the text box. The exception applies to the folder you specify and all its subfolders. Then select the file groups to exclude from screening. If necessary, you can create a new file group by clicking Create. When you're finished, click OK to close the dialog box.

To create a file screen template, you follow the same procedure as you do for creating a file screen but click Create File Screen Template in the FSRM console. All the options are the same as for creating a file screen except you enter a name for the template and don't specify a file screen path.

File Groups   A file group is a list of the types of files that define a file screen. For example, in Activity 3-7, you chose the Compressed Files file group to create a file screen. FSRM includes predefined file groups that should meet most needs, but you might need to create custom file groups or create exceptions to your file screens. To create custom file groups, expand File Screening Management in the left pane of the File Server Resource Manager console, and click File Groups. In the center pane, you see a list of predefined file groups. Then follow these steps:

1. In the Actions pane, click Create File Group or right-click File Groups in the left pane and click Create File Group.

2. The Create File Group Properties dialog box opens (see Figure 3-25). Type a name for the file group.

Figure 3-25   Creating a custom file group

3. In the "Files to include" section, you can add specific filenames or filename patterns by using the * wildcard character (for example, *.mp4 or tmp*.*). After typing an entry, click the Add button to add it to the list. You can add as many filenames as you want.

4. Follow the same procedure in the "Files to exclude" section. After you have entered all the files or file types, click OK to close the dialog box.

3

Using Storage Reports

Setting quotas and creating file screens are the start of the storage management process. Next, you need to see how storage is being used, which might require creating more quotas or screens and auditing violations of existing quotas and screens. You can run a variety of storage reports (which are saved in the C:\StorageReports\Scheduled folder) to check on the file server's state and the use of quotas and file screens. The following reports are available:

- *Duplicate Files*—Lists files of the same size and same last modified date.

- *File Screening Audit*—Lists audit events generated by users' file screen violations.

- *Files by File Group*—Sorts files by FSRM-defined file groups.

- *Files by Owner*—Lists files sorted by the file owner. This report helps you determine which users are consuming a lot of disk space.

- *Files by Property*—Lists files by classification property. This report is new in Windows Server 2012 R2. Classification properties are discussed later in the chapter in "File Classification Management."

- *Folders by Property*—Lists folders by secure classification property. This report is new in Windows Server 2012 R2.

- *Large Files*—Lists files larger than a specified size.

- *Least Recently Accessed Files*—Lists files not accessed for a specified number of days. Use this report to identify files that can be archived or deleted.

- *Most Recently Accessed Files*—Lists files accessed most recently. Use this report to identify files that need to be highly available.

- *Quota Usage*—Lists quotas that exceed a specified level of disk space use. This report is used to identify quotas that might be exceeded soon. You can notify users so that they can clean up unneeded files, if necessary.

Scheduling Storage Report Tasks   Although you can run storage reports on demand whenever you like, you might find it useful to schedule some to run at specified times. Follow these steps to schedule storage report tasks:

1. Open the File Server Resource Manager console. In the left pane, right-click Storage Reports Management and click Schedule a New Report Task.

2. The Storage Reports Task Properties dialog box opens (see Figure 3-26). In the Settings tab, enter a report name, and you can select from the list of reports to generate. Some reports

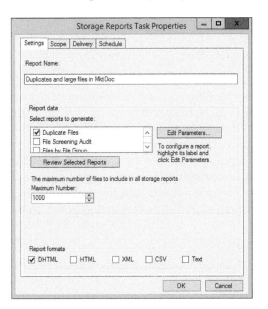

Figure 3-26   The Storage Reports Task Properties dialog box

have parameters you can edit. For example, if you select Files by Owner and click Edit Parameters, a dialog box opens where you can change the report from the default All owners to Selected owners.

3. In the Scope tab, click Add to select the folder on which to generate a report. You can also use the options at the top to report on the predefined file types listed in all folders.

4. Click the Delivery tab to have the report e-mailed to an administrator, and then click the Schedule tab to set a schedule for the report. When you're finished, click OK.

To use the e-mail notification features, you must enter the e-mail server information in the FSRM console as follows:

1. In the left pane, right-click File Server Resource Manager and click Configure Options.

2. In the E-mail Notifications tab, enter the SMTP server name or IP address and the default administrator recipients. You can then click Send Test E-mail, and when the test is successful, click OK to close the dialog box.

File Classification Management

Because the number and size of files organizations store on file servers keeps increasing, users have more difficulty finding the files they want, even with advanced search algorithms to help with the task. File classification management is a fairly new feature, introduced in Windows Server 2008 R2. This topic is covered in more detail in *MCSA Guide to Configuring Advanced Windows Server 2012/R2 Services, Exam 70-412* (Cengage Learning, 2015), but this section covers the basics.

In the past, the only way to classify a file was to organize files with descriptive filenames and folder names. With indexing, files can be searched based on file content, but finding certain words in a file doesn't tell you whether the file contains sensitive information or is related to a particular vendor or customer. File classification by file naming or folder storage is often left up to users, which can result in inconsistencies and errors. FSRM's file classification feature helps you develop a consistent, reliable classification system for file management tasks. File classification management involves three basic steps:

1. Create file classification properties.

2. Create classification rules to apply to files and folders.

3. Carry out file management tasks based on the classified files.

 File classification is also used by dynamic access control (DAC), a new feature in Windows Server 2012/R2 for setting access permissions on files. DAC is covered in *MCSA Guide to Configuring Advanced Windows Server 2012/R2 Services, Exam 70-412* (Cengage Learning, 2015).

Classifying Files   To begin classifying files, you need to create classification properties that are applied by using classification rules. A classification property is a file attribute containing a value that's used to categorize the data in a file or an aspect of the file, such as its location or creation time. For example, you want to classify all files containing Social Security numbers so that they can be flagged for special handling. You start by creating a classification property in the FSRM console by expanding the Classification Management node, clicking Classification Properties, and clicking Create Local Property in the Actions pane to open the Create Local Classification Property dialog box (see Figure 3-27). In this dialog box, you give the property a name and description and then select a property type from the eight available types. If you want to flag a file based only on whether it contains certain information, for instance, you use the Yes/No property type.

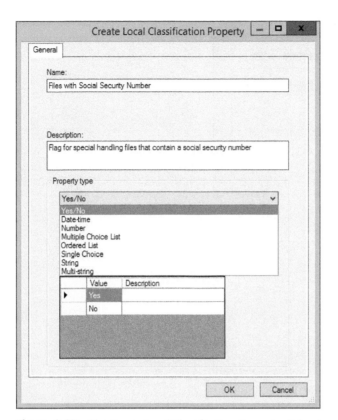

Figure 3-27 The Create Local Classification Property dialog box

The description of all the property types is beyond the scope of this book, but you can find more information by visiting *http://technet.microsoft.com/en-us/library/dd759215.aspx* or by clicking each property in the dialog box.

Next, you create a classification rule to set the property in files containing a Social Security number. Users can access the property in the Classification tab of a file's Properties dialog box and set the property manually. For example, a user who creates a spreadsheet containing Social Security numbers can right-click the spreadsheet file in File Explorer and click Properties, and then click the Classification tab (see Figure 3-28).

You can also create classification rules that set classification properties automatically. To do so, expand the Classification Management node in the FSRM console, click Classification Rules, and click Create Classification Rule in the Actions pane to open the Create Classification Rule dialog box. In this dialog box, you enter the rule name and an optional description. Next, click the Scope tab and specify the folders the rule should apply to and, if necessary, the types of files. The interesting part comes when you click the Classification tab and specify the classification parameters to configure how FSRM should recognize the type of data you're looking for. In this example, you're looking for SSNs, which have the pattern DDD-DD-DDDD (with D representing a digit). In the Classification tab, click Configure to open the Classification Parameters dialog box (see Figure 3-29) where you can set strings or regular expressions used to search for data in files. In this example, the regular expression $\hat{}\backslash d\{3\}-\backslash d\{2\}-\backslash d\{4\}\$$ is used; the $\backslash d$ indicates a digit, the number in braces indicates how many digits, and the $\hat{}$ and $ symbols indicate the beginning and ending of the expression. This regular expression matches an SSN. If you create multiple expressions for the same rule, all expressions must match for the rule to assign the property to the file.

Figure 3-28   The Classification tab

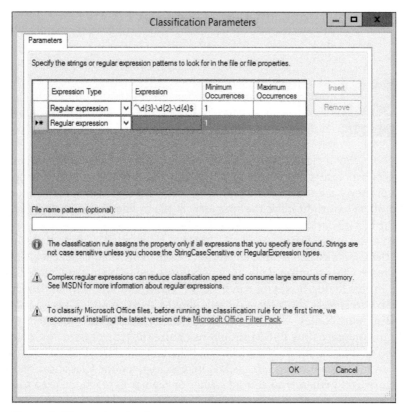

Figure 3-29   Setting classification parameters

After creating the classification rule, you can run it manually or schedule it to run periodically. If you run it manually, a report is created showing how many property matches were found and how many files were affected. Figure 3-30 shows the file used to test this example and the results after running the rule. From this simple example, you can get an idea of how powerful classification management can be.

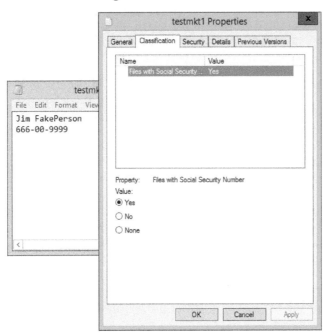

Figure 3-30   Viewing file contents in the Classification tab

Creating File Management Tasks

In any network, you can find files that are no longer being used or work files for a specific short-term process that didn't get removed. Over time, these files can consume a lot of space and add unnecessary overhead to the file system in the form of indexing, file classification, and general file system maintenance tasks. In addition, you might have files containing sensitive information that need special handling. FSRM includes the File Management Tasks feature to help automate processes for identifying these files and performing some needed action on them. Five properties are used to define files to be processed by a file management task: creation time, modification time, last accessed time, filename pattern, and classification property. Three types of actions can be performed on files matching the selected properties:

- *File expiration*—A file expiration task moves matching files to a folder you specify. You can base the expiration on any of the five properties mentioned in the preceding paragraph, but the last accessed time is usually selected if this task is actually being used for file expiration. Alternatively, you can use this action to move files that meet the criteria to an encrypted or a compressed folder, among other possibilities.

- *RMS encryption*—The Rights Management Services (RMS) server role is required for this option. RMS and RMS encryption are beyond the scope of this book, but if you're using RMS in your network, you can encrypt files meeting the specified criteria automatically.

- *Custom*—You create a custom task that runs a program or script when a file matches the criteria. For example, the file expiration action might not suit your needs for all types of files. You might want to delete matching files, for instance, instead of moving them to a folder.

File management tasks can be run manually in the FSRM console, and they can be scheduled to run at a particular time on a daily, weekly, or monthly basis. You can also set a task to run continuously on new files created in target folders so that if they meet classification criteria, they're processed right away.

Like other functions in FSRM, when a file management task runs, you have the option of creating a notification. Notifications can generate an e-mail message or a log event or cause a command or script to run. For example, for a file expiration task, you can send an e-mail to owners of affected files to let them know that their files will expire in a certain number of days. Notifications can also be generated before running the file management task so that users can take care of any files they want to keep. In addition, reports can be generated when a task runs, and events can be logged in the Application log based on a task starting and any errors that occurred. Reports are stored in the C:\StorageReports\Scheduled folder.

Configuring File and Disk Encryption

Part of any file management strategy includes securing the data contents to make sure unauthorized users can't access it. File and folder permissions are used to secure files from unauthorized users in a network, but they're mostly intended to prevent accidental deletion of files or to keep curious users from attempting to access files they aren't authorized to see. File and folder permissions aren't intended to prevent a determined hacker from accessing files containing sensitive data.

The old adage in computer and network security is "If there's physical access to a system, there's no security." This adage is particularly true when you're trying to protect files only with permissions. Almost every system has a method for bypassing file and folder permissions after physical access has been gained. For example, in a Windows system, all that's needed is booting the computer to a different OS from a DVD, flash drive, or other removable media. After another OS is running, permissions on the internal hard disk are rendered ineffective. In addition, there are ways to change the local Administrator password after you have physical access to a Windows system.

So how do you protect files from prying eyes if permissions can be bypassed? Use file and disk encryption. Encryption prevents unauthorized users from interpreting the data in files. In this context, "unauthorized" means someone without a decryption key. Even if a user is able to open an encrypted file or use brute-force methods of reading data on a disk sector by sector, the data is still unintelligible if the user doesn't have the decryption key. Windows has two built-in methods for encrypting data on a disk: Encrypting File System (EFS) and BitLocker Drive Encryption. However, before getting into these encryption solutions, review the following section to familiarize yourself with some methods and terms used in the world of cryptography.

Cryptography Terminology

The following terms used in cryptography are useful for understanding file and disk encryption:

- *Cryptography*—**Cryptography** is the practice and study of methods used to protect information by encoding or encrypting it to an unreadable format, which can be decoded later to its original format.

- *Encryption*—**Encryption** is the process of encoding data to a format unusable to anyone who doesn't have the decryption key. Encrypted text data is called "ciphertext."

- *Decryption*—**Decryption** is the process of decoding data, usually by using a decryption key. For text data, decryption converts ciphertext to plaintext.

- *Plaintext*—**Plaintext** is data that has been unaltered; as used in cryptography, this term defines the state of information before it's encrypted or after it has been decrypted.

- *Ciphertext*—**Ciphertext** is data that has been encrypted; it's the result you get when plaintext is transformed by an encryption algorithm.

- *Cryptographic algorithm*—A **cryptographic algorithm** is a mathematical computation used to encrypt and decrypt data.

- *Encryption key*—An **encryption key** (or simply "key") is a numeric value that a cryptographic algorithm uses to change plaintext to ciphertext (encrypt) and ciphertext back to plaintext (decrypt).

- *Hash*—A **hash** is a fixed-size value produced by running a string of data through a mathematical function called a hash algorithm. A hash is a type of one-way encryption because it can't be used to produce the original data.

- *Digital certificate*—A **digital certificate** is a digital document containing identifying information about a person or system. Information in the certificate typically includes a person's or organization's name or a system's URL and IP address as well as a key and a digital signature.

- *Digital signature*—A **digital signature** is a numeric string created by a hash algorithm that's used to validate a message or document's authenticity.

- *Secret key*—A **secret key** is used to both encrypt and decrypt data in a secure transaction. It must be known by both parties because it's used in both ends of the cryptography process. The terms "symmetric key" and "shared secret key" are also used. Secret keys are used in symmetric encryption (defined later in this list) and provide a lower-overhead secure transaction than using a public/private key pair.

- *Private key*—A **private key** is held by a person or system and is unknown to anyone else. It's part of a key pair used in asymmetric encryption (defined later in this list) and is most often used by the owner to decrypt data that has been encrypted with the corresponding public key. Private keys are also used to create digital signatures.

- *Public key*—A **public key** is owned by a person or system and is available as part of a user's or system's digital certificate. The public key, part of the key pair used in asymmetric encryption, is used to encrypt data, which can then be decrypted only by using the owner's private key. A public key is also used to verify a digital signature.

- *Symmetric encryption*—**Symmetric encryption** is an encryption/decryption process that uses a single key to encrypt and decrypt data (also called "private key cryptography" or "secret key cryptography").

- *Asymmetric encryption*—**Asymmetric encryption** is an encryption/decryption process that uses both a public key and a private key. It's more complex and requires more computing resources than symmetric encryption, but it's also more secure. Because of its higher resource requirements, asymmetric encryption is often used along with symmetric encryption. It's often used to encrypt keys, which are then used symmetrically for the bulk of data encryption and decryption.

This list is just a sampling of terms used in cryptography; you encounter several more as you learn methods for protecting data stored on a Windows system.

Encrypting File System

File encryption on NTFS volumes is made possible by Encrypting File System (EFS). Files encrypted with EFS can be opened only by the holder of an encryption key, which is stored in a digital certificate. You can encrypt files or entire folders by simply setting or clearing the encryption attribute in the file or folder's properties. To do so, use this procedure:

1. Right-click the file or folder and click Properties.

2. In the General tab of the Properties dialog box, click the Advanced button.

3. In the Advanced Attributes dialog box, click the "Encrypt contents to secure data" check box.

4. Click OK twice. If you're encrypting a single file, you have the option to encrypt only the file or encrypt the file and parent folder. If you're encrypting a folder, you have the option to encrypt its contents.

5. To decrypt a file or folder, clear the "Encrypt contents to secure data" check box.

Another method of encrypting and decrypting files and folders is the `cipher.exe` command. To encrypt a file or folder, enter `cipher /e` *filename* at a command prompt. To decrypt a file or folder, enter `cipher /d` *filename*.

After a file is encrypted, a user can open it by using the normal means for the file type, such as double-clicking the file in File Explorer to open it in the associated application. The data in the file is decrypted automatically before it's loaded in the application, but the data remains encrypted on the disk.

You can set the encryption attribute on a file or folder but not on a volume. If encryption is set on a folder, you're prompted with the option to set the attribute on the folder only or on the folder, subfolders, and files. After the encryption attribute is set on a folder, all files created in or moved to the folder are encrypted. By default, encrypted folders and files can be identified by their filenames displayed in green.

EFS Process   When a user encrypts a file by setting its encryption attribute or by creating a file in or moving a file to an encrypted folder, the following takes place:

1. The file is encrypted by using a symmetric key called a file encryption key (FEK).

2. The public key in the user's digital certificate is used to encrypt the FEK. If the user doesn't have a digital certificate, one is created automatically and stored on the system.

3. The encrypted FEK is stored with the encrypted file.

   When a user attempts to open the encrypted file, the following takes place:

1. The encrypted FEK stored with the file is decrypted by using the user's private key, which is associated with the user's logon account. (The FEK was encrypted by using the user's public key.)

2. The file is decrypted by using the decrypted FEK.

Encrypted files can usually be opened only by the user account that encrypted the file because the user's private key is used in the process. However, the user can designate other accounts that are allowed to access the file. In addition, in a domain environment, the domain administrator account is designated as a recovery agent, which can open all encrypted files. Recovery agents are used, for example, if the user account that encrypted the file can no longer access it. This can happen if an administrator resets a user's password, the user account is deleted, or the user leaves the company.

A user must have a valid EFS certificate to be added to an encrypted file's access list. EFS is set up to issue an EFS certificate automatically to any user who encrypts a file. Users can also be issued a certificate from a certificate server.

When working with EFS, keep the following points in mind:

- EFS is supported only on NTFS volumes.

- Encrypted files that are copied or moved always stay encrypted, regardless of the destination folder's encryption attribute. The exception is if the file is copied or moved to a FAT or ReFS volume, in which case the file is decrypted because neither FAT nor ReFS support encryption.

- Unencrypted files that are moved or copied to a folder with the encryption attribute set are always encrypted.

- Encrypted files are unencrypted when they're transferred across a network and remain unencrypted on the destination server unless they're saved to an encrypted folder.

- If a user's private key is corrupted or damaged, the user can't decrypt files. For this reason, the user's EFS certificate and private key should be archived so that they can be imported later to recover files.

- EFS keys are associated with a user's logon account. Anyone with access to a user's logon ID and password can decrypt files this user has encrypted.

- Instead of encrypting files, it's better to set the encryption attribute on folders and place files that should be encrypted in these folders.

Activity 3-8: Encrypting Files with EFS

Time Required: 10 minutes
Objective: Encrypt files with EFS.

Required Tools and Equipment: 411Server1
Description: In this activity, you create a folder, create a file in the new folder, and set the encryption attribute on the file. Then you encrypt the folder and create a file to see that it's encrypted automatically.

1. Log on to 411Server1 as **Administrator**, if necessary, and open File Explorer.

2. Create a folder on the **C** volume named **Secret**.

3. Create a text file in the Secret folder named **File1**. Right-click **File1** and click **Properties**. Click the **Advanced** button, click the **Encrypt contents to secure data** check box, and then click **OK**. Click **OK** again. In the Encryption Warning message box, click **Encrypt the file only**, and then click **OK**.

4. In File Explorer, the filename of **File1** is green, indicating that the file is encrypted. Double-click **File1** to open it in Notepad. Type your name in the file, save the file, and exit Notepad.

5. Double-click **File1**. Notice that the file opens, and you can read your name because data decryption occurs automatically. Exit Notepad.

6. In File Explorer, right-click the **Secret** folder, and click **Properties**. Click **Advanced**, click the **Encrypt contents to secure data** check box, and click **OK**. Click **OK** again, and in the Confirm Attribute Changes dialog box, click **OK**.

7. Create a user in Active Directory in the Users folder with the logon name **EFStest1** and the password **Password01**, and set the password to never expire. You can use Active Directory Users and Computers, PowerShell, or Active Directory Administrative Center.

8. You need to set a group policy to allow EFStest1 to log on to the server. In Server Manager, click **Tools, Group Policy Management** from the menu. Right-click **Default Domain Controllers Policy** and click **Edit**.

9. In the Group Policy Management Editor, navigate to **Computer Configuration, Policies, Windows Settings, Security Settings, Local Policies,** and **User Rights Assignment**. In the right-pane, double-click **Allow log on locally**, if necessary. Click **Define these policy settings**, if necessary, and click **Add User or Group**.

10. In the Add User or Group dialog box, type **Domain Users** and click **OK**. Click **OK** again. Open a command prompt window, type **gpupdate**, and press **Enter**.

11. Log off 411Server1 and log back on as **EFStest1**. In File Explorer, navigate to the **Secret** folder you created and try to open **File1**. Notepad opens, but you see an "Access is denied" message. Click **OK**. In Notepad, type anything you like, and then save the file in the Secret folder as **File2**. Close Notepad. In File Explorer, notice that the filename for **File2** is green because it inherited the encryption attribute from the Secret folder.

12. Open a command prompt window. Type **cipher /?** at the command prompt and press **Enter**. Review the options for the **cipher** command. Type **cipher /d c:\secret\file2.txt** and press **Enter**. You see a message stating that the file was decrypted. Type **cipher /e c:\secret\file2.txt** and press **Enter** to encrypt the file again. A message informs you that sections of the plaintext file might still be on the volume because when a file is encrypted, the original plaintext file is deleted and a new ciphertext file is created. The data from the deleted file, however, is not erased from the disk. The command **cipher /w:*directory*** erases data from the deleted file.

13. Log off 411Server1.

Allowing Other Users Access to an Encrypted File   As discussed, you can allow other users to access files you encrypt, as long as they have EFS certificates. To add a user to the list of those who can access a file you encrypted, you must import the user's EFS certificate, or the user must have a certificate stored on the system. Activity 3-9 shows how to give other users access to your encrypted files.

Activity 3-9: Sharing an Encrypted File with Another User

Time Required: 5 minutes
Objective: Share an encrypted file with another user.

Required Tools and Equipment: 411Server1
Description: In this activity, you share `File1.txt`, which is encrypted, with the EFStest1 user account.

1. Log on to 411Server1 as **Administrator,** and open File Explorer.
2. Open the **Secret** folder, and then right-click **File1** and click **Properties.** Click the **Advanced** button. Click the **Details** button to open the User Access to File1 dialog box (see Figure 3-31).

Figure 3-31   The User Access dialog box for an encrypted file

3. The top pane of the User Access dialog box shows who has access to the file. The bottom pane shows the recovery agents, if any. Because this computer is in a domain, the domain administrator is the recovery agent by default. Click **Add.**
4. In the Encrypting File System dialog box, you see accounts that have EFS certificates on the system. Because EFStest1 has encrypted a file on the server, the account's certificate is listed. If necessary, click **EFStest1** and click **OK.** EFStest1 is added to the list of users who can access the file. Click **OK** three times.
5. Log off, log back on as **EFStest1,** and try to open **File1.** You should be successful.
6. Log off 411Server1.

EFS Recovery Agent   A recovery agent is a user account with a recovery agent certificate. Recovery agents can open all encrypted files for which they're the designated recovery agent. In a domain, the Administrator account is the default recovery agent and can open and decrypt all encrypted files created by domain users. Additional recovery agents can be added by using

Group Policy. On a workgroup computer, there's no default recovery agent, but you can create one with the Local Security Policy console. Recovery agents on a workgroup computer can open and decrypt files only on that computer.

To be added as a recovery agent, the user account must have a recovery agent certificate issued by a certification authority. Configuring a certification authority is beyond the scope of this chapter, but assuming there are one or more user accounts that have a recovery agent certificate, follow these steps to add an account as a recovery agent for the domain:

1. Open the Default Domain Policy in the Group Policy Management Editor.

2. Navigate to Computer Configuration, Policies, Windows Settings, Security Settings, and Public Key Policies.

3. Right-click Encrypting File System and click Add Data Recovery Agent (see Figure 3-32). Follow the instructions in the Add Recovery Agent Wizard. Any recovery agent certificates that were published in Active Directory are listed in the Select Recovery Agents window. Otherwise, you can browse to a folder where the certificate is stored.

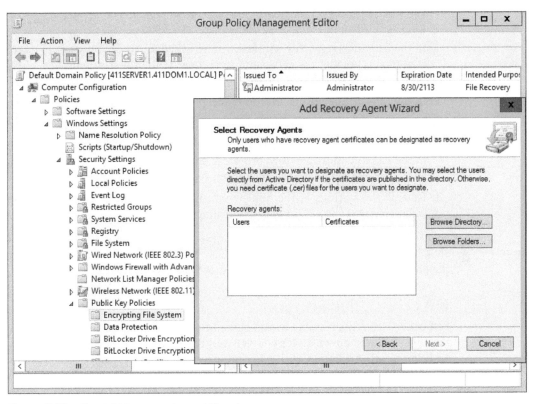

Figure 3-32   The Add Recovery Agent Wizard

EFS Certificates   If you have encrypted files, you should back up your EFS certificate and private key in case they're damaged or lost. The EFS certificate can be lost if a user account is deleted or if a user's profile on the computer is deleted or corrupted. Ideally, the certificate should be backed up on removable storage, such as a flash drive. Certificates for recovery agents should also be backed up. To back up an EFS certificate, export it by using this procedure:

1. Open the Certificates snap-in by adding it to an MMC or by entering `certmgr.msc` at a command prompt or in the Run dialog box.

2. In the left pane, click to expand Personal, and then click Certificates (see Figure 3-33). The Administrator account shown in Figure 3-33 has both an EFS certificate and a File Recovery certificate.

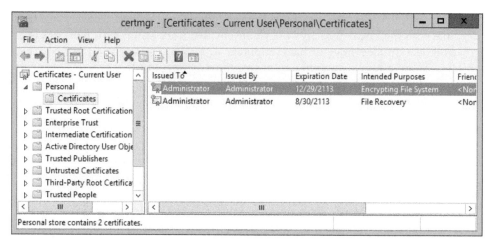

Figure 3-33   Managing certificates

3. Right-click the certificate and click All Tasks, and then click Export to start the Certificate Export Wizard. In the welcome window, click Next.

4. In the Export Private Key window, you're asked whether you want to export the private key. If you're exporting the certificate to recover from a lost private key, click "Yes, export the private key," and then click Next.

5. In the Export File Format window, accept the default options, and then click Next.

6. In the Security window, click Password, and then type a password and confirm it. The password is needed if you want to import the certificate with the private key later. Click Next.

7. In the File to Export window, browse to the location where you want to export the certificate, and enter a filename for the certificate, such as EFScert. Click Save, and then click Next.

8. Review the settings in the final window, and then click Finish. Click OK in the message indicating that the export was successful.

To restore a certificate and private key, use a similar procedure, but right-click Certificates, click Import, click All Tasks, and then follow the Certificate Import Wizard. You're prompted for the password you entered when you exported the certificate.

BitLocker Drive Encryption

BitLocker Drive Encryption, as the name implies, encrypts entire drives or volumes. It encrypts the entire volume on which it's enabled and can be used to encrypt the Windows boot volume in addition to other volumes. BitLocker mitigates the risk of a lost or stolen computer and is useful when decommissioning computers because data on the disk remains encrypted even if the disk is removed and placed in another system.

To secure the Windows boot volume (the volume where the \Windows folder is installed) with BitLocker, you must make sure your system meets these requirements:

- The Windows boot volume and the Windows system volume (the active partition containing the files needed for the computer's BIOS to start Windows) must be on separate partitions. The system volume must remain unencrypted so that the BIOS can read it.

- The computer must have a Trusted Platform Module (TPM), or a USB flash drive must be accessible during system boot. The TPM module or USB flash drive stores the encryption key.

To secure a drive that doesn't hold the Windows OS, there are no special requirements. After the drive is encrypted with BitLocker, you have the option to unlock it with a password or smart card or unlock it automatically when you log on to the system. You select the method when you first encrypt the drive.

Trusted Platform Module   A Trusted Platform Module (TPM) is a microchip built into some computer motherboards that's used to create and store cryptographic information for the purposes of securing a computer against unauthorized use. Used with BitLocker on a Windows system, it can prevent the system from booting without authentication. Even if the Windows boot volume is removed from the computer, it can't be used on another computer because the TPM holds the encryption keys needed to decrypt the volume.

Installing and Configuring BitLocker Drive Encryption   In Windows Server 2012/R2, BitLocker Drive Encryption is a feature installed with the Add Roles and Features Wizard in Server Manager or with PowerShell. After the BitLocker Drive Encryption feature is installed, you must restart the server, and then you configure BitLocker on the volumes you want to protect.

In some editions of Windows 7 and later, BitLocker is installed by default but must be enabled for each volume you want to protect.

The options vary depending on whether you're configuring BitLocker for a volume containing the Windows OS or a data volume and whether your computer has a TPM. To find out whether you have a TPM, go to the BitLocker control panel and click TPM Administration, or load the TPM Management snap-in in an MMC console. If you attempt to enable BitLocker on the Windows boot volume without a TPM, you see the error message shown in Figure 3-34.

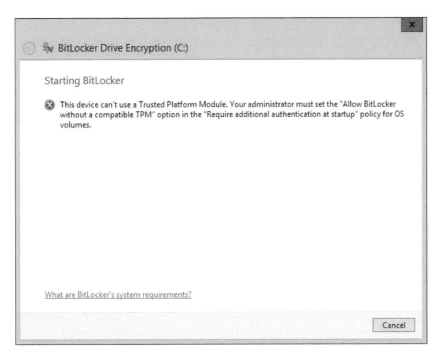

Figure 3-34   Error message when no TPM is available

If your system doesn't have a TPM, you need to take another step before you can configure BitLocker on the volume containing Windows: configuring the "Require additional authentication at startup" policy. You can set this policy in a GPO linked to an OU containing the relevant computer accounts. The policy is at Computer Configuration, Policies, Administrative Templates, Windows Components, BitLocker Drive Encryption, Operating System Drives.

During BitLocker configuration on a volume with the Windows OS, you have the following options for unlocking the drive to allow the system to boot:

- *TPM-only*—In this mode, the system boots normally, with no special user interaction. If the drive is removed from the system or the TPM detects changes to OS files, the system enters recovery mode, which requires a recovery password.

- *TPM with PIN*—The user must enter a personal identification number (PIN) to boot the system.

- *TPM with startup key*—A startup key stored on a USB drive must be available for the system to boot.

- *TPM with startup key and PIN*—This option uses multifactor authentication, meaning two authentication methods are required: a USB drive with startup key and a PIN.

- *Startup key only*—If the system doesn't have a TPM, this option can be used if the right policy is configured.

Installing and Configuring BitLocker with PowerShell   The following PowerShell cmdlets are available for installing and configuring BitLocker:

- `Install-WindowsFeature BitLocker -IncludeManagementTools`—Installs the BitLocker Drive Encryption feature.

- `Enable-BitLocker -MountPoint` *DriveLetter*—Enables BitLocker on a volume.

- `Disable-BitLocker -MountPoint` *DriveLetter*—Disables BitLocker on a volume.

- `Enable-BitLockerAutoUnlock -MountPoint` *DriveLetter*—Enables the automatic unlocking feature on a non-Windows volume.

Activity 3-10: Installing BitLocker Drive Encryption

Time Required: 10 minutes
Objective: Install the BitLocker Drive Encryption feature.

Required Tools and Equipment: 411Server1
Description: You want to experiment with BitLocker Drive Encryption, so you install this feature and then access the BitLocker control panel.

1. Log on to 411Server1 as **Administrator,** if necessary.

2. Open Server Manager, and start the Add Roles and Features Wizard. In the Features window, click to select **BitLocker Drive Encryption.** Accept the defaults for the remainder of the wizard.

3. After BitLocker Drive Encryption is installed, shut down 411Server1. (Don't just restart it because a complete shutdown is often necessary to enable BitLocker.) Start 411Server1.

4. Log on to 411Sever1 as **Administrator.** Open Control Panel, click **System and Security,** and click **BitLocker Drive Encryption** (see Figure 3-35).

5. Click **TPM Administration** to open the TPM Management console. In the middle pane, you see a message indicating whether the system has a TPM. Close the TPM Management console. Perform this next step only if there was no TPM found on your system! In the Operating system drive list box, click **Turn on BitLocker,** and then click **Yes.** You see the error message shown earlier in Figure 3-34 stating that you must configure a policy to use BitLocker on OS volumes on systems without a TPM. Click **Cancel.**

6. Notice in Figure 3-35 that you can enable BitLocker on removable drives, a feature called BitLocker To Go. If you insert a USB drive, you can enable BitLocker on it by using this feature. Close the BitLocker Drive Encryption control panel.

7. Log off or shut down 411Server1.

Figure 3-35   The BitLocker Drive Encryption control panel

Configuring Bitlocker with Group Policies   You might want to use BitLocker Drive Encryption throughout your organization or for only selected parts of it. There are dozens of BitLocker-related policies you can configure in Group Policy (by navigating to Computer Configuration, Policies, Administrative Templates, Windows Components, BitLocker Drive Encryption). After you configure the policies you need, you can link the GPO to the domain to configure all computers or to selected OUs to configure certain computers in the domain. Browse through the policies with the Group Policy Management Editor and read the descriptions to see the available settings.

Using Network Unlock   Network Unlock is a new feature in Windows Server 2012/R2 that makes it easier to manage BitLocker on OS volumes in a domain environment. With the Network Unlock feature enabled, OS volumes are unlocked automatically when they're connected to the network, so users don't need to supply a PIN or startup key each time their system boots. If their system becomes disconnected from the network, they need to supply the PIN or startup key. To use Network Unlock, first install the BitLocker Network Unlock feature by using the Add Roles and Features Wizard or PowerShell. Additional requirements include the following:

- A Windows 8/8.1 or Windows Server 2012/R2 computer with a NIC that has a Universal Extensible Firmware Interface (UEFI)–compatible DHCP driver
- A Windows Server 2012/R2 computer running WDS
- A DHCP server on a separate server from the one running WDS
- A Network Unlock certificate for the WDS server and each client computer
- Network Unlock settings configured in Group Policy

The Network Unlock feature requires clients to be connected via a wired network interface; wireless networks aren't supported.

Assuming the client computers meet the requirements, follow these steps to configure Network Unlock:

1. Install the Windows Deployment Services role.

2. Install the BitLocker Network Unlock feature.

3. Create a Network Unlock certificate on the WDS server from an existing certification authority or use a self-signed certificate.

4. Deploy the certificate and private key to the WDS server.

5. Configure Network Unlock settings in Group Policy by going to this node: Computer Configuration, Policies, Administrative Templates, Windows Components, BitLocker Drive Encryption, Operating System Drives.

You can find more details on configuring Network Unlock at *http://technet.microsoft.com/en-us/library/jj574173.aspx.*

Chapter Summary

- Distributed File System is a role service under the File and Storage Services role that enables you to group shares from different servers into a single logical share called a namespace. Users see each namespace as a share with subfolders, giving them access to files that are actually stored on different servers.

- DFS uses two technologies: DFS namespaces and DFS replication. They can be used together to provide fault tolerance and load balancing for files

- DFS namespaces create a hierarchy of shared folders to provide access to shared files from a single logical reference point across an organization.

- There are two types of DFS namespaces: domain-based and stand-alone. Domain-based information is stored in the Active Directory and namespaces are available even if server names change. Stand-alone information is stored on the server where it was created.

- If Active Directory is at a Windows Server 2008 functional level, you can choose from Windows Server 2008 mode or Windows Server 2000 mode. Windows Server 2008 mode supports up to 50,000 folders and access-based enumeration. Windows 2000 Server mode supports 5000 folders.

- Referrals are prioritized lists of folder targets. They can be configured by using lowest cost, random order, and excluding targets outside the client's site.

- File security is managed with share permissions and NTFS permissions. Access-based enumeration allows users to see only files and folders they have permissions to.

- DFS replication provides fault tolerance by replicating folders to multiple servers. It requires a minimum of two targets. DFS replication can be scheduled to optimize bandwidth use.

- Space must be planned to accommodate the Staging and Conflict and Deleted folders when configuring DFS replication groups.

- File Server Resource Manager helps manage file servers through the use of quotas (to limit how much data can be stored) and file screens (to specify what types of data can be stored).

- Quotas can be set manually, or a template can be defined and applied. Hard and soft quotas can be defined to restrict creating files beyond the quota and to send a notification.

- File screens can be set manually, or a template can be defined and applied. Active and passive screens can be defined to restrict creating certain types of files or to just send a notification.

■ Storage reports offer insight into how storage is being used, where you might need to set or change quotas or file screens, and which files are being used the most and the least. There are 10 different criteria for creating these reports.

■ Files and folders can be classified and file management tasks can be created to perform actions on groups of files of specified classifications or attributes.

■ File and disk encryption add a layer of security to protect sensitive information. Windows includes Encrypting File System for file-level encryption and BitLocker for disk-level encryption.

3

Key Terms

active screening   A file-screening method that prevents users from saving unauthorized files on the server. *See also* file screen.

asymmetric encryption   An encryption/decryption process that uses both a public key and a private key.

ciphertext   Data that has been encrypted; it's the result you get when plaintext is transformed by an encryption algorithm. *See also* cryptography.

cryptographic algorithm   A mathematical computation used to encrypt and decrypt data. *See also* cryptography.

cryptography   The practice and study of methods used to protect information by encoding or encrypting it to an unreadable format, which can be decoded later to its original format.

decryption   The process of decoding data, usually with a decryption key.

digital certificate   A digital document containing identifying information about a person or system.

digital signature   A numeric string created by a hash algorithm that's used to validate a message or document's authenticity. *See also* hash.

Distributed File System (DFS)   A role service under the File and Storage Services role that enables you to group shares from different servers into a single logical share called a namespace.

encryption   The process of encoding data to a format unusable to anyone who doesn't have the decryption key.

encryption key   A numeric value that a cryptographic algorithm uses to change plaintext to ciphertext (encrypt) and ciphertext back to plaintext (decrypt). *See also* ciphertext *and* plaintext.

file group   A list of the types of files that define a file screen. *See also* file screen.

file screen   A method of limiting the types of files a user can store on a server.

File Server Resource Manager (FSRM)   A role service with services and management tools for monitoring storage space, managing quotas, controlling the types of files users can store on a server, creating storage reports, and classifying and managing files.

folder target   A UNC path configured on a DFS namespace folder that points to a shared folder hosted on a server.

hard quota   A type of quota that prevents users from saving files if their files in the target folder already meet or exceed the quota limit.

hash   A fixed-size value produced by running a string of data through a mathematical function called a hash algorithm.

namespace   A name given to a grouping of folders maintained on a DFS server that facilitate access to shares on multiple servers, using a single UNC path.

namespace root   A folder that's the logical starting point for a namespace. *See also* namespace.

namespace server   A server with the DFS Namespaces role service installed. *See also* namespace.

passive screening   A file-screening method that monitors and notifies when unauthorized files are saved but doesn't prevent users from saving unauthorized files on the server. *See also* file screen.

plaintext   Data that has been unaltered; as used in cryptography, it's the state of information before it's encrypted or after it has been decrypted. *See also* cryptography.

private key   A key that's held by a person or system and is unknown to anyone else.

public key   A key owned by a person or system that's available as part of a user's or system's digital certificate.

quota   A limit placed on the amount of storage on a server volume or share available to a user.

referral   A prioritized list of servers used to access files in a namespace. *See also* namespace.

remote differential compression (RDC)   An algorithm used to determine changes that have been made to a file and replicate only those changes.

replication   The process of creating redundant copies of files on multiple servers.

replication group   Two or more servers, known as members, that synchronize data in folders so that when a change occurs, all replication group members are updated at once. *See also* replication.

replication topology   A DFS replication setting that describes the connections used to replicate files between servers. *See also* replication.

secret key   A key used to both encrypt and decrypt data in a secure transaction.

soft quota   A type of quota that alerts users when they have exceeded the quota but doesn't prevent them from saving files.

symmetric encryption   An encryption/decryption process that uses a single key to encrypt and decrypt data (also called "private key cryptography" or "secret key cryptography"). *See also* cryptography, private key, *and* secret key.

Review Questions

1. The Distributed File System role service provides which of the following? (Choose all that apply.)

   a. Access to files across the network

   b. Replacement for regular backups

   c. Copies of files created automatically for redundancy

   d. Fault-tolerant access to files

2. Which of the following is true about the two types of namespaces?

   a. Stand-alone namespaces always use more bandwidth.

   b. Domain-based namespaces remain regardless of the server status where the share resides.

   c. Domain-based namespace includes the current server name for faster name resolution.

   d. Stand-alone namespace can't be replicated.

3. Folders added to a namespace can be described as which of the following?

   a. Copies of existing folders

   b. Copies of existing folders that are initially empty

   c. Pointers to existing shared folders

   d. Copied to a staging area automatically

4. In DFS, what are the differences between Windows Server 2008 mode and Windows Server 2000 mode?

   a. Server 2008 mode supports 15,000 folders and access-based enumeration, and Server 2000 mode supports 5000 folders.

   b. Server 2008 mode supports 75,000 folders, and Server 2000 mode supports 10,000 folders.

   c. Nothing a user can see.

   d. Server 2008 mode supports 50,000 folders and access-based enumeration, and Server 2000 mode supports 5000 folders.

5. Where does a referral originate when a client accesses a DFS namespace?

    a. From the namespace server

    b. From the domain controller

    c. From the namespace server for a stand-alone type and from the domain controller for a domain-based type

    d. From a cached copy of referrals on the server where the share is located

6. What's the default ordering method for referrals?

    a. No default; you must choose an ordering method during initial configuration.

    b. Random order to ensure load balancing.

    c. Lowest cost, selecting the closest server first.

    d. The order in which the target servers were defined.

7. If a client is on the same site as a particular target, what will it do?

    a. Follow the referral ordering method.

    b. Always go to that target.

    c. Ignore the targets on the same site.

    d. Go to a target randomly.

8. How can referral order be customized?

    a. There's no way to customize the referral order.

    b. Exclude targets in the client's site.

    c. Use the Override Referral Ordering option.

    d. Put in nonexistent targets, forcing the system to follow your custom order.

9. When should share permissions be set?

    a. Before DFS configuration.

    b. During DFS configuration.

    c. After DFS configuration is finished.

    d. Never; DFS handles all permissions.

10. DFS replication configuration requires a minimum of how many targets?

    a. 1

    b. 2

    c. 3

    d. 4

11. Which is the best method of synchronization to reduce bandwidth with a DFS replication group made up of a main office and eight branch offices?

    a. Full mesh topology

    b. Hub and spoke topology

    c. Round robin topology

    d. Random synchronization

12. What's the algorithm used to replicate only changes made in files?

    a. Remote replication connection

    b. Remote change comparison

    c. Remote differential compression

    d. Remote change compression

13. Where are changed files cached until replication is finished?

    a. Caching folders in the C:\DFScache folder on the namespace server.

    b. The Staging folder on the target server.

    c. No caching is done.

    d. The Staging folder for the folder being replicated.

14. What's the model used when there's an update conflict?

    a. Last writer wins; losing file is cached.

    b. First writer wins; losing file is cached.

    c. First writer wins; losing file is deleted.

    d. Last writer wins; losing file is deleted.

15. What are the two types of quotas you can create with File Server Resource Manager?

    a. Hard and soft

    b. Hard and notify

    c. Limit and notify

    d. Final and minimum

16. Which of the following is an advantage of using quota templates? (Choose all that apply.)

    a. They can't be applied to new volumes that come online later.

    b. Quotas can be changed in the template and applied to all volumes using that quota previously.

    c. The template can be named and have a description included for future reference.

    d. Properties can be copied from an existing template.

17. What are the two types of file screens you can create with File Server Resource Manager?

    a. Hard and soft

    b. Active and passive

    c. Active and notify

    d. Restrict and notify

18. A file screen is used to do which of the following? (Choose all that apply.)

    a. Limit access to certain types of files.

    b. Screen files for malware and viruses.

    c. Analyze file use and restrict use to maximize network bandwidth.

    d. Send a notification about access to certain types of files.

19. Which of the following is a method for defining elements in a file group? (Choose all that apply.)

    a. Filenames

    b. Namespaces

    c. Folder names

    d. Filename patterns

20. Storage reports can show which of the following? (Choose all that apply.)

    a. File-screening violations

    b. Files by owner

    c. Files by permissions

    d. Quota use

21. Which FSRM feature should you use if you want to set certain attributes of a file automatically based on its content?

    a. File Screening Management

    b. Quota Management

    c. Classification Management

    d. Storage Reports Management

22. Which of the following should you create if you want all files that haven't been accessed in more than six months moved to a special folder?

    a. File-screening action

    b. File expiration task

    c. File storage job

    d. Quota report

23. Which of the following is true about EFS?

    a. An EFS certificate is created automatically, if necessary.

    b. It's supported only on NTFS and ReFS volumes.

    c. Encrypted files that are moved to another folder must be encrypted again.

    d. EFS can be configured only on files.

24. Which of the following is true about BitLocker Drive Encryption?

    a. It can't be used to encrypt the Windows boot volume.

    b. Only computers with a TPM can use it.

    c. Network Unlock allows a system to boot without a PIN.

    d. A startup key is stored in the \Windows folder.

Case Projects

CASE PROJECTS

Case Project 3-1: Managing Referrals

Your organization has expanded dramatically, and suddenly there's heavy file server use. All the file servers are fairly close to clients, and you're adding several more, creating a large group. The number of name servers has also expanded. Your initial configuration used default settings for the referral ordering method and polling. What changes should you consider?

Case Project 3-2: Optimizing Replication

The Marketing Department for CSM Tech Publishing is busy producing videos and print materials (stored in PDF format) for distribution and use by the Sales Department. With new products being introduced and a good bit of marketing testing, marketing materials change often, and there's often a substantial delay before the Sales Department gets access to these changes. The Sales Department is in another site and wants access to the marketing materials, but given the size of files and the number of updates, you're reluctant to give the Sales Department direct access to files across the WAN link. What DFS replication group configuration could you consider for replication and frequency of access?

Case Project 3-3: Using File Screens

You discover that employees are storing music, video, and games in their user folders, which raises copyright issues. You want to prevent these files from being stored on company computers. At the same time, Human Resources wants to have training materials available in video and audio formats. Using file screens, how can you meet both needs?

chapter 4

Server Monitoring and Auditing

After reading this chapter and completing the exercises, you will be able to:

- Monitor Windows Server events
- Configure and use tools to perform network monitoring
- Use auditing to improve network security

Although installing a server and never having to worry about performance would be great, that simply isn't realistic. Server use changes when users are added and applications are installed, and problems with hardware and application updates can cause unexpected events. For these reasons, Windows Server 2012/R2 includes tools, such as Task Manager, and Performance Monitor, to help you check and analyze server performance. In this chapter, you learn how to use these tools to troubleshoot problems and to evaluate performance to see whether and where changes to system configuration are needed.

Security also improves when server events are monitored. Auditing gives you information on violations of security policies and warnings of attempted unauthorized access. Windows Server 2012/R2 has the auditing features you need, such as logging access to restricted directories or files, to protect your network. You learn how to configure auditing and what actions to take based on audit events.

Monitoring a Windows Server

Table 4-1 summarizes what you need for the hands-on activities in this chapter.

Table 4-1   Activity requirements

Activity	Requirements	Notes
Activity 4-1: Creating a Custom View	411Server1	
Activity 4-2: Creating an Event Subscription	411Server1, 411Server2	
Activity 4-3: Exploring Task Manager	411Server1	
Activity 4-4: Using Performance Monitor	411Server1	
Activity 4-5: Creating a Performance Baseline Report with a Data Collector Set	411Server1	
Activity 4-6: Creating a Performance Alert	411Server1	
Activity 4-7: Creating a Capture with Microsoft Network Monitor	411Server1	Microsoft Network Monitor downloaded and installed
Activity 4-8: Auditing Folder Access	411Server1	

© 2015 Cengage Learning®

In networks, any number of things can go wrong or affect the performance and availability of servers and their resources, so network administrators should monitor which users are logged on, what they're doing, and what resources they're using. Some problems reveal themselves over time, so reviewing past data to detect trends is the best type of analysis to perform. If you're troubleshooting an ongoing problem or responding to a complaint about current performance, however, most likely you want to see what's happening on the system in real time, instead of reviewing old log data. Luckily, you can find many types and sources of information on the health of a server and the network. The categories of information you can monitor includes events occurring on the system, tasks running on the system, resources being used, and network traffic. The following sections explore the available information and the tools you can use to collect and analyze this information.

Monitoring Events

As events occur on a Windows server, they're recorded in one of several event logs. Windows Server 2012/R2 includes Event Viewer, an MMC snap-in, to review the events recorded in logs on your local computer as well as other computers on the network. You can also use Event Viewer to get more detailed information on a specific event. This tool is useful for tracking down system or application problems and investigating security violations. It can also react to events, so you can create a task that runs a program or script when a specific type of event occurs.

Viewing Events   After events have been logged, Event Viewer reads a log and formats the information in a form that's easy to read and interpret. You can start Event Viewer with the

Computer Management console, the Tools menu in Server Manager, or the `eventvwr.msc` command. At startup, Event Viewer looks like Figure 4-1.

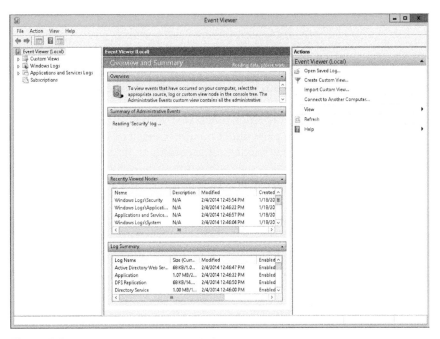

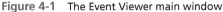

Figure 4-1   The Event Viewer main window

A busy system might log hundreds or even thousands of events, and if you're trying to isolate a particular problem, going through every item in an event log can be daunting. For this reason, Event Viewer offers many ways to search, filter, and sort event logs.

To search an event log, expand the log group the event log belongs to (for example, Windows Logs), click the event log (such as Application) you want to find an event in, and then click Find in the Actions pane. Basic search features are limited to text occurrences—using keywords such as "error" or phrases such as "did not start." For an event to be included in the search results, an exact text match is required. For example, "did start" doesn't match "did not start," and vice versa.

To create a filter, select a log in the left pane, and then click Filter Current Log in the Actions pane. Filters give you more flexibility in specifying criteria than the basic Find function does; however, they're limited to a single event log. Here are the criteria for filtering:

- *Logged*—The time and date range an event occurred in. You can select from a list of periods or specify a custom range.

- *Event level*—Select from these levels of event severity: Critical, Error, Warning, Information, and Verbose.

- *Event sources*—Select one or multiple sources of events (for example, the Task Scheduler service).

- *Event IDs*—You can enter a single ID or multiple IDs separated by commas. Placing a minus sign in front of an ID excludes it from the filter results.

- *Task category*—A list of categories becomes available only if you select an event source with corresponding tasks.

- *Keywords*—Select from a list of predefined keywords, such as Audit Failure or Audit Success.

- *User*—Use specific user accounts as filters. You can enter a single user or a list of users separated by commas.

- *Computer*—Use a specific computer or groups of computers as filters. For multiple computers, separate the list items with commas.

To remove a filter, click Action, Clear Filter from the menu.

Clicking a column header sorts an event log based on the column's contents. For example, clicking the Date and Time column header sorts the display from the earliest event to the latest. Click again to display the most recent event at the top. Sorting might take a while if the log is large. To return a list of events to its default order, right-click the column header and click Remove Sorting.

Each event has detailed information associated with it. When you click an event in the center pane, details are displayed in a pane under the list of events. For example, a user disconnecting a Remote Desktop session without logging off generates an information event with a specific code. Double-clicking the event opens a separate window showing details (see Figure 4-2), which is useful when you want to compare details of multiple events at once.

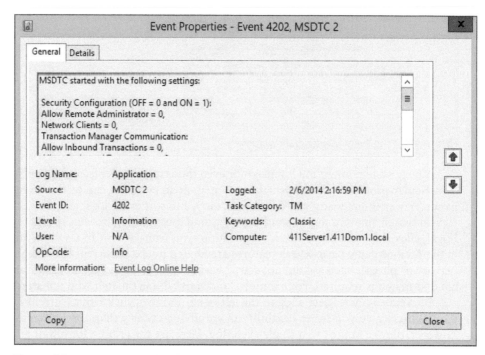

Figure 4-2   Viewing event details

Notice the two tabs in this window: General and Details. The General tab formats information about the event in an easy-to-read table format. The Details tab formats information in XML view or "friendly view," with the data in a tree structure and the event name bolded. You can save event log information in these formats: an event file that can be opened and displayed in Event Viewer; an XML file, similar to the XML view in the Details tab; and a tab-delimited or comma-delimited file.

Creating Tasks from Events   Responding to events manually can be time consuming and inefficient because an administrator would have to review the logs constantly. However, you can create a task in Event Viewer that runs whenever a particular event is logged. Follow these steps:

1. Right-click an event in a log and click Attach Task To This Event to start the Create Basic Task Wizard.

2. You can enter a name for the task (see Figure 4-3) or use the name that's assigned automatically. The assigned name begins with the log name followed by the source and event ID.

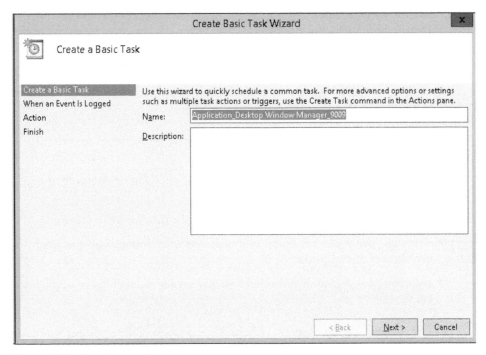

Figure 4-3   Entering a task name

3. The next window shows details about the type of event that triggers the task: log name, source, and event ID. This information can't be changed.

4. In the Action window, you select from these options: Start a program, Send an e-mail (deprecated), or Display a message (deprecated). To run a program or script, click the Start a program option button, if necessary, and then click Next.

Sending an e-mail and displaying a message are deprecated options. They're still available, but they might be removed in later versions, so using them isn't recommended.

5. In the Start a Program window, type the program or script name you want to run (or browse to and select the name) when the event is generated. You can also enter command-line arguments and a working directory.

6. In the Finish window, you can review the details.

Using Log Categories   Events are logged in two main categories: Windows logs, containing events that apply system wide and events from applications, and Applications and Services logs, containing events from specific applications or system services. Windows logs contain these five log files:

- *System*—This log stores events generated by Windows system components, such as a device driver that fails to load. Windows determines the events and the information on each event a particular component logs.

- *Application*—This log stores events generated by applications. For example, a database-driven accounting system might generate an Application log entry when a write operation to the database fails. Application developers determine what events and information an application logs.

- *Security*—This log stores events related to security policies, such as logon attempts, file accesses, and file creation or deletion. Administrators can determine and set the security policies that create log entries.

- *Setup*—This log stores events occurring during Windows setup.

- *Forwarded Events*—This log stores events collected from other systems. An event subscription (discussed later in "Event Subscriptions") must be created to collect events from other systems.

Each event is assigned a level that classifies it in terms of severity. In the Windows logs (except for the Security log) and the Applications and Services logs, there are four levels:

- *Error*—A problem that can affect how the application or component logging the event functions

- *Critical*—An unrecoverable failure in an application or a component

- *Warning*—An issue that doesn't immediately affect operations but might cause future problems if not addressed

- *Information*—A change not related to any problems, such as an application finishing successfully

The Security log has these two levels: Audit Success (a file or object was accessed successfully) and Audit Failure (a file or object was accessed unsuccessfully).

Although the basic information in Windows logs can be helpful in troubleshooting Windows system and application problems, the information in Applications and Services logs is usually more useful in troubleshooting. There are four subtypes of these logs: Admin, Operational, Analytic, and Debug.

The Admin subtype shows a problem and a solution with instructions on how to fix the problem. The detail and guidance it supplies make it a good source of troubleshooting information for users, administrators, and support staff. Operational logs aren't as straightforward, and determining solutions might require more analysis; typically, users don't have the knowledge or expertise to use an Operational log. Analytic logs record a series of events related to a problem. Because the volume of events logged can be quite high, sifting through information in Analytic logs requires more effort than with Admin or Operational logs. Debug logs contain events software developers can evaluate to troubleshoot programs. By default, the Analytic and Debug logs are hidden and disabled. To make them visible, click View, Show Analytic and Debug Logs from the menu. To enable them after they have been made visible, right-click the one you want to enable and click Enable Log.

Creating Custom Views Now that you know where different types of events are stored, you might be thinking of situations in which grouping different types of events makes it easier to see relationships or simply have an overall view. The problem is that Event Viewer typically shows information from only one log at a time. So how can you mix a variety of data from different logs? You can create custom views to pull data from multiple logs based on the criteria listed previously in "Viewing Events." Event logs are XML based, which enables you to construct XML queries, but the selections in the Filter tab allow you to create views that should answer most needs without requiring XML coding knowledge. You create a custom view in Activity 4-1.

Activity 4-1: Creating a Custom View

Time Required: 10 minutes

Objective: Create a custom view to see data from multiple logs.

Required Tools and Equipment: 411Server1

Description: Create a custom view by using available filtering options.

1. Start 411Server1, and log on as **Administrator,** if necessary. Open Server Manager, and click **Tools, Event Viewer** from the menu.

2. Click **Create Custom View** in the Actions pane to open the Create Custom View dialog box. Click the **Filter** tab, if necessary.

3. Leave the default **Any time** option in the Logged list box. Leave the Event level check boxes (Critical, Warning, Error, Information, and Verbose) unselected so that all event levels are recorded. (If you select a level here, only events meeting this level are recorded.)

4. If necessary, click the **By log** option button, click the **Event logs** list arrow, and click to expand **Applications and Services Logs.** Click the **DFS Replication** and **DNS Server** check boxes (see Figure 4-4), click the list arrow to close the list box, and then click **OK.**

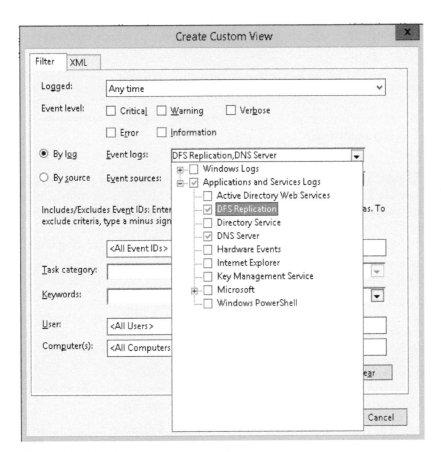

Figure 4-4   Selecting logs for a custom view

5. In the Save Filter to Custom View dialog box, type **Test View** in the Name text box.

6. In the "Select where to save the Custom view" section, click **Custom Views,** and then click **OK.**

7. To view the results, click to expand **Custom Views**, if necessary, in the left pane of Event Viewer, and click **Test View**. Events related to DFS replication and DNS should be displayed in the center pane (see Figure 4-5).

8. Close Event Viewer, and stay logged on for the next activity.

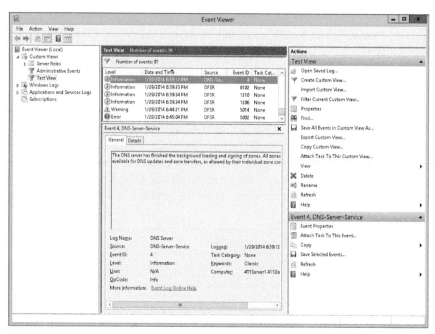

Figure 4-5   Using a custom view

Using Event Subscriptions   Instead of going from system to system to check event logs, you can use the Forwarded Events log to view event information from remote computers in a single log, which can save a lot of time. To create this log, you need an event subscription. An **event subscription** specifies what server to collect events from, what events to collect, and the local event log to write them to. Activity 4-2 guides you through creating one.

Activity 4-2: Creating an Event Subscription

Time Required: 15 minutes
Objective: Create an event subscription.

Required Tools and Equipment: 411Server1 and 411Server2
Description: You have been asked to collect event data from two different systems in the Forwarded Events log so that they can be viewed in Event Viewer.

1. Log on to 411Server1 as **Administrator**, and start 411Server2, if necessary.

2. On 411Server1, open Event Viewer. In the left pane, right-click **Subscriptions** and click **Create Subscription**. In the message about starting the Windows Event Collector Service, click **Yes**.

3. In the Subscription Properties dialog box, type **411Server2 errors and warnings** in the Subscription name text box. The Destination log drop-down list is set to Forwarded Events by default (see Figure 4-6); leave this default setting.

4. Verify that the **Collector initiated** option button is selected, and click the **Select Computers** button.

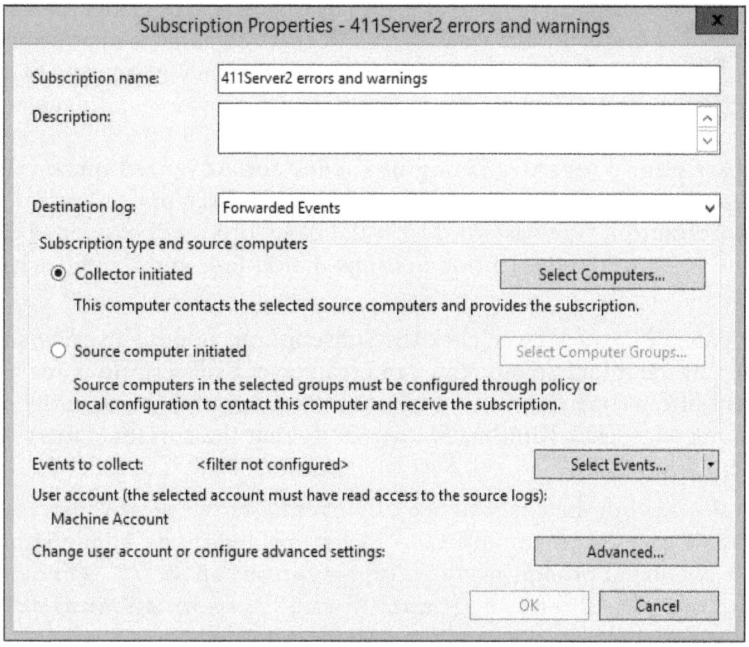

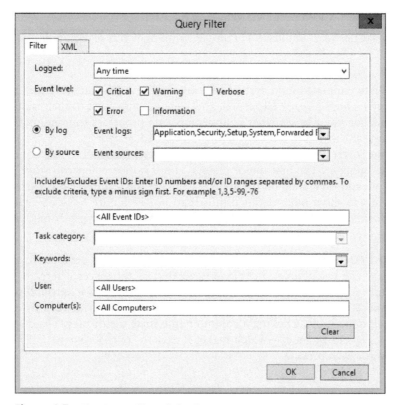

Figure 4-6   The Subscription Properties dialog box

5. Click **Add Domain Computers**. In the Select Computer dialog box, type **411Server2**, click **Check Names,** and then click **OK**. Click **Test** to verify connectivity with 411Server2. Click **OK** in the "Connectivity test succeeded" message box, and then click **OK** again.

6. In the Subscription Properties dialog box, click the **Select Events** button. In the Query Filter dialog box, click to select the **Critical, Error,** and **Warning** check boxes. Click the **By log** option button, if necessary. Click the **Event logs** list arrow, and click **Windows Logs** to collect events from the main log files. Notice that you can filter the subscription even more by event ID, keywords, user, and computer (see Figure 4-7). Click the list arrow again to close the list box, and then click **OK**.

Figure 4-7   The Query Filter dialog box

 You might notice that the Query Filter dialog box looks the same as the Create Custom View dialog box. That's because the same parameters for determining what data is shown in a custom view are used to determine what data is included in a query filter.

7. In the Subscription Properties dialog box, click the **Advanced** button. In the Advanced Subscription Settings dialog box, click the **Specific User** option button. Click the **User and Password** button, type **Password01** in the Password text box, and click **OK**. Click **OK** to close the Advanced Subscription Settings dialog box and the Subscription Properties dialog box.

8. In the left pane of Event Viewer, click the **Subscriptions** node. The event subscription name is displayed in the middle pane. You can create event subscriptions for other servers and use different filter properties. Click to select the subscription name in the middle pane, and in the Actions pane, click **Runtime Status**. Verify that the current status is Active, and then click **Close**.

9. It might take a while before you see any events. However, to test your subscription, you can create an event manually. On 411Server2, log on as **Administrator**, if necessary, and open a command prompt window. Type **eventcreate /T Error /ID 1000 /L Application /D "Event to test Event Viewer subscriptions"** and press Enter to create an Error-level event in the Applications log.

10. Sending the event to the Forwarded Events log on 411Server1 might take a few minutes. In Event Viewer on 411Server1, expand **Windows Logs** and click **Forwarded Events**. If the event isn't listed, wait a few minutes, and then right-click **Forwarded Events** and click **Refresh**. Eventually, the event should be listed.

11. You can also have an alert sent when a subscribed event arrives. In Event Viewer, right-click the **Forwarded Events** log and click **Attach a Task To this Log**.

12. The Create Basic Task Wizard starts. Accept the default task name, and then click **Next**. Click **Next** again. In the Action window, the Start a program option is the only one available; the other two have been deprecated. You could run a simple PowerShell or Visual Basic script that shows a message if you just want to be informed that a new event has arrived. For now, click **Cancel**. Close Event Viewer.

13. Shut down 411Server2, but leave 411Server1 running if you're continuing to the next activity.

Using Task Manager

Viewing what has happened on a system by looking at events that were generated is valuable but reactive; events have already happened, and you can only react to the results of these events. With Task Manager, you can see what's happening with processes running on the system in real time, so you can take action in a timely manner, if needed.

In Windows Server 2012/R2, Task Manager has been enhanced to make it even more useful for system management. The first major change you'll notice when you start Task Manager is the view of applications running on the system. Clicking the "More details" arrow at the bottom expands the view to show more detailed information (see Figure 4-8). This view has five tabs: Processes, Performance, Users, Details, and Services. In the following sections, you look at different tasks to see how you might use the data in these tabs.

Monitoring Processes   The Processes tab is an easy-to-read perspective of what processes are consuming which resources and the load generated on the server. There are three sections of the Processes tab: Apps, which are applications such as Notepad; Background processes, such as DNS Server; and Windows processes, such as Desktop Window Manager. By default, each section is sorted alphabetically. Clicking a column name sorts the display. The display is limited to two metrics—CPU and Memory—which makes it easy to see the system's CPU and memory use as a whole and for each process.

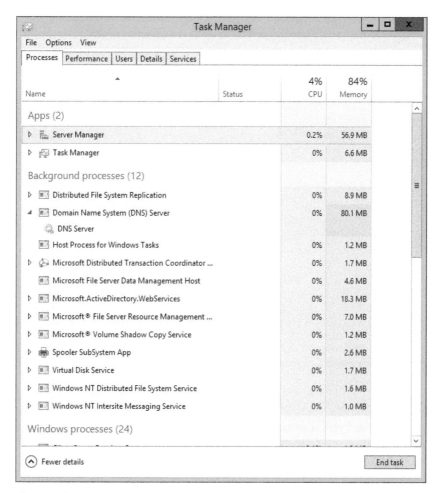

Figure 4-8   The Processes tab

If more information for a process is available (indicated by the arrow next to the process name), you can expand the process to view the additional information, as shown previously for Domain Name System (DNS) Server in Figure 4-8. You can also expand background processes to see what services are running, which can be useful in troubleshooting. In previous versions of Task Manager, processes and services were shown separately, so seeing a relationship between them was more difficult. Right-clicking a service gives you the option to stop the service or open the service's control panel. Right-clicking a process gives you the option to end the task, go to that process in the Details tab, or go to the program file's location. The Details tab has more information on each process, including the process ID (PID), the status of the process, what username it's running under, CPU and memory use for the process, and a brief description of the process.

Basic Performance Monitoring   Although there are many specialized tools you can use for performance monitoring, you can do basic monitoring in the Performance tab of Task Manager (see Figure 4-9) on three important performance components: CPU, memory, and network adapters (Ethernet in the figure). These components are listed on the left with basic current information.

A server usually handles a lot of network traffic. When the network adapter component is selected on the left, a graph on the right shows the network throughput over a 60-second period. Above the graph, you see the type of NIC. This graph makes it easy to see problems such as excessive network use. The information under the graph shows the network adapter name, connection type, and the IPv4 and IPv6 addresses. Right-clicking this graph gives you the option

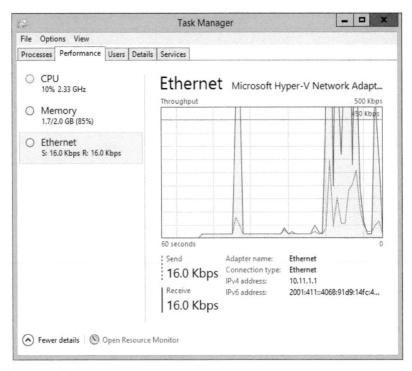

Figure 4-9 The Performance tab

"View network details," which displays real-time details about the network traffic, including percent utilization, bytes sent and received, and throughput. Depending on the number of tasks a server is called on to perform, memory use can be a critical resource to monitor. Clicking Memory displays the view shown in Figure 4-10.

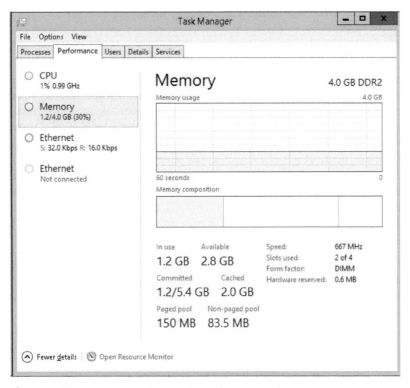

Figure 4-10 The Memory view of the Performance tab

In this view, you see statistics on how much memory is being used, how much is available, and what percentage of the total it represents. On the right are two graphs: Memory usage, which shows the memory use over a 60-second period, and Memory composition, which divides how the memory is being used into four categories:

- *In use*—Memory used by the OS, applications, and other processes
- *Modified*—Memory containing content that must be written to disk before being released for other purposes
- *Standby*—Memory containing cached information
- *Free*—Memory available for use

You have to hover your mouse over parts of the Memory composition graph to see the In use, Modified, Standby, and Free labels.

Below the graphs on the right is hardware information, including the memory's speed, how many memory slots are being used, the form factor (indicating the type of memory), and how much memory is reserved for use by hardware. More data is available under the graphs, including the following:

- *In use*—Total amount of memory currently allocated by the OS and running processes.
- *Available*—The amount of physical memory that can be used by the system and running processes.
- *Committed*—Measures the demand for virtual memory. As the amount of committed memory exceeds available physical memory, paging increases, and if it becomes excessive, it can have a serious effect on performance.
- *Cached*—The sum of modified and standby memory, described in the preceding list.
- *Paged pool*—The amount of memory currently required by the OS kernel and drivers that can be written to virtual memory.
- *Non-paged pool*—The amount of memory currently required by the OS kernel and drivers that must remain in physical memory.

The third metric you can monitor in the Performance tab is CPU use, as shown in Figure 4-11.

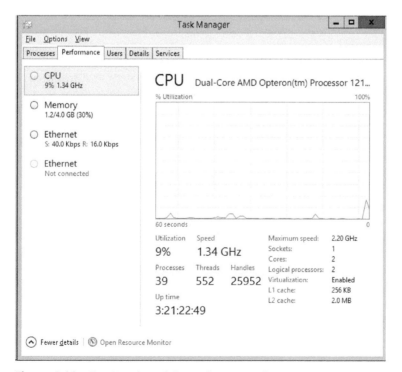

Figure 4-11   The CPU view of the Performance tab

Under the CPU component on the left is the percentage currently being used and the processor speed. The graph on the right shows the percentage of the CPU used in the most recent 60-second period. Above the graph is the processor make, model, and speed. Under the graph on the right are the CPU's physical details, including maximum speed (in GHz), number of sockets, number of cores, number of logical processors, whether virtualization is enabled, and the size of the L1 and L2 caches.

 Some systems include an L3 cache in addition to the L1 and L2 caches.

The details on the left under the graph are more operational and include the current percentage utilization of the CPU, the current processor speed, how many processes are running, how many threads are in use, how many handles are in use, and the system's current uptime. A **thread** is the smallest piece of program code that Windows can schedule for execution. For example, Microsoft Word is an application and is listed in Task Manager in the Processes tab, but several threads can be scheduled to run within this larger process, such as the spell checking and autocorrect features. A **handle** is a reference to a resource on the computer. Handles are often associated with open files but can also be associated with a block of memory or other data structures an application is using. Handles help processes and the OS keep track of open and used resources.

Monitoring Logged-on Users   Besides the system processes and background tasks running on a server, users logged on to a server consume resources, too. The Users tab in Task Manager shows the CPU and memory use for each logged-on user as well any processes he or she might be running on the server. If you click to expand the user, you see a list of processes the account is running. Right-clicking a user gives you the options of disconnecting the user and managing the user in the User Accounts control panel.

Monitoring Services   The Services tab of Task Manager lists services, much like what you see in the Services MMC opened via Server Manager. However, there are limits to what you can manage here. Services can be started, stopped, or restarted. You can also open the Services MMC, search online, or jump back to the Details tab.

Using Resource Monitor

Another tool for real-time monitoring is Resource Monitor, which shows CPU, memory, disk, and network use information for separate processes or the system as a whole in real time. You can go beyond the simple system resource monitoring Task Manager offers. With Resource Monitor, you can review processes that have stopped responding and close them if needed, check current file use by applications, and start, restart, pause, and end services. You start Resource Monitor from the Tools menu in Server Manager or by typing resmon.exe at a command prompt. The first time you start Resource Monitor, it opens to the Overview tab shown in Figure 4-12. This tab and others in Resource Monitor are formatted similarly, with data in tables on the left and graphs on the right.

The left side of the Overview tab is divided into four sections—CPU, Disk, Network, and Memory—that show current utilization and activity. Right-clicking a process in the CPU section gives you options to end, suspend, or resume it. If an application has stopped responding, for example, you can analyze the wait chain to see whether the application might be waiting on another process to release needed resources. If an application is consuming a lot of CPU or disk I/O resources, you could pause or end it to give other applications a chance to run. On the right are real-time graphs of CPU and memory use and disk and network activity. You can resize the graphs as small, medium, or large.

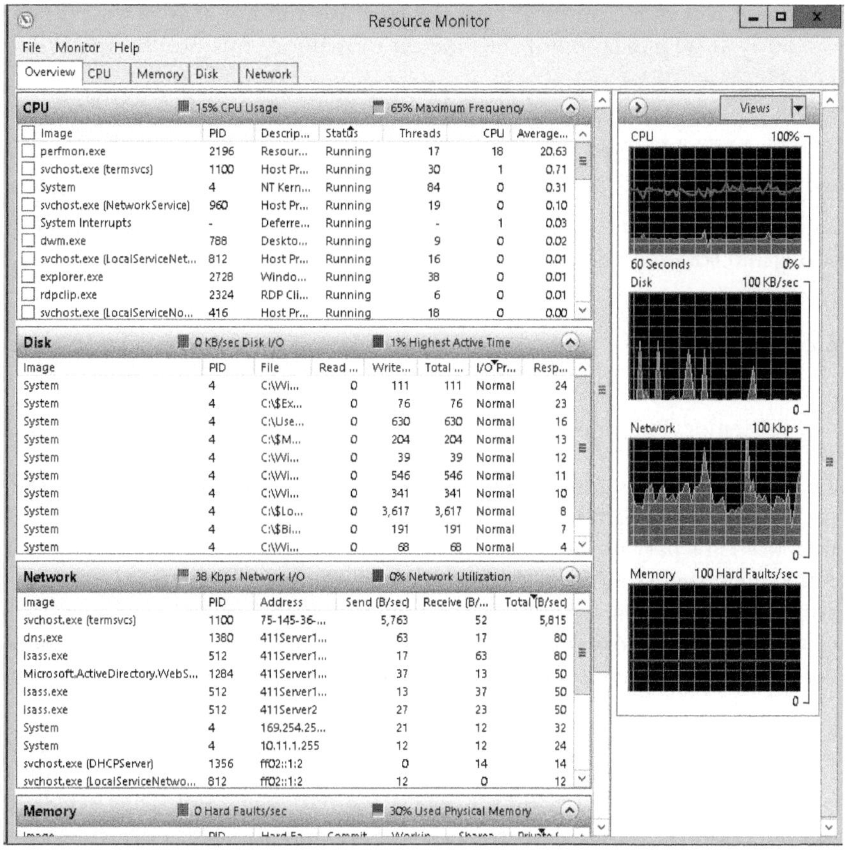

Figure 4-12 The Overview tab of Resource Monitor

The CPU tab is divided into four sections: Processes, Services, Associated Handles, and Associated Modules. The Processes section displays the name of the program executable file, the process ID (PID), a short description of the process, its status, the number of threads in use, the percentage of the CPU it's currently using, and an average of CPU use for the past 60 seconds. The Services section displays a service's name, PID, description, and status as well as the service group it belongs to, the current percentage of CPU being used, and the average CPU use. Right-click a service to start, stop, or restart it. The Associated Handles section shows the file handles in use by selected processes, and the Associated Modules section shows files, such as dynamic link libraries (DLLs), used by selected processes as part of their operation. When you click a check box next to a process name in the Processes section, the results in the lower sections are filtered. Only the services, file handles, and module names associated with this process are shown.

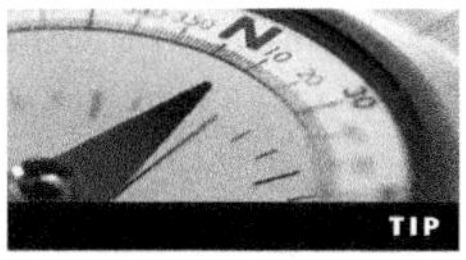

The PID is useful in linking the information in each section to a particular process or image.

In the Memory tab, the graphs on the right show overall memory use. The left side is divided into Processes and Physical Memory sections. In the Processes section, each process's memory use is divided into these categories:

- *Commit*—How much physical memory plus pages from the paging file the OS reserves for the process
- *Working Set*—How much physical memory is currently in use
- *Shareable*—How much physical memory is in use and shared with other processes

- *Private*—How much physical memory is in use and not shared with other processes, which is a fairly close indication of the amount of memory this process requires to run

- *Hard Faults/sec*—The number of times the process must read memory written to the paging file

The Physical Memory section has a color-coded bar graph of overall memory allocation divided into these sections:

- *Hardware Reserved*—Memory reserved by hardware components, such as buses, video cards, and sound cards, used to communicate with the OS

- *In Use*—Memory used by OS processes, drivers, and other processes

- *Modified*—Pages of modified memory that haven't been accessed for some time

- *Standby*—Memory still linked to a process but available for reuse

- *Free*—Memory not in use by any processes or released when a process ended

The totals under the graph in this section show available, cached, total, and installed memory. The total memory is the amount installed minus the amount of hardware reserved memory (because this memory isn't part of the available pool.) If you're troubleshooting performance problems, especially when there's a heavy load on a server, the graphs and displays in the Memory tab can be particularly useful. Watch for frequent periods of high levels of hard faults, which can indicate a problem with how memory is being used. (Keep in mind, however, that some hard faults are normal and don't reflect a problem.) If a lot of memory is consistently in use (shown by the size of the green bar), you might want to consider adding memory. Remember to examine the actual values as well the percentages; if a lot of physical memory was available, there might still be enough memory for the system to perform adequately, even at high percentages of use. In the Disk tab, graphs on the right show overall disk activity and the queue length for each disk. The left side is divided into three sections: Processes with Disk Activity, Disk Activity, and Storage. For each process, the Disk Activity section shows the files in use (one per line), read activity, write activity, total activity (read + write), priority, and response time. To filter the display, you click the check box next to a process. The Storage section shows logical disks with their physical drive numbers. Metrics in both sections can help you troubleshoot performance problems. For example, in the Storage section, a consistently high value in the Active Time column (showing the percentage of time a disk is actually servicing requests) can indicate a bottleneck, and adding disk storage and distributing the load could alleviate this problem. In the Disk Activity section, response times consistently higher than 20 milliseconds (ms) warrant attention, and consistent response times higher than 50 ms indicate a serious problem.

In the Network tab, graphs on the right show overall network bandwidth use over the past 60 seconds, the number of TCP connections, and the current utilization of Ethernet connections (determined by the number of NICs). The left side is divided into these sections: Processes with Network Activity, which shows the processes currently accessing the network and how much data is being sent and received; Network Activity, which lists the amount of data processes are sending and receiving as well as their network addresses; TCP Connections, which lists local and remote addresses and ports associated with programs (executable images) accessing the network; and Listening Ports, which lists all ports currently listening. To filter the display, you can click the check box next to a process. Metrics in this tab that are especially useful for troubleshooting include Ethernet connection use graphs. Watch for consistent utilization higher than 40%, which can indicate a network bottleneck that might be improved with some changes to the network layout (such as adding subnets). Consistent utilization in the 60% to 70% range is a good indicator that you should reexamine the network layout. If you're seeing utilization consistently higher than 90%, there's definitely a problem that should be solved as soon as possible.

Using Performance Monitor

Although general data can point you in the right direction, more detailed metrics are helpful in identifying a specific problem. Performance Monitor can collect and combine data from three sources:

- *Performance counters*—Performance metrics from OS components and applications. Depending on what's being reported, they can be counts (such as physical disk reads per second) or percentages (for example, CPU utilization).

- *Configuration information*—Changes to values of Windows Registry keys. A data collector set (covered later in this section) is used to determine which keys are monitored.
- *Event trace data*—Log files created by applications and device drivers that incorporate Event Tracing for Windows (ETW). This data is different from events shown in Event Viewer and is usually used only by software developers.

Performance Monitor can monitor real-time activity and review logs for historical information, and you can customize the data that's collected in logs. You can also trigger alerts and tasks based on user-defined thresholds and generate a variety of reports. Access to this tool is determined by what groups a user belongs to. Administrators can access all features, and other groups have access but with certain limits:

- *Users*—This group can view log files and modify display properties but can't access real-time data and can't create or modify data collector sets.
- *Performance Monitor Users*—This group can view log files and real-time data and modify display properties but can't create or modify data collector sets.
- *Performance Log Users*—This group can use all features available to the other two groups. If this group is given the "Log on as a batch user" right, members can create and modify data collector sets; however, data collector sets must run under their own credentials. This group can't use the Windows Kernel Trace provider in data collector sets.

The next two activities guide you through using Task Manager and Performance Monitor to monitor real-time activity.

Activity 4-3: Exploring Task Manager

Time Required: 10 minutes
Objective: Explore Task Manager's features.

Required Tools and Equipment: 411Server1
Description: You have recently hired a junior administrator who will be responsible for monitoring server performance. You ask him to watch as you review Task Manager features.

1. Log on to 411Server1 as **Administrator**, if necessary.

2. Right-click the taskbar and click **Task Manager**. Click the **Processes** tab, if necessary. Click the **CPU** column header to change the ordering of CPU utilization from lowest to highest.

3. Click the **Name** column to sort processes by name. Under Background processes, click to expand **Domain Name System (DNS) Server**, and you see the DNS Server service. Right-click **Domain Name System (DNS) Server** and click **Go to details**. The Details tab opens with dns.exe highlighted. Click the **CPU** column header again to change the ordering of processes. Scroll to the top of the list in the Details tab. You see System Idle Process, which wasn't listed in the Processes tab. This process runs when no other processes require CPU time, so it often shows CPU % utilization near 100%.

4. To add or remove columns from the Details tab, right-click any column header and click **Select columns**. Click the **Page faults** and **I/O writes** check boxes, and then click **OK** to add these columns to the display.

5. Start Notepad. In Task Manager, click the **Processes** tab. Right-click the **Notepad** task and click **Go to details**.

6. Right-click the **notepad** process and point to **Set priority**. You can use this method to increase or decrease a process's priority manually. For example, if you're running an application that tends to have high CPU use, but you don't want it to affect server performance adversely, you can set the application's priority to Below normal or Low. The application might respond more sluggishly, but server performance for other tasks is better.

Use the Set Priority feature with care. Setting a higher priority can sometimes have unexpected and undesirable results. In particular, never set priority to Realtime unless an application's instructions specify it.

7. Click **End task**. When prompted to confirm, click **End process**. Notepad is removed from the running process list. Ending a process is useful when a task is exhibiting problems and doesn't terminate on its own.

8. Click the **Performance** tab. Click **Open Resource Monitor** to see more detailed graphs of CPU, disk, network, and memory utilization. Explore each tab so that you're familiar with the information you can gather from this tool. Close Resource Monitor.

9. Click the **Users** tab, which lists users who are currently logged on interactively through a console connection, a remote desktop connection, or a Terminal Services connection. Click to expand **Administrator**. You see a list of processes started by the Administrator account. You can right-click any process to see the same menu available in the Processes tab.

10. Close Task Manager, and stay logged on for the next activity.

Activity 4-4: Using Performance Monitor

Time Required: 10 minutes
Objective: Use Performance Monitor to do a real-time check on CPU, memory, and disk use.

Required Tools and Equipment: 411Server1
Description: You use Performance Monitor to create reports (line graph, histogram, and text report) showing real-time system utilization.

1. Start 411Server1 and log on as **Administrator**, if necessary. Open Server Manager, and click **Tools, Performance Monitor** from the menu.

2. Click to expand **Monitoring Tools** in the left pane, if necessary, and click **Performance Monitor**. The view changes to a line graph of the % Processor Time counter showing the percentage of processor use (see Figure 4-13).

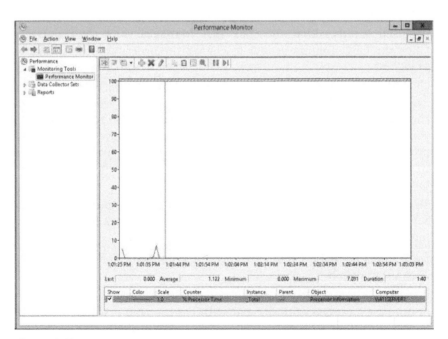

Figure 4-13 The % Processor Time graph in Performance Monitor

3. Right-click the graph and click **Add Counters**. In the Add Counters dialog box, shown in Figure 4-14, you can add counters from the local computer or remote computers; leave the default **<Local computer>**. Under this text box is a list of counters in alphabetic order. Click to expand **LogicalDisk**. Ctrl+click **% Disk Read Time** and **% Disk Write Time** to select both counters.

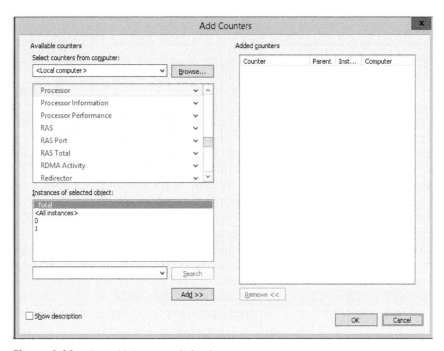

Figure 4-14   The Add Counters dialog box

4. Click **_Total** in the "Instances of selected object" list box, and then click the **Add** button. Scroll through the counter list again, and click to expand **Memory**. Click **% Committed Bytes In Use**, click the **Add** button, and then click **OK**.

5. Performance Monitor displays a line graph with different colors representing the different metrics. Click the **Change graph type** icon (to the left of the green plus sign above the graph) to toggle from Line Chart to Histogram to Report and finally back to Line Chart.

6. Under the graph, click to clear the **% Committed Bytes In Use** check box. Notice that the line representing this metric is no longer in the line graph. Click to select the **% Committed Bytes In Use** check box again.

7. Leave the graph open to review information in the following paragraphs and to begin the next activity.

To customize a view even more, you can open the Performance Monitor Properties dialog box by right-clicking the graph and clicking Properties. There are five tabs with options for customizing the display:

- *General*—Control display elements, such as the legend explaining graphs, the value bar (showing the last, average, minimum, and maximum values for a selected metric), and the length of time the graph covers. You can also decide whether to display the minimum, maximum, or average value for the graph's duration and specify how often samples of data are taken and how long to display data.

- *Source*—Specify whether to display current activity on the system, which is good for troubleshooting an immediate problem, or activity from log files or a database, which is a good option when you're looking for trends or a recurring problem. With log files and databases, you can also set a time range for viewing data.

- *Data*—Select which performance counters to display and configure line or bar color, scale, and style for each counter. With the scale setting, you can show both smaller and larger numbers on the same graph (for example, CPU and memory use).

- *Graph*—Select the type of view (Line Chart, Histogram, or Report) and do some customizing, if you like. For example, you can configure scrolling and wrapping for a line graph or add vertical and horizontal grids to a histogram.

- *Appearance*—Control colors for the graph background, control background (the area around the graph), text labels, and grid lines. You can also change the font for text labels and add a border.

Viewing performance data in real time is helpful if you want to see the impact certain actions have on selected counters. For example, you might want to see whether Active Directory replication results in unacceptably high CPU and network use. After adding the necessary counters, you can force replication to occur or make a change to Active Directory to trigger automatic replication and observe the changes in CPU and network use. Real-time monitoring of performance counters in Performance Monitor can also be useful for tracking the cause of a sluggish system. Unless you have a good idea what part of the system to examine, however, finding the cause could be a hit-and-miss proposition. You might have better results checking the graphs in Resource Monitor, which give you an overall view of the resources being used, instead of having to guess which ones to observe in Performance Monitor.

One reason tracking causes of poor performance with real-time monitoring is difficult is that you have no point of reference for comparing data. This point of reference, called a "performance baseline" or simply a "baseline," is a record of performance data gathered when a system is performing well under normal operating conditions. Generally, baseline data is collected shortly after a system is put into service and then again each time changes are made, such as installing or removing a server role or when many users are added. The baseline data collected during normal operation conditions can then be compared with data collected during peak resource demands to give you insight into your system's capabilities and limitations.

To create a baseline of performance data, you create a **data collector set** that specifies the performance counters you want to collect, how often to collect them, and how long to collect them. You can create multiple data collector sets that capture different aspects of system performance and measure performance during different periods. For example, if you know a database application is used heavily between 10:00 a.m. and 3:00 p.m., you can collect CPU, disk, memory, and network performance data during that period. If Active Directory is used heavily between 7:00 a.m. and 10:00 a.m. because users are starting work, logging on, and changing passwords during these hours, you can collect Active Directory–related data during these hours. You should also collect data for critical resources over an entire day so that you can spot usage trends.

A data collector set can contain a variety of types of information collected and displayed as a graph or report. Information types in a data collector set include the following:

- *Performance counters*—These system performance indicators used to view real-time data are also used in data collector sets.

- *Counter alerts*—Events generated when a counter falls below or exceeds a specified threshold. For example, you can create an alert to log an entry in the Application log if the % Processor Time counter exceeds 90%.

- *Event traces*—Logs information based on system or application events.

- *System configuration*—Monitors and records changes to Registry keys.

Predefined data collector sets can be run as they are or used as templates to create user-defined data collector sets. These data collector sets include Active Directory Diagnostics, LAN Diagnostics, System Diagnostics, and System Performance. Data collector sets can be scheduled to run at certain times and certain days for a specified period of time. To specify how long a data collector set runs, you set a stop condition, explained later in "Scheduling Data Collector Sets." For now, Activity 4-5 guides you through the process of creating a DCS.

Be aware that performance monitoring uses system resources. It takes memory to run Performance Monitor, CPU cycles to collect and display counter data, and disk resources to update log files. With Performance Monitor, however, you can select a remote computer as the target for monitoring. By monitoring remotely, you lessen the monitoring session's impact on the computer being monitored. You can also adjust the counter sampling interval to collect counter data less often than the default values. The more often counter data is collected, the greater the impact the monitoring session has on system resource use.

Activity 4-5: Creating a Performance Baseline Report with a Data Collector Set

Time Required: 10 minutes
Objective: Use data collector sets to create a performance baseline report.

Required Tools and Equipment: 411Server1
Description: In this activity, you create a data collector set containing some performance metrics, and then review the results as a report to see what utilization was like during the time data was collected.

1. Log on to 411Server1 as **Administrator,** and open Performance Monitor, if necessary.

2. Click to expand **Data Collector Sets** in the left pane.

3. Right-click the **User Defined** node, point to **New,** and click **Data Collector Set** to start the Create new Data Collector Set Wizard.

4. Type **Test Data Collector Set** in the Name text box. Accept the default setting **Create from a template (Recommended),** and then click **Next.**

5. Click **System Performance** in the Template Data Collector Set list box, and then click **Next.**

6. In the "Where would you like the data to be saved?" window, accept the default setting **%systemdrive%\PerfLogs\Admin\Test Data Collector Set,** and then click **Next.**

7. In the "Create the data collector set?" window, accept the default settings, and then click **Finish.**

8. In the left pane, click **User Defined,** if necessary. Right-click **Test Data Collector Set** and click **Start** to begin collecting data. The data collection should finish in about 60 seconds. In the middle pane, you see the status change to Running. When the data collection is finished, the status changes to Complete.

9. Click to expand **Reports, User Defined,** and **Test Data Collector Set.** Click the log file to see the report in the right pane.

10. Close Performance Monitor. Stay logged on for the next activity.

Scheduling Data Collector Sets   Running data collectors manually is fine when you're doing a quick real-time performance analysis, but to conduct longer-term studies, to measure performance during off hours, or to run them at times you're not available, you need to create a scheduled data collector set with these steps:

1. In the left pane of Performance Monitor, right-click the data collector set to schedule and click Properties. You can use a data collector set you created in the User Defined node or the predefined data collector set Server Manager Performance Monitor under the User Defined node. More predefined data collector sets are available under the System node.

2. Click the Schedule tab, and then click the Add button.

3. In the Folder Action dialog box, you can choose a beginning date, an expiration date, days of the week it should run, and the start time. A new report is created each time the data collector set runs, with the date and time appended to the report name.

4. If you want to run the data collector set for only a certain number of days, click the Expiration date check box, and enter the date the data collector set should stop running.

If a data collector set is still running when the expiration date is reached, it continues to run but doesn't start again.

5. Click OK, and then click the Stop Condition tab (see Figure 4-15). You can specify how long the data collector set should run each time it starts in units of seconds, minutes, hours, days, and weeks. The duration is set to 1 minute by default for the Test Data Collector Set. In the Limits section, you have the following options:

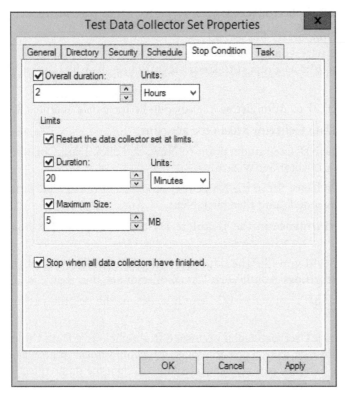

Figure 4-15 Setting a stop condition for a data collector set

- *Restart the data collector set at limits*—If this check box is selected, the data collector set saves a report when either limit has been reached and restarts to create a new report. This process continues until the overall duration is reached or the data collector set is manually stopped.
- *Duration*—If this check box is selected, the data collector set runs for the specified period within the overall duration. Enabling this limit makes sense only if you select the restart option.
- *Maximum Size*—If this check box is selected, the data collector set runs until it reaches a maximum size. However, if an overall duration is specified, it takes precedence.

If you have set an overall duration, clicking the "Stop when all data collectors have finished" check box allows the most recent counter data to be recorded before the data collector set stops.

Performance Alerts   Using a data collector set isn't limited to creating a log file for later analysis and reporting. You can configure one so that when a particular performance counter value falls below or above a certain threshold value, an alert is triggered. Alerts can write an entry to the Application event log and run a specific program or script. An alert can also trigger another data collector set to start collecting related data. An alert data collector set checks or "samples" the counter value at user-defined intervals. You want to sample often enough to make sure a problem doesn't go unnoticed for too long, but sampling too frequently can put an unnecessary load on the system.

Activity 4-6: Creating a Performance Alert

Time Required: 10 minutes
Objective: Create a performance alert.

Required Tools and Equipment: 411Server1
Description: You have been asked to create an alert that fires whenever CPU utilization exceeds 50%.

1. Log on to 411Server1 as **Administrator**, if necessary.

2. Open Performance Monitor, and click to expand **Data Collector Sets**. Right-click **User Defined**, point to **New**, and click **Data Collector Set**.

3. Type **Alert Data Collector Set** in the Name text box, click the **Create manually (Advanced)** option button, and then click **Next**.

4. Click the **Performance Counter Alert** option button, and then click **Next**. Click **Add** to add performance counters.

5. Click to expand **Processor** in the list of counters, and then click **% Processor Time**. Click the **Add** button, and then click **OK**.

6. In the Alert when list box, accept the default **Above**, type 50 in the Limit text box (see Figure 4-16), and then click **Next**.

Figure 4-16   Selecting a performance counter to monitor

7. Click **Finish** to return to Performance Monitor. Click **Alert Data Collector Set** in the left pane, and in the right pane, right-click **DataCollector01** and click **Properties** (see Figure 4-17).

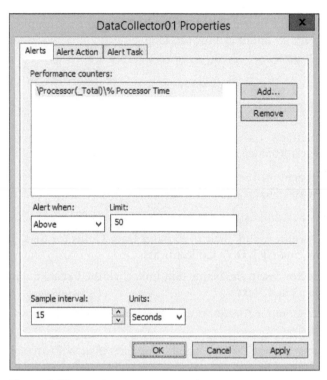

Figure 4-17   Configuring properties for a data collector set

8. In the Sample interval list box, leave the default value of 15 seconds. Click the **Alert Action** tab, and click **Log an entry in the application event log**.

9. Click **OK** to return to Performance Monitor. Right-click **Alert Data Collector Set** in the left pane and click **Start.**

10. Create some CPU activity by opening and closing Server Manager, Internet Explorer, and other applications. Check the Application event log occasionally in Event Viewer to see whether CPU utilization has exceeded 50%.

11. After an event has been generated, right-click **Alert Data Collector Set** and click **Stop.**

12. Stay logged on to 411Server1 if you're continuing to the next activity.

Network Monitoring

A network, for the purposes of this discussion, connects multiple computers so that they can easily communicate and transfer information. Servers are key members of networks because they provide services to all other computers in that network (and possibly other networks). Because network problems can limit the availability of services just as surely as performance issues on servers, you need to be able to monitor and troubleshoot network performance. Windows Server 2012/R2 includes some basic tools for this purpose. You have already learned about using three tools for system performance monitoring. In this section, you review their use for network monitoring.

The Performance tab in Task Manager shows valuable real-time information about the status, activity, type, and IP address of network adapters. In addition, a graph shows the network throughput over a 60-second period. You can right-click this graph and click "View network details" to see real-time details about network traffic.

Next, the Network tab in Resource Monitor shows what's generating network traffic on a per-process basis and what connections, ports, and network protocols these processes are using. Because this data is on a per-process basis, Resource Monitor is an excellent tool for spotting processes using a disproportionate share of network resources by design (because of malware, for example) or by accident (caused by a poorly written or buggy program, for instance).

Finally, you can use Performance Monitor to create real-time monitors that can be customized to show specific data on hardware, protocols, and applications. You can configure data collector sets to create log files for later analysis, baseline reports to help determine which situations are truly anomalous, and generate alerts that can take action to remedy a problem and add it to the event log.

Protocol Analyzers   Although the basic tools covered so far have their place and can give you valuable information about the status of a network, sometimes you need to dig deeper and get a more detailed view of traffic passing through the network. To determine the actual packet content in a transmission, for example, you need to use a protocol analyzer or "packet sniffer," as it's called sometimes. This tool enables you to examine the data being passed along on the network and trace its flow, and then save these captured sessions as files to analyze later. Microsoft has two protocol analyzers available as free downloads: Microsoft Network Monitor and Microsoft Message Analyzer. Another tool that's widely used is Wireshark, a third-party tool. All these tools use the network adapter on the computer where they're installed to capture packets. So if you want to collect data across an entire network from a single computer, its network adapter must be set to **promiscuous mode**. In this mode, a network adapter accepts all network packets, not just the ones addressed to it, so it can pass these packets to the protocol analyzer.

Although explaining the purpose of every network protocol and the performance implications of particular kinds of traffic is beyond the scope of this book, the following list defines a few terms to help you understand how to use these tools:

- *Packet*—A piece of data in a specific format that's being sent through the network.
- *Frame*—A packet and all signals preceding and following it that are required to move the packet through the network.
- *Protocol*—A specification for how data is structured and used in the network to perform a particular task. For example, FTP is a protocol for transferring files.
- *Parser*—A feature of a protocol analyzer that identifies the type of packet being examined and labels the packet's components correctly.
- *Capture*—A packet collected from the network and recorded by the protocol analyzer.
- *Trace*—A set of captured network traffic.

The monitor you choose is largely a matter of preference. All the monitors discussed in the following sections help you monitor and analyze traffic on your network. You might even want to combine two or more of these monitors. In the end, the choice of tool is less important than getting familiar with and using the tool to maintain network performance and reliability.

Microsoft Network Monitor   Like all protocol analyzers, Microsoft Network Monitor's main function is to capture network packets so that you can examine their contents. To use Network Monitor, you must be able to connect to the network via the network adapter to capture packets. In Activity 4-7, you configure a capture and collect some sample traffic.

Activity 4-7: Creating a Capture with Microsoft Network Monitor

Time Required: 10 minutes

Objective: Use Microsoft Network Monitor to capture network traffic.

Required Tools and Equipment: 411Server1, Microsoft Network Monitor downloaded and installed

Description: Capture multiple frames of network traffic and view the packets making up these frames.

1. Log on to 411Server1 as **Administrator**, if necessary.

2. Start a Web browser, go to **www.microsoft.com/en-us/download/details.aspx?id=4865**, and download Microsoft Network Monitor. Install it on your system.

3. Start Microsoft Network Monitor, and click the **Start Page** tab, if necessary.

4. In the Select Networks pane at the lower left, click the **Ethernet** check box, if necessary. In the Recent Captures pane at the upper left, click the **New capture tab** link. If necessary, click the new **Capture** tab (see Figure 4-18).

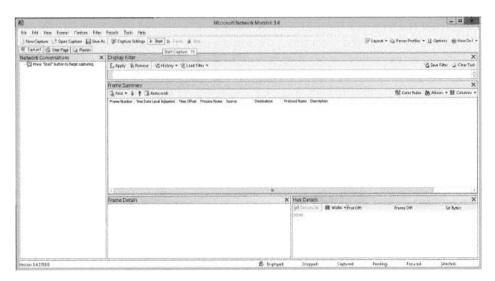

Figure 4-18 The Capture tab

New tabs are generally numbered "Capture1," but your tab name might differ.

5. Click the **Start** button on the toolbar to start the capture. After 1 minute, click **Stop** to end the capture.

6. Exit Network Monitor, and stay logged on if you're continuing to the next activity.

After you have a capture, you can begin analyzing it in the Frame Summary pane (see Figure 4-19). Click a frame in this pane to see its parts in the Frame Details pane and view each byte in hexadecimal format in the Hex Details pane. You can also expand each part of a frame in the Frame Details pane. (If you wanted to create a capture file for later review, you could click File, Save As from the menu.)

Network Monitor offers the following additional features and capabilities:

- In new capture tabs, you can load display filters to focus on specific packets.

- Click Color Rules in the Frame Summary pane to define color coding for frames so that they're easier to identify.

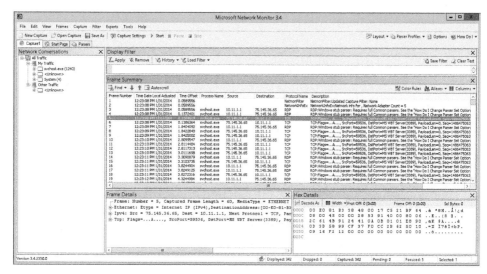

Figure 4-19   The Frame Summary pane

- Optional parser profiles give you more details about a packet's components. Parsers range from a simple capture of network traffic with no breakdown of packet components to a Windows parser that can break down packet components for many Windows protocols.

- Downloadable Experts are external analysis tools you can use on open capture files. See *http://nmexperts.codeplex.com* for more information.

Microsoft hosts the Codeplex site (*www.codeplex.com*) for open-source projects. This site includes numerous projects for Network Monitor parsers and Experts on Codeplex that can be downloaded free. For example, if you're trying to analyze encrypted data, you can download NmDecrypt, which enables you to import a certificate to decrypt packets.

Microsoft Message Analyzer   Like Network Monitor, Microsoft Message Analyzer captures, displays, and analyzes network traffic, but it can also capture data from Windows sources, including event logs, Network Monitor capture files, and Speech Server event trace files. Message Analyzer also makes it easier to set up and analyze traces. Data can be captured live or loaded from saved message collections from multiple data sources. This tool has excellent report capabilities and a range of default viewers. You can also configure custom viewers. Message Analyzer offers more assistance in interpreting network capture activities, so it's a better tool for those who don't have much experience in analyzing network traffic.

As of this writing, Microsoft Message Analyzer doesn't support collecting packets from a network adapter in promiscuous mode. However, you can capture packets in Network Monitor with promiscuous mode and then import them into Message Analyzer.

When you start Microsoft Message Analyzer, the Start page is displayed, where you can find articles and announcements, available downloads, guidance on using Message Analyzer, and current settings. The Quick Trace pane offers predefined traces you can create with one click. Clicking File on the menu gives you options for opening a saved trace (such as Quick Open), browsing to find data files and filters to import, and starting a new custom trace. Traces are managed in the Home tab, where you can view trace data and customize the view. Consistent with many Microsoft applications, Message Analyzer uses a ribbon interface for easy access to important view and data options. You can use it to define filters, change or customize the view, and get additional message information from the Tool Windows section.

Using a predefined Quick Trace, capturing traffic with Message Analyzer is easy. Just follow these steps:

1. Download Microsoft Message Analyzer from *www.microsoft.com/en-us/download/details.aspx?id=40308* and install it.

2. Start Microsoft Message Analyzer. If the Start page isn't displayed, click File, Start Page from the menu.

3. In the Quick Trace section, click Local Link Layer (Windows 8.1/Windows Server 2012 R2).

4. To end the trace, click the Stop button on the toolbar.

The data for a trace is displayed in the Home tab. Click a message (what Message Analyzer calls frames) to see more detailed information in the Details and Diagnostics panes at the bottom (see Figure 4-20). The information displayed in these panes is determined by options in the Tool Windows list in the ribbon. The Details pane breaks down a message into its components, such as name, type, bit offset, and so forth. The Diagnostics pane displays diagnostic messages contained in captured messages so that you don't need to search for them.

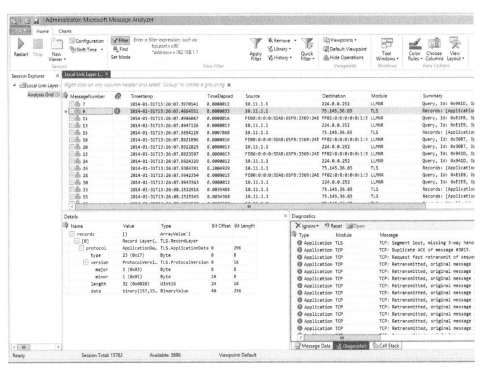

Figure 4-20 The Home tab

Other options in the Tool Windows list are available:

- *Message Data*—Highlights the hexadecimal value of a field you select in the Details pane or the analysis grid that displays the message in a capture. Hex format enables you to see data exactly as it looks going over the network, which is useful when parts of a packet have byte values that might not represent printable characters.

- *Field Data*—Shows the decimal value of any field selected in the Details pane.

- *Bookmarks*—Creates a reference to messages so that they're easier to find later.

- *Comments*—Enables you to add a comment to a message for future reference.

- *Call Stack*—Displays the fragments (called a "message stack") that make up a message in the capture.

- *Column Chooser*—Allows you to add data columns to the analysis grid. For example, you could add a column to the display of TCP data that would give you more information on the segment, such as whether it was retransmitted.

- *Session Explorer*—Lists the viewers currently displayed in the central pane. You can also add or remove viewers in this pane.

In the Charts tab, you can create, edit, save, and share chart viewers that can contain customized pie chart, bar graph, timeline, and grid components. For example, you can create a protocol dashboard that shows the distribution of protocols (TCP, DHCP, and so forth) in the capture data.

Wireshark   Wireshark is a widely used third-party network protocol analyzer. Available since 1998, it's open source and free to download (*www.wireshark.org*). It has extensive features, and the open-source community keeps it updated.

   Wireshark can read capture information from Network Monitor.

When you start Wireshark, it opens to the main page, shown in Figure 4-21, which is divided into four panes: Capture Help, Files, Online, and Capture. The Capture Help pane has links to information about setting up captures and information to capture on different network media. The Files pane lists previous capture files and a link to sample captures. The Online pane has links to the Wireshark Web site, the user's guide, and information on using Wireshark securely.

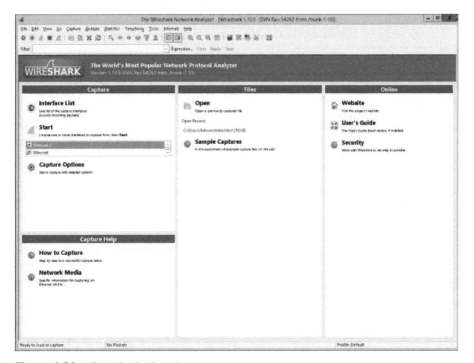

Figure 4-21   The Wireshark main page

The Capture pane is where you actually begin configuration: selecting the interface (typically a server NIC), starting the capture, and setting options for the capture. Clicking Capture, Options from the menu opens a dialog box with the following choices:

- View interfaces and manage their status in Wireshark.

- Use promiscuous mode in captures (so that selected interfaces are set to record all packets, whether packets are addressed to them or not).

- Select capture filters.
- Specify a filename for saving the capture.
- Set a size or time for when captures should be written to multiple files.
- Configure when to stop a capture.
- Configure display options.
- Configure name resolution options, such as translating addresses in numeric format to a more understandable form, including a hostname (for example, www.domain.com) or a device name.

The capture display is divided into three sections. The top section shows the packet list, the middle section shows a selected packet in text, and the bottom section shows details in hexadecimal format. You can specify colors to highlight packets meeting certain conditions. Wireshark's default color rule highlights packets matching the condition tcp.analysis.flags in red. This condition indicates a problem such as a packet being received out of order or traffic indicating dropped packets. An example of a trace with packet highlighting is shown in Figure 4-22.

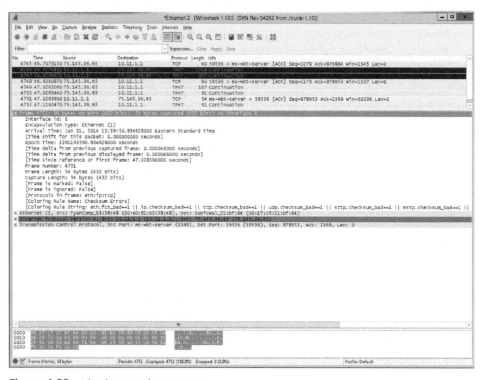

Figure 4-22   Viewing a packet capture

Using Auditing to Improve Network Security

Configuring policies to protect a network and the information stored on it is just the first step. You also need to verify that security measures have been carried out and determine whether there are gaps in the policies you've configured. This is where auditing comes in: to give you an overview of security policies, notify you when attempts are made to violate a security policy, and help determine what went wrong when security policies fail.

Auditing in Windows Server 2012/R2 includes the basic auditing features available in previous versions and adds the following improvements:

- Target specific files and users in audit policies to reduce the volume of auditing information logged.

- Combine global object access auditing with Dynamic Access Control (DAC) to zero in on specific activities. DAC, a new feature in Windows Server 2012, is covered in *MCSA Guide to Configuring Advanced Windows Server 2012/R2 Services, Exam 70-412* (Cengage Learning, 2015).

- Data access events contain more information, so you can conduct more precise searches to find audit information.

- Audit removable storage devices to increase security.

Configuring Auditing with Group Policies

When auditing is in use, events are sent to the Security log based on audit policies defined with the Group Policy tool on a domain or with local policies on a stand-alone system and can be viewed in Event Viewer. In Windows Server 2012/R2, you can configure a multitude of policies, but you need to be cautious about trying to capture too much information. If you're auditing many items or have enabled auditing indiscriminately, the overwhelming number of events being recorded might make meaningful review impossible. To keep the amount of data manageable, start with a minimum of information and then add to it as needed. Two of the most important and most often used policies affect logon/logoff events and object access events, so the following sections start with them.

Auditing Object Access   Every organization has sensitive files or folders that need restricted access, and some organizations might want to restrict access to printers or other devices. Creating an object access policy allows tracking both successful and unsuccessful attempts to access these non-Active Directory objects. Creating a policy to audit object access isn't enough to have access events logged, however; the object must also have a system access control list (SACL) associated with it. Without an SACL limiting who can access an object, there can be no unsuccessful attempts and, therefore, no reason to audit access attempts.

Activity 4-8: Auditing Folder Access

Time Required: 15 minutes
Objective: Create an audit policy for a folder.

Required Tools and Equipment: 411Server1
Description: Auditing access to folders is an essential part of security measures. In this activity, you create an audit policy that records an event each time a designated folder is accessed successfully.

1. Log on to 411Server1 as **Administrator**, if necessary.

2. Open File Explorer, and create a folder named **Audit Test** on your C drive.

3. Open Server Manager, and click **Tools, Group Policy Management** from the menu. In the Group Policy Management console, right-click **Default Domain Policy** and click **Edit** to open the Group Policy Management Editor.

4. In the left pane, expand **Computer Configuration, Policies, Windows Settings, Security Settings, Local Policies,** and click **Audit Policy.** Double-click **Audit object access** in the right pane to open the Properties dialog box.

5. Click the **Define these policy settings** check box, click the **Success** and **Failure** check boxes, and then click **OK**.

6. Open a command prompt window. Type **gpupdate** and press **Enter** to refresh the security policy immediately. Close the command prompt window.

7. Open File Explorer, and then right-click the **Audit Test** folder created in Step 2 and click **Properties**.

8. Click the **Security** tab, and then click the **Advanced** button at the bottom to open the Advanced Security Settings dialog box (see Figure 4-23).

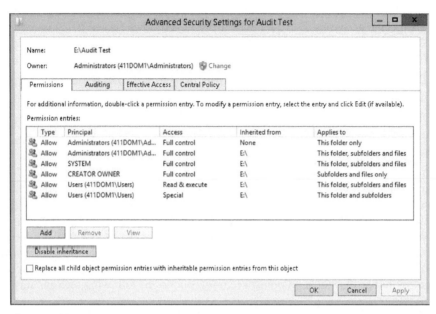

Figure 4-23   The Advanced Security Settings dialog box

9. Click the **Auditing** tab and click **Add** to open the Auditing Entry for Audit Test dialog box.

10. Click the **Select a principal** link to open the Select User, Computer, Service Account, or Group dialog box. Type **Authenticated Users** in the "Enter the object name to select" text box, and then click **OK** to return to the Auditing Entry for Audit Test dialog box.

11. Click **Success** in the Type drop-down list, if necessary.

12. Click the **Full control** check box so that all successful accesses are logged, and then click **OK** to add the entry. Close all open dialog boxes.

13. To verify audit settings, navigate to and open the Audit Test folder. Start Event Viewer, expand **Windows Logs,** and click the **Security** log. You should find a successful access event.

14. Log off 411Server1.

Auditing Logon and Logoff Events   Seeing who has been logging on to—or, even more important, attempting to log on to—a system or network is essential information for security purposes. Many unsuccessful logon attempts, particularly for administrative accounts, can indicate a network attack. You might also want to know that certain users are logging off, especially when leaving an unattended computer logged on to a privileged account could be a security risk.

The Logon Events policy refers to logons and logoffs to a particular computer and is easily confused with the Account Logon Events policy, which refers to an attempt to authenticate a user through a domain controller or a local Security Accounts Manager.

To monitor these attempts, you can configure a policy to audit logon attempts and logoffs:

1. In the Group Policy Management console, right-click Default Domain Policy and click Edit.

2. In the left pane, expand Computer Configuration, Policies, Windows Settings, Security Settings, Local Policies, and Audit Policy.

3. Double-click the "Audit logon events" policy in the right pane to open the Properties dialog box. Click the "Define these policy settings," Success, and Failure check boxes, and then click OK.

 Policies defined in the Default Domain Policy node are inherited by all OUs at lower levels; however, a GPO linked to a lower-level OU can override them.

Additional Audit Policies   Now that you're familiar with the basic audit policies and how to apply them, you can investigate additional audit policies. Remember that as you increase the number of auditing policies you're using, you increase the size of the Security log, which can make analysis more time consuming. Here are the nine basic auditing policies; you examine some in the following sections:

- *Object Access*—Attempts to access or change non–Active Directory objects, such as files, folders, and printers
- *Logon Events*—Attempts at user logons to and logoffs from a computer and attempts at logons to a network
- *Account Management*—Attempts to change user, computer, and group accounts by changing passwords or adding or deleting accounts, for example
- *Privilege Use*—Use of sensitive user rights, such as the "Act as part of the operating system" policy
- *Policy Change*—Attempts to change security policies
- *Directory Service Access*—Attempts to access or change Active Directory objects
- *Account Logon Events*—Attempts to authenticate a user through a domain controller or a local Security Accounts Manager
- *Process Tracking*—Events, such as creation and termination, related to specific processes
- *System Events*—Changes that could affect security and aren't covered in other policies

Viewing Auditing Events with Event Viewer   Creating audit events isn't of much use if there's no way to review them. After policies have been defined and events are being logged, you can view the results in Event Viewer. Using the policy you configured in Activity 4-8 as an example, follow these steps to view auditing results:

1. Copy a file to the Audit Test folder, or open the folder and create a file with Notepad.
2. To make sure the log file has been updated, wait a few minutes before opening Event Viewer and navigating to the Security log (under the Windows Logs node).
3. Click Find in the Actions pane, type "file system" in the "Find what" text box, and click the Find Next button.
4. In the top pane, you should see an event related to copying or creating the file that's highlighted. For this example, you'd see "File System" displayed in the Task Category column. The lower pane displays more detailed information in the General tab.

Advanced Auditing Policies   One disadvantage of collecting auditing data from basic auditing policies is that the amount of data generated can be enormous, and some of it (or most of it) might not be applicable to your analyses. Sifting through this data can be time consuming and frustrating. With advanced auditing policies, however, you can narrow the scope of what's being audited to a subset of the basic policy. For example, under the Logon/Logoff basic policy are these 10 subcategories:

- Account lockout
- User/device claims
- IPsec extended mode

- IPsec main mode
- IPsec quick mode
- Logoff
- Logon
- Network policy server
- Other logon/logoff events
- Special logons

For example, if you're focusing on attempts to log on to accounts that have been locked out, choosing only the advanced policy for auditing account lockouts results in far fewer audit events being written to the Security log. This way, finding the events you want to investigate is much easier. Advanced auditing policies can be set in a GPO with the Group Policy Management Editor by expanding Computer Configuration, Policies, Windows Settings, Security Settings, Advanced Audit Policy Configuration, Audit Policies, and then clicking one of the basic policies. The advanced policies are listed in the right pane when you select the basic category in the left pane, as shown in Figure 4-24 for the Object Access basic policy.

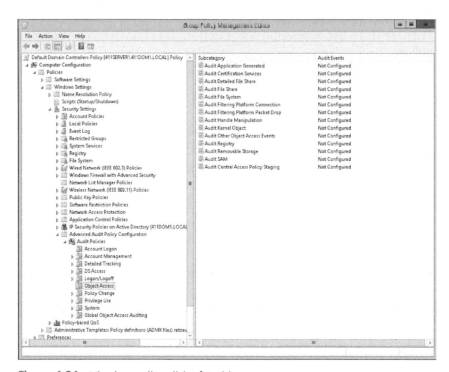

Figure 4-24   Viewing audit policies for object access

When using advanced auditing policies, keep two cautions in mind. First, advanced auditing policies can be overridden by a broader basic policy, such as the Logon/Logoff basic policy overriding the Account lockout advanced policy. To make sure the advanced policies you set aren't overridden by broader basic policies, follow this procedure:

1. Open the GPO in the Group Policy Management Editor.

2. Navigate to Computer Configuration, Policies, Windows Settings, Security Settings, Local Policies, and Security Options.

3. In the right pane, double-click Audit: Force audit policy subcategory settings (Windows Vista or later) to override audit policy category settings. In the dialog box that opens, click the "Define this policy setting" check box, click Enable, and then click OK.

Using Auditing to Improve Network Security

Second, if you decide to return to basic auditing policies, you need to follow these steps to disable an advanced auditing policy:

1. Set all Advanced Audit Policy subcategories to Not Configured.

2. Delete all `audit.csv` files from the SYSVOL folder on the domain controller.

3. Reconfigure and apply the basic audit policy settings you want to use.

Auditing Removable Devices   USB flash drives are convenient, but they can pose a security risk for an organization because they make it easy to copy confidential information from the network or upload viruses and malware to the network. Creating an access policy to deny the use of removable devices might not be practical. However, you can create an audit policy to track attempts to use a removable device:

1. In the Group Policy Management console, right-click Default Domain Policy and click Edit.

2. Navigate to Computer Configuration, Policies, Windows Settings, Security Settings, Advanced Audit Policy Configuration, Audit Policies, and Object Access.

3. Double-click Audit Removable Storage in the right pane. In the Properties dialog box, click the "Configure the following audit events," Success, and Failure check boxes. Click OK to apply the policy.

Global Object Access Auditing   Although you might need to audit access to every folder and file on a disk occasionally, this task could be overwhelming if you have thousands of folders that need policies assigned because each would need its own SACL. Global object access auditing solves this problem by making it possible for you to apply an audit policy to all object types in the file system or Registry; in other words, you can create a **global system access control list (SACL)** that applies to all files and folders. You can have both a file or folder SACL and a global SACL that's applied to a folder or file. Any activity matching the conditions defined for the global SACL or the file/folder SACL triggers the corresponding audit event. Here are the steps to set up global object access auditing:

1. In the Group Policy Management console, right-click Default Domain Policy and click Edit.

2. Navigate to Computer Configuration, Policies, Windows Settings, Security Settings, Advanced Audit Policy Configuration, Audit Policies, and Global Object Access Auditing.

3. Double-click File system in the right pane to open the File system Properties dialog box.

4. Click the "Define this policy setting" check box, and then click Configure to open the Advanced Security Settings for Global File SACL dialog box.

5. Click Add to open the Auditing Entry for Global File SACL dialog box. Click the "Select a principal" link, enter a user, computer, service account, or group to define who's affected by the policy, and then click OK.

6. In the Type list box, click Success, Fail, or All. In the Permissions section, click the one you want to create events for, and then click OK. Click OK in the Advanced Security Settings for Global File SACL dialog box, and click OK again to close the File system Properties dialog box.

7. In the Group Policy Management Editor, navigate to Computer Configuration, Policies, Windows Settings, Security Settings, Advanced Audit Policy Configuration, Audit Policies, and Object Access, and then double-click Audit File System in the right pane.

8. In the Properties dialog box, click "Configure the following audit events." Click the Success and Failure check boxes, and then click OK.

Expression-Based Auditing   One major stumbling block in configuring audit policies is the need to create groups users must belong to so that a policy can be assigned. As access rules get more complex, new groups need to be defined to make sure users meet all the qualifications. For example, access to payroll files might be restricted to certain members of the Accounting group. If you want to create a policy for auditing access to payroll files, you need to create a group made up of only those members of the Accounting group. Managing many groups can be time consuming and makes adding users more complicated because you must ensure that each user belongs to the right groups so that auditing works correctly. In the past, some access rules were impossible to carry out in auditing. Expression-based audit policies, introduced in Windows 8 and Windows Server 2012, enable you to build complex filters based on a variety of criteria to limit audit events to a very specific group of users and a specific set of data being accessed. **Expression-based auditing** uses user claims, device claims, and resource properties to set conditions for limiting auditing. A claim is a statement about a user's or device's identity, usually verified by a third party. The statement is packaged in a token and presented to any service or application that requires identity authentication. As an analogy, when you enter an amusement park, you present your ticket and sometimes your ID, if needed. You are then issued a wrist band so that you can access amusements in the park without having to verify your identity at each one. The wrist band is the token, and the "claim" it represents is that you had a valid entrance ticket.

Dynamic Access Control must be configured to use expression-based auditing. This topic is covered in more detail in *MCSA Guide to Configuring Advanced Windows Server 2012/R2 Services, Exam 70-412* (Cengage Learning, 2015).

For example, you can use a user's department property to create a condition that restricts auditing an object to access attempts by a member of the Finance Department. Any new user joining the Finance Department is included in the policy automatically instead of having to be assigned to a group. Figure 4-25 shows this auditing condition entered, with the user's department attribute being equal to "finance."

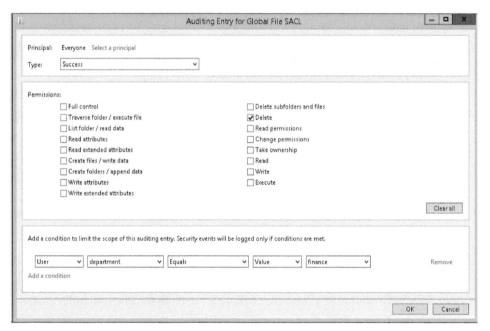

Figure 4-25   Configuring expression-based auditing

Configuring Auditing with `auditpol.exe`

If you do a lot of audit configuration or review, using the command line or creating scripts to review audit policies or effect policy changes can be more efficient than using a GUI tool. Here's the basic syntax of the `auditpol` command-line utility:

```
auditpol command subcommand options
```

With `auditpol`, you can handle the following tasks, among others:

- Back up and restore audit policies to comma-separated value (CSV) files.
- Set system and per-user audit policies and their options.
- Display current audit policies.
- Configure global resource SACLs.

For example, to back up all audit policies to a `.csv` file, enter the following command:

```
auditpol /backup /file:auditpolicybackup.csv
```

4

Chapter Summary

- Monitoring performance is critical to maintaining server health. Windows Server 2012/R2 includes tools such as Event Viewer, Task Manager, Performance Monitor, Network Monitor, and Message Analyzer to assist with this task.

- Event Viewer is useful for tracking down system or application problems and investigating security violations. Events are logged in two main categories: Windows logs, containing events that apply system wide and events from applications, and Applications and Services logs, containing events from specific applications or system services.

- To help you isolate a problem or review log files more efficiently, Event Viewer offers several ways to search, filter, and sort event logs.

- Administrators can create event subscriptions to have logs from other systems written to a single log file, the Forwarded Events log.

- With Task Manager, you can see what's happening with processes running on the system in real time, so you can take action in a timely manner.

- Another tool for real-time monitoring is Resource Monitor, which shows CPU, memory, disk, and network use information for separate processes or the system as a whole in real time. You can also review processes that have stopped responding, check current file use by applications, and control services.

- Performance Monitor can monitor real-time activity and review logs for historical information, and you can customize the data that's collected in logs. Alerts and tasks can be triggered based on user-defined thresholds, and a variety of reports can be generated.

- Data collector sets specify the performance counters you want to collect, how often to collect them, and how long to collect them. You can create multiple data collector sets that can be scheduled to capture different aspects of system performance and measure performance during different periods. You can also have alerts triggered when a performance counter value falls below or above a certain threshold value.

- To get a detailed view of traffic passing through a network, use a protocol analyzer, which enables you to examine the data being passed along the network and trace its flow, and then save these captured sessions as files to analyze later. Microsoft has two tools, Network Monitor and Message Analyzer, for this purpose, and Wireshark is a widely used third-party network protocol analyzer.

- Creating an object access policy allows tracking both successful and unsuccessful attempts to access files, folders, printers, and other devices.

- Seeing who has been logging on to—or attempting to log on to—a system or network is essential information for security purposes.

- There are nine basic auditing policies: Object Access, Logon Events, Account Management, Privilege Use, Policy Change, Directory Service Access, Account Logon Events, Process Tracking, and System Events.

- After policies have been defined and events are logged, you can view the results in Event Viewer.
- With advanced auditing policies, you can narrow the scope of what's being audited to a subset of the basic policy.
- Global object access makes it possible for you to apply an audit policy to all object types in the file system or Registry.
- Expression-based audit policies, introduced in Windows 8 and Windows Server 2012, enable you to build complex filters based on a variety of criteria to limit audit events to access from a very specific group of users.
- Using the auditpol command-line utility to review audit policies or effect policy changes can be more efficient than using a GUI tool.

Key Terms

data collector set   Settings that specify the performance counters you want to collect, how often to collect them, and how long to collect them.

event subscription   A feature in Event Viewer that allows an administrator to collect events from other systems.

expression-based auditing   A method for specifying conditions, based on object properties in Active Directory, that must be met to trigger an audit event.

global system access control list   An ACL that applies to all file system object types, not just a single file or folder.

handle   A reference to a resource on the computer; often associated with open files but can also be associated with a block of memory or other data structures an application is using.

promiscuous mode   A setting on a network adapter that allows it to accept all network packets, not just the ones addressed to it.

thread   The smallest piece of program code that Windows can schedule for execution.

Review Questions

1. You can set filters in Event Viewer for multiple logs. True or False?

2. You can save event log information as a file in which format? (Choose all that apply.)

   a. Event log file format

   b. Log file format

   c. Tab delimited

   d. Comma delimited

3. Which subtype of the Applications and Services logs in Event Viewer is hidden and disabled by default? (Choose all that apply.)

   a. Analytic

   b. Admin

   c. Debug

   d. Operational

4. Which of the following logs in Event Viewer do you use to create an event subscription?

   a. System

   b. Forwarded Events

   c. Security

   d. Setup

5. In the Performance tab of Task Manager, which of the following components can you monitor? (Choose all that apply.)

   a. CPU use

   b. Process use

   c. Memory use

   d. Network adapters

6. In addition to monitoring system resources, you can do which of the following with Resource Monitor? (Choose all that apply.)

   a. Review and close processes that have stopped responding.

   b. Delete files.

   c. Control services.

   d. See what files are in use by applications.

7. Which of the following is a source of data for Performance Monitor? (Choose all that apply.)

   a. Configuration information

   b. Event trace data

   c. Task Manager data

   d. Performance counters

8. Performance Monitor displays statistics in which of the following formats? (Choose all that apply.)

   a. Pie chart

   b. Histogram

   c. Report

   d. Line graph

9. What should you do to get a better idea of normal and abnormal system performance on your network?

   a. Talk to your users every day.

   b. Create a baseline by recording monitor sessions at random times for later comparison.

   c. Watch for certain thresholds to be exceeded.

   d. Create a baseline by recording monitor sessions at peak and off-peak times for later comparison.

10. An alert in Performance Monitor can write an event to which log?

    a. Security

    b. System

    c. Application

    d. Error

11. When can thresholds in a data collector set be configured to trigger an alert? (Choose all that apply.)

    a. The value in the counter falls below the threshold.

    b. The value in the counter is equal to the threshold.

    c. The value in the counter rises above the threshold.

    d. The value in the counter differs from the threshold by some percentage up or down.

12. Protocol analyzers provide information on which of the following? (Choose all that apply.)

    a. Network throughput

    b. Network speed

    c. Protocols in use on the network

    d. Contents of network packets

13. The Users group has permission to do which of the following in Performance Monitor? (Choose all that apply.)

    a. View log files

    b. Access real-time data

    c. Create data collector sets

    d. Modify display properties

14. Performance-monitoring tools can't be used for network monitoring. True or False?

15. An object must have an associated SACL to be audited. True or False?

16. Advanced auditing policies can't be overridden by broader basic policies. True or False?

17. Global object access auditing allows you to do which of the following?

    a. Audit computers outside your domain.

    b. Audit computers over a WAN.

    c. Increase the number of objects that can be audited.

    d. Configure a single policy to audit access to all folders and files on a disk.

18. You can use `auditpol` to handle which of the following auditing tasks? (Choose all that apply.)

    a. Back up and restore audit policies to CSV files.

    b. Disable advanced auditing policies to return to basic policies.

    c. Display current audit policies.

    d. Configure global resource SACLs.

Case Projects

CASE PROJECTS

Case Project 4-1: Using System-Monitoring Tools

You recently became the server administrator for a company. As soon as you walked in the door, users were telling you the network is running slowly quite often, but they couldn't tell you when it happened or how much it slowed down. What tests and measurements could you use to try to determine what's going on?

Case Project 4-2: Protecting the Network

You work for a company that hasn't been too concerned about network security and performance, but as more employees are hired, management is beginning to worry that employees are using the Internet for purposes that aren't work related. What types of network monitoring could you do to make sure Internet access is being used correctly in the company?

Case Project 4-3: Auditing Sensitive Data Access

You're the network administrator for a company that has contracts to store sensitive data for other companies, and clients want reassurance that you're protecting their data. The company has groups of employees who will be working with clients, and several contractors need access to the data, too. To make managing data easier, each client has been assigned his or her own disk volume. What types of auditing can you set up to reassure clients their data is protected and to check which files employees and contractors are accessing?

chapter 5

Remote Access Configuration

After reading this chapter and completing the exercises, you will be able to:

- Describe remote access
- Install and configure the Remote Access server role
- Configure the DirectAccess role service

All screenshots, unless otherwise noted, are used with permission from Microsoft Corporation.

The old work model of throngs of workers going to an office and staying there from 9 to 5 no longer applies to many businesses. With remote access technology, employees can work from home or on the road and still have access to all the resources and applications they would have sitting at a desk in the company office. With the Remote Access server role, network administrators can offer options to employees for accessing network resources remotely. The Remote Access server role also has features that enable you to configure a Windows server as a local area network (LAN) router or Network Address Translation device. In this chapter, you learn how to install and configure the Remote Access server role and its three role services. This chapter also focuses on configuring virtual private networks and the DirectAccess role service.

An Overview of Remote Access

Table 5-1 describes what you need for the hands-on activities in this chapter.

Table 5-1   Activity requirements

Activity	Requirements	Notes
Activity 5-1: Installing the Remote Access Role	411Server2	
Activity 5-2: Configuring a VPN	411Server2	Two NICs must be installed in 411Server2
Activity 5-3: Creating a VPN Connection and Testing the VPN	411Server2, 411Win8	
Activity 5-4: Configuring Routing	411Server2	
Activity 5-5: Configuring DirectAccess	411Server1, 411Server2	
Activity 5-6: Testing DirectAccess	411Server1, 411Server2, 411Win8	
Activity 5-7: Removing the Remote Access Configuration	411Server1, 411Server2, 411Win8	

© 2015 Cengage Learning®

Remote Access is a server role that provides services to keep a mobile workforce and branch offices securely connected to resources at the main office. Some reasons businesses, large and small, use a remote access solution include the following:

* *Work from home employees*—Employees' physical locations might not be as important as their ability to produce the required work. In addition, teleconferencing applications can often meet the need for personal interactions with other employees and team members.

* *Frequent travelers*—Employees who are on the road a lot, such as salespeople and product support specialists, and people who need to make contact with customers or the product in the field need up-to-date access to company resources.

* *Business partners*—You might need to provide limited access to the company network for partners who need real-time information on inventory and product delivery.

* *Branch offices*—With the widespread availability of high-speed Internet connections, branch offices can often use less expensive, but still secure, virtual private networks (VPNs) to connect to the main office.

No matter how remote access is set up, the goal is usually the same: giving remote users access to network resources in a way that's much like being on the network premises. The Remote Access server role has several services and tools to help achieve this goal, including the following:

* *Virtual private network*—A VPN uses the Internet to create a secure connection from a client computer or branch office to the company network. It has largely replaced remote dial-in for client computers.

- *Remote dial-in*—This technology is less common but still used when broadband Internet isn't available. It uses the phone system and modems to connect remotely.

- *Routing*—This service configures a Windows server as a router with support for static and dynamic routing.

- *Network Address Translation (NAT)*—NAT is used with routing to translate private IP addresses to public IP addresses to facilitate hosts accessing the Internet in a private network.

- *Web Application Proxy*—A new feature in Windows Server 2012 R2, Web Application Proxy allows users outside the network to access select internal Web applications by using a reverse proxy.

- *DirectAccess*—Similar to VPNs, DirectAccess provides a more convenient and manageable secure remote connection using features available in IPv6.

The Remote Access server role has some additional features, but the ones in the preceding list are the core services for most remote access needs and are discussed in the following sections.

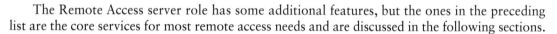

Installing and Configuring the Remote Access Role

To install the Remote Access server role, use Server Manager or the `Install-WindowsFeature` PowerShell cmdlet. Under the main Remote Access server role, there are three role services to choose from:

- *DirectAccess and VPN (RAS)*—This role service has the features needed for dial-in, VPN, and DirectAccess remote access.

- *Routing*—This role service provides routing and NAT. The Routing role service requires the DirectAccess and VPN (RAS) role service.

- *Web Application Proxy*—Allows publishing Web-based applications for use by clients outside the network.

Activity 5-1: Installing the Remote Access Role

Time Required: 10 minutes
Objective: Install the Remote Access role and role services.

Required Tools and Equipment: 411Server2
Description: You want to configure a variety of remote access solutions, including dial-in, VPN, routing, NAT, and Web Application Proxy, so you install the Remote Access server role and associated role services. The Web Server role is required for the Remote Access role, so you're prompted to install it, too.

1. Start 411Server2 and log on as **Administrator**, if necessary.

2. Open Server Manager, and click **Manage, Add Roles and Features** from the menu. In the Add Roles and Features Wizard, click **Next** until you get to the Server Roles window.

3. Click **Remote Access,** and then click **Next** twice. In the Remote Access window, read the information describing the features of the Remote Access role, and then click **Next**.

4. In the Role Services window, click to select all three role services. When prompted, click the **Add Features** button, and then click **Next**.

5. In the Web Server Role (IIS) window, read the information, and click **Next**. Accept the default role services for the Web Server role, and then click **Next**. (*Note:* If you don't see this window, IIS is already installed, so go to the next step.)

6. Click **Install**. The installation might take a while. When it's finished, click **Close**.

7. The next step is to configure routing and remote access in the Routing and Remote Access console accessed via Server Manager, which you do in the next activity. Stay logged on for the next activity.

Virtual Private Networks

A **virtual private network (VPN)** is a network connection that uses the Internet to give mobile users or branch offices secure access to a company's network resources on a private network. VPNs use encryption and authentication to ensure that communication is secure and legitimate, so while data travels through the public Internet, the connection remains private—hence the name "virtual private network."

Privacy is achieved by creating a "tunnel" between the VPN client and VPN server. A **tunnel** is a method of transferring data across an unsecured network in such a way that the actual data in the transmission is hidden from all but the sender and receiver. Tunnels are created by encapsulation, in which the inner packet containing the data is encrypted, and the outer headers contain the unencapsulated addresses that Internet devices need to route packets correctly. To use a mail delivery analogy, suppose you have an ultra-secure package to deliver, but you must use a courier. In a separate transaction, you deliver a key to the office manager at the package recipient's location. Next, you place the secret package containing the recipient's name in a lockbox. You put the lockbox inside an envelope and address the envelope to the office manager of the company where the recipient works. The courier can read the addressing on the envelope, but if the envelope is opened, the package contents can't be accessed without the key to the lockbox. The envelope is delivered, and the office manager removes the lockbox from the envelope and opens it with the key delivered earlier. The office manager can then deliver the package to the final recipient. In this analogy, the lockbox and outer envelope make up the VPN tunnel, and the office manager is the VPN server to which messages are delivered.

Figure 5-1 shows a VPN tunnel between a client computer and a company network. The tunnel connection is made between the client computer and the VPN server. After the VPN server opens the packet, the inner packet is decrypted (unlocked) and delivered to the resource the client requested. From the client computer's standpoint, access to network resources is little different than if the client were physically connected to the company network. In fact, the VPN network connection on the client OS is assigned an IP address on the network.

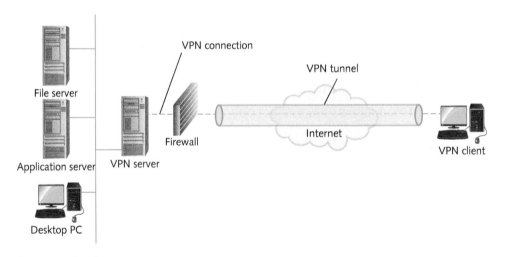

Company network

Figure 5-1   A typical VPN connection
© 2015 Cengage Learning®

VPN Tunnel Types   Windows Server 2012/R2 has a VPN server solution with Routing and Remote Access Service (RRAS), a component of the Remote Access server role, and supports three types of VPN tunnels:

- *Point-to-Point Tunneling Protocol (PPTP)*—A commonly used VPN protocol that encapsulates Point-to-Point Protocol (PPP), using a modified version of Generic Routing Encapsulation (GRE). The data in encapsulated PPP frames is compressed, encrypted, or both. Frames are encrypted with Microsoft Point-to-Point Encryption (MPPE) by using encryption keys from the authentication process. Authentication uses Microsoft Challenge Handshake Authentication Protocol version 2 (MS-CHAP v2) or Extensible Authentication Protocol-Transport Layer Security (EAP-TLS) (described later). An advantage of using PPTP is that it's well supported by most OSs and network devices and doesn't require exchanging a preshared key or certificates. Because of its widespread support, this tunnel type is often used when a variety of clients are used to connect to the VPN.

- *Layer 2 Tunneling Protocol with Internet Protocol Security (L2TP/IPsec)*—Developed in cooperation with Cisco Systems and Microsoft, L2TP with IPsec generally provides a higher level of security than PPTP. L2TP doesn't use MPPE for encryption; instead, it uses the encryption technology built into IPsec. IPsec uses Data Encryption Standard (DES) or Triple DES (3DES), using encryption keys generated by the Internet Key Exchange (IKE) process. L2TP/IPsec requires certificates or preshared keys for authentication. Certificates issued to both client and server computers from a public key infrastructure (PKI) is recommended. In addition to securing data through encryption, L2TP/IPsec provides data integrity and identity verification. This tunnel type is most often used when an organization has an established PKI, and client computers are members of the organization's network (as opposed to being employee home computers).

- *Secure Socket Tunneling Protocol (SSTP)*—SSTP has the advantage of working behind most firewalls without firewall administrators needing to configure the firewall to allow VPN. It uses the standard TCP port 443 used for Secure Sockets Layer (SSL) communication (HTTPS). SSTP is supported only on Windows clients, starting with Vista SP1, and as a VPN server, starting with Windows Server 2008. It requires the VPN server to have a valid digital certificate issued by a certification authority (CA) for server identification. This tunnel type is gaining in popularity because of its ease of use and compatibility with firewalls but only when client computers run Windows Vista SP1 and later.

All three types are enabled by default when you configure Windows Server 2012/R2 as a VPN server, so any type of client that tries to connect will be successful, as long as each tunnel type is configured correctly. VPN server configuration in Windows Server 2012/R2 is fairly straightforward. After the Remote Access server role is installed, you configure it in the Routing and Remote Access console, accessed from the Tools menu in Server Manager.

VPN Requirements   Before you can configure a VPN with RRAS, your server and network must meet the requirements for the type of VPN you want to set up:

- *Two or more NICs installed on a server*—One NIC is connected to the private network you're allowing remote access to, and the other is connected to the Internet. The VPN server acts as a kind of router, receiving traffic on the interface connected to the Internet from VPN clients and routing it to the private network. The VPN server decrypts, authenticates, and validates the traffic as the tunnel type requires before sending it to the private network. Traffic from the private network is received on one or more other NICs and routed to the Internet-connected NIC, where it's made secure for transmission to the VPN client.

- *Correctly configured firewall*—The network firewall must be configured according to the requirements of the VPN tunnel type. When the VPN is configured on the Windows server, Windows configures Windows Firewall for the VPN tunnel type, but the firewall protecting the network must also be configured to allow VPN traffic to reach the VPN server. Firewall configurations are discussed later in this section.

- *Authentication*—Depending on which tunnel types your VPN supports, you might need to configure one or more authentication methods, such as a Remote Authentication Dial In User Service (RADIUS) server to handle user authentication. RADIUS is a service that's part of the Network Policy Server (NPS) server role, which provides centralized authentication for remote access and wireless clients. (NPS and RADIUS are discussed in Chapter 6.)

If the VPN supports SSTP connections, the server must have a digital certificate assigned by a public CA, such as VeriSign. L2TP/IPsec tunnels that don't use preshared keys need both client and server certificates, which can be issued from a Windows-based PKI with Windows Certificate Services.

- *DHCP configuration*—Clients that connect to the VPN server are usually assigned an IP address dynamically. Although the server can be configured with a pool of addresses to assign to clients, a Dynamic Host Configuration Protocol (DHCP) server is recommended for centralized IP address management. When a DHCP server is used, the VPN server requests a small pool of 10 addresses from the DHCP server and then allocates these addresses to clients when they connect. If the VPN server runs out of addresses, it requests another small pool of addresses to lease to clients.

Network Firewall Configuration for a VPN   Configuring the perimeter network firewall is critical for VPN operation. A perimeter network is a boundary between the private network and the public Internet and is where most resources available to the Internet, such as mail, Web, DNS, and VPN servers, are located. Although these resources can be accessed from the Internet, they're still guarded by a firewall to prevent malicious packets from entering the network.

Most firewalls are configured to allow only limited types of incoming traffic. For example, if you have a company Web server, the firewall must allow TCP port 80 for incoming Web traffic to reach the Web server. If you're running a DNS server for Internet resources, the firewall must allow UDP port 53 for DNS queries. For VPNs, the firewall must be configured to allow the following types of traffic to the VPN server, according to the VPN tunnel type:

PPTP tunnels

- Inbound destination TCP port 1723 for PPTP maintenance traffic from VPN client to server
- Inbound destination IP protocol ID 47 (GRE) for tunneled data transfers from VPN client to server
- Outbound source TCP port 1723 for PPTP maintenance traffic from VPN server to client
- Outbound source IP protocol ID 47 (GRE) for tunneled data transfers from VPN server to client

L2TP/IPsec tunnels

- Inbound destination User Datagram Protocol (UDP) port 500 for IKE traffic from VPN client to server
- Inbound destination UDP port 4500 for IPsec NAT traversal traffic from VPN client to server
- Inbound destination IP protocol ID 50 for IPsec Encapsulating Security Payload (ESP) traffic from VPN client to server
- Outbound source UDP port 500 for IKE traffic from VPN server to client
- Outbound source UDP port 4500 for IPsec NAT traversal traffic from VPN server to client
- Outbound source IP protocol ID 50 for IPsec ESP traffic from VPN server to client

SSTP tunnels

- Inbound destination TCP port 443 for HTTPS traffic from VPN client to server
- Outbound source TCP port 443 for HTTPS traffic from VPN server to client

VPN Configuration

After meeting the requirements for a VPN server and network, it's time to configure a VPN. If the VPN server is a domain member, its computer account must first be added to the RAS and IAS Servers group in Active Directory. (IAS stands for "Internet Authentication Service.") The RAS and IAS Servers group is in the Users folder.

Although you can use PowerShell cmdlets to configure RRAS, the following steps use the Routing and Remote Access console. By default, all remote access functions are disabled, indicated by a red down arrow on the server icon. To enable these functions, right-click the server icon and click Configure and Enable Routing and Remote Access. After the Welcome window, the Configuration window gives you the following options for the type of remote access server you want to configure (see Figure 5-2):

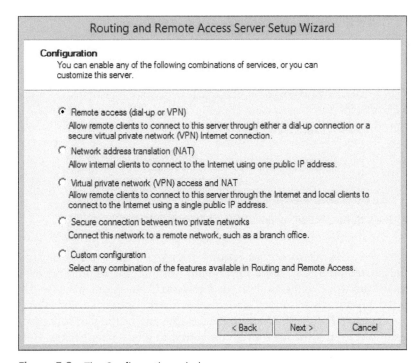

Figure 5-2   The Configuration window

- *Remote access (dial-up or VPN)*—Configures the server as a VPN server, a dial-up server, or both. Select this option if the server will provide incoming VPN or dial-up services for remote clients but not act as a NAT device for outgoing Internet connections.

- *Network address translation (NAT)*—Configures the server as a NAT router to allow computers on the private network to access the Internet with a public IP address.

- *Virtual private network (VPN) access and NAT*—Configures the server as both a remote access (VPN or dial-up) server and a NAT router. This option combines the first two options.

- *Secure connection between two private networks*—Configures the server as a VPN router between two networks, such as between a main office and branch office. With this configuration, all traffic between the two networks is secure, but the server doesn't accept client connections.

- *Custom configuration*—Allows you to manually configure the routing and remote access features you need if one of the standard options doesn't meet your requirements.

For a standard VPN server, select the "Remote access (dial-up or VPN)" option. In the next window, you can choose VPN, dial-up, or both. For a VPN server without dial-up support, select the VPN option. In the VPN Connection window, select the network interface that connects the server to the Internet (see Figure 5-3). This interface must be connected to the Internet and the correct firewall ports must be open to allow VPN traffic to this interface's IP address.

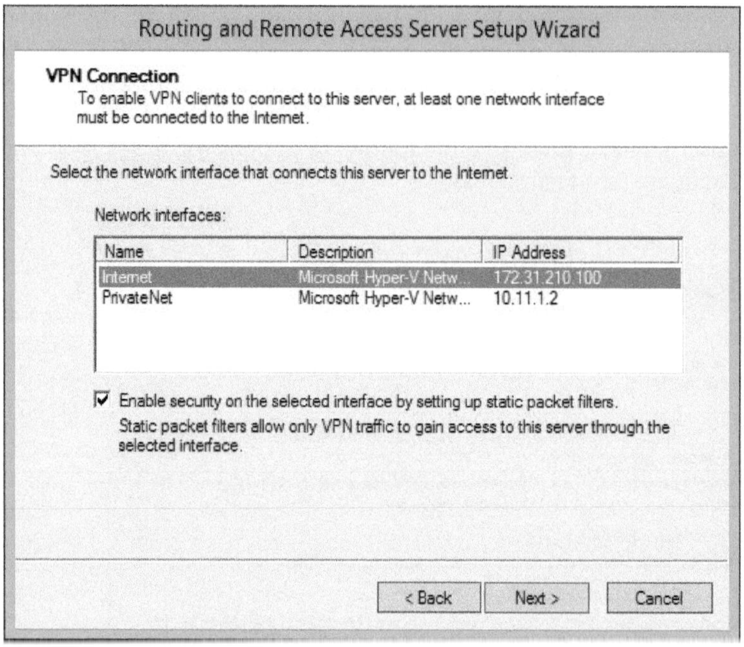

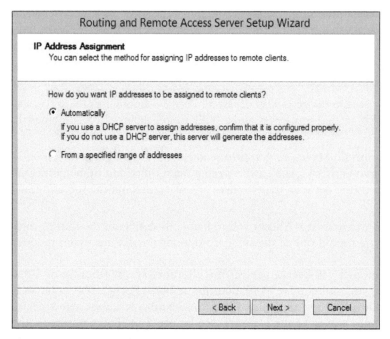

Figure 5-3   The VPN Connection window

In Figure 5-3, the network connections are named descriptively; although this naming convention isn't required, it's a good idea on any computer with multiple network connections. You can rename network connections in the Network Connections window. The "Enable security on the selected interface by setting up static packet filters" option is enabled by default. It prevents the interface connected to the Internet from accepting any traffic that isn't part of a VPN connection. For example, even if the firewall is configured to allow ping packets into the network, the packet filters created by this option deny these packets unless they originate from a VPN client.

Next, you decide how VPN client connections are assigned an IP address when they connect to the VPN (see Figure 5-4):

Figure 5-4   The IP Address Assignment window

- *Automatically*—This option is preferred and requires a correctly configured DHCP server on the network. The VPN server gets a pool of 10 addresses at a time to allocate to VPN clients. If the DHCP server is on a different subnet from the VPN client, the DHCP relay agent must be configured. Both IPv4 and IPv6 addresses can be assigned. If you select this option and no DHCP server can be contacted to assign IPv4 addresses, the VPN server assigns APIPA addresses to clients. If a DHCP server can't be contacted to assign IPv6 addresses, the client uses the IPv6 prefix configured on the VPN server and a locally generated interface ID.

- *From a specified range of addresses*—If no DHCP server is available, choose this option to specify a range of IPv4 addresses for allocating to clients. For IPv6 addresses, only the prefix is assigned by the VPN server; the client uses a locally generated interface ID.

Next, you decide how clients are authenticated to the VPN server and specify whether you want to use RADIUS to handle authentication for client connection requests (see Figure 5-5):

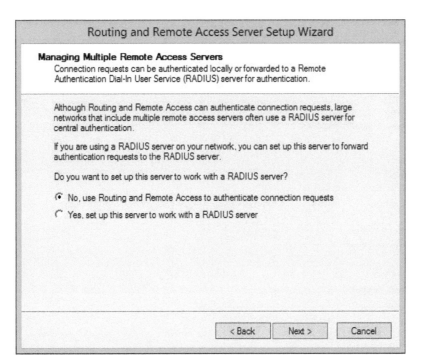

Figure 5-5 Configuring authentication

- *No, use Routing and Remote Access to authenticate connection requests*—With this option, the VPN server authenticates connection requests by contacting a domain controller if the server is a domain member. If it isn't a domain member, it uses accounts from the local SAM database. For security reasons, a domain-joined VPN server isn't recommended.

- *Yes, set up this server to work with a RADIUS server*—Choose this option when there are multiple remote access servers that aren't joined to a domain. A RADIUS server performs centralized authentication, as you learn in Chapter 6.

After you click Finish in the summary window, you see a message stating that you must configure the DHCP relay agent. You need to do this only if you configured automatic IP address assignment and the DHCP server isn't on the same subnet as the server's private network connection.

Finishing VPN Configuration

After you have finished the RRAS Setup Wizard, the VPN server is ready to start accepting VPN client connections. However, first you need to define who's allowed to connect via remote access.

By default, all users are denied remote access. There are two ways to allow users to connect via remote access: configuring dial-in settings in user accounts and configuring a network policy in the Network Policy Server (NPS) console.

Configuring Dial-in Settings in User Accounts If you have only a few users who should be able to access the network remotely, you can configure each user's account properties in Active Directory or Local Users and Groups to allow remote access. In the account's Properties dialog box, click the Dial-in tab (see Figure 5-6). By default, the Network Access Permission attribute is set to "Control access through NPS Network Policy." The NPS Network Policy is configured to deny access to all users by default, so select the Allow access option to give the user permission to connect remotely via dial-in, VPN, and DirectAccess.

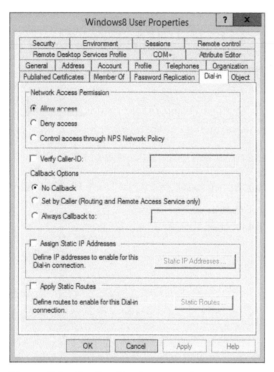

Figure 5-6 Configuring the Network Access Permission attribute for a user account

The remaining settings on the Dial-in tab are as follows:

- *Verify Caller-ID*—This option is used only for dial-in remote access. When the user attempts to log on, the phone number attempting the remote connection is verified against the phone number entered in the text box by using caller ID. If the number doesn't match or caller ID isn't supported, the connection is denied.

- *Callback Options*—This option is used only for dial-in remote access and by default is set to No Callback. If Set by Caller is selected, the remote access client enters a number, and the server calls the client back to make the connection, thereby saving client phone charges. If "Always Callback to" is selected, the server attempts to call the number specified to make the connection.

- *Assign Static IP Addresses*—Use this option to assign static IPv4 and IPv6 addresses the client uses for remote access connections rather than dynamic addresses assigned by the VPN server.

- *Apply Static Routes*—Select this option to configure routes the client's connection uses when accessing certain network resources.

Activity 5-2: Configuring a VPN

Time Required: 15 minutes
Objective: Configure a VPN.

5

Required Tools and Equipment: 411Server2 with two NICs installed
Description: Configure a VPN with the network set up as shown in Figure 5-7. (For this activity, only 411Server2 needs to be on.) 411Server2 is the VPN server. In the VPN configuration, the interface in the 10.11.0.0/16 network acts as the interface connected to the private network, and the interface connected to the 203.0.113.0/24 network acts as the interface connected to the Internet network. You might want to rename your network connections on 411Server2 accordingly; for example, name the interface connected to 10.11.0.0 "PrivateNet" and the other one "Internet."

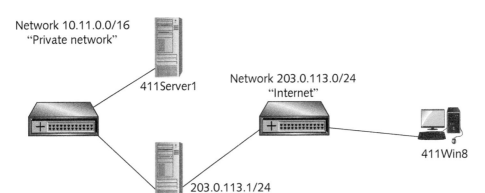

Figure 5-7   Network setup for Activities 5-2 and 5-3
© 2015 Cengage Learning®

1. Log on to 411Server2 as **Administrator**, if necessary. Right-click **Start** and click **Network Connections.** On the second network interface, set the IP address to **203.0.113.1** with subnet mask **255.255.255.0.** Leave the default gateway and DNS server settings blank.

2. Open Server Manager, and click **Tools, Routing and Remote Access** from the menu.

3. In the Routing and Remote Access console, right-click **411Server2 (local)** and click **Configure and Enable Routing and Remote Access.** Click **Next.**

4. In the Configuration window, accept the default setting **Remote access (dial-up or VPN),** and click **Next.**

5. In the Remote Access window, click **VPN** to configure the server to accept VPN connections, and then click **Next.**

6. In the VPN Connection window, click to select the interface that connects to the Internet. In this case, it's the interface with the IP address 203.0.113.1. Leave the **Enable security on the selected interface by setting up static packet filters** check box selected, and click **Next.**

7. In the IP Address Assignment window, click **From a specified range of addresses** (because 411Server1, your DHCP server, isn't running during this activity), and click **Next.**

8. In the Address Range Assignment window, click **New.** In the Start IP address text box, type **10.11.0.100,** and in the Number of addresses text box, type **10.** Click **OK,** and then click **Next.**

9. In the Managing Multiple Remote Access Servers window, accept the default setting **No, use Routing and Remote Access to authenticate connection requests.** Click **Next,** and then click **Finish.**

10. In the message stating that the computer can't be added to the list of valid remote access servers in Active Directory, click **OK,** and then click **OK** in the message box about supporting the relaying of DHCP messages.

11. Stay logged on for the next activity.

VPN Client Configuration   The VPN client is configured by setting up a new connection in the Network and Sharing Center. When you set up a new connection, you choose "Connect to a workplace," and then you have the option to use your existing connection to the Internet, if you have one, or create a dial-up connection. After you choose the connection, you enter the address of the VPN server you'll connect to and enter a name for the connection. You create a VPN connection in Activity 5-3 with this method. You can also create a VPN connection by using the following PowerShell cmdlet in Windows 8.1 and Windows Server 2012 R2 and later:

```
Add-VpnConnection -Name "VPN to Work" -ServerAddress
  "203.0.113.1"
```

If you need to set up a VPN connection to several computers in your network, you can do so with group policy preferences. Open a GPO in the Group Policy Management Editor and navigate to Computer Configuration, Preferences, Windows Settings, and Control Panel Settings. Right-click Network Options, point to New, and click VPN Connection. In the New VPN Properties dialog box, fill in the information shown in Figure 5-8.

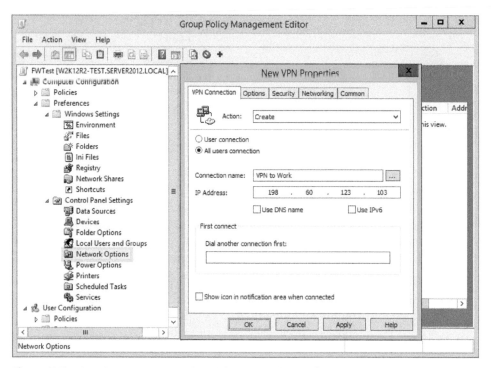

Figure 5-8   Creating a VPN connection with group policy preferences

When you create a VPN connection, the default tunnel type is Automatic. This means the VPN client attempts to make the connection by using each tunneling method until it's successful or the connection fails. You can configure the client to use a particular tunnel type in the connection's properties.

Activity 5-3: Creating a VPN Connection and Testing the VPN

Time Required: 15 minutes
Objective: Create and test a VPN connection.

Required Tools and Equipment: 411Server2 and 411Win8
Description: Test the VPN configuration by creating a VPN client connection on 411Win8 and attempting to connect to the VPN server. For this activity, you need to move 411Win8 to the 203.0.113.0/24 network and set the IP address on the 411Win8 network interface to 203.0.113.10/24.

1. Log on to 411Server2 as **Administrator,** if necessary.

2. Open the Computer Management MMC, and start Local Users and Groups. Create a user on 411Server2 with the username **VPNTest1** and the password **Password01.** Set the **Password never expires** option.

3. Double-click **VPNTest1** to open the Properties dialog box. Click the **Dial-in** tab, click **Allow access** in the Network Access Permission section, and then click **OK.**

4. On 411Win8, log on as **Win8User,** if necessary. If necessary, click **Desktop.** Right-click **Start** and click **Network Connections.** Change the IPv4 address to **203.0.113.10** with subnet mask **255.255.255.0.** Close the Network Connections window.

5. Open the Network and Sharing Center. Click **Set up a new connection or network.** In the Choose a connection option window (see Figure 5-9), click **Connect to a workplace,** and then click **Next.**

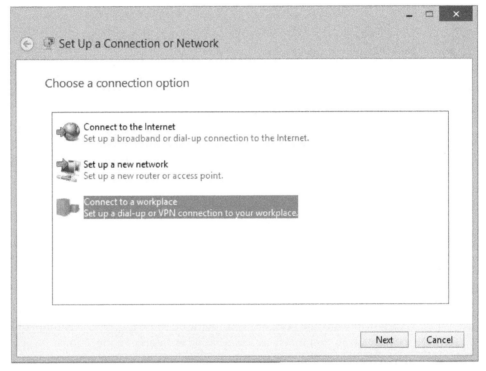

Figure 5-9 Setting up a VPN connection

6. In the How do you want to connect? window, click **Use my Internet connection (VPN).** (If you see a window asking whether you want to set up an Internet connection before continuing, click **I'll set up an Internet connection later.**) In the "Type the Internet address to connect to" window, type **203.0.113.1** in the Internet address text box. (*Note:* You could also use the server's FQDN.) Click **Create.**

7. A Networks panel opens on the right. Click **VPN Connection,** and then click **Connect.** When prompted to sign in, type **411server2\vpntest1** in the User name text box and **Password01** in the Password text box, and then click **OK.** In the Networks panel, you should see the VPN connection status listed as "Connected" (see Figure 5-10).

Figure 5-10   The Networks panel showing the VPN connection

 If the VPN doesn't connect and you see Error 850, open the VPN Connection Properties dialog box, click the Security tab, and click Use Extensible Authentication Protocol (EAP). Click OK, and try the connection again.

8. In the Network and Sharing Center, click **Change adapter settings**. Right click **VPN Connection** and click **Status**. Click **Details** to see the IPv4 address assigned, which should be 10.11.0.101. Click **Close** twice.

9. Right-click **VPN Connection** and click **Connect/Disconnect**. In the Networks panel, click **VPN Connection** and click **Disconnect**. Reconnect 411Win8 to the **10.11.0.0/16** network, and set its IP address to **Obtain an IP address automatically**.

10. Log off 411Win8. Stay logged on to 411Server2 for the next activity.

Configuring Remote Dial-in

As discussed, remote dial-in (called "dial-up networking" in the past) uses the phone system to connect a computer with a remote network. Each connection requires a modem and a phone line on both ends of the connection. So a server supporting remote dial-in must have one modem connected to a phone line for each simultaneous remote access user. It's not a very efficient system, which is why it has been largely replaced by VPN and, more recently, DirectAccess in Windows environments. Nevertheless, it might be the only option available for some clients in remote locations who don't have access to reliable Internet connections.

Remote dial-in is configured almost the same way as VPN configuration, but in the Network Selection window, you choose the private network from which dial-in clients are assigned an IP address. After the Routing and Remote Access Server Setup Wizard is finished, you need to configure the modems used for servicing dial-in connections. This configuration is beyond the scope of this book, however.

 Remote dial-in supports both plain old telephone service (POTS) and ISDN connections.

Configuring Remote Access Options

The default settings for VPN and dial-up might be adequate in many circumstances, but you might need to support different OSs and VPN clients over a variety of tunneling methods, which could require security settings different from the default. In addition, although RRAS allows multiple tunneling types by default for VPN connections, you might want to restrict connections to a particular tunneling method.

As you've learned, you can configure remote access settings in the properties of a user account, but this method can prove inefficient when many users need remote access permission. Instead, you can allow or disallow remote access to users based on connection-related group policies. The following sections cover tasks you might need to perform after configuring RRAS.

Configuring Remote Access Security   To configure security settings for remote access, right-click the server in the Routing and Remote Access console and click Properties. In the Security tab (see Figure 5-11), you can configure the following settings:

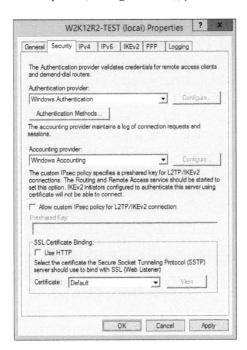

Figure 5-11   Security settings for remote access

- *Authentication provider*—Choose Windows Authentication or RADIUS Authentication. If you choose Windows Authentication, Windows tries to authenticate users attempting to log on via VPN or dial-in from the local SAM account database or a DC. If you choose RADIUS, you must specify which RADIUS servers the RRAS server should use.

- *Authentication methods*—Whether you're using Windows Authentication or RADIUS Authentication, you can select the authentication methods available to the user account trying to log on. Authentication is attempted by using the enabled methods in the order you see in Figure 5-12:

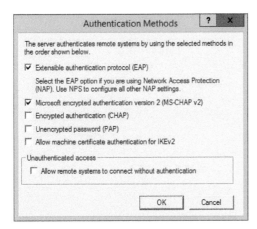

Figure 5-12   Authentication methods

o Extensible authentication protocol (EAP): Selected by default, it's the most flexible authentication method because it works with non-Windows clients, and third-party providers can develop custom authentication schemes. EAP is required for the use of smart cards and can be used for biometric authentication.

o Microsoft encrypted authentication version 2 (MS-CHAP v2): This mutual authentication protocol encrypts both authentication information and data. A different encryption key is used each time a connection is made and on both ends of the connection. MS-CHAP v2 is compatible with most Windows clients, going back to Windows 98. This method has the advantage of being able to prompt the user to change an expired password.

o Encrypted authentication (CHAP): This method provides compatibility with non-Windows clients and encrypts authentication data but not connection data.

o Unencrypted password (PAP): This method has no encryption of user credentials or data, so it's not recommended for most applications.

o Allow machine certificate authentication for IKEv2: This method authenticates the client computer with a digital certificate and can be used only when the tunnel type is L2TP/IPsec.

o Allow remote systems to connect without authentication: This method allows anonymous authentication, meaning no user credentials are required. It should be used only to test other aspects of the remote access connection.

- *Accounting provider*—Options are Windows Accounting, RADIUS Accounting, and none. If you leave Windows Accounting selected (the default), the server logs information about remote access connections in the log files configured in the Logging tab. If you select RADIUS Accounting, connection information is sent to a RADIUS server for logging.

- *Allow custom IPsec policy for L2TP/IKEv2 connection*—If you select this option, you must supply a preshared key for all connections using the custom IPsec policy.

- *SSL Certificate Binding*—If you're using the SSTP tunneling type, you can click the Use HTTP check box to specify that SSTP should use the same certificate as the HTTP server. Otherwise, you select the certificate in the Certificate drop-down list. The certificate must already be installed.

Configuring Available Tunnel Types   When a VPN client attempts to connect to a VPN, it tries to use each of the tunneling types until it's successful or the connection fails. By default, each tunneling type is enabled in the RRAS service when you configure a VPN, and each type allows up to 128 connections or ports. You can configure the number of ports in the Routing and Remote Access console by right-clicking Ports and clicking Properties. In the Ports Properties dialog box, double-click a tunnel type to see the Configure Device dialog box, where you can change the maximum number of ports (see Figure 5-13). Changing the number of ports to 0 effectively disables the tunnel type. You can also disable inbound remote access connections for that tunnel type, which also disables the tunnel type.

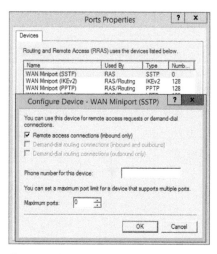

Figure 5-13   Configuring port properties

Configuring Network Policies As discussed, you can configure a user's account to allow connecting to the network via remote access, but controlling remote access permissions with network policies is more efficient. Network policies are discussed more in Chapter 6, but this section gives you a brief introduction. By default, a user account's Network Access Permission attribute is set to "Control access through NPS Network Policy" in the Dial-in tab of the user account's Properties dialog box, and the default NPS Network Policy disallows all remote access. So to make a remote access server useful, you must change the Network Access Permission attribute to "Allow access" on user accounts or configure an NPS network policy.

You configure a network policy in the Network Policy Server console (accessed via the Tools menu in Server Manager). Follow these steps to configure a remote access policy for RRAS:

1. In the Network Policy Server console, click to expand Policies in the left pane (see Figure 5-14). Right-click Network Policies and click New to start the New Network Policy Wizard.

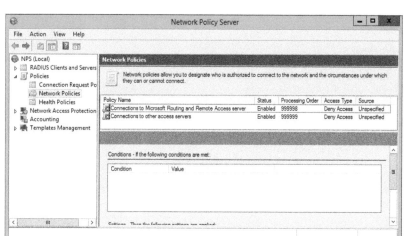

Figure 5-14   The Network Policy Server console

2. In the Specify Network Policy Name and Connection Type window, type a name for the policy. Click the "Type of network access server" list arrow, and click Remote Access Server (VPN-Dial up) in the list (see Figure 5-15). Click Next.

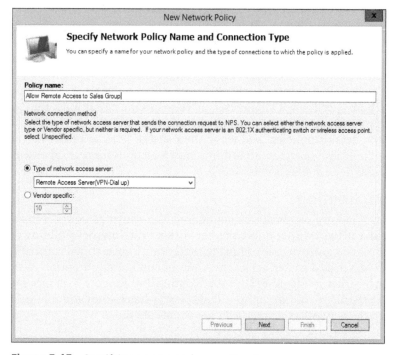

Figure 5-15   Specifying a name and connection type

3. In the Specify Conditions window, click Add, and you can choose from a list of conditions (see Figure 5-16). There are many types of conditions, including group membership, IP address, authentication type, and tunnel type, and you can combine conditions in a single policy. Click the User Groups condition, and then click Add.

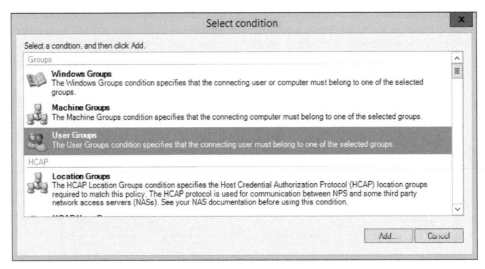

Figure 5-16 Selecting a condition

4. Add the group or groups in the User Groups dialog box, and click OK. Click Next, and then specify whether access should be granted or denied.

5. Next, you specify the authentication method, which can be any of the methods discussed earlier in "Configuring Remote Access Security."

6. In the Configure Constraints window, you can specify other restrictions, such as day and time restrictions and timeouts.

7. In the Configure Settings window, you can configure RADIUS attributes, Network Access Protection (NAP) enforcement, filters, and encryption settings.

8. After reviewing your settings, click Finish in the last window to create the policy.

After you create network policies and an attempt is made to connect via remote access, the policies are evaluated to determine whether the connection should be permitted. If the connection attempt doesn't match any of the policies that allow a connection, or if it matches a policy that denies the connection, the connection is denied. Policies are evaluated in the order you see them in the Network Policy Server console, so it's always a good idea to list the most specific policies first (those specifying a single user or very specific conditions, for example). You can change a policy's order in the list by right-clicking it and clicking Move Up or Move Down. Don't delete the default policies, and leave them at the bottom of the list because they're a safeguard: Any policies you create that don't match a connection attempt are matched by the default policies, and the connection is denied.

Configuring Routing

Using RRAS, a Windows server can be configured as a router to connect multiple subnets (see Figure 5-17) in a network or connect the network to the Internet. Windows Server 2012/R2 supports static routing and dynamic routing with Routing Information Protocol Version 2 (RIPv2). To configure a server as a router, select the Custom configuration option in the Configuration window (shown earlier in Figure 5-2) of the Routing and Remote Access Server Setup Wizard, and then select the LAN routing option. If the server has two or more interfaces, packets are routed between the networks the interfaces are connected to.

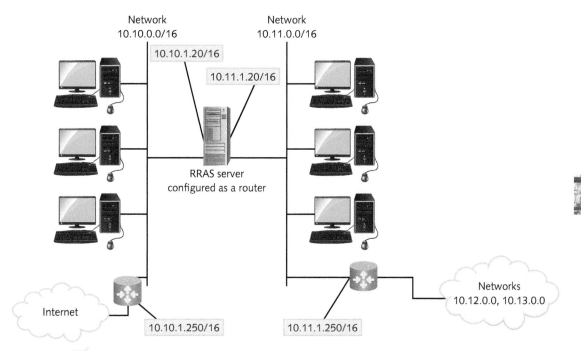

Figure 5-17   An RRAS server configured as a router
© *2015 Cengage Learning*®

By default, only IPv4 routing is enabled. If you want to route IPv6 packets, right-click the server in the Routing and Remote Access console and click Properties. In the General tab, click the IPv6 Router check box.

Routing Tables   A router determines where to send packets it receives by consulting a routing table. A **routing table** is a list of network destinations, along with information on which interface can be used to reach the destination (see Figure 5-18). The routing table in this figure matches the drawing in Figure 5-17. The routing table has the following columns of information:

W2K12R2-TEST - IP Routing Table						☒
Destination	Network mask	Gateway	Interface	Metric	Protocol	
0.0.0.0	0.0.0.0	10.10.1.250	Ethernet	261	Network management	
10.10.0.0	255.255.0.0	0.0.0.0	Ethernet	261	Local	
10.10.1.20	255.255.255.255	0.0.0.0	Ethernet	261	Local	
10.10.255.255	255.255.255.255	0.0.0.0	Ethernet	261	Local	
10.11.0.0	255.255.0.0	0.0.0.0	Ethernet 2	261	Local	
10.11.1.20	255.255.255.255	0.0.0.0	Ethernet 2	261	Local	
10.11.255.255	255.255.255.255	0.0.0.0	Ethernet 2	261	Local	
127.0.0.0	255.0.0.0	127.0.0.1	Loopback	51	Local	
127.0.0.1	255.255.255.255	127.0.0.1	Loopback	306	Local	
224.0.0.0	240.0.0.0	0.0.0.0	Ethernet 2	261	Local	
255.255.255.255	255.255.255.255	0.0.0.0	Ethernet 2	261	Local	

Figure 5-18   A routing table

- *Destination*—The destination network or host address. In most cases, this column is a network address but can also be a host or broadcast address. A value of 0.0.0.0 indicates a default route or default gateway. The **default route** is where the router sends all packets that don't match any other destinations in the routing table. If there's no default route, the router discards packets that don't match a destination in the table. The destination 255.255.255.255 is the local broadcast address. Destination 224.0.0.0 is for multicast packets, and entries beginning with 127 are for the loopback address.

- *Network mask*—The subnet mask for the corresponding address in the Destination column. A mask of 0.0.0.0 is used for the default route, and a mask of 255.255.255.255 indicates a host address rather than a network address; it's sometimes referred to as a "host route."

- *Gateway*—The address to which packets are forwarded that matches the destination address/network mask; also referred to as the "next hop address." If there are two or more identical Destination and Network mask columns, the Metric column is used to decide which gateway address to use. If the Gateway column is 0.0.0.0, the destination address is connected directly to an interface.

- *Interface*—The interface used to reach the destination address.

- *Metric*—The value assigned to the route. Lower metrics take precedence when there are two or more routes to the same destination.

- *Protocol*—Reports how the route was derived. The value "Local" indicates the route is connected directly to an interface. The value "Network management" means the route was derived internally, usually by a default gateway assignment in the interface's IP address configuration. Other values include "Static," which indicates an administrator added the route to the table, and "RIP," which means the route was derived from the RIP routing protocol.

Configuring Static Routes

After routing is enabled, you can add routing protocols and configure static routes. When a router receives packets on one interface, it consults its routing table to determine where to send the packet to get the packet to its destination. If there's no entry in the routing table that matches the destination network in the packet, the router forwards the packet via the default route, if it's configured. If no default route is configured, the router discards the packet. Examine Figure 5-17 and Figure 5-18 again. The RRAS server can route packets between the 10.10.0.0 and 10.11.0.0 networks because it has an interface configured in both networks. It can also route packets to the Internet because it has a default route configured for the router at 10.10.1.250. However, it can't route packets to 10.12.0.0 or 10.13.0.0 because it doesn't have a route to those networks. In fact, the RRAS server attempts to send packets to the 10.10.1.250 router to get packets to the 10.12.0.0 or 10.13.0.0 networks. The solution to this problem is **static routes**, which instruct the router where to send packets destined for particular networks. An IPv4 static route has the following pieces of information, as shown in Figure 5-19:

- *Interface*—Select which interface should be used to reach the destination network.

- *Destination*—The network address. If you're creating a static default route, use 0.0.0.0 as the destination network.

- *Network mask*—The subnet mask for the destination network. For a static default route, use 0.0.0.0 as the subnet mask.

- *Gateway*—The address of the router to which packets should be sent to reach the destination network. An address of 0.0.0.0 indicates the destination is directly connected.

- *Metric*—A value assigned to the route; used by the router to determine which gateway to use if there are identical routes.

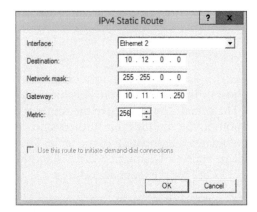

Figure 5-19   An IPv4 static route

In Figure 5-19, a static route is created for network 10.12.0.0, shown previously in Figure 5-17. A similar route should be added to reach network 10.13.0.0 to arrive at the routing table shown in Figure 5-20.

W2K12R2-TEST - IP Routing Table						
Destination	Network mask	Gateway	Interface	Metric	Protocol	
0.0.0.0	0.0.0.0	10.10.1.250	Ethernet	261	Network management	
10.10.0.0	255.255.0.0	0.0.0.0	Ethernet	261	Local	
10.10.1.20	255.255.255.255	0.0.0.0	Ethernet	261	Local	
10.10.255.255	255.255.255.255	0.0.0.0	Ethernet	261	Local	
10.11.0.0	255.255.0.0	0.0.0.0	Ethernet 2	261	Local	
10.11.1.20	255.255.255.255	0.0.0.0	Ethernet 2	261	Local	
10.11.255.255	255.255.255.255	0.0.0.0	Ethernet 2	261	Local	
10.12.0.0	255.255.0.0	10.11.1.250	Ethernet 2	261	Static (non demand-...	
10.13.0.0	255.255.0.0	10.11.1.250	Ethernet 2	261	Static (non demand-...	
127.0.0.0	255.0.0.0	127.0.0.1	Loopback	51	Local	
127.0.0.1	255.255.255.255	127.0.0.1	Loopback	306	Local	
224.0.0.0	240.0.0.0	0.0.0.0	Ethernet 2	261	Local	
255.255.255.255	255.255.255.255	0.0.0.0	Ethernet 2	261	Local	

Figure 5-20   A routing table with static routes

Static routes can be configured at the command line, too. The following command adds a route to network 10.12.0.0, using gateway 10.11.1.250. The interface doesn't need to be included because the interface connected to the gateway network is used by default. The metric uses the default value for the interface:

```
route add 10.12.0.0 mask 255.255.0.0 10.11.1.250
```

Here's the PowerShell cmdlet to add a static route:

```
New-NetRoute -DestinationPrefix "10.12.0.0/16" InterfaceAlias
  "Ethernet 2" -NextHop 10.11.1.250
```

Routes created at the command line aren't listed as static routes in the routing table in RRAS; they're listed as network management routes.

Configuring Routing Information Protocol   As mentioned, Windows Server 2012/ R2 supports dynamic routing with RIPv2. To configure RIPv2, you must have configured routing on the RRAS server first. In the Routing and Remote Access console, under the IPv4 node, right-click General and click New Routing Protocol. Select RIP Version 2 for Internet Protocol in the New Routing Protocol dialog box, and then RIP is added under the IPv4 node.

Next, you need to configure RIP by enabling it on interfaces that RIP uses to send and receive routing information. Right-click the RIP node and click New Interface, and then select the interface. Repeat this step for each interface RIP uses. RIP should be enabled only on interfaces connected to the internal network, not interfaces connected to the Internet.

RIPv2 works by communicating with other routers on the internetwork. Each router that uses RIPv2 sends a copy of its routing table to other RIPv2 routers on the same network; these routers are called "neighbors." Routing table information is passed along from neighbor to neighbor until all routers on the internetwork know about each network and how to get there. RIPv2 uses the **hop count** metric for determining the best path to a network; it's the number of routers a packet must go through to reach the destination network.

Several other routing protocols are used by commercial routers in large internetworks; they're more complex and more efficient than RIP. One example is Open Shortest Path First (OSPF), a routing protocol that determines the best path by using the speed (or cost) of each link in the path from source network to destination network.

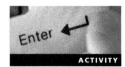

Activity 5-4: Configuring Routing

Time Required: 15 minutes
Objective: Configure routing in the Routing and Remote Access console.

Required Tools and Equipment: 411Server2

Description: In this activity, you disable RRAS, and then you enable and configure routing. You also create a static route and configure the RIPv2 routing protocol.

1. Log on to 411Server2 as **Administrator**, if necessary.

2. Open the Routing and Remote Access console. Right-click **411Server2** and click **Disable Routing and Remote Access.** When prompted, click **Yes.** The RRAS service stops, and you see the red down arrow on the 411Server2 icon to indicate that the service is disabled.

3. Right-click **411Server2** and click **Configure and Enable Routing and Remote Access.** Click **Next** in the Welcome window.

4. In the Configuration window, click **Custom configuration**, and then click **Next.**

5. In the Custom Configuration window, click **LAN routing**, and then click **Next.**

6. Click **Finish.** When prompted, click **Start service.**

7. The server routes between known networks in its routing table by default. Click to expand the **IPv4** node, and then right-click **Static Routes** and click **Show IP Routing Table.** You see entries for the default route, the 10.11.0.0 network, the 203.0.113.0 network, the loopback network, and other host and broadcast routes. Close the routing table.

8. To create a static route, right-click **Static Routes** and click **New Static Route.** In the Destination text box, type **203.0.114.0**, and in the Network mask text box, type **255.255.255.0.** In the Gateway text box, type **203.0.113.1**, and then click **OK.** The route is added to the list of static routes.

9. Right-click **Static Routes** and click **Show IP Routing Table** to verify that the route is in the routing table. Close the routing table.

10. To enable RIPv2, right-click **General** under IPv4 and click **New Routing Protocol.** In the New Routing Protocol dialog box, click **RIP version 2 for Internet Protocol**, and then click **OK.**

11. By default, no interfaces are enabled for RIP. In the Routing and Remote Access console, right-click **RIP** under IPv4 and click **New Interface.** Click the first interface listed, and then click **OK.** In the RIP Properties dialog box, you can change settings for the RIPv2 routing protocol. For this activity, just click **OK.** Repeat this step, selecting the second interface.

12. Right-click **RIP** and click **Show Neighbors.** Any other routers in the networks connected to either of 411Server2's interfaces are listed here. Close the RIP Neighbors dialog box.

13. Disable Routing and Remote Access. To reset your network interfaces, restart 411Server2, and leave it running for the next activity.

Configuring Network Address Translation

Network Address Translation (NAT) is a process whereby a router or other type of gateway device replaces the source or destination IP addresses in a packet before forwarding the packet. It's used mainly to allow networks to use private IP addressing while connected to the Internet. It does this by replacing private IP addresses with public IP addresses in outgoing packets and replacing public IP addresses with private IP addresses in incoming packets.

This process allows any number of companies to use private IP addresses in their own network, requiring a public IP address only when a workstation attempts to access the Internet. Therefore, NAT reduces the number of public IP addresses needed. A drawback of NAT is that one public address is required for every computer with an active connection to the Internet. However, it's usually used only for Web servers and other devices that must be accessed through the Internet.

An extension of NAT, called **Port Address Translation (PAT)**, allows several hundred workstations to access the Internet with a single public Internet address. This process relies on each packet containing not only source and destination IP addresses, but also source and destination TCP or UDP port numbers. With PAT, the address is translated into a single public IP address for all workstations, but a different source port number (which can be any value from 1024 to 65,535) is used for each communication session, allowing a NAT device to differentiate between workstations. The device configured as a NAT router keeps track of the active translations using a NAT table. When you configure Windows RRAS for NAT, you're actually configuring PAT.

To configure NAT in the Routing and Remote Access Server Setup Wizard, select the "Network address translation (NAT)" option in the Configuration window. For LAN-based Internet access, choose the interface connected to the Internet in the NAT Internet Connection window (see Figure 5-21). If the Internet connection is dial-up, you can choose the option to create a new demand-dial interface to the Internet. A **demand-dial interface** is an interface that's activated when a client attempts to connect to the Internet, such as a dial-up modem or Point-to-Point Protocol over Ethernet (PPPoE) connection. The IP address of the interface you choose is used for all address translations.

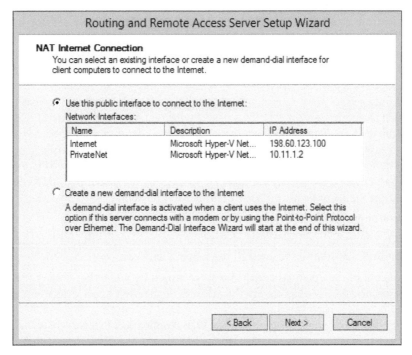

Figure 5-21   The NAT Internet Connection window

Figure 5-22 shows what a NAT configuration might look like along with the NAT table. In this figure, when a computer on the private network tries to access the Internet, the source address and source port number in the packet are translated to the public address of the NAT router's Internet interface and a port number before being delivered to the Internet. The port number may or may not stay the same in the private and public addresses. When a device on the Internet responds, the destination public address and port number are translated back to the private address and port number before being delivered to the host on the private network.

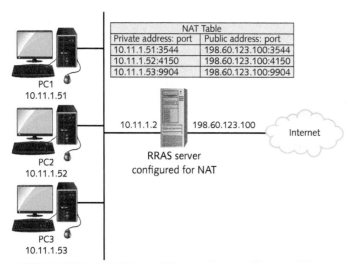

NAT Table	
Private address: port	Public address: port
10.11.1.51:3544	198.60.123.100:3544
10.11.1.52:4150	198.60.123.100:4150
10.11.1.53:9904	198.60.123.100:9904

PC1
10.11.1.51

PC2
10.11.1.52

PC3
10.11.1.53

10.11.1.2   198.60.123.100   Internet

RRAS server
configured for NAT

Figure 5-22   A Windows server configured as a NAT router
© *2015 Cengage Learning®*

Configuring Web Application Proxy

Web Application Proxy is a new Routing and Remote Access role service in Windows Server 2012 R2. It allows remote users to access network applications from any device that supports a Web browser. Applications made available to users with this method are said to be "published applications." Published applications can also be accessed from an Office client or a Windows store app.

Web Application Proxy works with Active Directory Federation Services (AD FS) to enable features such as single sign-on. AD FS is used to authenticate and authorize users who attempt to access a published application and protects the network from unmanaged devices, such as smartphones and tablets. AD FS is a complex server role that requires multiple servers to deploy and is beyond the scope of this book; however, it's covered in *MCSA Guide to Configuring Advanced Windows Server 2012/R2 Services, Exam 70-412* (Cengage Learning, 2015). Some requirements for configuring Web Application Proxy include the following:

- A functioning AD FS deployment on the network
- Two NICs installed on the Web Application Proxy server with one NIC accessible to the Internet and the other connected to the private network
- A certificate in the Personal certificate store issued by a CA that covers the federation service name and one that covers the address of the Web application you publish

Here are the basic steps for configuring Web Application Proxy:

1. Install the Remote Access server role and the Web Application Proxy role service.
2. Open the Remote Access Management console from the Tools menu in Server Manager, and click Web Application Proxy in the left pane (see Figure 5-23).
3. Click the Run the Web Application Proxy Configuration Wizard link, and then click Next in the Welcome window.
4. In the Federation Server window, enter the FQDN of the server running AD FS, and enter the credentials of the local administrator account on the federation servers. Click Next.
5. In the AD FS Proxy Certificate window, select the certificate to be used by the AD FS proxy. The certificate must have already been installed in the server's Personal certificate store. Click Next.
6. Click Configure in the Confirmation window.

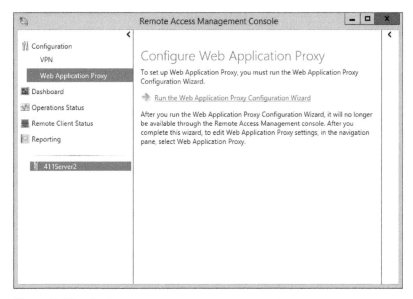

Figure 5-23   The Remote Access Management console

After Web Application Proxy is configured, you can begin publishing applications. To do so, in the Remote Access Management console, click Web Application Proxy, and click Publish to start the Publish New Application Wizard, which guides you through the process. You enter a name for the application, an external URL for users to access the application, a certificate for the application, and the URL of a backend server (if it's different from the external URL). The external and backend server URLs must be able to be resolved through DNS to the IP address of the Web Application Proxy server's external interface.

The DirectAccess Role Service

The DirectAccess role service is part of the DirectAccess and VPN role service under the Remote Access server role. It became available with Windows Server 2008 R2 and has become more streamlined in Windows Server 2012/R2. Most implementations of DirectAccess in Windows Server 2008 R2 were made with the software platform Forefront Unified Access Gateway (UAG), which required installing a downloaded software package separately. DirectAccess in Windows Server 2008 R2 is a separate server role, but it's now combined with Remote Access and is configured in the Remote Access Management console.

As mentioned, DirectAccess provides many of the same features as a VPN but adds client management and always-connected capability. DirectAccess uses IPv6 and IPsec to create secure connections to the network and almost eliminates client connection problems caused by firewall settings. On networks that don't yet fully support IPv6, transition technologies, such as 6to4, Teredo, and IP-HTTPS, are used to allow IPv6 clients to access IPv6 resources across an IPv4 Internet or intranet.

IPv6 transition technologies are discussed in *MCSA Guide to Installing and Configuring Windows Server 2012/R2, Exam 70-410* (Cengage Learning, 2015).

DirectAccess Requirements

In Windows Server 2008 R2, with Windows 7 clients, setting up DirectAccess was a fairly complex task. In Windows Server 2012/R2, when using only Windows 8/8.1 clients, a basic DirectAccess configuration is only slightly more complicated than setting up a VPN. The following sections list requirements for the DirectAccess server and clients. These requirements are for a basic configuration, using Windows Server 2012/R2 and Windows 8/8.1 and the Getting Started Wizard in the Remote Access Management console. Optional configurations are listed, too.

DirectAccess Server Requirements The following are requirements for DirectAccess in Windows Server 2012/R2:

- *Two NICs, as for a VPN server*—Although a single-NIC setup is possible, the two-NIC solution is preferred. Like a VPN server, one NIC is connected to the private network, and the other is connected to the Internet.

- *The server must be a domain member*—DirectAccess is a remote access solution best suited for enterprise networks, and tight control over servers and clients is one of the goals. In addition, much of the server and client configuration is done with group policies.

- *A public IP address*—When configuring DirectAccess, you need to enter a public IP address or a FQDN that can be resolved to a public IP address associated with the DirectAccess server. The public address can be configured on the interface connected to the Internet or an address that's translated by a NAT router to an address assigned to the DirectAccess Internet-connected interface.

You might be asking "What about encryption and authentication?" A big improvement in DirectAccess in Windows Server 2012/R2 and Windows 8/8.1 is the option for the DirectAccess server to use self-signed certificates and Kerberos proxy for authentication and encryption. **Kerberos proxy** allows a client computer to authenticate to a domain controller, using the DirectAccess server as a proxy. The client computer is issued a certificate through Kerberos, which is used with the user's domain credentials to establish an authenticated and secure communication session with IPsec and IPv6.

Optional Server Configurations The preceding server requirements are for a basic DirectAccess configuration. The following is a list of recommended enhancements for production environments or when there are multiple DirectAccess servers providing remote access connectivity.

- *An internal PKI*—A PKI is a system for managing digital certificates for use in public key cryptography. At the heart of a PKI is a CA that issues certificates. It can be a public entity, such as VeriSign, that issues certificates to organizations for use in public key encryption applications, such as HTTPS, or you can set up an internal PKI with Active Directory Certificate Services.

- *SSL certificate issued by a public CA for IP-HTTPS*—**Internet Protocol-Hypertext Transfer Protocol Secure (IP-HTTPS)** is a tunneling protocol used to transport IPv6 packets over an HTTPS connection. The DirectAccess Getting Started Wizard issues a self-signed certificate if you don't install one issued by a CA. Self-signed certificates are okay for testing, but they can be spoofed easily and generally shouldn't be used for production networks.

- *SSL certificate issued by an internal PKI for Network Location Server*—A **Network Location Server (NLS)** is a basic Web server used by DirectAccess client computers to determine whether they're on the main network or a remote network. If the client determines it's on the main network, it turns off the connection to the DirectAccess server. The DirectAccess Getting Started Wizard installs NLS on the DirectAccess server and issues a self-signed certificate by default; however, a separate server with a certificate issued by an internal PKI is recommended.

- *Computer certificate issued by an internal PKI for IPsec authentication*—DirectAccess uses IPsec for secure packet transport and computer authentication. Both the client computer and the server must have a certificate for authentication and encryption. However, because Kerberos proxy is used in Windows Server 2012/R2 and Windows 8/8.1, there's no need for computer certificates issued by a PKI. This solution works only with a single DirectAccess server, however, meaning you can't have multisite DirectAccess or use DirectAccess in a server cluster.

- *Two consecutive public IP addresses*—This configuration is recommended for optimal operation. It was a strict requirement with Windows Server 2008 R2 because UAG relied on Teredo for the IPv4-to-IPv6 transition technology. With Windows Server 2012/R2, the DirectAccess server needs only one public IP address or even none if the server will be behind a NAT router because it can use IP-HTTPS.

DirectAccess Client Requirements   There's nothing special about the client configuration because no special software needs to be installed on clients. DirectAccess works by using standard Windows client software and IPv6 technology built into current Windows OSs. The following is a list of requirements for DirectAccess clients:

- Must be running at least Windows 7 Enterprise or Ultimate or Windows 8/8.1 Enterprise, Windows Server 2008 R2, or Windows Server 2012/R2. To use the basic configuration generated by the Getting Started Wizard, you need Windows 8/8.1 Enterprise or Windows Server 2012/R2 clients.

- The client must be a domain member. Client configuration is done strictly with the Group Policy tool, so the client must be a member of a domain so that it can download group policy settings from a DC.

- IPv6 must be enabled on the client. By default, IPv6 is enabled on the supported client OSs, so this is a concern only if IPv6 was disabled or unbound from the NIC.

How DirectAccess Connections Work

Before you learn more about deploying DirectAccess, take a look at how a DirectAccess connection is established from client to DirectAccess server. As mentioned, users don't have to do anything to initiate a DirectAccess connection. The built-in Windows software with IPv6 attempts to connect whenever the computer is connected to the Internet rather than the company network. The following steps explain this process:

1. The DirectAccess client computer detects that it has a valid network connection.

2. Using an NLS server, the client determines whether it's connected to the Internet or the company network by attempting to connect to the URL of the NLS server via HTTPS (this URL is configured in a group policy), which is available only on the company network. If it can connect to the NLS, the computer knows it's on the company network. In this case, no DirectAccess connection is made, and the process stops. If it isn't connected to the company network, the process continues to the next step.

3. The DirectAccess client attempts to connect to the DirectAccess server via IPv6 and IPsec. Depending on the server configuration, the client uses 6to4, Teredo, or IP-HTTPS, in that order, to try to connect over an IPv4 Internet connection. If a native IPv6 connection to the DirectAccess server is available, no transition technology is needed. The 6to4 or Teredeo technology is preferred but can be blocked by a firewall or if the client is using a proxy server to connect to the Internet. 6to4 is used only if the client is using a public IPv4 address. Teredo is used only if the DirectAccess server has two consecutive public IP addresses.

4. The DirectAccess client and server authenticate with each other, using computer certificates issued by a PKI or Kerberos proxy.

All these steps take place when the client computer is turned on or connected to a new network. A user doesn't need to be logged on. At this point, the **infrastructure tunnel** has been created between the client computer and the DirectAccess server. When a user logs on, the DirectAccess client establishes the **intranet tunnel** with user account credentials, which provides access to resources on the company network. When a client requests access to a network resource, traffic is forwarded from the DirectAccess server to the resource.

If you have set up Network Access Protection configured for health validation, the DirectAccess client must get a valid health certificate before it's connected to the network. NAP is discussed in Chapter 6.

Installing and Configuring DirectAccess

This section describes a basic DirectAccess configuration, which requires only a domain controller, a member server for installing the DirectAccess role service, and a client computer. For this basic test configuration, the network is configured similar to Figure 5-24. The Internet is simulated by a router with connections to two interfaces: one for the network the DirectAccess client is on and one for the network the DirectAccess server's public interface is on. The DirectAccess server has two interfaces, one connected to the network and the other to the Internet with a public IP address. The DirectAccess server is not behind a NAT router.

These steps use the Getting Started Wizard, which is fine for a test environment. However, this wizard configures DirectAccess in a very basic way, using self-signed certificates for authentication and disabling Teredo. For security and the most flexible client configuration, it's recommended that you run the Remote Access Setup Wizard and use certificates issued by a CA.

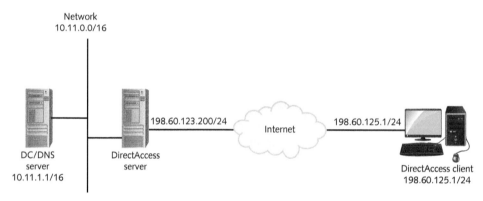

Figure 5-24   A DirectAccess test network

© 2015 Cengage Learning®

Here are the steps for configuring DirectAccess with the Getting Started Wizard, using the network configuration in Figure 5-24:

1. On the domain controller, create a global security group named DA-Computers (or a similar name). Add to this group the computer accounts you want to be able to connect to the network via DirectAccess. This step isn't required, but it's recommended because the default settings apply DirectAccess client settings to all mobile computers in the domain.

2. Install the DirectAccess role service, if necessary. If the Remote Access server role is installed for VPN connections, the DirectAccess role service is already installed.

3. Open the Remote Access Management console from the Tools menu in Server Manager. Under Configuration in the left pane, click DirectAccess and VPN. Click the Run the Getting Started Wizard link in the right pane.

4. In the Configure Remote Access window, click Deploy DirectAccess only (see Figure 5-25). The wizard verifies that your server meets the prerequisites for deployment.

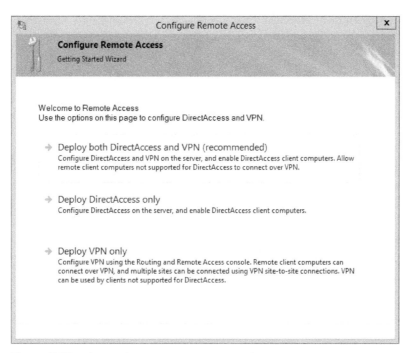

Figure 5-25   The Configure Remote Access window

5. In the Remote Access Server Setup window, you choose the network topology and enter the server's name or IPv4 address. The default option, Edge, is similar to Figure 5-24, where one interface of the DirectAccess server is connected to the network and the other directly to the Internet. The next option, "Behind an edge device (with two network adapters)," is similar, but one adapter is connected to a perimeter network behind a firewall and the other to the company network. For the last option, "Behind an edge device (with one network adapter)," the DirectAccess server is connected only to the network, and NAT is used to translate a public address to the private address assigned to the interface. For the purposes of this example, choose Edge. In the text box, type the DirectAccess server's public IPv4 address, which is 198.60.123.200 for this example (see Figure 5-26).

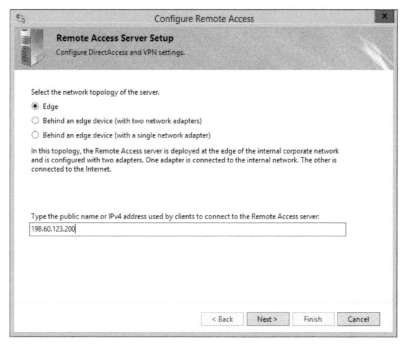

Figure 5-26   The Remote Access Server Setup window

6. In the next window, click the link to edit the wizard settings. You see a summary of the configuration settings (see Figure 5-27).

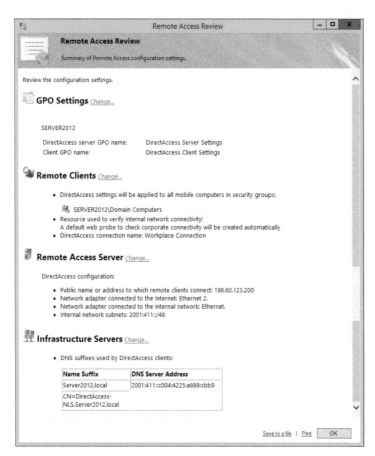

Figure 5-27   The Remote Access Review window

7. Click the Change link next to Remote Clients. In the DirectAccess Client Setup window, you can change the default group. Click the Remove button to remove the Domain Computers group, click Add, type DA-Computers, and click OK. Then click to clear the "Enable DirectAccess for mobile computers only" check box (see Figure 5-28). This setting changes

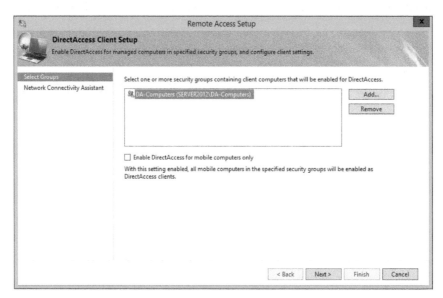

Figure 5-28   The DirectAccess Client Setup window

the scope of the group policy so that only computers in the DA-Computers group are affected by the DirectAccess Client Settings GPO. If you leave this check box selected, a Windows Management Instrumentation (WMI) filter is applied to the GPO so that only computers identified as laptops are enabled for DirectAccess. For a production deployment, this setting might be what you want, but not for testing. Click Next, and then click Finish.

8. Back in the Remote Access Review window, click OK, and then click Finish. The necessary GPOs are created, and settings for the DirectAccess server are applied. The NLS server is configured, and self-signed certificates are generated for IP-HTTPS and the NLS server. Click Close, and you're back in the Remote Access Management console (see Figure 5-29). If necessary, you can click the Edit button to change any settings for DirectAccess components.

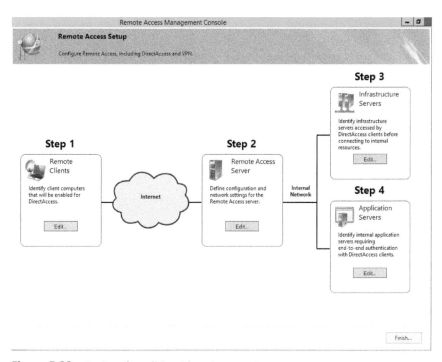

Figure 5-29 Options for editing DirectAccess components

9. The only step left is verifying and testing the configuration. If you click Operations Status in the left pane of the Remote Access Management console, you see the window shown in Figure 5-30, assuming everything is working as planned. If any component doesn't

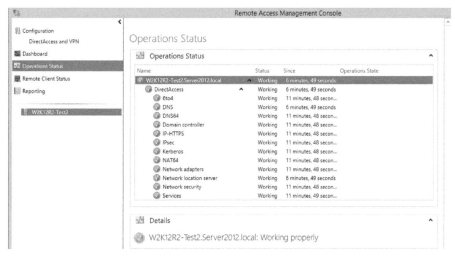

Figure 5-30 Viewing the status of DirectAccess operation

show a check mark in a green circle, you can click it to see additional information and troubleshooting suggestions. A question mark in a blue circle means the status can't yet be determined. Press F5 or click Refresh in the Tasks pane to refresh the screen; it might take a while for DirectAccess to determine a component's status.

To test the DirectAccess configuration with a client computer, follow these steps:

1. Use domain credentials to log on to a Windows 8/8.1 Enterprise computer that's a domain member. The client computer needs to be connected to the network at this point.

2. If the client computer was already on, open a command prompt window and enter the gpupdate command to be sure the computer gets the client configuration settings from group policies.

3. Open a PowerShell prompt, type Get-DAConnectionStatus, and press Enter. You should see output similar to Figure 5-31, showing that the DirectAccess Connection Assistant (DCA) has determined you're on the company network (connected locally). If you see an error stating that the Network Connectivity Assistant isn't responding, restart the computer, and make sure you're running Windows 8 or later Enterprise Edition.

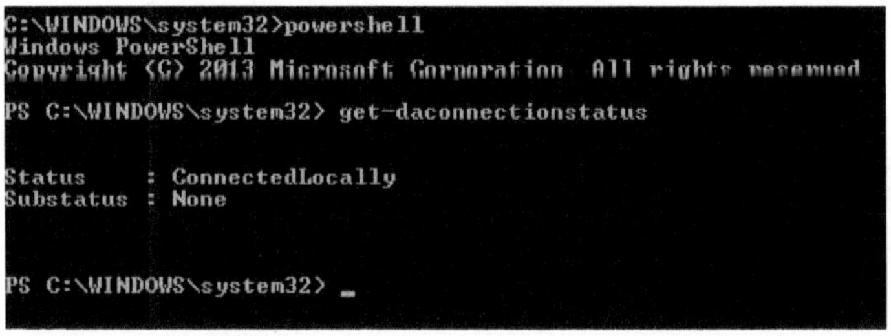

```
C:\WINDOWS\system32>powershell
Windows PowerShell
Copyright (C) 2013 Microsoft Corporation. All rights reserved.

PS C:\WINDOWS\system32> get-daconnectionstatus


Status     : ConnectedLocally
Substatus  : None


PS C:\WINDOWS\system32> _
```

Figure 5-31   Results of the Get-DAConnectionStatus cmdlet

4. Shut down the client computer, and connect it to the public (Internet) side of the network. Make sure it can get an IP address configuration via DHCP and can communicate with the public interface on the DirectAccess server.

5. Turn on the client computer, and log on with domain credentials. Open a PowerShell prompt, type Get-DAConnectionStatus, and press Enter. Then type ping *server* (replacing *server* with the name of the domain controller in the network). You should see output similar to Figure 5-32 for both commands, showing that you're connected via DirectAccess, and the connection is using IPv6.

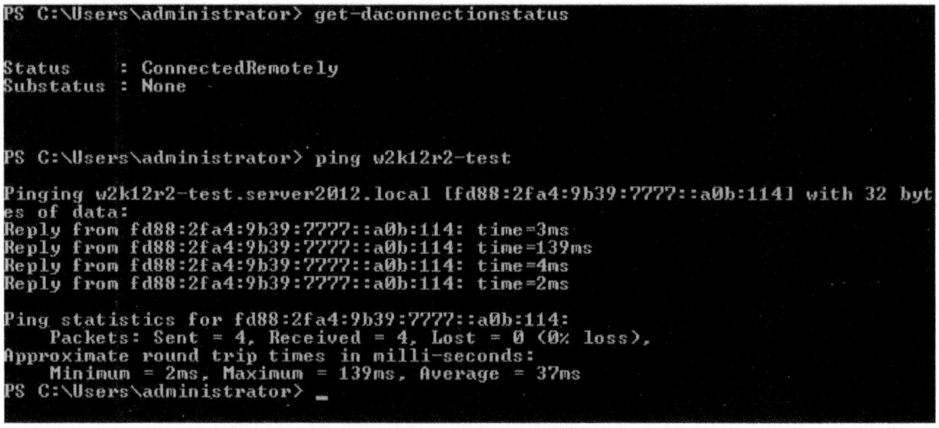

```
PS C:\Users\administrator> get-daconnectionstatus


Status     : ConnectedRemotely
Substatus  : None



PS C:\Users\administrator> ping w2k12r2-test

Pinging w2k12r2-test.server2012.local [fd88:2fa4:9b39:7777::a0b:114] with 32 byt
es of data:
Reply from fd88:2fa4:9b39:7777::a0b:114: time=3ms
Reply from fd88:2fa4:9b39:7777::a0b:114: time=139ms
Reply from fd88:2fa4:9b39:7777::a0b:114: time=4ms
Reply from fd88:2fa4:9b39:7777::a0b:114: time=2ms

Ping statistics for fd88:2fa4:9b39:7777::a0b:114:
    Packets: Sent = 4, Received = 4, Lost = 0 (0% loss),
Approximate round trip times in milli-seconds:
    Minimum = 2ms, Maximum = 139ms, Average = 37ms
PS C:\Users\administrator> _
```

Figure 5-32   The DirectAccess connection status and ping results

6. Last, click the network icon in the notification tray. You see the list of connected networks (see Figure 5-33). The Workplace Connection is the DirectAccess connection.

Figure 5-33   List of connected networks

Activity 5-5: Configuring DirectAccess

 This activity requires moving the 411Win8 computer from the "private" network to the "public" network to simulate a mobile device. You also need to assign a public IP address to the "Internet" connection on the DirectAccess server. The wizard won't continue if you try to use a private IP address.

Time Required: 20 minutes
Objective: Configure DirectAccess.

Required Tools and Equipment: 411Server1 and 411Server2
Description: First, you create a security group to identify which computers in the domain can connect to the network via DirectAccess. Next, you run the Getting Started Wizard, and then verify and test the configuration. At first, the client computer is attached to the network. After DirectAccess has been configured and the client configuration has been downloaded via Group Policy, you move the client to the "public" network to simulate an Internet connection and then verify connectivity on the client. Figure 5-34 shows the topology for this activity. You use 203.0.113.0/24 for the public network, which is technically a public address. However, RFC 5737 has defined it for use in documentation and testing, and it shouldn't be used in a real public network. 411Win8 should be turned off for this activity. You use it in the next activity to test DirectAccess.

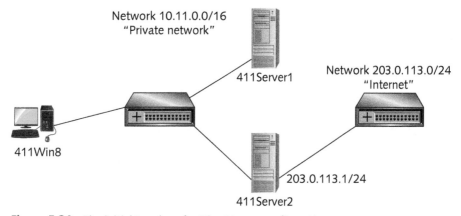

Figure 5-34   The initial topology for DirectAccess configuration
© 2015 Cengage Learning®

1. On 411Server1, log on as **Administrator**, and create a global security group in the Users folder named **DA-Computers**. Add the **411Win8** computer account as a member of this group. (When you're adding the computer to the group, be sure you add **Computers** to the list of object types in the Select Users dialog box).

2. On 411Server2, log on to the domain as **Administrator**, if necessary. (You must be logged on with the domain administrator account, not the local computer administrator account.)

3. Open Server Manager, and click **Tools, Remote Access Management** from the menu. Click **DirectAccess and VPN** under the Configuration node in the left pane. In the middle pane, you should see links to the Getting Started Wizard and the Remote Access Setup Wizard. If you don't see these links, you must disable Routing and Remote Access first. Click **Run the Getting Started Wizard.**

4. In the Configure Remote Access Window, click **Deploy DirectAccess Only.** You see a message indicating that prerequisites are being checked. If prerequisites are met, you see the Remote Access Server Setup window; if they aren't met, read the description of the problem, fix it, and restart the wizard.

5. In the Remote Access Server Setup window, leave the default topology setting **Edge**, type the public IPv4 address **203.0.113.1** in the text box, and click **Next.**

6. In the Configure Remote Access window, there are options to click Finish or click the link to edit the wizard settings. For this activity, click the **here** link to edit the settings you've made. In the Remote Access Review window, click **Change** next to Remote Clients.

7. In the DirectAccess Client Setup window, click **Domain Computers**, and then click the **Remove** button. Click the **Add** button. In the Select Groups dialog box, type **DA-Computers**, click **Check Names**, and then click **OK**. Click to clear the **Enable DirectAccess for mobile computers only** check box, and then click **Next.**

8. In the Network Connectivity Assistant window, click **Finish**. Click **OK** in the Remote Access Review window. In the Configure Remote Access window, click **Finish**. Watch some of the tasks the wizard performs, such as creating GPOs and self-signed certificates. In the Applying Getting Started Wizard Settings window, click **Close** when it's finished applying settings.

9. Back in the Remote Access Review window, click **Edit** in the Step 2 box to open the Remote Access Server Setup window and view what you can change. You can't change the topology, but you can change the IP address, the certificate used for IP-HTTPS, and the user and computer authentication method. When you have finished browsing the settings, click **Cancel**, and then click **OK.**

10. Click the **Edit** button in the Step 3 box to open the Infrastructure Setup window, where you can change the certificate for the NLS server or change the NLS deployment from the DirectAccess server to a remote Web server. Scroll through the information in the rest of the boxes, and click **Cancel** and then **OK.**

11. In the Remote Access Management console, click **Dashboard** in the left pane. You see a summary of the operations status, configuration status, and client status. All functions in the Operations Status section should display a check mark in a green circle.

12. Click **Operations Status** in the left pane. If any function doesn't have a check mark, click it to see a description of the problem in the Details pane. Assuming everything is working correctly on the DirectAccess server, it's time to see whether a client can connect, which you do in the next activity. If something isn't working, attempt to troubleshoot the problem by clicking the function and reading a description of the problem. You might also see suggestions for solving the problem. Stay logged on to 411Server2 and leave 411Server1 running.

Activity 5-6: Testing DirectAccess

Time Required: 20 minutes
Objective: Test DirectAccess.

Required Tools and Equipment: 411Server1, 411Server2, 411Win8
Description: You have installed DirectAccess on 411Server2. Everything checks out on the server, and you want to test the configuration. 411Win8 must have Windows 8.1 Enterprise Edition installed; DirectAccess isn't supported in Windows 8.1 Professional.

1. Start 411Win8 and log on to the domain as **Administrator**. Open a PowerShell prompt by right-clicking **Start**, clicking **Run**, typing **powershell**, and pressing **Enter**.

2. Type **Get-DAConnectionStatus** and press **Enter**. You should see output indicating that you're connected locally (refer back to Figure 5-31).

3. Unless there's a DHCP server on the Internet network, you need to set 411Win8's IP address. The best thing to do is set the alternate configuration, which is used if Windows can't get an address via DHCP. Right-click **Start** and click **Network Connections**. Right-click **Ethernet** and click **Properties**. Double-click **Internet Protocol Version 4 (TCP/IPv4)**, and then click the **Alternate Configuration** tab. Configure the IP settings as follows:

   IP address: **203.0.113.10**

   Subnet mask: **255.255.255.0**

   Default gateway: None or an address provided by your instructor

   Primary DNS server: None or an address provided by your instructor

4. Shut down 411Win8. Disconnect it from the domain network and connect it to the Internet network (the same network the Internet interface of 411Server2 is connected to) so that the network looks similar to Figure 5-35.

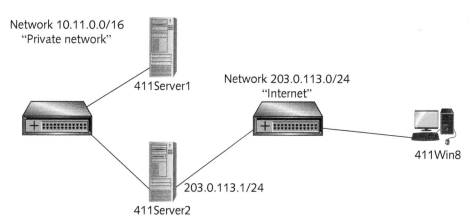

Figure 5-35   A DirectAccess network with a client connected to the "Internet"
© 2015 Cengage Learning®

5. Start 411Win8 and log on to the domain as **Administrator**.

6. Open a PowerShell prompt. Type **Get-DAConnectionStatus** and press **Enter**. You should see output indicating that you're connected remotely, similar to Figure 5-32 shown earlier. If your client isn't connected to the Internet, the output might display an error indicating that Internet connectivity is down. To show that you're connected to the private network, type **ping 411server2** and press **Enter**. You should see IPv6 ping replies.

7. Close the PowerShell window, and shut down 411Win8. Reconnect 411Win8 to the **10.11.0.0/16** network. Leave 411Server1 and 411Server2 running for the next activity.

Advanced DirectAccess Deployment Options

After you have established a basic DirectAccess configuration, you might want to add some features for security or convenience. Some options discussed in the following sections include the following:

- Setting up a PKI
- Configuring NLS on a separate Web server
- Configuring the name resolution policy table (NRPT)
- Configuring forced tunneling
- Configuring ISATAP

Setting Up a PKI   As discussed, you can configure a DirectAccess server without using a PKI but only if you're using a Windows Server 2012/R2 DirectAccess server and all your clients are Windows 8 or later. As you've learned, self-signed certificates present a security risk in production environments, and if you want to use multiple DirectAccess servers, a PKI is required because Kerberos proxy doesn't work with multiple DirectAccess servers. This section doesn't go into details of setting up a PKI, but here are the basic steps to follow:

1. On a server separate from the DirectAccess server, install Active Directory Certificate Services configured as an Enterprise Certificate Authority.

2. Issue an SSL certificate to the NLS server, set up on a server separate from the DirectAccess server (discussed in the next section).

3. Issue machine certificates to the DirectAccess server and each DirectAccess client computer. It's best to configure auto-enrollment so that each client computer can automatically request and be issued a machine certificate.

An internal PKI is highly recommended for a production DirectAccess deployment because it widens your configuration options, offering the following:

- Support for Windows 7 clients.
- Better security than self-signed certificates.
- Support for multisite DirectAccess and DirectAccess server clusters. **Multisite DirectAccess** just means there are two or more DirectAccess servers, each providing a secure entry point into the network. For example, companies with multiple locations can have a DirectAccess server in each one. A DirectAccess cluster uses Windows clustering technology for fault tolerance and load balancing.
- Support for two-factor authentication, such as smart cards.

Configuring NLS on a Separate Web Server   Even the Getting Started Wizard suggests that the NLS server should be on a separate machine from the DirectAccess server. All you need is IIS installed on any server in the network. DirectAccess clients connect to it with HTTPS, so it requires an SSL certificate. The certificate can be issued by an internal PKI because it won't be publicly accessible. You also need to make sure a DNS record is created on internal DNS servers that points to the NLS server, using a name such as nls.csmtech.local. The name is published to DirectAccess clients with a group policy. Creating a simple `Default.htm` file instead of using the IIS default home page is recommended but not necessary. You can change the NLS server in the Remote Access Management console by clicking DirectAccess and VPN under the Configuration node, and then clicking the Edit button in the Step 3 box for infrastructure servers in the Remote Access Setup window (refer back to Figure 5-29).

Configuring the Name Resolution Policy Table   When DirectAccess clients are connected to the Internet, the **name resolution policy table (NRPT)** makes sure DNS requests for network resources are directed to internal DNS servers, not Internet DNS servers. For example, if the internal DNS domain name is csmtech.local, a DNS query for server1.csmtech.local is directed to the network DNS servers. A DNS query for www.google.com, however, is sent to the DNS servers configured in the client's IP settings, usually on the ISP's network. All these settings are configured by default. However, some companies have an Internet and an intranet version of certain resources, such as Web servers. For example, internal DNS servers might return the address 10.11.1.25 when www.csmtech.local is queried, and Internet DNS servers return 203.0.113.100 for the same URL. If you want DirectAccess clients to use the Internet address, you create an exemption rule in the NRPT on client computers. Creating NRPT exemptions is referred to as "split-brain DNS." You create exemptions by following these steps:

1. On a domain controller, open the Group Policy Management console.

2. Right-click DirectAccess Client Settings and click Edit. Expand Computer Configuration, Policies, and Windows Settings, and click Name Resolution Policy. In the right pane, click the DNS Settings for DirectAccess tab, and then click the "Enable DNS settings for DirectAccess in this rule" check box (see Figure 5-36).

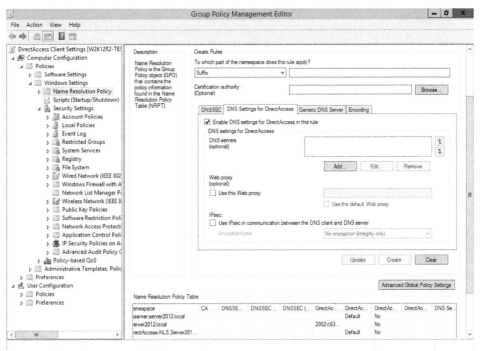

Figure 5-36 Creating an NRPT exemption

3. Add one or more rules or edit existing rules. To create a new rule, you specify which part of the DNS namespace the rule applies to (suffix, subnet, prefix, FQDN, or any), fill in information for the type of rule, and click Create. To edit an existing rule, click the rule in the Name Resolution Policy Table section (at the bottom of Figure 5-36), and click the Edit Rule button (not shown in the figure).

4. Run `gpupdate` on the clients, or wait until the client downloads new computer group policies.

Configuring Force Tunneling The default DirectAccess client configuration is **split tunneling,** a remote access method in which only requests for resources on the network are sent over the DirectAccess tunnel. Requests for Internet resources are sent out through the regular Internet connection. Split tunneling is usually preferred from the client and network administrator's standpoint because the client's Internet traffic doesn't have to traverse the network. It usually means faster response times for clients and less consumption of network bandwidth. If you configure force tunneling, all traffic from the client goes over the DirectAccess tunnel. When using force tunneling, the only tunnel option is IP-HTTPS. Because the connection from the client to the DirectAccess server uses IPv6, clients using force tunneling can access only IPv6 resources on the Internet unless an IPv6-to-IPv4 proxy is configured on the company network that provides IPv4 Internet access. Therefore, force tunneling is usually used only when you want to limit DirectAccess clients' access to the Internet.

You configure force tunneling by using group policies with the same procedure for configuring NRPT exemptions, but expand Computer Configuration, Policies, Administrative Templates, Network, and Network Connections, and enable the "Route all traffic through the internal network" policy (see Figure 5-37).

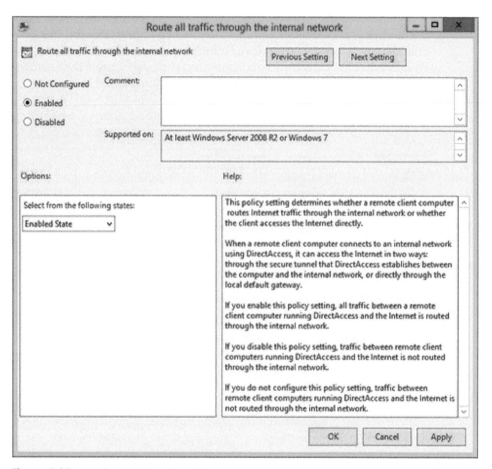

Figure 5-37   Configuring force tunneling

 You can also enable force tunneling during DirectAccess setup if you use the Remote Access Setup Wizard instead of the Getting Started Wizard.

Configuring ISATAP   ISATAP allows computers on the network to access DirectAccess clients that are connected via the Internet. For example, suppose a user on a DirectAccess client computer is having problems with an application on her laptop. The help desk personnel can open a Remote Desktop Protocol (RDP) session with the client and help solve the problem. For this situation to occur on an IPv4 network, ISATAP must be in place. The tunnels created by DirectAccess work only when a client connects to the DirectAccess server and establishes the communication session. The IPv6 IPsec tunnel created between the client and DirectAccess server is used by devices on the network to respond to the client. However, if a computer inside the network tries to initiate communication with the DirectAccess client, it will likely fail because there's no existing tunnel for the communication session to use. This is where ISATAP comes in. ISATAP is discussed in more detail in *MCSA Guide to Installing and Configuring Windows Server 2012/R2, Exam 70-410* (Cengage Learning, 2015), but here are two ways to enable it on the network:

- *Enable ISATAP for all computers on the network*—Create a DNS A record with the hostname ISATAP and the IP address of the DirectAccess server's internal interface. This record sets the DirectAccess server up as an ISATAP router, and any attempts to connect to clients connected to the DirectAccess server go through the DirectAccess server. If you use this method, you also need to configure DNS by entering `dnscmd /config / globalqueryblocklist wpad` at a command prompt. By default, DNS ignores queries to resolve the name `isatap`, and this command removes `isatap` from the list of names that are blocked by default.

- *Enable ISATAP for only certain computers*—The problem with the preceding method for enabling ISATAP is that all computers on the network are ISATAP enabled, which can put a strain on the DirectAccess server. To prevent this problem, you can select computers to initiate communication with DirectAccess clients. To selectively enable ISATAP, follow these steps:

1. Create a DNS A record with a hostname something like "DA-ISATAP," using the IP address of the DirectAccess server's internal interface.

2. Create a security group and add the computer accounts you want to enable ISATAP for.

3. Create a GPO and enable this policy: Computer Configuration, Policies, Administrative Templates, Network, TCPIP Settings, IPv6 Transition Technologies, Set ISATAP Router Name. In the "Enter a router or relay name" text box, type the name of the DNS record you created in Step 1.

4. Enable the ISATAP State policy setting (in the same path as the Set ISATAP Router Name policy in Step 3).

ISATAP is a good solution on networks that don't support IPv6 by default if you need to initiate communication with DirectAccess clients. You probably also need to set policies to configure the Windows firewall on client computers to allow the particular types of communication you configured ISATAP for in the first place. For example, if you want network computers to connect via RDP to DirectAccess clients, you need to open port 3389 on the client firewall and allow edge traversal if the client is using Teredo.

ISATAP doesn't work reliably with multisite DirectAccess because computers on the network don't know which DirectAccess server a particular client is connected to.

Activity 5-7: Removing the Remote Access Configuration

Time Required: 20 minutes
Objective: Remove the Remote Access configuration.

Required Tools and Equipment: 411Server1, 411Server2, 411Win8
Description: You're finished working with DirectAccess, so you remove the Remote Access configuration settings. Make sure that 411Win8 is connected to the same network as 411Server1 and 411Server2. 411Server1 needs to be running so that the group policy changes can be made when DirectAccess is uninstalled.

1. Start 411Win8, 411Server1, and 411Server2, if necessary. On 411Server2, log on to the domain as **Administrator**.

2. Open Server Manager, and click **Tools, Remote Access Management** from the menu.

3. In the left pane, expand **Configuration**, if necessary, and click **DirectAccess and VPN**. In the Tasks pane, click **Remove Configuration Settings**.

4. In the Confirm Remove Configuration message box, click **OK**. After the removal is finished, click **Close**, and then close the Remote Access Management console.

5. On 411Win8, log on as **Administrator**, and open a command prompt window. Type **gpupdate** and press **Enter**. The DirectAccess policies are removed from 411Win8.

6. Shut down all three computers.

Chapter Summary

- Remote Access is a server role that provides services to keep a mobile workforce and branch offices securely connected to the main office. Services include VPN, remote dial-in, routing, NAT, Web Application Proxy, and DirectAccess.

- When you install the Remote Access server role, you can install three role services: DirectAccess and VPN, Routing, and Web Application Proxy.

- A VPN is a network connection that uses the Internet to give users or branch offices secure access to a company's network resources on a private network. VPNs use encryption and authentication to ensure that communication is secure and legitimate, so although data travels through the public Internet, the connection remains private.

- Windows Server 2012/R2 supports three tunnel types: PPTP, L2TP/IPsec, and SSTP. After you finish the VPN server configuration, you need to define who's allowed to connect via remote access. You can do this with a user's account settings or by configuring a network policy.

- Remote dial-in uses the telephone system to connect a computer with a remote network. Each connection requires a modem and a phone line on both ends of the connection.

- The default settings for VPN and dial-up might be enough in many circumstances, but you might need to support different OSs and different VPN clients over different tunneling methods, which could require security settings different from the defaults.

- Using RRAS, a Windows server can be configured as a router to connect multiple subnets in the network or connect the network to the Internet. After routing is enabled, you can add routing protocols and configure static routes.

- Network Address Translation (NAT) is a process whereby a router or other type of gateway device replaces the source or destination IP addresses in a packet before forwarding the packet. An extension of NAT, called Port Address Translation (PAT), allows several hundred workstations to access the Internet with a single public Internet address.

- Web Application Proxy is a new Routing and Remote Access role service in Windows Server 2012 R2. It allows users to access applications from any device that supports a Web browser from outside the network.

- The DirectAccess role service is part of the DirectAccess and VPN role service under the Remote Access server role. It provides many of the same features as a VPN but adds client management and always-connected capability.

- A basic DirectAccess deployment requires only a domain controller, a member server to install the DirectAccess role service, and a client computer. After basic DirectAccess configuration, you might want to add some features for security or convenience, such as setting up a PKI, configuring NLS on a separate Web server, configuring the name resolution policy table, configuring force tunneling, and configuring ISATAP.

Key Terms

default route   The network where the router sends all packets that don't match any other destinations in the routing table.

demand-dial interface   An interface that's activated when a client attempts to connect to the Internet, such as a dial-up modem or Point-to-Point Protocol over Ethernet (PPPoE) connection.

hop count   The number of routers a packet must go through to reach the destination network.

infrastructure tunnel   A tunnel created between the client computer and the DirectAccess server, used for control of the DirectAccess connection.

Internet Protocol-Hypertext Transfer Protocol Secure (IP-HTTPS)   A tunneling protocol used to transport IPv6 packets over an HTTPS connection.

intranet tunnel   The tunnel created when a user logs on to the DirectAccess client; it provides access to resources on the network.

Kerberos proxy   An authentication method that allows a client computer to authenticate to a domain controller by using the DirectAccess server as a proxy.

multisite DirectAccess   A DirectAccess configuration with two or more DirectAccess servers, each providing a secure entry point into a network.

name resolution policy table (NRPT)   A table configured on a DirectAccess client that makes sure DNS requests for network resources are directed to internal DNS servers, not Internet DNS servers.

Network Address Translation (NAT)   A process whereby a router or other type of gateway device replaces the source or destination IP addresses in a packet before forwarding the packet.

Network Location Server (NLS)   A basic Web server used by DirectAccess client computers to determine whether they're on the main network or a remote network.

Port Address Translation (PAT)   A variation of NAT that allows several hundred workstations to access the Internet with a single public Internet address.

Remote Access   A server role that provides services to keep a mobile workforce and branch offices securely connected to resources at the main office.

routing table   A list of network destinations and information on which interface can be used to reach the destination.

split tunneling   A remote access method in which only requests for resources on the network are sent over the DirectAccess tunnel; requests for Internet resources are sent out through the regular Internet connection.

static route   A manually configured route in the routing table that instructs the router where to send packets destined for particular networks.

tunnel   A method of transferring data across an unsecured network in such a way that the data is hidden from all but the sender and receiver.

virtual private network (VPN)   A network connection that uses the Internet to give mobile users or branch offices secure access to a company's network resources on a private network.

Review Questions

1. Which of the following is a service provided by the Remote Access server role? (Choose all that apply.)

    a. Network Address Translation

    b. Web Application Proxy

    c. Windows Server Update Services

    d. Internet Information Services

2. Which role service should you install if you want client computers to be able to authenticate an IPsec connection with Kerberos proxy?

    a. DirectAccess and VPN

    b. Web Application Proxy

    c. Routing

    d. Remote dial-in

3. Which VPN tunnel type requires the firewall to allow TCP port 443?

   a. PPTP

   b. SSTP

   c. L2TP/IPsec

   d. PPP

4. Which VPN tunnel type uses an Internet Key Exchange?

   a. PPP

   b. PPTP

   c. SSTP

   d. L2TP/IPsec

5. Which tunnel type needs to authenticate client and server computers with a preshared key or a digital certificate?

   a. PPTP

   b. SSTP

   c. L2TP/IPsec

   d. PPP

6. Which of the following needs to be configured on the firewall to allow PPTP VPN connections? (Choose all that apply.)

   a. UDP port 4500

   b. TCP port 1723

   c. IP protocol ID 50

   d. IP protocol ID 47

7. Which remote access configuration option should you choose if you want mobile users to be able to make a secure connection to the main network and allow computers on the private network to access the Internet with a public IP address?

   a. Remote access (dial-up or VPN)

   b. Network Address Translation

   c. VPN access and NAT

   d. Secure connection between two private networks

8. The Network Access Permission attribute for a user account is set to which of the following by default?

   a. Control access through NPS Network Policy

   b. Allow access

   c. Deny access

   d. Control access through Group Policy

9. When you create a VPN connection on a client computer, what's the default tunnel type?

   a. SSTP

   b. PPTP

   c. Automatic

   d. L2TP/IPsec

10. Which authentication method should you choose if users authenticate with smart cards?

    a. MS-CHAPv2

    b. PAP

    c. EAP

    d. RADIUS

11. What should you configure if you want only users who are members of particular groups to be able to connect to the VPN?

    a. Connection Request Policy

    b. Network Policy

    c. Remote Authentication Rule

    d. Network Access Rule

12. What do you configure in Routing and Remote Access that specifies the server should send its routing table to its neighbors?

    a. Static routing

    b. L2TP

    c. RIPv2

    d. Default route

13. What's the metric used by the dynamic routing protocol you configure in Routing and Remote Access?

    a. Least cost

    b. Bandwidth

    c. Ping time

    d. Hop count

14. What should you configure in Routing and Remote Access if you want computers using a private IP address to access the public Internet?

    a. Demand-dial interface

    b. NAT

    c. Dynamic routing

    d. Web Application Proxy

15. Which of the following is a requirement for using Web Application Proxy? (Choose all that apply.)

    a. Active Directory Federation Services

    b. A RADIUS server

    c. A NAT router

    d. A digital certificate

16. Routing Information Protocol should be enabled on interfaces connected to the Internet. True or False?

17. Which of the following does a router do if it receives a packet for a destination network that's not in its routing table and no default route is configured?

    a. Broadcasts the packet

    b. Discards the packet

    c. Returns the packet to the sender

    d. Sends a route query to the next router

18. Remote access is denied to users by default. Which of the following must you do to allow users to connect via remote access? (Choose all that apply.)

    a. Configure settings in the Routing and Remote Access console.

    b. Configure dial-in settings in user accounts.

    c. Configure a network policy in the Network Policy Server console.

    d. Set up a VPN.

19. Which DirectAccess IPv6 transition technology uses Secure Sockets Layer over port 443?

    a. 6to4

    b. Teredo

    c. IP-HTTPS

    d. ISATAP

20. Which DirectAccess component allows clients to determine whether they're on the company network or a remote network?

    a. NLS

    b. PKI

    c. Kerberos proxy

    d. ISATAP

21. Which of the following is a benefit of using a PKI instead of self-signed certificates when configuring DirectAccess? (Choose all that apply.)

    a. Better security

    b. Support for multisite configurations

    c. Two-factor authentication support

    d. Simpler DirectAccess client deployment

22. Which of the following should you configure if you want DirectAccess clients to access the Internet through the company network?

    a. Split tunneling

    b. NLS

    c. Force tunneling

    d. Intranet tunnel

Case Projects

Case Project 5-1: Deploying Remote Access

You're consulting for a company that uses Windows Server 2012 R2 servers in a domain environment. All computers are running Windows 8.1. You have been told to come up with a remote access solution for the company's mobile workforce. Employees will be using company-issued laptops that they can use when they're on the premises, too. The solution should provide access to the company network when employees have an Internet connection without them having to specifically initiate a connection. The solution should be secure and allow IT staff to perform maintenance tasks via Remote Desktop sessions on the laptops when they're connected locally or remotely. What remote access solution do you recommend, and why? Are there any configuration options you should consider for this solution?

Case Project 5-2: Solving a Router Problem

CSM Tech Publishing has four buildings connected by fiber-optic cabling and 12 subnets connected by several routers running RIP. One building has flooded, so employees and their equipment have moved to a temporary building on the same site. A router with three interfaces in the flooded building was also damaged. There are no spare routers, and the router can't be replaced for several days. Five servers running Windows Server 2012 R2 have been moved to the temporary building. One of these servers is available as a spare or for other purposes. What can you do to solve your routing problem? Be specific about how you would carry out your solution, and state whether you would use static or dynamic routing.

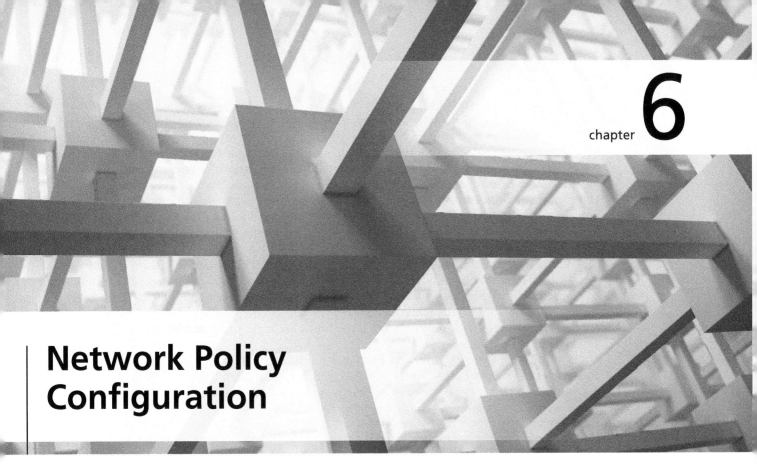

chapter 6

Network Policy Configuration

After reading this chapter and completing the exercises, you will be able to:

- Describe the components and flow of Network Policy Server and configure RADIUS

- Configure Network Access Protection

Although good internal security policies are a must, ensuring that unauthorized access to the network is blocked is the first line of defense, so you should pay particular attention to this task. Knowing who is allowed access and by what methods can help limit network attacks and make creating and monitoring security policies easier. Incorporating industry standards for authentication and authorization, Windows Server 2012/R2 includes ways to protect a network at the gate. With Network Policy Server, for example, you can create policies to determine who can access your network and how they can connect. Even if users are authorized to access the network and authenticated successfully, they can still be a threat without knowing it. A computer coming into your network could be harboring viruses, malware, and spyware that could infect the network and spread to all the users. Along with authentication and authorization, Windows Server 2012/R2 gives you ways to evaluate the health of a client attempting access, and then decide whether to block access, reroute the client to another server, or even take corrective action. By using Network Access Protection with Network Policy Server, you can create policies that require computers attempting to access your network to have a firewall running and up-to-date antivirus and antispyware protection.

In this chapter, you learn how to configure centralized authentication and authentication policies with Network Policy Server and RADIUS. You also learn how to configure Network Access Protection to protect the health of the network from computers that don't meet policies set for security configuration and malware protection.

Network Policy Server Overview

Table 6-1 summarizes what you need for the hands-on activities in this chapter.

Table 6-1   Activity requirements

Activity	Requirements	Notes
Activity 6-1: Installing the Network Policy Server Role Service	411Server1	
Activity 6-2: Configuring a VPN Server to Test RADIUS	411Server2	
Activity 6-3: Configuring a RADIUS Server	411Server1, 411Server2	
Activity 6-4: Configuring a RADIUS Proxy	411Server1, 411Server2	
Activity 6-5: Configuring RADIUS Accounting	411Server1	
Activity 6-6: Creating a Connection Request Policy	411Server1	
Activity 6-7: Creating a VPN Client Network Policy	411Server1	
Activity 6-8: Creating a Shared Secret Template	411Server1	
Activity 6-9: Configuring a System Health Validator	411Server1	
Activity 6-10: Configuring Health Policies	411Server1	
Activity 6-11: Configuring NAP with the DHCP Enforcement Method	411Server1	A DHCP server installed and active on 411Server1
Activity 6-12: Configuring NAP Clients with Group Policies	411Server1, 411Server2	A DHCP server installed and active on 411Server1
Activity 6-13: Uninstalling NPS and RRAS	411Server1, 411Server2	

© 2015 Cengage Learning®

With **Network Policy Server (NPS),** a role service of the Network Policy and Access Services (NPAS) server role, you can define and enforce rules that determine who can access your network and how they can access it (via VPN, dial-up, and so forth). NPS also includes an infrastructure to incorporate client system health checks and restrict access to systems that don't meet minimum health requirements, such as not having up-to-date antivirus protection and the latest system and security updates installed. Access attempts, both successful and unsuccessful, can be logged, so NPS has authentication, authorization, and auditing capabilities. The NPS architecture includes four features: **Remote Authentication Dial In User Service (RADIUS)** server, RADIUS proxy, RADIUS accounting, and Network Access Protection (NAP).

The RADIUS Infrastructure

Network Policy Server is Microsoft's implementation of the RADIUS protocol, a proposed IETF standard that's widely used to centralize authentication, authorization, and accounting to network services. To use NPS, you need to understand the types of messages used in a RADIUS infrastructure carried out in an NPS environment. The following list describes the process and what types of messages are sent:

1. An **access client** (for example, a user on a laptop) makes a connection request to a **network access server (NAS)**, which handles access to a network. An NAS can be, for example, a wireless access point, a VPN server, or a dial-up server. In the RADIUS infrastructure, an NAS is configured as a RADIUS client.

The term "client" can be a bit confusing. Only an NAS that's already part of the network can be a RADIUS client. Access client devices, such as users' desktops, laptops, or tablets that are requesting access to the network, aren't RADIUS clients.

2. The RADIUS client sends an Access-Request message, including a username/password combination or a certificate from the user, to an NPS server acting as a RADIUS server. This message can include other information about the user, such as the network address.

3. The NPS server evaluates the Access-Request message. This process can include authenticating the username and password (along with other user information) via a domain controller or client certificate.

4. The NPS server can respond with one of three types of messages:

   • *Access-Reject*—The request is rejected, and access is denied to the network or resources.

   • *Access-Challenge*—More information is requested, such as a secondary password or other access code or credential.

   • *Access-Accept*—Access is granted, and authorization is given to certain resources, based on defined network policies.

5. The connection is completed, and the NAS sends an Accounting-Request message to the NPS server to be logged. This message is sent to collect information about the user, such as his or her IP address, method of connecting to the network, and a session identifier, so that additional information that's sent can be attributed to this user's connection.

6. The NPS server sends an Accounting-Response message, which acknowledges that the request was received, to the NAS.

7. During the session, additional Accounting-Request messages containing information about the current session are sent. Each Accounting-Request message is acknowledged by an Accounting-Response message.

8. When the user's connection ends, one last Accounting-Request message with information about the overall use during the session is sent. This final message is acknowledged by an Accounting-Response message.

A RADIUS proxy can be inserted between Network Access Servers and NPS servers to help manage the load on the NPS servers. The proxy receives the Access-Request and Accounting-Request messages from an NAS and directs them on to the NPS server. Figure 6-1 shows the overall RADIUS message flow between access clients, RADIUS clients, and RADIUS servers, and access clients, RADIUS clients, RADIUS proxies, and RADIUS servers.

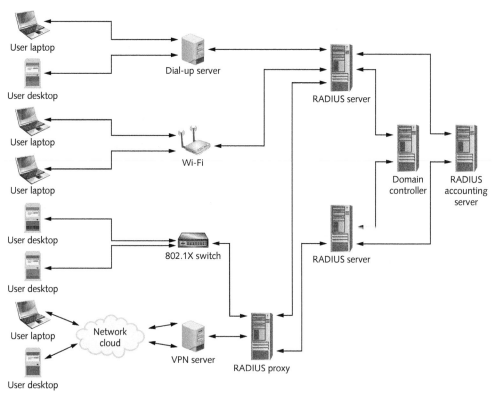

Figure 6-1   The RADIUS infrastructure
© 2015 Cengage Learning®

There are two main reasons you should set up an NPS architecture with RADIUS when you have different connection paths to your network. First, RADIUS centralizes control over authentication and authorization. No matter which path a user uses to access the network, a single point of contact—the NPS server acting as a RADIUS server—handles authenticating the user and determining the level of authorization. Next, standardizing on RADIUS requires all NAS devices to be RADIUS clients so that only one protocol performs authentication and authorization, and only one standard configuration process is used, regardless of the kind of device connecting to the network. To begin configuring an NPS/RADIUS environment, you must install the NPS role.

Activity 6-1: Installing the Network Policy Server Role Service

Time Required: 10 minutes
Objective: Install the Network Policy Server role service.

Required Tools and Equipment: 411Server1
Description: You want to begin using a RADIUS infrastructure in your network for authentication and authorization, so you install the Network Policy Server role service.

1. Start 411Server1, and log on as **Administrator**, if necessary. Open Server Manager, and click **Manage, Add Roles and Features** from the menu.

2. Click **Next** in the Before You Begin window, and in the Installation Type window, click **Role-based or feature-based installation**, if necessary, and then click **Next**.

3. In the Server Selection window, click **Select a server from the server pool**. Click **411Server1** in the Server Pool section, and then click **Next** to continue.

4. In the Server Roles window, click the **Network Policy and Access Services** check box. In the dialog box asking you to confirm the additional features needed for this role service, click the **Add Features** button, and then click **Next**.

5. In the Features window, click **Next**. Read the description of the role service in the next window, and then click **Next**.

6. In the Role Services window, accept the default selection **Network Policy Server**, and click **Next**.

7. In the Confirmation window, click **Install**.

8. After the installation is finished, click **Close** in the Results window to close the wizard.

9. Leave Server Manager running, and stay logged on to 411Server1 for the next activity.

Activity 6-2: Configuring a VPN Server to Test RADIUS

Time Required: 10 minutes
Objective: Configure a VPN server to test RADIUS.

Required Tools and Equipment: 411Server2
Description: You want to begin using a RADIUS infrastructure in your network for authentication and authorization and have installed the Network Policy Server role service. Now you configure a VPN server on 411Server2 so that you can configure it as a RADIUS client in Activity 6-3.

1. Start 411Server2, and log on to the domain as **Administrator**. Open Server Manager, and click **Tools**, **Routing and Remote Access** from the menu.

2. In the Routing and Remote Access console, right-click **411Server2** and click **Configure and Enable Routing and Remote Access**. Continue with the Routing and Remote Access Server Setup Wizard, making sure to configure a VPN using the network connection with address 203.0.113.1 as the Internet connection. Accept the default selections for the rest of the settings.

3. Stay logged on to 411Server2 if you're continuing to the next activity.

After NPS is installed, you can configure the server to be a RADIUS server, RADIUS proxy, or both. In a small environment with few network logon requests, a single RADIUS server is usually enough. After you have installed the NPS Server role, you can manage NPS in the Network Policy Server console. You need to configure a couple of settings: which NASs can connect and the authentication method each one uses. NPS gives you the choice of standard or advanced configuration options. The advanced configuration option requires you to set up the components for a RADIUS server or proxy. The standard configuration has wizards to walk you through these policy settings:

- *Network Access Protection (NAP)*—This option configures NPS as an NAP policy server (covered later in the "Configuring Network Access Protection" section).

- *RADIUS server for Dial-Up or VPN Connections*—This option defines network policies for authenticating and authorizing connections from these RADIUS clients: dial-up or VPN network access servers.

- *RADIUS server for 802.1X Wireless or Wired Connections*—This option defines network policies for authenticating and authorizing connections from these RADIUS clients: wireless access points and authenticating switches.

A policy must be defined for each type of RADIUS client, such as VPN NAS, in the NPS console. To create these policies, you need to consider several factors. Just as you want to authenticate clients attempting to access the network, you need to validate communication between a RADIUS client and a RADIUS server or proxy with a **shared secret**, a text string that acts as a password between RADIUS clients, servers, and proxies. Here are a few guidelines for creating shared secrets:

- A shared secret should be at least 22 characters to make guessing or using brute-force techniques more difficult. It should include uppercase and lowercase letters, numbers from 0 to 9, and symbols such as !, &, and @.
- A shared secret can be up to 128 characters.
- Use a random combination of letters, numbers, and symbols rather than a phrase.

The credentials the NAS passes need to be authenticated. Depending on the type of NAS, two general types of authentication methods are used: password based and certificate based. Four password-based methods are supported:

- *Microsoft Challenge Handshake Authentication Protocol*—**Microsoft Challenge Handshake Authentication Protocol (MS-CHAP)** starts with a challenge-response with the access client, and then sends the username and a password with a one-way encryption (meaning the password can't be unencrypted) to be authenticated against the stored credentials.
- *Microsoft Challenge Handshake Authentication Protocol version 2*—**Microsoft Challenge Handshake Authentication Protocol version 2 (MS-CHAP v2)** is an update to MS-CHAP with stronger security. Of the four password-based methods, it's the preferred one.
- *Challenge Handshake Authentication Protocol*—**Challenge Handshake Authentication Protocol (CHAP)** is similar to MS-CHAP, but the password must be able to be unencrypted, making it less secure than MS-CHAP.
- *Password Authentication Protocol*—**Password Authentication Protocol (PAP)** is the least secure method. The password is sent in plaintext, and there's no challenge and response. Because the password could be captured easily, PAP isn't recommended.

The certificate-based authentication method is **Extensible Authentication Protocol (EAP)**. Certificate-based authentication is more secure than password-based methods. Depending on the method you choose, there are two authentication types. The authentication type for EAP is **Transport Layer Security (TLS)**. Certificates and options for using them are discussed later in "Using Certificates for Authentication."

Protected Extensible Authentication Protocol (PEAP) is a special way to encrypt a password being sent via MS-CHAP v2. With PEAP, you can check the server's certificate, but user authentication is still done through passwords.

The groups a user belongs to can control access based on the network policy's access permission setting. With user groups and IP filters, you can create policies that restrict users to using specific protocols and specific servers. For example, you could restrict a VPN user to have access only to certain servers via certain protocols, such as FTP. Several other authentication settings can be configured. If the client is encrypting its messages to the NAS, you can specify what level of encryption is supported. For example, with a Routing and Remote Access Service (RRAS) server such as VPN or dial-up, Encryption, Strong Encryption, and Strongest Encryption are all supported.

Another part of the network policy is the **realm**. By default, it's the domain where the NPS server is located. If connection requests require authentication from another domain controller, they can be sent to an NPS server acting as a RADIUS proxy, and the realm determines which server the request is routed to.

Activity 6-3: Configuring a RADIUS Server

Time Required: 15 minutes
Objective: Configure a RADIUS server to authenticate VPN access requests.

Required Tools and Equipment: 411Server1 and 411Server2
Description: You want to authenticate and authorize VPN traffic coming into the network, so you need to configure a RADIUS server to accept access requests from VPN clients.

1. Log on to 411Server1 as **Administrator,** and open Server Manager, if necessary. Click **Tools, Network Policy Server** from the menu to open the Network Policy Server console.

2. In the Standard Configuration section of the Getting Started window shown in Figure 6-2, click **RADIUS server for Dial-Up or VPN Connections,** and then click the **Configure VPN or Dial-Up** link to start the corresponding wizard.

6

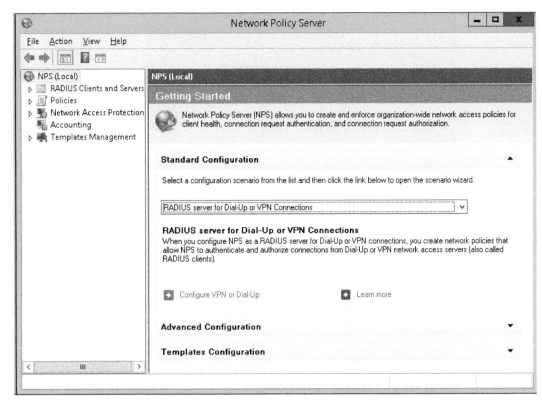

Figure 6-2 Selecting a configuration option for the RADIUS server

3. In the Select Dial-up or Virtual Private Network Connections Type window, click the **Virtual Private Network (VPN) Connections** option button. This option adds text to the Virtual Private Network (VPN) Connections text box that's used as part of the name of all policies created with the wizard. Leave this text, and click **Next.**

4. In the Specify Dial-Up or VPN Server window, click **Add** to open the New RADIUS Client dialog box. In the Friendly name text box, type **411Server2.411dom1.local**, and in the Address (IP or DNS) text box, type **10.11.1.2** (see Figure 6-3). You can click the **Verify** button to make sure you entered the correct address. Type **password1** in the Shared secret and Confirm shared secret text boxes.

Figure 6-3   The New RADIUS Client dialog box

 For the purposes of this activity, you're using a simple password. For a production server, you should use a password that's at least 22 characters and contains a random mix of uppercase and lowercase letters, numbers, and symbols.

5. Click **OK**, and then click **Next** to continue. In the Configure Authentication Methods window, click **Microsoft Encrypted Authentication version 2 (MS-CHAPv2)**, if necessary, and then click **Next**.

6. In the Specify User Groups window, you can add Active Directory user groups that the policy affects. You want this policy to apply to all users, so leave this window blank, and click **Next** to continue.

7. In the Specify IP Filters window, you can add IPv4 and IPv6 inbound and outbound filters, but you do not need to add filters for this activity. Click **Next** to continue.

8. Because Routing and Remote Access Service supports all three types of encryption, all are selected in the Specify Encryption Settings window. Leave them selected, and click **Next** to continue.

If you want to connect a non-Microsoft RADIUS client, you need to verify that it supports the encryption type you select.

9. In the Specify a Realm Name window, leave the Realm name text box blank, and click **Next**. In the final window, you see a summary of the settings, including the RADIUS clients and the names of the connection request policy and the network policies to be generated. Click **Finish**.

10. Now you configure Routing and Remote Access to use RADIUS authentication and accounting. On 411Server2, open Server Manager, and click **Tools, Routing and Remote Access** from the menu.

11. Click **411Server2 (local)** in the left pane, open its Properties dialog box, and click the **Security** tab. In the Authentication provider drop-down list, click **RADIUS Authentication** (see Figure 6-4), and then click the **Configure** button to open the RADIUS Authentication dialog box.

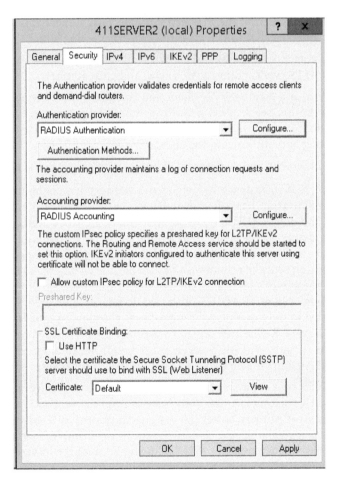

Figure 6-4 The Security tab

12. Click **Add** to open the Add RADIUS Server dialog box (see Figure 6-5). Type **411Server1** in the Server name text box, click the **Change** button, and type **password1** in the New secret and Confirm new secret text boxes.

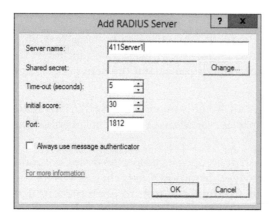

Figure 6-5   The Add RADIUS Server dialog box

13. Click **OK** three times to return to the Properties dialog box. Repeat this procedure for the accounting provider, and then click **OK** to close the Properties dialog box.

14. To restart the remote access service on 411Server2, go to the Routing and Remote Access console. Right-click **411Server2**, point to **All Tasks,** and click **Restart.**

15. Start 411Win8, log on, and create a VPN client and connect it to **411Server2.** (If you need a reminder of how to do this, see Activity 5-3.) You should be prompted for a username and password combination. Log on to the domain as **Administrator** to verify that the RADIUS server is authenticating and authorizing the client.

16. Stay logged on to 411Server1 and 411Server2 if you're continuing to the next activity.

Although a basic RADIUS infrastructure such as the one you just configured is adequate for most cases, a simple configuration has a few drawbacks. Lack of fault tolerance is the biggest disadvantage. If the one and only RADIUS server goes down, no network connection requests can be authenticated, which makes the network inaccessible to users. To eliminate this single point of failure, you can deploy multiple RADIUS servers. RADIUS clients can be configured to use a primary server and alternates, so if the primary isn't available, the client tries the alternates in turn.

Another concern is the server's load. In a network with hundreds or thousands of requests in extremely short periods, a single RADIUS server could be overwhelmed. One solution is to use RADIUS proxies (having only one proxy reintroduces the single-point-of-failure problem) with multiple RADIUS servers. Requests received by a proxy are forwarded to a **RADIUS server group**, composed of one or more RADIUS servers, for handling. In a server group of two or more RADIUS servers, the load can be balanced based on these properties:

- *Priority*—Tells the NPS proxy the order of importance of this server group member when passing on requests. This setting is a non-zero integer number (such as 1, 2, 3). The lower the number, the higher the priority, so servers assigned a priority of 1 get requests first. If the Priority 1 server is unavailable, the request is sent to the Priority 2 server, and so on. Setting just the priority doesn't result in load balancing because the lowest-priority server continues getting requests unless it becomes unavailable. However, a priority of 1 can be assigned to multiple servers, and the Weight setting can be used to force load balancing.

- *Weight*—Determines what percentage of connection requests are sent to a server group member when the priority is the same as other members. This setting is also a non-zero integer number between 1 and 100. For example, to distribute the load between two servers evenly, you could assign each a priority of 1 and a weight of 50 so that each server gets 50% of the connection requests. The sum of all weights in the server group must be 100.

- *Advanced settings*—Determines whether a server group member is unavailable and whether connection requests need to be routed to another server in the group. The settings include the number of seconds a proxy should wait for a response before deciding the request is dropped, the maximum number of requests dropped before the group server is considered unavailable, and the number of seconds between requests before the group server is considered unavailable.

Activity 6-4: Configuring a RADIUS Proxy

Time Required: 25 minutes

Objective: Configure 411Server2 as a RADIUS proxy.

Required Tools and Equipment: 411Server1 and 411Server2

Description: You want to manage traffic to the RADIUS server via a proxy and route accounting traffic.

1. Log on to 411Server1 as **Administrator,** and open Server Manager, if necessary. Log on to 411Server2 as **Administrator,** if necessary.

2. In Server Manager, click **Tools, Network Policy Server** to open the Network Policy Server console.

3. Expand **NPS (Local),** if necessary, and **RADIUS Clients and Servers** in the left pane. Right-click **Remote RADIUS Server Groups** and click **New.**

4. Type **Test Server Group** for the group name, and then click **Add** to open the Add RADIUS Server dialog box.

5. Type **10.11.1.1** (the IP address of 411Server1), and then click the **Authentication/ Accounting** tab.

6. Type **password1** as the shared secret, and click the **Request must contain the message authenticator attribute** check box.

7. Because you haven't changed the default ports, you can leave them as they are. Make sure the **Use the same shared secret for authentication and accounting** check box is selected.

8. Leave the default value for performance tuning, and click the **Load Balancing** tab (see Figure 6-6). Change your settings, if necessary, to match what's shown in Figure 6-6, and then click **OK** twice to finish.

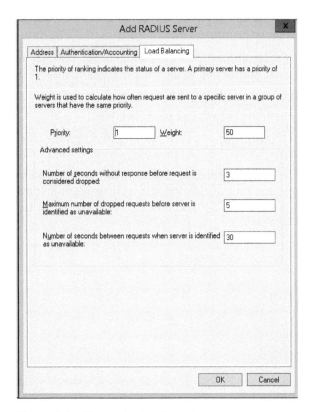

Figure 6-6   The Load Balancing tab

9. Using the VPN client you created in Activity 6-3, connect to 411Server2 again. Make sure you're prompted for a username and password and can log on with the **411dom1\Administrator** account. There should be no discernible difference between logging on with the RADIUS proxy and connecting directly through the RADIUS server, as you did in Activity 6-3.

10. Stay logged on to 411Server1 and 411Server2 if you're continuing to the next activity.

Configuring RADIUS Accounting

RADIUS accounting is essentially a log of the different access and accounting requests and responses sent between RADIUS clients and RADIUS servers that were outlined previously in "The RADIUS Infrastructure." NPS logs requests and responses by using one of these methods:

- *Event logging*—Events that occur while NPS is running are written to event logs.

- *Local text file*—Each user authentication and accounting request is logged to a text file.

- *Microsoft SQL Server XML-compliant database*—Logged data is written to a SQL Server database. Multiple servers can write to a single database. One advantage of this method is that the accounting data is stored in an easily accessible container (a SQL Server database), and the data for multiple systems is combined in this container, which makes reporting more flexible.

The default setting is to log accounting information in a local text file in C:\Windows\System32\LogFiles. You can change this setting in the Network Policy Server console.

Activity 6-5: Configuring RADIUS Accounting

Time Required: 5 minutes
Objective: Configure RADIUS accounting to write to an XML-formatted text file.

Required Tools and Equipment: 411Server1 and 411Server2
Description: You want to keep track of all access attempts to the network, so you decide to set up RADIUS accounting to have it write information to a standard XML-formatted text file.

1. Log on to 411Server1 as **Administrator,** if necessary. Open the Network Policy Server console, if necessary, and click **Accounting** in the left pane. Make sure 411Server2 is running.

2. Click **Configure Accounting** in the right pane to start the Accounting Configuration Wizard.

3. Read the information in the first window, and then click **Next.**

4. In the Select Accounting Options window, click the **Log to a text file on the local computer** option, and then click **Next.**

5. In the Configure Local File Logging window, click the **Accounting requests, Authentication requests, Periodic accounting status,** and **Periodic authentication status** check boxes, if necessary (see Figure 6-7), and then click **Next** twice. Click **Close** in the Conclusion window.

Figure 6-7   Selecting information to log

6. On 411Win8, connect to 411Server2 with the VPN client you created in Activity 6-3. Navigate to **C:\Windows\System32\LogFiles** on 411Server1. You should see the `INyymm.log` file, with *yy* representing the year and *mm* representing the month, such as `IN1512.log`. You can open it to see a record of your connection attempts in XML.

7. Disconnect the VPN connection. Stay logged on to 411Server1 if you're continuing to the next activity.

Using Certificates for Authentication

The easiest authentication method to set up is password based. Unfortunately, easy authentication methods often have less security. For stronger security, **certificate-based authentication** is recommended, which uses a certificate (a digital document) containing information that establishes an entity's identity, such as an NPS server or an access client. With this authentication method, a server's or client's identity can be verified. You have seen this type of authentication in action on the Internet. When you connect to a Web site by using https:// in the URL instead of http://, the server is asked for the Web site certificate to prove that you're connecting to the site you requested. If the server doesn't present the certificate, the connection fails. If the certificate has expired or information such as the requested URL doesn't match what's on the certificate, the connection fails. With NPS, the certificate is presented when the client is attempting to connect, and the server, the client, or both are asked to prove their identity.

Certificates are created and distributed by a **certification authority (CA)**, which is given information that can uniquely identify the server or client. There are two types of CAs: public and private. Examples of public CAs are VeriSign and Thawte. You purchase certificates from these companies and give them information to prove that you are who you say you are. A private CA, such as Active Directory Certificate Services, allows you to produce as many certificates as you want.

For a certificate to be used for authentication, the CA must be trusted by the client or server, and to be trusted, it must have a **root certificate** (also called the "CA certificate") in the Trusted Root Certification Authorities certificate store. Think of the root certificate as the master certificate for a CA. After the root certificate is installed, all other certificates from this CA are trusted automatically by the client or server. The process of requesting a certificate, having it approved, and downloading it is called "enrollment." Clients can be enrolled automatically for some certificates in a domain. For example, if the client is a member of the same domain as the CA, the CA certificate is autoenrolled. Besides the root certificate, there are three other important certificate types:

- *Client computer certificate*—This certificate verifies a client computer's identity to an NPS server. It's enrolled automatically for domain members and imported manually for non-domain members.
- *Server certificate*—This certificate verifies a server's identity to a client. It can be set for autoenrollment in Active Directory.
- *User certificate*—This certificate can be put on a smart card to verify a user's identity, and the smart card reader is attached to the client computer. If you're using smart cards, you don't autoenroll client computer certificates.

When a certificate is presented for authentication, it must meet these three criteria for authentication to succeed:

- It must be valid (for example, hasn't expired).
- It must be configured for the purpose it's presented for.
- It must be issued by a trusted CA.

For a client to accept a certificate from an NPS server, the certificate must meet these requirements:

- The subject name can't be blank.
- The certificate is linked to a trusted root CA.
- The purpose of the certificate is server authentication.
- The algorithm name is RSA, and the minimum key size is at least 2048.
- If the subject alternative name (SubjectAltName) extension is used, which allows multiple servers to use the certificate, the certificate must contain the NPS server's DNS name.

You can select certificate-based authentication—EAP—when you're setting the authentication method. EAP requires both the server and the access client to present valid certificates, which is the most secure authentication method. However, in a large organization, maintaining potentially thousands of client certificates can be a daunting administrative job, even with autoenrollment for new access clients. Selecting PEAP as the authentication method doesn't involve using a client certificate; instead, it uses MS-CHAP v2 for client authentication. It's not as secure, however, as a pure certificate-based authentication method (such as EAP) because users still enter passwords, which can be guessed or stolen. However, PEAP can be configured to require a server certificate. This method protects clients from connecting to a server that's pretending to be the server they want to connect to, and PEAP encrypts the information it's passing.

Configuring NPS Policies

NPS policies define who can connect, when they can connect, and how they can connect to the network. Three policy types are available:

- *Connection request policies*—Specify which RADIUS servers handle connection requests from RADIUS clients.

- *Network policies*—Specify which users and groups have access, the times they can access the network, and any conditions that apply.

- *Health policies*—Used with Network Access Protection, these policies create System Health Validators (SHVs) that define client computer configuration requirements (for example, a current antivirus program installed). NAP-capable computers that attempt to connect must comply with these policies, or they can't connect.

Configuring Connection Request Policies   Connection request policies are used to specify which RADIUS servers perform authentication and authorization of RADIUS clients' connection requests. These policies can also specify which servers RADIUS accounting requests are sent to. They're applied to NPS servers configured as RADIUS servers or RADIUS proxies. Requests are authenticated and authorized by NPS acting as a RADIUS server or forwarded by NPS acting as a RADIUS proxy for authentication and authorization by another RADIUS server only if settings in the Access-Request message match at least one of the connection request policies that have been configured. You can define connection request policies for the following NAS types:

- *Unspecified*—Process or forward connection requests from any type of NAS, depending on whether the server receiving the message is configured as a RADIUS server or RADIUS proxy.

- *Remote Desktop Gateway*—Process or forward connection requests from an NAS that's managing connections from Remote Desktop clients.

- *Remote access server (VPN-dial up)*—Process or forward requests from an NAS that's managing dial-up and VPN connections.

- *DHCP server*—Process or forward requests from an NAS that's giving network IP addresses to access clients.

- *Health Registration Authority (HRA) server*—Process or forward requests from an NAS that supplies a certificate for the access client to use when connecting to the network, based on the client's health status. (Client health is covered in more detail in "Configuring Network Access Protection.")

- *Host Credential Authorization Protocol (HCAP) server*—Works with Cisco Network Admission Control to provide interoperability between Cisco network access servers and NAP.

- *Vendor specific*—Process or forward requests from an NAS with proprietary RADIUS attributes not included in RFC 2865 and 2866, which list the standard RADIUS attributes.

 For a policy to apply to an 802.1x authenticating switch (such as several types of Cisco switches that can act as RADIUS clients) or a wireless access point, the NAS type must be Unspecified.

When a RADIUS server receives a RADIUS Access-Request message from a RADIUS client, the client's attributes are checked against the connection request policy's conditions. The attributes in the Access-Request message must match at least one of the conditions in the policy before the NPS server acts as a RADIUS server (authenticating and authorizing the connection request) or a RADIUS proxy (passing the request on to a RADIUS server for authentication and authorization). Creating conditions allows you to control who can access the network, how they can access it, and when they can access it, based on the NAS the client is using to request access. For example, you might decide that dial-in users should be allowed to connect anytime on Sunday but only during certain times on other days of the week. The condition you set up would specify that users can connect on Monday through Saturday, 7:00 a.m. to 6:00 p.m., and from midnight Saturday to midnight Sunday. You could also limit access to certain usernames or usernames starting with certain characters (such as an abbreviation for a project group or a company).

The following groups of condition attributes can be used in a connection request policy to compare with the attributes of the RADIUS Access-Request message:

- *Day and time restrictions*—Restrict access to specific days and times.
- *Username*—Restrict access to certain usernames, which can be partial names or a pattern to match.
- *Machine identity*—Specify the method to identify clients in the policy.
- *Connection properties*—Restrict access to certain connection types, such as Point-to-Point Tunneling Protocol (PPTP) or Layer Two Tunneling Protocol (L2TP) for clients connecting by creating a tunnel.
- *Gateway properties*—Specify where a client is connecting from, such as the NAS phone number (if the client is dialing in), IP address, or port type (for example, analog phone lines, ISDN, or wireless).
- *RADIUS client properties*—Specify information about the RADIUS client, such as phone number, IP address, RADIUS client computer name, and RADIUS client vendor name.

In Activity 6-3, you created a connection request policy automatically when you were setting up and configuring a RADIUS server, but you can also add policies after a server has been configured.

Activity 6-6: Creating a Connection Request Policy

Time Required: 10 minutes
Objective: Create a connection request policy.

Required Tools and Equipment: 411Server1
Description: In a previous activity, you created a connection request policy by configuring a RADIUS server with a wizard, but in this activity, you create a connection request policy manually.

1. Log on to 411Server1 as **Administrator**, if necessary. Open Server Manager, if necessary, and click **Tools, Network Policy Server** to open the NPS console.

2. In the left pane, expand **Policies,** and then right-click **Connection Request Policies** and click **New** to start the New Connection Request Policy Wizard. Enter **Test** for the name of the policy. Leave **Unspecified** selected in the "Type of network access server" drop-down list, and click **Next.**

3. In the Specify Conditions window, click **Add** to open the Select condition dialog box (see Figure 6-8).

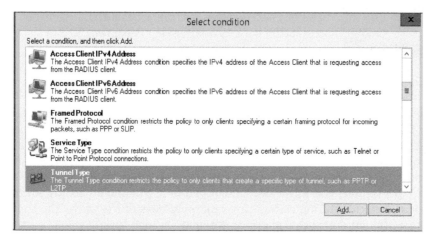

Figure 6-8   The Select condition dialog box

4. Scroll down and click **Tunnel Type**, and then click **Add** to open the Tunnel Type dialog box. Click **PPTP, SSTP, L2TP**, and **GRE** to allow a wide variety of VPN tunnels, and then click **OK**. Click **Next**.

5. In the Specify Connection Request Forwarding window, leave the **Authenticate requests on this server** option selected, and leave the default accounting settings (see Figure 6-9). You can also use this window to forward requests to a RADIUS server group if you want these functions to be performed elsewhere. Click **Next**.

Figure 6-9   The Specify Connection Request Forwarding window

6. In the Specify Authentication Methods window, you can override the authentication methods specified in the network policy, if needed. For this activity, leave the **Override network policy authentication settings** check box cleared, and click **Next**.

7. In the Configure Settings window, you can enter a realm name or a RADIUS attribute, if needed. Click **Next**, and then click **Finish** in the Completing Connection Request Policy Wizard window.

8. Stay logged on to 411Server1 for the next activity.

Policies are processed until a matching one is found. To make sure more specific policies are evaluated, place them higher in the list than general policies.

Configuring Network Policies   After you have configured RADIUS servers and clients defined in connection request policies, you need to specify who can connect to the network and under what conditions. To do this, you create network policies. Connection request policies are specific to an NAS type, but network polices affect all clients who are trying to connect. For these policies, you must configure at least one condition. As with connection request policies, there are groups of conditions for determining access, each with attributes to compare the incoming request with:

- *Groups*—Specify user or computer groups created in Active Directory Domain Services that the client must be a member of to match the policy. Using this condition, you can restrict access to users or computers belonging to a particular Windows group, computers belonging to a particular machine group, or users who are members of a particular user group.

- *Day and time restrictions*—Specify days and times clients can or can't access the network.

- *RADIUS client*—Specify RADIUS attributes the client must have to match the policy. For example, you could restrict access to RADIUS clients that have a certain IP address or fall in a specified range of addresses.

 A RADIUS client's IP address isn't the same as an access client's IP address. This condition applies to all access clients connecting via a particular NAS type, such as a VPN server.

- *Connection*—Specify attributes for how the access client is connecting to the network. This condition compares attributes such as the access client's (not the RADIUS client's) IP address, the authentication method being used, the framing protocol (for example, PPP), the service being used (such as Telnet or PPTP), and the tunnel type (PPTP or L2TP). This condition could be used to restrict access for clients with a particular IP address yet allow access for other clients using the same NAS.

- *Gateway*—Specify NAS attributes, such as the phone number, name, IP address, and port type. For example, this condition can limit access to connection requests from an NAS with a particular IP address or clients requesting access via a wireless connection.

- *Network Access Protection*—Specify attributes related to NAP, such as whether the client has met the health policy criteria or whether the computer is NAP capable. For example, this condition can require an access client to have health checks performed, such as verification that a firewall is running, to match the policy.

- *HCAP*—Specify attributes related to Host Credential Authorization Protocol, which allows integrating Microsoft Network Access Protection with Cisco Network Admission Control. This condition requires using both NAP and Cisco Network Admission Control. For example, this condition can require the access client to be a member of a specific HCAP location group or user group to match the policy.

In addition to network policy conditions, you can specify network policy constraints. Constraints are similar to conditions, with one major difference. If a condition in a policy isn't met, NPS continues trying to find a match in the remaining conditions. If a constraint doesn't match the connection request, however, no further policies are checked, the request is rejected, and access to the network is denied. You can configure the following constraints, found in the Constraints tab of a network policy's Properties dialog box:

- *Authentication method*—The authentication method used when requesting access

- *Idle timeout*—The maximum number of minutes an NAS can be idle before dropping the connection

- *Session timeout*—The maximum number of minutes a user can remain connected to the network

- *Called station ID*—The phone number of the dial-up server (NAS) that access clients use

- *Day and time restrictions*—The schedule of days and times access is allowed

- *NAS port type*—The allowed access client's media type (such as phone lines or VPNs)

Configuring Network Policies for Virtual Private Networks   VPNs are common methods of accessing networks remotely and securely. Because VPNs access a network remotely, using a network policy to control how they can access your network is a natural choice. The authentication type for a VPN can be password based or certificate based. Certificate-based methods are more secure, but you must have a valid CA certificate installed on every computer connecting via the VPN and client certificates installed on each computer. Some of the settings made in the Routing and Remote Access console when you configure a network policy are particularly applicable to VPNs:

- *Multilink and Bandwidth Allocation Protocol (BAP)*—Handle connection types that include multiple channels (for example, ISDN). You can adjust how multilink connections are handled and modify BAP parameters to specify when to drop the extra connections.

- *IP filters*—Filter access based on the client computer's IP address. You can permit or disallow packets from a particular address or network and restrict access to certain ports and protocols.

- *Encryption settings*—Specify which encryption strengths you allow. The choices are Basic, Strong, Strongest, and No encryption (not recommended). All are supported by Routing and Remote Access Service, but some third-party clients might not support them. The connection tries the strongest type first, and then moves to the weaker choices, if needed.

- *IP settings*—Adjust how IP addresses are assigned to the access client. The choices are Server must supply an IP address, Client may request an IP address, Server settings determine IP address assignment (the default), and Assign a static IPv4 address.

Activity 6-7: Creating a VPN Client Network Policy

Time Required: 10 minutes
Objective: Create a network policy for VPN clients.

Required Tools and Equipment: 411Server1
Description: Network policies help determine what resources a client can access in the network. You decide to set up a network policy for VPN clients to give only domain users access to network resources.

1. Log on to 411Server1 as **Administrator**, if necessary. Open the Network Policy Server console, if necessary, and expand **Policies**. Right-click **Network Policies** and click **New** to start the New Network Policy Wizard.

2. Type **Test VPN policy** in the Policy name text box, click **Remote Access Server (VPN-Dial up)** in the "Type of network access server" drop-down list, and then click **Next**.

3. In the Specify Conditions window, click **Add** to open the Select condition dialog box. Click **Windows Groups**, and then click **Add** to open the Windows Groups dialog box. Click **Add Groups**, type **Domain Users**, and click **OK** twice. Click **Next**.

4. In the Specify Access Permission window, leave the default **Access granted** selected, and then click **Next**.

5. In the Configure Authentication Methods window, click the **Microsoft Encrypted Authentication version 2 (MS-CHAP-v2)**, **User can change password after it has expired**, **Microsoft Encrypted Authentication (MS-CHAP)**, and **User can change password after it has expired** check boxes, if necessary (see Figure 6-10), and then click **Next**.

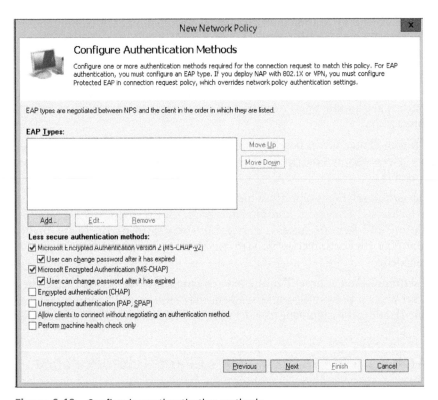

Figure 6-10   Configuring authentication methods

6. In the Configure Constraints window, click **Next** to go to the Configure Settings window, where you can specify settings such as standard and vendor-specific RADIUS attributes, NAP settings, and RRAS settings. Click **Next**.

7. In the Completing New Network Policy window, click **Finish**.

8. Stay logged on to 411Server1 for the next activity.

Managing NPS Templates

Templates can reduce the amount of work and minimize the chance of error, especially when many RADIUS servers and clients need to be configured. You can use NPS or RADIUS templates to reuse settings on the local server or export settings to other NPS servers. If you have many NPS servers and proxies to manage, templates can save time and prevent configuration errors when you're replacing a server or adding a new one.

Template settings apply only when the template is selected and actually applied in a RADIUS configuration; merely creating a template has no effect on a server's configuration.

Templates are in the Network Policy Server console under the Templates Management node. There are six template types:

- *Shared Secrets*—Specify a reusable password for validating a connection between RADIUS servers and proxies and NAS servers.

- *Remote RADIUS Servers*—Specify reusable RADIUS server settings.

- *RADIUS Clients*—Specify reusable RADIUS client settings.
- *IP Filters*—Specify reusable lists of the IPv4 and IPv6 addresses of allowed destinations.
- *Remediation Server Groups*—Specify reusable settings for remediation server groups.
- *Health Policies*—Specify reusable health policy settings.

Activity 6-8: Creating a Shared Secret Template

Time Required: 5 minutes
Objective: Create and apply a shared secret template.

Required Tools and Equipment: 411Server1
Description: In this activity, you create a template to set the shared secret between 411Server1 (the RADIUS server) and 411Server2 (the RADIUS client).

1. Log on to 411Server1 as **Administrator**, and open the Network Policy Server console, if necessary.
2. In the left pane, expand **Templates Management**, and then right-click **Shared Secrets** and click **New**.
3. Type **Test Shared Secret** as the template's name and **password1** as the shared secret. Confirm the password, and then click **OK**.
4. In the left pane, expand **RADIUS Clients and Servers**, and click **RADIUS Clients**. In the right pane, right-click **411Server2** (the RADIUS client) and click **Properties**. In the Shared Secret section, click **Test Shared Secret** in the drop-down list, and then click **OK**. You should see Test Shared Secret listed in the Templates Management node.
5. Stay logged on to 411Server1 for the next activity.

Exporting and Importing Templates   NPS can export templates to an XML file that can then be imported to another NPS server, which is particularly useful when you're setting up multiple NPS servers that should be configured the same way (for example, a server group). To export a template, open the Network Policy Server console. Right-click Templates Management and click Export Templates to a File. Select a location for the file, enter a name, and click Save.

To import a template, open the Network Policy Server console. Right-click Templates Management and click Import Templates from a File. Navigate to and select the XML file, and click Open. You can also click Import Templates from a Computer and enter the name of another NPS server on your network.

Importing and Exporting NPS Policies

After configuring policies and templates, you can back up the entire NPS configuration by exporting it to an XML file. You can keep it to restore the configuration, if needed, or use it to configure other NPS servers in your network. To export an NPS backup file, follow these steps in the Network Policy Server console:

1. In the left pane, right-click the NPS (Local) node and click Export Configuration. In the message box about exporting shared secrets, click the "I am aware that I am exporting all shared secrets" check box, and then click OK.
2. Choose a name and location to save the XML file, and click Save.
3. To restore the configuration, right-click the NPS (Local) node and click Import Configuration. Navigate to the XML file, and click Open.

To perform this same task from the command line, follow these steps:

1. Open a command prompt window. Type `netsh` and press Enter. At the `netsh` prompt, type `nps` and press Enter.
2. Type `export filename=`*path*`\NPSconfig.xml exportPSK=YES` (see Figure 6-11), replacing *path* with the location you specified and `NPSconfig.xml` with a name of your choosing, and press Enter.

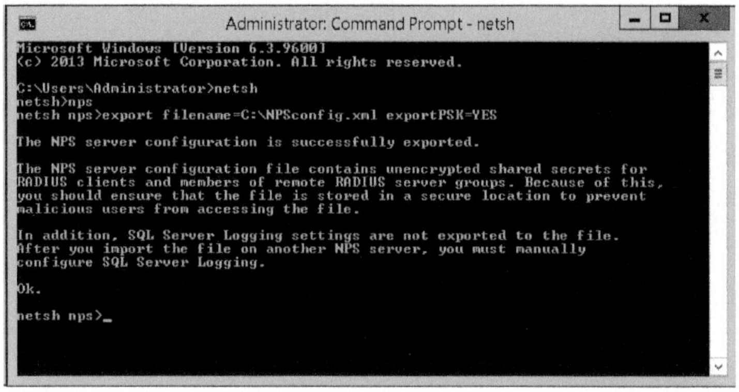

```
                    Administrator: Command Prompt - netsh            [-][□][X]
Microsoft Windows [Version 6.3.9600]
(c) 2013 Microsoft Corporation. All rights reserved.

C:\Users\Administrator>netsh
netsh>nps
netsh nps>export filename=C:\NPSconfig.xml exportPSK=YES

The NPS server configuration is successfully exported.

The NPS server configuration file contains unencrypted shared secrets for
RADIUS clients and members of remote RADIUS server groups. Because of this,
you should ensure that the file is stored in a secure location to prevent
malicious users from accessing the file.

In addition, SQL Server Logging settings are not exported to the file.
After you import the file on another NPS server, you must manually
configure SQL Server Logging.

Ok.

netsh nps>_
```

Figure 6-11   Exporting an NPS configuration from the command line

3. To import the file on this server or another server, type `netsh` and press Enter.

4. Type `nps` and press Enter, and then type `import filename="path\filename.xml"` and press Enter.

5. You get a message stating that the import was successful. Close the command prompt window.

Configuring Network Access Protection

Not every threat to your network can be stopped. After users gain authorized access to your network, if they decide to upload a virus or spyware, there's not much you can do to stop them. However, blocking access to computers that have no protection from viruses and spyware, such as remote users' laptops, can help prevent the spread of these threats. **Network Access Protection (NAP)** provides an infrastructure for checking client computers attempting to access the network to make sure they comply with health policies. For the purposes of NAP, "health" refers to computer settings, such as whether antivirus and antispyware software are up to date and whether recent security updates have been installed. Clients that aren't in compliance can be refused access or routed to restricted areas of the network where they have access to resources needed to bring them into compliance, such as an update server.

NAP requires certain components on both the client and server sides (see Figure 6-12). Computers requesting access to the network are called **NAP clients**. System health checks are

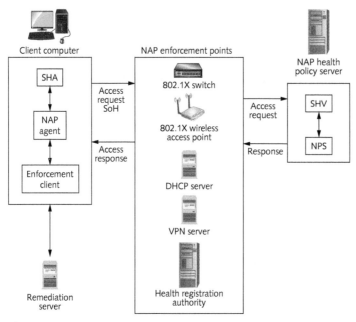

Figure 6-12   NAP components and functions

done via **system health agents (SHAs)** running on the client. An SHA monitors the client to determine whether specified security measures are in place (such as antivirus software being up to date). The Windows Security Health Agent (WSHA), included in Windows Vista and later, is an example of an SHA that communicates with the Windows Security Center to determine the status of security components, including antivirus and antispyware protection. The SHA creates a **statement of health (SoH)** that shows the client's current health status. Multiple SHAs can be installed on a client computer. The **NAP agent** collects multiple SoHs from the SHAs and creates a single **system statement of health (SSOH)** from them. An **NAP enforcement client** requests network access for the client, using a specific **NAP enforcement method,** and communicates the response to other NAP components. There are enforcement clients for these network technologies:

- *Remote access*—Enforces health policies for VPN connection attempts from clients running Windows Vista or later through an NAP-enabled VPN server.

- *Dynamic Host Configuration Protocol*—Gives noncompliant computers a different DHCP configuration that limits their access to the network and resources to servers that can help bring them into compliance. The drawback of this method is that it can be bypassed by using static IP addresses on the client computer.

- *Internet Protocol Security*—Uses a public key infrastructure to issue health certificates to computers meeting defined health standards. Only a compliant computer can initiate communication with IPsec-secured resources on the network. This method is the most secure way to ensure compliance.

- *Extensible Authentication Protocol*—Enforces health policies when a remote client running Windows 7 or later attempts to connect via a VPN, 802.1x network switches, and 802.1x wireless access points.

- *Wireless EAP over LAN (EAPOL)*—Enforces health policies for 802.1.x wireless connection attempts from clients running Windows XP SP3 or later.

- *Remote Desktop gateway enforcement*—Applies to Remote Desktop clients attempting to access the network.

The server running the NPS role validates NAP clients. This server is often called the NAP Health Policy server and uses a **System Health Validator (SHV)** to verify the statement of health made by the corresponding SHA on the client. Each SHV is paired with a client SHA. If there are several kinds of SHVs in a network, the data from all SHVs is taken into account to determine access for a noncompliant client computer. Updates that can bring a noncompliant client computer into compliance are hosted on a **remediation server.** The corresponding SHA, SHV, policy server, and remediation server work together to bring a client into compliance. (Remediation servers are an optional component.) Health policies are the rules the SHV has defined, and they're enforced as part of a network policy. If a client computer is deemed noncompliant, a **statement of health response (SOHR)** is sent to SHAs with instructions on how to bring the client into compliance. The connection process for a simple NAP configuration is as follows:

1. An NAP client attempts to connect to the network. Each of its SHAs generates an SoH.

2. The NAP agent on the NAP client combines these SoHs into a system statement of health and sends it to the enforcement clients to request validation.

3. The NAP Health Policy server evaluates the SSOH against its SHVs and health requirements policies to determine whether to grant access.

4. The NAP Health Policy server then sends a system state of health response (SSoHR) back to the NAP client.

5. Compliant computers are allowed to connect by the enforcement points. Noncompliant computers are denied access or connected to a **remediation network,** which is a group of remediation servers.

When clients connect by using the IPsec enforcement method, compliance is verified through a health certificate. The certificate is obtained from a CA by the Health Registration Authority server and then provided to the client.

System Health Validators

After NAP has been installed, you need to configure and enable SHVs. As mentioned, each SHV corresponds to an SHA on the client computers. By default, an SHV is already installed in Windows Server 2012/R2: Windows Security Health Validator (WSHV). This SHV is paired with the Windows Security Health Agent (WSHA), which can be enabled on clients running Windows XP SP3, Windows Vista, or later. WSHA builds its SoH based on monitoring applications' status through Windows Security Center (for example, Windows Firewall). Taking action to bring a system into compliance with a health policy, such as updating virus definition files, is called "remediation." Some security settings, such as enabling Windows Firewall, can be performed automatically by the system, which is called "auto-remediation."

Microsoft offers additional SHA-SHV sets for the System Center Configuration Manager (SCCM) (see *http://technet.microsoft.com/en-us/library/bb693725.aspx*). Many of the major third-party vendors in antivirus and security software include SHA-SHV sets with their enterprise-level products.

The WSHV handles security settings that are controlled through Windows Security Center:

- *Firewall settings*—Require a firewall that's enabled for all network connections. If the client has no firewall or one that isn't compatible with Windows Security Center, it's denied full access to the network. If you have enabled auto-remediation in the network policy, Windows Firewall is turned on.

- *Antivirus settings*—Require that antivirus software be installed, running, and up to date. There's no auto-remediation option for these settings. If the conditions aren't met, the client has limited access until antivirus software is running and up to date.

- *Spyware protection settings*—Require that antispyware software be installed, running, and up to date. If the client isn't running antispyware software and if auto-remediation is set, Windows Defender is turned on. (This option isn't available in Windows XP.)

- *Automatic updates settings*—Require automatic updating to be enabled. If auto-remediation is set, the WSHA turns on automatic updates.

- *Security updates settings*—Require installing all available security updates. You can specify the minimum severity level required for updates: Low and above, Moderate and above, Important and above, and Critical only.

Users must keep up to date with security updates. However, forcing users to download and install security updates as soon as they're released could interfere with daily operations. To minimize disruptions, you can specify in the SHV how long users have to check for updates before they're deemed noncompliant. The default is 22 hours, and the maximum time allowed is 72 hours.

Informing clients where they can download updates to bring them into compliance helps speed remediation. Windows Update is the default update location when you're configuring an SHV. If Windows System Update Service (WSUS) is running, you can specify it instead. Using WSUS gives you control over what updates are installed on computers in the network and when they should be installed. For example, you might want to test a new update to ensure compatibility with applications you're running before releasing the update.

Activity 6-9: Configuring a System Health Validator

Time Required: 5 minutes
Objective: Configure the default system health validator.

Required Tools and Equipment: 411Server1
Description: The system health validator is the server version of the system health agent on the client. In this activity, you configure the Windows Security Health Validator.

1. Log on to 411Server1 as **Administrator,** if necessary.

2. Open the Network Policy Server console, if necessary. Expand the **Network Access Protection** node in the left pane, and then expand **System Health Validators** and **Windows Security Health Validator.** Click the **Settings** node, and then double-click **Default Configuration** in the right pane.

3. In the left pane are two nodes, one for Windows 8/Windows 7/Windows Vista and the other for Windows XP. If necessary, click **Windows 8/Windows 7/Windows Vista.**

4. The right pane shows the settings that can be included in the policy. If necessary, click the check boxes for all entries in the Firewall Settings, Antivirus Settings, and Spyware Protection Settings sections (see Figure 6-13). You might need to scroll down to see the Automatic Updates Settings and Security Updates Settings sections. Click the **Automatic updating is enabled** check box. Leave the default security update settings, and click **OK.**

Figure 6-13   Policy settings for the Windows Security Health Validator

5. Keep the Network Policy Server console open and 411Server1 running for the next activity.

Health Policies and Enforcement Methods

With NAP installed and an SHV configured, you need health policies to apply the restrictions. Creating a health policy also creates a network policy and a connection request policy. As explained previously in "Configuring NPS Policies," a connection request policy specifies where the request is authenticated, and the network policy specifies the access an authenticated access client has. In the next activity, you create two health policies: one for compliant systems and another for noncompliant systems.

Activity 6-10: Configuring Health Policies

Time Required: 5 minutes
Objective: Create health policies for compliant and noncompliant clients.

Required Tools and Equipment: 411Server1
Description: In this activity, you create two health policies for the Windows Security Health Validator.

1. Log on to 411Server1 as **Administrator**, and open the Network Policy Server console, if necessary.

2. Expand **Policies** in the left pane. Right-click **Health Policies** and click **New** to open the Create New Health Policy dialog box. Type **Compliant** in the Policy name text box, and leave the default **Client passes all SHV checks** option (see Figure 6-14). In the "SHVs used in this health policy" list box, click the **Windows Security Health Validator** check box, and click **OK**.

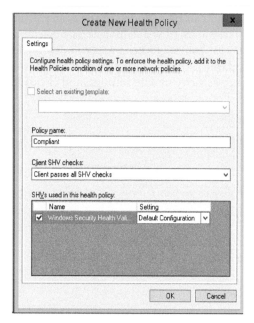

Figure 6-14   Creating a health policy

3. Right-click **Health Policies** and click **New** again. Enter **Noncompliant** in the Policy name text box, click **Client fails one or more SHV checks**, click the **Windows Security Health Validator** check box, and click **OK**.

4. Leave the Network Policy Server console open and 411Server1 running for the next activity.

Now that the basic configuration for NAP is in place, you need to configure enforcement. The enforcement client on the user's computer communicates with an enforcement point (the client's connection to the network) to coordinate the process of validating the client's health. The enforcement point communicates with the NAP health policy server to determine whether the access client should be given access, refused access, or given limited access. An enforcement point is related to the enforcement method being used. For example, a DHCP server is the enforcement point for the DHCP enforcement method. When you're configuring the enforcement method, you can also set options such as auto-remediation and groups of remediation servers. The available enforcement methods are as follows:

- *DHCP enforcement*—This method has the advantage of being the simplest to deploy. Enforcement is done when an access client requests an IP address via DHCP. This enforcement method has the disadvantage of being circumvented by the use of static IP addresses.

- *VPN enforcement*—Enforcement with this method is done by the VPN server when an access client attempts to connect through a VPN connection.

- *IPsec enforcement*—This method is the most secure and the most complex to deploy. Health certificates are issued to an access client when it's compliant, and these certificates allow access to the network.

- *802.1x wired and wireless enforcement*—Enforcement is done by an 802.1x authenticating switch (such as a Cisco switch) or an 802.1x-compliant wireless access point.

- *Terminal Services gateway enforcement*—Enforcement is done on the Terminal Services gateway server when an access client attempts to connect by using Terminal Services or Remote Desktop.

Enforcement methods can be combined for even stronger security, but doing so increases the complexity of an NAP deployment. The least complex, but still flexible, enforcement method is DHCP. With DHCP enforcement, you can specify scopes where NAP is enforced. This feature is useful when you're setting up NAP in a production environment because you can limit where it's applied to just a few IP addresses, giving you a chance to test policies without affecting the entire network. In addition, DHCP enforcement enables you to direct noncompliant access clients to a specific part of the network for remediation (as discussed later in "Remediation Server Groups and Networks"). Not all client computers can use NAP, however. If a computer can't install NAP components and create a statement of health for verification, it's considered NAP ineligible. In the next activity, you configure NAP with the DHCP enforcement method.

Activity 6-11: Configuring NAP with the DHCP Enforcement Method

Time Required: 15 minutes
Objective: Configure NAP with the DHCP enforcement method and set up a scope for DHCP.

Required Tools and Equipment: 411Server1 and a DHCP server installed and active on 411Server1
Description: In this activity, you configure the DHCP enforcement method so that client health is checked when a client requests its network IP address from the DHCP server.

1. Log on to 411Server1 as **Administrator,** if necessary. Open the Network Policy Server console, if necessary, and click the **NPS (Local)** node in the left pane. In the Standard Configuration section of the right pane, make sure **Network Access Protection (NAP)** is selected in the drop-down list, and click **Configure NAP** to start the Configure NAP Wizard.

2. In the Select Network Connection Method For Use with NAP window, click **Dynamic Host Configuration Protocol (DHCP)** in the "Network connection method" drop-down list. Keep the default policy name, **NAP DHCP,** and click **Next.**

3. In the Specify NAP Enforcement Servers Running DHCP Server window, you can add remote RADIUS clients as enforcement points. The local server is running DHCP, so click **Next.**

4. In the Specify DHCP Scopes window, you want to include all scopes, so click **Next.**

5. In the Configure Machine Groups window, you can add a computer group the policy is applied to, but leave it blank so that the policy is applied to all computers that connect with DHCP. Click **Next.**

6. In the Specify a NAP Remediation Server Group and URL window, you can specify a NAP remediation server group and a help page URL. For this activity, leave them blank, and click **Next.**

7. In the Define NAP Health Policy window, **Windows Security Health Validator** and **Enable auto-remediation of client computers** are selected by default. The network access restriction for NAP-ineligible client computers is set to **Deny full network access to NAP-ineligible client computers. Allow access to a restricted network only** by default (see Figure 6-15). Click **Next.**

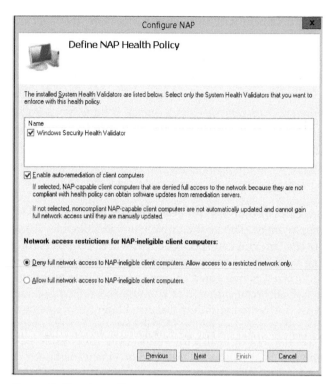

Figure 6-15 The Define NAP Health Policy window

8. The final window shows the policies to be created: two health policies, one for NAP DHCP–compliant clients and one for NAP DHCP–noncompliant clients; a single connection request policy, NAP DHCP; and three network policies—one for compliant computers, one for noncompliant computers, and one for non-NAP-capable computers. Click **Finish**.

9. Open the DHCP console by clicking **Tools, DHCP** from the Server Manager menu.

10. To enable the NAP health policy on all DHCP scopes (which you selected in Step 4), expand **411Server1.411dom.local** in the left pane, and then right-click **IPv4** and click **Properties**.

11. Click the **Network Access Protection** tab, and click the **Enable on all scopes** button (see Figure 6-16). When prompted to confirm your choice, click **Yes**. Accept the default option, **Full Access**, and then click **OK**.

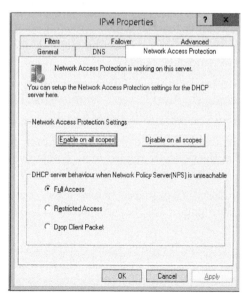

Figure 6-16 The Network Access Protection tab

12. Open an elevated command prompt, and then type **napclcfg.msc** and press **Enter** to start the NAP client configuration program (NAPCLCFG).

13. In the left pane of NAPCLCFG, click **Enforcement Clients**. In the center pane, click **DHCP Quarantine Enforcement Client**. In the Actions pane, click **Enable**.

14. Close the console to return to the elevated command prompt. Type **services.msc** and press **Enter** to open the Services console.

15. Scroll down to and double-click **Network Access Protection Agent**. In the Properties dialog box, change the startup type to **Automatic**, click **Start**, and then click **OK**.

16. Close the Services console and the command prompt window. Leave 411Server1 running for the next activity.

NAP VPN enforcement restricts access for remote VPN clients that aren't compliant with network health policies. This method affects only clients connecting through a VPN. To use it, you must configure the VPN server acting as the enforcement point to use PEAP authentication. To configure VPN enforcement, follow these steps in the Network Policy Server console:

1. Expand the NPS (Local) node in the left pane. In the center pane, click Configure NAP.

2. In the Select Network Connection Method For Use with NAP window, click Virtual Private Network (VPN) in the drop-down list, enter a name for the enforcement method policy, and then click Next.

3. In the Specify NAP Enforcement Servers Running VPN Server window, select the VPN server, and click Next.

4. In the Configure User Groups and Machine Groups window, you can specify Active Directory groups of users or machines to narrow down who the policy applies to. Leaving this option blank makes the policy apply to all VPN connections. Click Next.

5. In the Configure an Authentication Method window, leave the default option Secure Password (PEAP-MS-CHAP v2) selected. If you use smart cards on your network, you could also click the Smart Card or other certificate (EAP-TLS) option. Click Next.

6. In the Specify a NAP Remediation Server Group and URL window, you can add a group of servers, including WSUS and antivirus management servers. Click Next.

7. In the Define NAP Health Policy window, the Windows Security Health Validator and "Enable auto-remediation of client computers" check boxes are selected. You can also choose whether to allow access to NAP-ineligible clients. Then click Next.

8. The final window shows the names of the policies being created. Click Finish.

Remediation Server Groups and Networks

In a basic NAP configuration, if client computer health issues go beyond what auto-remediation can handle, there are two choices: Allow access to the network, or deny access to the network. Allowing an unhealthy computer in your network is risky. If, for example, its antivirus software isn't up to date, it could carry a virus into the main network. At the same time, users can't be productive if they aren't allowed access to the network. The solution is to isolate noncompliant computers from the rest of the network and give them the tools needed to achieve compliance. With DHCP enforcement or VPN enforcement, you can create a remediation network and restrict noncompliant computers' access to only those servers. To design a remediation network, first you should determine what servers to use in it. The following servers can be network members that can supply the needed resources for remediation:

- *Antivirus signature servers*—Many major third-party antivirus software vendors have update utilities that can be installed and configured to work with NAP. This server allows a noncompliant computer to download and install the latest antivirus signatures to get back into compliance.

- *Windows Server Update Services server*—Installing WSUS on a server makes it possible to control what updates are required and make them available for download and installation on noncompliant computers.
- *System Center component server*—A server running System Center Configuration Manager can host software updates to get a client computer compliant.

In addition, a client computer might need other resources to make the network connections for performing the remediation. The following servers should be considered additional remediation network members:

- *Domain controllers*—Noncompliant computers still need to authenticate, download group policies, and get their domain profile settings. If they can't access a domain controller, they might not be able to access the resources they need to get compliant.
- *DNS servers*—Without DNS, noncompliant computers can't resolve hostnames and might not be able to access remediation servers or outside servers, such as Windows Update.
- *DHCP servers*—Noncompliant computers might need to renew a DHCP lease while they're becoming compliant. They also need to change their IP profiles after they become compliant to access the main network.
- *Help servers*—You can set a help page URL when configuring a remediation server group that gives users instructions for bringing their computers into compliance. Each network policy can have a different URL. To be able to get these directions, noncompliant computers must be able to access the URL while on the remediation network.

Next, you need to limit the access of noncompliant computers to only the servers in the remediation network. When using DHCP or VPN enforcement, the easiest way to do this is to create a remediation server group in the NPS console, which limits noncompliant computers' access automatically to members of the group (the remediation network).

If you're using the VPN enforcement method, you can also restrict access to the remediation network by using IP packet filters to restrict access further to particular service port numbers. For example, you could create an IP packet filter that allows only port 80 (HTTP) access to a server in the remediation server group.

 When you're using VPN enforcement and allowing remediation, but no remediation server groups are specified, full network access is given to noncompliant clients unless IP packet filters are configured.

To create or update a remediation server group or to add or modify the help page URL, follow this procedure:

1. Open the Network Policy Server console, and in the left pane, expand Policies and then Network Policies.
2. Select the policy you want to modify and double-click it.
3. Click the Settings tab. Select the NAP Enforcement method, and enable the "Allow limited access" option. Click the Configure button.
4. In the Remediation Servers and Troubleshooting URL window, you can enter a remediation server group by clicking the New Group button or change an existing one by selecting it in the drop-down list. You can also add or modify the help page URL. Click OK when you're finished.

NAP Client Configuration

For NAP to function after the servers are configured, the client computers must be configured. There are three options for configuring clients; two are done on the client, and one is done in the Group Policy tool:

- The NAP Client Configuration console gives you a graphical interface for configuring the local system and saving the configuration file to be used on other clients.

- You can enter netsh commands to configure the local system and save the configuration file to be used on other clients.

- You can use the Group Policy Management console and the Group Policy Management Editor to specify that NAP-capable domain member clients have the NAP client settings updated when group policies are refreshed.

Unless there are reasons for configuring each NAP client separately, enabling Windows Security Center and the NAP agent with group policies is simpler and more efficient.

6

Activity 6-12: Configuring NAP Clients with Group Policies

Time Required: 5 minutes
Objective: Configure a group policy so that NAP clients can enable Windows Security Center and the NAP agent system service.

Required Tools and Equipment: 411Server1, 411Server2, and a DHCP server installed and active on 411Server1
Description: NAP requires both client and server configuration. In this activity, you configure a group policy that enables NAP on any NAP-capable domain client.

1. Log on to 411Server1 as **Administrator,** if necessary.

2. Open Server Manager, and click **Tools, Group Policy Management** from the menu.

3. In the left pane, expand the tree until you see the Default Domain Policy node. Right-click **Default Domain Policy** and click **Edit.** Expand **Computer Configuration, Policies, Administrative Templates, Windows Components,** and **Security Center.**

4. Double-click **Turn on Security Center (Domain PCs only),** click **Enabled,** and then click **OK.**

5. Expand **Computer Configuration, Policies, Windows Settings, Security Settings,** and **System Services.**

6. Scroll down and double-click **Network Access Protection Agent.** Click the **Define this policy setting** check box, and for the service startup mode, click **Automatic** (see Figure 6-17). Click **OK,** and then close the Group Policy Management Editor.

Figure 6-17   Configuring settings for NAP agents

7. Verify the policy configuration by opening a command prompt window, and then typing **netsh nap client show state** and pressing **Enter**. Open an elevated command prompt, type **gpupdate**, and press **Enter**. Log on to 411Server2 as **Administrator**.

8. Close all open windows, but stay logged on to 411Server1 and 411Server2 for the next activity.

Activity 6-13: Uninstalling NPS and RRAS

Time Required: 10 minutes
Objective: Uninstall NPS and RRAS.

Required Tools and Equipment: 411Server1, 411Server2
Description: You're done working with NPS and RRAS, so in this activity, you uninstall them and disable the second interface on 411Server2.

1. Log on to 411Server1 as **Administrator**, if necessary. Open Server Manager, and click **Manage, Remove Roles and Features** from the menu.

2. Click **Next** in the Before You Begin window and the Server Selection window. In the Server Roles window, click to clear the **Network Policy and Access Services** check box. Click the **Remove Features** button to confirm, and then click **Next**.

3. In the Features window, click **Next**. In the Confirmation window, click **Remove**. When the removal is finished, shut down 411Server1.

4. Log on to 411Server2 as **Administrator**, if necessary. Open Server Manager, and click **Manage, Remove Roles and Features** from the menu.

5. Click **Next** in the Before You Begin window and the Server Selection window. In the Server Roles window, click to clear the **Remote Access** check box. Click the **Remove Features** button to confirm, and then click **Next**.

6. In the Features window, click **Next**. In the Confirmation window, click **Remove**. When the removal is finished, click **Close**.

7. You don't need the second NIC on 411Server2 in subsequent activities, so right-click **Start** and click **Network Connections**. On the second network connection that was used for the Internet connection, right-click the connection and click **Disable**.

8. Shut down 411Server2.

Chapter Summary

- Ensuring that unauthorized access to the network is blocked is the first line of defense. Knowing who is allowed access and by what methods can help limit attacks on the network and make creating and monitoring security policies easier.

- Network Policy Server is Microsoft's implementation of the RADIUS protocol, a proposed IETF standard that's widely used to centralize authentication, authorization, and accounting.

- RADIUS accounting is essentially a log of access and accounting requests and responses sent between RADIUS clients and RADIUS servers.

- For stronger security, certificate-based authentication is recommended, which uses a certificate containing information that establishes an entity's identity. With this authentication method, a server's or client's identity can be verified.

- Connection request policies are used to specify which RADIUS servers perform authentication and authorization of RADIUS clients' connection requests. They can also specify which servers RADIUS accounting requests are sent to.

- After configuring RADIUS servers and clients defined in connection request policies, you need to specify who can connect to the network and under what conditions by creating a network policy.

- VPNs are common methods of accessing networks remotely and securely. A network policy should be used to control how they can access a network.

- Templates can reduce the amount of work and minimize the chance of error when configuring RADIUS servers and clients. You can use NPS or RADIUS templates to reuse settings on the local server or export settings to other NPS servers.

- NPS can export templates to an XML file that can then be imported to another NPS server, which is useful when you're setting up multiple NPS servers that should be configured the same way (for example, a server group).

- After configuring policies and templates, you can back up the entire NPS configuration by exporting it to an XML file. You can keep it to restore the configuration, if needed, or use it to configure other NPS servers in a network.

- Blocking access to computers that have no protection from viruses and spyware can help prevent the spread of these threats. Network Access Protection (NAP) supplies an infrastructure for checking clients attempting to access the network to make sure they comply with health policies.

- After NAP has been installed, you need to configure and enable System Health Validators (SHVs). Each SHV corresponds to a system health agent (SHA) on a client computer. The next step is adding health policies to apply the restrictions.

- After the basic NAP configuration is done, you need to configure enforcement. An enforcement point communicates with the NAP health policy server to determine whether the access client should be given access, refused access, or given limited access.

- If a computer is noncompliant with health policies, you should isolate it from the rest of the network and provide the tools for achieving compliance. Using DHCP enforcement or VPN enforcement, you can create a remediation network and restrict noncompliant computers' access to only these servers.

- For NAP to function after servers are configured, client computers must be configured.

Key Terms

access client   A user or device attempting access to the network.

certificate-based authentication   An authentication method that uses a certificate instead of a password to establish an entity's identity.

certification authority (CA)   An entity that issues digital certificates used for authentication.

Challenge Handshake Authentication Protocol (CHAP)   An authentication protocol that uses a series of challenges and responses to verify a client's identity.

Extensible Authentication Protocol (EAP)   A certificate-based authentication method.

Microsoft Challenge Handshake Authentication Protocol (MS-CHAP)   Microsoft's implementation of CHAP, used to authenticate an entity (for example, a user attempting access to the network). *See also* Challenge Handshake Authentication Protocol (CHAP).

Microsoft Challenge Handshake Authentication Protocol version 2 (MS-CHAP v2)   An authentication protocol used to authenticate a user or server. This newer version of MS-CHAP is more secure. *See also* Microsoft Challenge Handshake Authentication Protocol (MS-CHAP).

NAP agent   A system service on an NAP client computer that collects SoHs from the SHAs and forwards the information to NAP enforcement clients.

NAP clients   NAP-enabled computers attempting to access a network that can present their health status for evaluation.

NAP enforcement client   A component of an NAP client that presents a client computer's health status to the NAP server and requests access. Also communicates the result of the request to other NAP client components.

NAP enforcement method   A process used in NAP that specifies the type of network technology a client wants to connect to the network with.

Network Access Protection (NAP)   A Windows Server 2012 feature that supplies an infrastructure for checking clients attempting to access a network to make sure they comply with health policies.

network access server (NAS)   A protocol-specific device that aids in connecting access clients to the network.

Network Policy Server (NPS)   A role service that enables you to define and enforce rules that determine who can access your network and how they can access it.

Password Authentication Protocol (PAP)   An authentication protocol that uses passwords sent in plaintext to authenticate an entity.

Protected Extensible Authentication Protocol (PEAP)   A certificate based and password based authentication method designed to protect EAP messages by encapsulating them in a secure encrypted tunnel and using MS-CHAP v2 for user authentication. *See also* Extensible Authentication Protocol (EAP).

RADIUS server group   A group of RADIUS servers configured to accept authentication and authorization requests from a RADIUS proxy. *See also* Remote Authentication Dial In User Service (RADIUS).

realm   The Active Directory domain where a RADIUS server is located.

remediation network   A group of remediation servers that a noncompliant client computer can access. *See also* remediation server.

remediation server   A server that can help a noncompliant client computer become compliant by hosting software updates or giving instructions.

Remote Authentication Dial In User Service (RADIUS)   An industry-standard client/server protocol that centralizes authentication, authorization, and accounting for a network.

root certificate   A certificate establishing that all other certificates from that CA are trusted; also called a "CA certificate."

shared secret   A text string known only to two systems trying to authenticate each other.

statement of health (SoH)   A declaration from an NAP-enabled client computer about its status on having items such as antivirus protection and security updates installed.

statement of health response (SOHR)   A message from an NAP server indicating the status of a request about a client's health from a System Health Validator.

system health agents (SHAs)   An NAP client component that checks defined settings to see whether they are up to date and configured correctly; this component also creates a statement of health (SoH). *See also* statement of health (SoH).

System Health Validator (SHV)   An NAP server component that verifies the statement of health sent by a client. *See also* statement of health (SoH).

system statement of health (SSOH)   A group of SoHs collected by an NAP agent when there are multiple system health agents. *See also* statement of health (SoH).

Transport Layer Security (TLS)   A cryptographic protocol used to encrypt messages over a network.

Review Questions

1. Which of the following can function as a RADIUS client? (Choose all that apply.)

   a. A VPN server

   b. An unmanaged switch

   c. A wireless access point

   d. A dial-in server

2. What authentication methods does NPS use? (Choose all that apply.)

   a. Passwords

   b. Smart cards

   c. Certificates

   d. Biometrics

3. What's the maximum size of a shared secret?

   a. 128 characters

   b. 64 characters

   c. 32 characters

   d. 256 characters

4. What authentication methods does PEAP use? (Choose all that apply.)

   a. Passwords

   b. Certificates

   c. Biometrics

   d. None of the above

5. What criteria can a RADIUS proxy use to determine where to forward a request? (Choose all that apply.)

   a. The priority assigned the server

   b. The weight assigned the server

   c. The availability of the server

   d. The IP address of the server

6. What formats does RADIUS accounting write to? (Choose all that apply.)

   a. Event log

   b. SQL Server

   c. RADIUS accounting format

   d. Text file

7. What do connection request policies specify?

   a. Which RADIUS servers handle connection requests from RADIUS clients

   b. Which users and groups can connect, what times they can access the network, and what conditions apply

   c. a and b

   d. None of the above

8. What do network policies specify?

   a. Which RADIUS servers handle connection requests from RADIUS clients

   b. Which users and groups can connect, what times they can access the network, and what conditions apply

   c. a and b

   d. None of the above

9. To make a connection request policy apply to a wireless access point, the NAS type must be set to which of the following?

   a. Wireless access point

   b. 802.11

   c. Unspecified

   d. None of the above

10. Which of the following is *not* a template type?

   a. Certificates

   b. Shared secrets

   c. RADIUS clients

   d. Remote RADIUS servers

11. Authentication methods can be overridden in which of the following?

   a. Connection Request Policy node

   b. Network Policy node

   c. Override policy

   d. Templates

12. When all NPS policies on an NPS server are exported, what else is exported?

   a. The RADIUS accounting log

   b. Physical device names

   c. Shared secrets

   d. A list of client access devices

13. RADIUS proxies distribute requests equally between servers when which of the following is true?

   a. The load balancing attribute is set.

   b. The servers have the same priority.

   c. Each server has a different weight.

   d. The servers have the same weight.

14. Which of the following is a component of an NAP client? (Choose all that apply.)

   a. System health agent

   b. NAP agent

   c. System health validator

   d. Enforcement point

15. Remediation servers are an optional component of NAP. True or False?

16. What does an NAP agent do? (Choose all that apply.)

    a.   Pulls together all SoHs from the SHAs

    b.   Coordinates all NAP activity on the NPS server

    c.   Sends the SoH to the enforcement point

    d.   Sends the SoH to the enforcement client

17. What's the most secure NAP enforcement method?

    a.   DHCP enforcement

    b.   IPsec enforcement

    c.   VPN enforcement

    d.   802.1x enforcement

18. Some enforcement methods can be combined. True or False?

19. What is not considered a remediation server? (Choose all that apply.)

    a.   Domain controller

    b.   SQL server

    c.   DHCP server

    d.   NPS server

20. Which method is used to configure client computers to use NAP? (Choose all that apply.)

    a.   System health agents

    b.   NAP Client Configuration console

    c.   Group policies

    d.   `netsh` commands

Case Projects

Case Project 6-1: Adding a RADIUS Infrastructure

CSM Tech Publishing is growing. To keep building costs down, it's allowing more people to work from home and connect to the network via a VPN. For this reason, the CIO has asked you to propose a RADIUS infrastructure. The resources users access are about the same as though they were logged on at the office. The only external access to the network is through a VPN, and the internal infrastructure uses switches that don't perform any kind of authentication. Although not many people are currently working from home, the number is expected to grow quickly if things work out well. Given these considerations, what suggestions should you give the CIO?

Case Project 6-2: Setting Up Remote Access for Contractors

Several new projects are being staffed by outside contractors, who will be working on servers in the contractors' office, not in the company building, and will have their own VPN server. The contracting company has informed your company that none of its people will be working weekends. What controls can you set up to minimize contract employees' access to your network?

Case Project 6-3: Protecting a Network's Health

CSM Tech Publishing is allowing more employees to work from home. As the network administrator, your concern is that some of these employees are connecting to the network from their home computers rather than company-issued computers you have configured. You want to avoid viruses or spyware being brought into the network inadvertently, but you don't want employees' productivity reduced while they're trying to get their computers compliant, especially because many of them aren't computer savvy and would have trouble figuring out how to get needed updates. What's the most efficient configuration in this situation?

chapter 7

Domain Controller and Active Directory Management

After reading this chapter and completing the exercises, you will be able to:

- Describe Active Directory key concepts and components
- Clone a virtual domain controller
- Configure a read only domain controller
- Configure sites
- Work with operations master roles
- Maintain Active Directory

Domain controllers are the main physical component of Active Directory and must be used strategically to get the best performance and reliability from your domain. A single DC is rarely enough, even for a small domain. To provide fault tolerance and load balancing of the functions DCs provide, inevitably you need to install two or more DCs in your network. To facilitate creating DCs, you can use virtual domain controller cloning. In a multisite domain, you might want to use read only domain controllers. If you have multiple sites, it's important to understand how replication works between sites. When new DCs are deployed or DCs are taken offline, you need to be aware of the function and placement of DCs that hold operations master roles. This chapter covers all these topics so that you can manage domain controllers safely and efficiently in a variety of domains.

Although the Active Directory database is usually reliable, problems can occur because of accidental deletion of Active Directory objects as well as hardware and software failures. This chapter discusses how to back up and restore the Active Directory database and restore objects as needed.

Active Directory Review

Table 7-1 summarizes what you need for the hands-on activities in this chapter.

Table 7-1   Activity requirements

Activity	Requirements	Notes
Activity 7-1: Installing an RODC with Staging	411Server1, 411Server2	
Activity 7-2: Configuring the Password Replication Policy	411Server1, 411Server2	
Activity 7-3: Creating a Subnet in Active Directory Sites and Services	411Server1	
Activity 7-4: Viewing Site Properties	411Server1	
Activity 7-5: Changing an RODC to a Standard DC	411Server1, 411Server2	
Activity 7-6: Transferring FSMO Roles	411Server1, 411Server2	
Activity 7-7: Creating a System State Backup	411Server1	
Activity 7-8: Restoring Active Directory from a System State Backup	411Server1, 411Server2	
Activity 7-9: Restoring Deleted Objects from the Active Directory Recycle Bin	411Server1, 411Server2	
Activity 7-10: Compacting the Active Directory Database	411Server1, 411Server2	

© 2015 Cengage Learning®

As you learned from studying the objectives of the Installing and Configuring Windows Server 2012 exam (Exam 70-410), domain controllers (DCs) are the heart of the physical structure of a Windows Active Directory domain. The other physical component of Active Directory is a site. The logical components of Active Directory are forests, domains, and OUs. Before you learn about new topics related to DCs and Active Directory, review the following list of key points to keep in mind:

- DCs are servers that have a Windows Server OS installed with the Active Directory Domain Services server role installed and configured.

- DCs depend on Domain Name System (DNS) as part of the Active Directory infrastructure, and there must be at least one DNS server in a domain.

- One DC per domain is required, but having two DCs for each domain is recommended for reliability and availability. A DC can support only a single domain.

- DCs maintain data consistency in Active Directory with other DCs in the domain by using multimaster replication.

- Read only domain controllers (RODCs) are special DC configurations where Active Directory changes can't be written. Changes must always occur on a writeable DC, and the changes are replicated back to all RODCs, which is called "unidirectional replication."

- Some functions related to maintaining the Active Directory infrastructure are stored in certain DCs referred to as operations masters. These DCs are assigned a Flexible Single Master Operation (FSMO) role, which uses single master replication.

- A global catalog (GC) server is a DC configured to hold the global catalog. Every forest must have at least one GC server. GCs facilitate domain-wide and forest-wide searches and logons across domains, and they hold universal group membership information. Each site should have at least one GC server to speed logons and directory searches.

- Active Directory is based on the Lightweight Directory Access Protocol (LDAP) standard for accessing directory objects.

- An Active Directory tree is made up of one or more domains that share a common top-level and second-level domain name.

- An Active Directory forest consists of one or more trees with domains that share a common trust relationship and schema yet allow independent policies and administration.

- An Active Directory site is a physical location in which DCs communicate and replicate information frequently. A site is composed of one or more IP subnets connected by high-speed LAN technology. Replication between DCs in separate sites can be configured according to the available bandwidth.

Now that you're refreshed on the basics of DCs and Active Directory, turn your attention to a couple of new topics in the following sections: cloning a virtual domain controller and configuring RODCs.

Cloning a Virtual Domain Controller

Because of the benefits of virtualization, implementing DCs as virtual machines in Hyper-V is common practice. Unfortunately, with earlier versions of Windows Server, you couldn't take advantage of all the features and conveniences of virtualization when the virtual machine (VM) was a domain controller. For example, you couldn't create Hyper-V checkpoints without risk of Active Directory database corruption, and you couldn't export a DC for the purposes of creating a replica to use as another DC in the domain.

Windows Server 2012/R2 has eliminated many of the limitations on tasks you could perform on DCs in Hyper-V. Starting with Windows Server 2012, DCs running on Hyper-V are virtualization aware, and there are built-in safeguards to prevent the Active Directory database from being adversely affected when the VM is rolled back in time by applying a checkpoint.

These new safeguards not only allow checkpoints to be used with DCs, but also permit cloning virtual DCs safely, saving administrators from having to install the OS and configure Active Directory on each DC to be deployed. A DC clone is a replica of an existing DC and has the following benefits:

- Fast deployment of new DCs in a new or existing domain

- Fast DC restoration during disaster recovery

- Easy deployment of new branch office DCs

Domain Controller Cloning Prerequisites

To clone a DC, you need to verify the following prerequisites:

- The hypervisor must support virtual machine generation identifiers. Currently, this includes Hyper-V running on Windows Server 2012/R2, Microsoft Hyper-V Server 2012/R2, and VMware vSphere 5.0 Update 2 and later.

- The DC to be cloned must be running Windows Server 2012 or later.

- The PDC emulator FSMO role is running Windows Server 2012 or later.
- A GC server must be available.
- The following server roles must not be installed on the source DC: DHCP, Active Directory Certificate Services (AD CS), and Active Directory Lightweight Directory Services (AD LDS).

Steps for Cloning a Domain Controller

After you have verified the prerequisites, you clone a DC by following these steps:

1. Authorize the source DC for cloning by adding the DC's computer account to the Cloneable Domain Controllers group in the Users folder in Active Directory.

2. Run the PowerShell cmdlet `Get-ADDCCloningExcludedApplicationList` on the source DC to be sure it's not running any services that are incompatible with cloning. If any unsupported server roles are listed, they must be uninstalled. Other services or applications that are listed must be verified with the software vendor to determine whether they will be affected by a computer name or SID change. Listed software that's determined to be compatible must be added to the compatible list of programs by running the same command with the `-GenerateXml` option.

3. Run the PowerShell cmdlet `New-ADDCCloneConfigFile` on the source DC. This command creates an `.xml` file named `DCCloneConfig.xml` in the *%windir%*\NTDS folder. With this command, you can specify the computer name and IP address settings for the target DC.

4. Shut down the source DC.

5. Export the source DC virtual machine. You can export the VM to a share or a local drive by using the Hyper-V console or the `Export-VM` PowerShell cmdlet. If you export to a local drive, you must first copy the exported folder to a location where the other Hyper-V server can access it. Before you export the VM, make sure to delete all checkpoints first.

6. Import the virtual machine into Hyper-V. You can use the Hyper-V console or the `Import-VM` PowerShell cmdlet. If you're using the Hyper-V console, be sure to select the "Copy the virtual machine (create a new unique ID)" option, and when using PowerShell, make sure you use the `-GenerateNewId` option to create a VM-Generation ID on the new DC. Rename the VM.

7. Start the source DC and then the new DC. The cloned DC processes the `DCCloneConfig. xml` file created on the source DC because it was copied during the export/import process.

8. Both the source DC and the cloned DC are members of the Cloneable Domain Controllers group at this point. Best practices suggest removing both accounts and leaving the group empty until you're ready to clone again.

When you import the source DC, you can use the exported files in place or copy the exported files so that the original files can be used to create another DC. You can import the new DC to the same Hyper-V server or another Hyper-V server. The latter option is more common because having the DCs operate on two different Hyper-V hosts provides another level of fault tolerance. Try walking through an example of cloning a DC named DC1 on a server named HyperV-S1 to a new DC named DC2 running in HyperV-S2, all running Windows Server 2012 R2.

1. On DC1, add the DC1 computer account to the Cloneable Domain Controllers group.

2. On DC1, open an elevated PowerShell prompt and enter the `Get-ADDCCloningExcludedApplicationList` cmdlet. In this example, no incompatible applications or services are found.

3. Next, specify the new DC's configuration by using this cmdlet at the PowerShell prompt:

```
New-ADDCCloneConfigFile -CloneComputerName "DC2" -Static
  IPv4Address "10.11.1.102" -IPv4DNSResolver "10.11.1.101"
  -IPv4SubnetMask "255.255.0.0" -IPv4DefaultGateway "10.11.1.250"
```

If the new DC should be placed in a different Active Directory site, you can use the -SiteName option to specify a site.

4. Shut down DC1.

5. Export the DC1 VM. In this example, you use PowerShell to export it to a share named VMExports on a server named Server1:

```
Export-VM -Name DC1 -Path \\Server1\VMExports
```

The VM is copied to a subfolder of the specified path named DC1\Virtual Machines.

6. Import the DC1 VM. On HyperV-S2, issue the following command:

```
$vm = Import-VM -Path \\Server1\VMExports\DC1\Virtual Machines
  -Copy –GenerateNewID
```

The $vm parameter captures the name of the imported VM, which is the name of the exported VM plus a timestamp. This parameter is used in the next step. If you use the exported VM to create additional DCs, you also need to specify paths for the configuration file, VHD files, snapshot files, and the smart paging folder.

7. Rename the imported VM on HyperV-S2 with this cmdlet:

```
Rename-VM -VM $vm -New-Name "DC2"
```

8. Start DC1 and DC2. The new DC reads the DCCloneConfig.xml file and configures itself with the parameters specified in this file.

9. Remove DC1 and DC2 from the Cloneable Domain Controllers group.

 It's not necessary to use PowerShell for exporting, importing, and renaming the VM. You can perform these tasks in the Hyper-V management console. However, you do need PowerShell to check for compatible software and create the clone configuration file.

Configuring Read Only Domain Controllers

A read only domain controller (RODC) is simply an installation option of a server role you're already familiar with: Active Directory Domain Services. The RODC was developed to address the need to have a domain controller in a branch office where server expertise and physical security are often lacking. An RODC performs many of the same tasks as a regular domain controller, but changes to Active Directory objects can't be made on an RODC. An RODC maintains a current copy of Active Directory information through replication. However, there are some important differences in the information an RODC keeps that make it more secure than writeable DCs. These differences are discussed later in "RODC Replication." In addition, you should be aware of some factors before installing an RODC in your network. This section discusses the following aspects of using RODCs in a Windows network:

- RODC installation
- RODC replication
- The Password Replication Policy
- Read only DNS

RODC Installation

Before you can install an RODC, you must meet these prerequisites:

- A writeable DC running Windows Server 2008 or later must be operating in the domain. RODCs were introduced in Windows Server 2008, and they can't replicate with DCs running earlier versions of Windows Server.

- The forest functional level must be at least Windows Server 2003.

- In Windows Server 2008/R2, you must use the `adprep /rodcprep` command before installing the RODC if the forest functional level isn't Windows Server 2008 or later. This command is run automatically during Active Directory installation on a Windows Server 2012/R2 server.

Installing an RODC isn't too much different from installing a regular DC. You still install the Active Directory Domain Services role and run the Active Directory configuration wizard. In the Domain Controller Options window (see Figure 7-1), you select the "Read only domain controller (RODC)" check box.

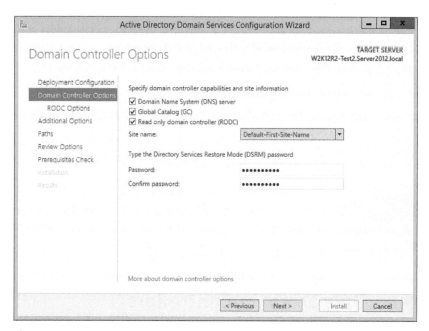

Figure 7-1   The Domain Controller Options window

If you select the RODC option, you move to the RODC Options window (shown in Figure 7-2), where you can select a **delegated administrator account**. A delegated administrator account has local administrative rights and permissions to the RODC, similar to members of the local Administrators group on a member computer or stand-alone computer. A delegated administrator account for an RODC doesn't have domain administrative rights and permissions, so the scope of the delegated permissions is limited to just the RODC computer. Delegated administration is useful if you need someone in a branch office to perform tasks on an RODC that require administrative capability without giving that user broader domain authority. Delegated administrators can perform tasks such as installing drivers and software updates, managing disk drives, installing devices, and starting and stopping Active Directory Domain Services.

In Figure 7-2, notice the two boxes listing group accounts:

- *Accounts that are allowed to replicate passwords to the RODC*—Contains the Allowed RODC Password Replication group, which has no members by default. You add accounts to this box or the Allowed RODC Password Replication group if you want account passwords to be replicated to the RODC.

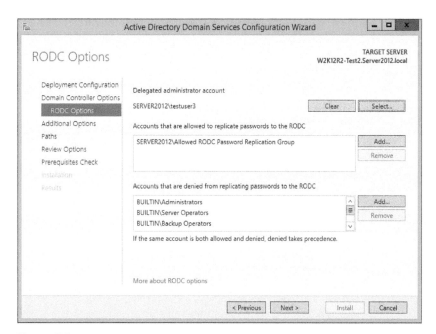

Figure 7-2   The RODC Options window

- *Accounts that are denied from replicating passwords to the RODC*—You add accounts to this box or the Denied RODC Password Replication group to specifically deny replication of account passwords.

Password replication is discussed more later in "Password Replication Policy."

Staged RODC Installation

Another option for installing an RODC that isn't available with a regular DC is a **staged installation** or "delegated installation," as it was called in Windows Server 2008. With staged installation, a domain administrator creates the RODC computer account in Active Directory, and then a regular user can perform the installation at any later time. To use this feature, you create a computer account for the server performing the RODC role in the Domain Controllers OU before installing the RODC. To do so in ADAC, click the Domain Controllers OU and click "Pre-create a Read-only domain controller account" in the Tasks pane to start the Active Directory Domain Services Installation Wizard (see Figure 7-3).

Figure 7-3   The Active Directory Domain Services Installation Wizard

In the next window, you enter credentials if you aren't already logged on as an administrator. In the Specify the Computer Name window, you enter the name of the new RODC computer account (see Figure 7-4). The target server must not be a domain member before you install Active Directory Domain Services on it.

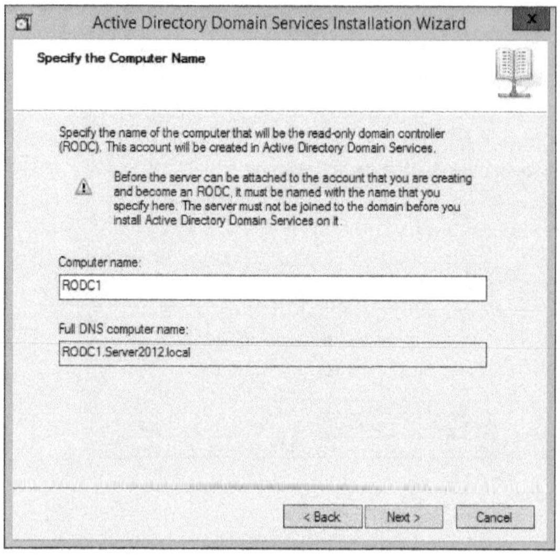

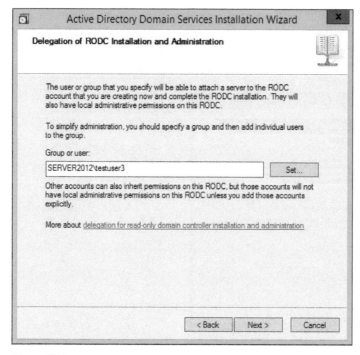

Figure 7-4   Specifying the computer name

Next, you select a site for the new RODC. The target server must have an IP address configuration that's suitable for the site. The next window looks much like Figure 7-1, where you specify whether the RODC should also be a DNS server or GC server. The "Read only domain controller (RODC)" option is selected and grayed out. In the Delegation of RODC Installation and Administration window, you specify the user or group who can perform the RODC installation (see Figure 7-5). This account should represent a user or users who are physically at the place where the RODC is to be installed. This account is also delegated administration of the RODC.

Figure 7-5   Delegating RODC installation and administration

Finally, you review your selections and finish the wizard. A computer account is created in the Domain Controllers OU, and ADAC shows the Domain Controller Type as Unoccupied Domain Controller until the RODC installation is finished. The rest of the process is done on the target server that will be the RODC. Make sure the target server's computer name is the name specified in the wizard and the server isn't currently a domain member.

The procedure for staging RODC installation can also be done in ADUC by right-clicking the Domain Controllers OU and clicking "Pre-create Read-only Domain Controller account."

Staged RODC Installation with PowerShell   As you might have expected, the procedure for staging an RODC installation can be done with a PowerShell cmdlet. At an elevated PowerShell prompt, use the following command to create an RODC computer account named RODC1 in the csmtech.local domain in a site named BranchOffice with a group named BranchOff-G as the delegated administrator account:

```
Add-ADDSReadOnlyDomainControllerAccount
  -DomainControllerAccountName RODC1 -DomainName
  csmtech.local -SiteName BranchOffice
  -DelegatedAdministratorAccountName BranchOff-G
```

Some PowerShell commands are lengthy. You can type them more easily by using the Tab key shortcut. Type a few letters of the command (enough letters to make it unique) and press the Tab key. PowerShell finishes the command for you. This method also works for options in the command. For example, you could type `Add-ADDSR<Tab> -DomainC<Tab>` for the first part of the preceding command.

Staged RODC Installation on the Target Server   To do the RODC installation on the target server, follow these steps:

1. Log on to the server as a local administrator.

2. Change the computer name to match the RODC account name, if necessary.

3. Install the Active Directory Domain Services role.

4. To configure the Active Directory Domain Services role, start the Active Directory Domain Services Installation Wizard by clicking the Alert flag and clicking Promote this server to a domain controller.

5. Next, click Add a domain controller to an existing domain. In this window, you specify the domain name and the credentials of an account that can perform the operation. Use the account credentials for an account that was delegated installation and administration for the RODC.

6. In the Domain Controller Options window, you see a message stating that a pre-created RODC account exists. The options are grayed out because they were specified when the computer account was created. However, you must supply a Directory Services Restore Mode (DSRM) password (see Figure 7-6). The "Reinstall this domain controller" option can be used if a DC is being replaced by another server because of hardware failure.

The remainder of the installation is the same as installing a regular DC or RODC.

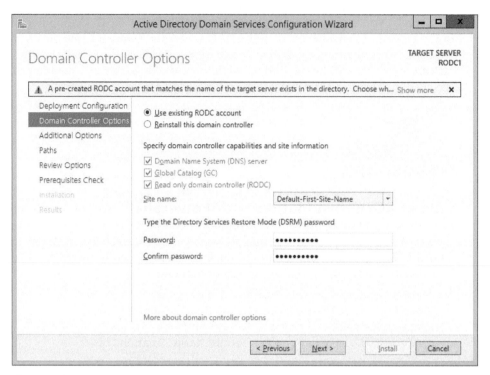

Figure 7-6   Entering a DSRM password

To use PowerShell for the staged RODC installation, first install the AD DS server role. Then type the following command at an elevated PowerShell prompt to configure RODC1 as an RODC in the 411Dom1.local domain, using credentials from BranchUser1:

```
Install-ADDSDomainController -DomainName csmtech.local
  -UseExistingAccount -credential (get-credential)
```

After you enter this command, you're prompted for the username and password of the delegated account and for the DSRM password.

 Because an RODC is meant to address the needs of a branch office, administrators can combine the RODC installation with another one that's designed for branch office installation: Server Core. This configuration often goes together because both optimize security and are meant for remote management.

 ## Activity 7-1: Installing an RODC with Staging

Time Required: 20 minutes
Objective: Install a domain controller with the RODC option.

Required Tools and Equipment: 411Server1 and 411Server2
Description: You're opening a branch office with about 20 users. No server administrators work in the branch office, and there's no designated equipment room to keep the DC secure. You opt to use an RODC so that branch office users have some benefits of a local DC without the security risks. You want to do RODC staging by using PowerShell, so first you create a group and an account you delegate administration to. 411Server2 will be the RODC, so it must be removed from the domain first.

1. Start 411Server1 and 411Server2, and log on to both as **Administrator**.

2. On 411Server2, open an elevated PowerShell prompt. Type **Remove-Computer -Restart -Force** and press **Enter**. 411Server2 restarts.

3. On 411Server1, open Active Directory Administrative Center. Create a new OU named **BranchOffice**. In the BranchOffice OU, create a global group named **BranchOff-G** and a user named **BranchUser1** with **Password01**. Make sure to set the password to never expire. Make BranchUser1 a member of the BranchOff-G group.

4. Click the **Domain Controllers** OU. Notice the option in the Tasks pane for "pre-creating" an RODC account. You can use this wizard to stage the RODC account, but you're using PowerShell.

5. On 411Server1, open an elevated PowerShell prompt. Type **Add-ADDSReadOnlyDomainControllerAccount -DomainControllerAccountName 411Server2 -DomainName 411Dom1.local -SiteName Default-First-Site-Name -DelegatedAdministratorAccountName BranchOff-G** and press Enter. You might see a warning message about default security settings, which you can ignore. The last part of the output should say "Operation completed successfully."

6. Make sure the **Domain Controllers** OU is selected and click the **Refresh** button. You should see 411Server2 in the middle pane with the Domain Controller Type showing Unoccupied Domain Controller Account (see Figure 7-7).

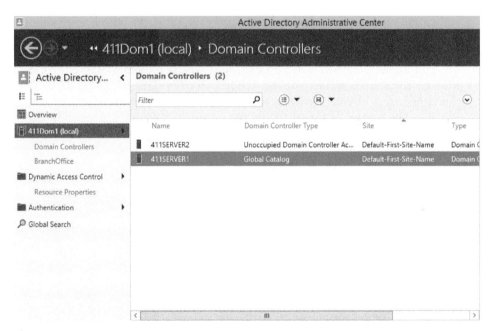

Figure 7-7   The staged RODC account in Active Directory Administrative Center

7. On 411Server2, open a PowerShell prompt. First you need to install the Active Directory server role. Type **Install-WindowsFeature -Name AD-Domain-Services -IncludeManagementTools** and press Enter. This installation takes some time.

8. At the PowerShell prompt, type **Install-ADDSDomainController -DomainName 411Dom1.local -UseExistingAccount -credential (get-credential)** and press Enter.

9. In the credentials dialog box, type **411Dom1\BranchUser1** in the User name text box and **Password01** in the Password text box, and then click **OK**.

10. When you're prompted for the SafeModeAdministratorPassword (which is the DSRM password), type **Password01**, press Enter, type it again, and press Enter.

11. When you're prompted to continue with the operation, press Enter.

12. You might see a warning that one of the network adapters doesn't have a static IP address assigned, which is because of the IPv6 settings. You can ignore this warning. The installation takes a while. When it's finished, you see a message stating that you'll be signed out. Click **Close** or just wait for Windows to restart.

13. While 411Server2 is restarting, refresh the screen in Active Directory Administrative Center on 411Server1 to see that 411Server2 is now listed as a read only, global catalog domain controller.

14. Close Active Directory Administrative Center on 411Server1. Stay logged on to both servers if you're continuing to the next activity.

If theft of an RODC is a likely risk, you can take further precautions to secure its sensitive data by using BitLocker Drive Encryption, which is installed as a server role in Server Manager. With BitLocker, you can secure data on the volume containing the Windows OS and Active Directory as well as on additional volumes.

RODC Replication

Replication on an RODC is unidirectional, meaning the Active Directory database is replicated from a writeable DC to an RODC, but data is never replicated from an RODC to another DC. RODCs can replicate only with Windows Server 2008 and later writeable DCs. **Unidirectional replication** provides an extra level of security for networks with branch office locations. Even if a server is compromised and someone is able to make malicious changes to Active Directory on the RODC, the changes can't be propagated to DCs in the rest of the network.

You already learned that you can limit which accounts' passwords are replicated to an RODC. To increase security of the Active Directory data stored on an RODC, administrators can configure a **filtered attribute set,** which specifies domain objects that aren't replicated to RODCs. The type of data to filter usually includes credential information that might be used by applications using Active Directory as a data store. Any data that might be considered security sensitive can be filtered, except objects required for system operation. Filtered attribute sets are configured on the schema master.

RODC placement in your site topology is important to ensure that replication occurs between an RODC and a writeable DC. A writeable DC is usually placed in the site nearest in the replication topology to the RODC's site. The nearest site is defined as the site with the lowest cost site link. If this placement isn't possible, you must create a site link bridge between the RODC site and a site with a writeable DC. Site links and site link bridges are discussed later in this chapter in "Understanding and Configuring Sites."

Password Replication Policy   As discussed, by default, account passwords are not stored on an RODC, which includes both user and computer account passwords. This arrangement makes the RODC more secure, in case an attacker tries to crack locally stored passwords. However, it also negates some advantages of having a domain controller on the local network. If the RODC stores no passwords, each user and computer authentication must be referred to a writeable DC, most likely located across a WAN link. To prevent this problem, as you learned, you can specify accounts for which passwords will be replicated. When an account password is replicated, its password is retrieved from a writeable DC the first time the account logs on, and thereafter, the password is retrieved from the RODC.

Password replication is also known as "credential caching."

Password replication is controlled by the Password Replication Policy (PRP), accessed in the Properties dialog box of the RODC computer account (see Figure 7-8). A PRP lists users and groups along with a setting of Allow or Deny. Account Operators, Administrators, Backup Operators, and Server Operators are built-in domain local groups added to the PRP with the Deny setting by default. Passwords of these groups' members aren't stored on the RODC.

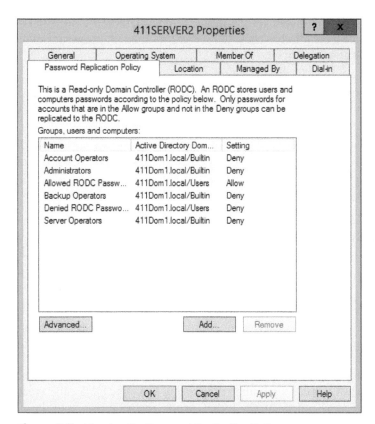

Figure 7-8   Viewing the Password Replication Policy

The PRP also contains groups named Allowed RODC Password Replication group and Denied RODC Password Replication group. These two groups are added to the PRP of all RODCs. These groups have no members at first, but administrators can add users or groups to these groups to control password caching on all RODCs centrally. If a user is a member of a group with the Allow setting and a group with the Deny setting, the Deny setting takes precedence. Generally, groups or users with permission to sensitive information should be added to the Denied RODC Password Replication group. Users who often visit where RODCs are used might be candidates for membership in the Allowed RODC Password Replication group.

Besides the default groups added to the PRP for all RODCs, an administrator can customize each RODC's PRP. For example, a group can be created for all users located at a branch office, and this group can be added to the PRP of the RODC at the branch office with an Allow setting. In addition, you can create a group for the computer accounts in the branch office and add this group to the PRP. Adding computer accounts to the PRP speeds up computer boot times and other actions that require the computer account to authenticate to the domain.

Activity 7-2: Configuring the Password Replication Policy

Time Required: 15 minutes
Objective: Add a group to the PRP of the 411Server2 computer account.

Required Tools and Equipment: 411Server1 and 411Server2
Description: You have installed an RODC at your branch office and lately have heard some complaints that logons are taking a long time. You suspect the problem is that the RODC isn't authenticating users because their passwords aren't replicated. You create a group and add it to the Allowed RODC Passwords Replication group.

1. Log on to 411Server1 as **Administrator,** if necessary.

2. Open Active Directory Users and Computers, click **Domain Controllers** in the left pane, and in the middle pane, double-click **411Server2** to open its Properties dialog box. Click the **Password Replication Policy** tab.

3. Click the **Advanced** button. The Advanced Password Replication Policy for 411Server2 dialog box shows you which account passwords are stored on the RODC. By default, the RODC computer account is replicated as is a special account used by the Kerberos authentication process. Click **Close** and then **Cancel**.

4. Open a PowerShell prompt. Add the BranchOff-G group to the Allowed RODC Password Replication Group by typing **Add-ADGroupMember "Allowed RODC Password Replication Group" BranchOff-G** and pressing **Enter**.

5. Log on to 411Server2 as **BranchUser1**.

6. On 411Server1, open the Properties dialog box for the 411Server2 account again, and click the **Password Replication Policy** tab. Click **Advanced** to see that BranchUser1 is now among the accounts whose passwords are stored on the RODC. Click **Close** and then **Cancel**.

7. Log off 411Server2. Stay logged on to 411Server1 if you're continuing to the next activity.

Read Only DNS

If you install DNS on an RODC, all Active Directory–integrated DNS zones are read only on the RODC. This is a departure from standard terminology because the zone is still considered a primary zone, even though it's read only. Zone information is replicated from other DNS servers, but zone changes can't be made on the RODC. Client workstations can still make name resolution queries to the RODC, but workstations in the branch office using Dynamic DNS can't create or update their DNS records on the RODC. Instead, the RODC sends a referral record to the client with the address of a DNS server that can handle the update. To maintain a current DNS database, the RODC requests a single-record replication from the DNS server that updated the client record. Note that if you attempt to create a new DNS zone on an RODC, you can create only a standard primary, secondary, or stub zone. You can't create a new Active Directory–integrated zone on an RODC.

Understanding and Configuring Sites

When studying the objectives for the Installing and Configuring Windows Server 2012 exam (Exam 70-410), you learned what an Active Directory site is and some of the differences in how replication occurs between DCs in different sites. As you know, a site is one of Active Directory's physical components, along with a domain controller. An Active Directory site represents a physical location where DCs are placed and group policies can be applied. When you're designing the logical components of Active Directory, such as domains and OUs, you don't need to consider the physical location of objects. In other words, an OU named Accounting could contain user accounts from both Chicago and New Orleans, and the DCs holding the Active Directory database could be located in San Francisco and New York. As long as there's a network connection between the location where a user logs on and the location of the DC, the system works.

Having said that, having a DC near the accounts using it makes sense. Authentication and resource access usually work fine across a reliable WAN link, but if a company location contains several users, placing DCs in that location is more efficient. Performance and reliability are less predictable on slower WAN links than on LAN links. So the extra cost of additional DCs can be outweighed by the productivity gained from faster, more reliable network access.

When the first DC of a forest is installed, a site is created named Default-First-Site-Name, but you can rename the site as something more descriptive. Any additional DCs installed in the forest are assigned to this site until additional sites are created. Figure 7-9 shows a single-site domain in two locations at the top and the same domain defined as two sites at the bottom.

There are three main reasons for establishing multiple sites:

- *Authentication efficiency*—When a user logs on to a domain, the client computer always tries to authenticate to a DC in the same site to ensure that logon traffic is kept in the same site and off slower WAN links.

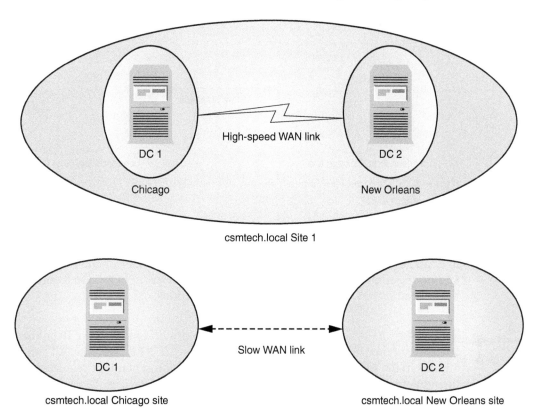

Figure 7-9   Active Directory sites
© 2015 Cengage Learning®

- *Replication efficiency*—A DC in every branch office facilitates faster and more reliable network access, but DCs must communicate with one another to replicate the Active Directory database. Using the default replication schedule, however, can create considerable replication traffic. Replication between DCs occurs within 15 seconds after a change is made and once per hour when no changes have occurred. In databases with several thousand objects, this schedule can take a toll on available bandwidth for other network operations. With multiple sites, intersite replication can be scheduled to occur during off-peak hours and at a frequency that makes most sense. For example, a small branch office site with a limited bandwidth connection to the main office can be configured to replicate less often than a larger branch office that requires more timely updates.

- *Application efficiency*—Some distributed applications, such as Exchange Server (an e-mail and collaboration application) and Distributed File System (DFS), use sites to improve efficiency. These applications ensure that client computers always try to access data in the same site before attempting to access services in remote sites via the WAN link.

Sites are created by using Active Directory Sites and Services. A site is linked to an IP subnet that reflects the IP addressing scheme used at the physical location the site represents. A site can encompass one or more IP subnets, but each site must be linked to at least one IP subnet that doesn't overlap with another site. When a DC is created and assigned an IP address, it's assigned to a site based on its address automatically. Figure 7-10 shows the relationship between sites and IP subnets.

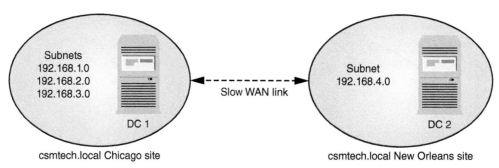

Figure 7-10   The relationship between sites and subnets
© 2015 Cengage Learning®

Site Components

Sites and connections between sites are defined by a number of components that can be created and configured in Active Directory Sites and Services. They include subnets, site links, and bridgehead servers, discussed in the following sections.

Subnets   As discussed, each site is associated with one or more IP subnets. In short, an IP subnet is a range of IP addresses in which the network ID is the same. All computers assigned an address in the subnet can communicate with one another without requiring a router. By default, no subnets are created in Active Directory Sites and Services. When a new site is created, all subnets used by the default site should be created and associated with the default site. Then the subnets for the new site should be created and associated with the new site. Figure 7-11 shows Active Directory Sites and Services with the Default-First-Site-Name Properties dialog box open.

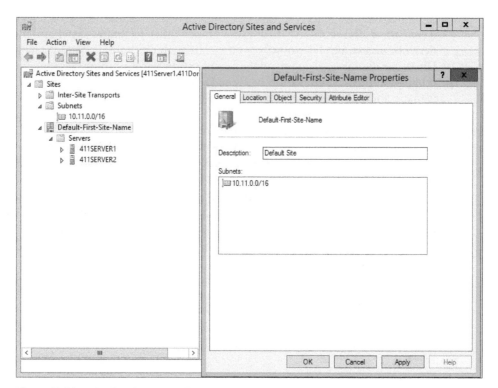

Figure 7-11   Viewing site properties

After creating a site, you must associate one or more subnets with it. Active Directory uses this information in two important ways:

- *Placing new domain controllers in the correct site*—Correct placement is necessary to determine the optimum intrasite and intersite replication topology and to associate clients with the nearest domain controllers. When a new DC is installed, it's automatically placed in the site corresponding with its assigned IP address. If the DC existed before the site was created, you need to move the DC manually from its existing site to the new site.

- *Determining which site a client computer belongs to*—When a client requests a domain service, such as logging on to the domain or accessing a DFS resource, the client request can be directed to a DC or member server in the same site. A local resource is usually preferable, especially when remote sites are connected via slower WAN links.

Defining your subnets is important when you have multiple sites. If a client's IP address doesn't match a subnet in any of the defined sites, communication efficiency could degrade because the client might request services from servers in remote sites instead of locally.

Activity 7-3: Creating a Subnet in Active Directory Sites and Services

Time Required: 5 minutes
Objective: Create a subnet in Active Directory Sites and Services and associate it with a site.

Required Tools and Equipment: 411Server1
Description: You're planning to create multiple sites for your Active Directory structure. Before you create new sites, however, you must configure the existing site to use the subnet already in use in your network. In addition, you rename the default site.

1. Log on to 411Server1 as **Administrator,** if necessary.

2. Open Server Manager, and click **Tools, Active Directory Sites and Services** from the menu.

3. Double-click to expand **Sites,** if necessary. Right-click **Subnets,** point to **New,** and click **Subnet.**

4. In the Prefix text box, type **10.11.0.0/16** (assuming you're following the IP address scheme used in this book; otherwise, ask your instructor what to enter).

5. In the "Select a site object for this prefix" list box, click **Default-First-Site-Name,** and then click **OK.**

6. In the left pane, click **Subnets.** Right-click **10.11.0.0/16** and click **Properties.** In the General tab, you can give the subnet a description and change the site the subnet is associated with. For now, leave it as is. Click **Cancel.**

7. In the left pane, right-click **Default-First-Site-Name** and click **Rename.** Type **Site11** and press **Enter.** You're using the second octet of the IP address as part of the site name.

8. In the left pane, right-click **Site11** and click **Properties.** In the Description text box, type **Site for the 10.11.0.0/16 subnet class,** and then click **OK.**

9. If you're continuing to the next activity, stay logged on to 411Server1.

Site Links   A **site link** is needed to connect two or more sites for replication purposes. When Active Directory is installed, a default site link called DEFAULTIPSITELINK is created. Until new site links are created, all sites that are added use this site link. Site links determine the replication schedule and frequency between two sites. If all locations in an organization are connected through the same WAN link or WAN links of equal bandwidth, one site link might be suitable. If the locations use different WAN connections at differing speeds, however, additional links can be created to configure differing replication schedules. You access the properties of a site link in Active Directory Sites and Services by expanding Sites and Inter-Site Transports and then clicking IP. Site links have three configuration options, as shown in Figure 7-12.

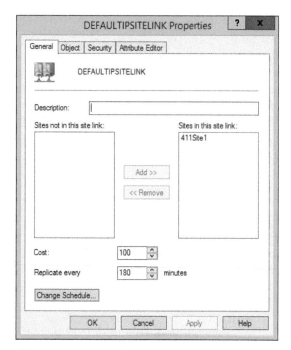

Figure 7-12   The Properties dialog box for DEFAULTIPSITELINK

The Cost field is an administrator-assigned value that represents the bandwidth of the connection between sites. The default value is 100. An administrator can alter this value to influence which path is chosen when more than one path exists between two sites. As shown in Figure 7-13, Site A replicates with Site B and Site C through the corresponding site links, but Site A has two options for replicating with Site D: the link with Site B or the link with Site C. The site link cost determines that Site A will use the link with Site B. Site link costs are additive, so the total cost for Site A to replicate with Site D through Site C is 400; the total cost to replicate with Site D via Site B is only 300. When you have more than one path option between two sites, the lower cost path is always used unless links in the path become unavailable. In this case, the replication process reconfigures itself to use the next lower cost path, if available. Site links are transitive by default, which means Site A can replicate directly with Site D, and Site C can replicate directly with Site B, without creating an explicit link between the two sites.

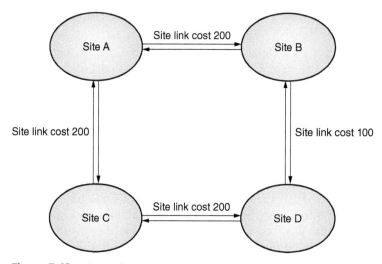

Figure 7-13   Site replication topology
© Cengage Learning®

Bridgehead Servers You learned when studying the objectives for the Installing and Configuring Windows Server 2012 exam (Exam 70-410) that intrasite replication occurs among several domain controllers after the Knowledge Consistency Checker (KCC) creates the topology. Intersite replication occurs between bridgehead servers. When the KCC detects that replication must occur between sites, one DC in each site is designated as the Inter-Site Topology Generator (ISTG). The ISTG then designates a **bridgehead server** to handle replication for each directory partition. Because bridgehead servers perform such a vital function in multisite networks, and this function can consume a lot of server resources, the administrator can override automatic assignment of a bridgehead server and assign the role to a specific DC.

Configuration of sites and site components is discussed in detail in *MCSA Guide to Configuring Advanced Windows Server 2012/R2 Services, Exam 70-412* (Cengage Learning, 2015). This chapter covers just enough so that you understand what a site is, particularly in relation to Active Directory replication and the global catalog.

The Global Catalog and Universal Group Membership Caching

As you've learned, the global catalog is a critical component for many Active Directory operations. It's the only place where universal group membership information is maintained, and it contains a partial replica of all domain objects. Access to a global catalog server must be considered when designing sites and configuring site replication. Having a global catalog server used to be critical in sites with more than a few users because it speeded logons and forest-wide searches for Active Directory objects. However, replication traffic is increased considerably in sites with global catalog servers, particularly if there are several large domains in your Active Directory forest.

Universal group membership caching, first available in Windows Server 2008, handles the potential conflict between faster logons and increased replication traffic. When this feature is enabled, the first time a user logs on to a domain in the site with no global catalog server, the user's universal group membership information is retrieved from a global catalog server in a different site. Thereafter, the information is cached locally on every DC in the site and updated every 8 hours, so there's no need to contact a global catalog server. Having this feature available, however, doesn't mean a global catalog server should never be placed in a site. Microsoft recommends placing a global catalog server in the site when the number of accounts (user and computer) exceeds 500 and the number of DCs exceeds 2. With 500 cached accounts, the traffic created by refreshing every 8 hours might be higher than global catalog replication traffic. In addition, you need to determine whether the other benefits of having a global catalog server (faster forest-wide searches, faster updates of universal groups) outweigh the reduced replication traffic of universal group membership caching.

To configure universal group membership caching, expand the site object in Active Directory Sites and Services, and then open the Properties dialog box of the NT Directory Service (NTDS) Site Settings object. In the Site Settings tab, click the Enable Universal Group Membership Caching check box. In addition, you can select which site is used for refreshing the cache.

Activity 7-4: Viewing Site Properties

Time Required: 10 minutes
Objective: View site properties.

Required Tools and Equipment: 411Server1
Description: You're trying to familiarize yourself with sites and site components, so you explore the properties of NTDS site settings, server NTDS settings, and connection objects.

1. Log on to 411Server as **Administrator**, and open Active Directory Sites and Services, if necessary.

2. Click to expand **Sites**, **Site11**, **Servers**, and **411Server1**. Under 411Server1 in the left pane, right-click **NTDS Settings** and click **Properties**.

3. In the General tab, you can select or clear the Global Catalog option to configure whether the server is a global catalog server. Click the **Connections** tab. You see 411Server2 in the Replicate To list box (see Figure 7-14). Click **Cancel**.

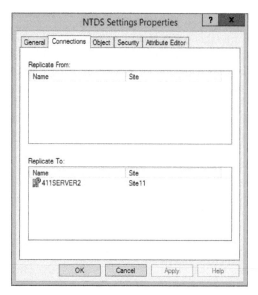

Figure 7-14 NTDS settings for 411Server1

4. In the left pane, click **Site11**. In the right pane, right-click **NTDS Site Settings** and click **Properties** to open the dialog box shown in Figure 7-15. There are NTDS settings associated with server objects and NTDS site settings associated with site objects.

Figure 7-15 The NTDS Site Settings Properties dialog box

5. Click the **Change Schedule** button to open the Schedule for NTDS Site Settings dialog box. As you can see, the regular schedule for intersite replication is once per hour. Click **Cancel**.

6. Notice the Enable Universal Group Membership Caching check box, which is where you enable this feature if the DC isn't a global catalog server. Because it is, enabling this feature has no effect. In the "Refresh cache from" list box, you can select a site for refreshing the cache. Click **Cancel**.

7. Close Active Directory Sites and Services, but stay logged on if you're continuing to the next activity.

Working with Operations Master Roles

Active Directory uses a multimaster replication scheme to synchronize copies of most information in the Active Directory database. However, some critical information is subject to a single master replication scheme to avoid any possibility of the information becoming unsynchronized. The servers that keep this critical information are assigned a Flexible Single Master Operation (FSMO) role. FSMO roles can be summarized as follows:

- *Forest-wide FSMO roles*—Only one DC per forest performs these roles: domain naming master and schema master.

- *Domain-wide FSMO roles*—Only one DC per domain performs these roles: PDC emulator, RID master, and infrastructure master.

This section discusses best practices for locating these DCs in your network for optimal reliability and replication efficiency and explains how to transfer and seize FSMO roles when you need to assign a role to a different DC.

Operations Master Best Practices

The decision of where to place an FSMO role holder is part of your overall Active Directory design strategy. If you build a new forest, the first DC installed performs all five FSMO roles. When a new domain is created in the forest, the first DC performs all three domain-wide FSMO roles for that domain, and a DC in the forest root domain handles the forest-wide roles. In a smaller network, having all these critical roles on a single server can work, but in a large network with multiple domains and sites, you might need to transfer some roles to different servers. Placement of the DCs functioning in these roles can affect replication and the capability to recover from a server failure. In addition, being able to restore the functioning of FSMO roles quickly after a server failure is critical. However, not all FSMOs have equal importance; some roles must be functioning almost continuously for correct domain operation, but other roles can be offline for a while with little disturbance to the network. Here are some common rules for operations masters:

- Unless your domain is very small, transfer some operations master roles from the first DC installed in the forest to other DCs because some FSMO roles require a lot of resources.

- Place the servers performing these roles where network availability is high.

- Designate an alternate DC for all roles. The alternate assumes the role if the original server fails, and it should be a direct replication partner with the original FSMO role holder. Document your plan to make sure alternate DCs aren't burdened with other services that could impede their performance as an FSMO role holder.

The following sections explain best practices with FSMO roles in more detail.

Domain Naming Master   The **domain naming master** is needed when a domain is added or removed from the forest. In most cases, neither users nor administrators notice its absence until one of these operations is attempted. If the DC performing this role goes offline, you should probably wait until it comes back online before attempting to add or remove a domain or DC. The exception, of course, is if you need to add a domain to the network immediately. If you decide to install this role on another DC, the original domain naming master server must not be put back into service unless you uninstall Active Directory.

When possible, the domain naming master should be a direct replication partner with another DC that's also a global catalog server in the same site. Ideally, the domain naming master should also be a global catalog server. If the role must be moved, the direct replication partner is the preferred choice because it should be most fully replicated with the original FSMO. The domain naming master and the other forest-wide FSMO role, the schema master, can be on the same server but need not be.

Schema Master   The **schema master** is needed when the Active Directory schema is changed, including raising the forest functional level. Its absence isn't apparent to users or administrators unless a schema change is attempted. Generally, the schema master should be transferred to another server only when you're certain the original server will be down permanently.

PDC Emulator   The **PDC emulator** processes password changes for older Windows clients (Windows 9x and NT) and is used during logon authentication. The DC performing this role should be centrally located where there's a high concentration of users to facilitate logons. The PDC emulator is the most heavily used of the FSMO roles and should be placed on a suitable DC. Unless your forest configuration has all DCs configured as GC servers, the PDC emulator should be on a DC that's not a global catalog server because global catalog servers are also used heavily. If the PDC emulator role fails, you might want to move the role to another server immediately. After the original server returns to service, the role can be transferred back to it. As mentioned earlier in "Domain Controller Cloning Prerequisites," the PDC emulator must be running Windows Server 2012 or later to perform DC cloning.

RID Master   All objects in a domain are identified internally by a **security identifier (SID)**. An object's SID is composed of a domain identifier, which is the same for all objects in the domain, and a **relative identifier (RID)**, which is unique for each object. Because objects can be created on any domain controller (except RODCs), there must be a mechanism that keeps two DCs from issuing the same RID, thereby duplicating an SID. The **RID master is** responsible for issuing unique pools of RIDs to each DC, thereby guaranteeing unique SIDs throughout the domain. The RID master must be available when adding a DC to an existing domain and should be placed in an area where Active Directory objects are created most often, such as near the server administrator's office. This FSMO role must be highly available to other DCs and is ideally placed with the PDC emulator because the PDC emulator uses the RID master's services frequently. Because the RID master doles out RIDs to DCs in blocks of 500, temporary downtime might not be noticed. However, if a DC has exhausted its pool of RIDs, and the RID master isn't available, new objects can't be created. If the RID master fails, moving this role to another server should be considered only if the original RID master is down permanently.

Infrastructure Master   This DC is responsible for ensuring that changes made to object names in one domain are updated in references to these objects in other domains. A temporary interruption of this role's services probably won't be noticed. This role is most needed when many objects have been moved or renamed in a multidomain environment. The **infrastructure master** role shouldn't be performed by a DC that's also a global catalog server, unless all servers in the forest have been configured as global catalog servers or there's only one domain in the forest. However, a global catalog server should be in the same site as the infrastructure master because there's frequent communication between these two roles. If an infrastructure master fails, the role can be moved to another DC, if necessary, and returned to the original server when it's back in service.

The only time the infrastructure master and global catalog can be on the same DC is when there's only one domain in the forest or all DCs are configured as global catalog servers. If neither is the case, and the infrastructure master is also a global catalog server, the infrastructure master never finds out-of-date data, so it never replicates changes to other DCs in the domain.

Managing Operations Master Roles

Because of the critical nature of the functions FSMO role holders perform, administrators should be familiar with two important FSMO management operations: transferring and seizing. These two functions enable administrators to change the DC performing the FSMO role to make the Active Directory design more efficient and to recover from server failure. Of course, system backups should always be part of managing disaster recovery.

Transferring Operations Master Roles Transferring an operations master role means moving the role's function from one DC to another while the original DC is still in operation. This transfer is generally done for one of the following reasons:

- The DC performing the role was the first DC in the forest or domain and, therefore, holds all domain-wide or domain- and forest-wide roles. Unless you have only one DC, distributing these roles to other servers is suggested.
- The DC performing the role is being moved to a location that isn't well suited for the role.
- The current DC's performance is inadequate because of the resources the FSMO role requires.
- The current DC is being taken out of service temporarily or permanently.

Aside from the best practices discussed previously, there's one restriction when transferring FSMO roles: An RODC can't be an FSMO role holder. Table 7-2 lists each FSMO role and its corresponding scope, the MMC used to work with the role, and the PowerShell command used to transfer the role to another DC.

In Table 7-2, you can replace the role name with a number to shorten the PowerShell command, as shown in the following list:

- PDC emulator: 0
- RID master: 1
- Infrastructure master: 2
- Schema master: 3
- Domain naming master: 4

Table 7-2 The MMCs and PowerShell cmdlets for transferring FSMO roles

FSMO role/scope	MMC	PowerShell cmdlet
Schema master/forest	Active Directory Schema	Move-ADDirectoryServerOperationMasterRole -Identity "*TargetDC*" -OperationMasterRole SchemaMaster
Domain naming master/forest	Active Directory Domains and Trusts	Move-ADDirectoryServerOperationMasterRole -Identity "*TargetDC*" -OperationMasterRole DomainNamingMaster
RID master/domain	Active Directory Users and Computers	Move-ADDirectoryServerOperationMasterRole -Identity "*TargetDC*" -OperationMasterRole RIDMaster
PDC emulator master/domain	Active Directory Users and Computers	Move-ADDirectoryServerOperationMasterRole -Identity "*TargetDC*" -OperationMasterRole PDCEmulator
Infrastructure master/domain	Active Directory Users and Computers	Move-ADDirectoryServerOperationMasterRole -Identity "*TargetDC*" -OperationMasterRole InfrastructureMaster

To seize the role by using PowerShell, add the `-Force` parameter to the command.

You can also use PowerShell to see which servers carry the FSMO roles:

- `Get-ADForest`—Shows which servers carry forest-wide roles and other forest information.
- `Get-ADDomain`—Shows which servers carry domain-wide roles and other domain information.

Before you begin to work with FSMO roles, you need another writeable DC. In the next activity, you demote your RODC to a member server and then promote it again to a standard DC.

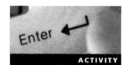

Activity 7-5: Changing an RODC to a Standard DC

Time Required: 20 minutes
Objective: Change an RODC to a standard writeable DC.

Required Tools and Equipment: 411Server1 and 411Server2
Description: You want to transfer some FSMO roles from 411Server1 to 411Server2, but first you must change 411Server2 from an RODC to a standard DC. You use PowerShell for this task.

1. Start 411Server1 and 411Server2, and log on to both as **Administrator**, if necessary.

2. On 411Server2, open a PowerShell prompt. First, uninstall DNS because it's also read-only. Type **Remove-WindowsFeature DNS -Restart** and press **Enter**. DNS is removed, and the server restarts.

3. Next, uninstall the domain controller function. This command doesn't remove the role; it just demotes 411Server2 back to being a member server. Type **Uninstall-ADDSDomainController** and press **Enter**.

4. When you're prompted for the local administrator password (which you need to log on to the server when it's no longer a DC), type **Password01**, press **Enter**, type **Password01** to confirm, and press **Enter**.

5. A message states that the server restarts automatically. When you're prompted to continue, press **Enter**. When the operation is finished, 411Server2 restarts.

6. Log on to 411Server2 as **Administrator**. When you installed Active Directory and DNS, the DNS server address in the IP address configuration was set to 127.0.0.1 because this server was a DNS server. You need to set it back to the address of 411Server1. Set the preferred DNS server address on the network interface to 10.11.1.1, and remove the alternate address. In the IPv6 Properties dialog box, click to select **Obtain an IPv6 address automatically**, if necessary, and then click the **Obtain DNS server address automatically** option.

7. To remove 411Server2 from the domain, right-click **Start** and click **System**. Next to "Computer name," click **Change settings**. Click the **Change** button, click **Workgroup**, and type **Workgroup** in the text box. Click **OK** in the Computer Name/Domain Changes message box, and then click **OK** again. When you're prompted to restart the system, click **OK**. Click **Close**, and then click **Restart Now**.

8. On 411Server1, open Active Directory Users and Computers, and click the **Domain Controllers** OU. Verify that the 411Server2 computer account has been removed. If it's still there, delete it.

9. Log on to 411Server2 as **Administrator**, and open a PowerShell prompt. Type **Install-ADDSDomainController -DomainName "411Dom1.local" -credential (get-credential)** and press **Enter**. When you're prompted for credentials, type **administrator** and **Password01**. The rest of the settings are the defaults for new DCs, which include installing DNS and configuring the paths to C:\Windows. The site is chosen based on the server's IP address, or if no subnets are defined, the default site is used.

10. When you're prompted for the safe mode administrator password, type **Password01**, press **Enter**, type **Password01** to confirm, and press **Enter**.

11. Press **Enter** to confirm. You see warning messages about default security settings, dynamic IP addresses, and DNS delegation, which you can ignore. When the configuration is finished, the server restarts.

12. Leave both servers running if you're continuing to the next activity.

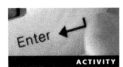

Activity 7-6: Transferring FSMO Roles

Time Required: 15 minutes
Objective: Transfer the schema master and infrastructure master roles.

Required Tools and Equipment: 411Server1 and 411Server2
Description: You want to distribute the FSMO load, so you're transferring the schema master and infrastructure master roles to 411Server2 by using PowerShell.

1. Make sure 411Server2 is running. Log on to 411Server1 as **Administrator**, if necessary.

2. On 411Server1, open a PowerShell prompt. Type **Get-ADForest** and press **Enter**. Find the output lines listing "DomainNamingMaster" and "SchemaMaster." Both indicate that 411Server1 is the FSMO role holder for the two forest-wide roles.

3. Type **Get-ADDomain** and press **Enter**. Find the FSMO roles and verify that 411Server1 is shown as the FSMO role holder for all three domain-wide roles.

4. To see what roles, if any, a server holds, type **Get-ADDomainController** and press **Enter**. Look for the output line "OperationMasterRoles," which lists the roles held by the current DC.

5. Now move the schema master role to 411Server2 by typing **Move-ADDirectoryServerOperationMasterRole -Identity "411Server2" -OperationMasterRole 3** and pressing **Enter**. The number 3 is the role number for the schema master.

6. When prompted to confirm, press **Enter**. When the operation is finished (no confirmation message, but the PowerShell prompt returns), type **Get-ADForest** and press **Enter**. Verify that the schema master role is now held by 411Server2. Another way to confirm is to type **Get-ADDomainController -Server "411Server2"** and press **Enter**. It might take a while to display the results.

7. Next, transfer the infrastructure master role by typing **Move-ADDirectoryServerOperationMasterRole -Identity "411Server2" -OperationMasterRole 2** and pressing **Enter**.

8. Press **Enter** to confirm. To view the domain-wide FSMO role holders in an easier-to-read format, type **Get-ADDomain | Format-Table PDCEmulator, RIDMaster, InfrastructureMaster** and press **Enter**. This command displays information about only these three items.

9. You need the schema master role on 411Server1 to enable the Active Directory Recycle Bin in a later activity, so transfer it back by typing **Move-ADDirectoryServerOperationMasterRole -Identity "411Server1" -OperationMasterRole 3** and pressing **Enter**.

10. Close the PowerShell window. If you're continuing to the next activity, stay logged on to both servers.

Seizing Operations Master Roles

An operations master role is seized when the current role holder is no longer online because of some type of failure. Seizing should never be done when the current role holder is accessible and should usually be done only when it's unlikely the original server can be restored to service. If a DC is scheduled to be decommissioned, you should transfer the role while the DC is still online. If the operations master DC becomes inaccessible because of network failure or a temporary hardware failure, you should wait until this server is back online rather than seize the operations master role.

An exception might be the PDC emulator role, which can affect user logons, or the RID master, which might be needed to create Active Directory objects. If either role holder is going to be offline for an extended period, seizing the role and then transferring it to the original DC when it's back online might be best for continued Active Directory operation. You can't use MMCs to seize a role. You must use the PowerShell cmdlets discussed previously with the -Force option or use ntdsutil, as shown in these steps:

1. Open a command prompt window, and type ntdsutil and press Enter.

2. Type roles and press Enter to get the FSMO Maintenance prompt.

3. Type connections and press Enter to get the Server Connections prompt.

4. Type connect to server *DCName*, replacing *DCName* with the domain controller where you're transferring the FSMO role.

5. Type quit to get back to the FSMO Maintenance prompt.

6. Type seize *RoleName* and press Enter, replacing *RoleName* with the name of the role you want to seize. Possible role names are domain naming master, schema master, PDC emulator, RID master, and infrastructure master.

7. Windows attempts to transfer the role first, and if a transfer fails, the role is seized. Type quit and press Enter to exit ntdsutil.

Maintaining Active Directory

You have learned how to configure Active Directory, install writeable and read only domain controllers, and work with FSMO roles. In the following sections, you learn how to maintain Active Directory whether you need to recover from accidental object deletion or recover Active Directory from catastrophic failure. You also learn how to optimize the Active Directory database, clean up metadata after DCs or domains are removed, and configure Active Directory snapshots.

Before getting into the details of how to maintain Active Directory, examine the two folders that hold most of the components of Active Directory:

- *NTDS*—By default, this folder is located in *%systemroot%* (usually C:\Windows). It contains the following files:

  o ntds.dit: The main Active Directory database.

  o edb.log: Holds a log of Active Directory transactions (changes). If Active Directory is shut down unexpectedly, changes that didn't get fully written to the database can be redone by using the data in this file to commit the changes. This file can grow to a maximum of 10 MB, and then new log files are created, named edb00001.log, edb00002.log, and so forth.

  o edb.chk: Stores information about the last committed transaction; used with edb.log to determine which transactions still need to be written to the database.

  o edbres00001.jrs: A placeholder file that simply takes up disk space. If the volume on which ntds.dit is stored fills up, this file and another named edbres00002.jrs are deleted to free up disk space so that pending transactions can be committed to the database. After the changes are made, the DC is shut down, and the administrator must make disk space available before Active Directory can operate again.

- *SYSVOL*—By default, this folder is located in *%systemroot%*. It contains group policy templates, logon/logoff scripts, and DFS synchronization data.

During Active Directory installation, you can change the default location for these folders rather than accept the default *%systemroot%*. If you do, you don't have to do anything special to back them up because Windows recognizes the new location as part of the Windows system state. The Windows system state on a DC is composed of the same elements as on a non-DC plus the SYSVOL folder and the ntds.dit file.

Active Directory Backup

Active Directory is backed up when you perform a full backup of a DC, when you back up the volumes containing system recovery information, and when you perform a system state backup. Backups can be created with one of three methods included with Windows Server 2012/R2:

- *Windows Server Backup*—A GUI backup tool that guides you through creating a number of backup types, including system state backups. This tool isn't installed by default. You install it with the Add Roles and Features Wizard or the Add-WindowsFeature PowerShell cmdlet.

- wbadmin.exe—A command-line tool for automating aspects of a backup. The Windows Server Backup tool must be installed for this command to work.

- *PowerShell*—The Start-WBBackup cmdlet has many of the same capabilities as wbadmin.exe. The Windows Server Backup tool must be installed for this cmdlet to work.

Although having a disaster recovery plan for all your servers that includes regular backups is a good idea, this chapter focuses on backing up Active Directory with system state backups. More general disaster recovery and server backup and recovery are covered in *MCSA Guide to Configuring Advanced Windows Server 2012/R2 Services, Exam 70-412* (Cengage Learning, 2015).

System State Backup

A system state backup on a DC includes the Registry, boot files, the Active Directory database, the SYSVOL folder, some system files, and other files, depending on roles installed on the server. A system state backup doesn't include user files and installed applications. To perform a system state backup, you can run the Windows Server Backup tool or the wbadmin command as described:

- *Recover the system state*—To start a system state recovery, including the Active Directory database, use the wbadmin start systemstaterecovery command.

- *Delete a system state backup*—The wbadmin delete systemstatebackup command deletes one or more system state backups.

- *Restore or delete a backup catalog*—A backup catalog is generated each time a backup is done. The catalog stores details about each backup and must be available when a recovery procedure is attempted. If the catalog becomes corrupt or deleted, it must be restored before backups can be accessed. To restore a catalog, use the wbadmin restore catalog command. To delete a catalog, use the wbadmin delete catalog command.

To perform most tasks with the wbadmin command, you must be a member of the Backup Operators or Administrators group. You must also open a command prompt window with elevated privileges by right-clicking Start and clicking Command Prompt (Admin) if you aren't logged on with the Administrator account.

Activity 7-7: Creating a System State Backup

Time Required: 25 minutes or longer
Objective: Create a system state backup.

Required Tools and Equipment: 411Server1
Description: You want to create a system state backup, but first you need to install the Windows Server Backup tool. You plan to store backups on a separate volume from Windows, so you create a new volume on Disk 1 on 411Server1 for this purpose. Then you create some objects in Active Directory and create the system state backup.

1. Log on to 411Server1 as **Administrator**, if necessary.

2. Open Disk Management. Create a 20 GB NTFS volume named **Backup** and assign it drive letter **B**. Close Disk Management. If prompted to format the disk, click **Cancel**.

3. Open Active Directory Users and Computers. First, you create some objects that you delete in a later activity to test the backup. Right-click the domain object, point to **New**, and click **Organizational Unit**. Type **TestOU1** in the Name text box. Click to clear the **Protect container from accidental deletion** check box. Click **OK**.

4. Create a user in TestOU1 with the full name **Test User1**, the logon name **testuser1**, and the password **Password01**. Set the password to never expire.

5. Open a PowerShell prompt. Type `Install-WindowsFeature Windows-Server-Backup` and press **Enter**.

6. Even though wbadmin isn't a PowerShell cmdlet, you can still run it from PowerShell. Type `wbadmin start systemstatebackup -backuptarget:B:` and press **Enter** to start a system state backup on the B drive.

7. When you're prompted to start the backup operation, type **y** and press **Enter**.

8. The backup must first identify all system state files, and you see progress displays as wbadmin finds the files. When the files are found, the backup begins. (It might take several minutes.) Progress lines are displayed periodically to show the percentage complete. When the backup is finished, a log of files backed up successfully is created in the C:\Windows\Logs\WindowsServerBackup folder. Close the PowerShell window.

9. To view files in the backup, open File Explorer and navigate to **B:\WindowsImage Backup\411Server1**. You see a folder named Backup *DateAndTime* where the backup you created is stored. You also see a folder named Catalog that holds the files composing the catalog of backups.

10. Close File Explorer, but stay logged on for the next activity.

Active Directory Restorations

An Active Directory restoration can be nonauthoritative or authoritative. A **nonauthoritative restore** restores the Active Directory database, or portions of it, and allows it to be updated through replication by other domain controllers. An **authoritative restore** ensures that restored objects aren't overwritten by changes from other domain controllers through replication. The restored objects are replicated to other domain controllers.

Nonauthoritative Active Directory Restore
A nonauthoritative restore of Active Directory is usually done when the Active Directory database is corrupt or when you're doing a full server recovery. For this restore, you can stop Active Directory Domain Services or restart the DC in Directory Services Restore Mode before restoring from backup. The first option is preferable because it doesn't require a server restart. To stop Active Directory Domain Services, use one of the following methods:

- In the Services MMC, right-click the Active Directory Domain Services service and click Stop.

- At a command prompt, type net stop ntds and press Enter.

- At a PowerShell prompt, type Stop-Service ntds and press Enter.

To restart the DC in DSRM, press F8 when the server begins to boot to access the Advanced Boot Options menu (see Figure 7-16).

After you have stopped Active Directory Domain Services or have booted into DSRM, run wbadmin to restore from a system state backup or from a backup that includes all critical volumes. After the restoration, restart the service or restart the server normally, and Active Directory replication updates the DC with any objects changed since the backup was created. If you have only one DC, any changes to Active Directory since the last backup are lost.

```
┌────────────────────────────────────────────────────────────────────┐
│                        Advanced Boot Options                         │
│                                                                      │
│ Choose Advanced Options for: Windows Server 2012 R2                   │
│ (Use the arrow keys to highlight your choice.)                       │
│                                                                      │
│     Repair Your Computer                                             │
│                                                                      │
│     Safe Mode                                                        │
│     Safe Mode with Networking                                        │
│     Safe Mode with Command Prompt                                    │
│                                                                      │
│     Enable Boot Logging                                              │
│     Enable low-resolution video                                      │
│     Last Known Good Configuration (advanced)                         │
│ ░░░ Directory Services Repair Mode ░░░                               │
│     Debugging Mode                                                   │
│     Disable automatic restart on system failure                      │
│     Disable Driver Signature Enforcement                             │
│     Disable Early Launch Anti-Malware Driver                         │
│                                                                      │
│     Start Windows Normally                                           │
│                                                                      │
│ Description: Start Windows in Directory Services Repair Mode.         │
│                                                                      │
│ ENTER=Choose                                              ESC=Cancel │
└────────────────────────────────────────────────────────────────────┘
```

Figure 7-16   The Advanced Boot Options menu

Authoritative Restore   With an authoritative restore, you can select specific Active Directory objects to be restored, or you can choose one or more containers and their contents, including the domain container. You can also choose to restore the SYSVOL folder authoritatively. A complete restore of an Active Directory domain should be a rare occurrence and a last-ditch effort to solve a major Active Directory problem because any changes made to objects on other DCs in the domain since the last backup will be lost. To perform an authoritative restore, follow these steps:

1. Boot the DC into DSRM.
2. Restore from the last system state backup by using the Recovery Wizard in Windows Server Backup or the `wbadmin` command.
3. Run `ntdsutil` to mark one or more objects as authoritative.
4. Restart the DC.

If you want the SYSVOL folder to be restored authoritatively, you have two options. If you're using the Recovery Wizard in Windows Server Backup, select the "Perform an authoritative restore of Active Directory files" option in the Select Location for System State Recovery window. If you're using `wbadmin`, include the `-authsysvol` parameter in the command.

After you have restored the system state from backup, you must use `ntdsutil` to mark one or more objects as authoritative before restarting the server. To mark an object or subtree as authoritative, enter these commands:

- `ntdsutil`
- `activate instance ntds`
- `authoritative restore`
- `restore object DistinguishedName` (to restore a single object)
- `restore subtree DistinguishedName` (to restore an entire OU and its child objects or specify the domain object if you want to restore the entire domain authoritatively)

Quit `ntdsutil`, and restart the server normally. After the server restarts, the Active Directory database is replicated to other domain controllers, overwriting any changes to objects since the last backup. Activity 7-8 guides you through restoring Active Directory and doing an authoritative restore. In Activity 7-9, you restore deleted objects with an easier method.

Activity 7-8: Restoring Active Directory from a System State Backup

Time Required: 30 minutes or longer
Objective: Restore Active Directory from a backup.

Required Tools and Equipment: 411Server1 and 411Server2
Description: You need to test the effectiveness of a system state backup and the capability to restore Active Directory. On a test DC where you have created a system state backup, you delete an OU from Active Directory, and then perform an authoritative restore on the deleted object.

1. Start 411Server2, if necessary. Log on to 411Server1 as **Administrator**, if necessary. Open Active Directory Users and Computers.

2. Click **TestOU1** and press **Delete**. When prompted to confirm the deletion, click **Yes**.

3. In the Confirm Subtree Deletion message box, click the **Use Delete Subtree server control** check box so that protected objects can be deleted, and then click **Yes**.

4. When the deletion is finished, restart 411Server1. When your server begins to restart, press **F8**. Press **F8** several times until the Advanced Boot Options menu is displayed.

5. In the Advanced Boot Options menu, press the down arrow key to highlight **Directory Services Repair Mode**, and then press **Enter**.

6. You must log on with the local administrator account and the DSRM password, which is Password01. To do so, click **Switch User**, and then type **411Server1\Administrator** in the User Name text box and **Password01** in the Password text box. It might take a while before you see the desktop. "Safe Mode" is displayed in the corner of the desktop.

7. Open a command prompt window. You must get a list of the available backups before you can restore the system state. Type **wbadmin get versions -backuptarget:B:** and press **Enter**. After a minute or so, a list of backups is displayed. Make a note of the version identifier of the most recent backup, which is the system state backup you created in Activity 7-7.

8. To begin the recovery, type **wbadmin start systemstaterecovery -version:*Version* -backuptarget:B:** (replacing *Version* with the version identifier you noted in Step 7) and press **Enter**. When prompted to start the recovery operation, type **y** and press **Enter**. You see a warning about replicated content causing latency or outage issues and are prompted to continue. Type **y** and press **Enter**.

9. The restoration will probably take several minutes. When it's finished, you're prompted to restart. However, don't restart the server because you must first mark deleted objects as authoritative. The prompt doesn't give you the option to enter "n" to prevent a restart, so press **Ctrl+C** to quit wbadmin. If this server were the only writeable DC, the next step isn't necessary, but 411Server2 is also writeable. With a nonauthoritative restore, you would simply restart the server to finish the restoration.

10. Type **ntdsutil** and press **Enter**. Type **activate instance ntds** and press **Enter** to make the Active Directory database the focus of the command. Type **authoritative restore** and press **Enter**. At the authoritative restore prompt, type **restore subtree ou=TestOU1,dc=411Dom1,dc=local** and press **Enter**. When the Authoritative Restore Confirmation Dialog message box opens, click **Yes**. Type **quit** and press **Enter**, and then type **quit** again and press **Enter**. The **restore** command specifies the object to restore authoritatively. The rest of the Active Directory database is stored nonauthoritatively.

11. Restart 411Server1 by typing **shutdown /r /t 0** and pressing **Enter**. Your server might restart several times to finish the restoration.

12. Log on as the domain administrator. The system state recovery performs some final tasks, opens a command prompt window, and displays a "Completed successfully" message. Press **Enter** to continue when prompted.

13. Open Active Directory Users and Computers, and click **TestOU1** to verify that the objects have been restored.

14. Close Active Directory Users and Computers, and stay logged on for the next activity.

That was a lot of time and energy to restore two Active Directory objects. Thankfully, there's an easier way.

Recovering Deleted Objects from the Recycle Bin   If the Active Directory Recycle Bin is enabled, the restore process is simple and straightforward and doesn't require a backup because like the Recycle Bin on a Windows desktop, the objects were never really deleted. They were just moved to a special folder called the Recycle Bin. You can restore objects from the Recycle Bin with any of these methods:

- In ADAC, navigate to the Deleted Objects container, and then right-click the object and click Restore.

- Use the `Restore-ADObject` PowerShell cmdlet. For details on using this cmdlet, enter `Get-Help Restore-ADObject -detailed`.

- Use the `ntdsutil.exe` command.

The Active Directory Recycle Bin isn't enabled by default. After it's enabled, it can't be disabled without reinstalling the entire Active Directory forest. To enable it, all DCs must be running Windows Server 2008 R2 or later, and the forest functional level must be at Windows Server 2008 R2 or higher. The Recycle Bin is enabled with Active Directory Administrative Center or the following PowerShell cmdlet on the 411Dom1.local forest:

```
Enable-ADOptionalFeature -Identity "cn=Recycle Bin
   Feature,cn=Optional Features,cn=Windows NT,
   cn=Services,cn=Configuration,dc=411Dom1,dc=local"
   -Scope ForestOrConfigurationSet -Target "411Dom1.local"
```

Activity 7-9: Restoring Deleted Objects from the Active Directory Recycle Bin

Time Required: 20 minutes
Objective: Restore deleted objects from the Active Directory Recycle Bin.

Required Tools and Equipment: 411Server1 and 411Server2
Description: You have seen that recovering deleted objects can involve quite a bit of time if the Active Directory Recycle Bin isn't enabled. To make the process easier, you enable and test this feature.

1. Start 411Server2, if necessary. Log on to 411Server1 as **Administrator**, if necessary.

2. On 411Server1, open Active Directory Administrative Center, and click **411Dom1 (local)** in the left pane.

3. In the right pane, click **Enable Recycle Bin**. You see a message explaining that the Recycle Bin can't be disabled after it's enabled. Click **OK**. (If you get a message about FSMO role ownership, click **OK**. Wait for replication to occur, or force replication in Active Directory Sites and Services.) You see a message telling you to refresh the Active Directory Administrative Center now. Click **OK**.

4. Click the **Refresh** icon to refresh Active Directory Administrative Center. You see a new folder named Deleted Objects. Log on to 411Server2, if necessary. Open Active Directory Administrative Center and click the domain object to verify that the Deleted Objects folder is there. If it is, the Recycle Bin is enabled on both DCs.

5. Now delete some objects. Right-click **TestOU1** and click **Delete**. Click **Yes** to confirm. Click **Use delete subtree server control** and click **Yes**.

6. On 411Server1, refresh Active Directory Administrative Center and verify that **TestOU1** has been deleted. Double-click the **Deleted Objects** folder. You see TestOU1 and Test User1.

7. To restore both objects, click **Test User1**, hold down the **Ctrl** key and click **TestOU1** so that both objects are highlighted, and then release the **Ctrl** key. In the right pane, click **Restore**.

8. In the left pane, click **411Dom1 (local)**. Double-click **TestOU1** and verify that Test User1 is also restored.

9. Next, you see how to restore an object with PowerShell. First you need a deleted object, so delete **Test User1** from TestOU1, but don't delete TestOU1 this time.

10. Open a PowerShell prompt. Type `Get-ADObject -Filter {DisplayName -eq "Test User1"} -IncludeDeletedObjects | Restore-ADObject` and press **Enter**.

11. Refresh Active Directory Administrative Center, and you see that Test User1 is restored.

12. Close the PowerShell window and Active Directory Administrative Center, but stay logged on to both servers for the next activity.

Active Directory Defragmentation

To maintain performance and efficiency, the Active Directory database requires periodic maintenance in the form of defragmentation and compaction. There are two methods of Active Directory defragmentation: online and offline. **Online defragmentation** occurs automatically when Active Directory performs garbage collection. Garbage collection runs every 12 hours on a DC and removes objects that have been deleted for more than 180 days. Objects that have been deleted but not removed are referred to as "tombstoned." When an Active Directory object is deleted, it's not actually removed from the database, much as a deleted file isn't physically erased from the file system. Instead, the object is marked for deletion and left in the database for a period called the **tombstone lifetime**, which by default is 180 days. During garbage collection, tombstoned objects older than the tombstone lifetime are removed from the database.

The tombstone lifetime has important implications for Active Directory backups. Suppose the tombstone lifetime is set to its default 180 days, and the Active Directory database is backed up on day 1. A user account, Julie, is deleted purposefully on day 3. On day 15, the database on a DC becomes corrupted and must be restored from backup with a nonauthoritative restore. The backup from day 1 is used for the restore, which is before the Julie account was deleted. However, because other DCs still have a record of the Julie account as being deleted, replication deletes the Julie account on the DC being restored. This is the result you want.

Now suppose the tombstone period is only 10 days. In the same situation, the Julie account is removed from the database during garbage collection on day 13. When the database is restored, the Julie account is restored with it, but the other DCs have no record of the Julie account being deleted, so the account remains, which isn't the result you want. Because of this potential database inconsistency, an Active Directory backup is considered invalid if it's older than the tombstone lifetime. The tombstone lifetime applies to the entire forest and can be changed by using Attribute Editor on the ForestRootDomain object. (Attribute Editor is a tab in the Properties dialog box of an Active Directory object.)

Online defragmentation removes deleted objects and frees up space in the database, but it doesn't compact the database to close up gaps that deleted objects create in the database. **Offline defragmentation** is necessary to keep the database lean and efficient. In Windows Server versions before Windows Server 2008, you had to restart the DC in DSRM to perform offline defragmentation, which interrupts other services running on the DC. Starting with Windows Server 2008, offline maintenance is possible because the Active Directory service can be stopped for performing maintenance and then restarted. Microsoft refers to this feature as **restartable Active Directory**. Using this feature, a server restart isn't required. However, another DC must be online before you can stop the Active Directory service so that users can continue to log on. While Active Directory is stopped, DNS on that DC stops servicing queries, so client computers should have the address of an alternate DNS server configured, too.

Like a file system, a database becomes fragmented over time because of object deletion and creation. Where deleted objects once were, gaps in the database are created, which makes the database less efficient in performance. Compacting the database removes the gaps, much as defragmenting a hard drive does for the file system.

Active Directory compaction is done with the `ntdsutil` command. The database can't be compacted in place, so a copy is made to a location you specify. After compaction is finished, the compacted database is copied to the original location.

Activity 7-10: Compacting the Active Directory Database

Time Required: 15 minutes
Objective: Compact the Active Directory database.

Required Tools and Equipment: 411Server1 and 411Server2
Description: You plan to compact the Active Directory database on 411Server1, but both DCs should be running. You create folders to hold temporary copies of the database, stop the Active Directory service, and then compact the database with one of the folders you created as the destination. First, you make a copy of the original database in case a problem occurs with compaction, and then you must delete the Active Directory log files and copy the compacted database to replace the original database.

1. Log on to 411Server1 as **Administrator**, if necessary. Start 411Server2, if necessary.

2. First, set the alternate DNS server address in the network connection IP address settings to the address of 411Server2 (10.11.1.2). This step is done as a precaution. Because DNS doesn't respond to DNS queries while Active Directory is stopped, 411Server1 might need to contact a DNS server if you have to log on after Active Directory is stopped. This can happen, for example, if your screen saver comes on and requires a password to access the desktop. Close any open dialog boxes.

3. Create two folders in the root of the C drive: **tempAD** and **backupAD**.

4. Open a command prompt window. Type **net stop ntds** and press **Enter** to stop the Active Directory service. When prompted to continue, type **y** and press **Enter**.

5. Type the following commands, pressing **Enter** after each one: **ntdsutil**, **activate instance ntds**, **files**, and **compact to c:\tempAD** (see Figure 7-17).

```
C:\Windows\system32>ntdsutil
ntdsutil: activate instance ntds
Active instance set to "ntds".
ntdsutil: files
file maintenance: compact to c:\tempAD
Initiating DEFRAGMENTATION mode...
     Source Database: C:\Windows\NTDS\ntds.dit
     Target Database: c:\tempAD\ntds.dit

                Defragmentation  Status  (% complete)

          0    10   20   30   40   50   60   70   80   90  100
          !----!----!----!----!----!----!----!----!----!----!
          ..................................................

It is recommended that you immediately perform a full backup
of this database. If you restore a backup made before the
defragmentation, the database will be rolled back to the state
it was in at the time of that backup.

Compaction is successful. You need to:
    copy "c:\tempAD\ntds.dit" "C:\Windows\NTDS\ntds.dit"
and delete the old log files:
    del C:\Windows\NTDS\*.log

file maintenance: _
```

Figure 7-17   Compacting the database with `ntdsutil`

6. The Defragmentation Status display shows the progress of compaction. When you see a message stating that you need to copy the new file over the old file and delete the log files, type **quit** and press **Enter**, and then type **quit** and press **Enter** again.

7. To copy the original database file to the backup folder you created, type **copy c:\windows\ntds\ntds.dit c:\backupAD** and press **Enter**.

8. To delete the log files, type **del c:\windows\ntds*.log** and press **Enter**.

9. To copy the compacted database over the original database, type **copy c:\tempAD\ ntds.dit c:\windows\ntds\ntds.dit** and press **Enter**. Type **y** and press **Enter** to confirm the copy.

10. Next, to verify the integrity of the new database, type the following commands, pressing **Enter** after each one: **ntdsutil, activate instance ntds, files,** and **integrity**. Assuming the integrity check was successful, type **quit** and press **Enter**. If it wasn't successful, copy the backup from C:\backupAD to **C:\Windows\Ntds**, and attempt the compaction process again, starting with Step 5.

11. To check the semantic database integrity (which is recommended), type **semantic database analysis** and press **Enter**, and then type **go fixup** and press **Enter**. Type **quit** and press **Enter**, and then type **quit** and press **Enter** again.

12. To restart Active Directory, type **net start ntds** and press **Enter**. You can verify a successful startup by checking the most recent events in the event log. Shortly after the service starts, a new event with ID 1000 should be created in the Directory Service log under Applications and Services Logs in Event Viewer, indicating a successful Active Directory start.

13. Close all open windows, and log off both servers.

Active Directory Metadata Cleanup

Active Directory metadata is data that describes the Active Directory database, not the actual Active Directory data. Metadata can get left over if a DC had to be removed forcibly from the domain, which can occur if the DC stops communicating correctly with other DCs, perhaps because of Active Directory corruption or hardware failure. The metadata is information about the failed DC that stays in the Active Directory database on the remaining DCs in the domain. Metadata might also have to be cleaned up if an attempt to install a new DC in the domain fails after a partial installation.

Metadata that's not cleaned up can have varying and unpredictable effects on the domain—some unnoticeable and some that cause replication and other functions to malfunction. In addition, any attempts to install a DC with the same name as the failed one will be unsuccessful until the metadata is cleaned up. Even after successful removal of a DC, it's a good idea to check for leftover metadata. There are three main methods for cleaning up metadata: Active Directory Users and Computers, Active Directory Sites and Services, and ntdsutil.

Using Active Directory Users and Computers is the simplest method but requires at least Windows Server 2008 or later. Locate the computer account of the failed DC in the Domain Controllers OU and delete it. You're asked to confirm the deletion, and then the message shown in Figure 7-18 is displayed, stating that you should try to remove the DC with the Remove Roles

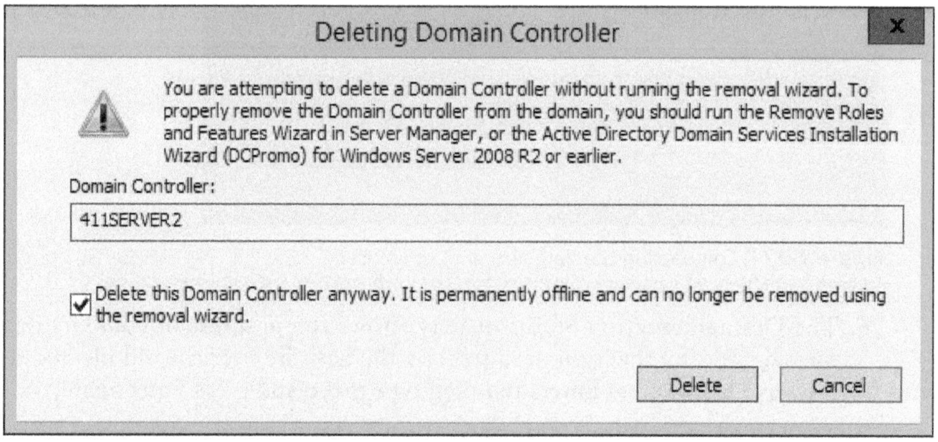

Figure 7-18 Warning about deleting a domain controller

and Features Wizard. Select the "Delete this Domain Controller anyway" check box, and then click Delete. If the server is a GC server, you're prompted again to continue with the deletion. If the server is a FSMO role holder, you're asked to confirm moving the roles to another DC. This procedure should clean up all remaining metadata for the selected DC.

To use Active Directory Sites and Services, you expand the site name, the Servers folder, and then the failed DC. Right-click NTDS Settings and click Delete, and then click Yes to confirm. You see the same message as in Figure 7-18, along with messages about a GC server and FSMO role holder, if needed. After the NTDS Settings node is deleted, right-click the computer object and delete it.

To clean up metadata with `ntdsutil`, follow these steps:

1. Open a command prompt window and type the following commands, pressing Enter after each one:

```
ntdsutil
metadata cleanup
remove selected server DomainController
```

2. In the warning message, click Yes to confirm the removal.

3. Type `quit` and press Enter twice to exit `ntdsutil`.

4. Open Active Directory Sites and Services and delete the computer object, if necessary.

Working with Active Directory Snapshots

An **Active Directory snapshot** is just what it sounds like: an exact replica of the Active Directory database at a specific moment. It's similar to a snapshot (or "checkpoint," as it's called in Hyper-V) of a virtual machine. You can browse through Active Directory snapshots to view Active Directory's state at different times. You can also export Active Directory objects from a snapshot and import them with `ldifde`. The basic procedure for working with snapshots is as follows:

1. Create and mount the snapshot with `ntdsutil`.

2. Activate the snapshot with `dsamain`.

3. Browse the snapshot with Active Directory Users and Computers or another LDAP tool.

4. Dismount the snapshot.

Creating and Mounting Snapshots   To use a snapshot, create one first and then mount it with `ntdsutil`, using the following procedure (shown in Figure 7-19):

1. Open a command prompt window, and type `ntdsutil` and press Enter.

2. Type `snapshot` and press Enter.

3. Type `activate instance ntds` and press Enter.

4. Type `create` and press Enter.

```
C:\>ntdsutil
ntdsutil: snapshot
snapshot: activate instance ntds
Active instance set to "ntds".
snapshot: create
Creating snapshot...
Snapshot set {5a5bdb36-168d-4e7b-a32a-cc9eb591a726} generated successfully.
snapshot: mount 5a5bdb36-168d-4e7b-a32a-cc9eb591a726
Snapshot {4d60d4a5-008f-4aa5-8a14-09489b6bbb6d} mounted as C:\$SNAP_201401302053
_VOLUMEC$\
snapshot:
```

Figure 7-19   Creating an Active Directory snapshot

5. `Ntdsutil` names the snapshot by using a GUID. You need the GUID, so instead of having to type it, right-click it and click Mark. Use your mouse to highlight the number between the braces and press Enter.

6. Type `mount` and press the spacebar. Right-click at the cursor and click Paste, and then press Enter.

7. Copy the part of the output starting with `C:\$SNAP` and ending with `VOLUMEC$\` because you need it in the command in the following section. It's the path to the snapshot, which includes a timestamp. If you open File Explorer, you see a volume mounted in the root of the C drive with that name.

8. Type `quit` and press Enter twice to exit `ntdsutil`.

Activating a Snapshot   After you've created a snapshot, you need to let the Active Directory service know about it by using the following steps:

1. At a command prompt, type `dsamain /dbpath` *SnapshotPath*`\windows\ntds\ ntds.dit /ldapport 20000` and press Enter. The *SnapshotPath* is the output you copied in the previous section, and `ldapport` is the port number you use when browsing the snapshot.

2. When you see the line beginning with `EVENTLOG` and ending with `1000`, the process is done. Leave the command prompt window open.

3. To browse the snapshot, open Active Directory Users and Computers, and then right-click the domain object and click Change Domain Controller. In the Change Directory Server dialog box, click "<Type a Directory Server name[:port] here>," type *DCName*:20000 (see Figure 7-20), and press Enter (replacing *DCName* with the name of the domain controller). Click OK.

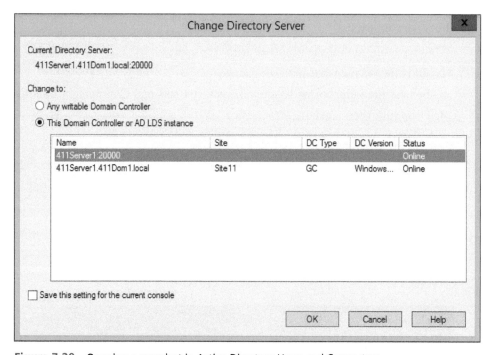

Figure 7-20   Opening a snapshot in Active Directory Users and Computers

You can browse the snapshot of Active Directory in Active Directory Users and Computers. Just realize that if you make any changes, they're made to the snapshot, not to the live Active Directory database.

Exporting a Snapshot You can export Active Directory objects from the snapshot by using `ldifde` and import these objects into another instance of Active Directory. To export the users in the TestOU1 OU to the `testOU1users.txt` file, enter the following command at a command prompt:

```
ldifde -t 20000 -f testOU1users.txt -d
  "ou=TestOU1,dc=411Dom1,dc=local" -r (ObjectClass=user)
```

Unmounting and Deleting a Snapshot When you use `dsamain` to activate a snapshot, you leave the command prompt window open until you're finished with the snapshot. To stop `dsamain` and unmount the snapshot, use the following steps:

1. In the command prompt window where `dsamain` is running, press Ctrl+C.

2. Type the following commands, pressing Enter after each:

```
ntdsutil
snapshot
unmount SnapshotGUID
quit
quit
```

In these commands, *SnapshotGUID* is the GUID that was generated when you mounted the snapshot. If you need to see the GUID, type `list all` in `ntdsutil` while in snapshot mode. Unmounting the snapshot doesn't delete it. To delete the snapshot, type `delete` *SnapshotGUID* after you enter snapshot mode.

Chapter Summary

- DCs and sites are the physical components of Active Directory, and forest, domains, and OUs are the logical components. DCs use multimaster replication, but RODCs use unidirectional replication.

- A global catalog server is a DC configured to hold the global catalog. Every forest must have at least one GC server. GC servers facilitate domain-wide and forest-wide searches, enable logons across domains, and hold universal group membership information. Each site should have at least one GC server to speed logons and directory searches.

- Because of the benefits of virtualization, implementing DCs as virtual machines in Hyper-V is common practice. Starting with Windows Server 2012, DCs running on Hyper-V are virtualization aware, and there are built-in safeguards to prevent the Active Directory database from being adversely affected when the VM is rolled back in time by applying a checkpoint.

- To clone a Windows Server 2012/R2 DC, you need to verify that the hypervisor supports virtual machine generation identifiers, the PDC emulator FSMO role is running Windows Server 2012 or later, a GC server is available, and only supported roles are installed on the DC to be cloned.

- RODCs were developed to provide secure Active Directory support in branch office installations where physical server security is lax and there are no on-site server administrators. Before installing an RODC, make sure there's a writeable Windows Server 2008 DC or later the RODC can replicate with. The forest functional level must be at least Windows Server 2003, and you must use `adprep /rodcprep` if the functional level isn't Windows Server 2008.

- Replication on an RODC is unidirectional, and user passwords aren't stored on the RODC by default. You can configure credential caching if you want the RODC to store passwords of selected users locally.

- With staged RODC installation, a domain administrator creates the RODC computer account in Active Directory, and a regular user can then perform the installation.

- An Active Directory site represents a physical location where domain controllers reside. Multiple sites are used for authentication efficiency, replication efficiency, and application efficiency. Site components include subnets, site links, and bridgehead servers.

- Universal group membership caching handles the potential conflict between faster logons and additional replication traffic.

- Deciding where to place the FSMO role holder is part of the overall Active Directory design strategy. Two important operations for managing FSMOs are transferring and seizing operations master roles.

- Active Directory is composed of two important folders: %*systemroot*%\NTDS and %*systemroot*%\SYSVOL. When you back up the system state, both folders are included in the backup. A system state backup on a domain controller includes the Registry, boot files, the Active Directory database, the SYSVOL folder, some system files, and other files, depending on roles installed on the server.

- You can restore Active Directory by using a nonauthoritative restore or an authoritative restore. A nonauthoritative restore restores the Active Directory database, or portions of it, and allows it to be updated through replication by other domain controllers. An authoritative restore ensures that restored objects aren't overwritten by changes from other domain controllers through replication.

- The Active Directory Recycle Bin isn't enabled by default, and after it's enabled, it can't be disabled without reinstalling the entire Active Directory forest. It's enabled in ADAC, and objects that are deleted can be restored from the Deleted Folders container.

- The Active Directory database becomes fragmented over time. Online defragmentation simply deletes deleted objects that have been deleted longer than the tombstone lifetime, a process called "garbage collection." You can't restore a backup that's older than the tombstone lifetime. Offline defragmentation compacts the database for more efficient operation. Offline defragmentation can be performed by stopping the Active Directory service without having to restart the server.

- Active Directory metadata is data that describes the Active Directory database, not the actual Active Directory data. Metadata can get left over if a DC has to be forcibly removed from the domain. Metadata that isn't cleaned up can have varying and unpredictable effects on the domain.

- An Active Directory snapshot is an exact replica of the Active Directory service at a specific moment. Active Directory snapshots can be browsed to view the state of Active Directory when the snapshot was taken. You can export objects from a snapshot by using `ldifde`.

Key Terms

Active Directory snapshot   An exact replica of the Active Directory database at a specific moment.

authoritative restore   A method of restoring Active Directory data from a backup to ensure that restored objects aren't overwritten by changes from other domain controllers through replication.

bridgehead server   A DC at a site the Inter-Site Topology Generator designates to replicate a directory partition with other sites.

delegated administrator account   A user account with local administrative rights and permissions to the RODC, similar to members of the local Administrators group on a member computer or stand-alone computer.

domain naming master   A forest-wide Flexible Single Master Operation role that manages adding, removing, and renaming domains in the forest.

filtered attribute set   A collection of attribute data configured on the schema master; used to specify domain objects that aren't replicated to RODCs, thereby increasing the security of sensitive information.

infrastructure master   A domain-wide Flexible Single Master Operation role that's responsible for making sure changes made to object names in one domain are updated in references to these objects in other domains.

nonauthoritative restore   A method of restoring Active Directory data from a backup that restores the database, or portions of it, and allows the data to be updated through replication by other domain controllers.

offline defragmentation   Defragmentation of the Active Directory database that also compacts the database to improve performance. The Active Directory service must be stopped before offline defragmentation can occur.

online defragmentation   Defragmentation of the Active Directory database that removes deleted objects and frees up space in the database but doesn't compact the database. Online defragmentation occurs automatically when Active Directory performs garbage collection.

PDC emulator   A domain-wide Flexible Single Master Operation role that processes password changes for older Windows clients (Windows 9x and NT) and is used during logon authentication.

relative identifier (RID)   A unique value combined with a domain identifier to form the security identifier for an Active Directory object. *See also* security identifier (SID).

restartable Active Directory   A feature introduced in Windows Server 2008 that makes it possible to take Active Directory offline to perform maintenance operations instead of requiring a server restart in DSRM.

RID master   A domain-wide Flexible Single Master Operation role that's responsible for issuing unique pools of RIDs to each DC, thereby guaranteeing unique SIDs throughout the domain.

schema master   A forest-wide Flexible Single Master Operation role that's responsible for replicating the schema directory partition to all other domain controllers in the forest when changes occur.

security identifier (SID)   A unique number assigned to every Active Directory object to identify it.

site link   A component of a site that's needed to connect sites for replication purposes.

staged installation   An RODC installation method that doesn't require domain administrator credentials; a regular user at a branch office can perform the installation. Called "delegated installation" in Windows Server 2008.

tombstone lifetime   A period of time in which deleted Active Directory objects are marked for deletion but left in the database. When the tombstone lifetime expires, the object is removed during garbage collection.

unidirectional replication   A replication method used with RODCs in which Active Directory data is replicated to the RODC, but the RODC doesn't replicate the data to other domain controllers.

universal group membership caching   This feature stores universal group membership information retrieved from a global catalog server, so the global catalog server doesn't have to be contacted for each user logon.

Review Questions

1. Which of the following is *not* a function of the global catalog?

    a.   Facilitates forest-wide searches

    b.   Keeps universal group memberships

    c.   Facilitates intersite replication

    d.   Facilitates forest-wide logons

2. You have an Active Directory forest of two trees and eight domains. You haven't changed any of the operations master domain controllers. On which domain controller is the schema master?

   a. All domain controllers

   b. The last domain controller installed

   c. The first domain controller in the forest root domain

   d. The first domain controller in each tree

3. Which of the following is a reason for establishing multiple sites? (Choose all that apply.)

   a. Improving authentication efficiency

   b. Enabling more frequent replication

   c. Reducing traffic on the WAN

   d. Having only one IP subnet

4. Users of a new network subnet have been complaining that logons and other services are taking much longer than they did before being moved to the new subnet. You discover that many logons and requests for DFS resources from clients in the new subnet are being handled by domain controllers in a remote site instead of local domain controllers. What should you do to solve this problem?

   a. Create a new site and add the clients and new GC server to the new site.

   b. Change the IP addresses of the clients to correspond to the network of the DCs that are handling the logons.

   c. Compact the Active Directory database because fragmentation must be causing latency.

   d. Create a new subnet and add the subnet to the site that maps to the physical location of the clients.

5. You want to decrease users' logon time at SiteA but not increase replication traffic drastically. You have 50 users at this site with one domain controller. Overall, your network contains 3000 user and computer accounts. What solution can decrease logon times with the least impact on replication traffic?

   a. Configure the domain controller as a domain naming master.

   b. Configure the domain controller as a global catalog server.

   c. Configure multiple connection objects between the domain controller in SiteA and a remote global catalog server.

   d. Enable universal group membership caching.

6. Which of the following configurations should you avoid?

   a. Domain naming master and schema master on the same domain controller

   b. PDC emulator and RID master on the same computer

   c. Infrastructure master configured as a global catalog server

   d. Schema master configured as a global catalog server

7. User authentications are taking a long time. The domain controller performing which FSMO role will most likely decrease authentication times if it's upgraded?

   a. RID master

   b. PDC emulator

   c. Infrastructure master

   d. Domain naming master

8. You're taking an older server performing the RID master role out of service and will be replacing it with a new server configured as a domain controller. What should you do to ensure the smoothest transition?

    a. Transfer the RID master role to the new domain controller, and then shut down the old server.

    b. Shut down the current RID master and seize the RID master role from the new domain controller.

    c. Back up the domain controller that's currently the RID master, restore it to the new domain controller, and then shut down the old RID master.

    d. Shut down the current RID master, and then transfer the RID master role to the new domain controller.

9. Which of the following is true about an RODC installation?

    a. A Windows server running at least Windows Server 2012 is required.

    b. The forest functional level must be at least Windows Server 2003.

    c. `Adprep /rodcprep` must be run in Windows Server 2008 forests.

    d. Another RODC must be available as a replication partner.

10. You need to install an RODC in a new branch office and want to use an existing workgroup server running Windows Server 2012 R2. The office is a plane flight away and is connected via a WAN. You want an employee at the branch office, Michael, to do the RODC installation because he's good at working with computers and following directions. What should you do?

    a. Add Michael to the Domain Admins group, and give him directions on how to install the RODC.

    b. Add Michael's domain account to the Administrators group on the server, and give him directions on how to install the RODC.

    c. Create the computer account for the RODC in the Domain Controllers OU, and specify Michael's account as one that can join the computer to the domain.

    d. Create a group policy that specifies that Michael's account can join RODCs to the domain. Then use the Delegation of Control Wizard on the Domain Controllers OU.

11. You have an application integrated with AD DS that maintains Active Directory objects containing credential information, and there are serious security implications if these objects are compromised. An RODC at one branch office isn't physically secure, and theft is a risk. How can you best protect this application's sensitive data?

    a. Configure the PRP for the RODC, and specify a Deny setting for the application object.

    b. Configure a filtered attribute set, and specify the application-related objects.

    c. Use EFS to encrypt the files storing the sensitive objects.

    d. Turn off all password replication on the RODC.

12. You maintain an RODC running Windows Server 2012 R2 at a branch office, and you want one employee with solid computer knowledge to perform administrative tasks, such as driver and software updates and device management. How can you do this without giving her broader domain rights?

    a. Assign the employee's account as a delegated administrator in the RODC's computer account settings.

    b. Create a local user on the RODC, and add it to the Administrators group. Have the user log on with this account when necessary.

    c. Create a script that adds the user to the Domain Admins group each day at a certain time, and then removes the user from the group one hour later. Tell the user to log on and perform the necessary tasks during the specified period.

    d. Send the user to extensive Windows Server 2012 R2 training, and then add the user to the Domain Admins group.

13. Users usually notice a failure of the domain naming master immediately. True or False?

14. You have installed an RODC at a branch office that also runs the DNS Server role. All DNS zones are Active Directory integrated. What happens when a client computer attempts to register its name with the DNS service on the RODC?

    a. The DNS service rejects the registration. The client must be configured with a static DNS entry.

    b. The DNS service passes the request to another DNS server. After registration is completed, the DNS server that performed the registration sends the record to the DNS service on the RODC.

    c. The DNS service creates a temporary record in a dynamically configured primary zone. The record is replicated to other DNS servers and then deleted on the RODC.

    d. The DNS service sends a referral to the client. The client registers its name with the referred DNS server.

15. You have three users who travel to four branch offices often and need to log on to the RODCs at these offices. The branch offices are connected to the main office with slow WAN links. You don't want domain controllers at the main office to authenticate these four users when they log on at the branch offices. What should you do that requires the least administrative effort yet adheres to best practices?

    a. Create a new global group named AllBranches. Add the four users to this group, and add the AllBranches group to the Allowed RODC Password Replication group.

    b. Add the four users to a local group on each RODC. Add the local groups to the PRP on each RODC with an Allow setting.

    c. Add each user to the PRP on each RODC with an Allow setting.

    d. Create a group policy and set the "Allow credential caching on RODCs" policy to Enabled. Add the four users to the policy, and link the policy to the Domain Controllers OU.

16. Which of the following is the term for a DC in a site that handles replication of a directory partition for that site?

    a. Inter-Site Topology Generator

    b. Knowledge Consistency Checker

    c. Bridgehead server

    d. Global catalog server

17. Where would you find files related to logon and logoff scripts in an Active Directory environment?

    a. C:\Windows\NTDS

    b. %systemroot%\SYSVOL

    c. %Windir%\ntds.dit

    d. C:\Windows\edb.log

18. Which of the following commands backs up the Registry, boot files, the Active Directory database, and the SYSVOL folder to the B drive?

    a. `robocopy C:\Windows /r /destination:B:`

    b. `wbadmin start systemstatebackup -backuptarget:B:`

    c. `backup %systemroot% -selectsystemstate > B:`

    d. `ntdsutil create snapshot -source C:\Windows\ntds -dest B:`

19. Which command must you use to restore deleted Active Directory objects in a domain with two or more writeable DCs if the Active Directory Recycle Bin isn't enabled?

    a. `wbadmin` with the `-authsysvol` option

    b. `wbadmin` with the `-restoreobject` option

    c. `ntdsutil` with the `authoritative restore` command

    d. `ntdsutil` with the `create snapshot` command

20. What's the term for removing deleted objects in Active Directory?

    a. Tombstoning

    b. Offline defragmentation

    c. Recycling objects

    d. Garbage collection

21. Which of the following is the period between an object being deleted and being removed from the Active Directory database?

    a. Tombstone lifetime

    b. Defragmentation limit

    c. Object expiration

    d. Restoration period

22. Your Active Directory database has been operating for several years and undergone many object creations and deletions. You want to make sure it's running at peak efficiency, so you want to defragment and compact the database. What procedure should you use that will be least disruptive to your network?

    a. Create a temporary folder to hold a copy of the database. Restart the server in DSRM. Run `ntdsutil` and compact the database in the temporary folder. Copy the `ntds.dit` file from the temporary folder to its original location. Verify the integrity of the new database, and restart the server normally.

    b. Create a temporary folder and a backup folder. Stop the Active Directory service. Run `ntdsutil` and compact the database in the temporary folder. Copy the original database to the backup folder, and delete the `ntds` log files. Copy the `ntds.dit` file from the temporary folder to its original location. Verify the integrity of the new database, and restart the server.

    c. Create a temporary folder and a backup folder. Restart the server in DSRM. Run `ntdsutil` and compact the database in the temporary folder. Copy the original database to the backup folder, and delete the `ntds` log files. Copy the `ntds.dit` file from the temporary folder to its original location. Verify the integrity of the new database, and restart the Active Directory service.

    d. Create a temporary folder and a backup folder. Stop the Active Directory service. Run `ntdsutil` and compact the database in the temporary folder. Copy the original database to the backup folder, and delete the `ntds` log files. Copy the `ntds.dit` file from the temporary folder to its original location. Verify the integrity of the new database, and restart the Active Directory service.

23. You have four DCs in your domain. Active Directory appears to be corrupted on one of the DCs, and you suspect a failing hard drive. You attempt to remove it from the domain, but the procedure fails. You take the DC offline permanently and will replace it with another DC of the same name. What must you do before you can replace the DC?

    a. Restore the system state.

    b. Perform metadata cleanup.

    c. Back up SYSVOL.

    d. Transfer the FSMO roles.

24. Your company has had a major reorganization, and you need to transfer several hundred user accounts to another domain. Which of the following can help with this task?

   a. Create a system state backup and restore `ntds.dit` to the new domain.

   b. In Active Directory Users and Computers, select each account and export it.

   c. Create a snapshot and export the accounts with `ldifde`.

   d. Use the `Export-ADUser` PowerShell cmdlet.

Case Projects

CASE PROJECTS

Case Project 7-1: Devising a DC Strategy

This project is suitable for group or individual work. You're the administrator of a network of 500 users and three Windows Server 2012 R2 DCs. All users and DCs are in a single building. Your company is adding three satellite locations that will be connected to the main site via a WAN link. Each satellite location will house between 30 and 50 users. One location has a dedicated server room where you can house a server and ensure physical security. The other two locations don't have a dedicated room for network equipment. The WAN links are of moderate to low bandwidth.

Design an Active Directory structure, taking into account global catalog servers, FSMO roles, sites, and domain controllers. What features of DCs and Active Directory discussed in this chapter might you put to use in your design?

Case Project 7-2: Recovering from Accidental Deletion

A junior administrator accidentally deleted the Sales OU, which contained 25 user accounts and 4 group accounts. You have five domain controllers in your network: two running Windows Server 2012 R2, two running Windows Server 2008 R2, and one running Windows Server 2008. Explain what you need and the procedure for recovering the deleted objects.

chapter 8

User and Service Account Configuration

After reading this chapter and completing the exercises, you will be able to:

- Configure user accounts and group policies
- Configure account policies
- Create password settings objects
- Work with service accounts

This chapter reviews user accounts and group policies so that you have a fresh context for learning how to configure account policies in a domain environment and on a local computer. Account policies help you maintain a secure authentication environment for your domain, but you need to find a balance between security and a system that works for all your users. You learn how to make exceptions in account policies so that you can designate more stringent or more lenient policies for groups of users as needed.

Services that run on your computer must also be authenticated to the network, and traditional methods for configuring service authentication have posed challenges in security, manageability, or both. This chapter discusses how you can configure service authentication with a variety of methods, allowing you to choose which method fits each service you install.

Overview of User Accounts and Group Policies

Table 8-1 describes what you need for the hands-on activities in this chapter.

Table 8-1   Activity requirements

Activity	Requirements	Notes
Activity 8-1: Creating User Accounts and OUs	411Server1	
Activity 8-2: Working with the Group Policy Management Console	411Server1	
Activity 8-3: Working with Domain Password Policies	411Server1	
Activity 8-4: Working with Local Password Policies	411Server1, 411Win8	
Activity 8-5: Applying Account Policies to an OU	411Server1	
Activity 8-6: Working with Account Lockout Policy	411Server1, 411Win8	
Activity 8-7: Creating a Password Settings Object	411Server1	

© 2015 Cengage Learning®

You have learned about creating, configuring, and managing user accounts in *MCSA Guide to Installing and Configuring Windows Server 2012/R2, Exam 70-410* (Cengage Learning, 2015) or in other sources. However, because you're learning about another aspect of user accounts—account policies—this section serves as a review of user accounts and their role in a domain. User accounts have two main functions:

- *Provide a method for user authentication to the network*—The user logon name and password serve as a secure method for users to log on to the network to access resources. A user account can also contain account restrictions, such as when and where a user can log on or an account expiration date.

- *Provide detailed information about a user*—For use in a company directory, user accounts can contain departments, office locations, addresses, and telephone information. You can modify the Active Directory schema to contain just about any user information a company wants to keep.

Of these two functions, this chapter focuses on account policies and how they affect a user's ability to authenticate to the network or a local computer. Recall that on local computers, user accounts are stored in the **Security Accounts Manager (SAM) database**, and users can log on to and access resources only on the computer where the account resides. A network running Active

Directory should limit the use of local user accounts on client computers, however, because they can't be used to access domain resources. Local user accounts are mainly used in a peer-to-peer network where Active Directory isn't running. Administrators can also log on to a computer with a local Administrator account for the purposes of joining the computer to a domain or troubleshooting access to the domain. Local user accounts are usually created in Control Panel's User Accounts applet or the Computer Management MMC's Local Users and Groups snap-in. Because these accounts don't participate in Active Directory, they can't be managed from Active Directory or be subject to group policies.

User accounts created in Active Directory are referred to as "domain user accounts." Generally, these accounts enable users to log on to any computer that's a domain member in the Active Directory forest. They also provide single sign-on access to domain resources in the forest and other trusted entities the account has permission to. Domain user accounts can be managed by group policies and are subject to account policies linked to the domain.

Creating and Modifying User Accounts

User accounts can be created with GUI tools, such as Active Directory Users and Computers (ADUC) and Active Directory Administrative Center (ADAC), and with command-line tools, such as `dsadd` and the PowerShell cmdlet `New-ADUser`. When you create a user account in an Active Directory domain, keep the following considerations in mind:

- A user account must have a unique logon name throughout the domain because it's used to log on to the domain. However, user accounts in different domains in the same forest can be the same.

- User account names aren't case sensitive. They can be from 1 to 20 characters and use letters, numbers, and symbols, with the exception of ", [,], :, ;, <, >, ?, *, +, @, |, ^, =, and,.

- Devise a naming standard for user accounts, which makes creating users easier and can be convenient when using applications, such as e-mail, that include the username in the address. The downside of using a predictable naming standard is that attackers can guess usernames easily to gain unauthorized access to the network. Common naming standards include a user's first initial plus last name (for example, kwilliams for Kelly Williams) or a user's first name and last name separated by a symbol (such as Kelly.Williams or Kelly_Williams). In large companies where names are likely to be duplicated, adding a number after the username is common.

- By default, a complex password is required. Passwords are case sensitive.

- By default, only a logon name is required to create a user account. If a user is created without a password and the password policy requires a nonblank password, the user is created but disabled. Descriptive information, such as first and last name, should be included for Active Directory searches.

Activity 8-1: Creating User Accounts and OUs

Time Required: 15 minutes
Objective: Create user accounts and OUs by using the GUI and command line.

Required Tools and Equipment: 411Server1
Description: You want to create some user accounts and OUs to use for future activities that configure account policies.

1. Log on to 411Server1 as **Administrator,** and open Active Directory Users and Computers.

2. Click to expand the domain node, if necessary. Click **TestOU1.** You should already have a user named Test User1 that you created in Chapter 7. Create two new users named **Test User2** and **Test User3** with the logon names **testuser2** and **testuser3.** Set the passwords to **Password01,** and set them to never expire. Close Active Directory Users and Computers.

3. Open Active Directory Administrative Center. In the left pane, right-click **411Dom1 (local)**, point to **New**, and click **Organizational Unit**.

4. In the Create Organizational Unit dialog box, type **TestOU2** in the Name text box, and then click **OK**.

5. In the middle pane, right-click **TestOU2**, point to **New**, and click **User**. Create two users named **Test User4** and **Test User5** with the logon names **testuser4** and **testuser5**. Set the passwords to **Password01** and set them to never expire. Close Active Directory Administrative Center.

6. Open a PowerShell prompt. Type **New-ADOrganizationalUnit TestOU3 -Path "dc=411Dom1,dc=local"** and press **Enter**.

7. Type **New-ADUser "Test User6" -SamAccountName "testuser6" -Path "ou=TestOU3,dc=411Dom1,dc=local" -PasswordNeverExpires $True** and press **Enter**.

8. Repeat the previous command, replacing the 6 with 7 to create **Test User7**. These user accounts are disabled because no password is set. For now, you don't need these accounts to be enabled.

9. Now you create a group and add members to it. You use this group in a later activity when you work with password settings objects. Type **New-ADGroup PSO-Group -Path "ou=TestOU1,dc=411Dom1,dc=local" -GroupScope Global** and press **Enter**.

10. Add members to the group by using `dsquery` and `dsmod` in a piped command. Type **dsquery user "ou=testou1,dc=411dom1,dc=local" | dsmod group "cn=pso-group,ou=testout1,dc=411dom1,dc=local" -addmbr** and press Enter.

11. To verify that users were added to the group, type **Get-ADGroupMember "cn=pso-group, ou=testou1,dc=411dom1,dc=local"** and press **Enter**. You see a list of the three users you added.

12. Stay logged on to 411Server1 if you're continuing to the next activity.

Creating and Configuring Group Policies

A GPO is a list of settings administrators use to configure user and computer operating environments remotely. Group policies can specify security settings, deploy software, and configure a user's desktop, among many other computer and network settings. They can be configured to affect an entire domain, a site, and, most commonly, users or computers in an OU. The **GPO scope** defines which objects a GPO affects.

You can link GPOs to sites, domains, and OUs, and GPOs linked to these containers affect only user or computer accounts in the containers. When Active Directory is installed, two GPOs are created and linked to two containers:

- *Default Domain Policy*—This GPO is linked to the domain object and specifies default settings that affect all users and computers in the domain. The settings in this policy are related mainly to account policies, such as password and logon requirements, and some network security policies.

- *Default Domain Controllers Policy*—This GPO is linked to the Domain Controllers OU and specifies default policy settings for all domain controllers in the domain (as long as the computer objects representing domain controllers aren't moved from the Domain Controllers OU). The settings in this policy pertain mainly to user rights assignments, which specify the types of actions users can perform on a DC.

You view, create, and manage GPOs by using the Group Policy Management console (GPMC). Each GPO has two main nodes in GPMC (shown in the right pane of Figure 8-1):

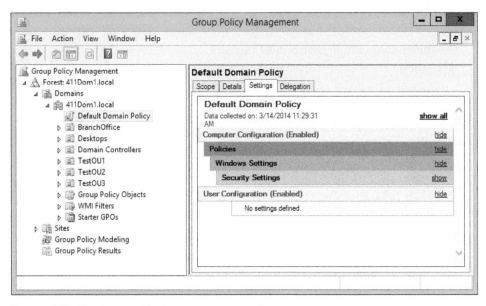

Figure 8-1   The Group Policy Management console

- *Computer Configuration*—Used to set policies that apply to computers in the GPO's scope. These policies are applied to a computer when the computer starts. Account policies are configured in this node.
- *User Configuration*—Used to set policies that apply to all users in the GPO's scope. User policies are applied when a user logs on to any computer in the domain.

The GPMC is used to create GPOs, view a GPO's settings, link and unlink GPOs with containers, and manage the inheritance settings of GPOs. To configure policy settings, you right-click a GPO in GPMC and click Edit to start the Group Policy Management Editor (GPME). When you change settings in a GPO that's linked to an Active Directory container, the change takes place as soon as the policy is downloaded to a computer. Computer Configuration policies are downloaded when a computer boots and about every 90 minutes on a running computer. User Configuration policies are downloaded when a user logs on and every 90 minutes for a logged-on user. You can also initiate a group policy update for both users and computers by entering gpupdate at a command prompt.

You learn more about working with GPOs in Chapters 9 and 10; in this chapter, you focus on user account policies.

The gpupdate command, when run with no arguments, updates changes to group policies. If you use gpupdate /force, the result is the same, but all group policies are downloaded whether they have changed or not. In a small network with few policies to download, using the /force option isn't a problem, but in a large network with many group policies, it can create a substantial processing burden on DCs and cause unnecessary network traffic. In a production network, use the /force option only if you suspect a problem with group policy processing.

Activity 8-2: Working with the Group Policy Management Console

Time Required: 10 minutes
Objective: Create a GPO in the Group Policy Management console.

Required Tools and Equipment: 411Server1
Description: In this activity, you create a GPO for configuring user account policies.

1. If necessary, log on to 411Server1 as **Administrator**, and open the Group Policy Management console.

2. Click to expand the **Forest** and **Domains** nodes and then the domain node, if necessary.

3. Click **Group Policy Objects**. In the right pane, you see existing GPOs, including the two default GPOs. To avoid confusion, you should unlink the WSUS-Desktops policy from the Desktops OU. In the left pane, expand **Group Policy Objects**, click **WSUS-Desktops**, and then right-click **Desktops** in the Links section of the right pane and click **Delete Link(s)**. Click **OK** to confirm.

4. Right-click **Group Policy Objects** and click **New**. In the Name text box, type **UserAcctPol**, and then click **OK**.

5. Click to expand **Group Policy Objects**, if necessary, and click **UserAcctPol**. In the right pane, click the **Scope** tab, if necessary. In the Links section, notice that the policy isn't linked to any objects yet.

6. Click the **Settings** tab. No settings are currently defined in the Computer Configuration or User Configuration sections.

7. In the left pane, right-click **UserAcctPol** and click **Edit** to open the Group Policy Management Editor.

8. Under Computer Configuration, click to expand **Policies, Windows Settings, Security Settings,** and **Account Policies**. The three nodes you see here—Password Policy, Account Lockout Policy, and Kerberos Policy—are the focus of this chapter. Close the Group Policy Management Editor.

9. Stay logged on if you're continuing to the next activity.

Configuring Account Policies

Account policies control settings related to user authentication and logon. They're found in a GPO in the path Computer Configuration, Policies, Windows Settings, Security Settings, Account Policies. It seems strange that account policies should be under the Computer Configuration node because they affect user accounts. The key is that account policies affect user accounts on the computer where the account is located. For example, domain user accounts are stored on domain controllers, so account policies applied to domain controllers affect all user accounts in the domain. Local user accounts are stored in the SAM database where the user account was created, so account policies applied to member computers affect the user accounts stored on these computers.

An important point to remember about account policies for domain user accounts is that they're effective only if the GPO where they're configured is linked to the domain. In other words, if you configure account policies on a GPO and link it to an OU, these policies don't affect domain users. However, the settings affect local user accounts on computers in the GPO's scope. Having said that, configuring settings only at the domain level is recommended so that both domain and local accounts are subject to the same policies. The Default Domain Policy GPO contains settings for many account policies so that a domain has secure settings defined when it's created. You can edit the Default Domain Policy GPO if you want to change the default settings, or you can create a GPO and link it to the domain to override the Default Domain

Policy settings. Creating a GPO is recommended instead of editing the Default Domain Policy so that you can revert to the original settings easily.

There are three subnodes under Account Policies. These subnodes and their settings are described in the following list. If the setting is configured in Default Domain Policy, the default setting value is given (see Figure 8-2):

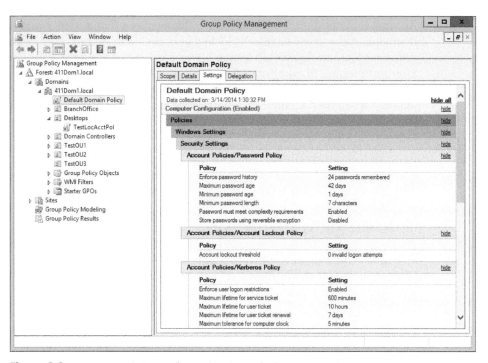

Figure 8-2   Account policies configured in the Default Domain Policy GPO

- *Password Policy*—Contains the following policies that control password properties. You can't enable a user account that has a password that doesn't meet the policy, and users can't change their passwords to one that doesn't meet the policy:

  o Enforce password history: Contains a value between 0 and 24, which indicates how many passwords Windows remembers before a user can reuse a password. A value of 0 means Windows doesn't keep a password history. To keep users from changing their passwords many times in succession to skirt this policy, you should set the "Minimum password age" policy. The Default Domain Policy sets it to 24 by default.

  o Maximum password age: A value between 0 and 999 indicates how many days a user can use a password before having to change it. If a user doesn't change his or her password within the required number of days, the password expires, and the user can't log on until the password is changed. A value of 0 means the password never expires. The default is 42 days.

  o Minimum password age: A value between 0 and 998 indicates how many days must elapse between successive password changes. A value of 0 means users can change their passwords as often as they want. The default is 1.

  o Minimum password length: A value between 0 and 14 indicates the minimum number of characters a user's password must be. A 0 means blank passwords are allowed. The default is 7.

  o Password must meet complexity requirements: If enabled (the default setting), a user's password must meet certain requirements: at least six characters (or meeting the "Minimum password length" policy, whichever is longer); doesn't contain more than two consecutive characters found in the user's account name or full name; and must contain characters from three of these categories—uppercase letters, lowercase letters, numbers, and symbols ($, @, !, #, and so on).

o Store passwords using reversible encryption: If enabled, passwords are stored with a method that's essentially plaintext and not secure. This policy should be set only if a critical application requires access to user passwords for authentication purposes. The default is disabled.

- *Account Lockout Policy*—Contains the following policies that control user account lockout. If a user account is locked, the user can't log on until the account is unlocked:

  o Account lockout duration: Contains a value between 0 and 99999 that indicates how many minutes a user's account is locked and, therefore, unable to be used for logon if the "Account lockout threshold" setting is exceeded. The account is unlocked automatically after this number of minutes passes. A value of 0 means the account remains locked until an administrator unlocks it. The default is "Not defined" because this setting has meaning only when the "Account lockout threshold" is defined and isn't 0. After the "Account lockout threshold" has a value other than 0 defined, the suggested setting for "Account lockout duration" is 30.

  o Account lockout threshold: Contains a value between 0 and 999 that determines how many times a user's password can be entered incorrectly before the account is locked out. The default is 0, which means accounts are never locked.

  o Reset account lockout counter after: Contains a value between 1 and 99999 that indicates the number of minutes that must elapse between failed logon attempts before the failed logon attempt counter is reset to 0. The default is "Not defined" because this setting has meaning only when the "Account lockout threshold" is defined and isn't 0. When "Account lockout threshold" has a value other than 0 defined, the suggested setting for "Reset account lockout counter after" is 30.

- *Kerberos Policy*—Administrators can use this suite of policies to fine-tune parameters for Kerberos, the default authentication protocol in a Windows domain. The policies deal mostly with the length of time Kerberos authentication tickets are active. Shortening the active time increases security but increases authentication overhead. In most cases, the default values shouldn't be changed. These settings are discussed more in "Kerberos Policy Settings."

Local Account Policies

As mentioned, account policies set in GPOs linked to an OU containing computer accounts affect only local user accounts defined in the computer's SAM database. Account policies set in GPOs linked to OUs take precedence over policies set at the domain level, unless the GPO linked to the domain has the Enforced setting enabled. Policies that aren't defined in a GPO linked to an OU use the policy setting defined in the domain-linked GPO, but if a policy is defined in both, the OU-linked policy is used.

Account policies are set in the Local Security Policy MMC on computers that aren't domain members because only domain members are affected by group policies. You can use the Local Security Policy MMC on domain members to view policy settings, but you can change only the ones that aren't defined by a group policy.

Activity 8-3: Working with Domain Password Policies

Time Required: 15 minutes
Objective: Change and test password policies for domain accounts.

Required Tools and Equipment: 411Server1
Description: You want to change some password policies from their default settings. Rather than edit the Default Domain Policy GPO, you edit the GPO you created earlier and link it to the

domain. The settings in the new GPO take precedence over the Default Domain Policy so that you can revert to the default account policies easily by unlinking the new GPO from the domain.

1. Log on to 411Server1 as **Administrator,** and open the Group Policy Management console, if necessary.

2. Click to expand **Group Policy Objects,** if necessary. Right-click **UserAcctPol** and click **Edit.**

3. In the Group Policy Management Editor, click to expand **Computer Configuration, Policies, Windows Settings, Security Settings,** and **Account Policies,** and then click **Password Policy.** In the right pane, double-click **Enforce password history.** Click the **Define this policy setting** check box, leave the "passwords remembered" value at 0, and then click **OK.**

 To see a detailed description of any account policy, double-click the policy, and click the Explain tab in its Properties dialog box.

4. Double-click **Minimum password age.** Click the **Define this policy setting** check box, set the value to 0 days so that passwords can be changed immediately, and then click **OK.** Windows provides a suggested value for "Maximum password age" because this policy must be defined if "Minimum password age" is defined. Click **OK** to accept the suggested value. Close the Group Policy Management Editor. Settings you didn't define, such as "Minimum password length," are still set because the Default Domain Policy defines them.

5. Before you test this policy, see how it works with the current policy in place. The default value for the policy you changed is 24, which means you shouldn't be able to change your password to the same value. Press **Ctrl+Alt+Del,** and then click **Change a password.** In the Old password text box, type your current password. In the New password and Confirm password text boxes, type your current password. Click the arrow next to the Confirm password text box. You see a message stating that Windows is unable to update the password because "Enforce password history" is set to 24, which means you can't reuse the same password until you have used 24 different passwords. Click **OK,** and then click the left arrow twice.

6. In the Group Policy Management console, link UserAcctPol to the domain by right-clicking **411Dom1.local** and clicking **Link an Existing GPO.** In the Select GPO dialog box, click **UserAcctPol** (see Figure 8-3) and click **OK.**

Figure 8-3   Selecting a GPO to link to the domain

8

7. Click **411Dom1.local,** and in the right pane, click **Linked Group Policy Objects.** The current link order causes the Default Domain Policy to take precedence over UserAcctPol. You want UserAcctPol to have precedence, so click **UserAcctPol** and click the up arrow to change UserAcctPol's link order to **1** (see Figure 8-4).

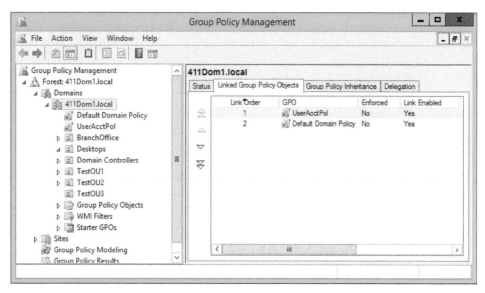

Figure 8-4   Changing a GPO's link order

8. Open a command prompt window, and then type **gpupdate** and press **Enter.** When the command finishes running, try to change your password again, using the same password for both the old and new passwords. You should be successful. Click **OK.** Close the command prompt window.

9. Leave the Group Policy Management console open if you're continuing to the next activity.

Activity 8-4: Working with Local Password Policies

Time Required: 15 minutes
Objective: Change and test password policies for local accounts.

Required Tools and Equipment: 411Server1 and 411Win8
Description: In this activity, you review current password policy settings on a member computer. You also set local password policies with Group Policy and verify changes by using a local user account.

1. Log on to 411Server1 as **Administrator,** and open the Group Policy Management console, if necessary.

2. Start 411Win8 and log on as **Administrator.**

3. On 411Win8, right-click **Start** and click **Run.** In the Open text box, type **secpol.msc,** and press **Enter** to open the Local Security Policy MMC. In the left pane, click to expand **Account Policies** and click **Password Policy.** Notice that the settings in the right pane match the settings for the Default Domain Policy and UserAcctPol combined, but the

UserAcctPol settings that are defined take precedence when a setting is defined in both GPOs (see Figure 8-5).

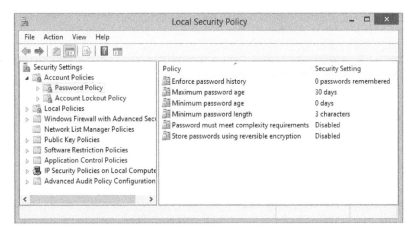

Figure 8-5   The Local Security Policy MMC

4. Double-click **Enforce password history** in the right pane. Note that you can't change the value because it has been set by a group policy, meaning it can't be overridden on the local computer. Click **Cancel.** Close the Local Security Policy MMC.

5. Right-click **Start** and click **Computer Management.** Click to expand **System Tools** and **Local Users and Groups,** and then click **Users.**

6. Right-click **Users** and click **New User.** In the New User dialog box, type **LocalUser1** in the User name text box, and click **Create.** In the error message stating that the user can't be created because the password doesn't meet complexity requirements, click **OK.**

7. Type **Password01** in the Password and Confirm password text boxes. Click to clear **User must change password at next logon,** and click **Password never expires.** Click **Create** and then **Close.**

8. On 411Server1, in the Group Policy Management console, right-click the **Desktops** OU (the 411Win8 computer account is in this OU) and click **Create a GPO in this domain, and Link it here.** In the New GPO dialog box, type **LocalUserAcctPol,** and click **OK.**

9. Under Desktops, right-click **LocalUserAcctPol** and click **Edit.** In the Group Policy Management Editor, click to expand **Computer Configuration, Policies, Windows Settings, Security Settings,** and **Account Policies,** and then click **Password Policy.**

10. In the right pane, double-click **Minimum password length.** Click **Define this policy setting** and set the length to **3.** Click **OK.**

11. Double-click **Password must meet complexity requirements.** Click **Define this policy setting,** if necessary. Click **Disabled,** if necessary, and then click **OK.**

12. On 411Win8, open a command prompt window, and then type **gpupdate** and press **Enter.** Close the command prompt window.

13. Open the Local Security Policy MMC and look at the Password Policy settings. Notice that the changes you made have been applied on the local computer.

14. In the Computer Management MMC, right-click **LocalUser1** and click **Set Password.** Click **Proceed.**

15. Type **pass** in the New password and Confirm password text boxes, and click **OK.** In "The password has been set" message box, click **OK.** (Notice you could set a password with only four characters and without meeting complexity requirements.) Close Computer Management.

16. Unlink the **LocalUserAcctPol** GPO from the **Desktops** OU.

17. Log off 411Win8, and stay logged on to 411Server1 if you're continuing to the next activity.

Activity 8-5: Applying Account Policies to an OU

Time Required: 10 minutes
Objective: Link a GPO to an OU to show that it has no effect on domain accounts.

Required Tools and Equipment: 411Server1
Description: In this activity, you unlink the UserAcctPol GPO from the domain and link it to the Domain Controllers OU. Next, you test to see which GPO's settings have an effect on domain accounts.

1. Log on to 411Server1 as **Administrator**, and open the Group Policy Management console, if necessary.

2. Click to expand **411Dom1.local**, if necessary. Right-click **UserAcctPol** and click **Delete**. Click **OK**.

3. Right-click the **Domain Controllers** OU and click **Link an Existing GPO**. In the Select GPO dialog box, click **UserAcctPol**, and then click **OK**.

4. The Domain Controllers OU contains the 411Server1 computer account, which holds the Active Directory database containing all domain users. Open a command prompt window, and then type **gpupdate** and press **Enter**. Close the command prompt window.

5. Press **Ctrl+Alt+Del**, and then click **Change a password**. In the Old password text box, type your current password. In the New password and Confirm password text boxes, type your current password.

6. You see a message stating that Windows is unable to update the password. This is because the Default Domain Policy is in effect. "Enforce password history" is set to 24 in the Default Domain Policy, so you can't change your password to the same value you used before. Because account policies can be set only at the domain level for domain accounts, the UserAcctPol GPO linked to the Domain Controllers OU has no effect on account policies for the Administrator user.

7. Unlink the **UserAcctPol** GPO from the **Domain Controllers** OU.

8. Stay logged on to 411Server1 if you're continuing to the next activity.

Activity 8-6: Working with Account Lockout Policy

Time Required: 10 minutes
Objective: Change and test account lockout policies.

Required Tools and Equipment: 411Server1 and 411Win8
Description: As a continuation of the previous activity, you change settings in the Account Lockout Policy node and test your changes.

1. Log on to 411Server1 as **Administrator**, and open the Group Policy Management console, if necessary.

2. Click **Group Policy Objects**, and then right-click **UserAcctPol** and click **Edit**. In the Group Policy Management Editor, click to expand **Computer Configuration**, **Policies**, **Windows Settings**, **Security Settings**, and **Account Policies**, and then click **Account Lockout Policy**. Double-click **Account lockout threshold**. Click the **Define this policy setting** check box, change the invalid logon attempts value to **2**, and then click **OK**.

3. The Suggested Value Changes dialog box suggests values for "Account lockout duration" and "Reset account lockout counter after." Click **OK** to accept these settings, and close the Group Policy Management Editor.

4. Link **UserAcctPol** to the domain node, and make sure it's first in the link order. (See Step 7 of Activity 8-3, if you need a reminder.)

5. Open a command prompt window, and then type **gpupdate** and press **Enter**. (Password policies that affect domain users are stored on domain controllers, not member computers, so the policy must be updated on the domain controller, even though you're logging on from 411Win8.) Close the command prompt window.

6. On 411Win8, attempt to log on twice as **testuser1** with an incorrect password. Attempt to log on a third time with the correct password (Password01). You should get a message stating that the account is currently locked out. Click **OK**.

7. On 411Server1, open Active Directory Users and Computers. Open the Properties dialog box for **Test User1,** located in TestOU1, and click the **Account** tab. Under the Logon Hours button is a message stating that the account is locked out. Click the **Unlock account** check box to unlock the account manually (see Figure 8-6), but be aware that the account unlocks automatically after the number of minutes in the "Account lockout duration" setting expires if it hasn't been unlocked manually. Click **OK**.

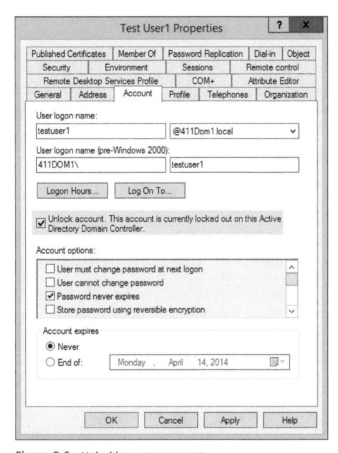

Figure 8-6   Unlocking a user account

8. Attempt to log on as **testuser1** from 411Win8 again. You should be successful.

9. Log off 411Win8, but stay logged on to 411Server1 if you're continuing to the next activity.

Kerberos Policy Settings

Kerberos is the authentication protocol used in a Windows domain environment to authenticate logons and grant accounts access to domain resources. An account can be a user or a computer because computers must also authenticate to the domain. Kerberos provides mutual authentication between a client and server or between two servers. **Mutual authentication** means the identity of both parties is verified. Kerberos is also the basis for authorization to network resources in a Windows domain.

Kerberos uses shared secret key encryption to ensure privacy, and passwords are never sent across the network. Kerberos authentication and authorization uses the following components:

- *Key Distribution Center*—Every domain controller is a **Key Distribution Center (KDC)**, which uses the Active Directory database to store keys for encrypting and decrypting data in the authentication process. The keys are based on an account's encrypted password.

- *Ticket-granting tickets*—When an account successfully authenticates with a domain controller (a KDC), it's issued a **ticket-granting ticket (TGT)**. A TGT grants the account access to the domain controller and is used to request a service ticket without having to authenticate again.

- *Service tickets*—A **service ticket** is requested by an account when it wants to access a network resource, such as a shared folder. It contains the account's access information, such as group memberships. A service ticket is sometimes called a "session ticket."

- *Timestamps*—A **timestamp** is a record of the time a message is sent. Timestamps are used in Kerberos to determine a message's validity and prevent replay attacks. When a computer receives a Kerberos message, the timestamp must be within 5 minutes of the current time on the receiving computer. The value of 5 minutes is the default and can be configured in Kerberos policy settings.

A replay attack occurs when an attacker captures a stream of packets transmitted between two computers and later replays the packets to one of the computers. Unless controls are put in place to detect the attack (such as a timestamp), the target computer is fooled into processing the packets as a legitimate communication session.

Here are the steps that take place when a user attempts to log on to a domain:

1. A user enters his or her username and password at a logon prompt.

2. A message is created containing the username and domain name. Part of the message is encrypted by using the shared secret key, which is based on the user's password. The encrypted message includes a timestamp.

3. A domain controller (a KDC) receives the message and retrieves the password from the Active Directory database for the username in the message. It then decrypts the message's encrypted part by using the user's password. If the message is decrypted successfully, the user's identity is verified. The timestamp is also decrypted. The time on it must be within the value specified in the Kerberos Policy setting "Maximum tolerance for computer clock synchronization" (5 minutes by default) for the server's current time. If the user's identity is verified and the timestamp is valid, the user is authenticated.

4. The domain controller sends the user a ticket-granting ticket (TGT), which includes a timestamp that authorizes the user to access the domain controller and request service tickets. The timestamp is again checked for validity. The user account caches the TGT information for future communication with the domain controller. A TGT is valid until it expires or the user logs off. By default, it's valid for 10 hours.

After an account has a TGT, it can request a service ticket to access a domain resource. For example, a user has just logged on to the domain and wants to access a shared folder on a file server. For this example, the KDC is DC1, and the file server is FS1. All messages include a timestamp, which is validated.

1. The user attempts to open a shared folder on FS1. The client computer sends a service ticket request to DC1 that includes the original TGT issued when the user authenticated and the name of the requested resource.

2. DC1 validates the request and sends a service ticket to the client, which contains the user's access information, including group memberships.

3. The client sends the service ticket to FS1, which validates the ticket and then checks the user's permissions, based on the access information in the ticket.

4. If the user has permissions to the resource, the user is granted access, and the service ticket is cached on the client computer. Future requests to access FS1 are sent directly to FS1, using the cached service ticket. A service ticket is valid until it expires or the user logs off. By default, it's valid for 10 hours.

The steps for Kerberos authentication and authorization left out some details about encryption and message contents, but they contain enough information for you to understand the purpose of these Kerberos policy settings:

- *Enforce user logon restrictions*—If this setting is enabled (the default), the KDC validates every request for service tickets against the rights granted to the requesting account. This process takes extra time, and although it's somewhat more secure, it might slow access to network resources, so it can be disabled if needed.

- *Maximum lifetime for service ticket*—This setting specifies in minutes how long a service ticket can be used before a new ticket must be requested to access the resource the ticket was granted for. The default is 600 minutes or 10 hours. The minimum allowed value is 10 minutes, and the maximum value is equal to the "Maximum lifetime for user ticket" setting.

- *Maximum lifetime for user ticket*—This setting is the maximum amount of time in hours a TGT can be used before it must be renewed or a new one must be requested. The default value is 10 hours.

- *Maximum lifetime for user ticket renewal*—This setting, specified in days, is the maximum period during which a TGT can be renewed. The default setting is 7 days. In this period, a TGT can be renewed without having to go through the full authentication process. After this period has expired (or the account logs off), a new TGT must be requested.

- *Maximum tolerance for computer clock synchronization*—This setting determines the maximum time difference allowed between a Kerberos message timestamp and the receiving computer's current time. If the time difference falls outside this limit, the message is considered invalid. The default is 5 minutes. Timestamp messages are corrected for time zone, so it's important to have the correct time zone set on all computers in the domain and have the domain controller clocks synchronized with a reliable source. By default, member computers are synchronized with the DC's clock.

Configuring Password Settings Objects

A **password settings object** (PSO) enables an administrator to configure password settings for users or groups that are different from those defined in a GPO linked to the domain. PSOs, introduced in Windows Server 2008, were somewhat awkward to create in ADSI Edit (available on the Tools menu in Server Manager) or with PowerShell. With Windows Server 2012/R2, you can create a PSO in Active Directory Administrative Center.

Another term for PSOs is "fine-grained password policies." Whichever term you use, they allow you to configure multiple password and account lockout policies for different sets of user accounts in the same domain. Recall that GPOs containing account policies are linked to the domain object, so all users in the domain are subject to the same account policies. Before PSOs, the only way to have different account policies affect different users was to have more than one domain you could apply the policies to. PSOs have the effect of overriding account policies set at the domain level, but they aren't configured like a GPO and linked to an OU or domain. PSOs are special objects that are assigned to users or groups. For example, you can set a different policy for members of the Domain Admins group, perhaps requiring their passwords to have a longer minimum length and be changed more often than other users' passwords.

Creating and Configuring a PSO

PSOs are created with Active Directory Administrative Center (ADAC), ADSI Edit, or PowerShell cmdlets. Using ADAC to create PSOs is new in Windows Server 2012/R2 and is the most convenient method. With PSOs, you can specify any settings under the Password Policy and the Account Lockout Policy nodes but not the Kerberos Policy node. You can create more than one PSO and configure different settings and assign them to different sets of users. If more than one PSO applies to a user (for example, two PSOs are assigned to two different groups, and some users are members of both groups), the PSO with the highest precedence value is applied to that user. The basic steps for creating and using a PSO are as follows:

1. Open ADAC, and expand the domain node. Double-click System, and then double-click Password Settings Container. In the Tasks pane, click New, and then click Password Settings.

2. In the Create Password Settings dialog box, give the PSO a name and precedence. The precedence is an integer value assigned to resolve conflicts if more than one PSO applies to a user. The lowest number has the highest priority. So if both PSO1 with the precedence value 1 and PSO2 with the precedence value 2 are linked to a user, the settings in PSO1 are applied to the user.

3. Configure password and account lockout policy settings.

4. Assign the PSO to one or more users or groups.

Like every Active Directory object, a PSO has security settings you can configure to allow or deny access to it. In the properties of the PSO in ADAC, simply scroll down to see the security settings. By default, the local Administrators group can make changes to a PSO, and both Domain Admins and Enterprise Admins have full control of a PSO. If you want other users or groups to manage a PSO, you can add them to the discretionary access control list (DACL) and give them read and write permissions.

Activity 8-7: Creating a Password Settings Object

Time Required: 15 minutes
Objective: Create a password settings object linked to a group.

Required Tools and Equipment: 411Server1
Description: You have a group of users who would benefit from a less stringent password policy than what's defined for the domain. You create a PSO, define the settings, and link it to the group. Last, you test the settings.

1. Log on to 411Server1 as **Administrator,** if necessary. Open Active Directory Administrative Center.

2. Click **411Dom1.local** to see the folders and OUs in the middle pane. Double-click **System** and then **Password Settings Container.** In the Tasks pane, click **New,** and then click **Password Settings.**

3. In the Create Password Settings dialog box, type **PSO1** in the Name text box and **5** in the Precedence text box. The Precedence value doesn't mean much until you have more than one PSO defined.

4. In the "Minimum password length (characters)" text box, type **4,** and in the "Number of passwords remembered" text box, type **5.** Click to clear the **Password must meet complexity requirements, Enforce minimum password age,** and **Enforce maximum password age** check boxes. Leave the **Enforce account lockout policy** at the default so that accounts are never locked out. Click to clear **Protect from accidental deletion** because you're deleting this PSO at the end of this activity.

5. Click the **Add** button, and type **PSO-Group**. Click **Check Names** and then **OK**. The settings should look like Figure 8-7. Click **OK**.

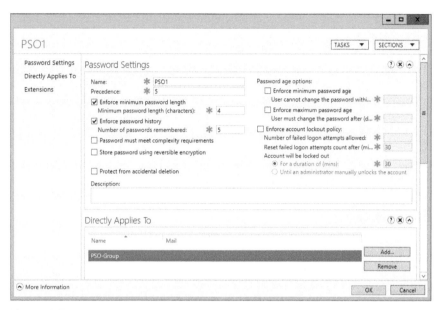

Figure 8-7 Creating a password settings object

6. In Active Directory Administrative Center, expand the **TestOU1** OU, and then click **Test User1**. In the Tasks pane, click **Reset password**. Type **pass1** in the Password and Confirm password text boxes, and then click **OK**. The new password is accepted. Navigate to **TestOU2** and click **Test User4**. In the Tasks pane, click **Reset password**. Type **pass1** in the Password and Confirm password text boxes, and then click **OK**. You see a message stating that the password doesn't meet complexity requirements. Click **OK** and then **Cancel**.

7. Log off 411Server1. Try to log on as **testuser1** with an incorrect password three times. The domain policy is set to lockout accounts after two incorrect attempts to log on. Then try to log on with **pass1**. You're successful because the PSO applied to PSO-Group (and testuser1 is a member) disables account lockout. Log out and log back on as **Administrator**.

8. Next, return account policies to their default values. On 411Server1, open the Group Policy Management console, if necessary. Expand the domain node, if necessary, so that you can see the two policies linked to it. Right-click **UserAcctPol** and click **Delete**. Click **OK** to confirm the deletion. That's it! No need to remember which policies to undo; by using a second GPO linked to the domain, you can simply link it or unlink it, depending on your policy requirements. In Active Directory Administrative Center, browse to the Password Settings Container, and then right-click **PSO1** and click **Delete**. Click **Yes** to confirm.

9. Log off and shut down 411Server1.

Service Accounts

A **service account** is a user account that Windows services use to log on to a computer or domain with a specific set of rights and permissions. A service needs to log on with a service account if it runs in the background because a user doesn't start it. When a user starts an application that runs interactively, the application uses the user's credentials to access the system, so there's no need for a service account.

In the past, two types of accounts have been used as service accounts: built-in and administrator-created. Built-in service accounts have few options for an administrator to configure different rights and permissions for different services, and the accounts are shared among several services. The OS manages the password for built-in service accounts automatically, much like the password for a computer account.

An administrator can also create a regular user account for use by a service (the administrator-created account) and manage rights and permissions for this account. However, the administrator would also have to manage password changes for each account created for that purpose, a task that can become unwieldy, especially when account policies require periodic password changes.

Starting in Window Server 2008 R2, Microsoft introduced managed service accounts and group managed service accounts. A **managed service account** (**MSA**) enables administrators to manage rights and permissions for services but with automatic password management. An MSA can be used on a single server. A **group managed service account** (**gMSA**) provides the same functions as managed service accounts but can be managed across multiple servers, as in a server farm or a load-balancing arrangement.

In this context, a service includes applications that run in the background, such as database or mail server applications.

Working with Service Accounts

There are three built-in service accounts, each with its own rights and permissions:

- *Local Service*—Intended primarily for services and background applications that need few rights and privileges. This account runs as a member of the local Users group or the Domain Users group in a domain environment. If network access is needed, Local Service runs as an anonymous user.

- *Network Service*—Intended primarily for services that need local and network access. This account runs as a member of the Users or Domain Users group and accesses the network as an Authenticated User member, which provides more privileges than for an anonymous user.

- *Local System*—This account should be used with caution because it has privileges that are in some ways more extensive than the Administrator account when accessing local resources. When accessing network resources, the Local System account uses the local computer account's credentials.

The advantage of using a built-in service account is that no management is needed, and the password is managed automatically. However, if a service requires more privileges than the Local Service or Network Service accounts have, you might need to use the Local System account, which in all likelihood offers more privileges than the service needs. The Services MMC (see Figure 8-8) shows services using all three types of built-in service accounts.

Name	Description	Status	Startup Type	Log On As
COM+ Event System	Supports Sy...	Running	Automatic	Local Service
COM+ System Application	Manages th...		Manual	Local System
Computer Browser	Maintains a...		Disabled	Local System
Credential Manager	Provides se...		Manual	Local System
Cryptographic Services	Provides thr...	Running	Automatic	Network Service
DCOM Server Process Laun...	The DCOM...	Running	Automatic	Local System
Device Association Service	Enables pair...		Manual (Trig...	Local System
Device Install Service	Enables a c...		Manual (Trig...	Local System
Device Setup Manager	Enables the ...		Manual (Trig...	Local System
DFS Namespace	Enables you...	Running	Automatic	Local System
DFS Replication	Enables you...	Running	Automatic	Local System
DHCP Client	Registers an...	Running	Automatic	Local Service
DHCP Server	Performs T...	Running	Automatic	Network Service

Extended / Standard

Figure 8-8   Viewing the Log On As setting in the Services MMC

Using Administrator-Created Service Accounts An administrator-created service account is simply a regular user account that you create for the purpose of assigning a logon account to a service. By using a regular user account, you can assign the service's logon account only the rights and permissions it needs to run correctly. Here are some guidelines to keep in mind when you use a regular user account as a service account:

- Assign only the rights and permissions the service needs.
- Use a very complex password because a user doesn't use this account to log on.
- Remove the account from the Users or Domain Users group if it doesn't need that group's rights and permissions.
- Set the password to never expire. If you leave the account subject to regular password policies, the service stops working if you fail to change the password when it expires. However, setting this option creates a security risk, which is why using managed service accounts, discussed next, is better.
- Never use the account to log on interactively.
- Use one account per service.

To configure a service with a logon account, open the Services MMC, double-click the service, and click the Log On tab. When you configure a service with a user account, you must enter and confirm the password, and then Windows automatically assigns the Log On As A Service right (see Figure 8-9).

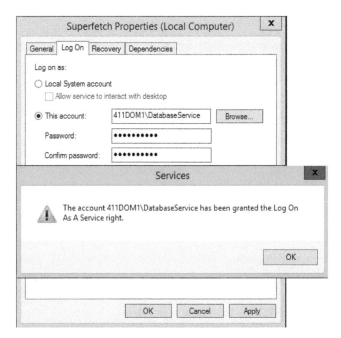

Figure 8-9   Configuring a service with a user account

Service Principal Names A service principal name (SPN) is a name that uniquely identifies a service instance to a client. Multiple instances of a service can be installed in a Windows Active Directory forest, and each instance must have a unique SPN. A service instance can also have multiple SPNs if clients can use different names to access it. An SPN is required for Kerberos authentication, and although administrators had to manage SPNs in the past, they're managed automatically for managed service accounts in a Windows Server 2008 R2 or later domain functional level.

When a client wants to connect to a service, it finds the service based on the SPN, which consists of the following elements:

- *Service type*—The service type is usually something like LDAP, MSSQLSvc, or HTTP.
- *Instance name*—This element is usually the hostname or IP address of the host running the service.
- *Port number*—The port number, such as 80 for HTTP or 389 for LDAP. If the service uses the standard port number, you don't need to specify this element.
- *Service name*—This element is usually the DNS name of the host providing the service. The service name and instance name are often the same, in which case the service name isn't needed.

The SPN is specified with the following syntax:

```
service type/InstanceName:port number/ServiceName
```

As mentioned, the service name can be omitted if it's the same as the instance name, and the port number can be omitted if it's the standard port number for a well-known service. So an SPN that provides Web services on the host www.csmtech.local, using the standard port, can be specified as follows:

```
HTTP/www.csmtech.local
```

If you're using user accounts rather than managed service accounts, you might need to manage SPNs, but in most cases they're created automatically. However, if you do have to change an SPN because, for example, a computer name changes or you need clients to be able to connect with a different name, you can do so with the setspn.exe command:

```
setspn.exe -s service/InstanceName ServiceAccount
```

For example, if you want to set the SPN for a service named LDAP on a server named ldsServ1.csmtech.local, using port 2300 and a service account called LDAPsvc, use the following command:

```
setspn.exe -s LDAP/ldsServ1.csmtech.local:2300 LDAPsvc
```

Working with Managed Service Accounts

An MSA is a new type of object in Active Directory that has the following attributes:

- Has a system-managed password
- Has automatic SPN support
- Is tied to a specific computer
- Can be assigned rights and permissions
- Can't be used for interactive logon
- Can't be locked out

The requirements for using an MSA include the following:

- It must be created in an Active Directory domain.
- The computer on which the MSA is used must be Windows 2008 R2 or Windows 7 or later.
- The Active Directory module for PowerShell must be installed.
- For automatic SPN support, you must be using a domain functional level of Windows Server 2008 R2 or later.

You create and manage MSAs with PowerShell; there's no GUI tool for working with them. Follow these steps to use MSAs:

1. Create an MSA in Active Directory in the Managed Service Accounts folder (which can be seen in Active Directory Users and Computers if you enable Advanced Features on the View menu). You can also set one or more SPNs on the account when you create it by using the

-ServicePrincipalNames option. To create an MSA named LDAPsvc, use the following PowerShell cmdlet on a DC:

```
New-ADServiceAccount -Name LDAPsvc
```

2. Associate the MSA with a member computer that will use the MSA. To allow a computer named ldsServ1 to use the service account, run this cmdlet on a DC:

```
Add-ADComputerServiceAccount -Computer ldsServ1 -ServiceAccount
    LDAPsvc
```

3. Install the MSA on the target computer by using the following cmdlet on the computer running the service. If the computer isn't a domain controller, you need to install the Active Directory module for Windows PowerShell.

```
Install-ADServiceAccount -Identity LDAPsvc
```

4. Configure the service on the target computer using the MSA. On the computer running the service, open the Services MMC, open the service's properties, and click the Log On tab. Specify the name of the account in the format *domain\MSAname*, or click Browse to select the account. Clear the password fields because the password is managed by the OS, and then stop and start the service.

Other PowerShell cmdlets you can use to work with MSAs include the following:

- Set-ADServiceAccount—Change an existing MSA's settings.
- Get-ADServiceAccount—Show an MSA's properties.
- Remove-ADServiceAccount—Delete an MSA.
- Reset-ADServiceAccountPassword—Reset the MSA's password on the computer where the account is installed.
- Uninstall-ADServiceAccount—Uninstall the account on the computer where the account is installed.
- Test-ADServiceAccount—Test the account to be sure it can access the domain with its current credentials or can be installed on a member computer.

Working with Group Managed Service Accounts   Managed service accounts can be used on only a single server. If a service is running on multiple servers, as in a server farm or load-balancing configuration, you can use a gMSA and still get all the benefits of an MSA. Group managed service accounts can be used only on computers running Windows Server 2012 or later with a domain functional level of Windows Server 2012.

gMSAs aren't actually different types of accounts from regular MSAs, but when you create them, you must use an additional option to specify which servers can use the account. You can specify server names or a group the servers are members of. This option wasn't available in PowerShell in earlier versions of Windows Server. To create a gMSA named LDAPsvc that's available to ldServ1, ldsServ2, and ldsServ3 (all members of the ldsServers global group), use the following cmdlet:

```
New-ADServiceAccount -Name LDAPsvc
 -PrincipalsAllowedToRetrieveManagedPassword ldsServers
```

You can also specify which servers can use the account after it's created by using the Set-ADServiceAccount cmdlet.

After the account is created, you need to go to each server using the account and run the Install-ADServiceAccount cmdlet, using the same syntax described in the preceding section.

Virtual Accounts Virtual accounts, introduced in Windows Server 2008 R2, are the simplest service accounts to use because you don't need to create, delete, or manage them in any way. Microsoft refers to them as "managed local accounts." To use them, you simply configure the service to log on as NT Service*ServiceName* with no password (as shown in Figure 8-10) because Windows manages the password. The service name isn't necessarily the name displayed in the Services MMC. You can find the service name in the General tab of the service's Properties dialog box.

Figure 8-10 Configuring a service to use a virtual account

Virtual accounts access the network with the credentials of the computer account where they're used. If the service needs to access network resources, you give permission for that resource to *ComputerName*$ (replacing *ComputerName* with the name of the computer). In most cases, it's better to use MSAs than virtual accounts if the service must access network resources because giving the computer account permission can be a security risk. For purely local services, however, virtual accounts are simple to use and effective.

Kerberos Delegation

Kerberos delegation is a feature of the Kerberos authentication protocol that allows a service to "impersonate" a client, relieving the client from having to authenticate to more than one service. In other words, if a client has authenticated to a service successfully, the service can then use the user's credentials to authenticate to another service on the client's behalf. For example, say a user logs on to an Outlook Web Access account. The user authenticates with the Outlook Web Access service, but the user's actual mailbox is on another server. Without delegation, the user would then have to authenticate to the server where the mailbox is located, too. With Kerberos delegation, the Outlook Web Access service can perform the authentication on the user's behalf.

Kerberos delegation is available when you use a domain account as a service account, and the account has been assigned an SPN. The Delegation tab is added to the account's Properties dialog box; this tab isn't available for a regular user account that hasn't been assigned an SPN. Figure 8-11 shows the properties of the LDAPsvc user account being used as a service account.

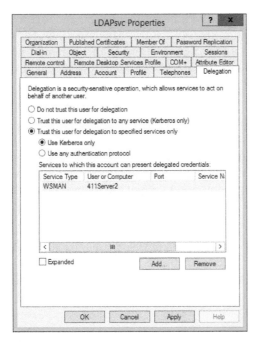

Figure 8-11   The Delegation tab for a service account

The Delegation tab has three main options:

- *Do not trust this user for delegation*—The account can't use Kerberos delegation.

- *Trust this user for delegation to any service (Kerberos only)*—The account can be used for delegation to any service but only by using the Kerberos authentication protocol.

- *Trust this user for delegation to specified services only*—This option is called **constrained delegation** because it limits the delegation to specific services running on specific computers. Constrained delegation can be limited to the Kerberos protocol, or you can specify using any authentication protocol.

Kerberos delegation is a convenient feature, especially when using multitiered applications where users connect only to a front-end interface, such as a Web server. It relieves administrators of having to find a way for users to authenticate to servers that might not be directly accessible to them.

Chapter Summary

- User accounts have two main functions: providing a method for user authentication to the network and providing detailed information about a user. On local computers, user accounts are stored in the SAM database, and users can log on to and access resources only on the computer where the account resides. User accounts created in Active Directory are referred to as "domain user accounts." Generally, these accounts enable users to log on to any computer that's a domain member in the Active Directory forest.

- User accounts can be created with GUI tools, such as Active Directory Users and Computers and Active Directory Administrative Center, and with command-line tools, such as dsadd and the PowerShell cmdlet New-ADUser.

- A GPO is a list of settings administrators use to configure user and computer operating environments remotely. Group policies can specify security settings, deploy software, and configure a user's desktop, among many other computer and network settings.

- Account policies control settings related to user authentication and logon. They're found in a GPO under Computer Configuration, Policies, Windows Settings, Security Settings, Account Policies. Account policies affect user accounts on the computer where the account is located. Account policies for domain user accounts are effective only if the GPO in which they're configured is linked to the domain.

- Account policies set in GPOs linked to an OU containing computer accounts affect only local user accounts defined in the computer's SAM database.

- Kerberos is the authentication protocol used in a Windows domain environment to authenticate logons and grant accounts access to domain resources. Kerberos is also the basis for authorization to network resources in a Windows domain. Kerberos authentication and authorization use the following components: Key Distribution Center, ticket-granting tickets, service tickets, and timestamps.

- A password settings object enables an administrator to configure password settings for users or groups that are different from those defined in a GPO linked to the domain.

- A service account is a user account that Windows services use to log on with a specific set of rights and permissions. A service needs to log on with a service account if it runs in the background because a user doesn't start it.

- A managed service account enables administrators to manage rights and permissions for services with automatic password management. A group managed service account provides the same functions but can be managed across multiple servers.

- A service principal name is a name that uniquely identifies a service instance to a client. Multiple instances of a service can be installed in a Windows Active Directory forest, and each instance must have a unique SPN.

- Virtual accounts are the simplest service accounts to use because you don't need to create, delete, or manage them in any way. They access the network with the credentials of the computer account where they're used.

- Kerberos delegation is a feature of the Kerberos authentication protocol that allows a service to impersonate a client, relieving the client from having to authenticate to more than one service.

Key Terms

constrained delegation   A type of delegation that limits the delegation to specific services running on specific computers. *See also* Kerberos delegation.

GPO scope   A property of GPO processing that defines which objects a GPO affects.

group managed service account (gMSA)   A specially configured managed service account that provides the same functions but can be managed across multiple servers. *See also* managed service account (MSA).

Kerberos   The authentication protocol used in a Windows domain environment to authenticate logons and grant accounts access to domain resources; also the basis for authorization to network resources in a Windows domain.

Kerberos delegation   A feature of the Kerberos authentication protocol that allows a service to impersonate a client, relieving the client from having to authenticate to more than one service.

Key Distribution Center (KDC)   A component of Kerberos that uses the Active Directory database to store keys for encrypting and decrypting data in the authentication process. *See also* Kerberos.

managed service account (MSA)   A service account that enables administrators to manage rights and permissions for services with password management handled automatically.

mutual authentication   A type of authentication in which the identities of both the client and server are verified.

password settings object (PSO)   An Active Directory object that enables an administrator to configure password settings for users or groups that are different from those defined in a GPO linked to the domain.

Security Accounts Manager (SAM) database   A database on stand-alone and member computers that holds local user and group account information.

service account   A user account that Windows services use to log on with a specific set of rights and permissions.

service principal name (SPN)   A name that uniquely identifies a service instance to a client.

service ticket   A digital message used by Kerberos; requested by an account when it wants to access a network resource, such as a shared folder. *See also* Kerberos.

ticket-granting ticket (TGT)   A digital message used by Kerberos; grants an account access to the issuing domain controller and is used to request a service ticket without having to authenticate again. *See also* Kerberos.

timestamp   A record of the time a message is sent; used in Kerberos authentication. *See also* Kerberos.

virtual account   A simple type of service account that doesn't need to be created, deleted, or managed by an administrator.

Review Questions

1. Which of the following is a main function of user accounts? (Choose all that apply.)

   a. User authentication

   b. Biometric identity

   c. Autonomous access

   d. Detailed information

2. Where are user accounts stored on a stand-alone computer?

   a. SQL database

   b. SAM database

   c. Active Directory

   d. A flat file

3. Which of the following can you use to create user accounts on a domain controller? (Choose all that apply.)

   a. `Create-Account user`

   b. `netsh user add`

   c. `New-ADUser`

   d. `dsadd user`

4. Which of the following is true about GPOs? (Choose all that apply.)

   a. They affect all groups in their scope.

   b. They can be linked to a site.

   c. The Default Domain Policy affects only user accounts.

   d. Account policies are under the Computer Configuration node.

5. Which of the following is included in account policies for a GPO? (Choose all that apply.)

   a. Password Policy

   b. Authorization Policy

   c. Account Lockout Policy

   d. Kerberos Policy

6. Which of the following best describes the "Account lockout threshold" setting?

   a. Specifies how many minutes a user's account is locked

   b. Defines the number of times a user can enter an incorrect username

   c. Specifies the number of minutes that must elapse between failed logon attempts

   d. Defines the number of times a user's password can be entered incorrectly

7. A junior administrator is configuring settings for the Password Policy of a new GPO he created and sets the minimum password length to 4. He links the GPO to the EngUsers OU containing the user and group accounts for the Engineering Department. A user in the Engineering Department calls and says he's trying to change the password on his domain user account to A$c1, but the system isn't taking the new password. What's the problem?

   a. The user doesn't belong to the Engineering group.

   b. The user's computer account isn't in the EngUsers OU.

   c. Password policies can be set only at the domain level.

   d. The user can't use the $ symbol in the password.

8. In a Windows domain running Windows Server 2012 R2, account lockout is enabled by default. True or False?

9. Which of the following is true about user accounts in a Windows Server 2012/R2 domain? (Choose all that apply.)

   a. The username can be from 1 to 20 characters.

   b. The username is case sensitive.

   c. The username can't be duplicated in the domain.

   d. Using default password policy settings, P@$$WORD is a valid password.

10. You discovered that a user changed his password 10 times in one day. When you ask why he did this, he replied that the system required him to change his password. He wanted to use his favorite password, but the system wouldn't accept it until he changed it 10 times. What should you do to prevent this user from reusing the same password for at least 60 days?

    a. Change the value for the "Enforce password history" setting.

    b. Change the value for the "Maximum password age" setting.

    c. Change the value for the "Minimum password age" setting.

    d. Enable the "Password must meet complexity requirements" setting.

11. An "Account lockout duration" setting of 0 means user accounts are never locked out. True or False?

12. A user is logged on to a Windows Server 2012 R2 domain from a Windows 8.1 computer and requests access to a shared folder. What must the user account request before the shared folder can be accessed?

    a. A service ticket

    b. A TGT

    c. A KDC

    d. An access code

13. You're the network administrator for several Windows Server 2012 R2 servers in New York. Your company just opened an office in California, and you sent one of the servers to the new office. The server was up and running within two days after you sent it. Now you're having authentication problems between the server in California and the domain controllers in New York. There's nothing wrong with the WAN connection, and you never had problems with the California server before, which seems to operate okay in every other way. What's a possible cause of this problem?

    a. The California server's hard drive was damaged in the move.

    b. The time zone needs to be changed on the California server.

    c. The computer account needs to be reset.

    d. The authentication protocol is incorrect.

14. A group of users in the Research Department has access to sensitive company information, so you want to be sure the group members' passwords are strong, with a minimum length of 12 characters and a requirement to change their passwords every 30 days. The current password policy requires passwords with a minimum length of 7 characters that users must change every 120 days. You don't want to inconvenience other users in the domain by making their password policies more stringent. What can you do?

    a. Create a GPO, configure the password policy for the Research Department, and link it to the domain. Block inheritance on all other OUs in the domain.

    b. Create a GPO, configure the password policy for the Research Department, and link it to the domain. Configure a security filter for the Research group.

    c. Create a PSO in ADAC, configure the password policy, and apply it to the Research Department group.

    d. Create a PSO in ADAC, configure the password policy, and link it to the Research Department OU.

15. Account policies configured in a GPO that's linked to an OU affect local user accounts on computers in the OU. True or False?

16. Which of the following is a built-in service account? (Choose all that apply.)

    a. Anonymous Logon

    b. Local system

    c. Network Service

    d. Authenticated Users

17. Which of the following is an advantage of using a managed service account instead of a regular user account for service logon? (Choose all that apply.)

    a. The system manages passwords.

    b. You can assign rights and permissions precisely.

    c. You can use the account to log on interactively.

    d. You can't be locked out.

18. Which of the following is used to uniquely identify a service instance to a client?

    a. SPN

    b. KDC

    c. Service ticket

    d. TGT

19. You have created an MSA on DC1 to run a service on the ldsServ1 server. What's the last thing you should do before using the Services MMC to configure the service to use the new MSA?

   a. On DC1, run the `Install-ADServiceAccount` cmdlet.

   b. On ldsServ1, run the `Install-ADServiceAccount` cmdlet.

   c. On DC1, run the `Add-ADComputerServiceAccount` cmdlet.

   d. On ldsServ1, run the `Add-ADComputerServiceAccount` cmdlet.

20. You have four servers running a service in a load-balancing configuration, and you want the services on all four servers to use the same service account. What should you do?

   a. Create a group and add the servers' computer accounts to it. Run the `New-ADServiceAccount` cmdlet.

   b. Run the `New-ADServiceAccount` cmdlet and configure constrained Kerberos delegation.

   c. Run the `New-gMSAServiceAccount` cmdlet and specify the four servers in the SPN.

   d. Move the four servers' computer accounts to the Managed Service Accounts folder in Active Directory.

21. In your Windows Server 2012 R2 domain, you have a member server also running Windows Server 2012 R2. You want to install the LocSvc service, which will be accessing only local resources. You need to configure authentication for this service but don't want to use one of the built-in service accounts and want to do this with the least administrative effort. What should you do?

   a. Create a local user on the server, and configure the service to log on as that user.

   b. Create an MSA with PowerShell, and configure the service to log on as the MSA.

   c. Create a domain user, and in the Delegation tab, select LocSvc.

   d. Configure the service to log on as NT Service\LocSvc.

22. You're configuring a Web-based intranet application on the WebApp server, which is a domain member. Users authenticate to the Web-based application, but the application needs to connect to a back-end database server, BEdata, on behalf of users. What should you configure?

   a. On the WebApp server, create a local user account, and grant it permission to BEdata.

   b. On the BEdata server, assign the Authenticate Users permission to the database files.

   c. On a domain controller, configure constrained delegation on the service account.

   d. Create an MSA on WebApp, and run `Add-ADComputerServiceAccount` with BEdata as the target.

Case Projects

CASE PROJECTS

Case Project 8-1: Solving a Password Policy Problem

You've been called in to solve a problem for CSM Tech Publishing, which is running Windows Server 2012 R2 Servers in a domain environment. Strict account policies that require password changes every 20 days, a password history of 24, complex passwords, and an account lockout threshold of 2 are in place because five high-level managers have access to information about future projects that must be kept secret. The problem is that the support team is constantly fielding calls to unlock accounts and reset passwords because users forget them. Worse, many users have taken to writing their passwords on notes stuck to their desks or monitors. What can you suggest to maintain a strict password policy for the five managers but loosen requirements for the remaining staff? What steps would you take?

Case Project 8-2: Working with Service Accounts

You're installing six new servers as members of a Windows Server 2012 R2 domain. All servers are also running Windows Server 2012 R2. Server 1 is running the NetServ1 network service, Server 2 is running the LocServ2 local service, and Servers 3 through 6 are a server farm, each running the LBServ service. Security policies forbid using built-in service accounts for configuring authentication on new services. You don't want to have to manage service account passwords, and you want to perform this task with the least administrative effort. Describe what type of service account you should use for each server, and explain your reasons.

8

chapter 9

Group Policy Settings and Preferences

After reading this chapter and completing the exercises, you will be able to:

- Describe the function of Group Policy
- Configure group policy settings
- Work with administrative templates
- Work with security templates
- Configure group policy preferences

Group Policy is a powerful tool for network administrators to manage the working environment of domain controllers, desktop computers, and users. You learned about several Group Policy topics while studying the objectives for Installing and Configuring Windows Server 2012, Exam 70-410, but this chapter delves into some different areas, including software installation policies, script deployment, folder redirection, administrative templates, security templates, and group policy preferences. First, however, you start with a quick review of Group Policy and how to create, configure, and link Group Policy objects. The hands-on activities in this chapter give you practice in working with policy settings and preferences, so be sure to place emphasis on them as you go through this chapter.

A Group Policy Primer

Table 9-1 describes what you need for the hands-on activities in this chapter.

Table 9-1   Activity requirements

Activity	Requirements	Notes
Activity 9-1: Creating, Linking, and Unlinking GPOs	411Server1	
Activity 9-2: Configuring and Testing a GPO	411Server1, 411Win8	
Activity 9-3: Deploying Software to a Computer	411Server1, 411Win8	Internet access required
Activity 9-4: Uninstalling a Deployed Package Automatically	411Server1, 411Win8	
Activity 9-5: Deploying Software to Users	411Server1, 411Win8	
Activity 9-6: Deploying a Shutdown Script to a Computer	411Server1, 411Win8	
Activity 9-7: Configuring a Folder Redirection Policy	411Server1, 411Win8	
Activity 9-8: Working with Computer Administrative Template Settings	411Server1, 411Win8	
Activity 9-9: Working with User Administrative Template Settings	411Server1, 411Win8	
Activity 9-10: Viewing Policy Settings with Filter Options	411Server1	
Activity 9-11: Creating a Security Template	411Server1, 411Win8	
Activity 9-12: Importing a Security Template	411Server1, 411Win8	
Activity 9-13: Configuring and Testing Preferences	411Server1, 411Win8	
Activity 9-14: Configuring Item-Level Targeting	411Server1, 411Win8	
Activity 9-15: Deploying a VPN Connection	411Server1, 411Win8	
Activity 9-16: Configuring Internet Explorer Settings	411Server1, 411Win8	An Internet connection is needed to test the preference settings.
Activity 9-17: Configuring Local Groups	411Server1, 411Win8	

Group Policy architecture, configuration, processing, and management were covered in *MCSA Guide to Installing and Configuring Windows Server 2012/R2, Exam 70-410* (Cengage Learning, 2015). This section serves as a review of group policies, and the remainder of the chapter covers group policy settings and group policy preferences in detail.

A Group Policy object (GPO) contains policy settings for managing many aspects of domain controllers, member servers, member computers, and users. There are two main types of GPOs: local GPOs and domain GPOs. **Local GPOs** are stored on local computers and can be edited with the Group Policy Object Editor snap-in. To use this tool, you add the Group Policy Editor snap-in to a custom MMC, or enter `gpedit.msc` at the command line to open an already configured MMC called Local Group Policy Editor. You use one of these tools to edit local GPOs on workgroup computers manually. The policy settings on domain members can be affected by domain GPOs linked to the site, domain, or OU in Active Directory. Settings in local GPOs that are inherited from domain GPOs can't be changed on the local computer; only settings that are undefined or not configured by domain GPOs can be edited locally.

Windows has an MMC called Local Security Policy that enables you to edit policies in just the Security Settings node of the local GPO. You access this MMC via the Tools menu in Server Manager or by entering `secpol.msc` at the command line.

Domain GPOs are stored in Active Directory on domain controllers. They can be linked to a site, a domain, or an OU and affect users and computers whose accounts are stored in these containers. A domain GPO is represented by an object stored in the Group Policy Objects folder in Active Directory.

Creating and Linking GPOs

The main tools for managing, creating, and editing GPOs are the Group Policy Management console (GPMC) and the Group Policy Management Editor (GPME). The purpose of using these tools is to carry out changes to the security and/or working environment for users or computers. There are several ways to go about this task:

- Edit an existing GPO that's linked to an Active Directory container.
- Link an existing GPO to an Active Directory container.
- Create a GPO while linking it to an Active Directory container.
- Create a GPO in the Group Policy Objects folder, which isn't linked to an Active Directory object.
- Create a GPO by using a Starter GPO.

If you edit an existing GPO that's already linked to an Active Directory container, keep in mind that changes in policy settings take effect as soon as clients download them. In other words, there's no Save option in the GPME; changes are saved immediately. By default, client computers download GPOs at restart, and user policies are downloaded at the next logon. Therefore, the best practice is usually creating GPOs in the Group Policy Objects folder, and then linking them to the target Active Directory container after all changes have been made and tested. When you're changing several policy settings at once or are unsure of the effect policy changes will have, you should test policies before enabling them by using a test OU and some test computers and users to test the policy settings.

Editing an Existing GPO   To edit an existing GPO, right-click it in the GPMC and click Edit, which opens the GPO in the GPME. In the GPMC, all GPOs are stored in the Group Policy Objects folder, and you can also find GPOs linked to an Active Directory container displayed as shortcut objects in the container to which they're linked. Checking whether and where a GPO is linked is a good idea before editing. To do this, select the GPO in the left pane of the GPMC and view the Scope tab in the right pane (see Figure 9-1). All Active Directory containers the GPO is linked to are listed for the selected location. In this figure, the domain is selected as the location, and you can also select "Entire forest" or "All sites" in the "Display links in this location" list box. You can also see whether the GPO is enforced and whether the link is enabled.

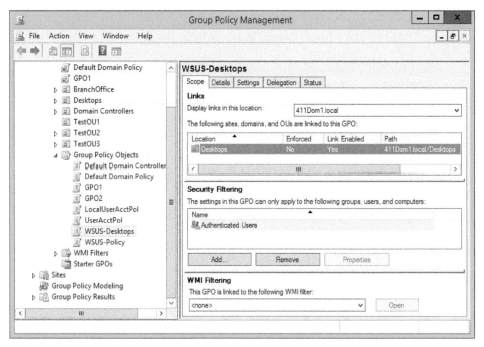

Figure 9-1   The Scope tab for a GPO

Editing the two default GPOs (Default Domain Policy and Default Domain Controllers Policy) isn't advisable. One reason is that you can't test the GPO adequately because it's already linked to the domain or the Domain Controllers OU. Another reason is that you might want to revert to the default settings, and you could have difficulty remembering what was changed. The recommended method for making changes to domain-wide policies is creating a new GPO and linking it to the domain. Remember that you can have multiple GPOs linked to the same container. Then if you need to revert to the original settings, you can unlink the GPO.

Creating a New GPO   There are two ways to create a GPO in the GPMC. You can right-click the container you're linking the GPO to and select "Create a GPO in this domain, and Link it here," or you can right-click the Group Policy Objects folder and click New. The latter method is preferable because it gives you a chance to test policies before enabling them. After creating a GPO, you can edit it and link it to an Active Directory container, if necessary. Because several GPOs can be linked to the same container, the best practice is to create GPOs that set policies narrowly focused on a category of settings, and then name the GPO accordingly. For example, if you need to configure policy settings related to the Network node under Computer Configuration, create a GPO named CompNetwork. If this policy will apply only to a certain container, you could include the container name in the GPO name—for example, Mktg-CompNetwork. Creating and naming GPOs in this manner make it easier to identify the GPO that sets a particular policy and to troubleshoot GPO-processing problems.

Activity 9-1: Creating, Linking, and Unlinking GPOs

Time Required: 10 minutes
Objective: Create, link, and unlink GPOs.

Required Tools and Equipment: 411Server1
Description: You want to be sure you know how to create and test GPOs, so you create a new GPO and experiment with linking and unlinking it to OUs.

1. Log on to 411Server1 as **Administrator**, if necessary.

2. Open the Group Policy Management console. Right-click **Group Policy Objects** and click **New**. In the New GPO dialog box, type **GPO1** in the Name text box, and then click **OK**. Create another GPO with the name **GPO2**.

3. If necessary, click the **Group Policy Objects** folder. In the right pane, notice that all the GPOs are listed as "Enabled" in the GPO Status column. Changes you make to an enabled GPO take effect on any users or computers in containers it's linked to.

4. Right-click **GPO1** and point to **GPO Status**. You can enable or disable the settings in a GPO or just disable the Computer Configuration or User Configuration settings.

5. Right-click the **Desktops** OU and click **Link an Existing GPO**. In the Select GPO dialog box, click **GPO1**, and then click **OK**. Repeat this procedure, but link **GPO2**. Click **Desktops** in the left pane, and in the right pane, notice that both GPO1 and GPO2 are linked to Desktops.

 If both GPOs had the same policy setting configured but with different values, the value of the policy setting in GPO1 would take precedence because it would be applied last, according to the link order. GPO1 has link order 1, and GPO2 has link order 2. The lowest number link order is applied last. GPO precedence is covered in detail in Chapter 10.

6. Right-click **GPO1** under Desktops and click **Delete**. Click **OK** in the message box asking you to confirm the deletion. Recall that this action deletes only the link to the GPO, not the GPO itself. Link **GPO1** to the **Desktops** OU again.

7. Click **GPO1** in the right pane. GPO1 now has link order 2, so GPO2 takes precedence. Click the **up arrow** to the left of the Link Order column. GPO1 now has link order 1, so it takes precedence again if any settings conflict.

8. Unlink **GPO1** and **GPO2** from the Desktops OU. No policies should be linked to Desktops now.

9. Stay logged on to 411Server1 if you're continuing to the next activity.

Activity 9-2: Configuring and Testing a GPO

Time Required: 10 minutes
Objective: Configure and test a GPO.

Required Tools and Equipment: 411Server1 and 411Win8
Description: Now that you have two test GPOs, you can configure and test some computer settings in them.

1. Start 411Win8. Log on to 411Server1 as **Administrator**, and open the Group Policy Management console, if necessary.

2. Click **Group Policy Objects** in the left pane. Right-click **GPO1** and click **Edit** to open it in the Group Policy Management Editor.

3. Click to expand **User Configuration, Policies, Administrative Templates,** and **Start Menu and Taskbar.** In the right pane, double-click **Go to the desktop instead of Start when signing in or when all the apps on a screen are closed.**

4. Click **Enabled,** and then click **OK.** Close the Group Policy Management Editor.

5. In the Group Policy Management console, click **GPO1,** and in the right pane, click the **Settings** tab. Click the **show all** link. You see the setting you just enabled.

6. Right-click the domain object (**411Dom1.local**) and click **Link an Existing GPO.** In the Select GPO dialog box, click **GPO1,** and then click **OK.**

7. On 411Win8, log on to the domain as **Win8User.** If the policy didn't take effect (in other words, you went to the Start screen when you logged on), open a command prompt window, type **gpupdate** to force an update of policies, and press **Enter.** Log off, and then log back on. You should go directly to the desktop instead of the Start screen.

8. Log off 411Win8. Stay logged on to 411Server1 if you're continuing to the next activity.

Group Policy Settings

The Group Policy Management Editor has a Computer Configuration node, with policies affecting all computer accounts in a GPO's scope, and a User Configuration node, with policies affecting all user accounts in a GPO's scope. Most policies in these two nodes affect different aspects of the working environment, but a few policies are the same. If the same policy is configured in both nodes and the settings conflict (for example, one disables a policy and the other enables it), the setting in Computer Configuration takes precedence.

Both nodes have a Policies folder and a Preferences folder (covered later in the "Group Policy Preferences" section). Under the Policies folder are these three folders: Software Settings, Windows Settings, and Administrative Templates. The Software Settings and Windows Settings folders include items called "extensions" because they extend the functionality of Group Policy beyond what was available in Windows 2000. The Administrative Templates folder contains categorized folders or nodes with settings that affect users' or computers' working environments, mainly by changing Registry settings.

Policy settings can be managed or unmanaged. A **managed policy setting** is applied to a user or computer when the object is in the scope of the GPO containing the setting. When the object is no longer in the GPO's scope or the policy is set to "Not configured," however, the setting on the user or computer reverts to its original state. An **unmanaged policy setting** is persistent, meaning it remains even after the computer or user object falls out of the GPO's scope until it's changed by another policy or manually. The policies already loaded in Active Directory are managed policies, but you can customize Group Policy by adding your own policies, which are unmanaged.

You learned about user account policies in Chapter 8 and learned about a variety of policy settings while studying the Exam 70-410 objectives. Administrative Templates are discussed later in "Working with Administrative Templates." The following sections focus on these categories of settings:

- *Software installation*—In the Software Settings folder under both the Computer Configuration and User Configuration nodes.
- *Folder redirection*—In the Windows Settings folder under the User Configuration node.
- *Scripts*—In the Windows Settings folder under both the Computer Configuration and User Configuration nodes.

Software Installation Policies

The Software installation extension is used to install software packages remotely on member computers. If it's configured under the Computer Configuration node, the software package is installed regardless of who logs on to the targeted computers. When it's configured under

User Configuration, the software package is available to targeted users when they log on to any domain computer.

Applications are deployed with the Windows Installer service, which uses installation packages called "MSI files." A **Microsoft Software Installation (MSI) file** is a collection of files gathered into a package with an `.msi` extension that contains the instructions Windows Installer needs to install an application.

You might want to install a software package that's available only as an executable (`.exe`) file. Depending on the software developer, an `.exe` file might contain an MSI file that you can extract with the command `filename.exe/extract` (replacing `filename` with the `.exe` file's name). If that's not possible, you might need to convert the `.exe` to an MSI. Although there's no Windows utility for this purpose, third-party programs are available, such as Advanced Installer (*www.advancedinstaller.com*) and Exe to MSI (*www.exetomsi.com*).

Configuring Software Installation for Computers   In the Computer Configuration node, software packages are assigned to target computers, meaning installation of the software is mandatory, and assigned packages are installed the next time the computer starts. To assign a software package to a computer, you must create a shared folder on a server that gives the computer the Read & execute permission. Typically, you do this by assigning the necessary permissions to the Authenticated Users special identity group. If you're deploying several applications through Group Policy, you can create a separate folder in the share for each package. After creating the shared folder and copying the installation package to it, you can create the deployment policy by using the Software installation extension.

Activity 9-3: Deploying Software to a Computer

Time Required: 20 minutes
Objective: Create a software installation policy and deploy a software package to a computer.

Required Tools and Equipment: 411Server1, 411Win8, Internet access
Description: You've learned about a utility that's available as a free download from the Microsoft Web site and realize all computers in a department will benefit from it. You decide to deploy the utility by using group policies. You link the GPO to the Desktops OU where the 411Win8 computer account is located.

1. Log on to 411Server1 and 411Win8 as **Administrator**, if necessary.

2. On 411Server1, open File Explorer, and create a folder called **SoftDeploy** on the C volume.

3. Right-click **SoftDeploy**, point to **Share with**, and click **Specific people**. In the File Sharing dialog box, type **Authenticated Users** in the text box at the top, and then click **Add**. Leave the default permission **Read** and the entries **Administrator** and **Administrators** in the permissions list. Click **Share**, and then click **Done**.

4. In File Explorer, double-click the **SoftDeploy** folder, and create a subfolder named **GPMCScripts**. (GPMC Sample Scripts is the name of the utility you're deploying.) Close File Explorer.

5. On 411Win8, start Internet Explorer and go to **www.microsoft.com/download**. In the Search text box, type **GPMC Sample Scripts**, and press **Enter**.

6. Click the **Group Policy Management Console Sample Scripts** link, and then click the **Download** button. In the message box asking whether you want to run or save the file, click **Save**. Click the **Open folder** button in the message box stating that the download has finished.

7. In the File Explorer window that opens, right-click **GPMCSampleScripts** and click **Copy**.

8. Right-click **Start** and click **Run**. Type **\\411Server1\SoftDeploy\GPMCScripts** in the Open text box, and click **OK**.

9. Right-click empty space in the File Explorer window that opens and click **Paste**. Close all open windows on 411Win8.

10. On 411Server1 in the Group Policy Management console, click the **Group Policy Objects** folder, and create a GPO in it named **SwInst**. Right-click **SwInst** and click **Edit**. In the Group Policy Management Editor, expand **Computer Configuration, Policies, Software Settings**, and **Software installation**.

11. Right-click empty space in the right pane, point to **New**, and click **Package**. In the Open dialog box, type **\\411Server1\SoftDeploy\GPMCScripts**, and press **Enter**. Click the **GPMCSampleScripts** file, and then click **Open**.

12. In the Deploy Software dialog box, leave the default option **Assigned**. Notice that the Published option is grayed out because you can publish a software package only in the User Configuration node. Click **OK**. The Advanced option enables you to set additional options for package deployment, but for now, stick with the default deployment options.

13. You see the Microsoft GPMC Sample Scripts file in the right pane (see Figure 9-2). Right-click **Microsoft GPMC Sample Scripts** and click **Properties**. Click each tab to get an idea of the available options for deploying a software package. (Some are discussed after this activity.) Click **Cancel** to close the Properties dialog box, and close the Group Policy Management Editor.

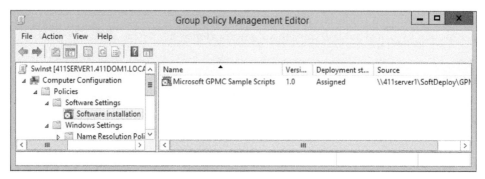

Figure 9-2   Configuring software installation settings

14. In the Group Policy Management console, link the **SwInst** GPO to the **Desktops** OU (where the 411Win8 computer account is).

15. For more reliable processing of software installation policies, you should configure another group policy setting. Right-click **GPO1**, which is linked to the domain, and click **Edit** to open it in the Group Policy Management Editor. Expand **Computer Configuration, Policies, Administrative Templates, System**, and **Group Policy**. In the right pane, double-click **Configure software Installation policy processing**. Click **Enabled**, and then click **Allow processing across a slow network connection** and **Process even if the Group Policy objects have not changed**. Click **OK**, and close the Group Policy Management Editor.

16. On 411Win8, open a command prompt window. Type **gpupdate** and press **Enter**. You might see a message stating that a restart is needed before the Computer Configuration policies can be processed. Restart 411Win8. Because of the way Group Policy processes Software installation extensions, two restarts are often needed. If necessary, restart 411Win8 again, and then log on to the domain as **Administrator**.

17. Right-click **Start** and click **Programs and Features**. You see Microsoft GPMC Sample Scripts in the list of installed programs. Close the Programs and Features window.

18. Microsoft GPMC Sample Scripts isn't actually an executable program; it's a collection of scripts that can be used with the Group Policy Management console. Open File Explorer, and navigate to **C:\Program Files\Microsoft Group Policy**. Double-click the **GPMC Sample Scripts** folder to see a bevy of scripts for managing Group Policy.

19. Log off 411Win8, but stay logged on to 411Server1 if you're continuing to the next activity.

Advanced Application Deployment Options   To access other options for deploying applications, click the Advanced option button in the Deploy Software dialog box or open the Properties dialog box for a package you've already added to the Software installation node. The Properties dialog box has several tabs with options for changing how the application is deployed:

- *General*—This tab is mostly just information about a package, including the name, version, language, publisher, and hardware platform. You can change the package name.

- *Deployment*—You can select whether a package is published or assigned. In the Computer Configuration node, software packages can only be assigned, so the Published option is disabled (see Figure 9-3). The deployment type selection determines what's available in the Deployment options section, including when and how an application is deployed. For example, an application can be installed at user logon or when a document used by the application is opened. Another deployment option uninstalls the application automatically if the user or computer falls out of the GPO's scope. In the Computer Configuration node, the only two deployment options are Auto-install and Uninstall. At the bottom of this tab, you can choose user interface options (Basic or Maximum), but these options are available only in the User Configuration node. Clicking the Advanced button shows other options for ignoring language when deploying the package and making a 32-bit application available on 64-bit machines (enabled by default).

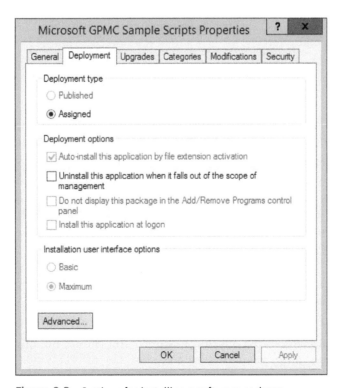

Figure 9-3   Settings for installing a software package

- *Upgrades*—You can deploy a package upgrade by specifying which existing packages should be upgraded by the new package and which packages can upgrade the current package.

- *Categories*—You use this tab to associate a published package with a category. Control Panel's Programs applet lists available applications under the specified categories. This option is used only for packages published in the User Configuration node.

- *Modifications*—You can use this tab to customize a package installation by using a transform file (.mst extension). Select transform files for customizing the installation of an MSI file. A transform file contains information about features and components that can be used to customize an application installation. For example, if you're installing Microsoft Office, you can use the Office Resource Kit to create a transform file that overrides the default installation path or specifies which Office components should be installed.

- *Security*—A standard DACL for the package object. By default, Authenticated Users have Read permission, and Domain Admins have Full control.

After a package is deployed to a computer, by default it's not installed again. However, if changes have been made to the original package, right-click the package in the Software installation extension and click All Tasks, and then click Redeploy application. This action reinstalls the package on target computers. To remove a deployed package, right-click the package and click All Tasks, and then click Remove. You have the option to uninstall the software immediately or simply prevent new installations yet allow users to use already deployed packages.

Activity 9-4: Uninstalling a Deployed Package Automatically

Time Required: 15 minutes
Objective: Configure a package to uninstall automatically when the GPO falls out of the target computer's scope.

Required Tools and Equipment: 411Server1 and 411Win8
Description: You have decided to uninstall an application that was deployed with Group Policy. You set the Uninstall option on the package, disable the policy link, and then restart the 411Win8 computer twice for it to take effect.

1. Log on to 411Server1 as **Administrator**, if necessary. Start 411Win8, if necessary, and log on as **Administrator**.

2. On 411Server1, open the Group Policy Management console, if necessary.

3. Open the **SwInst** GPO in the Group Policy Management Editor. Navigate to the **Software installation** node, and then right-click **Microsoft GPMC Sample Scripts** and click **Properties**.

4. Click the **Deployment** tab. Click **Uninstall this application when it falls out of the scope of management,** and then click **OK**. Close the Group Policy Management Editor.

5. Because 411Win8 doesn't yet have the Uninstall setting, you need to update the policy on it. Open a command prompt window, and then type **gpupdate** and press **Enter**. In a production environment, you should set the Uninstall option before deploying the GPO, or you can force a group policy update remotely (explained in Chapter 10).

6. On 411Server1, in the Group Policy Management console, navigate to the **Desktops** OU. Right-click **SwInst** and click to clear **Link Enabled**. (This step disables the link but doesn't remove the GPO shortcut under the OU.)

7. Shut down and restart 411Win8 twice. Log on to the domain as **Administrator**.

8. Right-click **Start** and click **Programs and Features**. You should no longer see Microsoft GPMC Sample Scripts in the list of installed programs. Log off 411Win8.

9. On 411Server1, unlink **SwInst** from the **Desktops** OU because you use it in the next activity. (Remember that you disabled only the link in Step 6.)

10. Stay logged on to 411Server1 if you're continuing to the next activity.

Configuring Software Installation for Users   The Software installation extension performs the same function in the User Configuration node as in the Computer Configuration node—deploying software to remote destinations—but has important differences in options and execution. A software package can only be assigned to a computer, but there are two options for deploying software to users:

- *Published*—A **published application** isn't installed automatically; instead, a link to install the application is available in Control Panel's Programs and Features by clicking the "Install a program from the network" link. Published applications can also be configured to install when the user opens a file type associated with the application.

- *Assigned*—**Assigned applications** can be installed automatically when the user logs on to a computer in the domain, or it can be set to install automatically if a user opens a file associated with the application.

Activity 9-5: Deploying Software to Users

Time Required: 20 minutes
Objective: Deploy a software package to a user account.

Required Tools and Equipment: 411Server1 and 411Win8
Description: You want to deploy a software package to certain users regardless of which computer they use to log on.

1. Log on to 411Server1 as **Administrator**, if necessary. Start 411Win8, if necessary.

2. On 411Server1, open the Group Policy Management console, if necessary.

3. Open the **SwInst** GPO in the Group Policy Management Editor. First, you delete the current software package in the Software installation node. Navigate to the **Software installation** node under the Computer Configuration node, right-click **Microsoft GPMC Sample Scripts**, point to **All Tasks**, and click **Remove**. You have the option of uninstalling the software from users and computers immediately or allowing users to continue using software already installed. Accept the default setting **Immediately uninstall the software from users and computers**, and click **OK**.

4. Navigate to **User Configuration, Policies, Software Settings**, and **Software installation**. Right-click in the right pane, point to **New**, and click **Package**. In the Open dialog box, type \\411Server1\SoftDeploy\GPMCScripts and press **Enter**. Click the **GPMCSampleScripts** file, and then click **Open**.

5. In the Deploy Software dialog box, click the **Advanced** option button, and then click **OK** to open the Microsoft GPMC Sample Scripts Properties dialog box. Click the **Deployment** tab.

6. Leave the Deployment type set at **Published**, and click to select **Uninstall this application when it falls out of the scope of management**. Leave the Installation user interface options at the default **Maximum** setting, and click **OK**. Close the Group Policy Management Editor.

7. Link the **SwInst** GPO to **TestOU1**.

8. On 411Win8, log on as **testuser1**. Right-click **Start** and click **Programs and Features**. Click the **Install a program from the network** link in the left pane. You should see a link to Microsoft GPMC Sample Scripts. If this were an executable program associated with a file type, it would install automatically if you tried to open a file of the specified type.

9. Next, you set the software installation policy to install automatically when the user logs on. On 411Server1, open **SwInst** in the Group Policy Management Editor. Navigate to **User Configuration, Policies, Software Settings**, and **Software installation**. In the right pane, right-click the package and click **Properties**. Click the **Deployment** tab.

10. Click the **Assigned** option button and click to select **Install this application at logon.** Click **OK.** Close the Group Policy Management Editor.

11. Log off 411Win8 and log back on as **testuser1.** Right-click **Start** and click **Programs and Features.** You see that Microsoft GPMC Sample Scripts is now installed. Log off 411Win8.

12. On 411Server1, unlink **SwInst** from **TestOU1.** Stay logged on to 411Server1 if you're continuing to the next activity.

Deploying Scripts

A **script** is a series of commands saved in a text file to be repeated easily at any time. For example, suppose you often use PowerShell to perform certain tasks. As you know, PowerShell commands can be long and complex. You can type the commands in a text file and save the file with a `.ps1` extension, such as `myscript.ps1`. To run this string of commands, type `PowerShell myscript.ps1` at a command prompt or just `myscript.ps1` at a PowerShell prompt. In addition to PowerShell scripts, you can create command scripts, which are just a series of commands saved in a file with a `.bat` extension, also known as a **batch file.** You can also create scripts with scripting languages such as VBScript and JScript. For the purposes of this section, you focus on deploying scripts with Group Policy that run when a computer starts up or shuts down or when a user logs on or logs off.

There's a Scripts extension in both the Computer Configuration and the User Configuration nodes in the path Policies, Windows Settings, Scripts. In the Computer Configuration node, you configure startup or shutdown scripts, and in the User Configuration node, you configure logon and logoff scripts. For example, to configure a logon script, navigate to User Configuration, Policies, Windows Settings, Scripts, and then right-click Logon and click Properties (see Figure 9-4). The properties of a logon script are the same as for the other three script types.

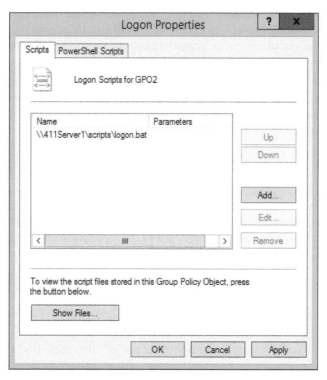

Figure 9-4   The properties of a logon script

This dialog box has two tabs:

- *Scripts*—This tab is used for command scripts (batch files), and scripts that can be run by Windows Scripting Host (WSH). WSH is used to run VBScript and JScript files.
- *PowerShell Scripts*—To run PowerShell scripts, the target computer must be running Windows 7 or later.

To add a script in the Scripts or PowerShell Scripts tabs, click the Add button. You can type the UNC path to a share where the script file is located or click Browse to search for the file. By default, Windows looks in the SYSVOL share on the DC in the folder containing the GPO where you're creating the script. The advantage of using the SYSVOL share is that scripts are replicated automatically and can be retrieved by clients from a DC in the domain. If you use a regular shared folder, the server hosting the share must always be available, and the script might have to run across a WAN link if the server is in a remote site.

If you want to store scripts in the SYSVOL folder with your GPO, you need the GUID of the GPO to locate the correct folder. You can find the GUID by looking in the System\Policies folder in Active Directory Users and Computers.

Activity 9-6: Deploying a Shutdown Script to a Computer

Time Required: 15 minutes
Objective: Create and deploy a shutdown script.

Required Tools and Equipment: 411Server1 and 411Win8
Description: You have several applications that create temporary files with a `.temp` extension that are slowly using up disk space on domain member computers. You write a shutdown script that deletes all files with a `.temp` extension, and you want to deploy this script to all computers in the domain by using group policies. First, you test the script and its deployment on your test OU.

1. Log on to 411Server1 as **Administrator**, if necessary.

2. Start Notepad and type **del /F /S c:*.temp**. The `/F` option forces deletion of read-only files, and the `/S` option deletes the file in the current directory and all subdirectories.

3. Click **File, Save As** from the menu. Choose the desktop as the location for saving your file. In the Save as type list box, click **All Files (*.*)**. Type **deltemp.bat** in the File name text box, and click **Save**. Exit Notepad.

4. Right-click **deltemp.bat** on your desktop and click **Copy**. (You paste the script into the SYSVOL share in Step 6.)

5. Open the Group Policy Management console. Click the **Group Policy Objects** folder and create a GPO named **Scripts**.

6. Right-click **Scripts** and click **Edit**. In the Group Policy Management Editor, click to expand **Computer Configuration, Policies,** and **Windows Settings,** and then click **Scripts**. Right-click **Shutdown** in the right pane and click **Properties**. In the Shutdown Properties dialog box, click **Show Files**. In the File Explorer window that opens, right-click the right pane and click **Paste**. Note the path where the script is stored—a folder in the SYSVOL share on your DC. Close the File Explorer window.

7. In the Shutdown Properties dialog box, click **Add**. In the Add a Script dialog box, click **Browse**. Click **deltemp**, and then click **Open**. Click **OK** twice.

8. Close the Group Policy Management Editor. Link **Scripts** to the **Desktops** OU.

9. Log on to 411Win8 as **testuser1**. You're going to create a few files on your desktop that have the `.temp` extension. Open a command prompt window, and then type **cd desktop**

and press **Enter**. Type `copy nul > file1.temp` and press **Enter** to create an empty file. Repeat the command two more times, changing `file1` to **file2** and then **file3**. You see the files on your desktop.

In the `copy nul > file1.temp` command, `nul` is a system device that's just an empty file, and the `>` redirects the empty file to a new file named `file1.temp`.

10. Type **gpupdate** and press **Enter**. After gpupdate is finished, restart your computer. (If you don't run gpupdate, you have to restart the computer to load the policy, and then shut it down again to make the shutdown script run.) The shutdown process will probably take a little longer than usual because the script has to run.

11. Log on to 411Win8 as **testuser1** again, and verify that the `.temp` files have been deleted. Log off 411Win8.

12. On 411Server1, unlink **Scripts** from the **Desktops** OU. Stay logged on to 411Server1 if you're continuing to the next activity.

Folder Redirection

Folder redirection enables an administrator to set policies that redirect folders in a user's profile directory. This feature is useful when you want users to store documents on a server for centralized backup, but you don't want to change the way they access their document folders. It's also quite useful when roaming profiles are used because it decreases the network bandwidth needed to upload and download a user's roaming profile.

Folder redirection applies strictly to user accounts and is found only under the User Configuration node in Policies, Windows Settings, Folder Redirection. There are 13 folders you can redirect, as shown in Figure 9-5.

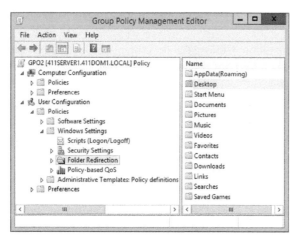

Figure 9-5   Folders that can be redirected

To redirect a folder, right-click it in the Folder Redirection node and click Properties. In the Target tab of a folder's Properties dialog box, you have the following options (see Figure 9-6):

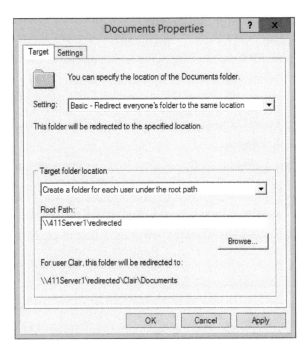

Figure 9-6   Configuring folder redirection for the Documents folder

- *Setting*—In this list box, you have the following options:
  - o Not configured: This default option means folder redirection isn't enabled for the folder.
  - o Basic - Redirect everyone's folder to the same location: This option redirects the selected folder to the same location for all user accounts in the GPO's scope.
  - o Advanced - Specify locations for various user groups: With this option, you can redirect folders to different locations based on group membership.
- *Target folder location*—In this list box, you have the following options:
  - o Create a folder for each user under the root path: The default setting; you specify the UNC path to a share in the Root Path text box. Each user has a folder under the root path. For example, the Documents folder for a user with the logon name jsmith is at \\411Server1\redirected\jsmith\Documents.
  - o Redirect to the user's home directory: If home directories are defined, the folder is redirected to the specified location.
  - o Redirect to the following location: The folder is redirected to the path you specify in the Root Path text box. If you use this option, multiple users have the same location for the folder.
  - o Redirect to the local userprofile location: The folder is located wherever the user's local profile is stored, which is usually in the C:\Users folder.

In the Settings tab, you specify options for redirection, including whether the folder should remain redirected or revert to its original location if the policy is removed.

Activity 9-7: Configuring a Folder Redirection Policy

Time Required: 15 minutes
Objective: Redirect the Documents folder.

Required Tools and Equipment: 411Server1 and 411Win8
Description: You want user's documents to be backed up in a central location, so you configure a folder redirection policy for the Documents folder.

1. Log on to 411Server1 as **Administrator**, if necessary.

2. Open File Explorer, and create a folder named **Redirected** in the C volume. Share the folder, giving the **Everyone** group **Read/Write** sharing permission, and leave the remaining permissions at their default settings.

3. Open the Group Policy Management console, and create a GPO named **FolderRedir** in the Group Policy Objects folder. Open **FolderRedir** in the Group Policy Management Editor. Expand **User Configuration, Policies, Windows Settings**, and **Folder Redirection**. Right-click the **Documents** folder and click **Properties**.

4. In the Documents Properties dialog box, click **Basic - Redirect everyone's folder to the same location** in the Setting drop-down list. Click the **Target folder location** list arrow to view the available options, and then, if necessary, click **Create a folder for each user under the root path** in the list. In the Root Path text box, type \\411Server1\Redirected.

5. Click the **Settings** tab, and review the available options. Click to clear the **Grant the user exclusive rights to Documents** check box. Click **Redirect the folder back to the local user-profile location when policy is removed**, click **OK**, and in the warning message box, click **Yes**. Close the Group Policy Management Editor.

6. In the Group Policy Management console, link the **FolderRedir** GPO to **TestOU1**.

7. On 411Win8, log on as **testuser1**, and run **gpupdate**. Then restart 411Win8, and log on again as **testuser1**.

8. On 411Win8, open File Explorer. Create a text file in the **Documents** folder named **TestRedirect**.

9. Right-click **Start**, click **Run**, type \\411Server1\redirected, and press **Enter**. You should see a folder named testuser1 in the share. Double-click the **testuser1** folder, and double-click the **Documents** folder. The TestRedirect file you created in the Documents folder should be there. Log off 411Win8.

10. On 411Server1, unlink the **FolderRedir** GPO from **TestOU1**. Stay logged on to 411Server1 if you're continuing to the next activity.

Working with Administrative Templates

Both the Computer Configuration and User Configuration nodes have an Administrative Templates folder. In the Computer Configuration node, the settings in Administrative Templates affect the HKEY_LOCAL_MACHINE Registry key. Settings in the User Configuration node affect the HKEY_LOCAL_USER Registry key.

Hundreds of settings are defined in the Administrative Templates nodes, and many more can be added through customization. The Administrative Templates folder uses policy definition files, called **administrative template files**, in XML format (with an .admx extension), which makes creating your own policies fairly easy if you need to control a setting not provided by default. The following sections cover these topics related to administrative templates:

- Computer Configuration settings
- User Configuration settings
- Administrative Templates property filters
- Custom administrative templates
- Migrating administrative template files
- Security templates

Computer Configuration Settings

This section doesn't attempt to cover all the settings in Administrative Templates, but it gives you a brief explanation of the types of settings in each folder under Administrative Templates. You're encouraged to spend some time browsing through the settings with the Group Policy

Management Editor so that you have a good idea where to look when you need to configure a particular type of policy setting. To see an explanation of a setting, double-click it and read the Help section of the dialog box for the policy's settings (see Figure 9-7).

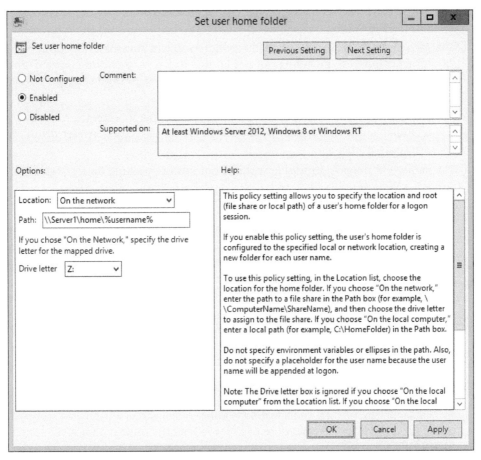

Figure 9-7   Configuring settings for a policy

Administrative Templates in the Computer Configuration node, where many aspects of the computer working environment are controlled, contains the following folders (see Figure 9-8), most with additional subfolders:

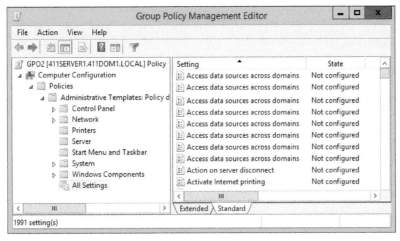

Figure 9-8   The Administrative Templates folders under Computer Configuration

- *Control Panel*—This folder has three subfolders: Personalization, Regional and Language Options, and User Accounts. Personalization has settings that affect the look of Windows, in particular the lock screen and background. Settings in Regional and Language Options allow administrators to set and restrict the language in the Control Panel user interface. The single policy in User Accounts configures a default user logon picture for all users on target computers.

- *Network*—There are 20 subfolders where you can control a host of network settings on target computers, including but not limited to Background Intelligent Transfer Service (BITS) parameters, DNS client settings, network connection settings, offline files configuration, and TCP/IP settings.

- *Printers*—Settings in this folder control how computers interact with network printers, including automatic printer publishing in Active Directory, printer browsing, and Internet printing parameters.

- *Server*—Settings in this folder control options for backing up a computer.

- *Start Menu and Taskbar*—Settings in this folder allow you to specify a Start screen layout and pin apps to the Start screen.

- *System*—This folder contains more than 35 subfolders with settings for controlling general computer system operation. Some computer functions that can be controlled include disk quotas, the file system, group policy processing, logon and shutdown, power management, and user profiles.

- *Windows Components*—This folder contains more than 50 subfolders with settings for configuring specific Windows components, such as app deployment, Event Viewer, File Explorer, Internet Explorer, Windows PowerShell, Windows Update, Work Folders, and many others. Some settings in this folder have an identical counterpart in the User Configuration node. When a conflict exists, the setting in Computer Configuration takes precedence.

An additional node under Administrative Templates called All Settings displays all Administrative Template settings and can be sorted in alphabetical order. You can select View, Filter Options from the GPME menu to list policies by certain criteria or keywords, too.

Activity 9-8: Working with Computer Administrative Template Settings

Time Required: 15 minutes

Objective: Become familiar with Administrative Template settings in Computer Configuration.

Required Tools and Equipment: 411Server1 and 411Win8

Description: In this activity, you explore Administrative Templates settings under Computer Configuration and configure some settings to see the effect they have on the computer operating environment.

1. Log on to 411Server1 as **Administrator,** and open the Group Policy Management console, if necessary. Start 411Win8, if necessary.

2. Open **GPO2** in the Group Policy Management Editor.

3. Under Computer Configuration, click to expand **Policies** and **Administrative Templates.** Browse through the folders under Administrative Templates to see the settings and subfolders under each one. Take your time to get a good feel for the types of settings available in each main folder.

4. Click the **All Settings** folder to see the full list of settings in Administrative Templates. The settings are arranged in alphabetic order by default. Click the **State** column to view the settings according to their state, which is Not configured, Enabled, or Disabled. Because GPO2 has no configured settings, the view doesn't change.

5. In the left pane, click to expand the **System** folder, and then click **Logon**. In the right pane, double-click **Run these programs at user logon**. This policy can be used in place of a logon script if you want more programs to run when any user logs on to certain computers.

6. In the "Run these programs at user logon" window, click **Enabled,** and then click **Show**. In the first row of the Show Contents dialog box, type **explorer.exe,** and in the second row, type **iexplore.exe** (see Figure 9-9). Now all target computers run File Explorer and Internet Explorer when a user logs on. Click **OK** twice, and close the Group Policy Management Editor.

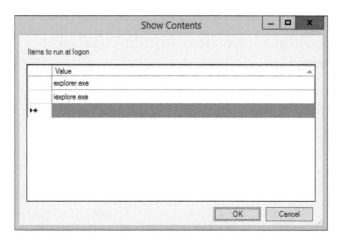

Figure 9-9   Configuring programs to run at user logon

7. Link **GPO2** to the **Desktops** OU.

8. On 411Win8, log on as **testuser1** and run `gpupdate`. Then log off 411Win8, and log on again as **testuser1**. After a few moments, File Explorer and Internet Explorer open. Leave 411Win8 running.

9. On 411Server1, unlink **GPO2** from the **Desktops** OU.

10. Open **GPO1** (which is linked to the domain) in the Group Policy Management Editor.

11. Expand **Computer Configuration, Policies, Administrative Templates,** and **Windows Components,** and click **Windows Logon Options**. In the right pane, double-click **Display information about previous logons during user logon**. Read the Help information about this policy setting. Click **Enabled,** and then click **OK**.

12. On 411Win8, run `gpupdate`, and then log off and log back on as **testuser1**. You see a message stating that it's the first time you have signed in to the account. Although you have signed in before, it's the first time since the policy was enabled. Click **OK**.

13. Log off 411Win8, and then log back on as **testuser1** but with an incorrect password. Then log back on with the correct password. A window opens showing the last successful sign-in and an unsuccessful sign-in attempt. This information is intended to let users know whether somebody has been trying to use their accounts to log on. Click **OK**.

14. Log off 411Win8. Stay logged on to 411Server1 if you're continuing to the next activity.

User Configuration Settings

Most of the previous information about Administrative Templates in the Computer Configuration node applies to the User Configuration node, too. Administrative Templates in User Configuration also contain the Control Panel, Network, Start Menu and Taskbar, System, and Windows Components subfolders, although most of the settings are different because they apply to specific users rather than all users who log on to a computer. With Administrative Templates in the User Configuration node, you can customize many aspects of a user's working environment. Policies in this node add the following subfolders to the previous list for the Computer Configuration node:

- *Desktop*—Controls the look of users' desktops, determines which icons are available, and can limit actions users can take on the desktop.

- *Shared Folders*—Controls whether a user can publish shared folders and Distributed File System (DFS) root folders in Active Directory.

Activity 9-9: Working with User Administrative Template Settings

Time Required: 10 minutes
Objective: Become familiar with Administrative Template settings in User Configuration.

Required Tools and Equipment: 411Server1 and 411Win8
Description: In this activity, you explore Administrative Templates settings under User Configuration, and then configure some settings to see the effect they have on a user's environment.

1. Log on to 411Server1 as **Administrator**, and open the Group Policy Management console, if necessary. Start 411Win8, if necessary.

2. Open **GPO2** in the Group Policy Management Editor.

3. Under User Configuration, click to expand **Policies** and **Administrative Templates**. Browse through the folders under Administrative Templates to see the settings and subfolders under each one. Take your time to get a good feel for the types of settings available in each main folder.

4. In the left pane, click to expand the **System** folder, and then click to select the **System** folder. In the right pane, double-click **Prevent access to the command prompt**.

5. Read the policy help information. Click **Enabled**, and then click **OK**. Close the Group Policy Management Editor.

6. Link **GPO2** to **TestOU1**.

7. On 411Win8, log on as **testuser1**. Right-click **Start** and click **Command Prompt**. A command prompt window opens, but you see a message stating that the administrator has disabled it. Press any key to close the command prompt window.

8. On 411Server1, unlink **GPO2** from **TestOU1**.

9. Log off 411Win8. Stay logged on to 411Server1 if you're continuing to the next activity.

Working with Filters

The number of settings in the Administrative Templates section of a GPO can be daunting when you're trying to find a particular policy to configure. As you saw when you expanded the All Settings node in Activity 9-8, there are several hundred policy settings under both Computer Configuration and User Configuration. If you know the name of the setting you need to configure or at least know the first word of the name, you can sort the settings alphabetically under All Settings and find it that way. However, if you don't know the name and perhaps know only the policy's general function, you could be searching a while. Thankfully, you can narrow the search by using a filter in the Group Policy Management Editor:

1. Open a GPO in the GPME, and click Policies, Administrative Templates under Computer Configuration or User Configuration. You see the filter icon on the toolbar.

2. Click Action, Filter Options from the menu to open the Filter Options dialog box (see Figure 9-10).

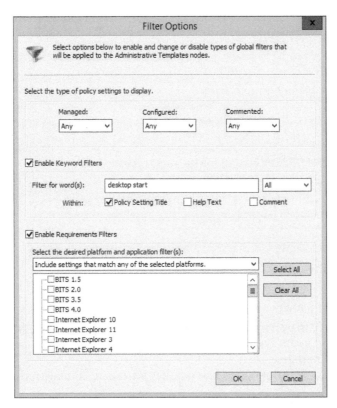

Figure 9-10   Configuring an Administrative Templates filter

3. You can configure a filter with the following criteria:

o *Managed*—Select Any, Yes, or No. If you select Any, both managed and unmanaged policies are included in the filter criteria. If you select Yes, only managed policies are included, and if you select No, only unmanaged policies are included.

o *Configured*—Select Any, Yes, or No to see only configured policies, unconfigured policies, or both.

o *Commented*—You can add a comment to any policy setting in Administrative Templates by double-clicking it and typing a comment in the Comment text box. This filter option allows you to view only policy settings with a comment, those without a comment, or both. By default, policy settings don't have a comment.

o *Enable Keyword Filters*—Select this check box, if needed, and in the Filter for word(s) text box, type one or more words that are part of the policy setting's title, help text, or comment field. You can specify how the words match by selecting Exact, All, or Any.

o *Enable Requirements Filters*—Narrow the search by OS or application platform. For example, you might want to see only policy settings that work with Windows Server 2012 R2.

Filters work only with settings in the Administrative Templates folders; you can't filter settings in the Software Settings or Windows Settings folders.

After you have configured filter options, you apply the filter by clicking Action, Filter On from the menu or clicking the Filter toolbar icon (see Figure 9-11). Only policies matching the criteria are displayed in the GPME.

Figure 9-11   The Filter toolbar icon

Activity 9-10: Viewing Policy Settings with Filter Options

Time Required: 10 minutes

Objective: Configure filter options to find a policy setting in Administrative Templates.

Required Tools and Equipment: 411Server1

Description: You want to configure the setting that displays the desktop instead of the Start screen when users log on. You can't remember the exact setting name, but you know it's in the User Configuration node of a GPO. You configure a filter to narrow down the search.

1. Log on to 411Server1 as **Administrator**, and open the Group Policy Management console, if necessary.

2. Open **GPO2** in the Group Policy Management Editor.

3. Under User Configuration, click to expand **Policies,** and click **Windows Settings**. Notice that there's no Filter icon on the toolbar because you can't filter settings in Windows Settings. Click **Administrative Templates**. You should see the Filter icon now.

4. Click **Action, Filter Options**. In the Filter Options window, click **Any**, if necessary, in the Managed, Configured, and Commented list boxes.

5. Click the **Enable Keyword Filters** check box. You remember that the policy setting title has the word "desktop" in it, so type **desktop** in the Filter for words(s) text box. If necessary, click **Any** in the list box next to the Filter for word(s) text box.

6. Click **Policy Setting Title,** and if necessary, click to clear the **Help Text** and **Comment** check boxes. Click **OK**. You see a filter icon on the Administrative Templates folder.

7. Under User Configuration, click to expand **Administrative Templates,** and click **All Settings**. You see a list of policy settings with the word "desktop" in the title. That's still quite a few settings to sift through.

8. Click **Action, Filter Options**. You remember that the word "start" was also in the title. In the Filter for word(s) text box, type the word **start** next to "desktop," making sure to leave a space between them. In the list box, click **All** so that the filter shows only policy settings with both words in them. Click **OK**.

9. Now you see only one policy setting, and it's the one you are looking for. Click the filter icon on the toolbar to remove the filter. You see all settings again. Close the Group Policy Management Editor.

10. Stay logged on to 411Server1 if you're continuing to the next activity.

Using Custom Administrative Templates

Administrative templates are a collection of policy definition files in XML format. These XML files, referred to as "ADMX files" because of their `.admx` extension, specify Registry entries that should be controlled and the type of data the entries take. Many software vendors provide administrative template files for controlling their applications' settings through group policies. For example, Microsoft offers administrative template files for the Microsoft Office suite.

Windows versions before Vista and Server 2008 used `.adm` files. This format can still be used on the same system as ADMX files, but you can create and edit ADMX files only on Windows Vista or later computers. ADMX files can also have an `.adml` extension, which provides a language-specific user interface in the Group Policy Management Editor. You can find all ADMX and ADML files under %*systemroot*%\PolicyDefinitions and open them in Notepad or an XML editor. However, you don't usually edit the standard ADMX files that ship with Windows.

Adding a Custom Administrative Template to Group Policy   If you create your
own ADMX file or download one for configuring settings on an installed application, you can simply add the ADMX file to the %*systemroot*%\PolicyDefinitions folder. The next time you open the GPME, the file is loaded. Any language-specific files (`.adml`) should be placed in the corresponding language folder. For example, if there's a U.S. English file, place it in the en-US folder under the PolicyDefinitions folder.

If you have created a central store for policy definition files, place your custom ADMX files in this location so that they're replicated to all domain controllers. The central store was discussed in *MCSA Guide to Installing and Configuring Windows Server 2012/R2, Exam 70-410* (Cengage Learning, 2015). It's a folder named PolicyDefinitions on the SYSVOL share of a DC that makes sure all policy definitions are replicated to other DCs.

Creating custom ADMX files is beyond the scope of this book, but you can read about the basics at *http://technet.microsoft.com/en-us/library/ cc770905(v=ws.10).aspx*.

9

Working with Older Administrative Templates   If you're using older ADM
administrative templates, you can add them manually by following these steps:

1. In the GPMC, open a GPO in the GPME. Right-click the Administrative Templates folder under Computer Configuration or User Configuration and click Add/Remove Templates.

2. In the Add/Remove Templates dialog box, click Add.

3. In the Policy Templates File Explorer window, browse to the ADM file's location. Select the ADM file and click Add.

4. In the Add/Remove Templates dialog box (see Figure 9-12), click Close.

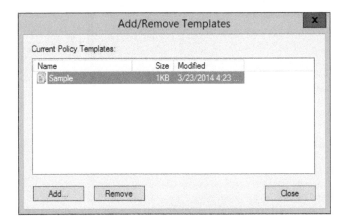

Figure 9-12   Adding a custom ADM administrative templates file

Migrating Administrative Templates

If you're running a Windows Server 2008 or later domain but still have to support clients older than Vista or are running older applications that use ADM files, you might want to migrate the older ADM files to ADMX format so that you can make use of the central store. As mentioned, the central store ensures that all policy definitions are replicated to other DCs. Because the central store can't work with ADM files, you need to convert the ADM files to ADMX files with ADMX Migrator, a snap-in tool available free from the Microsoft Download Center. To use this tool, follow these steps:

1. Download ADMX Migrator from the Microsoft Download Center.

2. Install ADMX Migrator on the computer with the ADM files; in most cases, it's a domain controller.

3. Navigate to the folder where you installed ADMX Migrator, and double-click the `faAdmxEditor.msc` file. An MMC opens with the ADMX Migrator snap-in.

4. Click Generate ADMX from ADM.

5. After the ADMX file is generated, move it to the *%windir%*\PolicyDefinitions folder or the central store.

Working with Security Templates

Security templates are text files with an `.inf` extension that contain information for defining policy settings in the Computer Configuration\Policies\Windows Settings\Security Settings node of a local or domain GPO. You can use them to create and deploy security settings to a local or domain GPO and to verify the current security settings on a computer against the settings in a template. There are three tools for working with security templates, discussed in the following sections: the Security Templates snap-in, the Security Configuration and Analysis snap-in, and `secedit.exe`.

The Security Templates Snap-in

You use the Security Templates snap-in to create and edit security templates. You can create templates for computers with differing security requirements, such as servers with different roles installed or different physical locations. Servers in branch offices that don't have tight physical security, for example, might require stronger security settings than servers in a secure location. Computers used by employees who have access to sensitive information often require tighter security than computers used by employees with limited access on the network.

Figure 9-13 shows the Security Templates snap-in with a new security template named LowSecurityWS. Notice that only a subset of the policies in a GPO are available in the template.

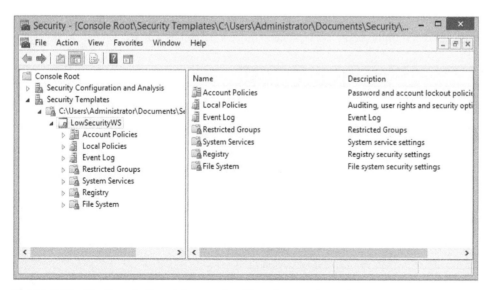

Figure 9-13   The Security Templates snap-in with an imported template

When a user creates a new template, it's stored in the user's Documents folder in Security\ Templates. After the template is created, it can be imported into a local or domain GPO or be used by the Security Configuration and Analysis snap-in. If you configure account policies in your template to import into a GPO, remember that settings in the Account Policies node are used only when linked to a domain or applied to a local GPO.

You create a security template in one of two ways:

- *Use the existing security settings on a computer*—If you want to create a security template using a baseline of settings from an existing desktop computer or server, open `secpol.msc`, and then right-click the Security Settings node and click Export policy. By default, policies are exported to the user's Documents folder in Security\Templates. Then you open the exported policy with the Security Templates snap-in, make changes as necessary, and save the template.

- *Create a security template from scratch*—Open the Security Templates snap-in in an MMC, and then right-click the folder under the Security Templates node and click New Template. This method creates a template with no defined settings.

The Security Configuration and Analysis Snap-in

The Security Configuration and Analysis snap-in is useful for checking a computer's existing security settings against the known settings in security template files that have been imported into a security database. You can also use this snap-in to apply a security template to a computer. Windows doesn't supply a configured MMC, so you have to add this snap-in to an MMC. If you'll be working with security templates quite a bit, you can create a custom MMC containing the Security Templates and Security Configuration and Analysis snap-ins.

When you analyze a template against the current security settings on a computer, a report is generated. For each policy setting, there are five possible results:

- An X in a red circle indicates that the template policy and current computer policy don't match.

- A check mark in a green circle indicates that the template policy and computer policy are the same.

- A question mark in a white circle indicates that the policy wasn't defined in the template or the user running the analysis didn't have permission to access the policy.

- An exclamation point in a white circle indicates that the policy doesn't exist on the computer.

- No indicator indicates that the policy wasn't defined in the template.

Activity 9-11: Creating a Security Template

Time Required: 15 minutes
Objective: Create a security template.

Required Tools and Equipment: 411Server1 and 411Win8
Description: You want to create a set of security baselines for your servers and computers. You start by exporting the current security settings on 411Win8 to a new security template and editing some settings that are suitable for computers that don't require a high level of security. Then you analyze the template settings against 411Win8's current security settings.

You create the security template on 411Win8 in this activity, but you could create all your templates on a server share, and then access them as needed from workstations to perform a security configuration analysis.

1. Start 411Server1 and 411Win8, if necessary. Log on to the domain from 411Win8 as **Administrator**.

2. On 411Win8, Open the Local Security Policy MMC by right-clicking **Start**, clicking **Run**, typing **secpol.msc**, and pressing **Enter**. Right-click **Security Settings** and click **Export policy**.

In the File name text box, type **LowSecurityWS**, and then click **Save**. Close the Local Security Policy MMC.

3. Open an MMC console. Add the **Security Templates** and **Security Configuration and Analysis** snap-ins to it, and save the console to your desktop with the name **Security**.

4. Click to expand **Security Templates**. Click to expand the folder under Security Templates, and then click **LowSecurityWS**. (If you want to create a template from scratch, you right-click the folder and click New Template.)

5. Click to expand **LowSecurityWS** and **Local Policies**, and then click **User Rights Assignment**. In the right pane, double-click **Back up files and directories**. In the Properties dialog box, verify that the **Define these policy settings in the template** check box is selected. Click **Add User or Group**. In the User and group names text box, type **Users**, and then click **OK** twice.

6. Double-click **Change the time zone**. Click **Users**, click the **Remove** button, and then click **OK**.

7. Double-click **Force shutdown from a remote system**. In the Properties dialog box, click **Add User or Group**. In the User and group names text box, type **Users**, and then click **OK** twice.

8. In the left pane, click **Security Options**. In the right pane, double-click **Accounts: Limit local account use of blank passwords to console logon only**. Click **Disabled**, and then click **OK**.

9. Double-click **Interactive logon: Do not require CTRL+ALT+DEL**. Click to select the **Define this policy setting in the template** check box. Click **Enabled**, and then click **OK**.

10. In the left pane of the Security console, right-click **LowSecurityWS** and click **Save**.

11. In the left pane, click the **Security Configuration and Analysis** snap-in, and then right-click it and click **Open Database**. In the File name text box, type **wslowsec**, and then click **Open**. In the Import Template dialog box, click **LowSecurityWS**, and then click **Open**. Read the message in the middle pane. You can configure the current computer with the settings from LowSecurityWS or analyze the computer's current settings against the settings from LowSecurityWS.

12. Right-click **Security Configuration and Analysis** and click **Analyze Computer Now**. In the Perform Analysis dialog box, click **OK**. The security analysis is performed. The results are saved to the `wslowsec.log` file you specified in Step 11.

13. Click to expand **Security Configuration and Analysis** and **Local Policies**, and then click **User Rights Assignment**. You should see a window similar to Figure 9-14. Each policy has a Database Setting column and a Computer Setting column. (The red and green indicators you see on some policies were explained previously.)

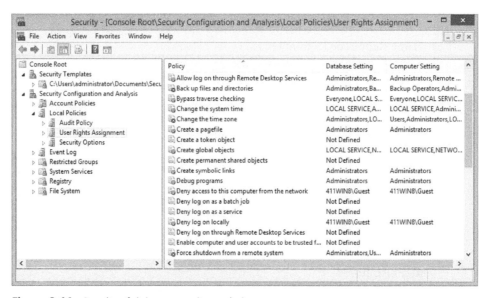

Figure 9-14   Results of doing a security analysis

14. Click the **Security Options** node to see the results of the analysis on that node.

15. Close the Security MMC. When prompted to save console settings, click **No**. Stay logged on to 411Win8 and leave 411Server1 running for the next activity.

Activity 9-12: Importing a Security Template

Time Required: 10 minutes
Objective: Import a security template into a GPO.

Required Tools and Equipment: 411Server1 and 411Win8
Description: You have created a security template. Next, you import the template into a GPO on the domain controller so that you can apply security settings to computers in the domain.

1. Start 411Server1 and 411Win8, if necessary. Log on to 411Server1 as **Administrator**, if necessary.

2. On 411Server1, create a folder on C:\ named **SecTempl**. Share this folder, making sure Administrators have Full control permission. (To do this, right-click the folder and click **Share with**, click **Specific people,** and then accept the default settings.)

3. On 411Win8, log on to the domain as **Administrator**, if necessary. Open File Explorer, and navigate to **Documents\Security\Templates**. Right-click **LowSecurityWS** and click **Copy**.

4. Right-click **Start**, click **Run**, type **\\411Server1\SecTempl** in the Open text box, and press **Enter**.

5. Right-click empty space in the resulting File Explorer window and click **Paste**. Log off 411Win8.

6. On 411Server1, open the Group Policy Management console, if necessary, and open **GPO2** in the Group Policy Management Editor.

7. Under Computer Configuration, click to expand **Policies** and **Windows Settings**. Right-click **Security Settings** and click **Import Policy**.

8. In the Import Policy From dialog box, navigate to **C:\SecTempl**. Click `LowSecurityWS.inf` and click **Open**.

9. In the Group Policy Management Editor, click to expand **Security Settings** and **Local Policies**, and then click **User Rights Assignment**. Scroll through the policy settings to see that the settings match the settings from the security template you created in Activity 9-11. You can link the GPO to an OU containing computer accounts you want the security settings applied to.

10. Close the Group Policy Management Editor and the Group Policy Management console. Stay logged on to 411Server1 if you're continuing to the next activity.

Using the Security Configuration Wizard

The **Security Configuration Wizard** (**SCW**) guides you through creating, editing, and applying a security policy on Windows servers. It creates an XML file that can be deployed to servers with Group Policy. The SCW does more than just apply settings; it analyzes the server environment, disables unnecessary services, and configures Windows Firewall settings. You can also include security templates in the security policy the SCW produces. To use the SCW, follow these steps:

1. In Server Manager, click Tools, Security Configuration Wizard from the menu. You have the option to create a new security policy, edit an existing policy, apply an existing policy, or roll back the last applied security policy.

2. Next, you select a server to act as a baseline for the policy. The server is analyzed for the roles and services it's running. If you plan to apply the policy to multiple servers, they should be configured with similar roles and services.

3. You can change the list of roles and features the server performs. If you're editing an existing policy to apply to a server with different roles configured, you can make the necessary changes (see Figure 9-15).

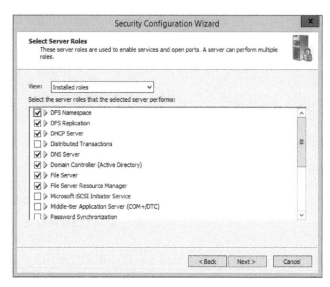

Figure 9-15   Selecting server roles

4. Other configuration windows include those for configuring network security rules, authentication rules, and auditing. Before you save the policy, you can specify one or more security templates to include in the policy. If you add multiple templates, you can prioritize them in case any settings conflict (see Figure 9-16).

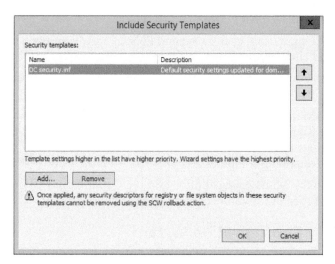

Figure 9-16   Including security templates

5. You assign a name to the policy, and it's saved by default in C:\Windows\security\msscw\ Policies.

6. Finally, you can apply the policy to the selected server or apply the policy later by running the wizard again and choosing to apply an existing policy.

If you want to use Group Policy to apply a saved policy created by the SCW, first use the scwcmd.exe command-line tool to convert the XML file to a GPO. For example, if you created a policy named DCSecPol.xml, enter the following command to convert the policy to a GPO named DCSecPol. The GPO is stored in the Group Policy Objects folder in the Group Policy Management console.

```
scwcmd transform /p:DCSecPol.xml /g:DCSecPol
```

Configuring Group Policy Preferences

Unlike user or computer policies that can't be changed by users, **group policy preferences** enable administrators to set up a baseline computing environment yet still allow users to make changes to configured settings. Both the Computer Configuration and User Configuration nodes have a Preferences folder with two subnodes—Windows Settings and Control Panel Settings—containing settings organized into categories (see Figure 9-17). With group policy preferences, you can perform many useful tasks, including the following:

Figure 9-17   Categories for preference settings

- Create and modify local users and groups.
- Enable and disable devices on a computer, such as USB ports, DVD drives, and removable media.
- Create drive mappings.
- Manage power options.
- Create and manage files, folders, and shortcuts.
- Create and modify printers.
- Configure custom Registry settings.
- Configure custom application settings.
- Configure Control Panel settings.
- Configure Internet Explorer.

Many of these tasks were managed by complex logon scripts in the past, but using group policy preferences should reduce the need for scripts substantially. In addition, new preferences can be created. For example, software vendors can create ADMX files for managing settings in their applications.

Computers need the Group Policy Preferences Client Side Extensions (GPP CSE) package installed to recognize and download settings in the Preferences folder when processing group policies. This package is already installed in Windows Server 2008 and later. For older clients (such as Windows XP, Windows Vista, and Windows Server 2003), you can download the client-side extensions package by going to *www.microsoft.com/download* and searching for "client-side extensions."

How Group Policy Preferences Are Applied

As mentioned, group policy preferences are simply preferences, which means users can usually change the settings configured here, as long as they have the permission to do so. However, preferences are refreshed on the same schedule as policies by default. This means Computer Configuration preferences are refreshed when the computer restarts and every 90 minutes thereafter, and User Configuration preferences are refreshed when the user logs on and then every 90 minutes. You can change this behavior by setting preferences to be applied only once. That way, preferences are used as a baseline configuration for the settings they affect, but users can still change them. Another difference between policies and preferences is management. If a managed policy setting is removed, unconfigured, or disabled, the original setting is restored on target users or computers. With preferences, the settings aren't restored by default, but you can change this behavior to make preferences act more like managed policies.

Creating Group Policy Preferences

There aren't hundreds of built-in preference settings to configure as there are with policies. In fact, there aren't any preferences at all—just preference categories. You must create each preference you want to deploy. The process of creating most preferences is similar. In this example, you create a folder preference under the User Configuration node:

1. Open the GPO in the Group Policy Management Editor, and navigate to User Configuration, Preferences, Windows Settings.

2. Right-click Folders, point to New, and click Folder to open the New Folder Properties dialog box.

3. In the New Folder Properties dialog box, select from the following actions in the General tab (which are common to most preferences categories):

   o *Create*—Creates a new folder.

   o *Replace*—Deletes and re-creates a folder. If the folder already exists, it's deleted along with its contents, and a new folder with the same name is created with the specified attributes. If the folder doesn't already exist, a new folder is created.

   o *Update*—Updates a folder's properties. If the folder doesn't exist, a new folder is created.

   o *Delete*—Deletes a folder.

 The General tab has different settings depending on the type of preference you're creating.

4. In this case, select Update. If the folder already exists, it's updated with any changes; otherwise, the folder is created.

5. Select the path of the folder or type the path in the Path text box. For this example, create a file named `TestPrefs` in the Documents folder of a user's profile. You can specify the %UserProfile% variable in the path. For example, if the user is testuser1, the %UserProfile% variable has the value C:\Users\testuser1, so the full path is %UserProfile%\Documents\TestPrefs (see Figure 9-18).

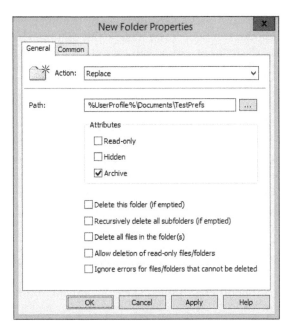

Figure 9-18   Creating a folder preference

6. Select attributes for the folder. You can choose from Read-only, Hidden, and Archive (the default setting).

7. If you choose Delete or Replace, you have additional options for deleting the folder. When the action is Create or Update, the delete options are grayed out.

8. Click the Common tab to see additional properties that are common to all preferences (see Figure 9-19).

Figure 9-19   Common preferences properties

- *Stop processing items in this extension if an error occurs*—If there's more than one preference in the extension (for example, you create two folder preferences), and this option is selected, no additional preferences are processed in the extension if there's an error.

- *Run in logged-on user's security context (user policy option)*—By default, preferences are processed with the SYSTEM account security context. Enable this option to have preference processing use the logged-on user's security context. This option ensures availability of resources the user has permission to and makes sure environment variables are set for the logged-on user.

- *Remove this item when it is no longer applied*—Select this option if you want preferences to be restored to their original values when the user or computer account falls out of the GPO's scope. For example, if you select this option and the user account falls out of the GPO's scope, the folder is removed. This option isn't available when the action in the General tab is set to Delete.

- *Apply once and do not reapply*—By default, preferences are applied on the same schedule as policies. Enable this option if you want users to be able to change the preference setting without their changes being overridden by the next Group Policy refresh.

- *Item-level targeting*—**Item-level targeting** enables you to target specific users or computers based on criteria, as described next in "Item-Level Targeting."

There are too many preference types to cover all of them thoroughly in one chapter, but the following activities walk you through creating a few types of preferences. You should explore the Preferences folders and try creating different preferences in a lab environment to get a good idea of what you can do with them.

Item-Level Targeting Preferences operate the same way as policies for default inheritance and scope. However, you can target users or computers for each preference based on certain criteria. For example, you can specify that only portable computers that are docked have a preference applied. Select the "Item-level targeting" option in the Common tab of the preference's Properties dialog box, and then click the Targeting button to define criteria that a computer or user must meet before the preference is applied. Figure 9-20 lists the properties that can be selected to define criteria.

Battery Present
Computer Name
CPU Speed
Date Match
Disk Space
Domain
Environment Variable
File Match
IP Address Range
Language
LDAP Query
MAC Address Range
MSI Query
Network Connection
Operating System
Organizational Unit
PCMCIA Present
Portable Computer
Processing Mode
RAM
Registry Match
Security Group
Site
Terminal Session
Time Range
User
WMI Query

Figure 9-20 List of criteria for item-level targeting

Criteria can be combined with the AND and OR operators. For example, if you want to target only mobile computers running Windows 8, you can create an item-level targeting statement that effectively says "If the operating system is Windows 8 AND a battery is present, apply this preference" (see Figure 9-21).

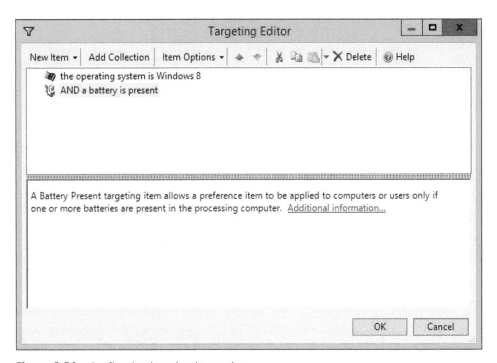

Figure 9-21   Configuring item-level targeting

Activity 9-13: Configuring and Testing Preferences

Time Required: 15 minutes
Objective: Configure and test preferences.

Required Tools and Equipment: 411Server1 and 411Win8
Description: You want all users to have a copy of policies and procedures in their Documents folders, so you create a file preference that copies the files and creates the necessary folder.

1. Log on to 411Server1 as **Administrator**, if necessary.

2. First, you create a share for the files to be copied in the preference. Open File Explorer, and create a folder named **PandP** on the **C** volume. Share this folder, and give the **Everyone** group **Read** permission.

3. In the PandP folder, create two text files: Name the first file **Policy.txt** and the second one **Procedure.txt**. Close File Explorer.

4. Open the Group Policy Management console, if necessary. Create a GPO named **Prefs** in the Group Policy Objects folder, and open it in the Group Policy Management Editor.

5. Under User Configuration, click to expand **Preferences** and **Windows Settings**. Right-click **Files**, point to **New**, and click **File**.

6. In the Action list box, click **Create**.

7. In the Source file(s) text box, type **\\411Server1\PandP*.***. Using a wildcard copies all files in the PandP folder. In the "Destination folder" text box, type **%UserProfile%\Documents\ PandP**. The PandP folder is created automatically. Leave the default **Archive** attribute selected (see Figure 9-22).

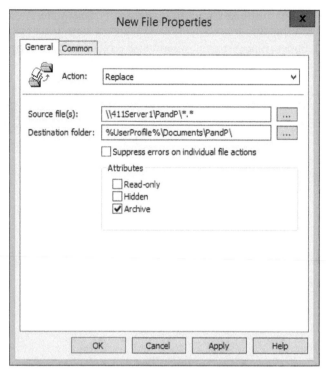

Figure 9-22   Creating a file preference

8. Click the **Common** tab. Review the available options, and then click **OK**. Note that you can change the processing order of preferences, so if you need one preference to be processed before another, you can arrange them in the order you want. Close the Group Policy Management Editor.

9. In the Group Policy Management console, link the **Prefs** GPO to the domain object.

10. Log on to 411Win8 as **testuser1**. Open File Explorer, and in the left pane, click **Documents** under This PC. Double-click the **PandP** folder, and you should see the two files you created.

11. Log off 411Win8, but stay logged on to 411Server1 if you're continuing to the next activity.

Activity 9-14: Configuring Item-Level Targeting

Time Required: 10 minutes

Objective: Configure a preference with item-level targeting.

Required Tools and Equipment: 411Server1 and 411Win8

Description: You want to limit the file preference to users in a particular OU, but you might have other preferences defined that should apply to all users. You configure item-level targeting for the file preference so that you can still have the policy linked to the domain, and other preferences affect all users.

1. Log on to 411Server1 as **Administrator,** if necessary.

2. Open the **Prefs** GPO in the Group Policy Management Editor. Under User Configuration, expand **Preferences** and **Windows Settings,** and then click **Files.**

3. Double-click the file preference in the right pane. In the Properties dialog box, click the **Common** tab.

4. Click the **Item-level targeting** check box, and then click the **Targeting** button.

5. In the Targeting Editor window, click **New Item,** and then click **Organizational Unit.**

6. In the Organizational Unit text box, click the browse button, click **TestOU1**, and then click **OK**. Click **OK** twice to get back to the Group Policy Management Editor.

7. Log on to 411Win8 as **testuser1**, and delete the **PandP** folder. Log off 411Win8.

8. Log back on to 411Win8 as **testuser1**, and verify that the PandP folder and the two files were created again.

9. Log off 411Win8, and log back on as **testuser4**. (This user account should be in TestOU2.) Open File Explorer, and in the left pane, click **Documents** under This PC. The PandP folder is there, but there are no files in it because item-level targeting limited this preference to user accounts in TestOU1.

10. Unlink the **Prefs** GPO from the domain. Log off 411Win8, but stay logged on to 411Server1 if you're continuing to the next activity.

Activity 9-15: Deploying a VPN Connection

Time Required: 15 minutes
Objective: Configure a preference to deploy a VPN connection.

Required Tools and Equipment: 411Server1 and 411Win8
Description: You have just set up a VPN server, and you want to deploy a VPN connection to all the desktop computers. You create a Network Options preference and link it to the Desktops OU.

1. Log on to 411Server1 as **Administrator**, if necessary.

2. Open the **Prefs** GPO in the Group Policy Management Editor. Under Computer Configuration, click to expand **Preferences** and **Control Panel Settings**. Right-click **Network Options**, point to **New**, and click **VPN Connection**.

3. In the Action drop-down list, leave the default setting **Update**. Click the **All users connection** option button so that all users logging on to target computers have access to the connection. In the Connection name text box, type **WorkVPN**. In the IP Address text box, type **10.11.1.2** (see Figure 9-23).

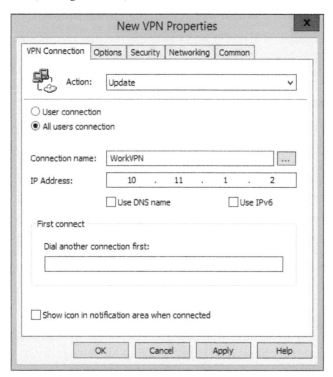

Figure 9-23   Creating a VPN connection preference

If the VPN connection was already created on the server, you could select it by clicking the browse button, and the preferences settings would be populated from the existing connection.

4. Click the **Options** tab, and review the available settings. Click the **Security** tab, which is where you set authentication options. Leave the settings at their defaults, however.

5. Click the **Networking** tab, where you can choose the VPN tunnel type. Leave the default setting **Automatic**.

6. Click the **Common** tab, and click **Remove this item when it is no longer applied**. In the warning message stating that the preference will be set to Replace mode, click **OK**. Click **OK** again.

7. Link the **Prefs** GPO to the **Desktops** OU. Log on to 411Win8 as **testuser1**. Because it's a Computer Configuration policy, you have to restart the computer or run `gpupdate` for it to be applied. Open a command prompt window, and then type **`gpupdate`** and press **Enter**.

8. Right-click **Start** and click **Network Connections**. You see the WorkVPN connection.

9. Because you selected the "Remove this item when it is no longer applied" option, you should test it. On 411Server1, unlink **Prefs** from the **Desktops** OU. On 411Win8, run **`gpupdate`** again.

10. Look in the Network Connections window to verify that the VPN connection has been removed. Log off 411Win8, but stay logged on to 411Server1 if you're continuing to the next activity.

Activity 9-16: Configuring Internet Explorer Settings

Time Required: 10 minutes
Objective: Configure a preference for Internet Explorer settings.

Required Tools and Equipment: 411Server1 and 411Win8; Internet connection
Description: You want to configure default home page tabs for domain users when they open Internet Explorer so that they always see the company home page when they start Internet Explorer. This page often has important announcements and links to related pages. To do this, you create an Internet Settings preference under User Configuration.

1. Log on to 411Server1 as **Administrator**, if necessary.

2. Open the **Prefs** GPO in the Group Policy Management Editor. Under User Configuration, click to expand **Preferences** and **Control Panel Settings**. Right-click **Internet Settings**, point to **New**, and click **Internet Explorer 10**. (*Note*: Windows 8.1 and Windows Server 2012 R2 ship with Internet Explorer 11, but most of the Internet Explorer 10 preference options work with Internet Explorer 11.)

3. Settings with a red dotted line under them or a red circle in front of them aren't applied, but settings with a green underline or green circle are applied. You can change which settings get applied. If you press F5, all settings in the current tab are applied. If you press F6, the last setting you edited is enabled. If you press F7, the last setting you edited is disabled. If you press F8, all settings in the current tab are disabled. Press **F8**, and all settings are displayed with a red dotted line under them. Now press **F5** to enable all settings.

4. In the Home page text box, type **www.cengage.com** and press **Enter**, and then type **books.tomsho.com** and press **Enter**. Click the **Start with home page** option button, and then click the **Delete browsing history on exit** check box (see Figure 9-24).

Figure 9-24 Creating an Internet Explorer preference

5. Review the available options in the General tab and other tabs to see all the settings you can configure. Click **OK**.

6. Link the **Prefs** GPO to the **TestOU1** OU. Log on to 411Win8 as **testuser1**.

7. Start Internet Explorer. You should see the *www.cengage.com* and *books.tomsho.com* Web sites open in two tabs. Click the **Settings** icon and click **Internet options** to see the settings you configured. Notice that you can still change the options, which you couldn't do if these settings were configured with a policy rather than a preference. Click **Cancel**, and log off 411Win8.

8. On 411Server1, unlink the **Prefs** GPO from **TestOU1**. Stay logged on to 411Server1 if you're continuing to the next activity.

Activity 9-17: Configuring Local Groups

Time Required: 15 minutes
Objective: Configure local groups by using a preference.

Required Tools and Equipment: 411Server1 and 411Win8
Description: You want to be able to give certain domain users administrative capabilities on any Windows desktop computer they log on to, so you create a global group in the domain called Local_Admins. Then you set a preference to add this group to the local Administrators group on all computers in the Desktops OU.

1. Log on to 411Server1 as **Administrator**, if necessary.

2. Open Active Directory Users and Computers. Click the **Users** folder, and then create a global security group named **Local_Admins** in this folder. Add **testuser1** to this group.

3. Open the Group Policy Management console, and open the **Prefs** GPO in the Group Policy Management Editor. First, do a little cleanup of preferences you don't need anymore. Delete the **Network Options** preference under the Computer Configuration node and the **Files** and **Internet Settings** preferences under the User Configuration node.

4. Click to expand **Preferences** and then **Control Panel Settings** under Computer Configuration, and then right-click **Local Users and Groups**, point to **New**, and click **Local Group**.

5. Make sure **Update** is the selected action. Click the **Group name** list arrow, and click **Administrators (built-in)** in the list.

6. Click the **Add** button, and then click the browse button next to the Name text box. In the Select User, Computer, or Group dialog box, type **Local_Admins**, click **Check Names**, and then click **OK**. Make sure the action is **Add to this group**, and then click **OK** twice.

7. Link the **Prefs** GPO to the **Desktops** OU.

8. Log on to the domain from 411Win8 as **Administrator**. Open a command prompt window, type **gpupdate**, and press **Enter**. Close the command prompt window.

9. Right-click **Start** and click **Computer Management**. Click to expand **Local Users and Groups**, click **Groups**, and then double-click **Administrators** to open the Properties dialog box. You should see Local_Admins in the Members text box. Click **OK**. Now any domain user you add to the Local_Groups group has local administrator access to all computers in the Desktops OU.

10. Unlink the **Prefs** GPO from the **Desktops** OU. Log off or shut down 411Win8 and 411Server1.

Chapter Summary

- A Group Policy object (GPO) contains policy settings for managing many aspects of domain controllers, member servers, member computers, and users. There are two main types of GPOs: local GPOs and domain GPOs. Domain GPOs are stored in Active Directory on domain controllers.

- The main tools for managing, creating, and editing GPOs are the Group Policy Management console and the Group Policy Management Editor. The purpose of these tools is to carry out changes to the security and working environments for users or computers.

- The Group Policy Management Editor has a Computer Configuration node, with policies affecting all computer accounts in a GPO's scope, and a User Configuration node, with policies affecting all user accounts in a GPO's scope. Most policies in these two nodes affect different aspects of the working environment, but a few policies are the same.

- The Software installation extension is used to install software packages remotely on member computers. If it's configured in the Computer Configuration node, the software package is installed regardless of who logs on to the targeted computers. When it's configured in User Configuration, the software package is available to targeted users when they log on to any domain computer.

- After a package is deployed to a computer, by default it's not installed again. However, if changes have been made to the original package, you can redeploy it.

- A script is a series of commands saved in a text file to be repeated easily at any time. There's a Scripts extension in both the Computer Configuration and the User Configuration nodes in the path Policies, Windows Settings, Scripts. In the Computer Configuration node, you configure startup or shutdown scripts, and in the User Configuration node, you configure logon and logoff scripts.

- Folder redirection enables administrators to set policies that redirect folders in a user's profile directory. This feature is useful when you want users to store their documents on a server for centralized backup, but you don't want to change the way they access their document folders.

- Both the Computer Configuration and User Configuration nodes have an Administrative Templates folder. In the Computer Configuration node, the settings in Administrative Templates affect the HKEY_LOCAL_MACHINE Registry key. Settings in the User Configuration node affect the HKEY_LOCAL_USER Registry key.

- You can create a filter in the Group Policy Management Editor to find a particular policy setting under Administrative Templates. After you have configured and applied filters, only policies matching the criteria are displayed in the Group Policy Management Editor.

- Administrative templates are a collection of policy definition files in XML format. These XML files, referred to as "ADMX files" because of their `.admx` extension, specify Registry entries that should be controlled and the type of data the entries take.

- If you're running a Windows Server 2008 or later domain but still have to support clients older than Vista or are running older applications that use ADM files, you might want to migrate the older ADM files to ADMX format with ADMX Migrator.

- Security templates are text files with an `.inf` extension that contain information for defining policy settings in the Computer Configuration, Policies, Windows Settings, Security Settings node of a local or domain GPO. The Security Configuration and Analysis snap-in is useful for checking a computer's existing security settings against the known settings in security template files.

- The Security Configuration Wizard (SCW) guides you through creating, editing, and applying a security policy on Windows servers. It creates an XML file that can be deployed to servers with Group Policy.

- Unlike user or computer policies that can't be changed by users, group policy preferences enable administrators to set up a baseline computing environment yet still allow users to make changes to configured settings. You must create each preference you want to deploy.

- Preferences operate the same way as policies for default inheritance and scope. However, you can target users or computers for each preference based on a set of criteria, a feature called item-level targeting.

Key Terms

administrative template files   XML-formatted text files that define policies in the Administrative Templates folder in a GPO. Custom ADMX files can also be created.

assigned application   A method of software deployment in which an application can be installed automatically when the computer starts, a user logs on to the domain, or a user opens a file associated with the application.

batch file   A text file containing a series of commands that's saved with a `.bat` extension.

domain GPOs   Group Policy objects stored in Active Directory on domain controllers. They can be linked to a site, a domain, or an OU and affect users and computers whose accounts are stored in these containers.

folder redirection   A Group Policy feature that allows an administrator to set policies that redirect one or more folders in a user's profile directory.

group policy preference   A feature of Group Policy that contains settings organized into categories, which enables administrators to set up a baseline computing environment yet still allows users to make changes to configured settings.

item-level targeting   A feature of group policy preferences that allows an administrator to target specific users or computers based on criteria.

local GPOs   Group Policy objects stored on local computers that can be edited by the Group Policy Object Editor snap-in.

managed policy setting   A type of group policy setting whereby the setting on the user or computer account reverts to its original state when the object is no longer in the scope of the GPO containing the setting.

Microsoft Software Installation (MSI) file   A collection of files gathered into a package with an `.msi` extension that contains the instructions Windows Installer needs to install an application.

published application   A method of software deployment in which the application isn't installed automatically; instead, a link to install the application is available in Control Panel's Programs and Features.

script   A series of commands that have been saved in a text file to be repeated easily at any time.

Security Configuration Wizard (SCW)   A tool that guides you through creating, editing, and applying a security policy on Windows servers.

security templates   Text files with an `.inf` extension that contain information for defining policy settings in the Computer Configuration, Policies, Windows Settings, Security Settings node of a local or domain GPO.

unmanaged policy setting   A type of group policy setting that persists on the user or computer account, meaning it remains even after the computer or user object falls out of the GPO's scope.

Review Questions

1. Which of the following is true about GPOs? (Choose all that apply.)

    a. Local GPOs override domain GPOs.

    b. Domain GPOs are stored on member servers.

    c. Domain GPOs can be linked to Active Directory sites.

    d. The gpedit.msc tool can be used to edit local GPOs.

2. Which of the following is a method for creating a GPO? (Choose all that apply.)

    a. Use Active Directory Users and Computers.

    b. Link it to a container.

    c. Use the Group Policy Objects folder in the Group Policy Management console.

    d. Use an XML editor.

3. You create GPOs in the Group Policy Management console and change them in the Group Policy Management Editor. True or False?

4. You have configured a policy setting in the User Configuration node of a domain GPO and linked the GPO to OU-X. Later, you discover you linked it to the wrong OU, so you unlink it from OU-X and link it to OU-Y, which is correct. A few days later, you find that users in OU-X still have the policy setting applied to their accounts. What's the most likely cause of the problem?

    a. Group policy settings haven't been refreshed.

    b. The policy setting is unmanaged.

    c. Users in OU-X have an item-level target filter configured.

    d. The GPO is disabled.

5. You want to deploy a software package that's available to all users in the domain if they want to use it, but you don't want the package to be installed unless a user needs it. How should you configure the software installation policy?

    a. Publish the package under the Computer Configuration node.

    b. Assign the package under the Computer Configuration node.

    c. Publish the package under the User Configuration node.

    d. Assign the package under the User Configuration node.

6. You want to deploy a logon script by using Group Policy. You have several sites connected via a WAN with a DC at each site. You want to make sure the script is always available when users log on from any computer at any location. What should you do?

   a. Create a share on the fastest DC in the network and save the script there.

   b. Send the script via e-mail to all users and have them save it locally.

   c. Save the script in the SYSVOL share.

   d. Copy the script to cloud storage.

7. You want to centrally back up the files users store in the Documents folder in their user profiles, but you don't want users to have to change the way they access their files. What's the best way to go about this?

   a. Deploy a script that copies files from the Documents folder to a share on a server.

   b. Configure folder redirection in the User Configuration node of a GPO.

   c. Deploy a Mapped Drive preference, and tell users to save their files to the mapped drive.

   d. Configure a backup policy in the Computer Configuration node of a GPO.

8. Which of the following is best described as policy definition files saved in XML format?

   a. Administrative templates

   b. Security templates

   c. Group Policy objects

   d. Group Policy templates

9. Which of the following is a subfolder in the User Configuration node but not the Computer Configuration node of a GPO?

   a. Network

   b. Windows Components

   c. System

   d. Desktop

10. Settings in the Computer Configuration node of a GPO affect the HKEY_CURRENT_CONFIG Registry key. True or False?

11. You need to find a policy related to an application that was installed a couple years ago. You know that the policy is persistent when the computer it's applied to falls out of scope, but you can't remember its name. You remember a word or two that might be in the policy name or comments. What can you do to find this policy quickly?

    a. In the Group Policy Management console, create a policy search term; set Persistent to Any, and enable Full Text search.

    b. In the Group Policy Management Editor, configure a filter; set Managed to No, and enable Keyword Filters.

    c. In the Group Policy Management console, configure a search script; set Managed to Yes, and enable Requirements Filters.

    d. In the Group Policy Management Editor, configure a policy screen; set Persistent to Yes, and enable Title and Comments.

12. You have created a custom administrative template. You want this template to be available to all DCs so that policies can be configured with it from any DC. Where should you save it?

    a. In %*systemroot*%\PolicyDefinitions

    b. In the central store

    c. In the root of the C drive

    d. In ADUC

13. You have installed an application that can be configured with Group Policy. The application came with a custom ADM file that must be replicated to all DCs. What should you do first?

    a. Copy the file to %*windir*%\PolicyDefinitions.

    b. Open the file with an XML editor and save it.

    c. Open the file with ADMX Migrator.

    d. Change the extension to `.inf`.

14. You're concerned that some domain controllers and workstations don't meet security requirements. What should you do to verify security settings on a computer against a list of known settings?

    a. Run Security Configuration and Analysis on the computer to compare its security settings against a security database.

    b. Open the Group Policy Management console on the computer, click the Security node, and run Group Policy Results.

    c. Run `secpol.msc` on the computer, and use Group Policy Modeling.

    d. Use `secedit /configure` on the computer, and read the report that's generated.

15. You have six servers on your network that run Active Directory, DNS, and DHCP. You want to use the Group Policy tool to configure all with the same security settings, including firewall settings, and disable all unnecessary services. What should you do?

    a. Run `secpol.msc` and then Security Configuration and Analysis.

    b. Run the SCW and then `scwcmd`.

    c. Configure a Service and Control Panel preference.

    d. Create a custom ADMX file and deploy it with ADMX Migrator.

16. You want to set a group policy preference that affects only computers with a CPU speed of at least 4.0 GHz. What's the best way to do this?

    a. Configure item-level targeting.

    b. Move all computers meeting the criteria to a separate OU.

    c. Configure the group policy client on each computer with this type of CPU.

    d. Create a WMI filter with the Group Policy Management Editor.

17. You have configured a group policy preference that creates a VPN connection for all computers in the GPO's scope. One user says the connection was there yesterday, but it's no longer showing in his Network Connections window. You suspect he might have deleted the connection accidentally. What can you do to make sure the VPN connection is re-created even if a user deletes it?

    a. Disable the "Remove this item when it is no longer valid" option.

    b. Configure the Read-only option.

    c. Configure item-level targeting.

    d. Disable the "Apply once and do not reapply" option.

18. You want all users to have the company home page and two other Web sites loaded in tabs when they start Internet Explorer, but you want them to be able to change their home pages if they like. What should you do?

    a. Configure an IE policy, and set it to unmanaged.

    b. Configure an Internet Options preference, and accept the default options in the Common tab.

    c. Configure an IE policy and enable the Allow user changes option.

    d. Configure an Internet Options preference, and change the defaults in the Common tab.

Case Projects

Case Project 9-1: Configuring Users' Working Environments

You have been told that all users in the Marketing Department must have a computer working environment that meets certain criteria. Marketing Department users don't always log on to the same computer every day, so these requirements should apply wherever they log on. You have a Windows Server 2012 R2 domain, and all computers are domain members. All Marketing Department user and computer accounts are in the Marketing OU. All desktops run Windows 8.1.

- Marketing users must be able to access documents they save in the Documents folder in their profiles from any computer they log on to.

- A company marketing application must be installed automatically whenever they log on if it's not already installed.

- The marketing application they run leaves behind temporary files named `mktapp.tmp` *X* in the C:\MktApp folder (with the *X* representing a number). These files contain sensitive information and must be deleted when the user logs off.

How can you make sure all these criteria are met? What should you configure to meet each criterion? Be specific about any options that should be enabled or disabled and how the configuration should be applied.

Case Project 9-2: Configuring Preferences

Users in the Engineering Department need a higher level of access on their local computers than other users do. In addition, you want to set power options on mobile computers that Engineering users use. All Engineering Department user and computer accounts are in the Engineering OU. What should you configure to meet the following criteria?

- When an Engineering user logs on to a computer, the user account is added to the local Administrators group on that computer.

- Enable the hibernation power mode but only if the user's computer is identified as a portable computer. Set the power scheme to hibernate mode if the laptop's lid is closed or the power button is pressed.

chapter 10

Managing Group Policies

After reading this chapter and completing the exercises, you will be able to:

- Configure group policy scope, precedence, and inheritance
- Configure group policy client processing
- Configure the Group Policy Results and Group Policy Modeling tools
- Manage GPOs

Different aspects of group policies were covered in Chapter 8 and Chapter 9 in this book as well as in *MCSA Guide to Installing and Configuring Windows Server 2012/R2, Exam 70-410* (Cengage Learning, 2015). Aside from understanding how to configure policy and preference settings, however, it's important to understand GPO scope, precedence, and inheritance so that you can make sure the right objects are configured with the right settings. In this chapter, you learn about these topics and see how to change the default group policy client processing.

Sometimes you need to confirm that the settings you think are being set are actually being set on the target accounts. The Group Policy Results tool can show you the actual results of group policy processing, and the Group Policy Modeling tool enables you to create "what-if" scenarios so that you know what policies will be applied if you move an account to an Active Directory container or change an account's group memberships. Finally, you learn how to back up, restore, copy, and migrate GPOs.

Configuring Group Policy Processing

Table 10-1 summarizes what you need for the hands-on activities in this chapter.

Table 10-1   Activity requirements

Activity	Requirements	Notes
Activity 10-1: Working with GPO Inheritance Blocking	411Server1, 411Win8	
Activity 10-2: Working with GPO Enforcement	411Server1, 411Win8	
Activity 10-3: Using GPO Security Filtering	411Server1, 411Win8	
Activity 10-4: Using GPO Security Filtering for a Computer Account	411Server1, 411Win8	
Activity 10-5: Creating WMI Filtering	411Server1, 411Win8	
Activity 10-6: Configuring Loopback Policy Processing	411Server1, 411Win8	
Activity 10-7: Using Remote Group Policy Updates	411Server1, 411Win8	
Activity 10-8: Using Group Policy Results and Group Policy Modeling	411Server1, 411Win8	
Activity 10-9: Backing Up and Restoring a GPO	411Server1	

© 2015 Cengage Learning®

Group policy processing can be confusing because there are so many exceptions to normal processing and inheritance behavior. When you configure and link a GPO to an Active Directory container, you need to be aware of how that GPO affects objects in the container and subcontainers. To do so, you need to have a solid understanding of how GPOs are processed, how settings are inherited, and the exceptions to normal processing and inheritance. This section discusses the following topics related to group policy processing:

- *GPO scope and precedence*—Defines which objects are affected by settings in a GPO and which settings take precedence if conflicts exist
- *GPO inheritance*—Defines how settings are applied to objects in subcontainers
- *GPO filtering*—Creates exceptions to the normal scope by using security and WMI filtering
- *Loopback processing*—Changes how settings in the User Configuration node are applied

GPO Scope and Precedence

GPO scope defines which objects are affected by settings in a GPO. As you've learned, policies and preferences defined in a GPO's Computer Configuration node affect computer accounts, and policies and preferences in the User Configuration node affect user accounts. In addition, GPOs are applied in this order: local computer, site, domain, and OU. Policies that aren't defined or configured are not applied at all, and the last policy applied is the one that takes precedence. For example, a GPO linked to a domain affects all computers and users in the domain, but settings in a GPO linked to an OU override the settings in a GPO linked to the domain if there are conflicts.

When OUs are nested, the GPO linked to the OU nested the deepest takes precedence over all other GPOs. When a policy setting isn't configured, its status is Not defined or Not configured. When a GPO is applied to an object, only the configured settings have any effect on that object. If two GPOs are applied to an object, and a certain setting is configured on one GPO but not the other, the configured setting is applied.

Understanding Site-Linked GPOs GPOs linked to a site object affect all users and computers physically located at the site. Because sites are based on IP address, GPO processing determines from where a user is logging on and from what computer, based on that computer's IP address. So users who log on to computers at different sites might have different policies applied to their accounts. In addition, mobile computers can have different policies applied, depending on the site where the computer connects to the network. Keep in mind that if a site contains computers and domain controllers from multiple domains, a site-linked GPO affects objects from multiple domains. For simplicity, when you have only one site and one domain, domain GPOs should be used rather than site-linked GPOs. As you might imagine, using site-linked GPOs can be confusing for users, particularly with a lot of user mobility between sites, so site-linked GPOs should be used with caution and only when there are valid reasons for different sites to have different policies.

Understanding Domain-Linked GPOs GPOs set at the domain level should contain settings that you want to apply to all objects in the domain. The Default Domain Policy is configured and linked to the domain object by default and mostly defines user account policies. Account policies that affect domain logons can be defined only at the domain level, as you learned in Chapter 8. Typically, they're configured by using the Default Domain Policy but can use a different GPO, as long as it's linked to the domain object.

Active Directory folders, such as Computers and Users, are not OUs and, therefore, can't have a GPO linked to them. Only domain-linked GPOs and site-linked GPOs affect objects in these folders. If you need to manage objects in these folders with group policies, moving the objects to OUs is recommended instead of configuring domain or site GPOs to manage them.

It might be tempting to define most group policy settings at the domain level and define exceptions at the OU level, but in a large Active Directory structure, this strategy could become unwieldy. Best practices suggest setting account policies and a few critical security policies at the domain level and setting the remaining policies on GPOs linked to OUs.

Understanding OU-Linked GPOs Most fine-tuning of group policies, particularly user policies, should be done at the OU level. Because OU-linked policies are applied last, they take precedence over site and domain policies (with the exception of account policies, which can be applied only at the domain level). Because the majority of policies are defined at the OU level, a well-thought-out OU design is paramount in your overall Active Directory design. Users and computers with similar policy requirements should be located in the same OU or have a common parent OU when possible.

Because OUs can be nested, so can the GPOs applied to them. When possible, your OU structure should be designed so that policies defined in GPOs linked to the top-level OU apply to all objects in that OU. GPOs applied to nested OUs should be used for exceptions to policies set at the higher level OU or when certain computers or users require more restrictive policies. For example, all full-time employees in the Engineering Department need complete access to Control Panel, but part-time employees should be restricted from using it. You can configure a policy allowing Control Panel access in a GPO linked to the Engineering OU. Then you create an OU under the Engineering OU that contains part-time employees' accounts and link a GPO to it that restricts use of Control Panel.

Group Policy Inheritance

By default, GPO inheritance is enabled and settings linked to a parent object are applied to all child objects. Therefore, settings in a GPO linked to the domain object are inherited by all OUs and their child objects in the domain. Settings in a GPO linked to the site are inherited by all objects in that site. To see which policies affect a domain or OU and where the policies are inherited from, select a container in the left pane of the Group Policy Management console (GPMC) and click the Group Policy Inheritance tab in the right pane. There are two main ways to change default GPO inheritance:

- Blocking inheritance
- GPO enforcement

Blocking Inheritance   Although the default inheritance behavior is suitable for most situations, as with NTFS permission inheritance, sometimes you need an exception to the default. One method is blocking inheritance, which prevents GPOs linked to parent containers from affecting child containers. To block inheritance, in the GPMC, right-click the child domain or OU and click Block Inheritance. You can enable this setting on a domain or an OU. On a domain object, this setting blocks GPO inheritance from a site, and on an OU, it blocks inheritance from parent OUs (if any), the domain, and the site. If inheritance blocking is enabled, the OU or domain object is displayed with an exclamation point in a blue circle. Inheritance blocking should be used sparingly; if you find that you need to block GPO inheritance frequently, it's an indication that your OU design is probably flawed and should be reexamined.

What happens if you have a nested OU and want to block GPO inheritance from its parent OU, but you still want domain- and site-linked GPOs to apply? This is where GPO enforcement, discussed next, comes in.

GPO Enforcement   GPO enforcement forces inheritance of settings on all child objects in the GPO's scope, even if a GPO with conflicting settings is linked to a container at a deeper level. In other words, a GPO that's enforced has the strongest precedence of all GPOs in its scope. If multiple GPOs have the Enforced option set, the GPO that's highest in the Active Directory hierarchy has the strongest precedence. For example, if both a GPO linked to an OU and a GPO linked to a domain have the Enforced option set, the GPO linked to the domain has stronger precedence. GPO enforcement also overrides GPO inheritance blocking.

GPO enforcement is configured on the GPO, not the Active Directory container. To configure enforcement in the GPMC, right-click the shortcut to a linked GPO and click Enforced.

Remember that the Block Inheritance option is set on a domain or OU, and the Enforced option is set on a GPO linked to a site, domain, or OU.

Activity 10-1: Working with GPO Inheritance Blocking

Time Required: 20 minutes
Objective: Enable the Block Inheritance option on an OU.

Required Tools and Equipment: 411Server1 and 411Win8
Description: In this activity, you configure a policy to bring the user straight to the desktop at logon. Then you block inheritance to see that the policy doesn't affect objects below where inheritance blocking is enabled. Finally, you unblock inheritance to see the policy take effect.

1. Log on to 411Server1 as **Administrator**, and open the Group Policy Management console. Start 411Win8, if necessary.

2. In Chapter 9, you created a GPO named GPO1 and configured a policy under the User Configuration node that causes users to go to the desktop rather than the Start screen when a user logs on. Right-click **TestOU1** and click **Block Inheritance**. Now users in TestOU1 aren't affected by GPOs linked to the domain.

3. On 411Win8, log on as **testuser1**. This policy takes two logons before it's effective, so log off and log back on as **testuser1**. You go to the Start screen instead of the desktop.

4. On 411Server1, in Group Policy Management, right-click **TestOU1** and click to clear the **Block Inheritance** option to enable inheritance again.

5. On 411Win8, open a command prompt window. Type **gpupdate** and press **Enter**. Log off and log back on as **testuser1** to verify that you go straight to the desktop again.

6. Log off 411Win8, but stay logged on to 411Server1 if you're continuing to the next activity.

Activity 10-2: Working with GPO Enforcement

Time Required: 15 minutes
Objective: Enable the Enforced option on a GPO.

Required Tools and Equipment: 411Server1 and 411Win8
Description: You want to make sure information on the previous logon attempt is displayed when a user logs on to a computer in the domain, even if inheritance is blocked. In Chapter 9, you configured this policy setting in the Computer Configuration node of GPO1 and linked GPO1 to the domain.

10

1. Log on to 411Server1 as **Administrator**, and open the Group Policy Management console, if necessary.

2. Right-click the **Desktops** OU and click **Block Inheritance**.

3. Log on to 411Win8 as **testuser1**. Notice that information on the last successful and unsuccessful logon attempts is displayed. Click **OK**.

4. Open a command prompt window. Type **gpupdate** and press **Enter**.

5. Log off 411Win8, and log back on as **testuser1**. You no longer see information about the last logon attempts.

6. On 411Server1, in the Group Policy Management console, right-click **GPO1** under the domain node and click **Enforced**. You see a small padlock icon on the GPO to indicate that the Enforced setting is enabled.

7. On 411Win8, run **gpupdate**. Log off, and log back on as **testuser1**. You see information on the last logon attempt again. Click **OK**, and then log off 411Win8.

8. On 411Server1, in the Group Policy Management console, right-click the **Desktops** OU and click to clear **Block Inheritance** setting. Right-click **GPO1** and click to clear **Enforced**.

9. Stay logged on to 411Server1 if you're continuing to the next activity.

GPO Filtering

Blocking inheritance excludes all objects in an OU from inheriting GPO settings (unless they're enforced), but what if you want to exclude only some objects in the OU? This is where GPO filtering comes into play. There are two types of **GPO filtering**: security filtering and Windows Management Instrumentation (WMI) filtering.

Security filtering uses permissions to restrict objects from accessing a GPO. Like any object in Active Directory, a GPO has a discretionary access control list (DACL) that contains lists of security principals with assigned permissions to the GPO. User and computer accounts must have the Read and Apply Group Policy permissions for a GPO to apply to them. By default, the Authenticated Users special identity is granted these permissions to every GPO; Authenticated Users applies to both logged-on users and computers. You can see a GPO's DACL in Active Directory Users and Computers in the System\Policies folder and in the Delegation tab in the GPMC, but for basic GPO filtering, you can use the Scope tab in the GPMC. To view the current security filtering settings, click a GPO in the GPMC and click the Scope tab on the right (see Figure 10-1).

Figure 10-1   Viewing security filtering settings

You use the Security Filtering dialog box in the GPMC to add or remove security principals from the GPO access list. For example, if you want a GPO to apply to all users in a domain or OU except a few, follow these steps:

1. Create a security group in Active Directory Users and Computers.
2. Add all the users who should be subject to the GPO as members of the new group.
3. In the GPMC, click the GPO, and click the Scope tab in the right pane.
4. Use the Security Filtering dialog box to add the new group to this GPO.
5. In the Security Filtering dialog box, remove the Authenticated Users special identity from this GPO.

Remember that computer accounts are also affected by GPOs. So if the GPO you're filtering contains computer settings, you must add a group containing the computer accounts that should be subject to the GPO's policies.

Another way to use security filtering is to edit the GPO's DACL directly. This method is often easier when the GPO must be applied to many users or computers with just a few exceptions. In the GPMC, click the GPO in the Group Policy Objects folder, and click the Delegation tab in the right pane to see the complete list of access control entries (ACEs) for the GPO, as in Figure 10-2. You can add security principals to the DACL or click the Advanced button to open the Advanced Security Settings dialog box.

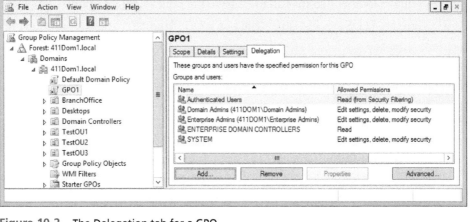

Figure 10-2   The Delegation tab for a GPO

By using the Advanced Security Settings dialog box, you can assign Deny permissions as well as Allow permissions. Assigning the Deny Read permission, for example, enables you to create exceptions to normal GPO processing. You can add a single user or computer account or a group to the DACL and prevent these security principals from being affected by the GPO.

For example, you have a GPO configuring some Internet Explorer settings in the Computer Configuration node that restricts access to advanced features. You have more than 500 computer accounts in different OUs, so you want to link the GPO to the domain so that it affects all computers in the domain. However, you have a dozen or so power users whose computers you want to exempt from these policies. You can create a group, add the power users' computers as members, add the group to the GPO's DACL, and then configure Deny Read permission.

Activity 10-3: Using GPO Security Filtering

Time Required: 25 minutes
Objective: Change the default security filtering on a GPO and examine the results.

Required Tools and Equipment: 411Server1 and 411Win8
Description: In this activity, you use GPO filtering to change the default inheritance behavior of GPO processing.

1. Log on to 411Server1 as **Administrator**, if necessary.

2. Open the Group Policy Management console, if necessary. Click to expand the **Group Policy Objects** folder, and then click **GPO1**. In the right pane, click the **Scope** tab, if necessary.

3. In the Security Filtering dialog box in the right pane, click the **Add** button. Type **testuser4**, click **Check Names**, and then click **OK**.

4. In the Name list box, click **Authenticated Users**, and then click the **Remove** button. Click **OK** to confirm that you want to remove the delegation privilege. Test User4 is now the only security principal with Read and Apply Group Policy permissions for GPO1.

5. GPO1 is still linked to the domain object, so there's no need to link it to a container. On 411Win8, log on to the domain as **testuser1**. The policy requires two logons before it takes effect. The first logon downloads the policy, and then it's effective for all future logons. Log off, and log back on as **testuser1**. You see that testuser1 no longer goes directly to the desktop, but instead goes to the Start screen because only testuser4 has permission to read the GPO1 Group Policy object.

6. Log off, and log on as **testuser4**; this time, you go directly to the desktop.

7. On 411Server1, change the security filtering for GPO1 to add **Authenticated Users** back and remove **testuser4** so that all users have the policy applied again.

8. Log off 411Win8, but stay logged on to 411Server1 if you're continuing to the next activity.

Activity 10-4: Using GPO Security Filtering for a Computer Account

Time Required: 25 minutes
Objective: Change the default security filtering on a GPO and examine the results.

Required Tools and Equipment: 411Server1 and 411Win8
Description: In this activity, you change the security filtering on a GPO for a computer account.

1. Log on to 411Server1 as **Administrator**, if necessary.

2. Open the Group Policy Management console, if necessary. Click to expand the **Group Policy Objects** folder, and then click **GPO1**. In the right pane, click the **Scope** tab, if necessary.

3. In the Security Filtering dialog box in the right pane, click the **Add** button. Click the **Object Types** button. By default, computer accounts aren't recognized in this dialog box. In the Object Types dialog box, click to select **Computers**. Click **OK**.

4. Type **411Win8**, click **Check Names**, and click **OK**. Click **Authenticated Users**, and then click the **Remove** button. Click **OK** to confirm that you want to remove the delegation privilege. 411Win8 is now the only security principal with Read and Apply Group Policy permissions for GPO1.

5. On 411Server1, run **gpupdate**. Log off 411Server1, and log back on as **Administrator**. You no longer see the last user logon attempt message, which is a policy that affects computer accounts.

6. On 411Win8, log on as **testuser4**; you see a message stating that security policies are set to show information about the last interactive sign-in, but the information can't be retrieved. The reason is that the information is stored on the DC, and the DC no longer has the policy applied. Click **OK**.

7. On 411Server1, change the security filtering for GPO1 to add **Authenticated Users** back and remove **411Win8** so that all accounts have the policy applied again. On 411Server1, run **gpupdate**. Log on to 411Win8 as **testuser4**. You see the sign-in information. Click **OK**.

8. Log off 411Win8, but stay logged on to 411Server1 if you're continuing to the next activity.

WMI Filtering   The second type of filtering is **WMI filtering**. Windows Management Instrumentation (WMI) is a Windows technology for gathering management information about computers, such as the hardware platform, the OS version, available disk space, and so on. WMI filtering uses queries to select a group of computers based on certain attributes, and then applies or doesn't apply policies based on the query's results. It's similar to the preference item-level targeting you learned about in Chapter 9. You need to have a solid understanding of the complex WMI query language before you can create WMI filters. Here's an example of using one to select only computers running Windows 8 Enterprise:

```
Select * from Win32_OperatingSystem where Caption =
  "Microsoft Windows 8 Enterprise"
```

This next example uses the OS version number. Windows 7 and Windows Server 2008 R2 have version numbers beginning with 6.1, and Windows 8 and Windows Server 2012 have version numbers beginning with 6.2. This command selects computers running an OS with a version number beginning with 6.2:

```
Select * from Win32_OperatingSystem where Version
  like "6.2%"
```

The next example uses `Version` and `ProductType`. `ProductType` differentiates between client and server OSs. A client OS, such as Windows 8, has a `ProductType` of 1, and a server OS, such as Windows Server 2012, has a `ProductType` of 3. This example selects Windows 8 systems:

```
Select * from Win32_OperatingSystem where Version
  like "6.2%" and ProductType = "1"
```

Suppose you want a policy that installs a large application on target machines with at least 2 GB of disk space available. You can use the following command:

```
Select * from Win32_LogicalDisk where FreeSpace > 2000000000
```

This example targets computers from a specific manufacturer and model:

```
Select * from Win32_ComputerSystem where
  Manufacturer = "Dell" and Model = "Optiplex 960"
```

You create WMI filters in the WMI Filters node of the GPMC. After creating a WMI filter, select it in the Scope tab of a GPO. Only one WMI filter can be selected per GPO, but you can use the same WMI filter in multiple GPOs.

To learn more about WMI and WMI filtering, search on the Microsoft TechNet Web site at *http://technet.microsoft.com.*

Activity 10-5: Creating a WMI Filter

Time Required: 25 minutes
Objective: Create and apply a WMI filter to limit a GPO's scope.

Required Tools and Equipment: 411Server1 and 411Win8
Description: In this activity, you create a WMI filter that limits a GPO's scope to only computers running an OS beginning with "Microsoft Windows Server."

1. Log on to 411Server1 as **Administrator**, if necessary.

2. Open the Group Policy Management console, if necessary. Right-click **WMI Filters** in the left pane and click **New**.

3. In the New WMI Filter dialog box, type **WindowsServer** in the Name text box. In the Description text box, type **Limit GPO scope to Windows Server OSs**.

4. Click the **Add** button. In the WMI Query dialog box, accept the default value in the Namespace text box. In the Query text box, type **Select * from Win32_OperatingSystem where Caption like "Microsoft Windows Server%"** (see Figure 10-3), and click **OK**. In the warning message, click **OK**.

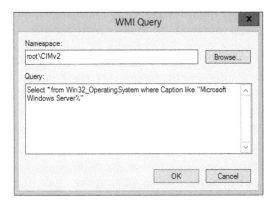

Figure 10-3　Creating a WMI query filter

5. The WMI filter now looks like Figure 10-4. Click **Save**.

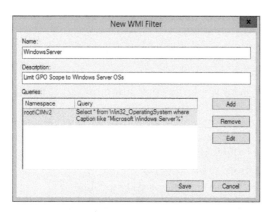

Figure 10-4   A completed WMI filter

6. Click **GPO1** in the Group Policy Objects folder, and in the WMI Filtering drop-down list box, click **WindowsServer** in the list of options. Click **Yes** to confirm.

7. Log on to 411Win8 as **testuser4**, and run **gpupdate**. Log off and log back on. Two things have occurred. First, you no longer go straight to the desktop, and second, you don't see the sign-in information. This is because your computer doesn't meet the criteria for the WMI filter and, therefore, has no access to the GPO.

8. Log off 411Server1, and log back on as **Administrator**. You still see the sign-in information because the OS meets the WMI filter's criteria.

9. To remove the WMI filter, open the Group Policy Management console, click **GPO1** in the Group Policy Objects folder, and in the WMI Filtering list box, click **<none>**. Click **Yes** to confirm.

10. Log off 411Win8, but stay logged on to 411Server1 if you're continuing to the next activity.

Loopback Policy Processing

By default, users are affected by policies in the User Configuration node, and computers are affected by policies in the Computer Configuration node. Furthermore, users are affected by GPOs whose scope they fall within, and the same goes for computers.

Normally, the policies that affect user settings follow users to whatever computer they log on to. However, you might want user policy settings to be based on the GPO within whose scope the computer object falls. To do this, you can use **loopback policy processing**. For example, you have an OU named ConfRoomComputers containing all computer accounts of computers in conference rooms. Perhaps you want standardized desktop settings, such as wallpaper, screen savers, Start screen, and so forth, so that these computers have a consistent look for visitors. All these settings are in the User Configuration node, however, so they can't apply to computer accounts. You don't want all users in the organization to be restricted to these settings when they log on to their own computers. The solution is to enable the "Configure user Group Policy loopback processing mode" policy setting under the Computer Configuration node. After this setting is enabled, all settings in the User Configuration node of the GPO apply to all users who log on to the computer. If you enable loopback policy processing, you have the option to replace the settings normally applied to the user or merge the settings in the GPO with settings normally applied to the user. If there's a conflict, the settings in the GPO take precedence.

To use loopback policy processing in the conference room computers example, you take the following steps:

1. Create a GPO (or edit an existing one), and enable the "Configure user Group Policy loopback processing mode" policy setting in the Computer Configuration\Policies\ Administrative Templates\System\Group Policy node.

2. In the User Configuration node of the GPO, edit policies to set wallpaper, screen saver, and Start screen options.

3. Link the GPO to the ConfRoomComputers OU.

When users log on to a computer in a conference room, they're now subject to the User Configuration policies you set in the GPO linked to the ConfRoomComputers OU. When users log on to any other computer, they're subject to whatever policies normally affect their user accounts.

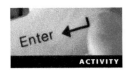

Activity 10-6: Configuring Loopback Policy Processing

Time Required: 25 minutes
Objective: Configure loopback policy processing.

Required Tools and Equipment: 411Server1 and 411Win8
Description: In this activity, you create a WMI filter that limits the scope of a GPO to only computers that have an OS name that begins with Microsoft Windows Server.

1. Log on to 411Server1 as **Administrator,** if necessary.

2. Open the Group Policy Management console, if necessary. Create a GPO named **GPO3,** and open it in the Group Policy Management Editor.

3. Expand **User Configuration, Policies, Administrative Templates,** and configure the following settings:

    Desktop\Remove Recycle Bin icon from desktop: **Enabled**

    Desktop\Desktop\DesktopWallpaper: **Enabled**

    Wallpaper Name: **C:\windows\web\wallpaper\theme1\img1.jpg** (or another image file if you don't have `img1.jpg`)

    Wallpaper Style: **Fill**

4. Link **GPO3** to the **Desktops** OU. Remember that these settings are User Configuration settings, so they don't normally have an effect on computer accounts.

5. Log on to 411Win8 as **testuser1.** Run `gpupdate`, log off, and log back on. The changes you made in GPO3 don't have any effect. The Recycle Bin is still on the desktop, and the wallpaper hasn't changed. Stay logged on to 411Win8.

6. On 411Server1, open **GPO3** in the Group Policy Management Editor, if necessary.

7. Expand **Computer Configuration, Policies, Administrative Templates, System,** and **Group Policy.** Double-click **Configure user Group Policy loopback processing mode.** Click **Enabled,** and in the Mode drop-down list box, click **Merge.** This option allows existing user settings that are normally applied to be applied as long as there's no conflict. Click **OK.**

8. On 411Win8, run `gpupdate`. Log off, and log back on as **testuser1.** The settings made in the User Configuration node of GPO3 should now be applied. The wallpaper has changed, and the Recycle Bin is no longer on the desktop.

9. Unlink **GPO3** from the **Desktops** OU.

10. Log off 411Win8, but stay logged on to 411Server1 if you're continuing to the next activity.

Configuring Group Policy Client Processing

Group Policy is a client/server system. Each Windows OS has a Group Policy client that contacts a domain controller to see whether any GPOs that apply to the computer or user have changed since the last time the client contacted the DC. When Group Policy determines that a GPO should be downloaded, the client activates client-side extensions. A **client-side extension (CSE)** is an extension to the standard group policy client that applies specific types of group policy settings to the client computer. For example, the Security CSE applies policy settings defined in a GPO's Security node, and the Software Installation CSE applies policies defined in the Software Installation node. CSEs are also used to apply group policy preferences.

As you have learned, group policies are processed when Windows boots and when a user logs on. Group policies are processed at these times by using **foreground processing**. Certain policies, such as Software Installation, are processed only during foreground processing. After Windows has booted and a user has logged on, most group policy settings are refreshed periodically with **background processing**.

Group policies are processed only if the client detects that a policy has changed. In addition, some policies aren't processed if the client detects that the network connection is slow. For many policies, you can change the way the client behaves by default. Settings for group policy processing behavior are found in Policies\Administrative Templates\System\Group Policy under both the Computer Configuration and User Configuration nodes. There are three main ways to change the default processing of certain types of policies, discussed in the following sections:

- Slow link processing
- Background processing
- Process even if the Group Policy objects haven't changed

Configuring Slow Link Processing

Processing certain policies across a slow WAN connection might not be desirable. For example, a software installation policy can use quite a lot of bandwidth if a large software package is being downloaded. A slow network link is, by default, a network connection that's less than 500 Kbps. Many types of policies aren't processed across a slow network link by default, including the following:

Slow link detection is a function of the Network Location Awareness (NLA) feature. Slow link estimates occur when a Group Policy client authenticates to a domain controller and determines the network name.

- Disk quota
- Folder redirection
- Internet Explorer maintenance
- Scripts
- Software installation
- Wireless network policies
- Wired network policies
- Most preferences

Administrative Templates policies are always applied because they control slow link processing and other client behavior. Security Settings policies are always applied to ensure that security settings are always in effect.

You might want to change the default behavior of slow link processing. You can do this in a couple of ways:

- *Configure the slow link detection policy*—You can configure the threshold value of what's considered a slow link. The range is between 0 and 4,294,967,200 Kbps; 0 indicates that no links are to be considered slow. If you set the value to 0, all policies are processed without attempting to detect whether the link is slow. The default value is 500 Kbps. You can also specify that wireless WAN (WWAN) connections are always considered slow. A WWAN is a 3G wireless link. To configure slow link detection, go to Policies\Administrative Templates\

System\Group Policy, and enable the "Configure Group Policy slow link detection" policy (see Figure 10-5). This policy is under both Computer Configuration and User Configuration and affects policy settings configured in these sections of a GPO.

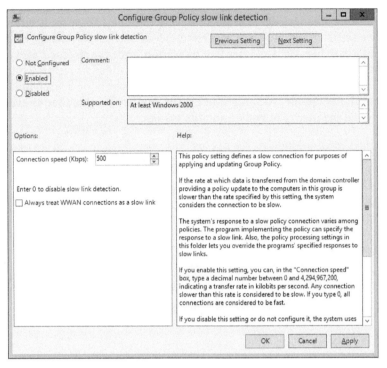

Figure 10-5   Configuring slow link detection

- *Allow slow link processing for selected policies*—The policies that aren't processed by default when a slow link is detected can be configured to allow processing. For example, if you want scripts to be processed even when a slow link is detected, enable the "Configure scripts policy processing" policy found in Policies\Administrative Templates\System\Group Policy (see Figure 10-6).

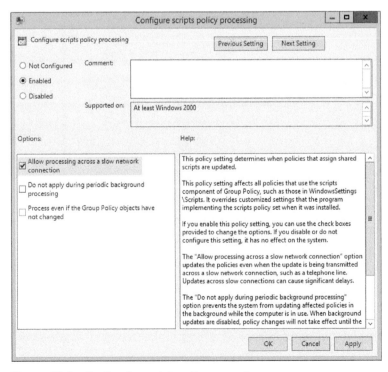

Figure 10-6   Configuring scripts policy processing

Changing Background Processing

After Windows is started, the Computer Configuration node of GPOs affecting the client is refreshed every 90 minutes with a random offset between 0 and 30 minutes. The random offset prevents all computers that were turned on at the same time from refreshing policies simultaneously. In some cases, changes occur immediately, while the computer is running, and in other cases, the policy setting is applied, but the system doesn't reflect the change until the next restart. Likewise, after a user logs on, the User Configuration node is refreshed every 90 minutes with the same random offset period. These settings work for most situations, but you might want certain policies to be applied only when a computer restarts or a user logs on, forgoing the periodic refresh. For example, you might not want a policy change that affects a user's working environment while the user is actively using the system.

 For domain controllers, the refresh period is 5 minutes with no random offset.

You have the option to turn off background processing for several types of policies and preferences, including but not limited to the following (see Figure 10-7):

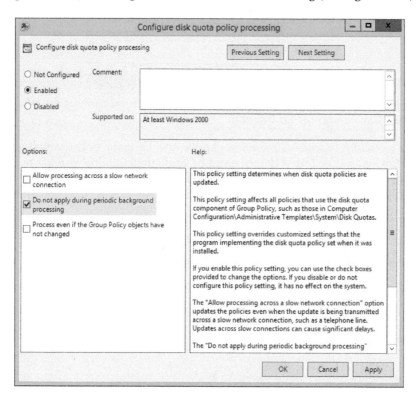

Figure 10-7   Disabling group policy background processing for disk quotas

- Application preference
- Devices preference
- Disk quota policy
- Files and folders preference
- Internet Explorer maintenance policy
- Internet settings preference
- Local users and groups preference

- Network options preference
- Scripts processing
- Wired and wireless policy

For the full list of policies and preferences that can have background processing disabled, look in the Computer Configuration\Policies\Administrative Templates\System\Group Policy node.

Some policies, such as software installation and folder redirection, are never processed in the background. For example, it might be quite surprising to a user if an application is updated or uninstalled while it's in use!

You can also change the background processing interval for computers, domain controllers, and users. The Set Group Policy refresh interval for computers (see Figure 10-8) policy lets you set the refresh interval for computers from 0 to 44,640 minutes and the random offset from 0 to 1440 minutes. There's a similar policy for domain controllers and users.

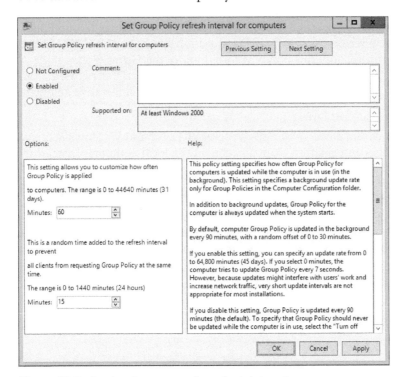

Figure 10-8   Setting the group policy refresh interval

You can turn off all background processing for all computers, domain controllers, and users in the scope of the GPO by enabling "Turn off background refresh of Group Policy." If this policy is enabled, policies are updated only when the computer starts and when the user logs on.

Processing Unchanged Policies

By default, the Group Policy client downloads and processes only policies that have changed. You can force policies and preferences to be processed even if they haven't changed since the last time they were processed. To do so, select the "Process even if the Group Policy objects have not changed" check box (shown earlier in Figure 10-7). This option isn't usually necessary because most settings configured by Group Policy can't be changed by regular users. However, if some users are logging on with administrative rights, they can change some policy settings. By enabling this setting, such as for security policies, you ensure that any settings the user changes are reapplied at the next refresh interval or system start. This setting can also be enabled for software installation policies, so if a user uninstalls an application, it's reinstalled the next time the computer restarts or the user logs on. If this option is set for a preference, it overrides the "Apply once and do not reapply" option in the Common tab of the preference's Properties dialog box.

Synchronous and Asynchronous Processing

Group policy processing can be synchronous or asynchronous. **Synchronous processing** forces group policy processing to finish before certain other system tasks can be performed. For example, during system boot, Computer Configuration policies are processed. If processing occurs synchronously, the user logon prompt isn't displayed until all processing is finished. **Asynchronous processing** allows displaying the user logon prompt while Computer Configuration policies are still being processed. Likewise, if User Configuration policies are processed synchronously, the user doesn't see the desktop until processing is finished. In short, asynchronous processing is better from a user experience standpoint because users don't have to wait as long for processing to finish.

Certain policies, however, require synchronous processing to ensure a consistent computing environment: Software Installation, Folder Redirection, Disk Quotas, and the Drive Mapping preference. After any of these policies are configured, the next system start or user logon might be noticeably slower because of synchronous processing.

When a slow link is detected, you can force asynchronous processing. To do this with policies that usually require synchronous processing, enable the "Change Group Policy processing to run asynchronously when a slow network connection is detected" policy. Like most of the policies discussed in this section, this policy is found under the Group Policy node. You can also force synchronous processing by enabling the "Always wait for the network at computer startup and logon" policy, under Computer Configuration\Policies\Administrative Templates\System\Logon.

Group Policy Caching

Group policy caching, new in Windows Server 2012 R2 and Windows 8.1, is a client-side feature that loads policy information from a cache on the local computer instead of always having to download it from a domain controller. It can speed system startup because the cache is used during synchronous foreground processing, which occurs when the system boots.

Group policy caching is enabled by default on Windows Server 2012 R2 and Windows 8.1 computers. A new policy setting, Configure Group Policy Caching, in the Computer Configuration\Administrative Templates\System\Group Policy path allows you to disable caching and configure some parameters (see Figure 10-9).

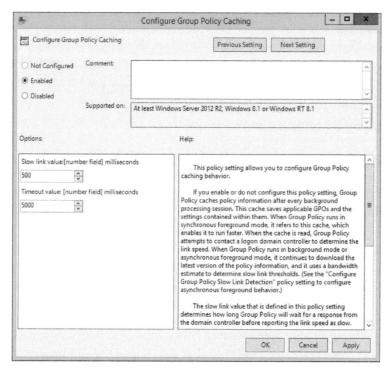

Figure 10-9   Configuring group policy caching

Group policy settings are cached each time background processing takes place. Note that the cache is used only when the system boots, not during background processing, and only GPOs that have caching enabled are saved. Figure 10-9 shows the Configure Group Policy Caching setting. If you enable caching (which is enabled by default, so you need to enable it only if you want to change these parameters or override a higher-precedence GPO that disables it), you can change two timing parameters:

- *Slow link value*—This value specifies the threshold for the response time from a domain controller to consider a link slow. When the group policy cache is read, the client contacts a DC and measures the response time. If the response time is slower than the specified value, the link is considered slow. In this case, only policies with slow link processing enabled are cached.

- *Timeout value*—This value is the maximum time the Group Policy client waits for a response from a DC before determining that there's no network connection to the DC. If a timeout occurs, group policy processing stops until a connection is established.

The group policy cache is on the local computer at %*systemroot*%\ System32\GroupPolicy\Datastore.

Forcing Group Policy Updates

As you know, you don't need to wait for a system reboot, user logon, or refresh interval to update group policies on a client computer. By now, you're quite familiar with the gpupdate.exe command you run on the client at a command prompt. However, additional options available with the gpupdate.exe command haven't been discussed yet. The following list describes this command and its options:

- *No options*—If you just type gpupdate and press Enter, the command's default behavior takes place: The Group Policy client contacts a DC, and then downloads and applies only changed policies for both the Computer Configuration and User Configuration nodes of all GPOs applicable to the computer and user account.

- /force—All settings from all applicable GPOs are reapplied, even if they haven't changed.

- /wait: *value*—Specifies the number of seconds the command should wait for policy processing to finish before returning to the command prompt. The default is 600 seconds. A value of 0 means don't wait. (You're returned to the command prompt immediately, but processing continues in the background.) A value of -1 means wait indefinitely. Even if the wait time is exceeded, group policy processing continues in the background.

- /logoff—The user is logged off after policy processing is finished.

- /boot—The computer restarts after policy processing is finished.

- /sync—Causes synchronous processing during the next computer restart or user logon.

- /target: Computer *or* User—You can specify that you want only computer or user policy settings to be updated.

Remote Group Policy Updates   The gpupdate.exe command is fine if you're simply testing group policies, and both the server where you're making changes and the client you're testing changes on are convenient. However, suppose you make an important policy change that you want a number of clients or even a single remote client to download and apply immediately? Starting with Windows Server 2012, you can cause a group policy refresh remotely on Windows Vista and later clients by using the GPMC or the PowerShell cmdlet Invoke-GPUpdate.

10

Using the GPMC, you can force a group policy refresh for all computers in an Active Directory OU and all logged-on users of those computers. Simply right-click an OU containing the computer accounts on which you want the refresh to occur and click Group Policy Update. All computers in the OU and child OUs are refreshed. This option isn't available on the domain node or the Computers folder, so the target computer accounts must be in an OU. When you force a group policy update from the GPMC, the following occurs:

1. A list of computers in the OU is created.

2. A list of users currently logged on to each computer is created.

3. A scheduled task that runs `gpupdate /force` is created on each computer for each logged-on user. The tasks are created with a random 10-minute offset to prevent all computers in the OU from initiating the update at the same time.

4. After the random delay period, users who are logged on see a command prompt open, and the `gpupdate /force` command runs.

The `Invoke-GPUpdate` PowerShell cmdlet performs similarly, except you specify a computer rather than an OU to update. By default, only changed policies are applied, but you can use the `-force` option to reapply all settings. In addition, you can cause the update to occur immediately or after a random delay specified in minutes. By using a pipe with the `Get-ADComputer` command, you can update several computers at once, including those in the Computers folder. The following two commands show examples of using `Invoke-GPUpdate`. The first example updates a single computer, and the second example forces updates on all computers in the Computers folder:

```
Invoke-GPUpdate -Computer 411Win8

Get-ADComputer -filter * -Searchbase "cn=computers,
  dc=411Dom1,dc=local" | foreach{ Invoke-GPUpdate
  -computer $_.name -force}
```

Configuring the Firewall for Remote Group Policy Updates   Target client computers must have the following inbound firewall rules enabled on the domain profile for a remote group policy update to be successful:

- Remote Scheduled Tasks Management (RPC)
- Remote Scheduled Tasks Management (RPC-EPMAP)
- Windows Management Instrumentations (WMI-In)

You can configure the firewall with the Group Policy tool or on the client computer. If you use Group Policy, a Starter GPO named Group Policy Remote Update Firewall Ports is available that already has the firewall settings configured correctly.

Activity 10-7: Using Remote Group Policy Updates

Time Required: 25 minutes
Objective: Configure the firewall and do a remote group policy update.

Required Tools and Equipment: 411Server1 and 411Win8
Description: Configure the firewall for a remote group policy update on 411Win8.

1. Log on to 411Server1 as **Administrator**, if necessary. Log on to 411Win8 as **Administrator**.

2. On 411Win8, open the Network and Sharing Center, and click **Windows Firewall** at the lower left.

3. In the Windows Firewall window, click **Advanced settings**. In the Windows Firewall with Advanced Security window, click **Inbound Rules**.

4. In the Actions pane, click **Filter by Profile** and click to select **Filter by Domain Profile**. Right-click the following settings and click **Enable Rule** for each one: **Remote Scheduled Tasks Management (RPC)**, **Remote Scheduled Tasks Management (RPC-EPMAP)**, and **Windows Management Instrumentations (WMI-In)**. Close all open windows.

5. On 411Server1, open the Group Policy Management console, if necessary. Right-click the **Desktops** OU and click **Group Policy Update**. When you're prompted to confirm, click **Yes**.

6. In the Remote Group Policy update results window, you should see 411Win8 in the list of computers (see Figure 10-10). Click **Close**. On 411Win8, a command prompt window opens after a while, and the gpupdate command runs.

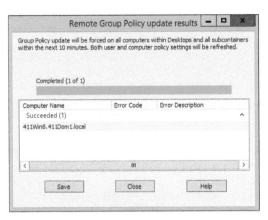

Remote Group Policy update results

Group Policy update will be forced on all computers within Desktops and all subcontainers within the next 10 minutes. Both user and computer policy settings will be refreshed.

Completed (1 of 1)

Computer Name	Error Code	Error Description
Succeeded (1)		
411Win8.411Dom1.local		

Save   Close   Help

Figure 10-10   Results of a remote group policy update

7. On 411Server1, open a PowerShell prompt. Type **Invoke-GPUpdate -Computer 411Win8 -RandomDelayInMinutes 0** and press **Enter**. A command prompt window opens immediately on 411Win8. On 411Server1, close the PowerShell prompt.

8. Log off 411Win8, but stay logged on to 411Server1 if you're continuing to the next activity.

Group Policy Results and Modeling

No matter how well you understand group policy processing and inheritance, determining exactly what GPOs and policy settings are applied to an object can be difficult. Windows includes the following tools to help you determine which policies are applied to a user or computer and which GPO supplied the policy. The information supplied by these tools can help you troubleshoot group policy processing:

- *Group Policy Results*—This wizard built into the GPMC creates a report to show administrators which policy settings apply to a user, computer, or both. To use this wizard, right-click the Group Policy Results node in the GPMC and click Group Policy Results Wizard. You have the option to display policy results for the current computer or another computer, and you can select which user to report on from a list of users who have logged on to the target computer. The wizard can show results only of policies that have already been applied to the computer or user. After the wizard finishes, the report has three tabs:

  o Summary: Shows information about which GPOs affect the specified computer and user. In addition, the report shows whether a fast or slow link was detected (see Figure 10-11). You can right-click this window and click Print or Save Report (which saves it in an HTML or XML file).

NOTE

In Figure 10-11, you see a warning and an alert message that says "AD/SYSVOL Version Mismatch." This is a known problem and can be solved on Windows Server 2012 R2 and Windows 8.1 machines by installing update 2919394. See *http://support.microsoft.com/kb/2866345* for more information.

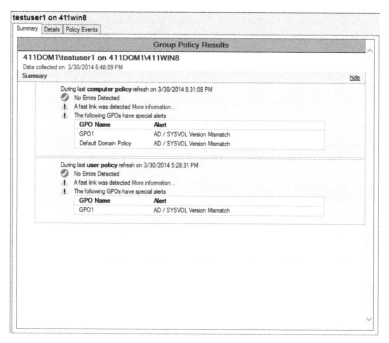

Figure 10-11   The Summary tab in Group Policy Results

○ Details: Displays information about the computer and Group Policy components, including when policies were last processed. All defined settings that were applied to the computer and user are listed. The Winning GPO column shows which GPO the setting came from (see Figure 10-12). You also see a list of GPOs that were denied, why they were denied, and the results of WMI filters. As with the Summary tab, you can right-click to print or save the report.

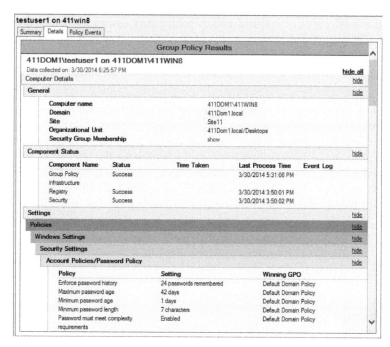

Figure 10-12   The Details tab in Group Policy Results

○ Policy Events: Displays all events in Event Viewer that are generated by group policies. To see the events on a remote computer, all three Remote Event Log Management rules must be enabled for inbound connections on the remote computer.

- `gpresult.exe`—This command-line version of the Group Policy Results Wizard outputs a report onscreen, or you can specify the name of a file with an `.html` extension. To produce a summary report for the 411Win8 computer and the testuser1 user, enter the following at a command prompt:

```
gpresult /s 411Win8 /user testuser1 /r
```

- *Group Policy Modeling*—This is a what-if tool for group policies. Like Group Policy Results, it's a wizard built into the GPMC that shows administrators which policy settings would apply to a computer and/or user account if it were moved to a different container. Essentially, the report shows which policy settings are in effect for a user whose account is placed in a particular OU and whose computer is placed in a particular OU. You can select user and computer membership in security groups so that GPO filtering is taken into account. In addition, you can select options for slow link processing and loopback processing and specify WMI filters. Group Policy Modeling produces a report similar to Group Policy Results with Summary and Details tabs. Instead of a Policy Events tab, the third tab, Query, summarizes the what-if choices that were made to produce the report.

- *Resultant Set of Policy (RSoP) snap-in*—This MMC snap-in functions much like Group Policy Results and Group Policy Modeling. RSoP has two modes: logging and planning. Logging mode produces a database of policy results that you browse similarly to using the Group Policy Management Editor. Planning mode is similar to Group Policy Modeling, producing a database of what-if results based on the same criteria you can choose from the Group Policy Modeling Wizard.

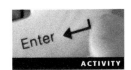

Activity 10-8: Using Group Policy Results and Group Policy Modeling

Time Required: 25 minutes
Objective: Use the Group Policy Results and Group Policy Modeling tools.

Required Tools and Equipment: 411Server1 and 411Win8
Description: In this activity, you use the Group Policy Results Wizard to see how user and computer accounts are affected by group policy settings. Then you use the Group Policy Modeling Wizard to create a "what-if" scenario to see how accounts are affected if they're moved to a different OU.

1. Log on to 411Server1 as **Administrator**, and open the Group Policy Management console, if necessary. Make sure 411Win8 is running, but you don't need to log on.

2. Link **GPO3** to the **TestOU2** OU.

3. Right-click **Group Policy Results** and click **Group Policy Results Wizard**. In the welcome window, click **Next**.

4. In the Computer Selection window, click the **Another computer** option button, and type **411Win8** in the text box. Click **Next**.

5. In the User Selection window, click **411DOM1\testuser1**, and then click **Next**.

6. In the Summary of Selections window, click **Next**, and then click **Finish**.

7. In the report generated in the right pane, examine the Summary and Details tabs. In the Details tab, click the **show all** link to see all applied settings. Click the **Policy Events** tab. You won't see the events unless you enable all three Remote Event Log Management rules in Windows Firewall on 411Win8.

8. In the left pane of the Group Policy Management console under Group Policy Results, you see a new icon named "testuser1 on 411Win8." You can right-click the icon to save the report, rerun the query, and see an advanced view. Right-click **testuser1 on 411Win8** and click **Advanced View**. The policy information opens in the RSoP snap-in. Close the RSoP console. When prompted to save the console, click **No**.

9. Right-click **Group Policy Modeling** and click **Group Policy Modeling Wizard**. In the welcome window, click **Next**.

10. In the Domain Controller Selection window, click the **This domain controller** option button, and then click **Next**.

11. In the User and Computer Selection window, click the **User** option button, and type **411Dom1\testuser1**. Click the **Computer** option button, type **411Dom1\411Win8** (see Figure 10-13), and click **Next**.

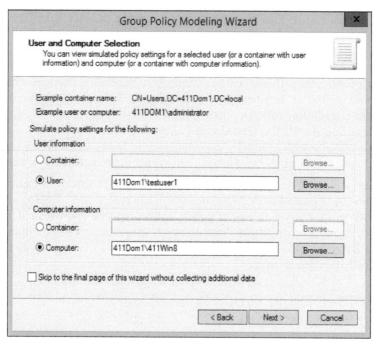

Figure 10-13   Selecting the user and computer

12. In the Advanced Simulation Options window (see Figure 10-14), accept the defaults, and click **Next**.

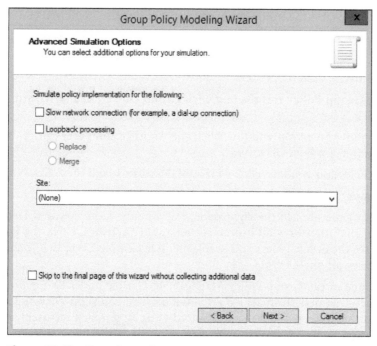

Figure 10-14   The Advanced Simulation Options window

13. In the Alternate Active Directory Paths window, in the User location text box, change TestOU1 to **TestOU2**. This change simulates the policies that would be applied to testuser1 if the user were in the TestOU2 OU. Click **Next**.

14. Click **Next** in the User Security Groups window, the Computer Security Groups window, the WMI Filters for Users window, and the WMI Filters for Computers window.

15. In the Summary of Selections window, click **Next**, and then click **Finish**.

16. The report is displayed in the right pane. Click the **Details** tab, and scroll down until you see User Details. Under the General section, notice that the User container shows 411Dom1.local/TestOU2 to indicate that the results are based on testuser1 being located in TestOU2. Look farther down and see GPO1 and GPO3 listed under Applied GPOs.

17. Scroll to the top of the report, and click **show all**. Scroll down again, and you'll see the policies that would be applied by GPO3 if testuser1 were in the TestOU2 OU.

18. Stay logged on to 411Server1 if you're continuing to the next activity.

Managing GPOs

You know how to create and link GPOs with the GPMC, and you have learned about group policy processing and inheritance. The following sections discuss GPO backup and restore, GPO import and copy, GPO migration, and GPO delegation.

GPO Backup and Restore

In a large, complex network, with many different policy needs for users, servers, and workstations, configuring and testing GPOs often takes many hours. Thankfully, Windows has a solution for backing up and restoring GPOs in case disaster strikes: GPO backups. GPO backups are also useful if you need to revert to an older version of a GPO or if you delete a GPO accidentally. For example, if many changes are made to a GPO and the changes cause unexpected problems, you might save time by restoring an older version instead of trying to undo the changes.

When you back up a GPO, the policy settings are backed up, but so are the security filtering settings, delegation settings, and WMI filter links. What's not backed up are the WMI filter files associated with the WMI links, IPsec policies, and GPO container links. Backing up a GPO is a simple three-step process:

1. In the GPMC, right-click the GPO in the Group Policy Objects folder (because you can't back up a GPO from the shortcut link to an Active Directory container) and click Back Up.

2. Select (or create) a folder where the GPO should be stored.

3. Enter a description of the GPO, if you want, and click Back Up.

Multiple GPOs can be stored in the same folder, so you don't need to create a folder each time you back up a GPO. The folder where you store GPO backups should be secure and backed up by a regular system backup routine. You can also right-click the Group Policy Objects folder and select options to back up all GPOs and manage backups.

The procedure for restoring a GPO varies, as follows:

- *Restore a previous version*—If the settings of a backed-up GPO have been changed and you need to revert to an older version, right-click the GPO in the Group Policy Objects folder, and click Restore from Backup. All policy and security settings in the current GPO are replaced by the backup GPO's settings.

- *Restore a deleted GPO*—Right-click the Group Policy Objects folder and click Manage Backups to open the Manage Backups dialog box (see Figure 10-15). You can select which GPO you want to restore, view a backed-up GPO's settings, or delete a backed-up GPO. Multiple versions of backed-up GPOs are listed by default, or you can specify seeing only the latest version of each GPO.

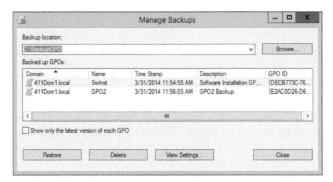

Figure 10-15   Restoring a deleted GPO

- *Import settings*—You can import settings from a backed-up GPO to an existing GPO by right-clicking the GPO and clicking Import Settings. This action is similar to restoring a GPO, except the existing GPO need not be the same GPO as the backed-up GPO. As with a GPO restore, all existing settings in the current GPO are deleted.

GPO Copy and Paste   If you simply want to copy the settings of a GPO into a new GPO, you can do so using the following steps from GPMC:

1. Right-click a GPO in the Group Policy Objects folder and click Copy.

2. Right-click the Group Policy Objects folder.

3. Click Paste. You're asked whether to use the default permissions for the new GPO or preserve the existing permissions of the copied GPO. Make your choice and click OK.

4. Click OK in the progress dialog box after the copy is finished. The new GPO is named "Copy of *OriginalGPOName*." For example, if you copied GPO1, the new GPO is named "Copy of GPO1."

5. Rename the copied GPO by right-clicking it and clicking Rename.

Resetting Default GPOs   Making changes to the two default GPOs (Default Domain Policy and Default Domain Controller Policy) isn't recommended. However, if you do make changes and need to revert to the original settings, you can do so without using a backup and restore operation. You can use the command-line program dcgpofix.exe to reset settings for either or both default GPOs. This command also resets permissions and any existing security or WMI filters:

- dcgpofix—Resets both the Default Domain Policy and the Default Domain Controllers Policy

- dcgpofix /target:DC—Resets the Default Domain Controllers Policy

- dcgpofix /target:domain—Resets the Default Domain Policy

Activity 10-9: Backing Up and Restoring a GPO

Time Required: 10 minutes

Objective: Back up and restore a GPO.

Required Tools and Equipment: 411Server1

Description: In this activity, you use PowerShell cmdlets to back up and restore a GPO.

1. Log on to 411Server1 as **Administrator**, and open the Group Policy Management console, if necessary.

2. Create a directory named **C:\backupgpo** to store backed-up GPOs.

3. Open a PowerShell prompt. Type `Backup-GPO -Name GPO1 -Path C:\backupgpo` and press **Enter**.

4. In the Group Policy Management console, open **GPO1** in the Group Policy Management Editor.

5. Expand **Computer Configuration, Policies, Windows Settings, Security Settings, Local Policies,** and **User Rights Assignment.** Double-click the **Add workstations to domain** policy.

6. Click **Define these policy settings.** Click the **Add User or Group** button, and type **Domain Users** in the User and group names text box. Click **OK** twice, and close the Group Policy Management Editor.

7. In the PowerShell window, type `Restore-GPO -Name GPO1 -Path C:\backupgpo` and press **Enter**.

8. In the Group Policy Management console, open **GPO1** in the Group Policy Management Editor.

9. Expand **Computer Configuration, Policies, Windows Settings, Security Settings, Local Policies,** and **User Rights Assignment.** Double-click the **Add workstations to domain** policy.

10. Verify the policy has been restored to its original setting, Not Defined.

11. Shut down or log off 411Server1.

GPO Migration

You might need to migrate GPOs from one domain to another for a variety of reasons. For example, you have a multidomain environment, and two domains have similar policy requirements. After perfecting the GPOs in one domain, you can migrate them to be used in the other domain. Migration is also useful when you have set up a test environment that's similar to one of your production domains. You can configure and test a GPO in the test environment thoroughly, and then migrate it to the production domain.

GPOs can be migrated across domains in the same or different forests by adding the domain to the GPMC. To add a domain in the same forest, right-click the Domains node in the left pane of the GPMC and click Show Domains to open the dialog box shown in Figure 10-16. Then select the domains you want to add to the GPMC.

Figure 10-16   Selecting domains to add to the GPMC

To add a domain from a different forest, right-click the Group Policy Management node in the left pane of the GPMC and click Add Forest. Then enter the name of the domain in the forest that you want to add.

When you have multiple domains in the GPMC, you can simply copy and paste a GPO from the source domain's Group Policy Objects folder to the target domain's Group Policy Objects folder. When you click Paste in the target folder, the Cross-Domain Copying Wizard starts. It gives you the option to use default permissions or preserve existing permissions on the GPO and translates any security principals or UNC paths in the GPO. Recall that security principals are assigned in policies such as User Rights Assignment and Restricted Groups, and UNC paths are used in policies such as Folder Redirection, Software installation, and Scripts. This information must be modified or translated during the migration process.

A second method for migrating GPOs uses the backup and import procedure. The biggest difference between these two methods is that the copy-and-paste method creates a new GPO, and the backup and import procedure overwrites settings in an existing GPO in the target domain.

Configuring a Migration Table If you're migrating several GPOs from one domain to another, you might want to use a migration table to map security principals and UNC paths. A **migration table** is a list of security principals and UNC paths in a GPO that can be mapped to the security principals and UNC paths in the destination domain (see Figure 10-17). The migration table can then be used when copying a GPO from one domain to another.

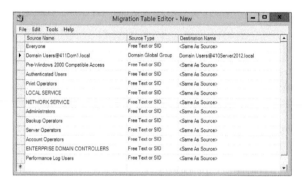

Figure 10-17 The Migration Table Editor

You create a migration table by right-clicking the Domains node in the GPMC and clicking Open Migration Table Editor or using the Cross-Domain Copying Wizard. In the Migration Table Editor, click Tools, and then choose Populate from GPO or Populate from Backup. All security principals and UNC paths used in the selected GPO are listed, as shown in Figure 10-17. By default, the Destination Name column is set to "<Same As Source>." You change this column to translate information, as in the second entry in this figure. Special identities and built-in groups don't need to be translated.

GPO Management Delegation

The possible permissions for GPO delegation depend on whether you're working with the GPO or the target the GPO is linked to. Eight possible permissions can be applied to GPOs and the container objects they're linked to through delegation:

- *Create GPOs*—This permission applies only to the Group Policy Objects folder where you can find all GPOs in the GPMC. When you click the Group Policy Objects folder and click the Delegation tab in the right pane, you can view, add, and remove security principals who are allowed to create GPOs in the domain (see Figure 10-18). By default, Domain Admins, Group Policy Creator Owners, and the System special identity have this permission.

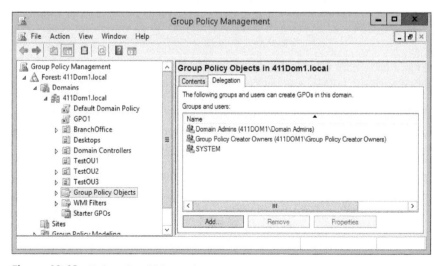

Figure 10-18 Delegating GPO creation

- *Link GPOs*—This permission can be set on sites, domains, and OUs and determines who can link or unlink a GPO to or from the container. Administrators, Domain Admins, Enterprise Admins, and the System special identity are granted this permission by default.

- *Perform Group Policy Modeling analyses*—This permission is set on domains and OUs and determines who can run the GPO Modeling Wizard (discussed in "Group Policy Results and Modeling" earlier in this chapter) on the specified container. The default users are the same as for the Link GPOs permission.

- *Read Group Policy Results data*—This permission is set on domains and OUs and determines who can run the Group Policy Results Wizard (discussed in "Group Policy Results and Modeling" earlier in this chapter) on users and/or computers. The default users are the same as for the Link GPOs permission.

- *Read*—This permission is set on GPOs; users with this permission can view settings and back up a GPO. By default, the Enterprise Domain Controllers universal group has this permission for all GPOs.

- *Read (from Security Filtering)*—This permission is used in group policy filtering. By default, the Authenticated Users group has this permission for all GPOs. It includes both the Read and Apply Group Policy permission and is generally set in the Scope tab of a GPO's Properties dialog box.

- *Edit settings, delete, modify security*—This permission is set on GPOs and determines who can edit, change status on, back up, delete, and change security on a GPO. By default, Domain Admins, Enterprise Admins, and the System special identity are granted this permission.

- *Edit Settings*—With this permission, security principals can change existing settings, import settings, and enable or disable a GPO. No users are granted this permission by default.

10

To configure delegation on a GPO, click the GPO in the GPMC and click the Delegation tab. You can add users and groups from the Delegation tab or click the Advanced button to add specific Allow and Deny permissions. The Advanced button opens the familiar DACL you have used to configure file and folder permissions.

PowerShell Cmdlets for Managing GPOs

A number of PowerShell cmdlets, described in Table 10-2, are available for managing GPOs. As with all PowerShell cmdlets, to find more information on using a cmdlet, type `Get-Help` *cmdletName* `-detailed` at a PowerShell prompt (replacing *cmdletName* with the name of the cmdlet).

Table 10-2   PowerShell cmdlets for managing GPOs

Cmdlet	Function	Example
`Backup-GPO`	Backs up one GPO or all the GPOs in a domain	`Backup-GPO -All -Path C:\BackupGPOs`
`Copy-GPO`	Copies the settings from an existing GPO and creates a new GPO with these settings	`Copy-GPO -SourceName GPO1 -TargetName NewGPO1`
`Get-GPO`	Gets information about one GPO or all GPOs in the domain	`Get-GPO -All`
`Get-GPResultantSetOfPolicy`	Gets the RSoP information for a user, computer, or both and saves it to a file	`Get-GPResultantSetOfPolicy -ReportType xml -Path C:\GPReports\RSoPReport.xml`
`Import-GPO`	Imports settings from a backed-up GPO to an existing GPO	`Import-GPO -BackupGPOName GPO1 -TargetName GPO2 -Path C:\BackupGPOs`
`New-GPLink`	Links a GPO to a site, domain, or OU	`New-GPLink -Name GPO1 -Target "ou=Desktops,dc=411Dom1,dc=Local"`
`New-GPO`	Creates a GPO	`New-GPO -Name GPO5`
`Remove-GPLink`	Deletes a GPO link	`Remove-GPLink -Name GPO1 -Target "ou=Desktops,dc=411Dom1,dc=Local"`

(continues)

Cmdlet	Function	Example
Remove-GPO	Deletes a GPO	Remove-GPO -Name GPO5
Rename-GPO	Renames a GPO	Rename-GPO -Name TestGPO -TargetName ScriptsGPO
Restore-GPO	Restores one GPO or all GPOs in the domain from GPO backup files	Restore-GPO -Name GPO1 -Path C:\BackupGPOs
Set-GPLink	Sets GPO link properties, such as enabled, disabled, enforced, and precedence order	Set-GPLink -Name GPO1 -Target "ou=Desktops,dc=411Dom1,dc=Local" -Enforced Yes
Set-GPPermission	Sets permissions for a security principal to a GPO or to all GPOs	Set-GPPermission -Name GPO1 -TargetName "Domain Users" -TargetType Group -PermissionLevel GpoRead
Get-Command -module GroupPolicy	Displays a list of all group policy–related cmdlets	

© 2015 Cengage Learning®

Chapter Summary

- Group policy processing can be confusing because there are so many exceptions to normal processing and inheritance behavior. When you configure and link a GPO to an Active Directory container, you need to be aware of how that GPO will affect the objects in the container and subcontainers.

- GPO scope defines which objects are affected by the settings in a GPO. GPOs are applied in this order: local computer, site, domain, and OU. When OUs are nested, the GPO linked to the OU nested the deepest takes precedence over all other GPOs.

- There are two main ways to change default GPO inheritance: blocking inheritance and using GPO enforcement.

- There are two types of GPO filtering: security filtering and Windows Management Instrumentation (WMI) filtering. Security filtering uses permissions to restrict objects from accessing a GPO. WMI filtering uses queries to select a group of computers based on certain attributes, and then applies or doesn't apply policies based on the query's results.

- If you enable loopback policy processing, all settings in the User Configuration node of the GPO apply to all users who log on to the computer.

- Group Policy is a client/server system. Each Windows OS has a Group Policy client that contacts a domain controller to see whether any GPOs that apply to the computer or user have changed since the last time the client contacted the DC.

- After Windows is started, the Computer Configuration node of GPOs affecting the client is refreshed every 90 minutes with a random offset between 0 and 30 minutes.

- Group policy processing can be synchronous or asynchronous. Synchronous processing forces group policy processing to finish before certain other system tasks can be performed. Asynchronous processing allows displaying the user logon prompt while Computer Configuration policies are still being processed.

- Group policy caching is a client-side feature that loads policy information from a cache on the local computer instead of always having to download it from a domain controller.

- Using the GPMC, you can force a group policy refresh for all computers in an Active Directory OU and all logged-on users of those computers.

- Group Policy Results is a wizard built into the GPMC that creates a report to show administrators which policy settings apply to a user, computer, or both. Group Policy Modeling is a what-if tool for group policies.

- When you back up a GPO, the policy settings are backed up, but so are the security filtering settings, delegation settings, and WMI filter links. What's not backed up are the WMI filter files associated with the WMI links, IPsec policies, and GPO container links.

- You might need to migrate GPOs from one domain to another for a variety of reasons. After perfecting GPOs in one domain, you can migrate them to be used in another domain.

- The possible permissions for GPO delegation depend on whether you're working with the GPO or the target the GPO is linked to. Eight possible permissions can be applied to GPOs and the container objects they're linked to through delegation.

Key Terms

asynchronous processing   A type of group policy processing that allows a user to log on and see the desktop while policies are still being processed.

background processing   Periodic group policy processing that occurs after a computer is running or a user is logged on.

client-side extension (CSE)   An extension to the standard group policy client that applies specific types of group policy settings to client computers.

foreground processing   Group policy processing that occurs when the system boots or a user logs on.

GPO enforcement   A setting on a GPO that forces inheritance of settings on all child objects in the GPO's scope, even if a GPO with conflicting settings is linked to a container at a deeper level.

GPO filtering   A method used to change the default inheritance settings of a GPO.

GPO scope   A combination of GPO linking, inheritance, and filtering that defines which objects are affected by the settings in a GPO.

group policy caching   A client-side feature that loads policy information from a cache on the local computer instead of having to always download it from a domain controller.

loopback policy processing   A Group Policy setting that applies user settings based on the GPO whose scope the logon computer (the one the user is logging on to) falls into.

migration table   A list of security principals and UNC paths in a GPO that can be mapped to the security principals and UNC paths in a destination domain a GPO is being copied to.

security filtering   A type of GPO filtering that uses permissions to restrict objects from accessing a GPO.

synchronous processing   A type of group policy processing that forces the processing to finish before certain other system tasks can be performed.

WMI filtering   A type of GPO filtering that uses queries to select a group of computers based on certain attributes, and then applies or doesn't apply policies based on the query's results.

Review Questions

1. Which of the following represents the correct order in which GPOs are applied to an object that falls within the GPO's scope?

   a.   Site, domain, OU, local GPOs

   b.   Local GPOs, domain, site, OU

   c.   Domain, site, OU, local GPOs

   d.   Local GPOs, site, domain, OU

2. Objects in an OU with the Block Inheritance option set are affected by a domain-linked GPO with the Enforced option set. True or False?

3. You have created a GPO named RestrictU and linked it to the Operations OU (containing 30 users) with link order 3. RestrictU sets several policies in the User Configuration node. After a few days, you realize the Operations OU has three users who should be exempt from the restrictions in this GPO. You need to make sure these three users are exempt from RestrictU's settings, but all other policy settings are still in effect for them. What's the best way to proceed?

   a. Move the three users to a new OU. Create a GPO with settings suitable for the three users, and link it to the new OU.

   b. Create an OU under Operations, and move the three users to this new OU. Create a GPO, and link it to this new OU. Configure the new OU to block inheritance of the RestrictU GPO.

   c. Create a global group, and add the three users as members. Configure GPO security filtering so that the global group is denied access to the GPO.

   d. Set the Enforced option on RestrictU with a WMI filter that excludes the three user accounts.

4. None of the computers in an OU seem to be getting computer policies from the GPO linked to the OU, but users in the OU are getting user policies from this GPO. Which of the following is a possible reason that computer policies in the GPO aren't affecting the computers? (Choose all that apply.)

   a. The GPO link is disabled.

   b. The Computer Configuration settings are disabled.

   c. The computer accounts have Deny Read permission.

   d. The OU has the Block Inheritance option set.

5. You need to move some user and computer accounts in Active Directory, but before you do, you want to know how these accounts will be affected by the new group policies they'll be subject to. What can you do?

   a. Run `secedit.exe` with the planning option.

   b. Run Group Policy Modeling.

   c. Run Group Policy Results.

   d. Run RSoP in logging mode.

6. You don't have policies that force settings for the look of users' computer desktops. Each user's chosen desktop settings are applied from his or her roaming profile to any computer he or she logs on to. You think it's important for users to have this choice, but you'd like a consistent look for computers used for product demonstrations to customers. What's the best way to do this without affecting users when they log on to other computers?

   a. Configure desktop policies in the Computer Configuration node of a GPO, and link this GPO to the OU containing the demonstration computers.

   b. Configure loopback policy processing in Computer Configuration. Configure the desktop settings in User Configuration, and link the GPO to the OU containing the demonstration computers.

   c. Create a user named Demo. Configure Demo's desktop settings, and use only this user account to log on to demonstration computers.

   d. Create a GPO with a startup script that configures desktop settings suitable for demonstration computers when these computers are started. Link the GPO to the OU containing the demonstration computers. Instruct users to restart demonstration computers before using them.

7. You want to create policies in a new GPO that affects only computers with Windows 7 installed. You don't want to reorganize your computer accounts to do this, and you want computers that are upgraded to Windows 8 to fall out of the GPO's scope automatically. What can you do?

   a. For each policy, use selective application to specify Windows 7 as the OS.

   b. Create a new OU, place all computer accounts representing computers with Windows 7 installed in this OU, and link the GPO to this OU.

   c. Create a group called Win7Computers. Place all computer accounts representing computers with Windows 7 installed in this group, and use this group in a security filter on the GPO. Link the GPO to the domain.

   d. Configure a WMI filter on the GPO that specifies Windows 7 as the OS. Link the GPO to the domain.

8. When a policy setting in Computer Configuration and User Configuration in the same GPO conflict, the Computer Configuration policy setting takes precedence. True or False?

9. An OU structure in your domain has one OU per department, and all the computer and user accounts are in their respective OUs. You have configured several GPOs defining computer and user policies and linked the GPOs to the domain. A group of managers in the Marketing Department need different policies from the rest of the Marketing Department users and computers, but you don't want to change the top-level OU structure. Which of the following GPO processing features are you most likely to use?

   a. Block inheritance

   b. GPO enforcement

   c. WMI filtering

   d. Loopback processing

10. You have created a GPO that sets certain security settings on computers. You need to make sure these settings are applied to all computers in the domain. Which of the following GPO processing features are you most likely to use?

   a. Block inheritance

   b. GPO enforcement

   c. WMI filtering

   d. Loopback processing

11. You have a branch office connected to the main office with a sometimes unreliable and slow WAN link. Users are complaining about long logon times. Which Group Policy client feature are you most likely to configure to solve the problem?

   a. Synchronous processing

   b. Background processing

   c. Slow link processing

   d. Remote update processing

12. You have just made changes to a GPO that you want to take effect as soon as possible on several user and computer accounts in the Sales OU. Most of the users in this OU are currently logged on to their computers. There are about 50 accounts. What's the best way to get these accounts updated with the new policies as soon as possible?

   a. Configure a script preference that runs `gpupdate` the next time the user logs off.

   b. Configure the GPO to perform foreground processing immediately.

   c. Run the `Get-ADComputer` and `Invoke-GPUpdate` PowerShell cmdlets.

   d. Use the `gpupdate /target:Sales /force` command.

13. You have just finished configuring a GPO that modifies several settings on computers in the Operations OU and linked the GPO to the OU. You right-click the Operations OU and click Group Policy Update. You check on a few computers in the Operations department and find that the policies haven't been applied. On one computer, you run `gpupdate`, and the policies are applied correctly. What's a likely reason the policies weren't applied to all computers when you tried to update them remotely?

    a. The Computer Configuration node of the GPO is disabled.

    b. A security filter that blocks the computer accounts has been set.

    c. The Operations OU has Block Inheritance set.

    d. You need to configure the firewall on the computers.

14. You want to create an HTML report that shows which policies and GPOs are applied to a particular user and computer. Which command should you use?

    a. `gpupdate`

    b. `gpresult`

    c. `rsop`

    d. `Invoke-GPReport`

15. When you restore a GPO, it's automatically linked to any containers it was linked to at the time you performed the backup. True or False?

16. A junior administrator deleted a GPO accidentally, but you had backed it up. What should you do to restore the deleted GPO?

    a. Right click the GPO backup file in File Explorer and click Restore.

    b. Open the Active Directory Recycle Bin, right-click the GPO object, and click Restore.

    c. Right-click the Group Policy Objects folder and click Manage Backups.

    d. Create a GPO, right-click the new GPO, and click Restore from Backup.

17. You were hired to fix problems with group policies at a company. You open the GPMC to look at the default GPOs and see that extensive changes have been made to both. You want to restore settings to a baseline so that you know where to start. What should you do?

    a. Delete the default GPOs and create new GPOs with the same names.

    b. Run `gpofix`.

    c. Create a domain and use GPO migration.

    d. Run `gpupdate /revert`.

18. You manage a multidomain forest with domains named DomainA and DomainB. You want to use the GPOs from DomainA in DomainB without having to reconfigure all GPOs. What do you need to configure?

    a. Migration table

    b. GPO backup and restore

    c. Delegation

    d. RSoP

19. What kind of group policy processing always occurs when a user is logged on to the computer at the time a group policy refresh occurs?

    a. Foreground processing

    b. Slow link processing

    c. Background processing

    d. Selective processing

20. Users who log on from a branch office connected to the DC via a slow WAN link are complaining of slow logon times whenever you assign applications via group policies. What can you do to speed their logons?

   a. Perform a remote group policy update.

   b. Disable group policy caching.

   c. Configure synchronous processing when a slow link is detected.

   d. Configure asynchronous processing when a slow link is detected.

Case Projects

CASE PROJECTS

Case Project 10-1: Dealing with Group Policies at a Branch Office

You have set up a branch office with 50 computers. The office is connected to the main office, where all the DCs are located, via a 128 Kbps ISDN connection. When you return to the main office, you run Group Policy Results on several users and computers in the branch office. You discover that several policies aren't being applied, including some software installation policies and folder redirection. What's the likely problem, and how can you solve it without incurring additional costs?

Case Project 10-2: Working with Power Users

You have several users who have local administrative access to their computers. Some of these users are changing certain policies that shouldn't be changed for security reasons. You don't want to take away their local administrative access, but you want to be sure these important policies are reapplied to computers if a user changes them. What can you do?

10

chapter 11

Managing and Configuring DNS

After reading this chapter and completing the exercises, you will be able to:

- Describe Domain Name System
- Configure DNS zones
- Configure DNS resource records
- Manage zones
- Configure zone storage
- Configure round-robin DNS

Domain Name System is a critical part of every network today. It translates computer and domain names to addresses, allowing network users to access network resources by name rather than by address. In this chapter, you learn how to configure zones, the main structural component of DNS. Zones hold resource records, which are the data component of DNS. You learn how to create and configure not only host resource records, but also mail server, name server, service locator, and start of authority records. Because DNS in an Active Directory environment can be stored in a traditional text file or an Active Directory partition, you learn the advantages of using an Active Directory–integrated zone and how to tune replication between DNS servers. Finally, you learn about round-robin DNS, which allows you to load-balance a variety of network services.

Domain Name System Overview

Table 11-1 summarizes what you need for the hands-on activities in this chapter.

Table 11-1   Activity requirements

Activity	Requirements	Notes
Activity 11-1: Installing DNS	411Server2	
Activity 11-2: Creating a Standard Primary FLZ	411Server2	
Activity 11-3: Creating a Standard Primary RLZ	411Server2	
Activity 11-4: Creating a Standard Secondary FLZ	411Server1, 411Server2	
Activity 11-5: Creating a Standard Stub Zone	411Server1, 411Server2	
Activity 11-6: Configuring a Conditional Forwarder	411Server1, 411Server2	
Activity 11-7: Configuring A and CNAME Records	411Server1, 411Server2	
Activity 11-8: Creating an MX Record	411Server2	
Activity 11-9: Creating a Zone and Using Zone Delegation	411Server1, 411Server2	
Activity 11-10: Configuring DNS Aging and Scavenging	411Server1	
Activity 11-11: Converting a Standard Zone to an Active Directory–Integrated Zone	411Server1	
Activity 11-12: Configuring Round-Robin DNS	411Server2	

© 2015 Cengage Learning®

Domain Name System (DNS) is a distributed hierarchical database composed mainly of computer name and IP address pairs. A distributed database means no single database contains all data; instead, data is spread out among many different servers. In the worldwide DNS system, data is distributed among thousands of servers throughout the world. A hierarchical database, in this case, means there's a structure to how information is stored and accessed in the database. In other words, unless you're resolving a local domain name that you have a local server for, DNS lookups often require a series of queries to a hierarchy of DNS servers before the name can be resolved.

This section serves as a brief review of the basic DNS structure and function. Additional details are covered in *MCSA Guide to Installing and Configuring Windows Server 2012/R2, Exam 70-410* (Cengage Learning, 2015).

The Structure of DNS

To better understand the DNS lookup process, reviewing the structure of a computer name on the Internet or in a Windows domain is helpful. Computer names are typically expressed as *host.domain.top-level-domain*; the *top-level-domain* can be .com, .net, .org, .us, .edu, and so forth. As you learned in *Guide to Installing and Configuring Windows Server 2012/R2, Exam 70-410*, this naming structure is called the fully qualified domain name (FQDN). The DNS naming hierarchy can be described as an inverted tree with the root at the top (named "."), top-level domains branching out from the root, and domains and subdomains branching off the top-level domains (see Figure 11-1).

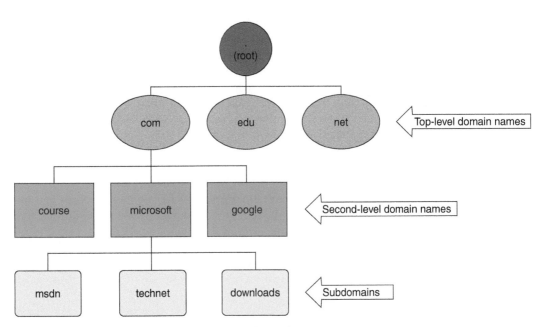

Figure 11-1   A partial view of the DNS naming hierarchy

© 2015 Cengage Learning®

The entire DNS tree is called the **DNS namespace**. When a domain name is registered, the domain is added to the DNS hierarchy and becomes part of the DNS namespace. Every domain has one or more servers that are authoritative for the domain, meaning the servers contain a master copy of all DNS records for that domain. A single server can be authoritative for multiple domains.

Each shape in Figure 11-1 has one or more DNS servers managing the names associated with it. For example, the root of the tree has 13 DNS servers called **root servers** scattered about the world that keep a database of addresses of other DNS servers managing top-level domain names. These other servers, aptly named, are called **top-level domain (TLD) servers**. Each top-level domain has servers that maintain addresses of other DNS servers. For example, the .com TLD servers maintain a database containing addresses of DNS servers for each domain name ending with .com, such as books.tomsho.com and microsoft.com. Each second-level DNS server can contain hostnames, such as www or server1. Hostnames are associated with an IP address, so when a client looks up the name www.microsoft.com, the DNS server returns an IP address. Second-level domains can also have subdomains, such as the technet in technet.microsoft.com.

The DNS Database   DNS servers maintain a database of information that contains zones. A **zone** is a grouping of DNS information that belongs to a contiguous portion of the DNS namespace, usually a domain and possibly one or more subdomains. Each zone contains a variety of record types called **resource records** containing information about network resources, such as hostnames, other DNS servers, domain controllers, and so forth; they're identified by letter codes. DNS resources records are discussed in more detail later in "Configuring DNS Resource Records."

Configuring DNS Zones

There are two DNS zone categories that define what kind of information is stored in a zone:

- *Forward lookup zone*—A **forward lookup zone (FLZ)** contains records that translate names to IP addresses. The zone name is based on the domain of the resource records it contains. For example, the zone name might be csmtech.local, and it might contain resource records for www, mail, db-server, vpnserver, and so forth, which are hostnames of computers in the domain. FLZs can contain a variety of resource record types, as discussed later in "Configuring DNS Resource Records." Forward lookup zones are used to perform forward lookups, which resolve computer names (FQDNs) to addresses. For example, the following ping command resolves the FQDN to an IP address before the ping program can send a packet to www.csmtech.local:

```
ping www.csmtech.local
```

- *Reverse lookup zone*—A **reverse lookup zone (RLZ)** contains records that map IP addresses to names and is named after the IP network address (IPv4 or IPv6) of the computers whose records it contains. For example, a typical name for an RLZ might be 1.10.in-addr.arpa, and it contains records for computers in the 10.1.0.0/16 subnet. An RLZ is queried when a network application has an IP address for a computer and needs the FQDN for that computer. A simple example of an application that queries an RLZ is ping, as in the following example:

```
ping -a 10.1.1.1
```

The -a option in the command tells ping to do a reverse lookup query. If the query is successful, ping displays the FQDN of the computer with IP address 10.1.1.1. This option might be useful if you need to know where packets are coming from and all you have is the IP address of the packet's source. For example, your DNS server is sluggish, so you begin to monitor traffic to and from this server. You find that the server is receiving queries from an unknown source. To learn about the domain where these packets are originating, you can do a reverse lookup query with ping -a.

On a Windows server, you can also choose how to store zone data, whether it's integrated with Active Directory or as a text file:

- *Active Directory–integrated zone*—An **Active Directory–integrated zone** is stored in an Active Directory partition on a domain controller and is replicated along with other Active Directory data.

- *Standard zone*—A **standard zone** is stored in a simple text file that can be edited with a text editor, such as Notepad. The text file is named *zone-name*.dns (with *zone-name* typically the domain name) and is in the *%systemroot%*\system32\dns folder on the DNS server. Standard zones are mostly installed on stand-alone servers that need to provide name resolution services for network resources outside the domain or in networks that don't use Active Directory at all, such as Linux- or UNIX-based networks. In addition, standard zones are used to resolve names for Active Directory domains in other forests.

Aside from determining how a zone is stored, both forward and reverse lookup zones can be one of three types: primary, secondary, or stub, discussed in the following sections.

Primary Zones

A **primary zone** contains a read/write master copy of all resource records for the zone. Updates to resource records can be made only on a server configured as a primary zone server. A primary DNS server is considered authoritative for the zone it manages. A primary zone can be an Active Directory–integrated or a standard zone. If a primary zone is a standard zone, there can be only one server that hosts the primary zone, referred to as the "primary DNS server." If a primary zone is Active Directory integrated, each DC in the replication scope of the Active Directory partition in which the zone is stored gets a copy of the zone, and changes can be made on any DC that hosts the zone, unless it's a read only domain controller (RODC).

Activity 11-1: Installing DNS

Note: Before beginning Chapter 11 activities, remove 411Server2 from the domain and uninstall AD DS and DNS.

Time Required: 10 minutes
Objective: Install the DNS Server role on 411Server2.

Required Tools and Equipment: 411Server2
Description: In this activity, you install the DNS Server role on 411Server2.

1. Log on to 411Server2 as **Administrator**, open Server Manager, and click **Manage, Add Roles and Features** from the menu.

2. In the Before You Begin window, click **Next**. In the Installation Type window, click **Next**. In the Server Selection window, click **Next**.

3. In the Server Roles window, click **DNS Server**. In the Add Roles and Features Wizard dialog box, click **Add Features**, and then click **Next**.

4. In the Features window, click **Next**. Read the information in the DNS Server window, and then click **Next**.

5. In the Confirmation window, click **Install**. After the installation is finished, click **Close**.

6. Stay logged on to 411Server2 if you're continuing to the next activity.

Activity 11-2: Creating a Standard Primary FLZ

Time Required: 10 minutes
Objective: Create a standard primary FLZ.

Required Tools and Equipment: 411Server2
Description: In this activity, you create and test a standard primary zone.

1. Log on to 411Server2 as **Administrator**, if necessary. Open Server Manager, and click **Tools, DNS** from the menu.

2. In DNS Manager, click to select **Forward Lookup Zones**, and then right-click **Forward Lookup Zones** and click **New Zone**.

3. In the Welcome to the New Zone Wizard window, click **Next**.

4. In the Zone Type window (see Figure 11-2), accept the default setting, **Primary zone**. Notice that the option to store the zone in Active Directory is grayed out because 411Server2 isn't a DC. Click **Next**.

11

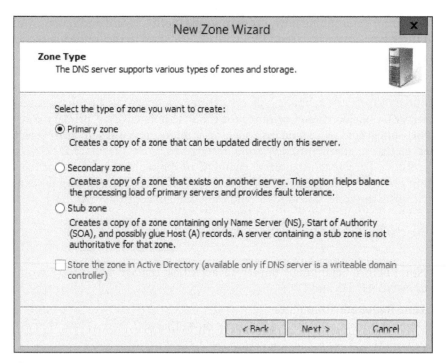

Figure 11-2   The Zone Type window

5. In the Zone Name window, type **csmtech.local**, and then click **Next**.

6. In the Zone File window, accept the default filename, **csmtech.local.dns**. (*Note*: If you like, you can use an existing file that was copied from another DNS server.) Click **Next**.

7. In the Dynamic Update window, accept the default option, **Do not allow dynamic updates**, and then click **Next**.

8. In the Completing the New Zone Wizard window, click **Finish**. The new zone is displayed in the right pane of DNS Manager.

9. In the right pane, double-click **csmtech.local**. You see two resource records that are created automatically for new zones: Start of Authority (SOA) and Name Server (NS).

10. Right-click **csmtech.local** and click **New Host (A or AAAA)**. In the New Host dialog box, type **www** in the Name text box, and type **10.11.1.150** in the IP address text box. Click **Add Host**. Click **OK** in the DNS message box, and then click **Done**.

11. To test the zone and new host record, open a command prompt window. Type **nslookup** and press **Enter**.

12. The DNS server is currently set to 10.11.1.1 (411Server1). To set the DNS server that nslookup uses to 411Server2, type **server 10.11.1.2** and press **Enter**.

13. Type **www.csmtech.local** and press **Enter**. Nslookup returns 10.11.1.150, which confirms that DNS is working on 411Server2. Stay logged on if you're continuing to the next activity.

Activity 11-3: Creating a Standard Primary RLZ

Time Required: 10 minutes
Objective: Create a standard primary RLZ.

Required Tools and Equipment: 411Server2
Description: In this activity, you create and test a standard primary reverse lookup zone (RLZ).

1. Log on to 411Server2 as **Administrator,** if necessary. Open Server Manager, and click **Tools, DNS** from the menu, if necessary.

2. In DNS Manager, click **Reverse Lookup Zones,** and then right-click **Reverse Lookup Zones** and click **New Zone.**

3. In the Welcome to the New Zone Wizard window, click **Next.**

4. In the Zone Type window, accept the default setting, **Primary zone,** and then click **Next.**

5. In the Reverse Lookup Zone Name window, click the **IPv4 Reverse Lookup Zone** option button, and then click **Next.**

6. In the Reverse Lookup Zone Name window, type **10.11** in the Network ID text box. Notice that the "Reverse lookup zone name" text box is filled in automatically with 11.10.in-addr. arpa, the standard format for an RLZ (see Figure 11-3). An RLZ inverts the network ID and adds "in-addr.arpa" to the name. Click **Next.**

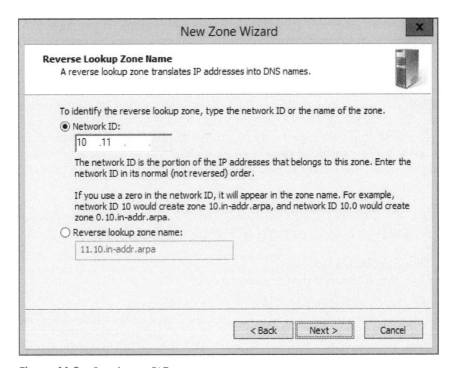

Figure 11-3   Creating an RLZ

7. In the Zone File name window, accept the default setting, **11.10.in-addr.arpa.dns,** and then click **Next.**

8. In the Dynamic Update window, click the **Allow both nonsecure and secure dynamic updates** option button, and then click **Next.**

9. In the Completing the New Zone Wizard window, click **Finish.** The new zone is displayed in the right pane of DNS Manager.

10. In the right pane, double-click **11.10.in-addr.arpa.** You see two resource records that are created automatically for new zones: Start of Authority (SOA) and Name Server (NS).

11. Right-click **11.10.in-addr.arpa** and click **New Pointer (PTR).** In the New Resource Record dialog box, the address has been started with 10.11., so add **1.150** to complete it. In the Host name text box, type **www.csmtech.local.** (*Note:* You can also click the Browse button and browse for the host.) Click **OK.**

12. To test the zone and new host record, open a command prompt window, if necessary. Type **nslookup** and press **Enter**.

13. The DNS server is currently set to 10.11.1.1 (411Server1). To set the DNS server that nslookup uses to 411Server2, type **server 10.11.1.2** and press **Enter**.

14. Type **10.11.1.150** and press **Enter**. Nslookup returns www.csmtech.local, which confirms that the RLZ is working.

15. Stay logged on if you're continuing to the next activity.

Secondary Zones

A **secondary zone** contains a read-only copy of all resource records for the zone. Changes can't be made directly on a secondary DNS server, but because it contains an exact copy of the primary zone, it's considered authoritative for the zone. A secondary zone can be only a standard zone, not an Active Directory–integrated zone. However, a file-based secondary zone can be created on a stand-alone server or a DC. Secondary zones are sometimes used to resolve names for domain-based resources outside the domain. For example, if you have two Active Directory forests, Forest1 and Forest2, you can create secondary zones on servers in Forest2 to resolve names for domains in Forest1, and vice versa. Secondary zones are also used in environments without Active Directory, such as for Internet domains and networks that are Linux/UNIX or Mac OS based.

When you're working with standard zones, a server that holds the primary zone is called the "master DNS server," and servers that hold secondary zones are called "slave DNS servers." You must configure zone transfer settings on the master DNS server that holds the primary zone to allow resource records to be transferred, or copied, to one or more slave DNS servers that hold secondary zones. Zone transfers are discussed in more detail in "Managing Zones."

Activity 11-4: Creating a Standard Secondary FLZ

Time Required: 10 minutes
Objective: Create a standard secondary FLZ.

Required Tools and Equipment: 411Server1 and 411Server2
Description: In this activity, you create a secondary zone on 411Server2 for the Active Directory domain on 411Server1.

1. Start 411Server1. Log on to 411Server2 as **Administrator**, open Server Manager, and click **Tools, DNS** from the menu, if necessary.

2. In DNS Manager, right-click **Forward Lookup Zones** and click **New Zone**.

3. In the Welcome to the New Zone Wizard window, click **Next**.

4. In the Zone Type window, click the **Secondary zone** option button, and then click **Next**.

5. In the Zone Name window, type **411Dom1.local**, and then click **Next**.

6. In the Master DNS Servers window, type **10.11.1.1** in the Master Servers text box, and press **Enter**. The address is resolved to 411Server1 (see Figure 11-4). (*Note:* You could have typed 411Server1 instead of the IP address, as long as 411Server2 could resolve the name to an address.) Click **Next**.

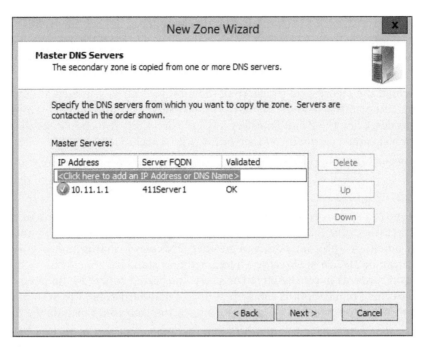

Figure 11-4   Specifying the master DNS server

7. In the Completing the New Zone Wizard window, click **Finish**. The new zone is displayed in the right pane of DNS Manager. Double-click the **411Dom1.local** zone. You see a message stating that there was a problem loading the zone.

8. Next, you need to configure 411Server1 to permit zone transfers to 411Server2. On 411Server1, log on as **Administrator**, and open DNS Manager. Click **Forward Lookup Zones**, if necessary, and in the right pane, right-click **411Dom1.local** and click **Properties**.

9. In the 411Dom1.local Properties dialog box, click the **Zone Transfers** tab.

10. Click **Allow zone transfers**, and then click the **Only to the following servers** option button.

11. Click the **Edit** button. In the Allow Zone Transfers dialog box, type **10.11.1.2** in the "IP addresses of the secondary servers" text box and press **Enter**. The name is resolved, but a message in the Validated column states that the server isn't authoritative for the required zone (see Figure 11-5). After records are transferred, the message goes away. Click **OK** twice.

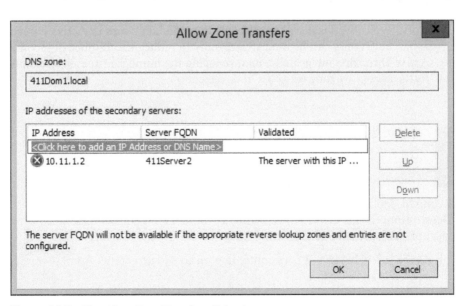

Figure 11-5   The Allow Zone Transfers dialog box

12. On 411Server2, click **411Dom1.local** in the left pane, and click the **Refresh** icon. If you don't see the records from 411Dom1.local, right-click **411Dom1.local** and click **Transfer from Master**, and then click the **Refresh** icon. You should see the records from the 411Dom1.local domain.

13. Now that the records are transferred, the message you saw in Step 11 about the server not being authoritative is gone. To verify, on 411Server1, right-click **411Dom1.local** and click **Properties**. Click the **Zone Transfers** tab and click **Edit**. You should see that OK is displayed in the Validated column on 411Server2. Click **Cancel** twice.

14. Stay logged on to both servers if you're continuing to the next activity.

Stub Zones

A **stub zone** is a special type of zone containing only an SOA record, one or more NS records, and the necessary glue A records to resolve NS records. A stub zone isn't authoritative for the zone. Essentially, a stub zone points to another DNS server that *is* authoritative for the zone. A stub zone can be an Active Directory–integrated or a standard zone. If it's Active Directory integrated, its records, as in other Active Directory–integrated zones, are updated regularly through Active Directory replication. If the stub zone is a standard zone, the SOA and NS records are updated through zone transfers. The reasons for using stub zones include the following:

- *Maintenance of zone delegation information*—If changes are made to addresses of the name servers hosting a delegated zone, the NS records on the parent DNS server must be updated manually. If a stub zone is created for the delegated zone on the parent DNS server, the NS records are updated automatically. The use of a stub zone effectively eliminates manual maintenance of the delegated zone's NS records. Delegated zones are discussed later in "Managing Zones."

- *In lieu of conditional forwarders*—If changes are made to addresses of domain name servers that are conditionally forwarded, the IP addresses for the conditional forwarder records must be changed manually. If a stub zone is created instead of using a conditional forwarder, the NS records in the stub zone are updated automatically. In addition, because stub zones can be Active Directory integrated, you need to create the stub zone only once on a DC, and it's replicated to all other DNS servers running on DCs.

- *Faster recursive queries*—When a DNS server receives a query for a resource record in the stub zone, it can make a recursive query by using the stub zone's NS records instead of accessing a root server.

- *Distribution of zone information*—When a network consists of many zones, distribution of these zones is necessary to make the entire DNS namespace accessible throughout the network. Typically, this distribution requires secondary zones or Active Directory–integrated zones. Stub zones can be used strategically to reduce the number of secondary zones or full Active Directory–integrated zones; reducing the number of these zones cuts down network traffic caused by zone transfers and replication.

Activity 11-5: Creating a Standard Stub Zone

Time Required: 10 minutes
Objective: Create a standard stub zone.

Required Tools and Equipment: 411Server1 and 411Server2
Description: In this activity, you create a stub zone on 411Server1 that points to the csmtech.local primary zone on 411Server2.

1. Make sure 411Server2 is running. Log on to 411Server1 as **Administrator**, if necessary, and open DNS Manager.

2. In DNS Manager, right-click **Forward Lookup Zones** and click **New Zone**.

3. In the Welcome to the New Zone Wizard window, click **Next**.

4. In the Zone Type window, click the **Stub zone** option button, and read the description. Click to clear the **Store the zone in Active Directory** check box, and then click **Next**.

5. In the Zone Name window, type **csmtech.local**, and then click **Next**.

6. In the Zone File window, accept the default filename, **csmtech.local.dns**, and then click **Next**.

7. In the Master DNS Servers window, type **10.11.1.2** in the Master Servers text box, and press **Enter**. The address is resolved to 411Server2. Click **Next**.

8. In the Completing the New Zone Wizard window, click **Finish**. The new zone is displayed in the right pane of DNS Manager, with the Type column set to Stub.

9. In the right pane, double-click **csmtech.local** to see the SOA and NS records. In the Data column, both records point to 411Server2. Before you can begin using the stub zone, you need to configure zone transfers on 411Server2.

10. On 411Server2, open DNS Manager, if necessary. Right-click **csmtech.local** and click **Properties**.

11. Click the **Zone Transfers** tab, and click the **Only to the following servers** option button. Click the **Edit** button, type **10.11.1.1** in the "IP addresses of the secondary servers" text box, and press **Enter**. Click **OK** twice.

12. On 411Server1, right-click **csmtech.local** in the left pane and click **Transfer from Master**.

13. Open a command prompt window, and then type `nslookup` and press **Enter**. Type `www.csmtech.local` and press **Enter**. The address should be resolved. Close the command prompt window.

14. Stay logged on to both servers if you're continuing to the next activity.

Configuring Forwarders

A **forwarder** is a DNS server to which other DNS servers send requests they can't resolve themselves. It's commonly used when a DNS server on an internal private network receives a query for a domain on the public Internet. The internal DNS server forwards the request recursively to a DNS server connected to the public Internet. This method prevents the internal DNS server from having to contact root servers and TLD servers directly because the forwarder does that on its behalf. Recall how a typical DNS query is processed: A DNS server receives a lookup request from a client, and if it's unable to satisfy the request, a recursive query ensues, starting with a root server. This process works well, but in situations such as the following, referring the query to a forwarder is more efficient:

- *When the DNS server address for the target domain is known*—Suppose a company has a department working on highly confidential research, and this department is segmented from the rest of the network by routers and firewalls. This department maintains its own domain controllers and DNS servers that aren't part of the organization's domain. However, department members often need access to resources on the network servers. In addition, the research department's DNS servers aren't permitted to contact the Internet. For computers in this department to resolve names for company resources, a forwarder can be configured on its DNS server that points to a company DNS server. The company DNS server not only resolves queries for company domain resources, but also performs recursive lookups for external domains on behalf of the research department's DNS server.

- *When only one DNS server in a network should make external queries*—A network consisting of several DNS servers might want to limit external queries to a single DNS server. This strategy has several benefits. First, network security can be enhanced by limiting exposure to the Internet to only one server. Second, because a single server is making all the queries to Internet domains, overall DNS performance can be enhanced because the server builds an extensive cache of Internet names. To use this strategy, all DNS servers on the network, except the actual forwarder, should be configured with the forwarder.

- *When a forest trust is created*—Windows requires DNS name resolution between the two forests involved in a trust relationship. Configuring conditional forwarders in the forest root name servers of both forests that point to each other is a good way to accomplish this.

- *When the target domain is external to the network and an external DNS server's address is known*—A company running a small network with limited bandwidth might find that the traffic caused by an internal DNS server's recursive lookups is excessive. The internal DNS server can provide name resolution for all internal resources and forward queries for external names to the DNS server of the company's ISP or a public DNS server, such as Google's at address 8.8.8.8.

You can configure two types of forwarders: traditional and conditional. A DNS server configured with a traditional forwarder means "If you can't resolve the query, forward it to this address." All queries that can't be resolved from the DNS server's zone data or cache are sent to the forwarder. Conditional forwarding enables administrators to forward queries for particular domains to particular name servers and all other unresolved queries to a different server.

Configuring Traditional Forwarders   Configuring a traditional forwarder is straightforward. Right-click the server node in DNS Manager, click Properties, and click the Forwarders tab (see Figure 11-6).

Figure 11-6   Configuring traditional forwarders

After clicking the Edit button, you can enter the IP address or FQDN of DNS servers that unresolved requests should be sent to. If more than one server is specified, they're queried in the order in which they're listed. Additional servers are queried only if no response is received from the first server. If no response is received from any forwarder, by default, the normal recursive lookup process is initiated, starting with a root server. If the "Use root hints if no forwarders are available" check box isn't selected and no forwarders respond, the DNS server sends a failure reply to the client.

Configuring Conditional Forwarders   A conditional forwarder is a DNS server to which other DNS servers send requests targeted for a specific domain. For example, computers in the csmtech.local domain might send a DNS query for a computer named server1.csmpub. local. The DNS server in the csmtech.local domain can be configured with a conditional forwarder that in effect says "If you receive a query for csmpub.local, forward it to the DNS server handling the csmpub.local domain." Servers that are forwarders or conditional forwarders require no special configuration, but the servers using them as forwarders must be configured to do so. Conditional forwarders are configured in DNS Manager. To create a conditional forwarder, click the Conditional Forwarders folder, and then right-click it and click New Conditional Forwarder.

Enter the domain name you want to forward queries for, and then add one or more IP addresses for DNS servers that are authoritative for the domain. After you enter an IP address, Windows attempts to resolve the IP address to the server's FQDN (see Figure 11-7).

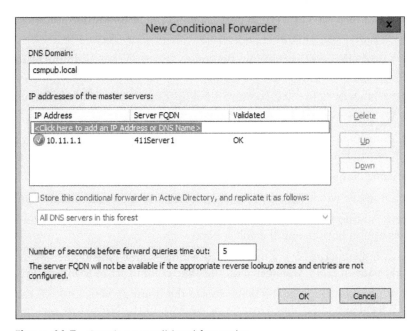

Figure 11-7   Creating a conditional forwarder

You can store the forwarder in Active Directory and have it replicated forest wide or domain wide by clicking the check box shown in Figure 11-7. This option is available only on a domain controller. If you choose this option, configuring the conditional forwarder on all DNS servers that are DCs isn't necessary because Active Directory replication does this automatically. The other option is a timeout. You can set the number of seconds until the server times out if no response is received from the forwarder.

With forwarders or conditional forwarders configured, the DNS server attempts to resolve DNS queries in this order:

1. From locally stored zone resource records

2. From the DNS cache

3. From conditional forwarders (if configured and the domain name matches)

4. From traditional forwarders (if configured)

5. Recursively by using root hints (only if no traditional forwarder is configured)

Conditional forwarders and stub zones perform much the same task. However, remember that if the IP address of the authoritative server for a zone changes, you must make a manual change to the conditional forwarder. DNS services for that domain might be interrupted for quite some time before you know that the change occurred and have the opportunity to fix it, especially if the target zone isn't under your management. With a stub zone, changes to the name servers for the zone are reflected in the stub zone during the next zone transfer or Active Directory replication.

Activity 11-6: Configuring a Conditional Forwarder

Time Required: 15 minutes
Objective: Configure a traditional forwarder.

Required Tools and Equipment: 411Server1 and 411Server2
Description: In this activity, you create a conditional forwarder. First, create a new zone on 411Server1, and then on 411Server2, create a conditional forwarder pointing to 411Server1 for that zone.

1. Make sure 411Server2 is running. Log on to 411Server1 as **Administrator**, and open DNS Manager, if necessary.

2. In DNS Manager, right-click **Forward Lookup Zones** and click **New Zone**.

3. In the Welcome to the New Zone Wizard window, click **Next**.

4. In the Zone Type window, click the **Primary zone** option button. Click to clear the **Store the zone in Active Directory** check box, and then click **Next**.

5. In the Zone Name window, type **csmpub.local**, and then click **Next**.

6. In the Zone File window, accept the default filename, **csmpub.local.dns**, and then click **Next**.

7. In the Dynamic Update window, click the **Allow both nonsecure and secure dynamic updates** option button, and then click **Next**.

8. In the Completing the New Zone Wizard window, click **Finish**. The new zone is displayed in the right pane of DNS Manager with the Type column set to Standard Primary.

9. Click **csmpub.local** in the left pane to see the familiar SOA and NS records. Right-click **csmpub.local** and click **New Host (A or AAAA)**. In the New Host dialog box, type **www** in the Name text box and **10.11.1.170** in the IP address text box. Click **Add Host**, and then click **OK**. Click **Done**.

10. On 411Server2, open a command prompt window, if necessary, and then type **nslookup** and press **Enter**. Type **server 10.11.1.2** and press **Enter** so that the DNS server is 411Server2.

11. Type **www.csmpub.local** and press **Enter**. You get a message indicating that **nslookup** can't find csmpub.local. Leave the command prompt window open.

12. Still on 411Server2, click the **Conditional Forwarders** folder in DNS Manager. Currently, there are no conditional forwarders. Right-click the **Conditional Forwarders** folder and click **New Conditional Forwarder**.

13. In the New Conditional Forwarder dialog box, type **csmpub.local** in the DNS Domain text box. In the "IP addresses of the master servers" text box, type **10.11.1.1** and press **Enter**. The address is resolved to 411Server1, and the entry is validated. Click **OK**.

14. In the command prompt window, type **www.csmpub.local** and press **Enter**. You get a reply indicating that 411Server2 forwarded the request to 411Server1. Close the command prompt window.

15. Stay logged on to both servers if you're continuing to the next activity.

Configuring DNS Resource Records

A DNS zone contains a number of resource records. Table 11-2 describes each record type briefly, and the following sections give you additional information. Resource records are added to a zone in one of two ways:

- *Static*—With this method, an administrator enters DNS record information manually. This method is reasonable with a small network of only a few resources accessed by name, but in a large network, creating and updating static records can be an administrative burden. Some records created by the system are also called static records, such as the SOA and NS records created automatically when a zone is created and records created automatically when Active Directory is installed.

- *Dynamic*—Referred to as **Dynamic DNS (DDNS)**, computers in the domain can register or update their own DNS records, or DHCP can update DNS on the clients' behalf when a computer leases a new IP address. Both the client computer and the DHCP server must be configured to use this feature.

Table 11-2   DNS resource record types

Record type (code)	Description
Host (A)	The most common resource record; consists of a computer name and an IPv4 address.
IPv6 Host (AAAA)	Like an A record but uses an IPv6 address.
Canonical Name (CNAME)	A record containing an alias for another record that enables you to refer to the same resource with different names yet maintain only one host record. For example, you could create an A record for a computer named "web" and a CNAME record that points to the A record but allows users to access the host with the name "www."
Pointer (PTR)	Used for reverse DNS lookups. Although DNS is used mainly to resolve a name to an address, it can also resolve an address to a name by using a reverse lookup. PTR records can be created automatically on Windows DNS servers.
Mail Exchanger (MX)	Contains the address of an e-mail server for the domain. Because e-mail addresses are typically specified as *user@domain*.com, the mail server's name is not part of the e-mail address. To deliver a message to the mail server, an MX record query supplies the address of a mail server in the specified domain.
Name Server (NS)	The FQDN of a name server that has authority over the domain. NS records are used by DNS servers to refer queries to another server that's authoritative for the requested domain.
Service Location (SRV)	Allows DNS clients to request the address of a server that provides a specific service instead of querying the server by name. This type of record is useful when an application doesn't know the name of the server it needs but does know what service is required. For example, in Windows domains, DNS servers contain SRV records with the addresses of domain controllers so that clients can request the logon service to authenticate to the domain.
Start of Authority (SOA)	Less a resource than an informational record, an SOA identifies the name server that's authoritative for the domain and includes a variety of timers, dynamic update configuration, and zone transfer information.

© 2015 Cengage Learning®

Host (A and AAAA) Records

Host records are the most abundant type of record in a typical DNS primary or secondary zone. A **host record** is fairly simple; it consists of a hostname and an IP address. A host record can be an A record, meaning it contains an IPv4 address, or an AAAA record, which contains an IPv6 address. When you configure a host record, an A or AAAA record is selected automatically, based on the IP address's format. As you have seen, when you create a host record, the only option by default is to update the associated PTR record in the RLZ, if it exists.

There are additional options for host records, however, if you enable the advanced view setting in DNS Manager. In DNS Manager, click View and then Advanced. If you open the properties of a host record, you see a dialog box similar to Figure 11-8. The following list describes the options you see in this figure:

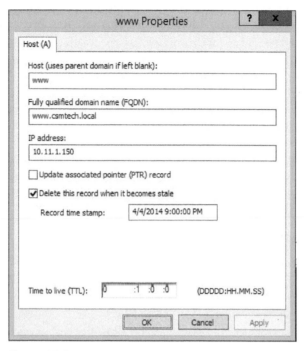

Figure 11-8 Properties of a host record with advanced view enabled

- *Update associated pointer (PTR) record*—If you enable this option, a PTR record is created or updated in the relevant RLZ, if it's present.
- *Delete this record when it becomes stale*—A stale record hasn't been updated in a period longer than its time to live (TTL) value. This option is set automatically on a dynamic record and can be set manually on a static record. If it's set, stale records are deleted (scavenged) from the database during aging and scavenging, a process discussed later in "Configuring Zone Scavenging."
- *Record time stamp*—For dynamic records, this field shows the date and time the record was created or updated. On static records, it's filled in automatically with the current date and time if the "Delete this record when it becomes stale" option is set and you click Apply in the Properties dialog box.
- *Time to live (TTL)*—The TTL tells the system how long the record should remain in the database after it was created or last updated. The default is 1 hour. This field is relevant only on zones that have scavenging enabled. It works with the "Record time stamp" option. If the actual time and date are past the "Record time stamp" value plus the TTL value, the record is eligible for scavenging.

Canonical Name (CNAME) Records

A **CNAME record** is an alias for another domain name record in the DNS database. It's often used when multiple services are running on the same server, and you want users to be able to refer to each service with a different name. For example, you might have an FTP service and a Web service hosted on the same server. You can set up DNS records as follows:

Record type	Name	Value
CNAME	www.csmtech.local	server1.csmtech.local
CNAME	ftp.csmtech.local	server1.csmtech.local
A	server1.csmtech.local	10.11.1.1

In this example, a reference to www.csmtech.local or ftp.csmtech.local returns server1.csmtech.local, which returns the IP address 10.11.1.1. A CNAME record must always point to another domain name; it can't point to an IP address. Although a CNAME record can point to another CNAME, it's not recommended, as it can result in circular logic. For example, you could have CNAME record X point to CNAME record Y, which points back to CNAME record X, in an unresolvable loop.

You can also create CNAME records that point to records in other domains. For example, you can create a CNAME record with the alias ftp.csmpub.local that points to www.csmtech.local, as long as the server you create the record on has a way to resolve ftp.csmpub.local (from local zone data, a forwarder, or recursion).

Activity 11-7: Configuring A and CNAME Records

Time Required: 10 minutes
Objective: Configure A and CNAME records.

Required Tools and Equipment: 411Server1 and 411Server2
Description: In this activity, you create A and CNAME records for a variety of settings.

1. Log on to 411Server1 as **Administrator**, and open DNS Manager. Make sure 411Server2 is running.

2. In DNS Manager, click **View**, **Advanced** from the menu to enable advanced view settings. The Cached Lookups folder that's now visible in the left pane enables you to browse and delete the cached records on the DNS server.

3. Right-click **csmpub.local** and click **New Alias (CNAME)**. In the New Resource Record dialog box, type **ftp** in the Alias name text box. The Fully qualified domain name (FQDN) text box is filled in automatically, and you can't change it. In the Fully qualified domain name (FQDN) for target host text box, type **www.csmpub.local**.

4. Click **Delete this record when it becomes stale**, and then click **OK** (see Figure 11-9). You can't type anything in the "Record time stamp" text box; the system fills it in automatically. Click **OK**. Double-click the CNAME record you just created to see that the "Record time stamp" text box has been filled in with the current date and time. Click **Cancel**.

Figure 11-9   Creating a CNAME record

5. Open a command prompt window, and then type **nslookup** and press **Enter**. Type **ftp.csmpub.local** and press **Enter**. The result is the address of www.csmpub.local.

6. In DNS Manager, right-click **csmpub.local** and click **New Alias (CNAME)**. In the New Resource Record dialog box, type **Win8** in the Alias name text box. In the Fully qualified domain name (FQDN) for target host text box, type **411Win8.411Dom1.local** and click **OK**.

7. At the command prompt, type **Win8.csmpub.local** and press **Enter**. The name is resolved to the address of 411Win8.411Dom1.local. Close the command prompt window.

8. Stay logged on to both servers if you're continuing to the next activity.

Pointer (PTR) Records

As discussed, PTR records are used to resolve a known IP address to a hostname. PTR records are used by some Web-based applications that limit their use to specific domains. When the application is accessed, a reverse lookup is performed, and the domain name of the host attempting to access the application is verified against the list of permitted domains. PTR records are also useful for certain applications when only the IP address is known and you want to find the hostname. For example, when you use the tracert command to map the route between your computer and a destination, each router along the way replies with its IP address. The tracert command can then do a reverse lookup to determine the router's FQDN, which often contains information for determining where the router is located and which ISP it belongs to. PTR records are found only in RLZs.

PTR records have much the same information as a host record, including a timestamp and TTL. When you create a host record, you have the option to create the related PTR record for the host automatically, as long as the RLZ already exists. In addition, you can edit an existing host record and select the "Update associated pointer (PTR) record" check box to create or update the PTR associated with the host.

Mail Exchanger (MX) Records

MX records are used by mail services to find the mail server for a domain. When a user writes an e-mail to mike@csmtech.local, for example, all that's known from the e-mail address is the recipient name and domain name. However, the mail protocol needs the name of a host in the domain that provides mail services, which is where the MX record comes in. When an outgoing mail server, usually an SMTP server, needs to deliver an e-mail message, it performs a DNS lookup for the MX record for the domain name contained in the e-mail address. The MX record points to an A record (much as a CNAME record does). So in this example, there might be records in the csmtech.local zone that look like the following:

Record type	Name	Value
A	mail.csmtech.local	10.11.1.20
MX	csmtech.local	mail.csmtech.local

© 2015 Cengage Learning®

When a client queries for an MX record for the csmtech.local domain, the DNS server returns the name of the server (mail.csmtech.local) and its IP address. The outgoing mail server can then deliver the mail to address 10.11.1.20, which contains a mailbox for the user account mike.

To create an MX record, right-click the zone where you want to create the record and click New Mail Exchanger (MX). There's only one required field: the target record, which can be a host or CNAME record (see Figure 11-10). The following list explains each option in this figure:

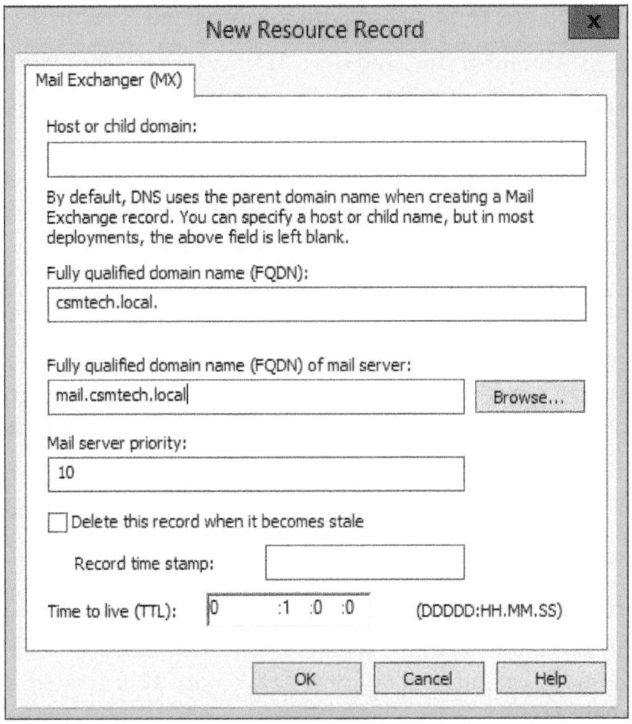

Figure 11-10   Creating an MX record

- *Host or child domain*—This field is usually left blank because the parent domain name is most often used. However, you can add a hostname or the name of a child domain. For example, if your primary domain name is csmtech.local, but you also have mail accounts in a child domain, such as europe.csmtech.local, you could enter europe in this text box.

- *Fully qualified domain name (FQDN)*—This is the name of the domain where you're creating the record. If you enter a value in the "Host or child domain" text box, it's added to the beginning of the default value. For example, if you enter "europe" in the "Host or child domain" text box, this field changes to europe.csmtech.local. You can't change its contents manually.

- *Fully qualified domain name (FQDN) of mail server*—This is the FQDN of the actual mail server, which is usually a host or CNAME record in the zone. In this example, the mail server is mail.csmtech.local.

- *Mail server priority*—If you have multiple mail servers in the zone, you can set a priority in this text box. Lower values have higher precedence. When a client queries for an MX record, the DNS server returns all MX records defined in it database for the zone. The client first tries the MX record with the lowest priority value. If it gets no response, it tries the next one, and so on. You can set the same priority value on two or more servers for a round-robin type of load balancing, as the equal-priority records are returned to the client in round-robin order.

- The last three fields are for scavenging stale records, as you have already learned.

Activity 11-8: Creating an MX Record

Time Required: 10 minutes

Objective: Create an MX record and a related A record.

Required Tools and Equipment: 411Server2

Description: In this activity, you create an MX record and a related A record.

1. Log on to 411Server2 as **Administrator**, and open DNS Manager, if necessary.

2. In DNS Manager, expand **Forward Lookup Zones**, if necessary. Right-click **csmtech.local** and click **New Mail Exchanger (MX)**.

3. Leave the "Host or child domain" text box blank, which is the default setting. In the "Fully qualified domain name (FQDN) of mail server" text box, type **mail.csmtech.local**. Leave the remaining values at their defaults, and click **OK**.

4. To create the host record the MX record points to, right-click **csmtech.local** and click **New Host (A or AAAA)**. Type **mail** in the Name text box and **10.11.1.170** in the IP address text box. Click **Add Host**, click **OK**, and then click **Done**.

5. Open a command prompt window, if necessary, and then type **nslookup** and press **Enter**. Type **server 10.11.1.2** and press **Enter**. You need to tell `nslookup` you're looking for MX records, so type **set type=mx** and press **Enter**.

6. Type **csmtech.local** and press **Enter**. The results show the domain name, the preference value, the target mail server (mail.csmtech.local), and the Internet address of mail.csmtech. local, 10.11.1.170.

7. Create another MX record, this time pointing it to **www.csmtech.local**.

8. Close and reopen the command prompt window. (`Nslookup` appears to remember the previous query and doesn't recognize that a new MX record was created until you quit the program and run it again.)

9. Type **nslookup** and press **Enter**. Type **server 10.11.1.2** and press **Enter**, and then type **set type=mx** and press **Enter**. Next, type **csmtech.local** and press **Enter**. You see that both MX records are returned. Type **csmtech.local** and press **Enter** again. Both records are returned but in a different order. This is how round-robin DNS works with multiple MX records of the same priority value. You can use this feature for load-balancing multiple mail servers. Close the command prompt window.

10. Stay logged on to both servers if you're continuing to the next activity.

Name Server (NS) Records

NS records specify FQDNs and IP addresses of authoritative servers for a zone. Each zone that's created has an NS record, which points to an authoritative server for that zone. For example, when a primary zone is created, the NS record points to the server it's created on. When a stub zone is created, however, the NS record points to the server that holds the primary zone data.

NS records are also used to refer DNS queries to a name server that has been delegated authority for a subdomain. For example, .com TLD servers refer queries for resources in the technet.microsoft.com subdomain to a DNS server that's authoritative for the microsoft.com domain. The microsoft.com domain name server can then refer the query to another DNS server that has been delegated authority for the technet subdomain of microsoft.com. Subdomains need not be delegated; they can simply be created under the zone representing their parent domain. If the subdomain has many resources and traffic on it is heavy, however, zone delegation (explained later in "Managing Zones") is a wise approach.

An NS record technically consists of just the name server's FQDN, but for the name to be useful, there must be a way to resolve it to an IP address. DNS does this with a **glue A record**, which is an A record containing the name server's IP address. In DNS Manager, glue records are created automatically, if possible, by a DNS lookup on the NS record's FQDN; they don't appear as an A record anywhere in the zone database. To create an NS record, right-click a zone, click Properties, and then click the Name Servers tab, which shows the current name servers for the zone. Click Add to add a name server (see Figure 11-11). If Windows fails to resolve the name server's FQDN, you can edit the record and add an IP address manually. You can add a TTL value for the record that tells other servers caching the NS record during recursive lookups how long they should keep it in cache. If no value is specified, the default TTL for the domain is used.

Figure 11-11   Creating an NS record

Service Location (SRV) Records

An SRV record specifies a hostname and port number for servers that supply specific services. For example, servers that provide Kerberos authentication or Lightweight Directory Access Protocol (LDAP) services can register an SRV record with a DNS server so that clients requiring these services can find them. SRV records are queried by client computers in the following format:

_*ServiceName*._*Protocol*.*DomainName*

For example, a client looking for an LDAP (Active Directory) server using the TCP protocol for the csmtech.local domain sends a query that looks like this:

_ldap._tcp.csmtech.local

In DNS Manager, several SRV records are in the _msdcs subdomain created for every Active Directory domain. Figure 11-12 shows DNS Manager with SRV records for the Kerberos, global catalog, and LDAP services in the 411Dom1.local domain.

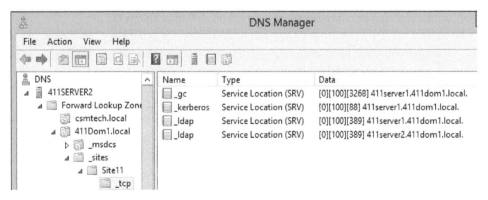

Figure 11-12   SRV records in an Active Directory domain

SRV records are critical to the operation of an Active Directory domain. Without the necessary SRV records, client computers couldn't find a domain controller or global catalog server to log on or join a domain. SRV records for Active Directory are usually created automatically when Active Directory is installed. If for some reason these records aren't created or updated correctly, you can register them by stopping and starting the Netlogon service on the domain controller or by restarting the server. You can also create or edit an SRV record manually. To create an SRV record, right-click the zone and click Other New Records, and then click Service Location (SRV) in the list of options. Figure 11-13 shows an SRV record for the LDAP service. The following list explains each option:

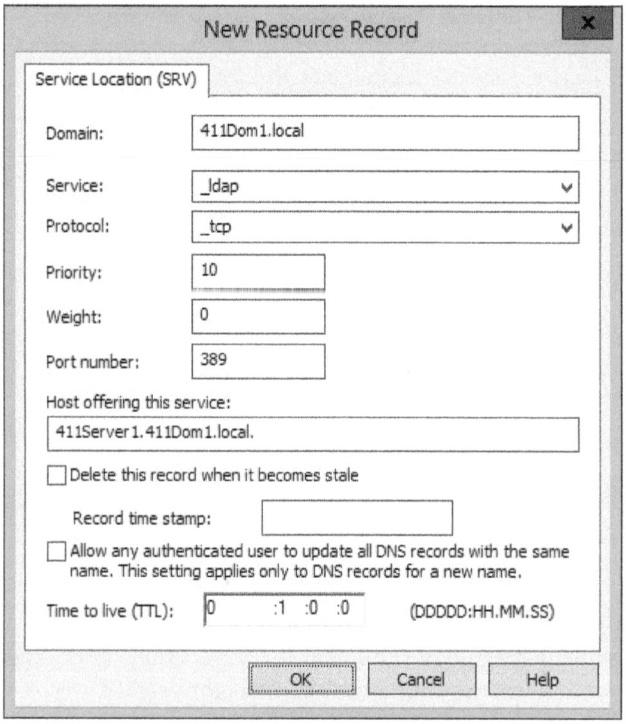

Figure 11-13 An SRV record for the LDAP service

- *Domain*—The name of the domain in which the service is located. This field is filled in for you, and you can't change it.
- *Service*—Choose a service in this list. The name is prefaced with an underscore character, so the Kerberos service, for example, is listed as _kerberos. Services you can choose from are finger, FTP, HTTP, Kerberos, LDAP, MSDCS, NNTP, Telnet, and Whois.
- *Protocol*—The Transport-layer protocol the service uses. The choices are TCP and UDP.
- *Priority*—The priority of this record if more than one server is providing the same service. Lower numbers are higher priority. The default value is 0.
- *Weight*—If two of the same service records have equal priority, the weight value determines which record the host should use. Unlike the priority, where the record with the highest priority (lowest value) is always used, the weight value is used more as a proportion. The higher the weight, the higher the proportion. So if there are two records with equal priority, and Record1 has a weight of 40 and Record2 has a weight of 20, Record1 is used twice as often as Record2. Records with equal weight are used equally. The default value is 0.
- *Port number*—This value is filled in automatically with the default port number for the selected service. However, you can change it if the service uses a nonstandard port number.
- *Host offering this service*—The FQDN of the host providing the service, ending with a dot.

Like all record types, if you have the Advanced View setting enabled, you can change the default TTL and select the option to delete the record when it becomes stale.

Start of Authority (SOA) Records

The SOA record, found in every zone, contains information that identifies the server primarily responsible for the zone as well as some operational properties for the zone. You can edit the SOA record by double-clicking it in the right pane of DNS Manager after selecting the zone or by viewing the zone's properties and clicking the Start of Authority tab. Shown in Figure 11-14, the SOA record contains the following information:

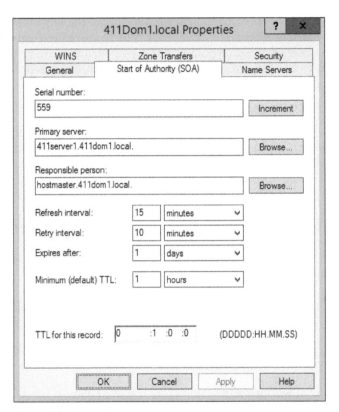

Figure 11-14   An SOA record

- *Serial number*—A revision number that increases each time data in the zone changes. This number is used to determine when zone information should be replicated or transferred.

- *Primary server*—On a primary Active Directory–integrated zone, this field displays the name of the server where DNS Manager is currently running. For a standard zone, it displays the primary DNS server's name.

- *Responsible person*—The e-mail address of the person responsible for managing the zone. A period rather than an @ sign is used to separate the username from the domain name (according to RFC 1183, which defines DNS resource record types).

- *Minimum (default) TTL*—This setting specifies a default TTL value for zone data when a TTL isn't supplied in a resource record. The TTL value tells other DNS servers and clients caching records from this zone how long they should keep cached data; this value should be adjusted according to how often data in the zone is likely to change. For example, a zone that maintains only static entries for resources that aren't changed, added, or removed often can specify a high TTL value. If a zone maintains dynamic records or records for resources that are going online and offline constantly, this value should be lower. If a redesign of your network will cause many changes to zone data, this value can be lowered temporarily.

Then wait until the previous TTL time has elapsed before making the changes. This way, devices that have cached records don't store them very long. The TTL set separately on resource records overrides this default value, which is 1 hour.

The other three fields—Refresh interval, Retry interval, and Expires after—control zone transfers and are discussed later in "Zone Transfer Settings."

Managing Zones

After you create a zone and some resource records, you might want to configure some management settings, depending on the type of zone. You might need to spread the DNS load if you have domains and subdomains defined in a zone, for example. If your network has frequent changes to IP addresses and hosts coming online and going offline often, you might need to change zone transfer settings for standard zones and configure zone scavenging to delete stale resource records. These settings and others are discussed in the following sections.

Zone Delegation

Zone delegation is transferring authority for a subdomain to a new zone, which can be on the same server or another server. Typically, you use zone delegation when a business unit in an organization is large enough to warrant its own subdomain and has the personnel to manage its own DNS server for the subdomain. Even if the business unit won't be managing the subdomain, delegating the handling of the subdomain to other servers might make sense for performance reasons.

When a subdomain has been delegated to a zone on another server, the DNS server hosting the parent zone maintains only an NS record pointing to the DNS server hosting the delegated zone. When the parent DNS server receives a query for the subdomain, it refers the query to the DNS server hosting the subdomain.

 If changes are made to the name servers hosting the delegated zone, the NS records on the server hosting the parent domain must be updated manually.

You might have noticed a zone called _msdcs.411Dom1.local on the DNS server. Every Windows domain zone has an _msdcs subdomain, which holds all the SRV records for Microsoft-hosted services, such as the global catalog, LDAP, and Kerberos. In the forest root domain, this subdomain is delegated to a new zone on the same server, not on a different server. For example, in DNS Manager in Figure 11-15, the _msdcs.411Dom1.local zone is under Forward

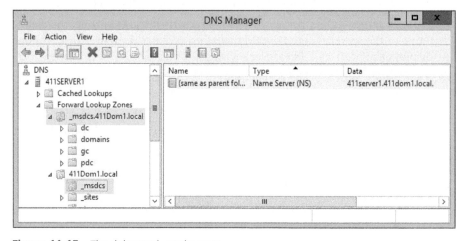

Figure 11-15   The delegated _msdcs zone

Lookup Zones, and you also see _msdcs under the 411Dom1.local folder. The _msdcs zone under the 411Dom1.local folder is grayed out, indicating it has been delegated. It contains a single NS record pointing to the server it has been delegated to.

The reason _msdcs is created as a subdomain is so that Windows clients and other clients specifically looking for a Microsoft service can query DNS for the service in the _msdcs subdomain. Remember: It's possible for non-Microsoft OSs to be operating in the same domain, and they might offer some of the same services, such as Kerberos and LDAP. The reason _msdcs is delegated to a separate zone in the forest root domain is to change the zone's replication scope from domain wide to forest wide. Because the forest root contains specialized functions, such as global catalog servers, replication of this domain's SRV records to the entire forest is critical. If the _msdcs subdomain isn't delegated to its own zone, the records it contains are replicated according to the parent zone's setting, which is often only domain wide, not forest wide.

Aside from using zone delegation in Active Directory, you can use it when you have a domain with several subdomains. The burden of handling the primary domain and subdomains could be substantial for both the server and administrator. You can delegate some or all of the subdomains to other servers (and perhaps administrators, too) to share the overall DNS load.

Activity 11-9: Creating a Zone and Using Zone Delegation

Time Required: 15 minutes
Objective: Create a zone and a delegation for the new zone.

Required Tools and Equipment: 411Server1 and 411Server2
Description: First, create a zone on 411Server2 named tech.csmpub.local, which is a subdomain of csmpub.local, a standard primary zone on 411Server1. Next, on 411Server1, you delegate the tech subdomain to 411Server1.

1. Log on to 411Server2 as **Administrator,** and open DNS Manager, if necessary.

2. Right-click **Forward Lookup Zones** and click **New Zone.** Click **Next.** Accept the default setting, **Primary zone,** and click **Next.**

3. In the Zone name text box, type **tech.csmpub.local,** and click **Next.**

4. In the Zone File window, accept the default zone filename, and click **Next.**

5. In the Dynamic Update window, accept the default setting, **Do not allow dynamic updates,** and click **Next.** Click **Finish.**

6. Create host (A) records in the tech.csmpub.local zone named **server1, server2,** and **server3.** Use the IP addresses **10.11.1.160, 10.11.1.161,** and **10.11.1.162.**

7. Log on to 411Server1 as **Administrator,** and open DNS Manager, if necessary.

8. Right-click **csmpub.local** in the left pane and click **New Delegation.** In the New Delegation Wizard, click **Next.**

9. In the Delegated Domain Name window, type **tech** in the Delegated domain text box. (The FQDN tech.csmpub.local has been filled in for you.) Click **Next.**

10. In the Name Servers window, click **Add.** In the New Name Server Record dialog box, type **411Server2.411Dom1.local,** and click **Resolve.** The IP address is shown as resolved in the Validated column. Click **OK.** Click **Next** and then **Finish.**

11. The tech subdomain is displayed with a gray folder icon under csmpub.local to indicate that it has been delegated. Click the **tech** folder. You see an NS record that points to 411Server2.

12. Open a command prompt window on 411Server1, if necessary. Type **nslookup** and press Enter, and then type **server1.tech.csmpub.local** and press Enter. An address is returned. 411Server1 sees that the tech subdomain is delegated to 411Server2 and uses the NS record to contact 411Server2 to retrieve the queried record. Close the command prompt window.

13. Stay logged on to both servers, and leave DNS Manager open for the next activity.

Zone Transfer Settings

Zone transfers occur between primary and secondary zones. The primary zone can be a standard zone or an Active Directory–integrated zone. The secondary zone is always a standard zone and can also be a standard stub zone. You configure zone transfers in two places: the Zone Transfers tab and the Start of Authority tab. The Zone Transfers tab (see Figure 11-16) in the zone's Properties dialog box specifies which servers the zone can be transferred to as well as notify settings.

 Zone transfers typically use TCP port 53, and most DNS queries from a client to a server use UDP port 53. If zone transfers must occur through a firewall, be sure to open TCP port 53 to allow master and slave servers to communicate.

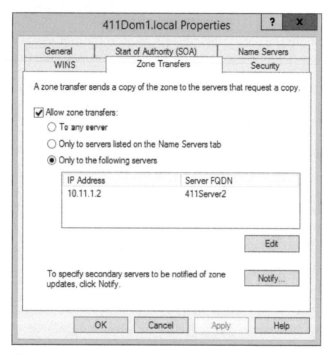

Figure 11-16   The Zone Transfers tab

The following are options for allowing zone transfers and specifying notifications:

- *To any server*—This option means just what it says: Any server (or any computer, for that matter) can request all the zone information. Normally, this option shouldn't be used, except perhaps for testing purposes, because it's a security risk. You don't want just anyone to have access to all your DNS data. For example, a user could run the `nslookup` command and then type `ls DomainName` to retrieve a list of all DNS records in the domain.

- *Only to servers listed on the Name Servers tab*—If you have added servers to the Name Servers tab, zone transfers are allowed to all of them.

- *Only to the following servers*—You can list the servers by name or IP address you want to allow zone transfers to.

- *Notify*—Clicking the Notify button opens a dialog box where you can add servers to notify of zone changes. If you use this option, zone transfers occur much sooner than the default polling period because they take place right after a change has happened. You might want to use this option when secondary servers are connected to the primary server via a high-speed link or when changes occur infrequently. However, if you have secondary servers connected over a WAN link, you must consider the effect on the link if zone transfers occur each time zone data changes. By default, notification is disabled.

You configure timing intervals of zone transfers in the Start of Authority tab, shown earlier in Figure 11-14. There are three timers related to zone transfers:

- *Refresh interval*—Specifies how often a secondary DNS server attempts to renew its zone information. When the interval expires, the server requests the SOA record from the primary DNS server. The serial number in the retrieved SOA record is then compared with the serial number in the secondary server's SOA record. If the serial number has changed, the secondary server requests a new copy of the zone data. After the transfer is completed, the refresh interval begins anew. The default value is 15 minutes. If notification is configured, the DNS server attempts to renew its zone information when it receives a notification and resets the Refresh interval timer.

- *Retry interval*—The amount of time a secondary server waits before retrying a zone transfer that has failed. This value should be less than the Refresh interval timer and defaults to 10 minutes. The Retry interval timer begins after the Refresh interval expires if the primary server can't be contacted or the zone transfer fails.

- *Expires after*—The amount of time before a secondary server considers its zone data obsolete if it can't contact the primary DNS server. If the Refresh interval timer expires without a successful zone transfer, this timer begins. If it expires without contacting the primary DNS server or without a successful zone transfer, the DNS server stops responding to queries. This value must be higher than the Refresh interval and Retry interval combined; the default is 1 day. This timer prevents a secondary server from responding to the DNS queries with data that might be stale.

Full Versus Incremental Zone Transfers   There are two types of zone transfers: full and incremental. A full zone transfer is often referred to as an "AXFR" because that's the query code used when the slave DNS server requests the transfer. An incremental zone transfer uses the code IXFR. An AXFR usually occurs when a secondary zone has just been set up on a DNS server, and all the records from the master server must be transferred. After that, the slave server sends a serial number indicating the version of the database it currently has. The master server uses the serial number to send only the changes to the zone that have occurred between the version of the database the slave has and the version the master has.

Configuring Zone Scavenging

When a dynamic resource record is created in a DNS zone, the record receives a timestamp based on the server's time and date. A static record can also be timestamped if you enable the option to delete the record when it becomes stale. When a resource using dynamic DNS goes offline, it should contact the DNS server to delete its resource records. Unfortunately, this process doesn't always occur, and records that are no longer valid are left in the database. In fact, Windows clients usually delete their DNS records only when they release or renew their IP addresses, not when they shut down.

Over time, these "stale" resource records can degrade server performance, provide incorrect information to DNS queries, and generally make DNS less reliable and efficient. To prevent stale resource records from accumulating in the DNS database, you need to enable scavenging. **Scavenging** is the process of scanning the records in each zone and deleting stale records.

Enabling Scavenging   Scavenging must be enabled in two places to occur. First, it must be enabled on the server, which allows scavenging to occur on all zones it's enabled on. To do this, right-click the server icon in DNS Manager, click Properties, and click the Advanced tab. Then click the "Enable automatic scavenging of stale records" check box (see Figure 11-17). You set the scavenging period in units of days or hours. The default value is 7 days. The scavenging period determines how often the server scans the zones on which scavenging is enabled and deletes stale records.

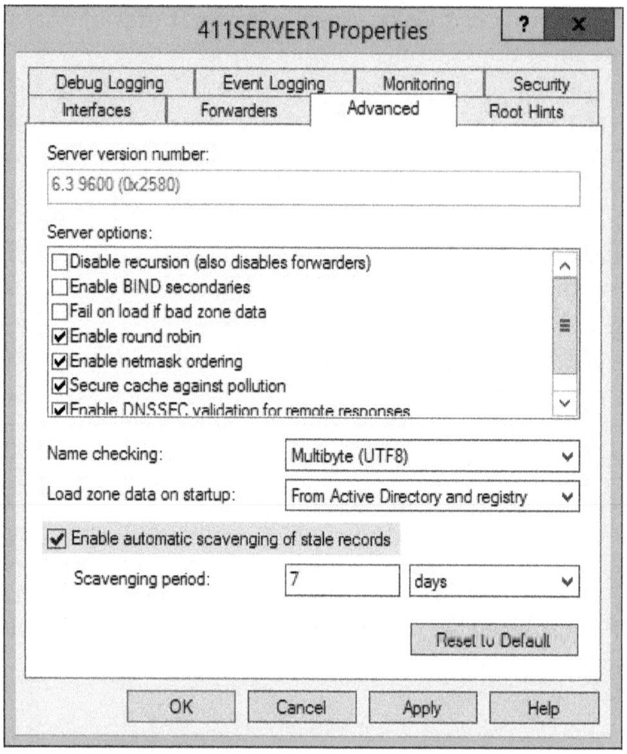

Figure 11-17   Enabling scavenging on the server

After you have enabled scavenging on the server, you enable it on zones. You can do this for all zones at once by right-clicking the server icon and clicking Set Aging/Scavenging for All Zones. If you choose this option, you can set scavenging parameters for all zones at once. Scavenging parameters include No-refresh interval and Refresh interval, discussed in the following list, and shown in Figure 11-18.

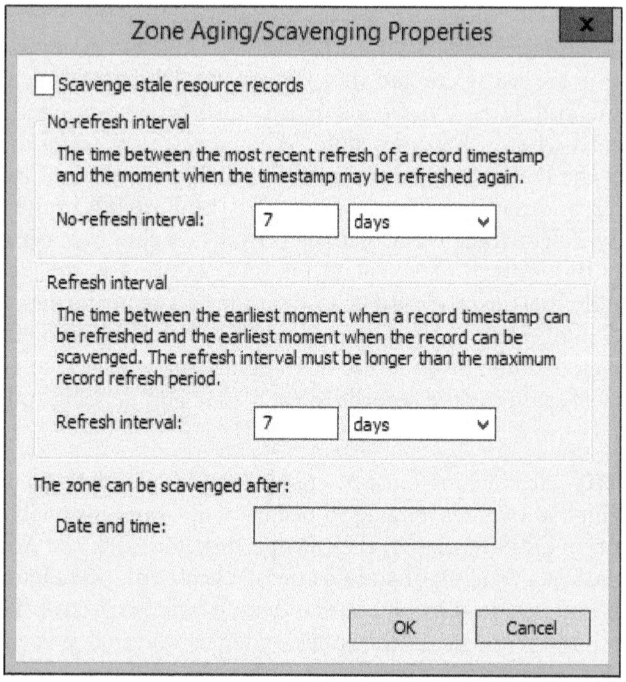

Figure 11-18   Configuring zone aging and scavenging

You can also enable scavenging for specific zones. Scavenging parameters set at the zone level override those set at the server level. Figure 11-18 shows the Zone Aging/Scavenging Properties dialog box. To open this dialog box, right-click a zone and click Properties, click the General tab, and then click the Aging button. By default, scavenging is disabled. When it's enabled, the server checks the zone file for stale records periodically and deletes those meeting the criteria for a stale record. The options in the Zone Aging/Scavenging Properties dialog box are as follows:

- *Scavenge stale resource records*—When this check box is selected, scavenging is enabled for the zone. Remember that scavenging must be enabled on the server in the Advanced tab of the DNS server's Properties dialog box. By default, scavenging on the server isn't enabled.

- *No-refresh interval*—To prevent DNS record timestamps from being updated too often, the No-refresh interval timer starts when a DNS record has been updated (refreshed). During this interval, DNS doesn't accept a timestamp change to the record. Timestamp changes can occur, for example, when a computer renews its IP address lease from DHCP, but no actual changes to DNS data occur. The No-refresh interval prevents excessive replication of DNS data because even a timestamp change requires record replication. The default No-refresh interval setting is 7 days.

- *Refresh interval*—After the No-refresh interval expires, the Refresh interval timer begins. During this interval, timestamp changes are accepted. If the Refresh interval timer expires, the record is considered stale and available for scavenging. If the record is refreshed during this period, the No-refresh interval timer begins again. The default Refresh interval setting is 7 days.

- *The zone can be scavenged after*—This setting is the earliest time and date that zone data can be scavenged. It's based on the current time and date plus the refresh interval. To see this information, you must have the Advanced View setting enabled in DNS Manager.

The process by which DNS records are aged and scavenged isn't obvious from reading descriptions of the No-refresh interval and Refresh interval timers, so a step-by-step example is in order, in which these timers are set to their default 7 days:

1. A DNS client computer gets a new IP address from a DHCP server and registers an A and a PTR record with the DNS server. Each record has its own set of timers, so the interval timers in this example apply to both the A and PTR records.

2. The No-refresh interval timer starts, and no timestamp refreshes are accepted for the record for 7 days.

3. The No-refresh interval timer expires.

4. The Refresh interval timer starts, and record refreshes are accepted for 7 days.

5. The computer doesn't refresh the DNS records, and it's shut down 1 day after the Refresh interval starts and isn't started again.

6. The Refresh interval timer expires.

7. The scavenging process deletes the expired DNS record.

The scavenging process, when enabled, is also set for 7 days by default. In the preceding example, the computer was shut down 1 day after the Refresh interval timer began, so 6 days elapsed before the record was available for scavenging. If the scavenging process had just finished a scavenging run before the refresh interval expired, the record could remain in the database for an additional 7 days, totaling 13 days from the time the computer was shut down and the time the record was actually deleted.

As mentioned, it's not enough to enable scavenging for zones. You must also enable scavenging on the server in the Advanced tab of its Properties dialog box. When using Active Directory–integrated zones, you don't need to enable scavenging on every DNS server. Because zone data, including aging/scavenging parameters, is replicated to all DNS servers, scavenging needs to be enabled on only one server. Scavenging does consume server resources, so enabling it on a DNS server with a fairly light workload is best.

Activity 11-10: Configuring DNS Aging and Scavenging

Time Required: 10 minutes
Objective: Configure aging and scavenging.

Required Tools and Equipment: 411Server1

Description: You have noticed quite a few stale DNS records in your zones, particularly for laptop computers that connect to the network briefly and then sometimes don't connect again for days, weeks, or longer. You want to reduce the number of stale records, so you enable and configure aging and scavenging.

1. Log on to 411Server1 as **Administrator**, and open DNS Manager, if necessary.

2. In the left pane of DNS Manager, right-click **411Server1** and click **Properties**. Click the **Advanced** tab, and click the **Enable automatic scavenging of stale records** check box, which enables scavenging on the server. Leave the scavenging period set to **7 days**, and then click **OK**.

3. Right-click **411Server1** in the left pane and click **Set Aging/Scavenging for All Zones**. Click the **Scavenge stale resource records** check box to enable scavenging on all zones. Leave the No-refresh and Refresh interval timers set at **7 days**, and then click **OK**.

4. In the Server Aging/Scavenging Confirmation dialog box, click **Apply these settings to the existing Active Directory–integrated zones**, and then click **OK**. Click the **Refresh** icon in DNS Manager so that the information you look at next reflects the change you just made.

5. Right-click the **411Dom1.local** zone and click **Properties**. Click the **Aging** button. The settings for the zone are the same as you set in Step 3. Notice also that the "Date and time" text box is filled in with a value approximately 7 days from now, which is the earliest any records will be scavenged. Click **OK** twice.

6. Stay logged on to 411Server1 if you're continuing to the next activity.

Configuring Zone Storage

As you have learned, standard zones are stored in text files, and Active Directory–integrated zones are stored in the Active Directory database. With standard zones, there aren't a lot of options for how zone data is stored, except perhaps the path and the filename. Active Directory–integrated zones, however, do have some storage configuration options.

Zone replication is the transfer of zone changes from one DNS server to another. For a standard zone, you've learned that zone replication is called "zone transfer." When DNS is installed on a domain controller, zone data is replicated automatically to other DCs. With standard zones, you need to create secondary zones on each DNS server that will host the zone. With Active Directory–integrated zones, a zone is created only once on a DC, and the zone is created automatically on every other DC in the zone replication scope.

For the purposes of zone replication, review the advantages an Active Directory–integrated zone has over a standard zone:

- *Automatic zone replication*—When DNS is installed on a new domain controller, zones are replicated to the new DNS server automatically. Standard zones require manual configuration of zone transfers.

- *Multimaster replication and update*—Multiple domain controllers can be configured as primary DNS servers, and changes can be made on any of these domain controllers. Multimaster replication provides fault tolerance because no single server is relied on to make DNS changes. Changes to DNS are replicated to all other DCs in the domain configured as DNS servers. In contrast, a standard zone has a single primary DNS server (and possibly one or more secondary servers), which is the only server where changes to the database can be made. If a standard primary server fails, DNS changes can't be made until another primary server is brought online.

- *Secure updates*—DNS can be configured to allow dynamic DNS updates only from DNS clients that have authenticated to Active Directory. This option prevents rogue clients from introducing false information into the DNS database.

- *Use permissions to restrict which users can modify zone data*—You can control which users or groups can change zone data by changing the permissions to the zone in the Security tab of the zone's Properties dialog box.

- *Efficient replication*—Replication of Active Directory–integrated zones can target only the DNS record properties that have changed and can target specific DNS servers to replicate with.

Active Directory Zone Replication Scope

The zone replication scope determines which partition the zone is stored in and which DCs the zone information is replicated to (see Figure 11-19). You can change the replication scope, if necessary, after a zone is created by selecting one of these options:

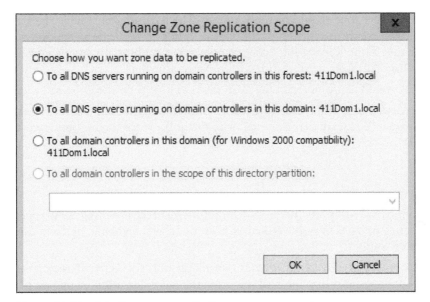

Figure 11-19 Selecting a zone replication scope

- *To all DNS servers running on domain controllers in this forest*—Stores the zone in the forest-wide DNS application directory partition ForestDNSZones. This partition is created when DNS is installed on the first DC in the forest.

- *To all DNS servers running on domain controllers in this domain*—Stores the zone in the domain-wide DNS application directory partition DomainDNSZones. It's the default option for new zones.

- *To all domain controllers in this domain (for Windows 2000 compatibility)*—Stores the zone in the domain partition, which is used to store most Active Directory objects. DNS zone information is replicated to all other DCs in the domain, regardless of whether the DNS Server role is installed. This option is the only one available for Windows 2000 DCs and should be selected if DNS information must be replicated to Windows 2000 DNS servers.

- *To all domain controllers in the scope of this directory partition*—A custom DNS application partition must be created before selecting this option, and the partition must use the same name on each DC hosting DNS that should participate in replication. Use this option to limit which DNS servers receive zone data to control replication traffic. By default, this option is grayed out and disabled until you have created a custom DNS application directory partition, discussed next.

Controlling Replication to Specific Domain Controllers

The "To all domain controllers in the scope of this directory partition" option for configuring the zone replication scope requires additional explanation and configuration. Normally, you want zones to be replicated to all other DCs that are DNS servers, but in some circumstances, you might want to limit replication to specific DCs. For example, you have set up a zone for testing purposes to be used by only a few departments in an Active Directory site that has three DCs. You can limit replication to just these three DCs so that zone data doesn't have to travel across WAN links when the zones aren't needed by users in other sites.

To limit replication to specific DCs, create a custom DNS application directory partition on each DC that the zone should be replicated to. The partition must have the same name on each DC. After you create the custom partition, the option to replicate to specific domain controllers in the Change Zone Replication Scope dialog box is enabled. To create a custom DNS application directory partition, use one of the following commands:

- At a PowerShell prompt, run the `Add-DnsServerDirectoryPartition` cmdlet.
- At a command prompt, enter the `dnscmd.exe /CreateDirectoryPartition` command. (Be aware that `dnscmd.exe` might be deprecated in future versions of Windows Server).

Dynamic Updates

As mentioned, a major advantage of using Active Directory–integrated zones is the ability to limit dynamic updates to only verified domain members. Dynamic updates can be configured in one of three ways:

- *Allow only secure dynamic updates*—Available only for Active Directory–integrated zones, this option ensures that the host initiating the record creation or update has been authenticated by Active Directory.
- *Allow both nonsecure and secure dynamic updates*—Both authenticated Active Directory clients and non–Active Directory clients can create and update DNS records. This option isn't recommended because it allows rogue clients to create DNS records with false information. A rogue DNS client can impersonate a server by updating the server's A record with its own IP address, thereby redirecting client computers to a fraudulent server.
- *Do not allow dynamic updates*—All DNS records must be entered manually. This option helps secure the environment, but on a network with many hosts that must be accessed by name and on networks using DHCP, it's an administrative nightmare. However, this option does work well for a DNS server that manages names for public resources, such as Web and mail servers with addresses that are usually assigned statically and don't change often.

What if you have a standard primary zone and want to ensure that dynamic updates are made only by known clients? The only option is to change the zone to an Active Directory–integrated zone. To do so, right-click the zone, click Properties, and in the General tab, click the Change button next to Type. Click the "Store the zone in Active Directory" check box. This option is available only on DNS servers that are domain controllers. The General tab also includes the option to disallow dynamic updates altogether so that all records are created manually.

Another form of DNS security, called DNSSEC, is mostly intended to protect DNS clients from invalid DNS data supplied by rogue or poisoned DNS servers. DNSSEC is covered in *MCSA Guide to Configuring Advanced Windows Server 2012/R2 Services, Exam 70-412* (Cengage Learning, 2015).

Activity 11-11: Converting a Standard Zone to an Active Directory–Integrated Zone

Time Required: 5 minutes
Objective: Convert a standard zone to an Active Directory–integrated zone.

Required Tools and Equipment: 411Server1
Description: You want to be sure dynamic updates to the csmpub.local domain can be made only by authenticated Active Directory domain members, so you convert a standard zone to an Active Directory–integrated zone.

1. Log on to 411Server1 as **Administrator,** and open DNS Manager, if necessary.

2. In the left pane of DNS Manager, right-click **csmpub.local** and click **Properties.**

3. In the General tab of the csmpub.local Properties dialog box, click the **Dynamic updates** list arrow. You see only two options: "Nonsecure and secure" and "None." There's no option to specify only secure updates until the zone is stored in Active Directory.

4. Click the **Change** button next to Type. Click the **Store the zone in Active Directory** check box, and then click **OK.** Click **Yes** to confirm.

5. Click the **Dynamic updates** list arrow. Click the **Secure only** option that's available now, and then click **OK.** Now only secure dynamic updates (and manual changes by an administrator) are allowed to the csmpub.local zone.

6. Stay logged on to 411Server1 if you're continuing to the next activity.

Configuring Round-Robin DNS

As you have seen, you can configure round-robin load-balancing for MX records and SRV records by creating multiple records with the same priority. You can also configure round-robin load-balancing for regular host records. In addition, you can configure load-balancing among servers running mirrored services. With a mirrored service, data for a service running on one server is duplicated on another server (or servers). For example, you can set up an FTP server or a Web server on servers that synchronize their content with one another regularly. Then configure DNS with multiple host records, using the server's name in both records but with each entry configured with a different IP address.

For example, suppose you have a Web server with the FQDN www.csmtech.local that's heavily used, responding slowly, and dropping connections. You can set up two additional Web servers and configure a mechanism for synchronizing files between the servers, such as Distributed File System Replication (DFSR) or a third-party file synchronization service. Next, you create two additional DNS A records (you already have one for the existing Web server) in the csmtech.local zone that use the same hostname, www, but different IP addresses. The Windows DNS service responds to queries for the www host by sending all three IP addresses in the response but varying the order of IP addresses each time. Figure 11-20 illustrates this setup.

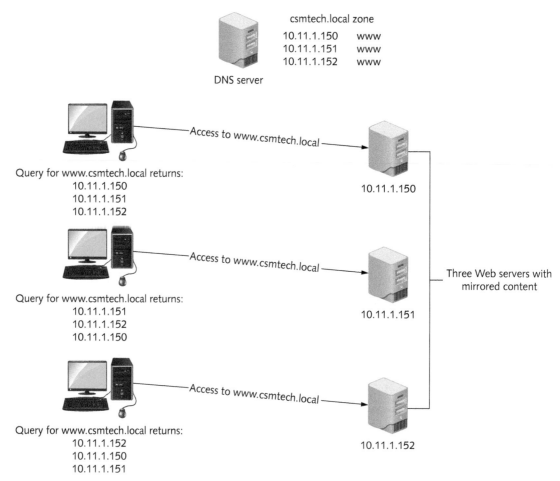

Figure 11-20   A round-robin DNS setup

© 2015 Cengage Learning®

This process is called **round-robin DNS** because each IP address is placed first in the list an equal number of times. Hosts receiving the DNS response always attempt to use the first address listed. You can improve the results of round-robin DNS by configuring a shorter TTL on the three A records so that remote DNS servers don't cache IP addresses for an extended period. By default, the round-robin option is enabled on Windows DNS servers, but you can disable it in the Advanced tab of the DNS server's Properties dialog box (see Figure 11-21).

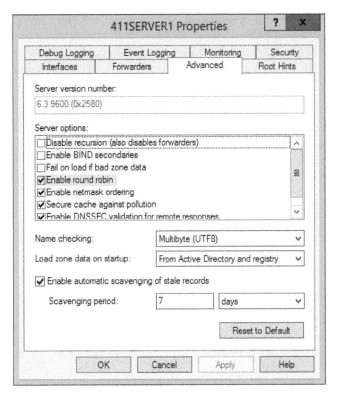

Figure 11-21   The round-robin DNS option

Unlike SRV records that have a weight parameter, you can't change the number of times a particular host record is used in round robin.

Activity 11-12: Configuring Round-Robin DNS

Time Required: 10 minutes

Objective: Create two host records with the same name but different IP addresses to enable round-robin load-balancing.

Required Tools and Equipment: 411Server2

Description: You have a Web server that has been performing slowly because of the number of hits. You build another Web server and mirror the content on both servers. Next, you create a new host record in DNS to use round-robin load-balancing.

1. Log on to 411Server2 as **Administrator**, and open DNS Manager, if necessary.

2. In the left pane of DNS Manager, right-click **csmtech.local** and click **New Host (A or AAAA)**.

3. In the New Host dialog box, type **www** in the Name text box and **10.11.1.151** in the IP address text box. Click the **Add Host** button. Click **OK** and then **Done**. You now see two www A records in the csmtech.local zone.

4. Open a command prompt window, if necessary, and then type **nslookup** and press **Enter**.

5. Type **www.csmtech.local** and press **Enter**. (If the request times out, press the up arrow and press **Enter** to repeat the command.) You see two IP addresses returned for www.csmtech.local.

6. Press the up arrow to repeat the command, and then press **Enter**. You see the same two IP addresses returned, but they're in reverse order. Each time a DNS lookup is made for www.csmtech.local, the records will alternate so that calls to the servers are load-balanced. You can have more than two records, and all records will be rotated accordingly.

7. Shut down or log off 411Server1.

PowerShell Cmdlets for Working with DNS

Table 11-3 describes some of the many PowerShell cmdlets for working with DNS. The last entry in the table lists all DNS-related cmdlets. As with all PowerShell cmdlets, to get help on using one, type Get-help *cmdletName* -detailed at a PowerShell prompt (replacing *cmdletName* with the name of the cmdlet).

Table 11-3 PowerShell cmdlets for working with DNS

Cmdlet	Function	Example
Add-DnsServerConditionalForwarderZone	Adds a conditional forwarder	Add-DnsServerConditionalForwarderZone -Name "csmpub.local" -MasterServers 10.11.1.2
Add-DnsServerDirectoryPartition	Creates a custom DNS application directory partition	Add-DnsServerDirectoryPartition -Name csmpart
Add-DnsServerForwarder	Adds a traditional forwarder	Add-DnsServerForwarder -IPAddress 10.11.1.2
Add-DnsServerPrimaryZone	Creates a primary zone	Add-DnsServerPrimaryZone -Name "csmpub.local" -ZoneFile "csmpub.local.dns"
Add-DnsServerResourceRecord	Creates a resource record of a specified type.	Add-DnsServerResourceRecord -ZoneName "csmpub.local" -A -Name "www" -IPv4Address "10.11.1.150"
Add-DnsServerSecondaryZone	Creates a secondary zone	Add-DnsServerSecondaryZone -Name "csmpub.local" -ZoneFile "csmpub.local.dns" -MasterServers 10.11.1.5
Add-DnsServerStubZone	Creates a stub zone	Add-DnsServerStubZone -Name "csmtech.local" -MasterServers 10.11.1.1 -ReplicationScope "Domain"
Add-DnsServerZoneDelegation	Creates a zone delegation	Add-DnsServerZoneDelegation -Name "csmpub.local" -ChildZoneName "tech" -NameServer "serv1.tech.csmpub.local" -IPAddress 10.11.1.5
Set-DnsServerResourceRecordAging	Starts aging of resource records in a specified zone	Set-DnsServerResourceRecordAging -ZoneName "csmtech.local"
Set-DnsServerScavenging	Sets scavenging settings	Set-DnsServerScavenging -RefreshInterval 3.00:00:00
Show-DnsServerCache	Shows the records in the DNS server cache, including the name, record type, timestamp, TTL, and record data	Show-DnsServerCache -ComputerName serv1.csmpub.local
Start-DnsServerScavenging	Starts the scavenging process to look for stale resource records	Start-DnsServerScavenging
Get-Command -module DNSServer	Displays a list of all DNS-related cmdlets	

Chapter Summary

- Domain Name System (DNS) is a distributed hierarchical database composed mainly of computer name and IP address pairs. A distributed database means no single database contains all data.

- The entire DNS tree is called the DNS namespace. When a domain name is registered, the domain is added to the DNS hierarchy and becomes part of the DNS namespace.

- There are two zone categories that define what kind of information is stored in the zone: forward lookup zones and reverse lookup zones.

- A primary zone contains a read/write master copy of all resource records for the zone. A secondary zone contains a read-only copy of all resource records for the zone. A stub zone is a special type of zone containing only an SOA record, one or more NS records, and the necessary glue A records to resolve NS records.

- A forwarder is a DNS server to which other DNS servers send requests they can't resolve themselves. A conditional forwarder is a DNS server to which other DNS servers send requests targeted for a specific domain.

- Resource records can be static or dynamic. There are A, AAAA, CNAME, PTR, MX, NS, SRV, and SOA records.

- Zone delegation is transferring authority for a subdomain to a new zone, which can be on the same server or another server.

- Zone transfers occur between primary and secondary zones. The primary zone can be a standard zone or an Active Directory–integrated zone.

- To prevent stale resource records from accumulating in the DNS database, you should enable scavenging.

- Zone replication is the transfer of zone changes from one DNS server to another. For a standard zone, replication is called "zone transfer." For Active Directory–integrated zones, the zone replication scope determines which partition the zone is stored in and which DCs zone information is replicated to.

- A major advantage of using Active Directory–integrated zones is the ability to limit dynamic updates to only verified domain members.

- You can configure round-robin load-balancing for DNS records. By default, the round-robin option is enabled on Windows DNS servers, but you can disable it in the Advanced tab of the DNS server's Properties dialog box.

- To see a list of all the PowerShell cmdlets for working with DNS, type `Get-Command -module DNSServer` at a PowerShell prompt.

Key Terms

Active Directory–integrated zone   A primary or stub zone with the DNS database stored in an Active Directory partition rather than a text file.

CNAME record   A record containing an alias for another record that enables you to refer to the same resource with different names yet maintain only one host record.

conditional forwarder   A DNS server to which other DNS servers send requests targeted for a specific domain.

DNS namespace   The entire DNS tree that defines the structure of the names used to identify resources in network domains. It consists of a root name (defined as a period), top-level domains, second-level domains, optionally one or more subdomains, and hostnames separated by periods.

Dynamic DNS (DDNS)   A DNS name-registering process whereby computers in the domain can register or update their own DNS records.

forwarder   A DNS server to which other DNS servers send requests they can't resolve themselves.

forward lookup zone (FLZ)   A DNS zone containing records that translate names to IP addresses, such as A, AAAA, and MX records. It's named after the domain whose resource records it contains.

glue A record   An A record used to resolve the name in an NS record to its IP address.

host record   A resource record in a DNS zone that consists of a hostname and an IP address.

primary zone   A DNS zone containing a read/write master copy of all resource records for the zone; this zone is authoritative for the zone.

resource records   Data in a DNS database containing information about network resources, such as hostnames, other DNS servers, and services; each record is identified by a letter code.

reverse lookup zone (RLZ)   A DNS zone containing PTR records that map IP addresses to names; it's named with the IP network address (IPv4 or IPv6) of the computer whose records it contains.

root servers   DNS servers that keep a database of addresses of other DNS servers managing top-level domain names.

round-robin DNS   A method of responding to DNS queries when more than one IP address exists for the queried host. Each IP address is placed first in the list of returned addresses an equal number of times so that hosts are accessed alternately.

scavenging   A process whereby the DNS server checks the zone file for stale records periodically and deletes those meeting the criteria for a stale record.

secondary zone   A DNS zone containing a read-only copy of all resource records for the zone.

standard zone   A primary, secondary, or stub zone that isn't Active Directory integrated.

stub zone   A DNS zone containing a read-only copy of only the zone's SOA and NS records and the necessary A records to resolve NS records.

top-level domain (TLD) servers   DNS servers that maintain addresses of other DNS servers that are authoritative for second-level domains.

zone   A grouping of DNS information that represents one or more domains and possibly subdomains.

zone delegation   The transfer of authority for a subdomain to a new zone, which can be on the same server as the parent zone or on another server.

zone replication   The transfer of zone changes from one DNS server to another.

Review Questions

1. The entire DNS tree is referred to as which of the following?

    a.   Zone hierarchy

    b.   Domain space

    c.   DNS namespace

    d.   Top-level domain

2. Which of the following accurately represents an FQDN?

    a.   host.top-level-domain.subdomain.domain

    b.   domain.host.top-level-domain

    c.   host.subdomain.domain.top-level-domain

    d.   host.domain.top-level-domain.subdomain

3. What type of DNS server maintains a database containing addresses of name servers for domains such as microsoft.com, yahoo.com, netacad.net, and data.gov?

    a. Root server

    b. TLD server

    c. Cache-only server

    d. Secondary server

4. A resource record containing an alias for another record is which of the following record types?

    a. A

    b. CNAME

    c. NS

    d. PTR

5. What type of resource record is necessary to get a positive response from the command `nslookup 192.168.100.10`?

    a. A

    b. CNAME

    c. NS

    d. PTR

6. What type of zone should you create that contains records allowing a computer name to be resolved from its IP address?

    a. RLZ

    b. FLZ

    c. Stub

    d. TLD

7. When you create a standard zone, you must specify the replication scope. True or False?

8. You have a DNS server running Windows Server 2012 R2 named DNS1 that contains a primary zone named csmtech.local. You have discovered a static A record for a server name DB1 in the zone, but you know that DB1 was taken offline several months ago. Aging and scavenging are enabled on the server and the zone. What should you do first to ensure that stale static records are removed from the zone?

    a. Change the default TTL on static records.

    b. Enable the Advanced View setting in DNS Manager.

    c. Configure the "Expires after" value in the SOA.

    d. Change the "No-refresh interval" timer to a lower number.

9. You have a DNS server outside your company's firewall that's a stand-alone Windows Server 2012 R2 server. It hosts a primary zone for the public Internet domain name, which is different from the internal Active Directory domain names. You want one or more of your internal servers to be able to handle DNS queries for the public domain and serve as a backup for the primary DNS server outside the firewall. Which configuration should you choose for internal DNS servers?

    a. Configure a standard secondary zone.

    b. Configure a standard stub zone.

    c. Configure a forwarder to point to the primary DNS server.

    d. Configure an Active Directory–integrated stub zone.

10. The IP address for the DNS server for the primary domain csmpub.local has just been changed. You have a stub zone named csmpub.local on another server. You need to update the NS record in the stub zone. True or False?

11. Which of the following is true about a stub zone? (Choose all that apply.)

    a. It's not authoritative for the zone.

    b. It holds mostly A records.

    c. It can't be Active Directory integrated.

    d. It contains SOA and NS records.

12. You have seven DNS servers that hold an Active Directory–integrated zone named csmpub.local. Three of the DNS servers are in the Chicago site, which is connected to three other sites through a WAN link with limited bandwidth. Only users in the Chicago site need access to resources in the csmpub.local zone. Where should you store the csmpub.local zone?

    a. ForestDNSZones partition

    b. csmpub.local.dns

    c. DomainDNSZones partition

    d. Custom application partition

13. The DNS server at your company's headquarters holds a standard primary zone for the abc.com domain. A branch office connected by a slow WAN link holds a secondary zone for abc.com. Updates to the zone aren't frequent. How can you decrease the amount of WAN traffic caused by the secondary zone checking for zone updates?

    a. In the SOA tab of the zone's Properties dialog box, increase the minimum (default) TTL.

    b. In the Advanced tab of the DNS server's Properties dialog box, increase the expire interval.

    c. In the SOA tab of the zone's Properties dialog box, increase the Refresh interval timer.

    d. In the Zone Transfers tab of the SOA Properties dialog box, decrease the Retry interval timer.

14. You have delegated a subdomain to a zone on another server. Several months later, you hear that DNS clients can't resolve host records in the subdomain. You discover that the IP address scheme was changed recently in the building where the server hosting the subdomain is located. What can you do to make sure DNS clients can resolve hostnames in the subdomain?

    a. Configure a forwarder pointing to the server hosting the subdomain.

    b. Edit the NS record in the delegated zone on the parent DNS server.

    c. Edit the NS record in the delegated zone on the DNS server hosting the subdomain.

    d. Configure a root hint pointing to the server hosting the subdomain.

15. You want a DNS server to be able to respond to queries for a domain in a standard primary zone hosted on another DNS server. You don't want the server to be authoritative for that zone. How should you configure the server? (Choose all that apply.)

    a. Configure a secondary zone on the DNS server.

    b. Configure a stub zone on the DNS server.

    c. Configure a conditional forwarder on the DNS server.

    d. Configure a delegation on the DNS server.

16. You're in charge of a standard primary zone for a large network with frequent changes to the DNS database. You want changes to the zone to be transmitted as quickly as possible after a change has been made to all secondary servers. What should you configure and where?

    a.   The notify option on slave servers

    b.   The Expires after timer on slave servers

    c.   The notify option on the master server

    d.   The Expires after timer on the master server

17. You have a server named DNS1 with a zone named csmtech.local. Several computers use DHCP for IP address assignment, and their IP addresses change often. Client computers are often unable to communicate with some of these computers until they clear their local DNS caches. What can you do to reduce the problem?

    a.   Set the minimum (default) TTL on the zone to a lower value.

    b.   Set the Expires after timer to a higher value.

    c.   Change the DNS records to static.

    d.   Change the "Record time stamp" setting to a lower value.

18. You have an Active Directory–integrated zone named csmtech.local on the DNS1 server. The forest root Active Directory domain is csmtech.local. Why is the _msdcs subdomain zone delegated on the DNS1 server?

    a.   To offload the DNS processing required of DNS1

    b.   To change the replication scope of _msdcs

    c.   To allow Windows clients to access Microsoft services

    d.   To allow dynamic updates to the _msdcs zone

19. You have a zone containing two A records for the same hostname, but each A record has a different IP address configured. The host records point to two servers hosting a high-traffic Web site, and you want the servers to share the load. After some testing, you find that you're always accessing the same Web server, so load sharing isn't occurring. What can you do to solve the problem?

    a.   Enable the load-sharing option on the zone.

    b.   Enable the round-robin option on both A records.

    c.   Enable the load-sharing option on both A records.

    d.   Enable the round-robin option on the server.

20. You have three servers providing the Kerberos authentication service—DC1, DC2, and DC3—and an SRV record for each server. You want to make sure DC1 handles 30% of the requests for the Kerberos server, DC2 handles 50% of the requests, and DC3 handles 20% of the requests. Currently, all settings for SRV records are at the default values. What should you configure?

    a.   The protocol on each SRV record

    b.   The priority on each SRV record

    c.   The weight on each SRV record

    d.   The TTL on each SRV record

21. You want to verify whether a PTR record exists for the Serv2.csmpub.local host, but you don't know the IP address. Which of the following commands should you use?

    a. `ping -a Serv2.csmpub.local` and then `ping` *IPAddress* returned from the first `ping`

    b. `nslookup Serv2.csmpub.local` and then `nslookup` *IPAddress* returned from the first `nslookup`

    c. `dnscmd /PTR Serv2.csmpub.local`

    d. `netsh /PTR Serv2.csmpub.local`

22. Which of the following is *not* an advantage of using Active Directory–integrated zones?

    a. Automatic zone replication

    b. Multimaster updates

    c. Can be stored on member servers

    d. Ability to configure secure updates

23. You have a primary zone stored in the myzone.local.dns file. Some devices that aren't domain members are creating dynamic DNS records in the zone. You want to make sure only domain members can create dynamic records in the zone. What should you do first?

    a. Configure the "Allow only secure dynamic updates" option.

    b. Configure permissions in the Security tab of the zone's Properties dialog box.

    c. Configure the "Store the zone in Active Directory" option.

    d. Configure the "Do not allow dynamic updates" option.

24. You have an application that needs to contact an LDAP server without knowing the name or address of the server. What kind of record can you create in DNS?

    a. MX

    b. SRV

    c. NS

    d. AAAA

25. You have two mail servers on your network named Mail1 and Mail2. You want clients to access Mail1 unless it's unresponsive, and then Mail2 should be accessed. What should you configure?

    a. The round-robin setting on the DNS server

    b. The priority value on the MX records

    c. The weight value on the SRV records

    d. The retry interval on the zone

Case Projects

CASE PROJECTS

Case Project 11-1: Configuring Zones

You have an Active Directory forest named csmtech.local and two Active Directory domains in the forest named csmpub.local and csmsales.local. You want the DNS servers in each domain to be able to handle DNS queries from client computers for any of the other domains. DNS servers in the csmtech.local and csmpub.local domains should be authoritative for their own domains and the csmsales.local domain. However, DNS servers in csmsales.local should be authoritative only for csmsales.local.

How should you set up the DNS servers and zones to handle this situation? Explain how the DNS servers in each domain should be configured with zones. Be sure to include information about replication scope and zone types.

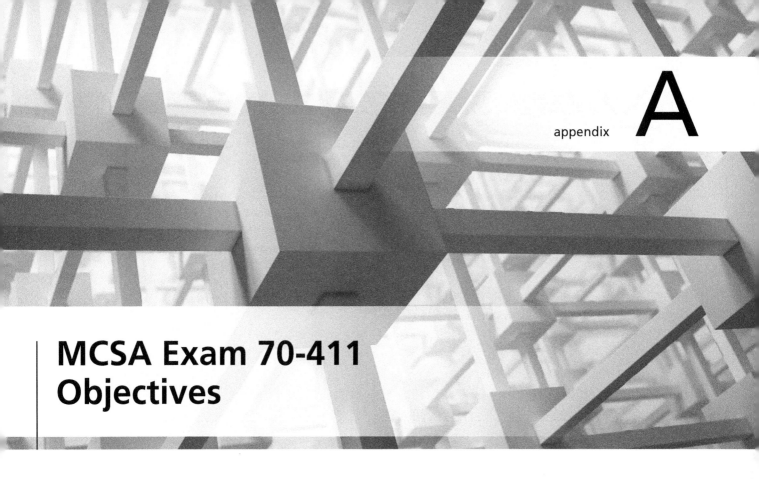

appendix **A**

MCSA Exam 70-411 Objectives

Table A-1 maps the Administering Windows Server 2012 (70-411) exam objectives to the corresponding chapter and section title where the objectives are covered in this book. Major sections are listed after the chapter number, and applicable subsections are shown in parentheses. After each objective, the percentage of the exam that includes the objective is shown in parentheses.

Table A-1   Objectives-to-chapter mapping

Objective	Chapter and section(s)
Deploy, manage, and maintain servers (16%)	
Deploy and manage server images	Chapter 1: An Overview of Windows Deployment Services
	Chapter 1: Windows Deployment Services Situations
	Chapter 1: Installing and Configuring the WDS Role
	Chapter 1: Working with WDS Images
	Chapter 1: Configuring DHCP for WDS
Implement patch management	Chapter 2: An Overview of Windows Server Update Services
	Chapter 2: Installing the WSUS Role
	Chapter 2: Configuring WSUS
	Chapter 2: WSUS Synchronization and Approval Rules
	Chapter 2: Additional WSUS Configuration Tasks
Monitor servers	Chapter 4: Monitoring a Windows Server
	Chapter 4: Network Monitoring
Configure file and print services (18%)	
Configure Distributed File System (DFS)	Chapter 3: An Overview of the Distributed File System
Configure File Server Resource Manager (FSRM)	Chapter 3: An Overview of File Server Resource Manager
Configure file and disk encryption	Chapter 3: Configuring File and Disk Encryption
Configure advanced audit policies	Chapter 4: Using Auditing to Improve Network Security

Objective	Chapter and section(s)
Configure network services and access (16%)	
Configure DNS zones	Chapter 11: Domain Name System (DNS) Overview
	Chapter 11: Configuring DNS Zones
	Chapter 11: Managing Zones
	Chapter 11: Configuring Zone Storage
Configure DNS records	Chapter 11: Domain Name System (DNS) Overview
	Chapter 11: Configuring DNS Resource Records
	Chapter 11: Configuring Round-Robin DNS
Configure VPN and routing	Chapter 5: An Overview of Remote Access
	Chapter 5: Installing and Configuring the Remote Access Role
Configure DirectAccess	Chapter 5: The DirectAccess Role Service
Configure a Network Policy Server infrastructure (20%)	
Configure Network Policy Server (NPS)	Chapter 6: Network Policy Server Overview
Configure NPS policies	Chapter 6: Network Policy Server Overview (Configuring NPS Policies)
	Chapter 6: Network Policy Server Overview (Importing and Exporting NPS Policies)
Configure Network Access Protection (NAP)	Chapter 6: Configuring Network Access Protection
Configure and manage Active Directory (13%)	
Configure service authentication	Chapter 8: Service Accounts
Configure Domain Controllers	Chapter 7: Active Directory Review
	Chapter 7: Cloning a Virtual Domain Controller
	Chapter 7: Configuring Read Only Domain Controllers
	Chapter 7: Understanding and Configuring Sites
	Chapter 7: Working with Operations Master Roles
Maintain Active Directory	Chapter 7: Maintaining Active Directory
Configure account policies	Chapter 8: Overview of User Accounts and Group Policies
	Chapter 8: Configuring Account Policies
	Chapter 8: Configuring Password Settings Objects
	Chapter 8: Service Accounts
Configure and manage Group Policy (15%)	
Configure Group Policy processing	Chapter 10: Configuring Group Policy Processing
	Chapter 10: Configuring Group Policy Client Processing
	Chapter 10: Group Policy Results and Modeling
Configure Group Policy settings	Chapter 9: A Group Policy Primer
	Chapter 9: Group Policy Settings
	Chapter 9: Working with Administrative Templates
	Chapter 9: Working with Security Templates
Manage Group Policy objects	Chapter 10: Managing GPOs
Configure Group Policy preferences	Chapter 9: Configuring Group Policy Preferences

Glossary

access client A user or device attempting access to the network.

Active Directory–integrated zone A primary or stub zone with the DNS database stored in an Active Directory partition rather than a text file.

Active Directory snapshot An exact replica of the Active Directory database at a specific moment.

active screening A file-screening method that prevents users from saving unauthorized files on the server. *See also* file screen.

administrative template files XML-formatted text files that define policies in the Administrative Templates folder in a GPO. Custom ADMX files can also be created.

answer file A text file containing information that answers the prompts and questions occurring during an OS installation.

assigned application A method of software deployment in which an application can be installed automatically when the computer starts, a user logs on to the domain, or a user opens a file associated with the application.

asymmetric encryption An encryption/decryption process that uses both a public key and a private key.

asynchronous processing A type of group policy processing that allows a user to log on and see the desktop while policies are still being processed.

authoritative restore A method of restoring Active Directory data from a backup to ensure that restored objects aren't overwritten by changes from other domain controllers through replication.

autonomous mode A WSUS server mode that decentralizes administration of update approvals and client groups; the default option when you install WSUS.

background processing Periodic group policy processing that occurs after a computer is running or a user is logged on.

batch file A text file containing a series of commands that's saved with a `.bat` extension.

boot image An image file containing the Windows Preinstallation Environment (PE) that allows a client computer to access a WDS server so that it can access an install image. *See also* Windows Preinstallation Environment (PE).

bridgehead server A DC at a site the Inter-Site Topology Generator designates to replicate a directory partition with other sites.

capture image A special boot image that creates an install image from a reference computer. *See also* install image *and* reference computer.

certificate-based authentication An authentication method that uses a certificate instead of a password to establish an entity's identity.

certification authority (CA) An entity that issues digital certificates used for authentication.

Challenge Handshake Authentication Protocol (CHAP) An authentication protocol that uses a series of challenges and responses to verify a client's identity.

ciphertext Data that has been encrypted; it's the result you get when plaintext is transformed by an encryption algorithm. *See also* cryptography.

client-side extension (CSE) An extension to the standard group policy client that applies specific types of group policy settings to client computers.

client-side targeting A method for adding computers to WSUS groups in which a Registry setting on the client machine instructs the client to add itself to the specified WSUS group.

CNAME record A record containing an alias for another record that enables you to refer to the same resource with different names yet maintain only one host record.

conditional forwarder A DNS server to which other DNS servers send requests targeted for a specific domain.

constrained delegation A type of delegation that limits the delegation to specific services running on specific computers. *See also* Kerberos delegation.

cryptographic algorithm A mathematical computation used to encrypt and decrypt data. *See also* cryptography.

cryptography The practice and study of methods used to protect information by encoding or encrypting it to an unreadable format, which can be decoded later to its original format.

data collector set Settings that specify the performance counters you want to collect, how often to collect them, and how long to collect them.

decryption The process of decoding data, usually with a decryption key.

default route The network where the router sends all packets that don't match any other destinations in the routing table.

delegated administrator account A user account with local administrative rights and permissions to the RODC, similar to members of the local Administrators group on a member computer or stand-alone computer.

demand-dial interface An interface that's activated when a client attempts to connect to the Internet, such as a dial-up modem or Point-to-Point Protocol over Ethernet (PPPoE) connection.

Deployment Image Servicing and Management (`dism.exe`) A command-line tool for updating an image file with patches, drivers, hot fixes, and service packs without having to re-create the entire image.

digital certificate A digital document containing identifying information about a person or system.

digital signature A numeric string created by a hash algorithm that's used to validate a message or document's authenticity. *See also* hash.

discover image An image file that can be used to boot a client computer that can't use PXE, usually from a CD/DVD or flash device.

Distributed File System (DFS) A role service under the File and Storage Services role that enables you to group shares from different servers into a single logical share called a namespace.

DNS namespace The entire DNS tree that defines the structure of the names used to identify resources in network domains. It consists of a root name (defined as a period), top-level domains, second-level domains, optionally one or more subdomains, and hostnames separated by periods.

domain GPOs Group Policy objects stored in Active Directory on domain controllers. They can be linked to a site, a domain, or an OU and affect users and computers whose accounts are stored in these containers.

domain naming master A forest-wide Flexible Single Master Operation role that manages adding, removing, and renaming domains in the forest.

downstream server A server in a multiple-server WSUS deployment that accesses other (upstream) WSUS servers for synchronizing updates.

driver group A collection of one or more driver packages you can restrict to specific client computers based on client hardware and software specifications.

Dynamic DNS (DDNS) A DNS name-registering process whereby computers in the domain can register or update their own DNS records.

encryption The process of encoding data to a format unusable to anyone who doesn't have the decryption key.

encryption key A numeric value that a cryptographic algorithm uses to change plaintext to ciphertext (encrypt) and ciphertext back to plaintext (decrypt). *See also* ciphertext *and* plaintext.

event subscription A feature in Event Viewer that allows an administrator to collect events from other systems.

expression-based auditing A method for specifying conditions, based on object properties in Active Directory, that must be met to trigger an audit event.

Extensible Authentication Protocol (EAP) A certificate-based authentication method.

file group A list of the types of files that define a file screen. *See also* file screen.

file screen A method of limiting the types of files a user can store on a server.

File Server Resource Manager (FSRM) A role service with services and management tools for monitoring storage space, managing quotas, controlling the types of files users can store on a server, creating storage reports, and classifying and managing files.

filtered attribute set A collection of attribute data configured on the schema master, used to specify domain objects that aren't replicated to RODCs, thereby increasing the security of sensitive information.

folder redirection A Group Policy feature that allows an administrator to set policies that redirect one or more folders in a user's profile directory.

folder target A UNC path configured on a DFS namespace folder that points to a shared folder hosted on a server.

foreground processing Group policy processing that occurs when the system boots or a user logs on.

forwarder A DNS server to which other DNS servers send requests they can't resolve themselves.

forward lookup zone (FLZ) A DNS zone containing records that translate names to IP addresses, such as A, AAAA, and MX records. It's named after the domain whose resource records it contains.

global system access control list An ACL that applies to all file system object types, not just a single file or folder.

glue A record An A record used to resolve the name in an NS record to its IP address.

GPO enforcement A setting on a GPO that forces inheritance of settings on all child objects in the GPO's scope, even if a GPO with conflicting settings is linked to a container at a deeper level.

GPO filtering A method used to change the default inheritance settings of a GPO.

GPO scope A combination of GPO linking, inheritance, and filtering that defines which objects are affected by the settings in a GPO.

group managed service account (gMSA) A specially configured managed service account that provides the same functions but can be managed across multiple servers. *See also* managed service account (MSA).

group policy caching A client-side feature that loads policy information from a cache on the local computer instead of having to always download it from a domain controller.

group policy preference A feature of Group Policy that contains settings organized into categories, which enables administrators to set up a baseline computing environment yet still allows users to make changes to configured settings.

handle A reference to a resource on the computer; often associated with open files but can also be associated with a block of memory or other data structures an application is using.

hard quota A type of quota that prevents users from saving files if their files in the target folder already meet or exceed the quota limit.

hash A fixed-size value produced by running a string of data through a mathematical function called a hash algorithm.

hop count The number of routers a packet must go through to reach the destination network.

host record A resource record in a DNS zone that consists of a hostname and an IP address.

image file A file containing other files, much like a zip file containing multiple files; WDS image files can be one of three formats: .wim, .vhd, and .vhdx.

image group A container for organizing images with common properties.

important updates Updates that usually solve a security or reliability issue in Windows.

infrastructure master A domain-wide Flexible Single Master Operation role that's responsible for making sure changes made to object names in one domain are updated in references to these objects in other domains.

infrastructure tunnel A tunnel created between the client computer and the DirectAccess server, used for control of the DirectAccess connection.

install image An image file containing the OS being deployed to client computers.

Internet Protocol-Hypertext Transfer Protocol Secure (IP-HTTPS) A tunneling protocol used to transport IPv6 packets over an HTTPS connection.

intranet tunnel The tunnel created when a user logs on to the DirectAccess client; it provides access to resources on the network.

item-level targeting A feature of group policy preferences that allows an administrator to target specific users or computers based on criteria.

Kerberos The authentication protocol used in a Windows domain environment to authenticate logons and grant accounts access to domain resources; also the basis for authorization to network resources in a Windows domain.

Kerberos delegation A feature of the Kerberos authentication protocol that allows a service to impersonate a client, relieving the client from having to authenticate to more than one service.

Kerberos proxy An authentication method that allows a client computer to authenticate to a domain controller by using the DirectAccess server as a proxy.

Key Distribution Center (KDC) A component of Kerberos that uses the Active Directory database to store keys for encrypting and decrypting data in the authentication process. *See also* Kerberos.

local GPOs Group Policy objects stored on local computers that can be edited by the Group Policy Object Editor snap-in.

loopback policy processing A group policy setting that applies user settings based on the GPO whose scope the logon computer (the one the user is logging on to) falls into.

maintenance window A set time of day at which your computer wakes up, if needed, to perform periodic maintenance tasks, including automatic updates if configured.

managed policy setting A type of group policy setting whereby the setting on the user or computer account reverts to its original state when the object is no longer in the scope of the GPO containing the setting.

managed service account (MSA) A service account that enables administrators to manage rights and permissions for services with password management handled automatically.

Microsoft Challenge Handshake Authentication Protocol (MS-CHAP) Microsoft's implementation of CHAP, used to authenticate an entity (for example, a user attempting access to the network). *See also* Challenge Handshake Authentication Protocol (CHAP).

Microsoft Challenge Handshake Authentication Protocol version 2 (MS-CHAP v2) An authentication protocol used to authenticate a user or server. This newer version of MS-CHAP is more secure. *See also* Microsoft Challenge Handshake Authentication Protocol (MS-CHAP).

Microsoft Software Installation (MSI) file A collection of files gathered into a package with an .msi extension that contains the instructions Windows Installer needs to install an application.

migration table A list of security principals and UNC paths in a GPO that can be mapped to the security principals and UNC paths in a destination domain a GPO is being copied to.

multicasting A network communication method for delivering data to multiple computers on a network simultaneously.

multisite DirectAccess A DirectAccess configuration with two or more DirectAccess servers, each providing a secure entry point into a network.

mutual authentication A type of authentication in which the identities of both the client and server are verified.

name resolution policy table (NRPT) A table configured on a DirectAccess client that makes sure DNS requests for network resources are directed to internal DNS servers, not Internet DNS servers.

namespace A name given to a grouping of folders maintained on a DFS server; it facilitates access to shares on multiple servers by using a single UNC path.

namespace root A folder that's the logical starting point for a namespace. *See also* namespace.

namespace server A server with the DFS Namespaces role service installed. *See also* namespace.

NAP agent A system service on an NAP client computer that collects SoHs from the SHAs and forwards the information to NAP enforcement clients.

NAP clients NAP-enabled computers attempting to access a network that can present their health status for evaluation.

NAP enforcement client A component of an NAP client that presents a client computer's health status to the NAP server and requests access. Also communicates the result of the request to other NAP client components.

NAP enforcement method A process used in NAP that specifies the type of network technology a client wants to connect to the network with.

Network Access Protection (NAP) A Windows Server 2012 feature that supplies an infrastructure for checking clients attempting to access a network to make sure they comply with health policies.

network access server (NAS) A protocol-specific device that aids in connecting access clients to the network.

Network Address Translation (NAT) A process whereby a router or other type of gateway device replaces the source or destination IP addresses in a packet before forwarding the packet.

network boot The process by which a computer loads and runs an OS that it retrieves from a network server.

Network Location Server (NLS) A basic Web server used by DirectAccess client computers to determine whether they're on the main network or a remote network.

Network Policy Server (NPS) A role service that enables you to define and enforce rules that determine who can access your network and how they can access it.

nonauthoritative restore A method of restoring Active Directory data from a backup that restores the database, or portions of it, and allows the data to be updated through replication by other domain controllers.

offline defragmentation Defragmentation of the Active Directory database that also compacts the database to improve performance. The Active Directory service must be stopped before offline defragmentation can occur.

online defragmentation Defragmentation of the Active Directory database that removes deleted objects and frees up space in the database but doesn't compact the database. Online defragmentation occurs automatically when Active Directory performs garbage collection.

passive screening A file-screening method that monitors and notifies when unauthorized files are saved but doesn't prevent users from saving unauthorized files on the server. *See also* file screen.

Password Authentication Protocol (PAP) An authentication protocol that uses passwords sent in plaintext to authenticate an entity.

password settings object (PSO) An Active Directory object that enables an administrator to configure password settings for users or groups that are different from those defined in a GPO linked to the domain.

patch management A procedure that enables administrators to control which product updates to allow as well as the source and timing of these updates.

PDC emulator A domain-wide Flexible Single Master Operation role that processes password changes for older Windows clients (Windows 9x and NT) and is used during logon authentication.

plaintext Data that has been unaltered; as used in cryptography, it's the state of information before it's encrypted or after it has been decrypted. *See also* cryptography.

Port Address Translation (PAT) A variation of NAT that allows several hundred workstations to access the Internet with a single public Internet address. *See also* Network Address Translation (NAT).

Preboot eXecution Environment (PXE) A network environment built into many NICs that allows a computer to boot from an image stored on a network server.

prestaging A feature that enables you to perform a basic unattended installation by specifying the computer name, selecting the boot and install images a client should receive, and joining the client to the domain.

primary zone A DNS zone containing a read/write master copy of all resource records for the zone; this zone is authoritative for the zone.

private key A key that's held by a person or system and is unknown to anyone else.

promiscuous mode A setting on a network adapter that allows it to accept all network packets, not just the ones addressed to it.

Protected Extensible Authentication Protocol (PEAP) A certificate-based and password-based authentication method designed to protect EAP messages by encapsulating them in a secure encrypted tunnel and using MS-CHAP v2 for user authentication. *See also* Extensible Authentication Protocol (EAP).

public key A key owned by a person or system that's available as part of a user's or system's digital certificate.

published application A method of software deployment in which the application isn't installed automatically; instead, a link to install the application is available in Control Panel's Programs and Features.

quota A limit placed on the amount of storage on a server volume or share available to a user.

RADIUS server group A group of RADIUS servers configured to accept authentication and authorization requests from a RADIUS proxy. *See also* Remote Authentication Dial In User Service (RADIUS).

realm The Active Directory domain where a RADIUS server is located.

recommended updates Updates that make minor improvements to Windows but aren't critical to security or reliability.

reference computer A computer that has been configured with the OS and applications you want to deploy; it's then used to create an install image that can be deployed to other computers by using WDS.

referral A prioritized list of servers used to access files in a namespace. *See also* namespace.

relative identifier (RID) A unique value combined with a domain identifier to form the security identifier for an Active Directory object. *See also* security identifier (SID).

remediation network A group of remediation servers that a noncompliant client computer can access. *See also* remediation server.

remediation server A server that can help a noncompliant client computer become compliant by hosting software updates or giving instructions.

Remote Access A server role that provides services to keep a mobile workforce and branch offices securely connected to resources at the main office.

Remote Authentication Dial In User Service (RADIUS) An industry-standard client/server protocol that centralizes authentication, authorization, and accounting for a network.

remote differential compression (RDC) An algorithm used to determine changes that have been made to a file and replicate only those changes.

replica mode A WSUS server mode that centralizes administration of update approvals and client groups.

replication The process of creating redundant copies of files on multiple servers.

replication group Two or more servers, known as members, that synchronize data in folders so that when a change occurs, all replication group members are updated at once. *See also* replication.

replication topology A DFS replication setting that describes the connections used to replicate files between servers. *See also* replication.

resource records Data in a DNS database containing information about network resources, such as hostnames, other DNS servers, and services; each record is identified by a letter code.

restartable Active Directory A feature introduced in Windows Server 2008 that makes it possible to take Active Directory offline to perform maintenance operations instead of requiring a server restart in DSRM.

reverse lookup zone (RLZ) A DNS zone containing PTR records that map IP addresses to names; it's named with the IP network address (IPv4 or IPv6) of the computer whose records it contains.

RID master A domain-wide Flexible Single Master Operation role that's responsible for issuing unique pools of RIDs to each DC, thereby guaranteeing unique SIDs throughout the domain.

root certificate A certificate establishing that all other certificates from that CA are trusted; also called a "CA certificate."

root servers DNS servers that keep a database of addresses of other DNS servers managing top-level domain names.

round-robin DNS A method of responding to DNS queries when more than one IP address exists for the queried host. Each IP address is placed first in the list of returned addresses an equal number of times so that hosts are accessed alternately.

routing table A list of network destinations and information on which interface can be used to reach the destination.

scavenging A process whereby the DNS server checks the zone file for stale records periodically and deletes those meeting the criteria for a stale record.

schema master A forest-wide Flexible Single Master Operation role that's responsible for replicating the schema directory partition to all other domain controllers in the forest when changes occur.

script A series of commands that have been saved in a text file to be repeated easily at any time.

secondary zone A DNS zone containing a read-only copy of all resource records for the zone.

secret key A key used to both encrypt and decrypt data in a secure transaction.

Security Accounts Manager (SAM) database A database on stand-alone and member computers that holds local user and group account information.

Security Configuration Wizard (SCW) A tool that guides you through creating, editing, and applying a security policy on Windows servers.

security filtering A type of GPO filtering that uses permissions to restrict objects from accessing a GPO.

security identifier (SID) A unique number assigned to every Active Directory object to identify it.

security templates Text files with an .inf extension that contain information for defining policy settings in the Computer Configuration, Policies, Windows Settings, Security Settings node of a local or domain GPO.

server-side targeting A method for adding computers to WSUS groups in which the server takes action to add the computer to the WSUS group.

service account A user account that Windows services use to log on with a specific set of rights and permissions.

service principal name (SPN) A name that uniquely identifies a service instance to a client.

service ticket A digital message used by Kerberos; requested by an account when it wants to access a network resource, such as a shared folder. *See also* Kerberos.

shared secret A text string known only to two systems trying to authenticate each other.

site link A component of a site that's needed to connect sites for replication purposes.

soft quota A type of quota that alerts users when they have exceeded the quota but doesn't prevent them from saving files.

split tunneling A remote access method in which only requests for resources on the network are sent over the DirectAccess tunnel; requests for Internet resources are sent out through the regular Internet connection.

staged installation An RODC installation method that doesn't require domain administrator credentials; a regular user at a branch office can perform the installation. Called "delegated installation" in Windows Server 2008.

standard zone A primary, secondary, or stub zone that isn't Active Directory integrated.

statement of health (SoH) A declaration from an NAP-enabled client computer about its status on having items such as antivirus protection and security updates installed.

statement of health response (SOHR) A message from an NAP server indicating the status of a request about a client's health from a System Health Validator.

static route A manually configured route in the routing table that instructs the router where to send packets destined for particular networks.

stub zone A DNS zone containing a read-only copy of only the zone's SOA and NS records and the necessary A records to resolve NS records.

symmetric encryption An encryption/decryption process that uses a single key to encrypt and decrypt data (also called "private key cryptography" or "secret key cryptography"). *See also* cryptography, private key, *and* secret key.

synchronous processing A type of group policy processing that forces the processing to finish before certain other system tasks can be performed.

system health agents (SHAs) An NAP client component that checks defined settings to see whether they are up to date and configured correctly; this component also creates a statement of health (SoH). *See also* statement of health (SoH).

System Health Validator (SHV) An NAP server component that verifies the statement of health sent by a client. *See also* statement of health (SoH).

System Image Manager (SIM) A tool in the Windows Assessment and Deployment Kit (ADK) that automates creating unattend files.

system statement of health (SSOH) A group of SoHs collected by an NAP agent when there are multiple system health agents. *See also* statement of health (SoH).

thread The smallest piece of program code that Windows can schedule for execution.

ticket-granting ticket (TGT) A digital message used by Kerberos; grants an account access to the issuing domain controller and is used to request a service ticket without having to authenticate again. *See also* Kerberos.

timestamp A record of the time a message is sent; used in Kerberos authentication. *See also* Kerberos.

tombstone lifetime A period of time in which deleted Active Directory objects are marked for deletion but left in the database. When the tombstone lifetime expires, the object is removed during garbage collection.

top-level domain (TLD) servers DNS servers that maintain addresses of other DNS servers that are authoritative for second-level domains.

Transport Layer Security (TLS) A cryptographic protocol used to encrypt messages over a network.

tunnel A method of transferring data across an unsecured network in such a way that the data is hidden from all but the sender and receiver.

unidirectional replication A replication method used with RODCs in which Active Directory data is replicated to the RODC, but the RODC doesn't replicate the data to other domain controllers.

universal group membership caching This feature stores universal group membership information retrieved from a global catalog server, so the global catalog server doesn't have to be contacted for each user logon.

unmanaged policy setting A type of group policy setting that persists on the user or computer account, meaning it remains even after the computer or user object falls out of the GPO's scope.

upstream server A server in a multiple-server WSUS deployment that other (downstream) WSUS servers use for synchronizing updates.

virtual account A simple type of service account that doesn't need to be created, deleted, or managed by an administrator.

virtual private network (VPN) A network connection that uses the Internet to give mobile users or branch offices secure access to a company's network resources on a private network.

wdsnbp.com A bootstrap program; a WDS component that a WDS client downloads when performing a network boot.

Windows Deployment Services (WDS) A server role that facilitates installing Windows OSs across a network.

Windows Imaging Format (WIM) The most common image file type used by WDS and the method used to store installation files on a Windows installation DVD.

Windows Preinstallation Environment (PE) A minimal OS that has only the services needed to access the network, work with files, copy disk images, and jump-start a Windows installation.

Windows Server Update Services (WSUS) A server role that makes it possible for administrators to take control of Microsoft product updates on computers running Windows.

WMI filtering A type of GPO filtering that uses queries to select a group of computers based on certain attributes, and then applies or doesn't apply policies based on the query's results.

zone A grouping of DNS information that represents one or more domains and possibly subdomains.

zone delegation The transfer of authority for a subdomain to a new zone, which can be on the same server as the parent zone or on another server.

zone replication The transfer of zone changes from one DNS server to another.

Index